RELIGIOUS HUMAN RIGHTS IN GLOBAL PERSPECTIVE

RELIGIOUS HUMAN RIGHTS IN GLOBAL PERSPECTIVE

Legal Perspectives

Edited by

Johan D. van der Vyver
I.T. Cohen Professor of International Law and Human Rights
Fellow, The Carter Center
Emory University

and

John Witte, Jr.
Director, Law and Religion Program
Jonas Robitscher Professor of Law
Emory University

MARTINUS NIJHOFF PUBLISHERS
THE HAGUE / BOSTON / LONDON

A C.I.P. Catalogue record for this book is available from the Library of Congress.

ISBN 90-411-0177-2 (Hb, Vol. 2)
ISBN 90-411-0176-4 (Hb, Vol. 1)
ISBN 90-411-0178-0 (Hb, Set of 2 volumes)
ISBN 90-411-0180-2 (Pb, Vol. 2)
ISBN 90-411-0179-9 (Pb, Vol. 1)
ISBN 90-411-0181-0 (Pb, Set of 2 volumes)

Published by Kluwer Law International,
P.O. Box 85889, 2508 CN The Hague, The Netherlands.

Sold and distributed in the U.S.A. and Canada
by Kluwer Law International,
675 Massachusetts Avenue, Cambridge, MA 02139, U.S.A.

In all other countries, sold and distributed
by Kluwer Law International,
P.O. Box 85889, 2508 CN The Hague, The Netherlands.

cover photograph: Corky Gallo, *Emory University*

Printed on acid-free paper

Kluwer Law International incorporates the publishing programmes of
Graham & Trotman Ltd, Kluwer Law and Taxation Publishers,
and Martinus Nijhoff Publishers.

Printed in the Netherlands

Contents

Acknowledgements

This volume and its companion, *Religious Human Rights in Global Perspective: Religious Perspectives,* are products of an ongoing project on religion, democracy, and human rights undertaken by the Law and Religion Program at Emory University. We wish to express our deepest gratitude to our colleagues on the Emory University Committee on Law and Religion for their enthusiastic support of this project—Dean Howard O. Hunter and Professors Frank S. Alexander, Harold J. Berman, and the late Donald W. Fyr of Emory Law School; Dean David F. Bright and Professors David R. Blumenthal and Paul B. Courtright of Emory College; and Dean R. Kevin LaGree, Dean Rebecca S. Chopp, and Professor Jon P. Gunnemann of the Candler School of Theology. We also wish to offer our warmest thanks to President William M. Chace and Provost Billy E. Frye of Emory University for their continued solicitude for the Law and Religion Program.

A number of colleagues at Emory Law School have contributed generously to the completion of this volume and its companion. Ms. Eliza Ellison served as principal administrator of this project and its publications. Mr. Daniel G. Ashburn served as research coordinator, with the assistance of Ms. M. Christian Green and Ms. Holliday Osborne. Ms. Anita Mann provided administrative support. Mr. Corky Gallo furnished technical support. Ms. Louise Jackson, Ms. Glennis O'Neal, Ms. Radine Robinson, and Ms. Marie Warren provided secretarial services. We are enormously indebted to each of these colleagues for their invaluable contributions to this project and volume.

We would like to express our appreciation to our friends at Martinus Nijhoff Publishers in The Hague, particularly Ms. Lindy Melman and Mr. Alan Stephens, for the privilege of publishing with them.

This project and its publications have been made possible by a generous grant from The Pew Charitable Trusts, Inc. in Philadelphia, Pennsylvania. On behalf of the Law and Religion Program, we wish to thank the Trusts, particularly President Rebecca M. Rimel and program directors,

Dr. Joel Carpenter and Dr. Kevin Quigley, for their gracious and unstinting support of our efforts.

Johan D. van der Vyver
John Witte, Jr.

Preface

JIMMY CARTER
The Carter Center, Emory University

The chapters in this volume inspire hope for the future of religious human rights. This is not because they report a universal reduction of abuses; these continue in too many places. However, the chapters demonstrate that the principles of religious human rights can no longer be ignored by any nation. In recent decades, virtually every nation has committed itself to international and domestic covenants that declare freedom of religion to be a fundamental right. Whatever the gap between principle and practice, it is a significant achievement for governments to recognize that people should be free to follow any religion, or no religion, without suffering discrimination.

To most Americans, religion and human rights are inextricably linked. The Declaration of Independence reflects our understanding that it is to the Creator that we should look for the origins of our rights, and therefore it seems only natural that many leading advocates of human rights are prominent members of religious communities. Yet we recognize that many atrocities have been and continue to be committed in the name of God. Because religion can be such a powerful force for good and evil, the protection of religious rights becomes critically important. How best to do this is a subject of debate, in the United States as well as in the rest of the world.

My own efforts in this area are channeled through The Carter Center. The Center's Conflict Resolution Program, in analyzing the more than thirty major wars taking place today, has determined that a failure to accommodate religious and ethnic differences is one of the foremost catalysts for violence. In Bosnia-Herzegovina, where the conflict is being waged among Muslims, Roman Catholics, and Orthodox Catholics, primary targets for destruction are churches and mosques. In Sudan, a major issue is whether Islamic law should apply to Christians and followers of traditional African beliefs. Our Human Rights Program has long been involved in seeking to protect victims of religious persecution. Now, working with the Law and Religion Program of Emory University, it is attempting to see if ways can be found to defuse religious conflicts before they result in violence.

This volume and its companion are important contributions to our understanding of religious human rights throughout the world. Through understanding, I hope will come improvement.

Introduction
Legal Dimensions of Religious Human Rights: Constitutional Texts

JOHAN D. VAN DER VYVER
Emory University

The United Nations seemingly succeeded in mustering universal support for the affirmation, testified to in the Preamble of its Charter[1] and in the Universal Declaration of Human Rights,[2] of "faith in fundamental human rights." Louis Henkin was perfectly right in proclaiming that: "[t]he idea of human rights is accepted in principle by all governments regardless of other ideology, regardless of political, economic, or social condition."[3]

All nations, large and small, those with commendable as well as the ones with deplorable track records in honoring the Organization's objective of promoting "universal respect for, and observance of, human rights and fundamental freedoms for all. . . ."[4] are *ad idem* in their stated commitment to the ideals embodied in the doctrine of human rights.

Jacques Maritain long ago sought to identify a certain public morality within a democratically constructed body politic, which he depicted as a kind of "*civic* or *secular* faith."[5] Perhaps a similar communal ethos, founded on the principle of human rights, has come to signify an international "secular faith." In that sense, Robert Traer unconditionally affirmed "faith in human rights" to be "a global concept."[6]

---

[1] Charter of the United Nations, 59 Stat. 1031, T.S. No. 993, 3 Bevans 1153, 1976 Y.B.U.N 1043.

[2] G.A. Res. 217 A (III) of 10 December 1958.

[3] Louis Henkin, The Rights of Man Today (Boulder/San Francisco, 1978), 28..

[4] U.N. Charter, art. 55(c).

[5] Jacques Maritain, *Man and the State* (Chicago, 1951), 110-111.

[6] Robert Traer, *Faith in Human Rights* (Washington, 1991), 216.

Included in the human rights values that thus acquired universal endorsement are the ones associated with the notion of religious freedom. In his chapter in this volume, Natan Lerner gives an impressive overview of such clauses in the leading international human rights instruments, which in general endorse the principle of religious freedom and non-discrimination on grounds of religious persuasion and penetrate almost the entire spectrum of the trans-national human rights agenda, such as gender issues, educational demands, employment practices and the plight of indigenous populations. The study concerning religious freedom undertaken by Special Rapporteur Arcot Krishnaswami in the late 1950s, and the culmination of efforts to promote religious human rights in the international arena as manifested in the UN's 1981 Declaration on Intolerance and of the Elimination of All Forms of Discrimination Based on Religion and Belief, received special attention in the Lerner essay and bear testimony of the universal significance of religiously based human rights concerns.

The universal appeal of human rights thinking also penetrated the world of religious institutions. In his informative survey on *Faith in Human Rights*, Traer set out to demonstrate that "human rights are the center of a global moral language that is being justified, elaborated, and advocated by members of different religious traditions and cultures."[7] He went on to proclaim: "This is true not merely in the West but also in Africa and Asia. It is true not only in the First and Second Worlds, where liberal and socialist human rights theories have evolved, but in the Third World as well. Jews, Christians, Muslims, Hindus, Buddhists, and advocates of religious traditions indigenous to Africa and Asia fundamentally agree about human rights."[8] In fact, it would be fair to endorse the judgment of Louis Henkin that "all major religions proudly lay claim to fathering" human rights[9]—but they do so on their own terms.

True enough, governments and religions alike would not want to be seen to contradict the salient appeal of human rights; yet, this universal adherence to its demands to a large extent signifies no more than rhetorical consensus.

Religion as the Basis of International Conflict

For many years, international politics was dominated by a power struggle that attended the East-West divide. An end to the Cold War that coincided with the collapse of the Soviet Union and the decline of social-

---

[7] Ibid., 10.

[8] Ibid.

[9] Henkin, *The Rights of Man Today*, xii.

ism in Eastern Europe, saw the emergence of a new dialectic in world relations: that between North and South.

As far as human rights are concerned, the polemics of South versus North are centered upon the question of economic and social demands. Emphasis in the developed regions of the world on the so-called "first generation" freedom rights provoked resentment of the developing South, whose main concerns are focussed on the second generation economic and social rights, and, as a matter of overriding urgency, on the third generation right to development. Dr. R.J. Vincent thus depicted the debate about human rights in North-South relations as a dispute between the "haves" and the "have-nots" of the world and one where "individualism and liberty are arranged against collectivism; civil and political rights against economic and social rights."[10]

At the same time, there is a new rivalry looming in international politics, founded, more or less, on an East-West contingent; and in this instance not centered upon the divergence of economic structures, but instead on the schism of religiously-based forces.[11] Eastern religions, with Islam in the lead, are increasingly questioning the Western perceptions of human rights and challenging the claim to prime authenticity of the liberal individualistic nuance of the human rights ideology as devised and understood in the West.

While Western traditions by and large founded the typical liberal perceptions of human rights on a secularized base, most Eastern proponents of human rights seek to construct an intimate link of the values embodied in that ideology with decidedly religious presuppositions. In the East, more so than in the West, human rights perceptions are accordingly conditioned by uncompromising tenets of religious belief. The result of these quite distinct points of departure—secular humanism in the West with a strong individualistic nuance, and religiously defined conditions of human rights observance—permeated the entire spectrum of particular rights, including the very notion of religious freedom per se.

Within the United Nations, the struggle for supremacy of different human rights perceptions has come to be marginally addressed in the debate as to the universality of human rights.

---

[10] R.J. Vincent, *Human Rights and International Relations* (Cambridge, 1986), 76. See in general, Rajni Kothari, "Human Rights as a North-South Issue," in Richard Pierre Claude & Burns H. Weston, eds., *Human Rights in the World Community: Issues and Actions* (Philadelphia, 1991), 134.

[11] See Peter Leuprecht, "Conflict Prevention and Alternative Forms of Dispute Resolution," in Kathleen E. Hamoney & Paul Mahoney, eds., *Human Rights in the Twenty-First Century: A Global Challenge* (Dordrecht/Boston/London, 1993), 959, 963 (singling out religious fundamentalism—not to be limited to Muslim fundamentalism—as one of several threats to the cause of human rights).

At the United Nations World Conference on Human Rights that was held in Vienna, Austria in June of 1993, the problem of universality, indivisibility, and interdependence of human rights emerged as an important stumbling block in East-West relations in the context, more precisely, of resentment on the part of Muslim-led "spoilers"[12] of attempts to enforce, throughout the world, the typical Western perceptions of human rights.[13] The East-West disputes that surfaced in Vienna acquired a particular dimension through its entanglement in the problem of religious fundamentalism. Particularly relevant in the present context are the conflicting views pertaining to the question as to the universality of human rights.

The principle proclaiming the universality of human rights is founded on the notion that all human rights apply uniformly and with equal force throughout the world. It thus opposes the doctrine of the so-called relativity of human rights, which maintains that in the application of human rights in concrete situations allowance should be made for particularities that attend cultural, ethnic or religious varieties. The principle of universality thus addresses the assumption that distinct cultural traditions or religious tenets provide justification for the denial to individual members of a group of certain basic human rights. It censures "adaptations" of human rights to suit non-libertarian practices founded on customs within indigenous, ethnic or religious communities.

Although the United Nations regime permits, in the language of the European human rights system, a "margin of appreciation"[14] in the practical application of human rights principles so as to accommodate ethnic, cultural and religious peculiarities, it does so only within the boundaries of basic human rights values. The Vienna Final Act thus proclaims:

> All human rights are universal, indivisible, interdependent and interrelated. The international community must treat human rights globally in a fair and equal manner, on the same footing, and with the same emphasis. While the significance of national and regional peculiarities and various historical, cultural and religious backgrounds must be borne in mind, it is the duty of

---

[12] Noticeable leaders in this field were Syria, Libya, Yemen, Iran, Iraq, Pakistan, India, Burma, China, Indonesia, Malysia and Cuba (mostly supported by Mexica and Colombia).

[13] Mr. Adrien-Claud Zoller, Director of the Geneva-based International Service Commission, published a particularly informative article outlining the events and controversies that attended the prelude to the World Conference. See Zoller, "The Political Context of the World Conference," *Human Rights Monitor* 21 (May 1993): 2-4.

[14] P. van Dijk and G.J.H. van 't Hoof, *Theory and Practice in the European Convention on Human Rights* (Denver/Boston, 1990), 585-606 .

> States, regardless of their political, economic and cultural systems, to promote and protect all human rights.[15]

There is one further aspect of the World Conference on Human Rights—also alluded to in the chapter in this volume by Jeremy Gunn—that requires special emphasis: the almost total absence of any reference to religious human rights. Religion featured most strongly in the NGO Forum, which coincided with the World Conference, in presentations of (mostly Muslim) human rights relativists; those who maintained that the norms of human rights as perceived in the West require adaptation to suit the distinct customs or scruples of indigenous, ethnic or religious communities: Human rights, it was claimed, must be adjusted to comply with the distinct demands of religious doctrine, and not *vice versa*; and when religious dogma differ, so too will the meaning attributed to particular human rights.

De Facto Relativism in Current Perceptions on Religious Human Rights

That is why—explains Said Arjomand in his contribution to this volume—Islamic countries are united in their insistence on relativism within the human rights arena: so as to uphold the dictates of Shari'a where it contradicts the accepted (Western) standards of human rights protection. It is worth noting in passing that state conduct of the United States renders that country as much prone to relativism as any Muslim community. This appears most vividly from the reservations, interpretations, and declarations that attended the ratification by the United States of the International Covenant on Civil and Political Rights in 1992,[16] exempting the U.S. from complying with every provision of the Covenant not in conformity with American perceptions and standards of human rights.[17]

Instead of uniformity in the definitions of human rights and of religious freedom, the world has come to know a radical diversity of perceptions as to these value structures. Cole Durham, in his historical and comparative analysis of religious liberty included in this volume, traced that diversity to several decisive forces: stability of the political regime, the nature and history of traditional relations between church and state,

---

[15] Vienna Declaration and Programme of Action, 25 June 1993, U.N. Doc. A/CONF 157/23, at Part I para. 5.

[16] Report of the Senate Committee on Foreign Relations, 102d Congress, 2nd Session, Senate Exec. Rep. 102-23, at 21-24 (1992).

[17] See M. Christian Green, "The "Matroishka" Strategy: US Evasion of the Spirit of the International Covenant on Civil and Political Rights," *South African Journal of Human Rights* 10 (1994): 357.

the degree of religious plurality within a community, the nature of the dominant religion and its commitment to or perception of religious liberty and tolerance, the history of interaction between religious groups, and the like. It therefore becomes necessary—as Hal Berman reminds us, in the context of the Russian experience—to evaluate religious human rights with a view to the positive law, moral theory, and historical contingencies of the places and countries where those rights are to be realized.

The Berman adage is borne out by several contributions included in this volume. Paul Mojzes thus points to political complications in the Balkans, cultivated by a tradition of distrust and repression, as the cause of rendering the realization of religious freedom and of sound state-church relations extremely problematic and dubious in that region. Reaction to the earlier repression of church and religion in Eastern Europe is likewise singled out by Tamás Földesi as a source of over-zealousness on the part of political authorities in the new democracies to regulate matters that ought to belong to the internal jurisdiction of the church.

These and other contributions also bear testimony, and contain striking details to show, that the dichotomy in the legal and political systems of the world is centered upon the fundamental question as to the function of the state in respect of religion and its relationship toward the institutional church or religious community. There is no single universal formula for reconciling religious rights and state authority, observes Judge John Noonan in his closing chapter to this volume. In their (historical) analysis of the American experiment in applying constitutional principles for the regulation of religious freedom, John Witte and Christy Green strikingly depict the theological forces that moulded that experiment and which culminated—perhaps through a misperception of those forces—in the adage of a separation of state and church which, as currently applied by the United States Supreme Court, seemingly inspires far more criticism than praise. A certain tradition in Germany, Martin Heckel tells us, prompted a legal arrangement of the interaction between state and church in that country that differs fundamentally from that which obtains in the United States. In Germany, the notion of religious freedom does not preclude the state from financing faculties of theology and religious education, from recognizing religious institutions as public-law corporations, from levying church taxes, from the sanctioning of religious holidays, or from providing for religious care in state prisons and in the military. Lourens du Plessis, commenting on the world's most recent bills of rights, explains how it came about that in the first democratic (interim) constitution of the Republic of South Africa the negotiators of that instrument deliberately decided not to erect a wall of separation between state and church but to construct a system of religious freedom that makes express allowance for religious observances in state and state-aided institutions and, in fact, for state-aided educational institutions founded on a distinct religious tradition. Peter Cumper's outline of the history and present state of affairs in regard to state/church relations in the United Kingdom—which includes establishment of the Church of England and proclaiming the monarch to be the defender of that faith—sketches a dispensation where the intertwinement of state and church takes on proportions that many might regard as a denial of religious freedom. Jeremy Gunn reminds us, however, that the institution of an established church (in this instance, the Lutheran Church in Sweden) was held not to violate the religion clauses of the European Convention of Human Rights. But then, again, Paul Sigmund seems to measure progress of the idea of religious freedom in Latin America with a view to the extent in which countries of that region, following Vatican II, have moved away from church establishment or the preferred status of certain religions.

The international community of states is not free from anomalies when it comes to the polemics of state and church relations. Israel is a case in point. There, according to Asher Maoz, the constitution does not proclaim a preferred state religion, but the practice and laws of Israel demonstrate quite the opposite.

Religious freedom finds itself under particular stress in countries where the state takes upon itself the function and power to enforce religious scruples. Dinah Shelton and Alexandre Kiss depict, with reference to Saudi Arabia, a perception of religious freedom that burdens the state with a competence to protect indigenous religions, which may be exemplified by the prohibition of apostasy in the Sudan and of proselytizing in Malaysia, or—to take an instance recorded in the chapter of Jeremy Gunn—the proscription of proselytizing in Greece. In Saudi Arabia, Said Arjomand tells us, the Basic Law of 1992 proclaimed Shari'a to be the law of the land, and there political authorities apply the state's power of the sword with full force to coerce subjects into religious submission and to punish conduct and beliefs regarded as acts of apostasy. Hal Berman gives the example of state resistance to foreign missionaries in Russia.

Intolerance seems to prevail in those countries where the functions of government are taken to include a special calling to uphold and to enforce religious scruples. Said Arjomand thus traces the persecution of Amadis in Pakistan and Baha'is in Iran to the theocratic constitutions of those countries. Other chapters in this volume reveal the many instances of such persecutions of religious dissidents by the powers that be. Shelton and Kiss record the banning of Jehovah's Witnesses in Indonesia and the repression of Amadis in Pakistan (who are even denied the right of being called Muslims). Michael Roan refers to NGO reports highlighting the repression of Buddhists in Vietnam and of Copts in the Sudan. James Finn depicts the neglect of religious human rights and of human rights violations in Cuba; David Little reminds the reader of the persecution of Baha'is in Iran, Jehovah's Witnesses in Singapore, the Tamil minority in Sri Lanka and the Buddhists of Tibet in China.

A special dimension of state-church relations emerges when political loyalties are founded on religious affiliation. David Little highlights such instances where conflicts that are essentially political in nature, such as those in Sri Lanka, Sudan and Tibet, acquire an apparent religious dimension due to the intertwinement of religious belief and ethnicity in those countries or regions. John Pobee, having alerted the reader to the multiplicity of religious affiliations in countries such as Nigeria, the Sudan, Ghana, and Namibia, notes the cultivation through that divide of political strife in the former two countries. Stanley Ibarra Muschett, writing about Central America, illustrates situations where dramatic changes in the religious demography of a country acquire political dimensions—often arising when religious sects that penetrated areas with a strong majoritarian religion begin to make political claims. To these examples may be added the current civil war in Bosnia-Herzegovina and other regions of the former Yugoslavia, and the bloody secessionist conflict in Chechnya.

The political dimensions of the spread of religion has also been particularly precarious in Africa. Makau wa Mutua depicts in his chapter opposition to proselytizing on that continent because of the destructive effects of the spread of religion upon indigenous African values. Evangelizing occurred in Africa while, in relation to traditional African religions, the playing fields were fundamentally unequal; and, instead of securing the peace advocated by the world's leading religions, the spread of Christianity and Islam was attended by colonization and violence and brought conflict within and between communities that had coexisted in relative tranquility.

Constitutional Arrangements of Church-State Relations

Legal perspectives of the state of religious human rights in the constitutional systems of the world require special emphasis of particular juridical mechanisms for the regulation of human rights with a religious base or substance. The constitutional mechanisms devised to this end will evidently differ in accordance with the premises of their founders as to the function of the state and the purport of the law in relation to religious belief and activity and concerning the institutional church.

Given the labyrinth of juridical and constitutional arrangements pertaining to religion, a feasible overview of these matters will be dependent on a credible classification of representative samples of the available material.

Classification is, as it were, in the eyes of the beholder. The classification of matters of law and religion preferred by Vernon van Dyke in his seminal work on *Human Rights, Ethnicity and Discrimination*[18]—distinguishing between systems where religious communities are afforded representation in government, those where the government supports religious activities (recognizing, for instance, the right of religious institutions to take care of education, or protecting religious communities against proselytizing), theocracies (where religion is the central feature of political life), and systems that recognize the autonomy of religious groups—was clearly informed by the subject-matter of that book.

Within the pages of this volume one finds several quite different points of departure applied by the respective authors to facilitate an understanding of the vast range of detail.

Paul Mojzes distinguishes, as a "theoretical framework" for various arrangements with a distinctly European origin and pertaining to religious human rights, (1) ecclesiastical absolutism, where one particular religion is given preferential treatment; (2) religious toleration, where the state is benign to all religions but affords preference to a particular dominant one; (3) secular absolutism, where all religions are rejected by the state in favor of a secular world view; and (4) pluralistic liberty, where the state is indifferent and neutral toward religion and non-religion alike.

Dinah Shelton and Alexandre Kiss classify different arrangements as to the relationship between state and religion with a view to (1) state control over religion; (2) state neutrality toward religion; (3) theocratic political perceptions, where a dominant religion controls the religious and secular spheres; (4) state hostility toward religion; and (5) division of authority between state and church by religious institutions being afforded autonomous control over certain activities.

Cole Durham has designed perhaps the most elaborate "comparative model for analyzing religious liberty." Based on "threshold conditions for religious liberty" (minimal pluralism, economic stability, political legitimacy and respect for the rights of those with different beliefs), he distinguishes among (1) absolute theocracies; (2) cooperationist regimes, where the state, without granting a special status to dominant churches,

---

[18] (Westport, CT, 1985), 53-77.

cooperate closely with religious institutions in various ways; (3) separationist regimes, which insist on a more rigid separation of church and state; (4) instances of inadvertent insensitivity, where the political authorities, though not inspired by deliberate anti-religious sentiments, remain unaware of the religious implications of their regulations; and (5) cases where the repositories of political power display hostility toward religion and embark upon persecution of particularly smaller religions.

For purposes of the following survey of legal provisions of state-church relations, four distinct dogmatic presuppositions reflected in the constitutions of the world will be our guide: As extreme positions, (1) the American notion of the impermeable wall between state and church, and (2) the Islamic Shari'a proclaiming the identity of law and religion; and somewhere in between, (3) the scholastic adage of subsidiarity alongside (4) the typical Calvinistic doctrine of sphere sovereignty.

The Separation of Law and Religion. There are many countries in the world that testify in their constitutions to being secular states: Angola;[19] Benin;[20] Burkina Faso;[21] Burundi;[22] Cameroon;[23] Chad;[24] the Congo;[25] France;[26] Guinea;[27] Guinea-Bissau;[28] Guyana;[29] India;[30] Ireland;[31] Ivory Coast;[32] Japan;[33] Kazakhstan;[34] Kyrghyzstan;[35] Madagascar;[36] Mali;[37] Mozambique;[38] Namibia;[39] Nicaragua;[40] Niger;[41] Nigeria;[42] Rus-

[19] Article 7 of the Constitution of the People's Republic of Angola (1980).

[20] Article 2 of the Constitution of the Republic of Benin (1990).

[21] Article 31 of the Constitution of Burkina Faso (1991).

[22] Article 1 of the Constitution of Burundi (1961).

[23] Article 1(2) of the Constitution of the Republic of Cameroon (1961), as amended by Law No. 84-1 (1984).

[24] Article 1 of the Constitution of the Republic of Chad (1989).

[25] Article 1 of the Constitution of the Republic of The Congo (1992).

[26] Article 2 of the Constitution of France (1958).

[27] Article 1 of the Federal Law of the Second Republic of Guinea (1992).

[28] Article 1 of the Constitution of the Republic of Guinea-Bissau (1984).

[29] Article 1 of the Constitution of the Co-operative Republic of Guyana (1980).

[30] Preamble to the Constitution of India (1949).

[31] Article 44.2.2. of the Constitution of Ireland (1937).

[32] Article 2 of the Constitution of the Republic of Côte d'Ivoire (1960).

[33] Article 20 of the Constitution of Japan (1947).

[34] Preamble to the Constitution of the Republic of Kazakhstan (1993).

[35] Article 1 of the Constitution of the Kyrghyz Republic (1993).

[36] Article 39 of the Constitution of the Democratic Republic of Madagascar (1975).

[37] Article 1 of the Constitution of the Republic of Mali (1974).

[38] Article 9 of The Constitution of the People's Republic of Mozambique (1975).

[39] Article 1(1) of the Constitution of the Republic of Namibia (1990).

[40] Article 14 of the Constitution of Nicaragua (1986).

[41] Article 6 of the Constitution of Niger (1960).

sia;[43] Sao Tome and Principes;[44] Senegal;[45] Togo;[46] Turkey;[47] Turkmenistan;[48] and Zaire.[49] There are those which in a similar vein proclaim their neutrality in respect of religion: Albania;[50] Australia;[51] Ireland;[52] Moldova;[53] Paraguay;[54] Slovakia;[55] and Spain.[56] And then there are the ones that expressly provide for the separation of state and church: Angola;[57] Brazil;[58] Cuba;[59] Ethiopia;[60] Gabon;[61] Guinea-Bissau;[62] Hungary;[63] Kazakhstan;[64] South Korea;[65] Latvia;[66] Liberia;[67] Macedonia;[68] Mexico;[69] Mongolia;[70] Mozambique;[71] the Philippines;[72] Poland;[73] Portugal;[74] Russia;[75] and the United States of America.

---

42 Article 10 of the Constitution of the Republic of Nigeria (1975).

43 Article 14 of the Constitution of the Russian Federation (1992).

44 Article 1(6) of the Constitution of the Democratic Republic of Sao Tome and Principes (1975).

45 Article 1 of the Constitution of the Republic of Senegal (1963).

46 Article 1 of the Constitution of the Fourth Republic of Togo (1992).

47 Article 2 of the Constitution of the Republic of Turkey (1982).

48 Article 1 of the Constitution of Turkmenistan (1992).

49 Article 1 of the Constitution of the Republic of Zaire (1978).

50 Article 37 of the Constitution of Albania (1976).

51 Preamble to, and sec. 116 of, the Constitution of Australia (1900).

52 Article 44.2.2. of the Constitution of Ireland (1937).

53 Article 5(2) of the Constitution of the Republic of Moldova (1994).

54 Article 24 of the Constitution of the Republic of Paraguay (1992).

55 Article 1 of the Constitution of the Slovak Republic (1992).

56 Article 16(3) of the Constitution of Spain (1978), but with special mention of the State maintaining "the appropriate relations of cooperation with the Catholic Church and other denominations."

57 Article 7 of the Constitution of the People's Republic of Angola (1980).

58 Article 19 of the Constitution of the Federal Republic of Brazil (1988).

59 Article 8 of the Constitution of the Republic of Cuba (1976, as amended in 1992).

60 Article 46(3) of the Constitution of the People's Democratic Republic of Ethiopia (1987).

61 Article 2 of the Constitution of Gabon (1975).

62 Article 6(1) of the Constitution of the Republic of Guinea-Bissau (1984).

63 Article 63(2) of the Constitution of Hungary (1949, as amended in 1989).

64 Article 58 of the Constitution of the Republic of Kazakhstan (1994).

65 Article 20(2) of the Constitution of the Republic of Korea (1980).

66 Article 35 of the Constitutional Law of the Republic of Latvia (1991).

67 Article 14 of the Constitution of Liberia (1984).

68 Article 19 of the Constitution of the Republic of Macedonia (1991).

69 Article 130 of the Constitution of the United Mexican States (1917, as amended in 1992).

70 Article 9 of the Constitution of Mongolia (1992).

71 Article 19 of the Constitution of the People's Republic of Mozambique (1975).

72 Section 6 of the Constitution of the Philippines (1987).

73 Article 82(2) of the Constitution of Poland (1989).

The Constitution of the United States of America succinctly proclaims in its First Amendment: "Congress shall make no law respecting the establishment of religion, or prohibiting the free exercise thereof." The two fundamental components of this provision, the Establishment Clause and the Free Exercise Clause, were both incorporated into the Fourteenth Amendment so as to also make them enforceable against state legislatures and administrations.[76] Their combined meaning was held to create "a wall of separation between state and church,"[77] which—in the celebrated words of Mr. Justice Black—"must be kept high and impregnable."[78]

Justice Black, speaking for the majority in the decisive case of *Everson v Board of Education*,[79] articulated what he regarded as the minimum impact of the Establishment Clause:

> Neither a state nor the Federal Government can set up a church. Neither can pass laws which aid one religion, aid all religions, or prefer one religion over another. Neither can force nor influence a person to go to or to remain away from church against his will or force him to profess a belief or disbelief in any religion. No person can be punished for entertaining or professing religious beliefs or disbeliefs, for church attendance or nonattendance. No tax in any amount, large or small, can be levied to support any religious activities or institutions, whatever they may be called, or whatever form they may adopt to teach or practice religion. Neither a state nor the Federal Government can, openly or secretly, participate in the affairs of any religious organization or group and *vice versa*.[80]

It is probably true to say that separatism in the strict sense took the religion clauses of the First Amendment well beyond the simple meaning

---

[74] Article 41(4) of the Constitution of Portugal (1982).

[75] Article 14 of the Constitution of the Russian Federation (1992).

[76] *Cantwell v. Connecticut*, 310 U.S. 296 (1940), in relation to the Free Exercise Clause; and *Everson v. Board of Education*, 330 U.S. 1 (1947), in relation to the Establishment Clause.

[77] The metaphor of "a wall of separation" is commonly attributed to Thomas Jefferson. See *Reynolds v. United States*, 98 U.S. 145, 164 (1879) (quoting Jefferson's letter of January 1, 1802 to the Danbury Baptist Association); A.P. Stokes and Leo Pfeffer, *Church and State in the United States* (New York, 1964), 335. It actually originated from a letter of Roger Williams to John Cotton, in which he referred to the "wall of separation between the garden of the Church and the wilderness of the world." See *The Complete Writings of Roger Williams* (n.p., 1963), 1: 392; on the origin and subsequent interpolations of the paradigm of "a wall of separation," see Mark D. Howe, *The Garden and the Wilderness: Religion and Government in American Constitutional History* (Chicago, 1965).

[78] Everson, at 18.

[79] Ibid.

[80] Ibid., 15-16.

and historical context of their wording.[81] It is also evident that American jurisprudence thus far has failed to come to terms with the seemingly simple directives of the religion clauses. Conflicts between the Establishment Clause and the Free Exercise Clause, inconsistencies in the final outcome of cases under either of these headings, and failure of the courts to maintain absolute neutrality in relation to religion, lead one to conclude—in the words of John Witte—that "[t]he U.S. Supreme Court has ensnared the First Amendment religion clauses in a network of antinomies."[82]

Application of the separatist position in the area of education has resulted in judgments which foreign observers might find difficult to understand. Particularly damnatory was the censure of Chief Justice Warren Burger in his dissenting judgment in *Aguilar v. Felton*[83]—a case in which the Court placed an embargo on the use of federal funds earmarked for elementary and secondary education to pay the salaries of public school employees who taught at parochial schools: "Rather than showing the neutrality the Courts boast of, it exhibits nothing less than hostility toward religion and the children who attend church-sponsored schools."

The U.S. Supreme Court has thus outlawed religious instruction on public school premises,[84] and declared unconstitutional state legislation that required the recitation of prayers and Bible reading in public schools.[85] It outlawed a daily period of silence in public schools for purposes of mediation or voluntary prayers,[86] and struck down a law requiring the Ten Commandments to be posted on the walls of public school classrooms.[87] It is not constitutional, decided the Court, to require the teaching of "creation science" in public schools whenever evolution was taught,[88] and state subsidies of programs and services from which secular schools would benefit are likewise constitutionally taboo.[89]

---

[81] See Robert L. Cord, "Church-State Separation: Restoring the 'No Preference' Doctrine of the First Amendment," *Harvard Journal of Law and Public Policy* 9 (1986): 129.

[82] John Witte, Jr., "The Integration of Religious Liberty," *Michigan Law Review* 90 (1992): 1363.

[83] 473 U.S. 402, 420 (1985).

[84] *McCollum v. Board of Education*, 333 U.S. 203 (1948).

[85] *Engel v. Vitale*, 370 U.S. 421; *Abington School District v. Schempp*, 374 U.S. 203 (1963).

[86] *Wallace v. Jaffree*, 472 U.S. 38 (1985).

[87] *Stone v. Graham*, 449 U.S. 39 (1980).

[88] *Edwards v. Aguillard*, 482 U.S. 578 (1987).

[89] See, for instance, *Lemon v. Kurtzman*, 403 U.S. 602 (1971) and *Aguilar v. Felton* (proscribing salary subventions to lay teachers in parochial schools); *Levitt v. Committee for Public Education*, 413 U.S. 472 (1973) (outlawing grants to non-public schools to reimburse them for expenses of examination and inspection services); *Committee for Public Education v. Nyquist*, 413 U.S. 756 (1973) and *Sloan v. Lemon*, 413 U.S. 825 (1973) (declaring unconstitu-

It was decided, on the other hand, that release time for public school students to receive religious instruction off public property was constitutional, provided no public funding was involved.[90] Religious colleges were allowed to use federal funds for capital projects, provided the facilities concerned were not used for sectarian purposes.[91] A program to aid a blind student in vocational education was upheld even though the student received instruction at a Christian college.[92] A religiously motivated rule prohibiting dancing by students on the school grounds was held not to be unconstitutional.[93]

In matters not related to education as such, application of the religion clauses is equally puzzling. For instance, in *County of Allegheny v. American Civil Liberties Union*,[94] the U.S. Supreme Court invalidated the display of a creche scene at a county courthouse, and at the same time upheld the display of a menorah next to a Christmas tree on city premises.[95] In *Bowen v. Kendrick*,[96] a federal grant to public and non-profit private organizations for services and research in the area of premarital adolescent sexual relations and pregnancy was found to be constitutionally in order, even though religious organizations were involved in conducting the counselling and education programs (subject to the proviso that the funds may not be used for family planning services or for promoting abortions); however, the Court at the same time remanded the matter for further consideration of whether the statute authorizing the grant in its *de facto* application violated the Establishment Clause.

Many reasons have been tendered to explain the difficulties experienced by American courts in producing a clear principle for defining the

---

tional the subsidizing of capital programs that have the effect of advancing the religious mission of sectarian schools and affording tax concessions to parents of perochial school children); *Meek v. Pittenger*, 421 U.S. 349 (1975); and *Wolmar v. Walter*, 433 U.S. 229 (1977) (striking down the provision to non-public schools of auxiliary services and loans of instructional material and equipment other than text-books—the loan of text-books was held not to violate the Establishment Clause, but the Supreme Court of California, in *California Teachers Association v. Riles*, 29 Cal. 3d 794; 632 P.2d 953 (1981), came to the opposite conclusion); *Grand Rapids School District v. Ball*, 473 U.S. 373 (1985) (prohibiting certain programs that provided classes, conducted by full-time or part-time school teachers, to non-public school students).

[90] *Zorach v. Clauson*, 343 U.S. 306 (1952).

[91] *Tilton v. Richardson*, 403 U.S. 672 (1971); see also *Hunt v. McNair*, 413 U.S. 734 (1973); *Roemer v. Board of Public Works of Maryland*, 426 U.S. 736 (1976).

[92] *Witters v. Washington Department of Services for the Blind*, 474 U.S. 481 (1986).

[93] *Clayton v. Place*, 884 F.2d. 192 (8th Cir., 1989). The petition for a rehearing was denied by the Court of Appeals for the 8th Circuit (884 F.2d. 376 (1989)), and certiorari was denied by the U.S. Supreme Court (494 U.S. 1081).

[94] 492 U.S. 573 (1989).

[95] Earlier, in *Lynch v. Donnelly*, 465 U.S. 668 (1984), the display of Christmas symbols by municipal authorities was held not to be unconstitutional.

[96] 487 U.S. 589 (1988).

impact of the religion clauses when applied to empirical contingencies and to achieve consistency in their application in practice. Historical analysis will show that from the outset, conflicting views prevailed amongst the personalities who, according to popular belief, constituted the key figures in the struggle of the seventeenth and eighteenth centuries for religious freedom in North America: The one view, represented by Roger Williams and James Madison, holding that the internal sovereignty of religious institutions ought to be respected by the state and that the government should abstain from enforcing religious scruples; and the other, represented by Thomas Jefferson, placing the emphasis upon protecting the state from religious influences.

Roger Williams (1603-1683), the founder of Rhode Island, persecuted for religious reasons in England and Massachusetts, and consecutively an Anglican, Baptist, and a Seeker, strongly believed that governments should not be called upon to enforce religious laws. According to the testimony of Stokes, Williams believed that "the State had no jurisdiction over the conscience of men."[97] He regarded the church as a distinct social entity, a voluntary association of people centered upon a particular objective and with its own legal personality: "Its internal affairs were no concern of the government so long as its members kept the peace and performed their obligations to the community at large."[98]

James Madison (1751-1836), reputed to have been the "leading architect of the religious clauses of the First Amendment"[99] and the fourth President of the United States, shared Williams's concerns regarding state interference in matters of religion. In the first paragraph of his well-known *Memorial and Remostrance against Religious Assessments*, he wrote:

> Above all are they to be considered as retaining an "equal title to the free exercise of Religion according to the dictates of conscience." Whilst we assert for ourselves a freedom to embrace, to profess and to observe the Religion which we believe to be of divine origin, we cannot deny an equal freedom to those whose minds have not yet yielded to the evidence which has convinced us. If this freedom be abused, it is an offense against God, not against man: To God, therefore, not to men, must an account be rendered. . . .[100]

At the First Congress called to consider the Bill of Rights, Madison reiterated that "there is not a shadow of a right in the general government to

---

[97] Stokes and Pfeffer, *Church and State*, 195.

[98] Ibid., 16.

[99] *Flast v. Cohen*, 392 U.S. 83, 103 (1968).

[100] Quoted by Mr. Justice Douglas (dissenting) in *Walz v. Tax Commission*, 397 U.S. 664, 705 (1970).

intermeddle with religion."[101] In a note in the *Harvard Law Review* it was said of Madison: "He believed . . . that both religion and government could best achieve their respective purposes if each was free within its proper area from interference by the other."[102] Careful consideration of Madison's views, statements and actions led Robert L. Cord to conclude that he and other supporters of the prohibitions concerned simply "wished to deny Congress the power to establish a national religion."[103]

Thomas Jefferson (1743-1826), a man with no religious affiliations and a major proponent of the "wall theory," was not so much engaged in protecting religious institutions against state interference as safeguarding the state from religious influences. He strongly opposed the status of the Episcopal Church as the established church of the state of Virginia and was particularly active in securing its disestablishment in 1786. This experience, perhaps more than anything else, convinced him of the need to separate state and church absolutely and completely.

There are many reasons in logic, history, practicality, and propriety why the U.S. Supreme Court in interpreting the religion clauses of the First Amendment might have sided with the socio-political convictions of Williams and Madison rather than with the radicalism of Mr. Jefferson. For one thing, Jefferson was not even there when the Bill of Rights was enacted. However, that was not to be. Instead, American jurisprudence paid lip-service to the wall paradigm while at the same time attempting to do justice to the divergent sentiments of both adversary camps.

John Witte thus attributed the dichotomy in American jurisprudence pertaining to the religion clauses to the influence of the separatist position of the evangelical and enlightenment traditions respectively.[104] Evangelical separatists, according to his testimony, "sought to free religion and the church from the intrusion of politics and the state,"[105] without wanting to sacrifice the influence of religion and the church upon politics; and, furthermore, not professing to forfeit the kind of state protection and privileges that had been afforded to the established church, but claiming such protection and privileges for all churches on an equal basis.[106] Enlightenment separatists, on the other hand, "sought to free re-

---

101 Quoted by Mr Justice Rutledge (dissenting) in *Everson*.

102 Note, "Towards a Constitutional Definition of Religion," *Harvard Law Review* 91 (1978): 1056, 1057.

103 Robert L. Cord, *Separation of Church and State: Historical Fact and Current Fiction* (New York, 1985), 15-16. See also the judgment of Mr. Justice Rehnquist (dissenting) *in Wallace v. Jaffree*, at 93-99.

104 John Witte, Jr."The Theology and Politics of the First Amendment Religion Clauses: A Bicentennial Essay," *Emory Law Journal* 40 (1990): 489, 494-95.

105 Ibid., 494.

106 Ibid. 494-95.

ligion and the church from the intrusions of politics and the state," while at the same time also seeking "to free politics and the state from intrusions of religion and the church."[107]

It is more important to note, though, that the Jeffersonian adage proceeds on the fallacious assumption that church and state, and law and religion, can indeed be isolated from one another in watertight compartments. That is not at all the case. Hal Berman on many occasions emphasized the religious, and in particular Christian, base of law in general and of specific legal standards, including those that obtain in the United States.[108] Chief Justice Burger, in *Lynch v. Donnelly*, pointed out that "the metaphor [of a wall between state and church] itself is not a wholly accurate description of the practical aspects of the relationship that in fact exists between church and state."[109] In *Aguilar v. Felton* he proclaimed:

> We have frequently recognized that some interaction between church and state is unavoidable, and that an attempt to eliminate all contact between the two would be both futile and undesirable.[110]

The intertwinement of state and church, and the inner cohesion of law and religion, constitute an undeniable and inescapable fact of actual reality. To again cite the contribution of Judge Noonan elsewhere in this volume: The neutrality option still requires the state to decide what is religion and what is not. Any constitutional arrangement that attempts to escape the implications of this *de facto* state of affairs will inevitably result in all kinds of anomalies.

Attempts of the U.S. Supreme Court to reduce the Establishment Clause to a single and consistent principle of application has thus far been unsuccessful. In *Lemon v. Kurtzman*, a three-pronged test was deduced from certain earlier judgments of the U.S. Supreme Court to establish whether a legislature has retained the measure of neutrality required by the Establishment Clause.[111] In order to withstand constitutional scrutiny, the enactment in question: (1) must have a secular purpose; (2) must have a principal or primary effect that neither advances nor inhibits re-

---

107 Ibid. 495.

108 Harold J. Berman, "The Interaction of Law and Religion," *Capital University Law Review* 8 (1979): 346; id., "Religious Foundations of Law in the West: An Historical Perspective," *Journal of Law and Religion* 1 (1983): 1.

109 *Lynch*, at 673.

110 *Aguilar*, at 420.

111 In *Schempp*, at 222-23, the Court initially laid down for this purpose a twofold test. See also *Board of Education v. Allen*, 392 U.S. 236 (1968). The third leg of the test emerged subsequently from *Walz*, at 74.

ligion; and (3) must avoid excessive governmental entanglement with religion.[112]

John Witte described the *Lemon* criteria of establishment as "unpursuasive in theory and unworkable in practice."[113] Justice O'Connor must have been of the same mind. In a series of judgments, commencing with her concurring opinion in *Lynch v. Donnelly*, she consequently transcribed the first two components of the three-pronged *Lemon* test.[114] Under the pretense of simply clarifying the establishment clause doctrine,[115] she in fact transformed the first leg of the test into an inquiry as to whether the government's *purpose* was to endorse religion;[116] and she restated the second prong of the *Lemon* test to mean "that a government practice not have the effect of communicating a message of government endorsement or disapproval of religion."[117] The question here is whether an objective observer, acquainted with the text, legislative history and implementation of a statute, would receive a message of the legislature having endorsed the effects of the statute.[118] In *Edwards v. Aguillard*, Justice Brennan, writing for the majority, endorsed Justice O'Connor's secular purpose requirement;[119] and in *Bowen v. Kendrick*, Chief Justice Rehnquist afforded the U.S. Supreme Court's sanction to Justice O'Connor's "no endorsement" criterion. Critical comment pertaining to the O'Connor alternative already indicates that it no more than shifted the goal posts to afford slightly greater latitude for religious interests to flourish in the United States.

Similar attempts to overcome the problem of religious freedom in the United States are numerous. Some years ago, Professor Philip Kurland suggested that dichotomies in the application of the religion clauses may be overcome by subjecting their application to the norm against discrimination:

---

112 *Lemon v. Kurtzman*, at 612-13; see also *Nyquist*; *Aguilar v. Felton*; *Bowen v. Kendrick*; *Estate of Thornton v. Caldor*, 472 U.S. 703 (1985);

113 Witte, "The Integration of Religious Liberty," 1364.

114 Lynch, at 687-89 (O'Connor, J., concurring); and see Carl H. Esbeck, "The *Lemon* Test: Should it be Retained, Reformulated or Rejected?" *Notre Dame Journal of Law, Ethics, and Public Policy* 4 (1990): 513; Joel T. Ireland, "The Transfiguration of the *Lemon* Test: Church and State Reign Supreme in *Bowen v. Kendrick*," *Arizona Law Review* 32 (1990): 365; Douglas C. Shimonek, "Using the *Lemon* Test as Camouflage: Avoiding the Establishment Clause," *William Mitchell Law Review* 16 (1990): 835.

115 *Lynch*, at 687 (O'Connor, J., concurring).

116 Ibid., 690 (O'Connor, J., concurring); see also *Wallace v. Jaffree*, at 69; *Edwards v. Aguillard*, at 585.

117 *Lynch*, at 692 (O'Connor, J., concurring); see also *Estate of Thornton v. Caldor*, at 711 (O'Connor, J., concurring).

118 *Lynch*, at 692-93 (O'Connor, J., concurring).

119 *Edwards v. Aguillard*, at 585.

> The proper construction of the religion clauses of the first amendment is that the freedom and separation clauses should be read as a single precept that government cannot utilize religion as a standard for action or inaction because these clauses prohibit classification in terms of religion either to confer a benefit or to impose a burden.[120]

This brings one back to the roots of the American dilemma: Failure to appreciate and/or to accommodate the empirical symbiosis, or—as Hal Berman prefers to call it—the "dialectical interdependence," of law and religion.[121]

The entanglement test, first enunciated in *Walz v. Tax Commission*, signifies acknowledgement by the Court of the intertwinement of state and church referred to earlier. In *Lemon v. Kurtzman*, the Court accordingly recognized that the "wall of separation" between state and church had become a "blurred, indistinct and variable barrier depending on all the circumstances of a particular relationship."[122] It stated that when called upon to decide whether the entanglement in any given case was excessive, the courts must take into account the "character and purpose of the institutions that are benefitted, the nature of the aid that the state provides, and the resulting relationship between the government and the religious authority."[123]

The U.S. Supreme Court could thus far find no fixed or principle-bound criterion for identifying excessiveness in the entanglement of state and church. In *Roemer v. Board of Public Works of Maryland* it was said in this regard: "There is no exact science in gauging the entanglement of church and state."[124]

This is undoubtedly so, but legal certainty could be served by facing up to the intertwinement of state and church as a normal fact of empirical reality and by coping with that fact of life in view of the function of the law to regulate, and of courts of law to adjudicate, conflicts that might arise from the co-existence of different persons and distinct social entities within one and the same body politic.

One final example will suffice to illustrate unbecoming state practice that might emerge from strict separation of state and church. It is a vital function of government to resolve, through its judicial arm, disputes in society. That, in the final analysis, is what "law and order" is all about. The semblance of religious neutrality in the United States has, however,

---

[120] P. Kurland, "Religion and the Law: Of Church and State and the Supreme Court," *University of Chicago Law Review* 29 (1961): 1, 6.

[121] Harold J. Berman, *The Interaction of Law and Religion* (Nashville, 1974), 78.

[122] *Lemon v. Kurtzman*, at 614.

[123] Ibid., 615.

[124] *Roemer*, at 766.

restrained the courts in the legitimate exercise of that function of state authority. Whenever an interdenominational quarrel or a conflict of interests between a church and any of its members cannot be resolved without an inquiry into doctrinal issues, civil courts decline to exercise jurisdiction in the matter.[125]

Identity of Law and Religion. The Universal Islamic Declaration of Human Rights of 1981 proudly proclaimed in its Preamble that "Islam gave to mankind an ideal code of human rights fourteen centuries ago."[126] An Islamic politician from Pakistan explained:

> When Muslims speak about human rights in Islam, they mean rights bestowed by Allah the exalted in the Holy Koran; rights that are divine, eternal, universal, and absolute; rights that are guaranteed and protected through the Shariah.[127]

In Islam there is no divide between state and church, and law and religion signifies one and the same modality of life. Donna Arzt thus noted: "Islamic law ... is a branch of a religious system, not a separate body of knowledge;"[128] and Ann Mayer, referring to the Islamic adage: *"al-Islam din wa dawla"* ("Islam is religion and State"), pointed out that "religion and the State are one in any truly Islamic system."[129]

The implications of this perception of the divine source of law, and of the identity of law and religion, are indeed startling. "It would be heretical," writes Abdullahi An-Na'im, "for a Muslim who believes that *Shariah* is the final and ultimate formulation of the law of God to maintain that any aspect of that law is open to revision and reformulation by mere mortal and fallible human beings. To do so is to allow human beings to correct what God has decreed."[130] Ann Mayer, again, pointed out that

---

[125] See *Watson v. Jones*, 80 U.S. (13 Wall.) 679 (1871); *Kedroff v. St. Nicholas Cathedral*, 344 U.S. 94 (1952); *Presbyterian Church v. Hull*, 393 U.S. 440 (1969); *Md. & Va. Churches v. Sharpsburg Church*, 396 U.S. 367 (1970); *Serbian Eastern Orthodox Diocese v. Milivojevich*, 426 U.S. 696 (1976). In *Jones v. Wolf*, 443 U.S. 595 (1979), a majority of the Court decided that a property dispute emanating from a church schism could indeed be decided on "neutral principles" and the Court consequently exercised jurisdiction to resolve the dispute.

[126] *Universal Islamic Declaration of Human Rights* (London, 1981).

[127] Khan Bahadur Khan, "The World of Islam," in *Proceedings of the Third World Congress on Religious Liberty* (Irla, 1989), 33, at 37.

[128] Donna E. Arzt, "The Application of International Human Rights Law in Islamic States," *Human Rights Quarterly* 12 (1990): 202, 203.

[129] Ann Elizabeth Mayer, "Law and Religion in the Muslim Middle East," *American Journal of Comparative Law* 35 (1987): 127, 130.

[130] Abdullahi A. An-Na'im, "Religious Minorities under Islamic Law and the Limits of Cultural Relativism," *Human Rights Quarterly* 9 (1987): 1, 10.

"whenever there is conflict between Islamic and international law [of human rights], Muslims are bound to follow their religious law."[131]

In seeking to uncover the constitutional status of religious human rights in Muslim countries, one must bear in mind that there is no uniformity in those countries as far as the practical manifestations of the Islamic perception of law and religion are concerned. In fact, after the death of the Prophet, there never was an "Islamic State" in the true sense where the government is constituted according to Islamic requirements and which is universally recognized by all Muslims.[132] Saudi Arabia perhaps comes closest to the traditional political arrangement where a single monarch rules and an *'uluma* class interprets the law in accordance with traditional doctrines of construction.[133] Those states which profess a special commitment to the doctrines of Islam, will be included in the present survey. Given the diversities that obtain in those states, one must inevitably resort to the art of stereotyping—which, like all generalizations, are bound to be inaccurate.

Several Muslim states testify in their constitutions to the overriding sovereignty of Allah. In the Preamble to the Constitution of the Islamic Republic of Pakistan (1973), it is thus proclaimed:

> Whereas sovereignty over the entire Universe belongs to Almighty Allah alone, and the authority to be exercised by the people of Pakistan within the limits prescribed by Him is a sacred trust. . . .[134]

It is also common practice for Muslim states to proclaim Islam to be the official state religion.[135] The Constitution of Yemen proclaims

---

131 Ann Elizabeth Mayer, "Current Muslim Thinking on Human Rights," in Abdullahi Ahmed An-Na'im & Francis M. Deng, eds., *Human Rights in Africa* (Washington, 1990), 133, at 136..

132 Ibid., 134.

133 Ibid.

134 See also art. 2(1) and 56 of the Constitution of the Islamic State of Iran (1979).

135 See, for example, art. 2 of the Constitution of the Republic of Afghanistan (1990); art. 2 of the Constitution of Algeria (1989); art. 2 of the Connstitution of Bahrain (1973); art. 2 of the Constitution of the People's Republic of Bangladesh (1972); Preamble to the Constitution of the Federal Islamic Republic of the Comores (1992), and see also id., art. 82 (rendering immutable the Islamic character of the state); art. 2 of the Constitution of the Arab Republic of Egypt (1980); art. 2 of the Constitution of Jordan (1952); art. 2 of the Constitution of Kuwait (1962); art. 2 of the Constitutional Proclamation of Libya (1969); art. 3 of the Federal Constitution of Malaysia (1963); art 3 of the Constitution of Maldives (1968); art. 5 of the Constitution of the Islamic Republic of Mauritania (1991); art. 6 of the Constitution of the Kingdom of Morocco (1972); art. 2 of the Constitution of the Islamic Republic of Pakistan (1973); art. 1 of the Constitution of Qatar (1970); art. 5 of the Constitution of the Kingdom of Saudi Arabia (1992) (instructing the sons of the Kingdom's founder to rule "under the guidance of the Holy Qu'ran and the Prophet's Sunnah"), and see also id., art. 7; art. 3 of the Constitution of the Democratic Republic of Somalia (1979); art. 3 of the Constitution of the Syrian Arab Republic

"defence of religion" to be a "sacred duty."[136] In some instances a particular sect of the Muslim faith is given preferential status. Article 12 of the Constitution of the Islamic Republic of Iran thus proclaims *Twelver Shi'ism* to be the country's official religion (with express testimony of tolerance in respect of certain other Muslim sects); and in Brunei Darussalam the established religion was proclaimed to be the *Shafeite* sect of the Muslim religion.[137]

There are four noticeable exceptions to the rule of Muslim states proclaiming Islam to be the established religion: Libya, Turkey, Syria and the Sudan.[138] In 1977, President Quahdhdafi of Libya, who gained power in 1969, replaced the Constitution of that country[139] with a "declaration on the power of the people," which purported to abolish the State so that, allegedly, the masses could rule themselves. Turkey under the reign of Kemal Atatürk (1923-38) opted for becoming a secular state, and Syria in its Constitution of 1973 also elected not to proclaim an established religion. The Sudan has been in a state of turmoil since the Civil War between North and South flared up in 1983 and, because that turmoil and Civil War was sparked by President Jaafer Mohammed al-Nemery's policy of Islamization, the question of a State religion was left open in the country's transitional Constitution of 1985.

In spite of the proclamation of an established religion, most Muslim states expressly uphold in their respective constitutions the principle of religious freedom and non-discrimination on basis of religion.[140] Article 35 of the Algerian Constitution succinctly provides: "The freedom of conscience and the freedom of opinion are inviolable;" Article 25(3) of the Syrian Constitution guarantees equality before the law of all citizens in their rights and duties, and article 35(1) asserts that "freedom of faith is paramount. The State respects all religions." Article 46 of the Egyptian Constitution states: "The State shall guarantee the freedom of belief and the freedom to practice religious rites," and guarantees in article 40

(1973); art. 1 of the Constitution of the Republic of Tunisia (1959); art. 7 of the Constitution of the United Arab Emirates (1971); and art. 1 of the Constitution of the Republic of Yemen (1994).

136 Article 59 of the Constitution of the Republic of Yemen (1994).

137 Section 3(1), read with the definition of "Muslim Religion" in sec. 2, of the Constitution of Brunei Darussalam (1984).

138 See Mayer, "Law and Religion in the Muslim Middle East," 135-38. Mayer also mentioned Saudi Arabia in the present context because, at the time when her article appeared, that country had no constitution other than the Qu'ran. Saudi Arabia did, however, enact a constitution in 1992, which does proclaim the Kingdom to be a Muslim state.

139 Article 2 of the Constitution of Lybia (1969) did proclaim Islam to be the religion of the State.

140 See Arzt, "The Application of International Human Rights Law," 223-24; An-Na'im, "Religious Minorities," 9.

equality before the law of all citizens, without discrimination due to religion, and so on.[141] In many instances, the constitutional guarantee of freedom of religion and/or of conscience are made subject to general conditions, such as public policy, public order, public health and/or morals.[142] The Constitution of Afghanistan of 1990 is particularly circumspect in its definition of the limitations that apply to freedom of religion:

> No individual has the right to abuse religion for anti-national and anti-people propaganda purposes, creation of enmity and commission of other deeds contrary to the interests of the Republic of Afghanistan.[143]

There are a few instances where the constitutions of Muslim countries expressly sanction discrimination against particular religious denominations.[144] The Iranian Constitution, for instance, upholds the distinction between Muslims, People of the Book (*kitabis*), that is non-Muslims who believe in the heavenly revealed scriptures (mostly Christians and Jews), and Unbelievers (*nasaara'hs*).[145] In terms of article 13 of the Iranian Constitution, Zoroastrians, Jews and Christians (the traditional *kitabis*) constitute "recognized religious minorities" with the right to practice their religious beliefs "within the limits of the law." In terms of article 14, non-Muslims "who refrain from engaging in conspiracy or activity against Islam and the Islamic Republic of Iran" are entitled to treatment "in conformity with ethical norms and the principles of Islamic justice and equity, and to respect [for] their human rights." Non-Muslims

---

141 See also sec. 3(1) (freedom of religion) of the Constitution of Brunei Darussalam (1984); arts. 28 and 29 (non-discrimination) and arts. 39 and 40 (freedom of conscience) of the Constitution of the People's Republic of Bangladesh (1972); art. 6 (non-discrimination) and art. 8 (freedom of conscience) of the Constitution of the Republic of Guinea (1982); art. 29(2) (freedom of religion) of the Constitution of Indonesia (1945); art. 9 (freedom of conscience) of the Constitution of Lebanon (1926); art. 11 of the Federal Constitution of Malaysia (1957) (freedom of religion); art. 9 (non-discrimination) of the Constitution of Qatar (1970); art. 6 (non-discrimination) and art. 31 (freedom of religion) of the Constitution of the Democratic Republic of Somalia (1979); art. 35 of the Constitution of the Syrian Arab Republic (1973); art. 47 (freedom of religion) of the Constitution of the People's Democratic Republic of Yemen (1978).

142 See, for example, art. 14 of the Constitution of Jordan (1952) (public order or decorum); art. 35 of the Constitution of Kuwait (1962) (public policy or morals); art. 11 of the Constitution of Mali (1974) (public order); art. 11(5) of the Federal Constitution of Malysia (1957) (public order, public health or morality); art. 20 of the Constitution of the Islamic Republic of Pakistan (1973) (law, public order and morality); art. 18 of the transitional Constitution of the Republic of Sudan (1985) (morality, public order and health as may be required by law); art. 5 of the Constitution of Tunisia (1959) (public order); art. 32 of the Constitution of the United Arab Emirates (1971) (public order and public morals).

143 Constitution of the Republic of Afghanistan, art. 40 (1990).

144 An-Na'im, "Religious Minorities," 1, 12-13; Mayer, "Current Muslim Thinking," 140-3.

145 An-Na'im, "Religious Minorities," 11.

such as Baha'is and Kurds, who are regarded in Iran as apostates from Islam, do not enjoy such rights.[146]

The Sudanese Constitution likewise protects Christians and members of "heavenly religions," but not apostates from Islam.[147]

Saudi Arabia imposed restrictions on religious practices of non-Muslims and prohibits non-Muslims from entering the holy areas of Medina and Mecca. It furthermore prohibits the construction of houses of worship by non-Muslims, and buildings used as places of worship by Christians may not be designated as churches.[148]

In many Islamic States it is expressly provided that the head of state,[149] and in some instances other high ranking officials,[150] shall be Muslims. In countries ruled by traditional Muslim dynasties, such as Jordan, Kuwait, Morocco and the United Arab Emirates, such provisions are, or would be, superfluous.[151]

Missionary work to convert Muslims to any other faith is generally restricted in Islamic countries, whereas missionary efforts to convert non-Muslims to Islam are encouraged.[152]

There is also a more subtle source of religious discrimination to be identified in those countries that proclaimed Shari'a (literally: "the way to follow") to be a source,[153] or in some instances the principal source,[154]

---

146 Ibid., 1, 12-13; Mayer, "Current Muslim Thinking," 140-42; Mayer, "Law and Religion in the Muslim Middle East," 147-49; Arzt, "The Application of International Human Rights Law," 223-24.

147 Art. 16.

148 Mayer, "Law and Religion in the Muslim Middle East," 148; Albeeb Abu-Sahlieh, "Les droits de l'homme et l'Islam," *Revue generale de droit international publique* 89 (1985): 626, 642.

149 See, for example, art. 74 of the Constitution of the Republic of Afghanistan (1990) (prescribing the presidential oath in the name of Allah); arts. 70 and 73 of the Constitution of Algeria (1989); art. 25 of the Constitution of the Federal Islamic Republic of the Comores (1992) (demanding an oath to be taken on the Quoran); art. 115 of the Constitution of the Islamic Republic of Iran (1979); art. 4 of the Constitution of Kuwait (1962); art. 23 of the Constitution of the Islamic Republic of Mauritania (1991); art. 41(2) of the Constitution of the Islamic Republic of Pakistan (1973); arts. 22 and 35 of the Constitution of Qatar (1970); art. 38 of the Constitution of the Republic of Tunisia (1959).

150 See, for example, sec. 3(2) and 4 of the Constitution of Brunei Darussalam (1984); and see also arts. 3, 7 and 64 of the Constitution of the Federal Islamic Republic of the Comores (1992); art. 66(2) of the Constitution of Kenya (1969).

151 Mayer, "Law and Religion in the Muslim Middle East," 148.

152 Ibid., 149; Aldeeb Abu Sahlieh, "Les droits de la homme," 642.

153 See art. 3 of the Constitution of Algeria (1990); art. 2 of the Constitution of Bahrain (1973): art. 2 of the Constitution of Kuwait (1962); art. 1 of the Constitution of Qatar (1970); art. 3(a) of the Constitution of the Democratic Republic of Somalia (1979); art. 4 of the transitional Constitution of the Republic of Sudan (1985); art. 3 of the Constitution of the Syrian Arab Republic (1973); art. 7 of the Constitution of the United Arab Emirates (1971).

154 See art. 2 of the Constitution of the Arab Republic of Egypt (1980), as amended in 1981. See also art. 64 of the Constitution of the Federal Islamic Republic of the Comores (1992)

of legislation.[155] Professor Abdullahi An-Na'im pointed out that the status of non-Muslims under Shari'a is inferior[156] and that constitutions which elevate Shari'a as a source of law therefore in effect sanction discrimination against religious minorities.[157] In his treatise on *Religious Minorities under Islamic Law,* Professor An-Na'im therefore speaks of "Islamic cultural impediments to the full and effective safeguards of the rights of religious minorities."[158] Ann Mayer compared the status in Islamic countries of non-Muslims who have not accepted the official state ideology with that of a non-communist [in bygone days] in a communist country.[159]

Flagrant violations of the rights of religious minorities were particularly evident in countries that embarked on a program of systematic Islamization of the community and constitutional structures;[160] that is, the process of "reinstating Islamic norms and values" in those societies.[161] Lybia after Colonel Qadhdhafi came to power in 1969; Pakistan following the *coup d'état* executed by General Mohammad Zia in 1977; Iran following the Iranian Revolution under the Ayatollah Khomeini in 1978-79; and the Sudan through the repressive regime of Major-General Jaafer Mohammed al-Nemery in the period 1969 to 1985. Religious repression under the banner of Islamization was especially aimed at sects regarded as

---

(proclaiming that "[j]ustice shall be given in every direction in the name of the Most Merciful, Compassionate Allah"); art. 8 and 26 of the Constitution of the Kingdom of Saudi Arabia (1992), and id., art. 21 (proclaiming that "[t]he State protects the Islamic creed, carries out its Sharia and undertakes its duty towards the Islamic call"); art. 3(2) of the Constitution of the Syrian Arab Republic (1973) (proclaiming Islamic jurisprudence to be a main source of legislation); art. 3 of the Constitution of the Republic of Yemen (1994) (proclaiming Shari'a to be the source of all legislation). The Constitutional Charter of the Military Committee of National Salvation of Mauritania (superceded by the Constitution of the Islamic Republic of Mauritania (1991)) proclaimed in even stronger terms: "The sole and unique source of law is Islamic Sharia."

155 In some instances only sections of the law are said to be regulated by Shari'a. Article 8 of the Constitutional Proclamation of Lybia (1969) thus provides that inheritance is governed by Islamic Shari'a; and in the Jordanian Constitution (1952), provision is made for religious courts (art. 99), which in turn are subdivided into the Sharia Courts and tribunals of other religious communities (art. 104), with Sharia courts being instructed to apply Shari'a Law (art. 106). See also arts. 6, 13 and 14 of the Constitution of Maldives (1968).

156 An-Na'im, "Religious Minorities," 10; see also Abdullahi Ahmed An-Na'im, "Cross-cultural Support for Equitable Participation in Subsaharan Africa," in Mahoney and Mahoney, eds., *Human Rights in the Twenty-First Century*, 133, 147.

157 An-Na'im, "Religious Minorities," 1; and see, in general, ibid., 10-14.

158 Ibid., 9.

159 Mayer, "Law and Religion in the Muslim Middle East," 179.

160 See ibid., 129-30, 135-37, 152-61 and 178-83; Mayer, "Current Muslim Thinking," 140-43.

161 Mayer, "Law and Religion in the Muslim Middle East," 129.

apostates from Islam, such as the Baha'is and Kurds in Iran,[162] the Ahmadi Muslims in Pakistan,[163] and the "Republican Brothers" in the Sudan.[164]

Human rights violations by Islamic authorities are often opposed and criticized by Muslims themselves. In its report of January 31, 1987, the Board of Trustees to the General Assembly of the Arab Organization for Human Rights thus noted that governments have used the Shari'a to support their "one-sided and self-serving interpretation of the Islamic doctrine."[165] In his treatise on *Faith in Human Rights,* Robert Traer collected an impressive list of Muslim protagonists of the human rights ideal.[166] The support for human rights in the Muslim world is, however, to a large degree conditioned by the relativist position, where "[j]udgments are based on experience, and experience is interpreted by each individual in terms of his own inculturation."[167]

The Principle of Subsidiarity. Islamic countries are not the only ones to found there constitutional priorities upon faith in the guidance and supreme authority of the Deity, or which afford a preferred status within the body politic to an established church.

The Evangelical Lutheran Church is an established church in Denmark,[168] Finland,[169] Iceland,[170] Norway,[171] and Sweden.[172] The Eastern Orthodox Church of Christ is singled out as "[t]he prevailing religion" in Greece,[173] and the "traditional religion" of Bulgaria.[174] The Church of

---

[162] See Elizabeth Odio Benito, Elimination of All Forms of Tolerance and Discrimination Based on Religion or Belief, E/CN.4/ Sub.2/1987/26, para. 47-50 (New York: United Nations 1989); Gianfranco Rossi, "Violations of Religious Freedom in Various Parts of the World," *Conscience and Liberty* 4(2) (1992): 58, 60.

[163] See Ilyas Khan, "The Ahmadiyya Movement in Islam," *Proceedings of the Third World Congress on Religious Liberty,* 85-88.

[164] Mayer, "Law and Religion in the Muslim Middle East," 180-82; see also, in general, An-Na'im, "Cross Cultural Support," 145-48.

[165] Mayer, "Current Muslim Thinking," 150, citing Human Rights in the Arab World IFDA Dossier 62 (November-December, 1987): 63, 70.

[166] Traer, *Faith in Human Rights,* 111-128.

[167] Melville J. Herskovitz, "Cultural Relativism," in Frances Herskovitz, ed., *Perspectives in Cultural Relativism* (New York, 1972), 15; and see An-Na'im, "Religious Minorities," 4-6.

[168] Section 4 of the Constitution of the Kingdom of Denmark (1953).

[169] See arts. 61, 83 and 90 of the Constitution of Finland (1919), where special mention is made of the Evangelical Lutheran Faith.

[170] Article 62 of the Constitution of Iceland (1944).

[171] Article 2 of the Constitution of the Kingdom of Norway (1814).

[172] Swedish Riksdag, Constitutional Documents of Sweden (1981), para. IV, 10.

[173] Article 3 of the Constitution of Greece (1975).

[174] Article 13(3) of the Constitution of the Republic of Bulgaria (1991).

England is the established church in England,[175] and the Presbyterian Church enjoys the same status in Scotland.[176] Buddhism is the established religion of Laos[177] and Sri Lanka.[178] Nepal proclaimed itself to be a Hindu State.[179] In the Preamble to the Constitution of Papua New Guinea (1975) the people proclaim "our noble traditions and the Christian principles that are ours now;" and the Constitution of Tonga (1875) contains the extraordinary commandment that "[t]he Sabbath Day shall be kept holy."[180] The Roman Catholic Church is an established church or is afforded special constitutional recognition in Argentina,[181] Bolivia,[182] Costa Rica;[183] El Salvador,[184] Guatemala,[185] Liechtenstein,[186] Malta,[187] Monaco,[188] Panama,[189] Paraguay,[190] and Peru.[191]

Traditionally, the typical Roman Catholic perception of religious freedom was founded on the scholastic doctrine of subsidiarity, which in turn emanated from the dualistic division of reality into the realms of nature and grace. In the natural order of things, the state was regarded as the *societas perfecta*, while the church constituted the perfect society in the supra-natural sphere of grace; and whereas in the realm of nature the

---

175 See Submission of the Clergy Act, 25 Hen. 8, c. 19 (1533); Act of Supremacy, 1 Eliz. I, c. 1 (1558); and see J.D. van der Vyver, *Die Juridiese Funksie van Saat en Kerk: 'n kritiese Analise van die beginsel van Soewereiniteit in eie Kring* (Durban, 1972), 134-40 .

176 See the Union with Scotland Act, 5 Ann, c. 8 (1706); and see also van der Vyver, Die Juridiese Funksie, 140-42.

177 Article 9 of the Constitution of the Lao People's Democratic Republic (1992).

178 Article 9 of the Constitution of the Democratic Socialist Republic of Sri Lanka (1978); and see also art. 7 of the Constitution of the Kingdom of Thailand (1991) (mandating the King to be "a Buddhist and Upholder of religions").

179 Article 4 of the Constitution of Nepal (1990).

180 Article 6 of the Constitution of Tonga (1875, as amended in 1971).

181 Article 2 of the Constitution of the Argentine People (1994).

182 Article 3 of the Constitution of Bolivia (1967).

183 Article 75 of the Constitution of the Republic of Costa Rica (1949).

184 Article 26 of the Constitution of El Salvador (1983).

185 Article 37 of the Political Constitution of the Republic of Guatemala (1985).

186 Article 37 of the Constitution of Liechtenstein (1921).

187 Article 2 of the Constitution of the Republic of Malta (1964).

188 Article 9 of the Constitution of the Principality of Monaco (1962).

189 Article 35 of the Political Constitution of the Republic of Panama (1972) (recognizing that the Catholic religion is that of the majority of Panamanians); and see also id., art. 103 (providing for Catholicism to be taught in schools).

190 Article 24 of the Constitution of Paraguay (1992) (proclaiming that relations between the State and the Roman Catholic Church are based on "independence, cooperation, and autonomy"); and see also id., art 82 (recognizing "[t]he role played by the Roman Catholic Church in the historical and cultural formation of the Republic").

191 Article 50 of the Political Constitution of Peru (1993) (recognizing the Catholic Church as "an important element in the historical, cultural, and moral development of Peru" and promissing cooperation with the Church).

state was seen to be subordinate to the church, so, again, was the state perceived to be subordinate to the church in the realm of grace.[192]

The traditional Thomistic view designating to the state the primary function of promoting the common good[193] is still expressly recognized in the Constitution of the Guatemala.[194]

Constitutional arrangements evidently regulate the affairs of state within the realm of nature, and here, as we have seen, the church was said to be subordinate to the state. As against the state, the church enjoyed no more than autonomous authority and competences in the sense of such authority and competences having been allocated to the church institution by the repositories of political power within the state structure.[195]

A particular constitutional manifestation of the autonomous subordination of the church to the powers of state authority may be gleaned from juridical provisions affording legal personality to the established church while in some instances denying the legal personality of non-established church institutions. El Salvador and Guatemala may be singled out as examples of countries where Roman Catholicism is recognized as the established religion and legal personality of the Roman Catholic Church has been constitutionally regulated as a *sine qua non* of that preferred status of the Church.[196] Uruguay no longer recognizes the Roman Catholic Church as an established church of the state but nevertheless still affords special constitutional recognition to property rights of that Church.[197] Spain also no longer afford "a state character" to any religion, but nevertheless promises in its Constitution to "maintain the appropriate relations of cooperation with the Catholic Church and other denominations."[198]

Further rather crude remnants of the principle of subsidiarity that still obtains in countries with a constitutional commitment to Roman Catholicism include the following arrangements: In Bolivia[199] and Liechtenstein,[200] recognition of the property rights of religious institutions are specially regulated as a constitutional matter; and in Panama similar con-

[192] See Herman Dooyeweerd, *A New Critique of Theoretical Thought*, David H. Freeman and H. de Jongste, trans. (Toronto, 1984): 3:220-222.

[193] Thomas Aquinas, *Summa Theologica* I-II, 21, 4, reply 3.

[194] Preamble to the Political Constitution of the Republic of Guatemala (1985).

[195] See Dooyeweerd, *A New Critique*, 220.

[196] See art. 26 of the Constitution of El Salvador (1983) and art. 37 of the Political Constitution of the Republic of Guatemala (1985).

[197] Article 5 of the Constitution of Uruguay (1967).

[198] Article 16(3) of the Constitution of Spain (1978).

[199] Article 28 of the Constitution of Bolivia (1967).

[200] Article 38 of the Constitution of Liechtenstein (1921).

stitutional recognition is afforded to the legal capacity of religious organizations.[201] In Argentina,[202] El Salvador,[203] Guatemala,[204] Panama[205] and Paraguay,[206] members of the clergy may not hold certain specified public offices. In Guatemala, religious processions outside churches are regulated by state-imposed law.[207] In Liechtenstein, the protection of religion is stipulated in the Constitution to be a function of the state.[208] In Panama, teaching of the Catholic religion in public schools is guaranteed in the Constitution, subject though to the proviso that parents or guardians may demand that their children or wards be excused from attending religious classes or participating in religious services.[209]

Although the established church thus, according to traditional scholastic teaching, owed its very existence as a legal entity, and its autonomous juridical functions and powers within the sphere of nature, to the state, Roman Catholicism nevertheless valued the principle of religious freedom. Jacques Maritain (1882-1973) thus included in the category of rights that belong to human persons as such (natural rights), the right to existence, to personal freedom, to pursue a natural and moral life, and to seek eternal life.[210] A contemporary scholar, Mgr. Roland Mennerath (Vatican Representative Professor in the University of Strasbourg) defined religious freedom as "a right to immunity against any constraint in religious matter,"[211] and in particular: "freedom of conscience and worship, freedom to teach and witness to the faith (in public and private), freedom to communicate with coreligionists, including those outside one's own country, freedom to engage in mission by acceptable means, and freedom of association and organization in an autonomous community."[212]

The scholastic theme of nature and grace filters through in the teaching of Professor Mennerath where he explains that the state, in regulating religious freedom, must place emphasis on individual con-

---

201 Article 36 of the Political Constitution of the Republic of Panama (1972).

202 Article 73 of the Constitution of the Argentine People (1994).

203 Article 82 of the Constitution of El Salvador (1983).

204 Articles 186, 197 and 207 of the Political Constitution of the Republic of Guatemala (1985).

205 Article 42 of the Political Constitution of the Republic of Panama (1972).

206 Articles 197(5) and 235(5) of the Constitution of the Republic of Paraguay (1992).

207 Article 33 of the Political Constitution of Guatemala (1985).

208 Article 14 of the Constitution of Liechtenstein (1921).

209 Article 103 of the Political Constitution of the Republic of Panama (1972).

210 Jacques Maritian, *Les droits de l'homme et la loi naturelle* (Paris, 1942), 110-113.

211 Roland Minnerath, "The Doctrine of the Catholic Church," *Proceedings of the Third World Conference on Religious Liberty*, 49, 50.

212 Ibid., 49.

science in the sense of every person being afforded freedom from outside constraints in the acceptance of a particular belief, whereas in a community of faith (the church), revealed truth is paramount and individual conscience must there be subordinated to a communal confession.[213]

The emphasis in contemporary Roman Catholic dogma upon religious freedom within the realm of nature derived special impetus from the Second Vatican Council (1962-65), and in particular from the Declaration on Religious Liberty (*Dignitatis Humanae Personae*). Here, the Vatican Council declared "that the human person has a right to religious freedom" and that "the right to religious freedom has its foundation in the very dignity of the human person,"[214] which the Declaration proclaims to be revealed in the Word of God and by reason itself.[215] Religious freedom, the Declaration goes on to assert, has its foundation, "not in the subjective disposition of the person, but in his very nature;"[216] and its protection "devolves upon the people as a whole, upon social groups, upon governments, and upon the Church and other religious communities."[217]

In response, several states that had proclaimed Roman Catholicism to be a state religion amended their constitutions to abandon the established status of the Church.[218] In conformity with the emphasis on religious freedom within the Roman Catholic communion, all the countries singled out earlier as the ones that continue to uphold special links with Roman Catholicism contain in their constitutions stipulations upholding the principle of religious freedom within the body politic.[219] These provisions

---

213 Ibid., 50.

214 Human dignity constituted the foundation of Roman Catholic social doctrine since the landmark encyclical, *Pacem in Terris* (1961). See Traer, *Faith in Human Rights*, 36. According to David Hollenbach, the principle of human dignity as the foundation of all human rights derives, first, from its accessibility to all human beings, whether they are religious or not, by virtue of "the person's transcendence over the world of things," and, secondly, as a matter of Christian faith, the belief that "all persons are created in the image of God, that they are redeemed by Jesus Christ, and that they are summoned by God to a destiny beyond history. . . ." *Justice, Peace, and Human Rights: American Catholic Social Ethics in a Pluralistic Context* (New York, 1988), 95-96..

215 *Dignitatis Humanae Personae*, no. 2.

216 Ibid.

217 Ibid., no. 6.

218 See Minnerath, "The Doctrine of the Catholic Church," 51.

219 Article 14 of the Constitution of the Argentine People (1994); art. 3 of the Constitution of Bolivia (1967); art. 75 of the Constitution of the Republic of Costa Rica (1949); art. 25 of the Constitution of El Salvador (1983); art. 36 of the Political Constitution of the Republic of Guatemala (1985); art. 21 of the Constitution of Liechtenstein (1921); art. 40 of the Constitution of Malta (1964), and see also id., art. 32; art. 23 of the Constitution of the Principality of Monaco (1962); art. 35 of the Political Constitution of the Republic of Panama (1972); art. 24 of the Constitution of the Republic of Paraguay (1992); art. 2(3) and (18) of the Political Constitution of Peru (1993).

are in many instances attended by reservations. For instance, in Guatemala the right to practice freedom of religion is subject to limitations dictated by the public order and "the respect due to the dignity of the hierarchy and the faithful of other beliefs;"[220] in Malta, freedom of conscience is subordinate to limitations "reasonably required in the interests of public safety, public order, public morality or decency, public health, or the protection of the rights and freedoms of others" and provided the restriction "is shown to be reasonably justifiable in a democratic society."[221] In Panama, freedom to profess any religion is subject to "respect for Christian morality and public order."[222] In Paraguay, freedom of religion, worship and ideology must be exercised subject to "this Constitution and the law."[223]

The Doctrine of Sphere Sovereignty. There seems to be a shift in Roman Catholic social theory toward recognizing a greater measure of sovereignty of state and church. Professor Ronald Minnerath almost said it in so many words. According to him, state-church relationships ought to be based on (1) the autonomy of each of the two parties, and (2) cooperation in areas of common interest;[224] and he went on to explain: "Recognition of the autonomy of church and state requires that each shall be sovereign and independent in its own sphere."[225]

The notion of sphere sovereignty finds expression in various forms in some of the constitutions of the world. Singapore confines the internal sovereignty of religious groups to managing their own religious affairs.[226] Romania permits the organization of religious sects "in accordance with their own statutes" but "under the conditions of the law."[227] Italy affords independence and sovereignty, "each within its own ambit," to the State and the Roman Catholic Church only.[228] Ireland more generously proclaims the right of every religious denomination to manage its own affairs.[229]

There is, of course, more to sphere sovereignty than just that.[230] First, in contradistinction to the Islamic presupposition of the identity of law

---

220 Article 36 of the Political Constitution of the Republic of Guatemala (1985).

221 Article 40(3) of the Constitution of Malta (1964).

222 Article 35 of the Political Constitution of the Republic of Panama (1972).

223 Article 24 of the Constitution of the Republic of Paraguay (1992).

224 Minnerath, "The Doctrine of the Catholic Church," 51.

225 Ibid.

226 Article 15(3) of the Constitution of the Republic of Singapore (1963).

227 Article 29(3) of the Constitution of Romania (1991).

228 Article 7 of the Constitution of Italy (1948).

229 Article 44.2.5. of the Constitution of Ireland (1937).

230 The Dutch expression "souvereiniteit in eigen sfeer" was first used in 1862 by a politician of the Netherlands, Guillaume Groen van Prinsterer (1801-1876), to designate the

and religion, it proclaims state and church to be distinct social structures, each with a unique identity and the one irreducible to the other. Second, as against the scholastic notion of subsidiarity, it stipulates in essence that social entities of different kinds, including state and church, do not derive their respective competences from one another, but are in each instance endowed with an internal enclave of domestic powers that emanate from the typical structure of the social entity concerned and as conditioned by the particular function that constitutes the special destiny of that social entity. Third, in opposition to the paradigm professing the separation of church and state, it recognizes the encaptic intertwinement of fundamentally different social structures,[231] and it accordingly emphasizes the mutual symbiosis of state and church as peculiarly different social structures and of law and religion as distinct modal aspects within the social environment.

The body politic, thus, by its very nature is charged with the duty of establishing and maintaining a legal order within a defined territory, while religious communities are essentially charged with fostering one's faith. In terms of the doctrine of sphere sovereignty, the nature of the internal authority of each social entity is determined by its leading function, and the doctrine requires every social entity to confine its activities to its characteristic objective.

Not every instance of authority being exercised within a social institution would qualify as a matter of sovereignty in the above sense. Sov-

---

range of competences of the church over against those of the state. G. Groen van Prinsterer, *Ter Nagedachtenis van Stahl* (Amsterdam, 1862), 30-1. The idea itself, however, preceded this descriptive phrase by approximately 300 years. According to Herman Dooyeweerd, "the first modern formulation of the principle of internal sphere-sovereignty in the societal relationship" is to be found in a statement of the Calvinistic jurist, Johannes Althusius (1557-1638). Dooyeweerd, *A New Critique*, 663; see also id., *De Strijd om het Souvereiniteit in de moderne Rechts- en Staatsleer* (Amsterdam, 1950), 7-8. Althusius proclaimed that all distinct social entities are governed by their own laws and that those laws differ in every instance according to the typical nature of the social institution concerned. Johannes Althusius, *Politica Methodiae Digesta*, 3d ed. (1614), 1.19. (at 7): Propriae leges sunt cujusque consociationis peculiares, quibus illa regitur. Atque hae in singulis speciebus consociationis iliae atque diversae sunt, prout natura cujusque postulat.

The doctrine, as currently defined, received its final touches through the Philosophy of the Cosmonomic Idea of Herman Dooyeweerd (1894-1977). See, in general, Dooyeweerd, *A New Critique*, 169-70; id., *Het Souvereiniteitbegrip*, 51; id., "Verkenningen in de Wijsbegeerte," in id., *De sociologie en de Rechtsgeschiedenis* (Amsterdam, 1962), 80; Jan Dengerink, *Critisch-Historisch Onderzoek naar de sociologische Ontwikkeling der Beginsel der "Souvereiniteit in eigen Kring" in de 19e en 20e Eeuw* (Amsterdam, 1948), 11; Gordon Spykman, "Sphere Sovereignty in Calvin and Calvinist Tradition," in David Holwerda, ed., *Exploring the Tradition of John Calvin* (Grand Rapids, 1976), 163; van der Vyver, *Die Juridiese Funksie*, 76-78, 91-99; id., "Sovereignty and Human Rights in Constitutional and International Law," *Emory International Law Review* 5 (1992): 321, 342-55.

[231] Dooyeweerd, *Verkenningen*, 102-03 (defining "encapsis" as "an intertwinement of intrinsically different structures").

ereign powers relate to the *inter*-relationships of structurally *different* kinds of social entities only. In the *intra*-relations of a social entity toward an assemblage of its own kind and constituting an integral component of itself, sovereignty would be out of the question. It is possible, of course, for such components of a community structure to be given authority to deal with matters falling within the domain of its domestic affairs. Such authority would then be a matter of delegated powers, emanating from the inner ties of a whole and its parts and being conditioned by a relationship of dominion and subordination, and constituted by a grant or concession of the superior social entity. In order to distinguish this kind of (delegated) authority from the sovereign powers of a societal institution, it might be called "autonomy."[232] The relationship between regional and local authorities of a state towards the central government, or between a particular congregation and the denomination of which it is part, would in this sense be a question of autonomy and not of sovereignty.

With these definitions and expositions in mind, one could propound that the Roman Catholic doctrine of subsidiarity proceeds on the assumption that relationships of authority that are in fact instances of sovereignty were matters of autonomy.[233]

In the constitutional context, the doctrine of sphere sovereignty requires the state to take cognizance of the existence of a great variety of social structures, each with its own body of internal rules of conduct. Those rules of conduct, and the power to make them, do not derive from the state but are enacted by the social entity concerned as a matter of internal sphere sovereignty. The state, by virtue of its function of maintaining law and order, may indeed be called upon, if need be and as a final resort, to uphold and enforce those internal rules of conduct of non-state institutions. However, the protective role of the state in the arena of the law does not in any way detract from the distinct nature and internal sovereignty of the non-state institution.

In the private enclave of a person's religious predilection and activity, sphere sovereignty likewise requires the state to confine its involvement to an enclave dictated by the appropriate juridical function of the state. It is not the function of the state to enforce any particular religious or moral

---

232 Dooyeweerd distinguished autonomy and sphere sovereignty as follows: "But autonomy is not identical with sphere-sovereignty of the different types of societal relationships. The fundamental difference between the two is that autonomy only occurs in the relation of a whole to its parts, whereas sphere-sovereignty pertains to the relation between social structures of a different radical or geno-type, which in principle lacks the character of a part-whole relation." Dooyeweerd, *A New Critique*, 221-22.

233 See van der Vyver, *Die Juridiese Funksie*, 91.

scruples *per se*.[234] Regulation of the conduct of subjects of the state ought to remain confined to resolving conflict situations in the community; but, on the other hand, when a conflict of interests does require state intervention, the state ought not to avoid its juridical responsibility simply because matters of faith or religious institutions might be involved.

The doctrine of sphere sovereignty thus opposes totalitarianism, which denotes state control of the internal affairs of institutions other than the state, as well as control of the affairs of government by non-state institutions. The interim Constitution of South Africa may be cited as an example where the state, from its side, promises not to prescribe to individuals how to live their private (religious) lives or to interfere in the internal affairs of the church and other non-state institutions.[235] The Chapter on Fundamental Rights[236] only applies, as far as "acts and decisions" (conduct) are concerned, to those of legislative and executive organs of state at all levels of government,[237] and, as far as "law" is concerned, to all the law of the state (including statutory law, the common law and customary law)[238] but not to the internal rules of conduct of organizations that do not form part of legislative or executive organs of state at any of the levels of government. However, should any non-state organization resort to practices amounting to "unfair discrimination," the state legislature would be entitled to outlaw that practice.[239] For these purposes, religious institutions clearly belong to the category not subject to state control—except in so far as their internal affairs may constitute "unfair discrimination" that constitutes a public menace of sufficient proportions to merit state intervention.

Conclusion

Religious human rights, according to international standards, primarily entail freedom of thought, conscience and religion, but also include the right of every person "to leave one religion or belief and to

---

[234] J.D. van der Vyver, "Law and Morality," in Ellison Kahn, ed., *Fiat Iustitia: Essays in Memory of Oliver Deneys Schreiner* (Cape Town/Wetton/Johannesburg, 1983), 305-369; id., "The Function of Legislation as an Instrument of Social Reform," *South African Law Journal* (1976): 56, 62-67; id., "The State, the Individual and Society," *South African Law Journal* (1977): 291, 303-305 .

[235] See J.D. van der Vyver, "The Private Sphere in Constitutional Litigation," *Tydskrif vir hedendaagse Romeins-Hollandse Reg* 57 (1994): 378.

[236] Chapter 3 of the Constitution of the Republic of South Africa (1993).

[237] Ibid., sec. 7(1).

[238] Ibid., sec. 33(2).

[239] bild., sec. 33(4).

adopt another, or to remain without any at all."[240] Several contributions included in this volume attempt to define ways and means whereby these minimum standards may be realized. John Pobee, thus, in general terms emphasizes the need for a theology of pluralism as the underpinning of a culture of religious pluralism. Tamás Földesi in a more restricted sense had the special needs of Eastern Europe in mind when he advocated a policy of state neutrality toward religion reminiscent of the American doctrine of separation.

With the "American experience" in mind, John Witte and Christy Green singled out several "essential rights and liberties of religion" as the minimum standards of religious freedom: liberty of conscience and non-discrimination on grounds of faith; free exercise of religion; accommodation of pluralism in the sense of confessional and institutional diversity; equality of all religions before the law; separation of church and state in order to protect religious bodies and believers from state interference in their internal affairs and private religious lives (respectively); and disestablishment of religion, foreclosing government from singling out any particular religion for preferential treatment. Dinah Shelton and Alexandre Kiss, more ambitiously, based their analysis of the presuppositions of religious freedom on a model statute drafted in terms that the authors believe might be acceptable throughout the world and containing guarantees of freedom of religion and belief, proclaiming the state to be secular and opposing establishment, securing equal rights irrespective of, and proscribing discrimination on grounds of, religion or belief, protecting the legal status of religious organizations and sanctioning their internal autonomy, prohibiting hate speech based on religious prejudice, and promising protection of religious sites.

The constitutions of many countries of the world do not live up to such standards.

When it comes to *de facto* violations of religious human rights by government agencies, the picture that emerges becomes even bleaker. And the above analysis only scraped the surface. Since 1990 alone, altogether 44 Member States of the United Nations have been under investigation by the Special Rapporteur on the Implementation of the Declaration on the Elimination of All Forms of Intolerance and of Discrimination based

---

[240] Odio Benito, Elimination of All Forms of Tolerance and Discrimination based on Religion or Belief, para. 21, with reference to art. 18 of the Universal Declaration of Human Rights (supra, note 2), art. 18 of the International Covenant on Civil and Political Rights, G.A. Res. 2200, 21 U.N. GAOR Supp. (No. 16) at 52, U.N. Doc. A/6316 (1967), and art. 1 of the Declaration on the Elimination of All Forms of Intolerance and of Discrimination based on Religion or Belief.

on Religion or Belief, Mr. Angelo Vidal d'Almeida Ribeiro.[241] Nine Member States featured in all three reports of the Special Rapporteur for the period 1990-1993 (China, Egypt, Greece, India, Indonesia, Iran, Pakistan, Saudi Arabia, and Viet Nam); specific incidents pertaining to violations of religious human rights came up twice in the case of 16 countries (Albania, Bulgaria, Burundi, Colombia, El Salvador, Ethiopia, Iraq, Israel, Malysia, Myanmar, Mauritania, Mexico, Nepal, Romania, Syria, and Turkey); and the religious human rights records of altogether 20 states were considered in one of the reports of the Special Rapporteur during the three years under consideration (Afghanistan, Canada, the former Czechoslovakia; the Dominican Republic, Cuba, Ghana, Italy, Malawi, Nicaragua, Somalia, Sri Lanka, Spain, the Sudan, Switzerland, the Ukraine, the former U.S.S.R., the United States of America, the United Kingdom, the former Yugoslavia, and Zaire). In 1989, Elizabeth Odio Benito, Special Rapporteur of ECOSOC's Sub-Commission on the Prevention of Discrimination and Protection of Minorities, concluded as follows as to the state of religious human rights in the world:

> There is a wealth of evidence to indicate that intolerance and discrimination based on religion or belief subsists in the contemporary world, and indeed that in some areas prejudice and bigotry have given rise to outright hatred, persecution and repression.[242]

Subsequent reports clearly indicate that, on the whole, nothing has changed.

It is also important to note that religious human rights cannot be seen in isolation. Violation of those rights almost invariably abridge other human rights, such as the right to life, liberty and security of the person; the right to freedom from torture or cruel, inhuman or degrading treatment or punishment; the right to freedom from discrimination; the right to a fair and public hearing by an independent and impartial tribunal; the right to freedom of movement and residence; the right to freedom of opinion and expression; freedom of assembly and association; and the right to privacy.[243]

The interdependence of human rights furthermore cuts both ways. Violations of other human rights often implicate religious freedom: repression of the right to equal treatment and non-discrimination, to life, to

---

[241] See the consecutive reports of the Special Rapporteur for the period 1990-1993 submitted to the Economic and Social Council of the United Nations: E/CN.4/1990/46; E/CN.4/1991/56; E/CN.4/1993/62.

[242] Odio Benito, Elimination of All Forms of Tolerance and Discrimination based on Religion or Belief, para. 45.

[243] Ibid., at para. 43.

human dignity, to freedom of expression, to freedom of assembly, to freedom of movement, to access to information, and to education may thus affect freedom of religion in general and in particular upon the right of religious minorities to profess and practice their own faith. One cannot do justice to evaluating the state of religious human rights in the constitutions of the world without also considering the status of those ancillary rights and freedoms.

Perspectives on Religious Liberty: A Comparative Framework[1]

W. COLE DURHAM, JR.
Brigham Young University

The right to religious freedom is the oldest of the internationally recognized human rights. As early as the Peace of Westphalia in 1648, the right to religious liberty was afforded international protection.[2] By the late 18th Century, religious liberty was afforded protection in a number of pathbreaking statutes,[3] and over the two centuries that followed, particularly in the period following World War II, it has found its way into most of the world's constitutions. In our increasingly secular world, it has tended to take a back seat to concern for more tangible encroachments on human dignity, such as torture, disappearances, and the like. As John Noonan has suggested, it has become "the neglected stepchild of the human rights movement." One could just as easily speak of it, in light of its age, as the "neglected grandparent" of human rights. Whatever the metaphor, recent events in the former Yugoslavia, Ireland, and Lebanon are a constant reminder that religious tensions can erupt as critical social problems, and the wave of new constitutions in Russia, Eastern Central Europe and other parts of the world has helped refocus attention on the importance of this fundamental freedom.

Increasingly, religious liberty needs to be reconceptualized not merely as a matter of fundamental national law, but as a genuinely inter-

1 An earlier and less fully developed version of this article was published in *First Amendment Freedoms and Constitution Writing in Poland*, Leszek Lech Garlicki, ed. (Warsaw, 1994), 61-72. The author wishes to express appreciation to Scott Ellsworth for assistance in the preparation of the final version of this article.

2 *See* William H. Maehl, *Germany in Western Civilization* (Birmingham, 1981), 194.

3 Virginia Bill of Rights of 1776, § 16; Austrian Act on Religious Tolerance of 1781; Virginia Bill Establishing Religious Freedom of January 1, 1786; Prussian Edict on Religion of 1788; Allgemeines Landrecht für die preussischen Staaten, part II, title 11, §§ 1-4.

J.D. van der Vyver and J. Witte, Jr. (eds.), Religious Human Rights in Global Perspective, 1-44.

national right. Like environmental issues, questions of religious affiliation extend across national boundaries. Injuries or burdens imposed in religious communities in one nation are felt by co-religionists in another. Moreover, the global perspective helps to humble and equalize. At the global level, everyone—whether Christian, Muslim, Jew, Buddhist, Hindu, adherent of any other religion, or unbeliever—is part of a minority group. However dominant a particular group may be in one country, it is part of a minority somewhere else in our very pluralistic world. These realities provide the background against which religious liberty rights must be analyzed and understood.

Legal protection of religious liberty varies significantly from country to country, depending on a variety of factors such as the stability of political regimes, the nature and history of traditional relationships between church and state, the degree of religious pluralism at the local level, the nature of the dominant religion or religions and its (their) internal commitment to religious liberty and toleration, the history of interactions between religious groups, and a variety of other factors. As one examines the issue of religious liberty cross-culturally, significant patterns of convergence are beginning to emerge with respect to the nature of religious liberty rights. This is particularly true in Europe and the Americas, where Western constitutional traditions and various international human rights agreements have had a significant impact on the articulation of religious liberty norms. At the same time, while the verbal formulas defining religious liberty are converging, substantial variation exists in the way that church-state relationships are institutionalized and religious freedom is achieved in various countries.

My aim in what follows is to elaborate a framework within which one can see the range of institutional possibilities for implementing religious freedom in legal systems around the world, and to consider in the process a series of philosophical and practical issues raised as one considers various aspects of the framework. I begin by describing what I call the "Tectonics of Religious Pluralism"—the underlying cultural differences that create rifts and tensions which can only be resolved by providing enhanced protection for religious freedom throughout the world. I next describe what I call the "Lockean Revolution in Religious Liberty"—the increasing tendency for religious traditions and more generally for what John Rawls has called "comprehensive doctrines"[4] to include freedom and mutual respect as central values. Once freedom and mutual respect are recognized as central notions in a constellation of moral or religious truths, the tension between commitment to truth and commit-

---

[4] John Rawls, *Political Liberalism* (Cambridge, MA 1993), 12-14.

ment to freedom of belief disappears, or is at least transformed. Against this background, I elaborate a comparative model of church-state systems that I have found useful in thinking about various church-state regimes around the world, and then trace what I call the "Archaeology of International Religious Liberty Norms." In this Section, I describe general developments in the international understanding of religious liberty rights, laying emphasis on some of the more detailed norms that have emerged under the European Convention for the Protection of Human Rights and Fundamental Freedoms and from the Helsinki process in Europe. Finally, I conclude by briefly summarizing some of the normative implications of emerging consensus on religious freedom.

The Tectonics of Religious Pluralism

Over the past five years, we have witnessed a period of extraordinary constitutional change. Beginning with the opening of Hungarian borders and the breaching of the Berlin wall, we have witnessed the collapse of communism. This collapse, and its ripple effects not only in the former USSR and East Central Europe, but in other areas as well, has ushered in an unparalleled period of constitutional change. New constitutions have either been adopted or are in process throughout the former communist bloc. The institutions of apartheid are being dismantled in South Africa. There is new hope for resolution of Palestinian questions. The tensions in Ireland may be working toward solution.

The euphoria of this period has brought with it substantial progress for the law of religious freedom. New constitutions uniformly include provisions on religious freedom,[5] and there has also been a pattern of adopting implementing legislation on freedom of conscience and religious associations that has high prestige because of the constitutional orbit in which it revolves.[6] Legal reforms of this nature have been evident not only in the former communist bloc countries, but also in Latin America, most notably with the recent repeal of anti-clerical provisions in the Mexican Constitution that date back to 1917.[7]

---

[5] See, e.g., Bulgaria Const. arts. 6, 13, 37 (1991); Hungary Const. § 63; Romania Const. arts. 4, 6, 29, 32 (1991); Russian Federation, arts 14, 19, 28, 29, 55, 56 (1993); Slovenia Const. arts 7, 14, 41 (1991).

[6] Ira C. Lupu, "Statutes Revolving in Constitutional Orbits," *Virginia Law Review* 79 (1993): 1-89.

[7] The religious provisions of the Mexican constitution were substantially altered in 1992 by amendment to articles 3, 5, 24, 27, and 130. These amendments, counteracting many of the anticlerical provisions of the 1917 Carranza constitution, forbid laws establishing or prohibiting any religion, grant religious associations legal personality and the power to acquire and hold property, restore to Mexican ministers the right to vote, allow non-Mexican ministers to enter the country, legalize parochial schools and monastic orders, and allow public worship

In short, this has been an extraordinary period both for constitutionalism in general and for religious freedom in particular. But as some of the initial post-1989 euphoria fades, it becomes clear that religious liberty will continue to face intense challenges, and that in the long-run, meeting this challenge is vital for international security and world peace. This becomes even more evident as one reflects on long-term sources of international tension. With the collapse of communism, we are witnessing the resurfacing of ancient cultural divides: what Professor Samuel Huntington has called "The Clash of Civilizations."[8] These cultural divides are similar to the vast tectonic plates beneath the surface of the earth that account for continental drift and that cause earthquakes where they collide. By analogy, tensions between fundamentally different civilizations underlie and increasingly explain patterns of strife in the contemporary world. Many such conflicts are merely the latest seismic activities in long-term historical struggles between rival civilizations that have continued for decades and even centuries.[9]

Perhaps the youngest of these civilization clashes has to do with the tensions tracing back to the Reformation between Protestantism and Roman Catholicism.[10] The fault lines of this cultural divide are still evident in Northern Ireland, and they remain a dominant feature of the background in the relations between North and South in the Western Hemisphere. To a large extent, modern conceptions of religious freedom were born in the crucible of warfare and social tension that flowed from this fundamental cultural divide. Implemented at first as a shaky experiment on American soil, these increasingly axiomatic notions of religious freedom have vindicated themselves as a vital antidote to religiously driven tensions between clashing civilizations.

Moving backwards through history and eastwards in political geography, the next major cultural divide is that separating Eastern (Orthodox) and Western Christianity. I remain optimistic that application of international human rights standards can help relieve tensions between these civilizations. Differing attitudes toward evangelizing and proselytizing have surfaced as a significant source of tension. The Orthodox East tends to view Western-based efforts at evangelization as a cultural affront. After all, these areas have been Christian for over a

---

services outside of church buildings. Legislation implementing these changes has been adopted as the Law of Religious Associations and Public Worship, officially published 15 July 1992, and implementing regulations are in process of being drafted.

[8] Samuel P. Huntington, "The Clash of Civilizations," *Foreign Affairs* 72 (1993): 22-49.

[9] David Martin, *Tongues of Fire: The Explosion of Protestantism in Latin America* (Oxford, 1990).

[10] For an insightful discussion of this cultural rift, see ibid., 1-26.

millennium. Why should missionaries be sent to this area? Western religious groups, in contrast, come from a civilization that has been far more thoroughly pluralized and tend to view restrictions on their activities as proof that the former communist lands have not yet succeeded in internalizing modern conceptions of freedom. These opposed perceptions are further exacerbated by worries about economic and political differentials. The Orthodox tradition, impoverished by fifty to seventy years under communism, feels threatened by expensive evangelizing campaigns that can use potent advertising techniques and modern media to spread its message. Western groups, on the other hand, are suspicious that Orthodox influence, reinforced by mounting strains of nationalism, is able to exert unfair and often hidden control on critical bureaucratic levers that control the ability of religious workers and volunteers to enter Orthodox countries and to register the religious entities through which they conduct their affairs. My sense is that many of these tensions are really part of the larger trauma of transition, and as time passes, implementation of sound principles of religious liberty and mutual respect will yield stable patterns of interaction similar to those that now prevail in Western Europe.

Still older in its provenance but even more critical today is the tension between Islam and Christianity. The collision of Western, Eastern, and Muslim tectonic plates is currently visible in the violent tremors in Bosnia. More generally, as former east bloc countries consolidate their ties with the West, polarization along Christian-Muslim lines at the international level seems increasingly likely. Tensions at national and local levels can also be anticipated. Growing Muslim minorities in Europe could provide the basis for political parties that could hold the key to coalition building. Over time, this could lead to increased divisiveness along religious lines, and corresponding increases in Christian-Muslim tensions within Western countries could result. These difficulties are compounded by the fact that fundamental axioms of liberal political culture such as equality and state neutrality with respect to religion often seem alien in Islamic contexts. In many respects, Islam has a better record of tolerance than Christianity, but those tolerated (the "people of the Book") were clearly in a second-class position, and there is no Qur'anic notion that other religions should be placed on a par with Islam. Partially due to the travail of Western imperialism in many Islamic countries, but also because of profound differences in theology, many Muslim leaders view international human rights norms as a subtle Western form of neoimperialism rather than as expressions of genuinely universal values.[11]

---

[11] See, e.g., Sultanhussein Tabandeh of Gunabad, *A Muslim Commentary on the Universal Declaration of Human Rights*, F.J. Goulding, trans. (1970); Alfred Taban, "Sudan Says U.N.

These problems, coupled with severe economic problems and the rise of Islamic fundamentalism, suggest that this civilization clash will be much more difficult to resolve.

As one moves still further back in time and to the east, one encounters still older cultural plates. The Jewish tectonic plate continues to collide with other world religions and to threaten world peace in the Middle East. It is also implicated in one of the greatest tragedies of this century: the holocaust. Other major world religions and outlooks mold other major cultures. In this regard, one could explore the significance of Hinduism, Sikhism, Buddhism, Confucianism, and so forth. Despite the impact of modernization, these traditions still continue to shape cultures in various parts of the world. Divisions within them generate tensions just as do the tensions between subdivisions of Christianity.

Now that Marxism is gone, or at least massively dismantled and transformed, one final tectonic plate deserves mention: Enlightenment secularism. This view often masquerades as a "neutral" and "scientific" position, but from the perspectives of the other religious world views, it is anything but neutral and is increasingly viewed as something that is profoundly threatening by various religious groups.[12] After all, post-Enlightenment anti-clericalism has often taken virulent forms. The rise of Christian and Muslim fundamentalism can be read at least in part as a reaction to this pervasive new cultural force. The sociologist James Davison Hunter has argued that in the contemporary United States, the major "culture wars" no longer involve tensions between Catholicism, Protestantism, and Judaism, but tensions between the more orthodox wings of these traditions and a "progressive" orientation linked to enlightenment secularism.[13] This is no doubt true in other parts of the world as well: tensions between various religious world views are now overlaid with a tension between more traditional religious outlooks and more secularist orientations. This tension cuts across all the traditional cultures to such an extent that the metaphor of tectonic plates (with its implicit assumptions of geographical homogeneity) breaks down. Perhaps the better image might be differing gravitational influences that pervade a culture and pull it in different directions. Whatever the appropriate metaphor, recognizing enlightenment secularism as one more cultural plate (or gravita-

---

Human Rights Report Insults Islam," *Reuters World Service* (Feb. 20, 1994).

12 See W. Cole Durham, Jr. and Alexander Dushku, "Traditionalism, Secularism, and the Transformative Dimension of Religious Institutions," *Brigham Young Law Review* (1993): 421, 461-63.

13 James Davison Hunter, *Culture Wars*: *The Struggle to Define America* (New York, 1991), 43-48.

tional influence) is vital if we are to avoid naively assuming that it can serve as the "neutral" foundation for a solution to tectonic pressures.

To the extent that the ideal of religious freedom is viewed as a mere emanation of enlightenment secularism, it will grow increasingly suspect within traditional cultures bent on maintaining their own hegemony. This explains to a considerable degree the resistance of Islamic cultures to acceptance of international religious human rights norms. What is needed is a notion of religious freedom that can be shown to be grounded as a shared value within both religious and secular traditions. But achieving any kind of consensus in this area—particularly consensus that goes beyond abstract platitudes and effectively protects minority groups—remains a remarkably difficult endeavor.

Despite this complexity, progressive implementation of ideals of religious freedom (even slightly differing ideals drawn from differing religious and secular traditions) holds the key to resolving the all-too-evident tensions between clashing civilizations in the contemporary world. One of the central questions of the post-communist era is whether the tensions associated with these resurfacing rifts can be resolved peacefully, or whether, like inexorably moving tectonic plates, they will necessarily lead to violence, dislocation, and warfare. If we do not find legal mechanisms for relieving tensions between these plates, I fear we will inevitably suffer mounting violence from internal terrorism and unrest and escalating armed conflicts, and world history will slip ineluctably toward Armageddon.

The Lockean Revolution in Religious Liberty

The resurfacing of ancient cultural divides that constitute the "tectonics of religious pluralism" provides the backdrop for renewed appreciation for what can appropriately be termed the Lockean revolution in religious liberty. For much of human history, it was assumed that religious truth required state implementation of religious beliefs and that political stability presupposed religious and cultural homogeneity. As a matter of logic, it was thought that if a particular set of religious beliefs are true, their truth provides a natural rationale for implementing them. Moreover, the assumption was that society could not be stable without an established homogeneous religion that could serve as a kind of social glue and ultimate motivation for loyalty and obedience to the regime. This impression was reinforced by the religious wars that had ravaged Europe until that time.

At least at the level of theory, the writings of John Locke in his *Letter Concerning Toleration*[14] represented a dramatic departure on both fronts. In this respect, Locke is probably best known for his powerful arguments that the machinery of state coercion is ineffective in the religious domain: the state can force no person to heaven.[15] The most it can do is cultivate outward hypocrisy.[16] But in many respects, a second insight buried toward the end of Locke's letter is even more significant for modern regimes of religious liberty. In the passage in question Locke states:

> Now if that church, which agrees in religion with the prince, be esteemed the chief support of any civil government, and that for no other reason, as has already been shown, than because the prince is kind and the laws are favorable to it; *how much greater will be the security of government, where all good subjects, of whatsoever church they be, without any distinction upon account of religion, enjoying the same favor of the prince, and the same benefit of the laws, shall become the common support and guard of it*; and where none will have any occasion to fear the severity of the laws, but those that do injuries to their neighbors, and offend against the civil peace![17]

Locke's contention in this passage was that far from destabilizing a regime, toleration and respect could have exactly the opposite effect. In the context of a pluralistic society, a regime that respects divergent beliefs will win support from those it respects, resulting in much greater stability than can be achieved by favoring the dominant group. The idea is that minority groups will be so grateful for this respect that instead of becoming centers of dissension and potential social disintegration, they will feel profoundly indebted and thus loyal to regime, thereby providing much greater social stability than can be derived from reinforcing the hegemony of the more powerful elements in society.

This insight has laid the foundation for religious liberty in contemporary regimes. Contrary to what might initially be thought (and what had been thought for centuries), Locke contended that respect for freedom of choice in matters of religion (and more generally with respect to comprehensive world views) is a source of both legitimacy and stability for political regimes. This insight constituted a kind of Copernican Revolution in political theory, akin in its magnitude to Kant's Copernican Revolution in epistemology and ethical philosophy.[18] Where Kant revolutionized

---

[14] John Locke, *A Letter Concerning Toleration* (First published in 1689; cited edition: Buffalo, NY, 1990).

[15] Ibid., 19-22, 35, 40-41.

[16] Ibid., 40-41.

[17] Ibid., 68-69 (emphasis added).

[18] See Lewis White Beck, *Early German Philosophy: Kant and His Predecessors* (Cambridge,

philosophy by shifting the locus of attention from the outer object to the inner subject, both in understanding the empirical world and in grounding ethics, Locke revolutionized politics by suggesting how religious (and by extension, political) freedom could sow political order from religious seeds that had always been assumed to be the ultimate source of anarchy. The Lockean insight thus opened up the possibility of seeing the political cosmos from a new perspective. By placing respect for freedom at the center of the constellation of values, and by recognizing that respect for freedom and dignity of individuals is itself a moral and religious truth of the highest order, this revolution transformed the grounds for legitimizing and stabilizing political communities.

Experience first with regimes of toleration in countries with established churches, and eventually with full scale religious liberty in religiously neutral states, has vindicated the Lockean insight. This idea was initially theoretical, but it became a central aspect of the "lively experiment"[19] with religious freedom in the United States. Over the past two centuries, the ideal of religious liberty has won extremely broad acceptance throughout the world. It is expressly recognized in every major international human rights declaration[20] and covenant,[21] as well as in the overwhelming majority of the world's constitutions.[22] Most European

---

MA 1969), 473-74, 479-80, 489.

[19] The phrase "lively experiment" actually antedates Locke. It originated with the Newport physician and clergyman, John Clarke, who wrote regarding the 17th Century situation in New England, "y[r] petitioners have it much in their hearts . . . to hold forth a lively experiment, that a flourishing civill State may stand, yea, and best be maintain'd . . . with full liberty in religious concernm[ts]." *Quoted in* Sidney E. Mead, *The Lively Experiment: The Shaping of Christianity in America* (New York, 1976), ii.

[20] Universal Declaration of Human Rights, art. 18, G.A. res. 217 (A(III), December 10, 1948, U.N. Doc. A/810, at 71 (1948); American Declaration of the Rights and Duties of Man, art. III, O.A.S. res. XXX, adopted by the Ninth International Conference of American States, Bogota (1948): *Novena Conferencia Internacional Americana, 6 Actas y Documentos* (1953), 297-302. *See also* United Nations Declaration on the Elimination of All Forms of Intolerance and of Discrimination Based on Religion or Belief, adopted 18 Jan. 1982, G.A. Res. 55, 36 U.N. GAOR Supp. (No. 51), U.N. Doc. A/RES/36/55 (1982) [hereinafter 1981 Declaration].

[21] International Covenant on Civil and Political Rights, G.A. Res. 2200A, U.N. GAOR, 21st Sess., Supp. No. 16, at 52, 55, U.N. Doc. A/6316 (1966), 999 U.N.T.S. 171 (1976) (art. 18) [hereinafter: Civil and Political Covenant]; [European] Convention for the Protection of Human Rights and Fundamental Freedoms, Nov. 4, 1950, art. 9, 213 U.N.T.S. 222 (entered into force Sept. 3, 1953), *as amended by* Protocol Nos. 3 & 5 [hereinafter: European Convention]; American Convention of Human Rights, O.A.S. Treaty Series No. 36, at 1, OEA/ser. L./V/II.23, doc. rev. 2 (entered into force July 18, 1978) [hereinafter: American Convention]. *See also* Concluding Document of the Vienna Meeting 1986 of Representatives of the Participating States of the Conference on Security and Co-Operation in Europe, Held on the Basis of the Provisions of the Final Act Relating to the Follow-Up to the Conference, Jan. 17, 1989, 28 I.L.M. 527, 534 (1989) [hereinafter: Vienna Concluding Document].

[22] See, e.g., Austl. Const. § 116; India Const. arts. 15, 16, 25, 26; Isr. Const. §§ 7, 22; Costituzione arts. 8, 19, 20 (Italy); Kenp arts. 19, 20 (Japan); Kenya Const. art. 78; Turk. Const. art

constitutions[23] and every constitution in the Western Hemisphere[24] expressly provide for the protection of religious liberty in some form. There is, of course, significant variation in the extent to which and in the manner this ideal is implemented in different countries.

Significantly, the principle of religious freedom is attracting increasing support within religious traditions as well as in increasingly pluralized societies and their governments and constitutions. One of the most significant developments in this regard was marked by the papal encyclical *Dignitatis Humanae Personae*,[25] which marked the internal recognition within the Roman Catholic tradition of the importance of recognizing religious freedom as an aspect of human dignity. The developments linked to Vatican II are representative of a much broader pattern within many religious traditions.[26] In general, there is growing consensus both that

---

24; Zaire Const. art. 17.

[23] Austria Const. arts. 7, 14 (1920); Belgium Const. arts. 14, 15, 16, 59 (1831); Bulgaria Const. arts. 6, 13, 37 (1991); Croatia Const. arts. 14, 40 (1990); Denmark Const. arts. 67, 68, 70, 71 (1953); Estonia Const. arts. 9, 14 (1937); Finland Const. arts. 8, 9 (1919); France Const. arts. 2, 77 (1958); German Basic Law arts. 4, 7, 140, 141 (1949); Greece Const. arts. 5, 13 (1975); Hungary Const. §63 (1972); Iceland Const. art. 63, 64 (1944); Ireland Const. arts. 40, 42, 44 (1937); Italy Const. arts. 8, 19, 20 (1948); Liechtenstein Const. arts. 37, 38, 39 (1921); Lithuania Const. arts. 18, 20, 27-31, 39 (1938); Luxembourg Const. arts. 19, 20 (1868); Malta Const. art. 40 (1964); Monaco Const. art. 23 (1962); Netherlands Const. arts. 6, 23 (1983); Norway Const. § 2 (1814); Poland Const., art. 82 (1952); Portugal Const. art. 41 (1982); Romania Const., arts. 4, 6, 29, 32 (1991); Russian Federation, arts. 14, 19, 28, 29, 55, 56 (1993); Slovenia Const. arts. 7, 14, 41 (1991); Spain Const. arts. 16, 27 (1978); Sweden Const. Chp. 2, arts. 1, 2 (1975); Switz. Const. arts. 27, 49, 50 (1874); Yugoslavia Const. arts. 155, 174 (1974). Some of the foregoing provisions are obviously dated at this point, but they confirm the general commitment to religious liberty.

[24] Antigua & Barbuda Const. sections 3, 11 (1981); Argentina Const. arts. 14, 19 (1853); Bahamas Const. arts. 15, 22 (1973); Barbados Const. §§ 11, 19 (1966); Belize Const. §§ 3, 11(1981); Bolivia Const. art. 3 (1967); Brazil Const. art. 5 (VI-VIII) (1988); Canada Const. art. 2 (1982); Chile Const. art. 19 (1980); Colombia Const. arts. 18-19 (1991); Costa Rica Const. art. 28 (1949); Cuba Const. art. 54 (1976); Dominica Const. art. 9 (1978); Dominican Repub. Const. 8 (1966); Ecuador Const. art. 19(6) (1979); El Salvador Const. art. 25 (1983); Grenada Const. §§ 1, 9 (1974); Guatemala Const. art. 36 (1985); Guyana Const. art. 1 (1980); Haiti Const. art. 30 (1987); Honduras Const. art. 77 (1982); Jamaica Const. 1-6 (1962); Mexico Const. arts. 3, 5, 24, 27, 130 (1992); Nicaragua Const. art. 29 (1986); Panama Const. art. 34 (1973); Paraguay Const. art. 70 (1967); Peru Const. art. 2(3) (1979); St. Christopher & Nevis Const. art. 11 (1983); St. Lucia Const. art. 9 (1978); St. Vincent Const. art. 9 (1979); Surinam Const. art. 8 (1987); Trinidad & Tobago Const. art. 9 (1976); United States Const. amend. I (1791); Uruguay Const. art. 5 (1967); Venezuela Const. art. 65 (1961).

[25] For an English version of the text of this encyclical, see *Declaration on Religious Freedom: On the Right of the Person and of Communities to Social and Civil Freedom in Matters of Religion*, in *The Documents of Vatican II*, Walter M. Abbott, S.J., ed. (The America Press, 1966), 675-700.

[26] See, e.g., The Report of the Conference at Oxford, July 1937, on Church, Community, and State; The First Assembly of the World Council of Churches, "A Declaration on Religious Liberty," Amsterdam, 22 August-4 September 1948; Third Assembly of the World Council of Churches, "Statement on Religious Liberty," New Delhi 19 November-5 December 1961; Ex-

freedom of religion should be respected and that protection of this fundamental human right is conducive to stability and peace.

Growing consensus on religious freedom reflects a more general need to address the reality of pluralism in the global setting. The increasingly free movement of labor, coupled with refugee movements, is resulting in much greater demographic pluralism in many parts of the world. Among other things, this is resulting in significant growth of Muslim populations in various European countries and substantial pressures for individuals from third world countries to move north and west. Even without the erosion of homogeneity such movements cause, globalization itself is enhancing our sense of pluralism. There are still enclaves of substantial religious homogeneity in some parts of the world, or at least, there are areas where one religious group or another is clearly in a majority position. But at the global level, there are no majority religions. In a shrinking and interconnected world adherents of religious traditions in one country have strong and direct connections to co-religionists in other parts of the world. Thus, not only are all religious traditions in minority positions; even adherents of majority traditions in one area are conscious of what it is like to be in a minority position, because they have direct ties to co-religionists who are in precisely that situation. These patterns of global demographic pluralism are likely to be conducive to religious freedom and application of the Lockean insight into the stabilizing force of respected pluralism in much the same way that American pluralism paved the way for meaningful institutions of religious freedom two centuries ago.

The influence of the Lockean revolution is still limited. It has not yet reached all legal systems or penetrated all systems of religious belief. Forces of nationalism, religious extremism and other anti-liberal forces often work against it. Even where it has taken root, the concrete implications of the right to religious freedom remain in dispute. Religious freedom can be given a broad range of interpretations, ranging from highly secularist versions that view state neutrality as the fundamental safeguard for religious freedom to versions in which minority religions are allowed to worship separately, but otherwise are merely tolerated.

---

ecutive Committee of the Commission of the Churches on International Affairs, Twentieth Executive Committee, World Council of Churches, "Human Rights and Religious Liberty," Geneva Switzerland, July 9-12, 1965; First Assembly of the World Council of Churches, "The Right to Religious Freedom," Nairobi, 23 November-10 December, 1975. For an overview of theological bases for mutual respect in a variety of traditions, see Harvey Cox & Arvind Sharma, "Positive Resources of Religion for Human Rights," in The Project on Religion and Human Rights, *Religion and Human Rights*, John Kelsay & Sumner B. Twiss, eds. (New York, 1994), 61-79; Robert Traer, *Faith in Human Rights: Support in Religious Traditions for a Global Struggle* (Washington, 1991).

Further, as Locke himself recognized, the ideal of religious liberty is not without limits. For a variety of historical and cultural reasons, Locke himself drew these limits in overly restrictive ways. For various reasons, he believed that his general principles of religious toleration did not apply to Catholics, Muslims and atheists.[27] However, while Locke got the application of his basic principles wrong, he rightly recognized at least three questions that suggest the outer limits of religious liberty and of liberalism itself: First, to what extent can a society tolerate those who do not share a commitment to principles of mutual toleration and respect? Second, to what extent can society tolerate those who will not keep their basic commitments, oaths, and promises (including the commitment to be bound by the social compact itself)? And third, to what extent can society tolerate those who are bent on destroying society, either through internal sedition or through international warfare? These questions suggest limits that even the most liberal and tolerant society must put to itself. They suggest the need for formulation, respectively, of a reciprocal toleration norm, an obligation fulfillment norm, and a societal self-preservation norm. This is not the place to articulate the content of these norms. Different societies will no doubt address these issues in different ways. What is significant is that they leave substantial room for recognizing that principles of community may be supported by different groups coming from different perspectives, and that these groups can be accepted into a community on their own terms. Affording maximal respect to such diversity can contribute in powerful ways to the achievement of social order, and to defusing pressures that would otherwise build up along the tectonic plates of the contemporary world's cultural divides.

A Comparative Model for Analyzing Religious Liberty

Up to this point, we have identified various cultural tensions that make religion potentially divisive and the countervailing considerations that have helped moderns since Locke to understand how respect for religion and its potential divisiveness can result in stabilization rather than disintegration of a society and its political institutions. We turn now to an effort to provide a comparative framework for possible configurations of religious and state institutions and resulting patterns of religious freedom.

Threshold Conditions for Religious Liberty. An initial consideration in any generalized reflection on religious liberty is the recognition that

[27] See Locke, *Letter Concerning Toleration*, 61-64.

there are certain threshold conditions that must be met before religious liberty can emerge. Briefly stated, there must be some measure of (1) pluralism, (2) economic stability, and (3) political legitimacy within the society in question. In addition, (4) there must be some willingness on the part of differing religious groups and their adherents to live with each other. Each of these threshold conditions deserves fuller analysis, but only a few comments are possible here.

Minimal Pluralism. Until some measure of divergence in fundamental belief systems emerges in a society, the question of religious liberty does not even arise. One can imagine a primitive society, for example, in which all the members of the community share assumptions about the nature of the physical and moral cosmos and in which agreement is so pervasive that questions of religious liberty and dissent would not arise.

Given human propensities to disagree and struggle with each other concerning fundamental issues, it seems difficult to imagine such pristine social homogeneity enduring for long. This difficulty is evident even within nuclear families, and is all the more likely to emerge in societies of any complexity. On the other hand, one can imagine societies enduring for substantial periods in which dominant religious views achieve effective consensus. Some medieval Christian communities no doubt functioned in this manner.

Similarly, one can imagine a society maintaining a sense of its own homogeneity by conceptualizing dissenters as strangers or foreigners. That is, group differentiation may obscure the emergence of incipient pluralism. Each group is committed to its own understanding of the world. Struggles between rival groups are understood as battles for the dominance of one outlook over another. Particularly if exit (or expulsion) from one group is easy, the home group remains homogeneous and the need for religious liberty is not perceived. Dissent appears as treason, betrayal, or at a minimum, as the mark of an outsider. Issues of religious liberty only begin to arise when differences between outlooks must be taken seriously as an unavoidable part of the relevant community.

Cultural blindness can play an analogous role in obscuring the need for religious liberty protections. Dominant European groups have often failed to show adequate respect for the belief systems of indigenous groups during periods of colonization. Similarly, even well-intended secular bureaucrats often fail to see how a seemingly routine regulation can have serious adverse consequences for a particular religious community. The distance between outsiders and marginalized insiders is very short.

Economic Stability. In situations of dire necessity, religious liberty concerns appear to have lower priority than meeting basic economic needs.

In Eastern Europe, for example, resolution of the economic crisis appears to be a more urgent concern than enhancing religious liberty. The fact that religious liberty can exist in countries with very weak economies suggests that this threshold is not very high. And it may simply be that when economic crisis is sufficiently acute, no regime is sufficiently stable to afford effective religious liberty guarantees. If differing religious orientations take differing views as to how the economic crisis can be resolved, this can exacerbate the problem of political instability and reduce the extent to which a regime is inclined to foster religious liberty. On the other hand, religious belief may help people to weather economic hardship (a partial truth behind Marx's notion of religion as "the opiate of the people") and may contribute to economic productivity (e.g., Weber's notion that the Protestant ethic contributed to the productivity of capitalism). Nonetheless, there appears to be some correlation between the level of economic productivity and effective religious liberty protections.

Political Legitimacy. Since religion can be a powerful legitimizing (or delegitimizing) force in a society, the likelihood of achieving religious liberty is reduced to the extent that a regime's political legitimacy is weak. Such a regime is likely either to exploit the legitimizing power of a dominant religion (with concomitant risks of oppression for dissenting groups) or to view religion in general as a threat. In either case, religious liberty suffers.

Public emergency situations can result either from economic or political instability or from natural or foreign threats (or any combination of the foregoing), but in any event, it is not surprising to find derogations of religious liberty rights during periods of emergency. I am not suggesting that this state of affairs is good[28]—just that it is not surprising.

Religious Respect for Rights of Those with Differing Beliefs. Religious liberty for all is not possible in a context in which one religious group not only rejects the beliefs of another group but is unwilling to live with that group. If the intolerant group is dominant, it will persecute adherents of other groups. If not, it is likely to attract persecution itself because of efforts to actualize its religious views. In either event, religious liberty will

---

[28] To the contrary, I support the notion of non-derogability of religious freedom rights called for by the International Covenant on Civil and Political Rights. Civil and Political Covenant, art. 4(2). Article 15 of the European Convention does not make freedom of thought, conscience and religion non-derogable. This may reflect the earlier adoption date of the European Convention. However, where states are parties to both agreements, articles 15(1) and 60 of the European Convention appear require that such states respect non-derogability as required by the Covenant. See Malcolm N. Shaw, "Freedom of Thought, Conscience and Religion," in *The European System for the Protection of Human Rights*, R. St. J. Macdonald, F. Matscher & H. Petzold, eds. (Dordrecht, 1993), 445, 446.

not be fully actualized in the community because there will be at least one group that feels inhibited in actualizing its religious beliefs.

This problem can only be solved if there are grounds within a religious tradition calling for toleration of or respect for the rights of others to have divergent beliefs. Fortunately, there are resources within most religious traditions that support according others such respect. Within the Roman Catholic tradition, there is the pronouncement from Vatican II in *De Libertate Religiosa*.[29] Within Islam, there is the doctrine of toleration of the "People of the Book."[30] Numerous pronouncements on religious liberty have been promulgated by the World Council of Churches.[31]

Religious teachings such as the foregoing which encourage toleration and respect are not always as expansive as one might wish, and are not always lived up to in practice. But they at least provide a starting point for making religious liberty possible.

The Relationship Between Religious Freedom Rights and Church-State Separation. With the foregoing analysis of threshold conditions for religious freedom in mind, we can turn to a comparative analysis of different types of church-state systems. The degree of religious liberty in a particular society can be assessed along two dimensions—one involving the degree to which state action burdens religious belief and conduct and another involving the degree of identification between governmental and religious institutions.[32] In the United States, because of the wording of the

---

[29] *Acta Synodalia Sacrosancti Concilii Oecumenici Vaticani II* (Vatican City, 1963). See also Enda McDonagh, *Freedom or Tolerance?* (New York, 1967), 13-32.

[30] See Huston Smith, *Religions of Man* (New York, 1958), 211.

[31] See, e.g., The Report of the Conference at Oxford, July 1937, on Church, Community, and State; The First Assembly of the World Council of Churches, "A Declaration on Religious Liberty," Amsterdam, 22 August-4 September 1948; Third Assembly of the World Council of Churches, "Statement on Religious Liberty," New Delhi 19 November-5 December 1961; Executive Committee of the Commission of the Churches on International Affairs, Twentieth Executive Committee, World Council of Churches, "Human Rights and Religious Liberty," Geneva Switzerland, July 9-12, 1965; First Assembly of the World Council of Churches, "The Right to Religious Freedom," Nairobi, 23 November-10 December, 1975.

[32] For the basic features of the model I describe in this section, I am indebted to the insights of a former student, George R. Ryskamp. For his description of the basic features of the model, see George R. Ryskamp, "The Spanish Experience in Church-State Relations: A Comparative Study of the Interrelationship Between Church-State Identification and Religious Liberty," *Brigham Young University Law Review* (1980): 616. I have always felt a degree of professorial involvement in the development of this model, in part because it was first worked out in a paper for a seminar I taught, and in part because the shift from thinking in terms of establishment to the German notion of identification (which I brought to Ryskamp's attention) helped him to work out the model. The notion of church-state identification "refers to the degree and type of interrelation between the state, as the governmental expression of society, and the church, as the institutional manifestations of society's religious expression." Ibid., 617.

religion clause of the First Amendment of the U.S. Constitution,[33] these two dimensions are thought of respectively as the "free exercise" and "establishment" aspects of religious liberty. But for comparative purposes, it is useful to think more broadly in terms of varying degrees of religious freedom and church-state identification.

At least in lay thought, there is a tendency to assume that there is a straightforward linear correlation between these two values that could be represented as shown in Figure 1:

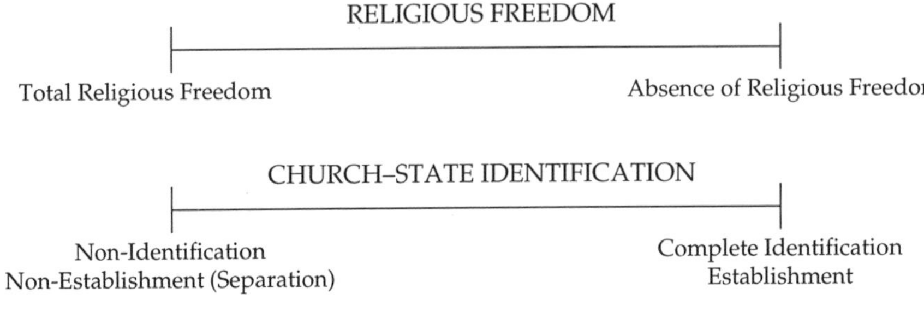

Figure 1

This picture considerably oversimplifies matters. The primary difficulties arise in connection with the church-state identification gradient and its correlation to the religious freedom continuum. Few religious establishments have ever been so totalistic as to achieve complete identification of church and state. To the extent that extreme situation is reached or approached, there is clearly an absence of religious freedom. This is obviously true for adherents of minority religions, and even the majority religion is likely to suffer because of extensive state involvement in or regulation of its affairs or due to the enervation that results from excessive dependence of religious institutions on the state.

At the other end of the church-state identification continuum, things seem more confused. The mere fact that a state does not have a formally established church does not necessarily mean that it has a separationist regime characterized by rigorous non-identification with religion. Moreover, there is considerable disagreement about the exact configuration of relationships between church and state that maximizes religious liberty, and it may well be that the optimal configuration for one culture may be different than that for another. Further, it is not clear whether "non-identification" accurately marks the end of this particular

[33] The First Amendment provides: "Congress shall make no law respecting an establishment of religion, or prohibiting the free exercise thereof." U.S. Const. amend. I.

continuum. Non-establishment and separation may mark intermediate points along a longer continuum that actually ends with "negative" identification: i.e., overt hostility or persecution. But if persecution lies at both ends of the church-state identification continuum, it is not at all clear how this continuum correlates with the religious liberty continuum.

The degree of confusion becomes evident when one considers one author's[34] attempt to plot countries along these two continua as shown in Figure 2:

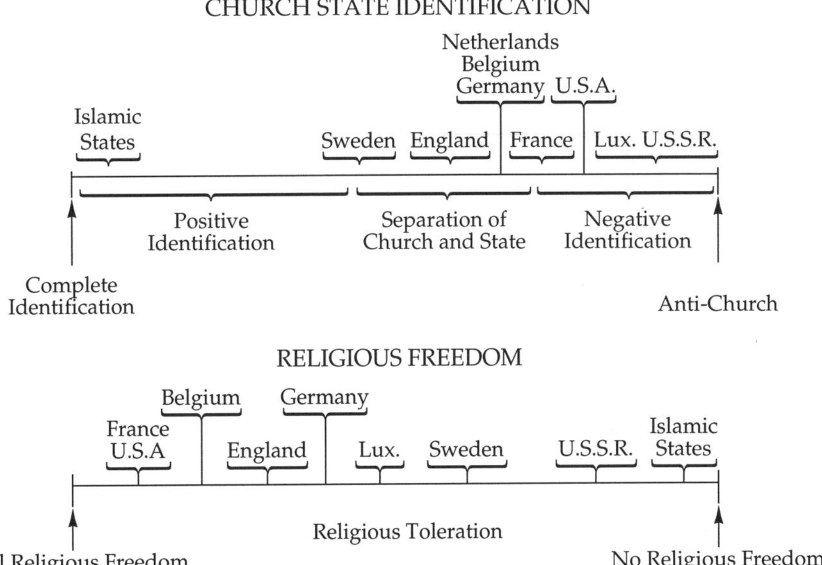

Figure 2

One can challenge several aspects of the foregoing diagram. For example, with respect to the identification continuum, it is not completely clear why there is a lesser degree of identification in Belgium than in England, or why the United States should be located between France and Luxemburg. Lumping all Islamic regimes together is unfair in that it fails to take account of variance across such regimes. It is also important to remember that through much of history, Islamic regimes were in fact more tolerant than their Christian counterparts. The U.S.S.R. is of course gone, but even at the beginning of the 1980s, when the diagram was originally framed, there was considerable variance within the communist bloc. In short, the rankings in the diagram with respect to degree of iden-

34 See Ryskamp, "The Spanish Experience," 620.

tification are oversimplified and to some extent based more on stereotypes than empirical realities. Many of the religious freedom rankings seem equally arbitrary. But minor reshuffling of some of these rankings fails to remove more fundamental puzzles, such as why states located at opposite ends of the identification gradient should be located so close to each other on the religious freedom gradient.

The answer to this seeming puzzle lies in reconceptualizing the church-state identification continuum as a loop that correlates with the religious freedom continuum as shown in Figure 3:[35]

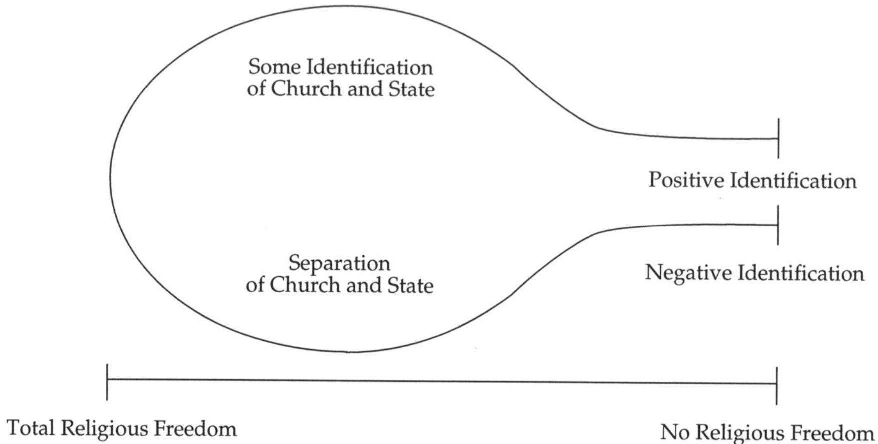

Figure 3

This model accurately reflects the fact that both strong positive and strong negative identification of church and state correlate with low levels of religious freedom. In both situations, the state adopts a sharply defined attitude toward one or more religions, leaving little room for dissenting views.

The model also captures a related but less obvious reality. Changes in political regimes often move back and forth between extreme positions near the ends of the identification gradients, skipping more moderate intermediate positions. Thus, the history of church-state experience in Spain reflects radical shifts from regimes strongly supportive of an established church to secularist, anti-clerical regimes.[36] In other settings, fun-

---

[35] See ibid., 652. I am indebted to Ryskamp for the recognition of the loop-like structure of the identification gradient. My analysis goes further in identifying some of the "way stations" along the continuum.

[36] Ibid., 620-36, 652-53. Ryskamp first worked out the loop-model of church-state identification in the context of a study of the Spanish experience. It was precisely the recognition

damentalist regimes may be replaced by radically secularist regimes, and vice versa.

Another significant aspect of religious liberty clarified by the model is that one cannot simply assume that the more rigidly one separates church and state, the more religious liberty will be enhanced. At some point, aggressive separationism becomes hostility toward religion. Mechanical insistence on separation at all costs may accordingly push a system toward inadvertent insensitivity and ultimately intentional persecution. Stalinist constitutions generally had very strong church-state separation provisions, but these can hardly be said to have maximized religious liberty. Rather, they were construed as a demand that religion should be excluded from any domain where the state was present. But in a totalitarian state, this became a demand in practice that religion be marginalized to the vanishing point. Secularist insistence in other countries that religion be confined to the ever-diminishing "private sphere," though typically less extreme, can have similar results in marginalizing religious life and reducing religious liberty.[37]

Once one recognizes the foregoing general features of the religious freedom and identification gradients, one can begin to introduce refinements that help describe significant subfeatures along the two continua. These subfeatures in turn help identify salient differences among national religious liberty systems.

Turning first to the identification continuum, one can conceive it as a representation of a series of types of church-state regimes. Beginning at the positive identification end of the continuum, one first encounters *absolute theocracies* of the type one associates with stereotypical views of Islamic fundamentalism. In fact, a range of regimes is possible in Muslim theory, depending on the scope given to internal Muslim beliefs about toleration and also depending on the extent to which flexible interpretation of Shari'a law creates normative space for modernization.[38]

---

that the two ends of the identification continuum must lie situated fairly close to each other to adequately model the pendulum shifts of Spanish that pointed to the need for the loop structure.

[37] *See* Frederick M. Gedicks, "Public Life and Hostility to Religion," *Virginia Law Review* 78 (1992): 671-696.

[38] The Qur'an contains an account according to which Muslims are to "fight those among the People of the Book [Christians, Jews, Zoroastrians, and Magians] who do not believe in Allah, [who do not believe] in the Last Day, who do not forsake what Allah and His Prophet forbid, and who do not abide in the True Religion . . . until such a time as they submissively render the *jizyah*." Qur'an 9:29. The *jizyah* is a tax that non-converting Jews and Christians are required to pay to demonstrate submissiveness to Islam. See also Qur'an 60:8 ("Allah does not forbid [the Muslim] from treating with kindness and justice those who refrain from fighting with you over religion . . . for Allah loves those who are just").

Established Churches. The notion of an "established church" is vague, and can in fact cover a range of possible church-state configurations with very different implications for the religious freedom of minority groups. At one extreme, a regime with an established church that is granted a strictly enforced monopoly in religious affairs is closely related to one with theocratic rule. Spain or Italy at some periods are classical exemplars. The next position is held by countries that have an established religion that tolerates a restricted set of divergent beliefs. An Islamic country that tolerates "people of the Book"[39] (but not others) would be one example; a country with an established Christian church that tolerates a number of major faiths, but disparages others would be another. The next position is a country that maintains an established church, but guarantees equal treatment for all other religious beliefs. Great Britain would be a fitting example.

Endorsed Churches. The next category consists of regimes that fall just short of formally affirming that one particular church is the official church of a nation, but acknowledge that one particular church has a special place in the country's traditions. This is quite typical in countries where Roman Catholicism is predominant and a new constitution has been adopted relatively recently (at least since Vatican II).[40] The endorsed church is specially acknowledged, but the country's constitution asserts that other groups are entitled to equal protection. Sometimes the endorsement is relatively innocuous, and remains strictly limited to recognition that a particular religious tradition has played an important role in a country's history and culture. In other cases, endorsement operates in fact as a thinly disguised method of preserving the prerogatives of establishment while maintaining the formal appearance of a more liberal regime.

Cooperationist Regimes. The next category of regime grants no special status to dominant churches, but the state continues to cooperate closely with churches in a variety of ways. Germany provides the prototypical example of this type of regime, though it is certainly not alone in this regard.[41] Most notably, the cooperationist state may provide significant funding to various church-related activities, such as religious education or maintenance of churches, payment of clergy, and so forth. Very often in such regimes, relations with churches are managed through special

---

[39] See Smith, *Religions of Man*, 211.

[40] See, e.g., Bolivia, art. 3; Costa Rica, art. 75; Panama, art. 34; Paraguay, art. 6; Spain, art. 16.

[41] For a valuable overview of the German church-state system, see Axel Freiherr von Campenhausen, *Staatskirchenrecht: Ein Studienbuch*, 2d ed., (Munich, 1983). A more comprehensive treatment is provided in the two volume *Handbuch des Staatskirchenrechts der Bundesrepublik Deutschland*, Ernst Friesenhahn, Ulrich Scheuner & Joseph Listl, eds. (Berlin, 1974-75).

agreements, concordats, and the like. Spain, Italy and Poland as well as several Latin American countries follow this pattern. The state may also cooperate in helping with the gathering of contributions (e.g., the withholding of "church tax" in Germany). Cooperationist countries frequently have patterns of aid or assistance that benefit larger denominations in particular. However, they do not specifically endorse any religion, and they are committed to affording equal treatment to all religious organizations. Since different religious communities have different needs, cooperationist programs can raise more complex interdenominational problems of equal treatment. It is all too easy to slip from cooperation into patterns of state preference. Also, vis-à-vis more separationist regimes, more complex questions of protecting the self-determination and internal autonomy of religious organizations arise.

Note that in some cases, a cooperationist approach may be necessary for a transition period. For example, because of the devastated condition of churches after communism in East Central Europe and the former U.S.S.R., corrective justice seems to require return of extensive properties wrongfully taken from various churches. This process of restoration will necessarily entail heavy cooperation on the part of the state with churches, but it is not completely clear whether this process should be handled in a way that will aim at restoration of patterns of cooperation, or whether the required cooperation will be merely transitional, while the long term policy is to establish a more voluntarist regime.

Accommodationist Regimes. A regime may insist on separation of church and state, yet retain a posture of benevolent neutrality toward religion. Accommodationism might be thought of as cooperationism without the provision of any direct financial subsidies to religion or religious education. An accommodationist regime would have no qualms about recognizing the importance of religion as part of national or local culture, accommodating religious symbols in public settings, allowing tax, dietary, holiday, Sabbath, and other kinds of exemptions, and so forth. Many scholars in the United States argue that the United States religion clause should be construed to allow a more accommodationist approach to religious liberty.[42] Note that the growth of the state intensifies the need for accommodation. As state influence becomes more pervasive and regulatory burdens expand, refusal to exempt or accommodate shades into hostility.

Separationist Regimes. As suggested by the earlier comments on Stalinist church-state separation, the slogan "separation of church and state"

---

42 *See, e.g.*, Michael W. McConnell, "Accommodation of Religion," *Supreme Court Review* (1985): 1-59; Michael W. McConnell, "Accommodation of Religion: An Update and a Response to Critics," *George Washington Law Review* 60 (1992): 685.

can be used to cover a fairly broad and diverse range of regimes. At the benign end, separationism differs relatively little from accommodationism. The major difference is that separationism, as it names suggests, insists on more rigid separation of church and state. Any suggestion of public support for religion is deemed inappropriate. Religious symbols in public displays such as Christmas creches are not allowed. Even indirect subsidies to religion through tax deductions or tax exemptions are either suspect or proscribed. Granting religiously-based exemptions from general public laws is viewed as impermissible favoritism for religion. No religious teaching or indoctrination of any kind is permitted in public schools (although some teaching about religion from an objective standpoint may be permitted). The mere reliance on religious premises in public argument is deemed to run afoul of the church-state separation principle. Members of the clergy are not permitted to hold public office.[43]

More extreme forms of separationism make stronger attempts to cordon off religion from public life. One form this can take is through tightening the state monopoly on certain forms of educational or social services. In the educational realm, the state can ban home schooling altogether, can proscribe private schools, or can submit either of the foregoing to such extensive accreditation requirements that it is virtually impossible for independent religious education to function. Different regimes make differing judgments about the extent to which religious marriages will be recognized. A range of social or charitable services (including health care) may be regulated in ways that make it difficult for religious organizations to carry out their perceived ministries in this area. "Separation" in its most objectionable guise demands that religion retreat from any domain that the state desires to occupy, but is untroubled by intrusive state regulation and intervention in religious affairs.

Inadvertent Insensitivity. Overlapping with some forms of separationism is a recurrent pattern of legislative or bureaucratic insensitivity to distinctive religious needs. Bureaucrats often fail to distinguish between conduct regulated in secular settings (e.g., regulating land use planning, labor discrimination, taxation with respect to secular business activities) and regulating similar conduct in religious settings. In many cases, fairly simple accommodations can satisfactorily solve religious concerns. Regulations as initially formulated often lack any anti-religious animus;

---

[43] Some interesting differences are evident with respect to this latter point. The Supreme Court of the more strictly separationist United States has held that a state constitutional provision barring the clergy from political office violated the first amendment. *McDaniel v. Paty*, 435 U.S. 618 (1978). A number of Latin American countries that are in other respects less separationist than the United States disqualify the clergy for higher elected positions. *See, e.g.*, Argentina, art. 65; Bolivia, art. 50; El Salvador, art 82; Guatemala, arts. 186, 197; Panama, art. 41.

those drafting the regulations were simply unaware of the religious implications of their regulations. At some point, those afflicted by the unintended burden bring the problem to the attention of government officials. At this point, a reasonable accommodation can be worked out, or inadvertent insensitivity shades into conscious persecution. The flip side of inadvertent insensitivity is subtle or not-so-subtle privileging of main-line or dominant groups. It is altogether too easy for state officials who work with major religious groups to be less concerned with the needs of smaller groups and to speak of them in disparaging ways.

Hostility and Overt Persecution. The test in this area is how smaller religious groups are treated. Government officials seldom persecute larger religious groups (though this was certainly not unheard of in communist lands). Persecution can take the form of imprisonment of those who insist on acting in accordance with divergent religious beliefs. In its most egregious forms, it involves "ethnic cleansing" or most extreme, genocide. More typical problems involve less dramatic forms of bureaucratic roadblocks which cumulatively have the effect of significantly impairing religious liberty. These can take the form of denying or delaying registration (granting entity status) and obstructing land use approvals.

With the foregoing categories in mind, the relationship between the more refined identification gradient and the religious freedom gradient can be modeled as shown in *Figure 4*:

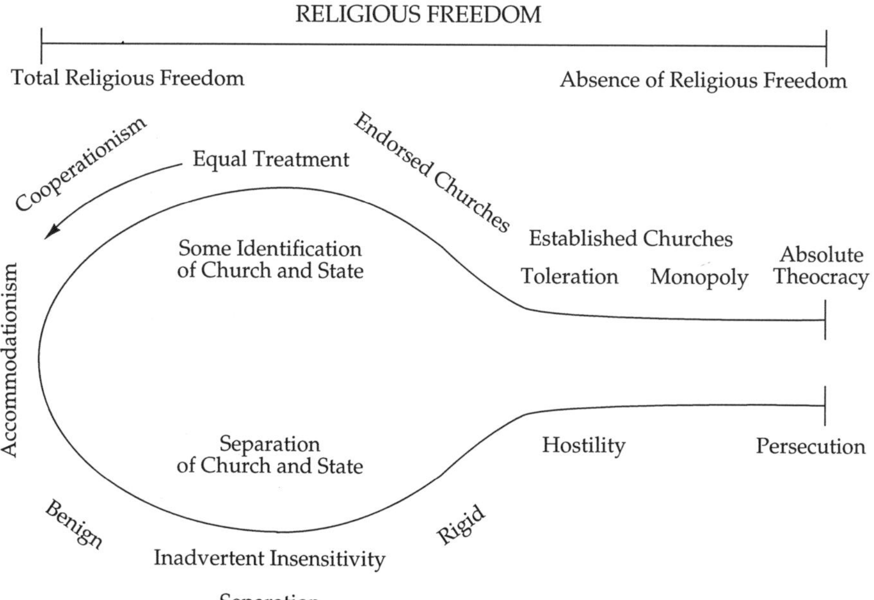

There is some room for argument about which type of regime should be displayed as the type most likely to maximize religious liberty. My contention is that accommodationist regimes have the best claim to this position. Historical experience suggests that maximal religious liberty tends to be achieved when church-state identification is in the accommodation or non-hostile separation mode. Of course, substantial religious liberty can also exist in cooperationist or endorsed church regimes, at least where genuine religious equality is present. However, there is always a sense in such regimes that smaller religious communities have a kind of second-class status, and to the extent that public funds are directly supporting programs of major churches, there is a sense that members of religious minorities are being coerced to support religious programs with which they do not agree. As between separationist and accommodationist regimes, accommodationism has the edge in contemporary settings where the modern secular "performance state" has emerged with its welfare and regulatory dimensions. As state action or influence pervades more and more of social life, wooden insistence on separation too easily slips into marginalization of religion. Moreover, as regulations proliferate, there is increased demand for exceptions that can sensitively accommodate religious needs. In the last analysis, if accommodation can be achieved without undue difficulty, a regime which fails to accommodate manifests a lesser degree of religious liberty.

Advocates of stricter separation tend to invoke notions of equality to argue against accommodation.[44] Accommodating a religious need or practice, the argument goes, inevitably involves giving religious individuals or groups special treatment, and this violates requirements of state neutrality and equal protection. This overlooks the fact that differential treatment does not necessarily violate equality norms if there is a rational basis for the differentiation. Protecting religious freedom rights provides not merely a rational basis but a compelling justification for reasonable accommodations. In the last analysis, making such accommodations (or alternatively, using the least burdensome means—from the standpoint of the religious practice affected—in pursuing state ends) is the best way to assure that the dignity of religiously different persons is afforded equal respect. Treating others with understanding of their differences shows far deeper respect than allocating everyone to equally Procrustean beds.

Differences in cultural or historical background may also affect the particular approach that best maximizes religious liberty in a particular

---

[44] William P. Marshall, "The Inequality of Anti-Establishment," *Brigham Young University Law Review* (1993): 63-71; id., "In Defense of Smith and Free Exercise Revisionism," *University of Chicago Law Review* 58 (1991): 308-28.

country. For example, accommodating religious instruction in schools may be more important in a country such as Germany, where school secularization is associated historically with the religious persecutions of Bismarck's *Kulturkampf*[45] and the Nazi *Kirchenkampf*.[46] In the United States, in contrast, introduction of indoctrination-style instruction in the public schools appears violative of long-entrenched church-state traditions. More generally, it is often the case that essentially similar conduct will have different cultural meaning in different national settings. Religious liberty must be sensitive to these shifting social realities.

The church-state identification loop is useful not only in comparing types of institutional configurations, but also in keeping institutional issues in perspective. It is useful to note, for example, that the often highly polarized constitutional debates in the United States are in fact debates about which of a fairly narrow range of institutional options is optimal. Seeing the different possible configurations as a continuum helps to alert one to risks of ways that one type of regime can gradually slip into another. Unfortunately, because religious and governmental institutions are striving for influence and prestige, and because accommodation is not necessarily the bureaucratic path of least resistance, the natural tendency in the system is in directions that drift away from optimal respect for religious freedom. This means that vigilance is necessary, and that legal remedies that can counter this drift are vital.

The Archaeology of International Religious Liberty Norms

The Broadening Scope of Religious Liberty. With the foregoing analysis of the identification continuum in place, it is time to turn to a more detailed analysis of the religious liberty continuum itself. The positions along this continuum reflect historical stages in the unfolding of religious freedom. The various stages in this development remain visible as "strata" in contemporary international human rights documents. A full account of the history of the unfolding of legal protections in this area

---

[45] See Maehl, *Germany in Western Civilization*, 464-467.

[46] Ulrich Scheuner, "Erörterungen und Tendenzen im gegenwärtigen Staatskirchenrecht der Bundesrepublik," *Essener Gespräche zum Thema Staat und Kirche* 1 (1969): 108, 110; Ernst Christian Helmreich, *Religious Education in German Schools: An Historical Approach* (Cambridge, MA, 1959), 9-10, 154-59, 163-69, 176-77; Paul G. Kauper & Rudolf Halberstadt, "Religion and Education in West Germany: A Survey and an American Perspective," *Valparaiso University Law Review* 4 (1969): 1, 21.

would trace back to the classic 18th century documents[47] that serve as the "grandparents" of most current religious liberty provisions. For present purposes, however, the basic "archaeology" of religious freedom rights (and a corresponding sense for the possible positions along the religious freedom continuum) can be sufficiently disclosed by unpacking Article 9 of the European Convention for the Protection of Human Rights and Freedoms.[48]

Article 9 is virtually identical to Article 18 of the International Covenant on Civil and Political Rights[49] and closely parallels Article 12 of the American Convention on Human Rights.[50] In short, it reflects emerging consensus on religious liberty. At the same time, one can discern in Article 9 the strata of older, narrower conceptions of religious liberty that have been deposited in the course of the historical broadening of religious freedom over time until the modern expansive protections have been attained. My aim in this section is to describe the archaeology of these successively broader conceptions of religious liberty so that the scope and meaning of modern provisions can be more fully appreciated.

Article 9 reads as follows:

> 1. Everyone has the right to freedom of thought, conscience, and religion; this right includes freedom to change his religion or belief and freedom, either alone or in community with others and in public or private, to manifest his religion or belief, in worship, teaching, practice, and observance.
> 2. Freedom to manifest one's religion or beliefs shall be subject only to such limitations as are prescribed by law and are necessary in a democratic society in the interests of public safety, for the protection of public order, health or morals, or for the protection of the rights and freedoms of others.

The first thing to notice about Article 9 is that it applies to "everyone." This is one of the most fundamental achievements of the law of religious freedom in this century, and in that sense represents a rela-

---

[47] Virginia Bill of Rights of 1776, § 16; Austrian Act on Religious Tolerance of 1781; Virginia Bill Establishing Religious Freedom of January 1, 1786; Prussian Edict on Religion of 1788; Allgemeines Landrecht für die preussischen Staaten, part II, title 11, §§ 1-4; *United States Constitution*, Amendment I; French *Declaration of the Rights of Man and Citizen*.

[48] European Convention for the Protection of Human Rights and Fundamental Freedoms, Nov. 4, 1950, U.N.T.S. 213: 222, entered into force Sept. 3, 1953, as amended by Protocol No. 3, entered into force Sept. 21, 1970, and Protocol No. 5, entered into force Dec. 21, 1971.

[49] G.A. res. 2200A (XXI), December 16, 1966, 21 U.N. GAOR Supp. (No. 16) at 52, U.N. Doc. A/6316 (1966), 999 U.N.T.S. 171, entered into force March 23, 1976.

[50] Nov. 22, 1969, O.A.S. Treaty Series No. 36, at 1, OEA/Ser. L./V/II.23 doc. rev. 2 entered into force July 18, 1978.

tively recent universalization of religious freedom claims. Contrary to earlier models of religious freedom, its protections are not limited to citizens. Resident aliens and those only temporarily in a country are also covered. Moreover, the right is not available only to believers. Particularly since World War II, it has come to be recognized that the right to freedom of thought, conscience, and religion, extends to philosophical *Weltanschauungen* as well as to more traditional religious orientations. Finally, while the term "everyone" could be construed as only applying to natural persons, the better contemporary readings also protect the rights of religious associations as entities or groups, for religious liberty can often be best protected by recognizing the rights of religious communities to autonomy.[51] In short, religious freedom has come to be understood as a universal value. This notion has come under increasing attack in recent years, particularly in Muslim circles where religious freedom norms have often been perceived as part of Western imperialism's attack on Islamic culture,[52] and it remains to be seen whether this "universalization" of religious freedom will remain as a permanent achievement—a kind of shared bedrock in all emerging regimes—or will succumb to pressures of nationalism (which often insists that religious freedom be guaranteed only for citizens) and particularism.[53]

Corresponding to the opening clause of Article 9, one can imagine a maximally restrictive regime that permits *only internal freedom of religion,* and limits religious freedom to its ineradicable psychological minimum: the freedom to think and believe as one will, so long as absolutely no external manifestation of such belief occurs. While it is now conceivable that even internal thought and belief processes can be impaired by drugs or other modern technologies, internal freedom of religion is an inner core of religious liberty that law simply cannot abolish without extraordinary measures. The "belief-action" dichotomy of 19th century religion clause case law in the United States tracks this maximally narrow conception of religious freedom and dates back to 17th and 18th century thinkers.[54] This notion is obviously unsatisfactory from a contemporary

---

[51] See discussion of Principle 16c of the Vienna Concluding Document hereafter.

[52] See, e.g., Kevin Dwyer, *Arab Voices: The Human Rights Debate in the Middle East* (Berkeley, 1991), 5-7; John L. Esposito, *Islam and Politics*, 3d ed. (Syracuse, NY, 1991), 77, 131-43.

[53] Consultation Group on Universality vs. Relativism, The Project on Religion and Human Rights, "Universitality vs. Relativism in Human Rights," in *Religion and Human Rights*, 32-59.

[54] In *Reynolds v. United States*, 98 U.S. 145, 163 (1878), the Court cites the preamble to Jefferson's Bill for Establishing Religious Freedom in articulating the limits of religious freedom as follows: "after a recital 'that to suffer the civil magistrate to intrude his powers into the field of opinion, and to restrain the profession or propagation of principles on supposition of their ill tendency, is a dangerous falacy which at once destroys all religious liberty,' [the pre-

perspective. A freedom that can be respected in the Gulag Archipelago is hardly a freedom deserving the name.

A slightly enlarged version of religious freedom can be described as *freedom of the hearth*—the type of freedom available to dissenters in Reformation times and still evident today in "house churches" in restrictive regimes such as the People's Republic of China.[55] This is akin to internal freedom of religion, except that internal beliefs can at least be externalized within the walls of the home, so long as they are not disclosed outside that setting. In the terms of Article 9, this would be a freedom of religion that could be practiced only "in private." Of course, Article 9 affords far broader protections, but the earliest beginnings of religious liberty are still visible in some of its phrases.

Closely related to the right to have a belief and to practice it in the privacy of the mind or the home is the *freedom to change religion or belief.* This freedom has often gone unrecognized, and to this day, conversion from Islam to another religion is not permissible in many Muslim countries. Most modern legal systems protect the general right to choose and change religious beliefs, but traces of older inflexibility are often evident. For example, conscription laws typically exempt conscientious objectors from military service (or provide for various forms of alternative service), but these laws are not always sensitive to changes of religious belief that occur once someone has entered the military.[56] Similarly, labor legislation will often make allowances for religious views held at the outset of employment, but not necessarily for subsequent changes in a worker's religious beliefs or for unanticipated implications of a worker's beliefs in subsequent work assignments.[57] In short, while modern legal systems are

---

amble to Jefferson's bill] . . . declared 'that it is time enough for the rightful purposes of civil government for its officers to interfere when principles break out into overt acts against peace and good order.' In these two sentences is found the true distinction between what properly belongs to the church and what to the State."

55 Human Rights Watch/Asia, *Freedom of Religion in China* (New York, 1992), 4, 8-9.

56 See generally European Consortion for Church-State Research, *Conscientious Objection in the EC Countries* (Milan, 1992)[*EC Conscientious Objection*]. Contributors to this volume noted that one can be released from military service for conscientious objections acquired after the start of service in Denmark, Erik Siesby, "Conscientious Objection in Danish Law," *EC Conscientious Objection* 159, 161, in the United Kingdom, Francis Lyall, "Conscience and the Law: UK National Report," in *EC Conscientious Objection*, 165, 170, and in the Netherlands, Ben. P. Vermeulen, "Conscientious Objection in Dutch Law," in *EC Conscientious Objection* 259, 277.

57 See, e.g., *Thomas v. Review Board of the Indiana Employment Security Division*, 450 U.S. 707 (1981)(holding that such changes *are* entitled to constitutional protection); W. Cole Durham, Jr., Mary Anne Wood, and Spencer J. Condie, "Accommodation of Conscientious Objection to Abortion Among Nurses: A Case Study of the Nursing Profession," *Brigham Young University Law Review* (1982): 253.

committed to the right to change religious beliefs in theory, they are often insufficiently sensitive to the implications of that right in practice.

It is very significant to note that under Article 9 and similar provisions of other human rights documents, freedom of religion (including internal freedom of religion, freedom of the hearth, and in general freedom to have and to change religion or belief), may not be regulated by the state in any manner. *Only manifestations of religion may be regulated,* and manifestations may only be regulated under the restricted conditions identified in subparagraph 2.[58] This is the more sophisticated 20th century version of the belief-action dichotomy. But this is getting ahead of the story.

The next enlargement of religious liberty discernible in Article 9 is protection of *freedom of worship*, narrowly construed. As a practical matter, the humblest versions of worship do not move far from the hearth. One believer may invite some neighbors or friends to join with him in worship within the walls of his home. At a more expansive level, freedom of worship might be construed to permit group services in churches or other edifices, without allowing any manifestation of belief outside of such "private" buildings. Worship narrowly construed extends protections only to actual worship services or formal acts of worship as opposed to other forms of religiously motivated behavior, such as visiting the sick or organizing an athletic program for youth. Achievement of the right to freedom of worship even in this narrow sense was, of course, a significant historical advance. To realize its limits, however, one need only reflect on the plight of believers in Stalinist systems, who could indeed go to church, but would lose their jobs (and educational opportunities for their children) if they did so. Moreover, the freedom of worship model reflects an excessively narrow conception of what religion is about. It may be as important to religious believers to engage in charitable practices or to observe dietary rules and religious days of rest as to join in formal worship services.

The presence of the term "worship" in Article 9 constituted a significant achievement at an earlier stage in the unfolding of religious freedom. But Article 9 has now moved far beyond this stratum. It clearly recognizes that religious liberty rights extend to both *communal and private* conduct ("freedom, either alone or in community with others . . . "). Part of what makes religious liberty distinctive is that it typically has a

---

58 See, e.g., Human Rights Committee, General Comment No. 22(48) concerning Article 18 (CCPR/C/21/Rev. 1/Add. 4, 27 September 1993 [hereinafter Human Rights Committee, General Comment No. 22(48)], ¶3; P. van Dijk & G.J.H. van Hoof, *Theory and Practice of the European Convention on Human Rights*, 2d ed. (Deventer, Netherlands, 1990), 397-98.

communal element. To afford the right to believe without protecting the communal ties and structures is a mockery of genuine religious liberty.[59]

Moreover, Article 9 extends religious liberty beyond the merely private sphere to public settings ("freedom . . . in public or private, to manifest his religion or belief . . ."). In contrast to other rights of freedom of expression, such as freedom of speech, protection of religious liberty in any modern regime must extend beyond belief and speech to conduct. Even to describe regimes which condone only internal religious freedom or freedom of the hearth is to call up reminders of past days when religious liberty was circumscribed in terrible and unacceptable ways. Just systems of religious liberty thus *protect religion in public or private.*

Finally, Article 9 extends religious liberty beyond mere manifestations of religion in belief and worship to protect "*teaching, practice and observance.*" Thus, individuals and religious groups should be left to teach and inculcate their religion in the manner that is appropriate within their traditions. This will often have significant institutional ramifications, because many religions have seminaries or other theological institutions for training their clergy. It is also vital that religious organizations and families have the right to teach the rising generation and new converts or potential converts. The independent right to freedom of speech will protect many of these practices, but the notion of freedom of religion more clearly implies the need to protect institutional structures needed to carry out processes of teaching and transmitting religious heritage and beliefs. Religious freedom also clearly entails the right to practice and observe religious beliefs—to follow dietary rules, to observe religious holidays and sabbaths, to participate in communal worship services and rituals, to abstain from medical treatment, to participate in ordinations, to hold church courts, to enjoy religious festivals, and so forth. Without this extension into the external world, religious liberty is largely meaningless.

Note that while religious liberty as articulated in Article 9 (and other human rights instruments) is very broad, it is not unlimited. Article 9 is fundamentally about religious belief or other deeply held convictions. It is not as broad as the general liberty described in phrases such as "life, liberty or property" in the United States' due process clause and that is one of the general assumptions of modern free societies. Religious liberty is a subset of general liberty and receives heightened protection because

[59] Early decisions of the European Commission on Human Rights suggested that legal entities could not assert rights under Article 9, and that such protections were derivative from the protections afforded natural persons. Later decisions have rejected that view and have recognized the right of religious organizations qua organizations to assert rights under Article 9. Malcolm N. Shaw, "Freedom of Thought, Conscience and Religion," in R. St. J. Macdonald, F. Matscher & H. Petzold, eds., *The European System for the Protection of Human Rights*, 445, 450.

most free societies have recognized the special role that religion plays in the lives of individuals, groups, and society. Article 9 protects manifestations of religion that are required or deeply and intimately linked to religious beliefs, but not necessarily everything that is motivated or permitted by religious beliefs.[60] Most religious beliefs permit individuals to run for and serve in political office, but the fact that this is permitted by religious beliefs does not imply that one has a religious liberty right to do so. The fact that someone's religious conscience will permit her to choose to have an abortion does not mean she has a religious liberty right to obtain one. The outer boundaries of religious liberty rights remain diffuse, but it is important to recognize there are some limits. Otherwise, there is a risk that fundamental religious liberty rights will be watered down and will lose the heightened protections they deserve.[61]

The Tightening Constraints on Permissible Limitations of Religious Liberty. Thus far, we have been discussing the archaeology of religious liberty rights as they have unfolded historically and as currently embodied in international human rights instruments. To gain a full sense for the structure of the religious freedom continuum, however, it is necessary to describe not only the expanding scope of religious liberty rights, but also the tightening constraints on governmental limitations on such rights that have emerged over time. As noted above, it is important to remember that the only permissible limitations are limitations on *manifestations* of religion, and probably only on public manifestations at that. No limitations on the right to hold or change religious beliefs are permissible. Again, historical strata in the unfolding story of religious liberty and its constraints are evident in the wording of Article 9.

The history of religious liberty in the period following the Reformation began with the principle of *cuius regio eius religio* enunciated in connection with the Peace of Augsburg in 1555[62] and continued in a more liberal form after the Peace of Westphalia.[63] Under this principle, the secular prince was given the right to dictate the religion of his realm to assure a religiously homogeneous population. Dissenters could move to a friendlier domain or possibly practice the freedom of the hearth, but they had little other recourse. In short, the secular ruler or the state under this regime had virtually unlimited discretion in imposing limitations on religious liberty, and was free to impose burdens or outright prohibitions on non-preferred religions.

---

60 Ibid., 458-59.

61 See W. Cole Durham, Jr., "Religious Liberty and the Call of Conscience," *DePaul Law Review* 42 (1992): 85-87.

62 Maehl, *Germany in Western Civilization*, 149.

63 Ibid., 194.

As compared with such absolute discretion, the requirement that emerged by the late 18th century that only generally applicable limitations could be imposed marked a considerable advance. The basic notion was that religious liberty would be recognized within the limits established by law, with the understanding that only neutral laws of general applicability would count as appropriate limiting laws. In a famous formulation that is still recognized in German constitutional law, "Every religious body shall regulate and administer its affairs independently *within the limits of the law valid for all.*"[64] The state was still free to impose any limitations on churches that it liked, but under this *rule of law constraint*, it could only do so if it was willing to impose the limitation generally on all religious groups, including those that were dominant or otherwise favored. Early versions of religious liberty, such as those enunciated toward the end of the 18th century, tended to assume that this rule of law constraint on religious liberty limitations would be adequate to safeguard religious liberty concerns.

The rule of law constraint is still evident in Article 9's insistence that "Freedom to manifest one's religion or beliefs shall be subject *only to such limitations as are prescribed by law. . . .*" The European Court of Human Rights has held that this phrase "does not merely refer back to domestic law but also relates to the quality of law, requiring it to be compatible with the rule of law, which is expressly mentioned in the preamble to the Convention."[65] Arguably, any law that specifically targets or imposes special burdens on a particular religious group, or that is retroactive or unduly vague, would run afoul of this requirement.

In the years since the end of the 18th century, as societies began to have more experience with genuine regimes of religious liberty, sensitivity grew concerning recurrent problem areas. Article 9's requirement that only those limitations can be permitted that are necessary for "interests of public safety, for the protection of public order, health or morals, or for the protection of the rights and freedoms of others" summarizes these problem areas. A variety of significant cases fall into these categories. Without evaluating the merits of such cases, a variety of problem situations come to mind: the legality of requiring immunizations,[66] the permissibility of objecting to blood transfusions,[67] the 19th century Mormon

---

[64] Article 137(3) of the Weimar Constitution, as incorporated in the current Basic Law of the Federal Republic of Germany by Article 140. The italicized phrase dates back to the 18th Century. For a description of its changing meaning over time, see Axel Freiherr von Campenhausen, *Staatskirchenrecht*, 85-95.

[65] *Malone Case*, 82 Eur. Ct. H.R. (ser. A) at 32 (1984).

[66] *Jacobson v. Massachusetts*, 197 U.S. 11 (1905).

[67] See, e.g., *In re President and Directors of Georgetown College, Inc.*, 331 F.2d 1000 (D.C. Cir.), *cert. denied*, 377 U.S. 978 (1964).

polygamy cases in the United States,[68] contemporary problems with "drug" churches,[69] problems associated with faith healing and human or animal sacrifice cases,[70] and so forth. Differing societies may draw differing conclusions about exactly where the borderline of religious liberty should be drawn, but I am aware of no society that does not recognize the need for some limitation.

At the same time, it did not take long to realize that the list of permissible grounds for encroachment on religious liberty summarized in Article 9 was so broad that it could justify almost as much intervention in religious liberty as the *cuius regio* principle. (It is hard to imagine any desired restriction of religious freedom in which one or more of the constraints set forth in Article 9, Section 2 does not apply.) While the rule of law constraint provided some assurance that governmental power would not be abused, history has demonstrated that this constraint is not enough to assure meaningful religious liberty. Many of the major religious persecutions of the last two centuries have been carried out under the guise of formally general and neutral laws. All that is necessary is to pass laws that prohibit everyone in the population from engaging in conduct that is only of concern to a particular religious group in order to pass a law that will fulfill the rule of law requirement but still encroach on religious liberty. Note that often, this will happen not because of intentional animus against a particular group, but because those passing the law are unaware of its adverse impact on a lesser known religious group.

Because of this deficiency in the rule of law constraint, most advanced systems have added an additional layer of constraint on state limitations on religious liberty. As phrased in Article 9, this is the requirement that freedom to manifest religion shall be subject only "to such limitations as . . . *are necessary in a democratic society* in the interests of public safety, [etc]." The Strasbourg Court has construed this to mean that the interference with a right must be motivated by a "pressing social need" and must be "proportionate to the legitimate aim pursued."[71] This constraint can accordingly be referred to as the *necessity* or *proportionality*

---

68 *Davis v. Beason*, 133 U.S. 333 (1890); *Reynolds v. United States*, 98 U.S. 145 (1878); see also *Cleveland v. United States*, 329 U.S. 14 (1946) (Mormon split-off group).

69 See, e.g., *United States v. Kuch*, 288 F. Supp. 439 (D.D.C. 1968), *cert. denied*, 386 U.S. 917 (1967); *North Carolina v. Bullard*, 148 S.E.2d 565 (N.C. 1966); cf. *People v. Woody*, 394 P.2d 813, 817 (Cal. 1964) (peyote use in long-established Native American Church).

70 *Church of Lukumi Babalu Aye, Inc. v. Hialeah*, 113 S. Ct. 2217 (1993). For an interesting discussion of the human sacrifice issue, challenging the assumption that this would necessarily be impermissible in all imaginable cases, see Stephen L. Pepper, "The Case of the Human Sacrifice," *Arizona Law Review* 23 (1981): 897.

71 See, e.g., *Case of Silver and Others*, 61 Eur. Ct. H.R. (ser. A) at 37-38 (1983).

requirement. While contracting States enjoy a certain "margin of appreciation" in determining how this applies in their own national setting,[72] interference with a right as fundamental as freedom of religion should be no greater than necessary and should utilize the least intrusive means possible. This corresponds to the requirement recognized until recently in the religion clause jurisprudence of the United States (and reinstituted by the Religious Freedom Restoration Act[73]) that infringements on religious liberty could be sustained only if justified by a "compelling state interest" that could not be attained by any less restrictive means.

If religious liberty is to have genuine practical meaning in the cases that count, this type of heightened requirement for any legislation (or other state action) that encroaches on religious liberty is vital. Failure to insist on this type of constitutional requirement implies that the majority, subject to the rule of law constraint, can override the religious liberty claims of minorities virtually at will. Moreover, if there is no necessity or proportionality requirement, it is far too easy for lower level officials and bureaucrats to assert their policies as general rules that are insensitive to genuine religious needs but that leave religious groups no effective recourse. It is simply too late in world history to be content with religious liberty protections that allow this kind of infraction.

In this regard, two recent developments are noteworthy. The first is what I regard as a tragic debacle in the constitutional law of the United States. In the 1990 case of *Employment Division v. Smith*,[74] the United States Supreme Court held that religious liberty must give way to any generally applicable, neutral law. In effect, the Supreme Court turned the clock back to the day when only the rule of law constraint prevented excessive limitations on religious liberty, ignoring in the process almost two centuries of history. There has been a tremendous outcry against this decision, with the result that Congress recently passed the Religious Freedom Restoration Act ("RFRA"),[75] which will have the effect of reinstituting a heightened standard of review in religious liberty cases in the United States. This enactment could of course be reversed by subsequent Congressional enactments, but under the supremacy clause of the

[72] Ibid.

[73] Pub. L. No. 103-141 (Nov. 16, 1993), 107 Stat. 1489, *codified at* 42 U.S.C.A. §§ 2000bb, 1988(b) and 5 U.S.C.A. § 504(b)(1)(C)(Supp. 1995). For analysis of this Act and its significance, see Douglas Laycock, "The Religious Freedom Restoration Act," *Brigham Young University Law Review* (1993): 221; id., "Free Exercise and the Religious Freedom Restoration Act," *Fordham Law Review* 62 (1994): 883-904; Rex E. Lee, "The Religious Freedom Restoration Act: Legislative Choice and Judicial Review," *Brigham Young University Law Review* (1993): 73.

[74] 494 U.S. 872 (1990).

[75] Pub. L. No. 103-141 (Nov. 16, 1993), 107 Stat. 1489, *codified at* 42 U.S.C.A. §§ 2000bb 1988(b) and 5 U.S.C.A. § 504(b)(1)(C)(Supp. 1994).

United States constitution, it will at least ensure that all state laws and other state action must pass a compelling state interest/least restrictive alternative test. Moreover, such enactments will need to explicitly indicate that they are cutting back on the religious freedom protections afforded by RFRA, which will be politically difficult.

Along these lines, a note of caution is in order. There is a tendency in much new legislation emerging in East Central Europe, the former Soviet Union, and other parts of the world to pass new religious liberty legislation that provides for protection of religious liberty "subject to compliance with law," or "in accordance with law," etc. Such locutions appear to be even more prevalent in civil law jurisdictions than elsewhere, because of lower comfort levels with judicially crafted exceptions and because of the instinctive sense that religious communities should comply with the "law valid for all." While there is substantial truth in this instinct, it is important to remember that appropriate allowance needs to be made for religious liberty, particularly where exceptions can be accommodated without undue injury to pressing social needs and where these needs can be met in other ways.

One final point should be mentioned about the American Convention of Human Rights. Article 12(3) of this convention is essentially similar to Article 9(2) of the European Convention in imposing constraints on limitations of manifestations of religious liberty. However, the wording is subtly different. Article 12(3) provides that the freedom to manifest religion "may be subject only to the limitations prescribed by law that are necessary to protect public safety, order, health, or morals, or the rights or freedoms of others." Missing is the phrase "necessary *in a democratic society*." Of course, there are many things that are not necessary if a democratic society is not assumed. Hopefully, the American Convention will be construed in light of a normative preference for democratic society, so this verbal difference in the key constraint on infractions of religious liberty will not in fact be a practical difference.[76]

A Comparative Framework for Religious Liberty. In light of the foregoing, the general model of religious liberty law in the various countries of the world can be represented as shown in Figure 5:

---

[76] A similar point could be made about the International Covenant on Civil and Political Rights, which also lacks explicit reference to the benchmark of what is necessary in a democratic society. However, the U.N. Human Rights Committee has now provided an official commentary on Article 18. Human Rights Committee, General Comment No. 22(48) concerning Article 18 (CCPR/C/21/Rev. 1/Add. 4, 27 September 1993 [hereinafter Human Rights Committee, General Comment No. 22(48)]. This effectively incorporates the proportionality constraint that has been developed under the European Convention. Ibid., ¶8.

RELIGIOUS FREEDOM CONTINUUM

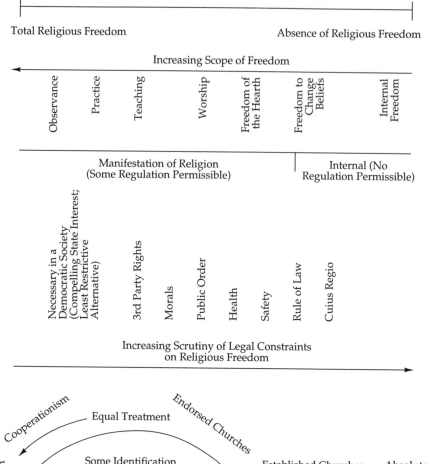

Total Religious Freedom

Absence of Religious Freedom

Increasing Scope of Freedom

Observance

Practice

Teaching

Worship

Freedom of the Hearth

Freedom to Change Beliefs

Internal Freedom

Manifestation of Religion (Some Regulation Permissible)

Internal (No Regulation Permissible)

Necessary in a Democratic Society (Compelling State Interest; Least Restrictive Alternative)

3rd Party Rights

Morals

Public Order

Health

Safety

Rule of Law

Cuius Regio

Increasing Scrutiny of Legal Constraints on Religious Freedom

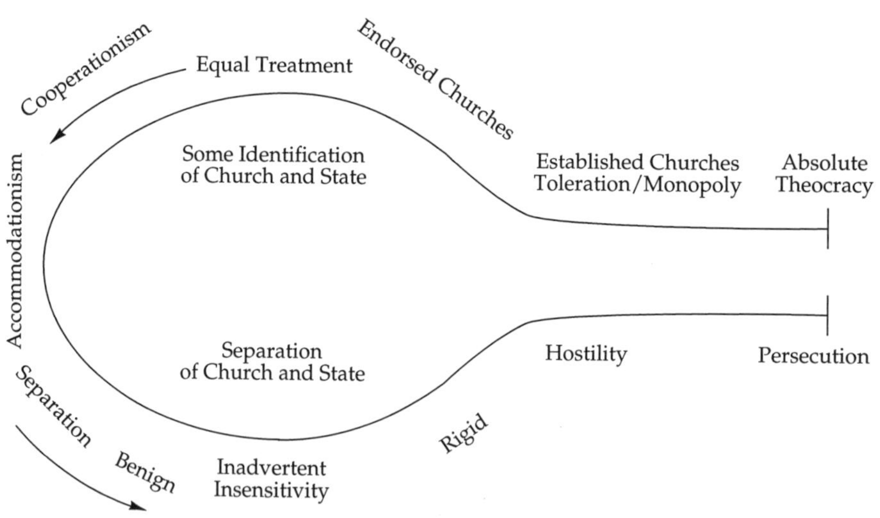

Figure 5

The Latest Deposits in the Archaelogy of Religious Freedom: Recent Developments in the Interpretation of International Religious Liberty Norms. With the opening of the new Europe, many things are happening that will have a significant impact on the ultimate contours of religious liberty in Europe and in many other parts of the world as well. Historical turning points of this magnitude cannot help leaving their own archaeological imprint. One form this imprint takes is the crystallization of concrete norms directed against recognized abuses of the past.

In this respect, the principles of religious liberty enunciated in Principles 16 and 17 of the Concluding Document of the Vienna Follow-up Meeting of Representatives of the Participating States of the Conference on Security and Co-operation in Europe that were promulgated in 1989 (hereinafter the "Vienna Concluding Document") are of particular interest. Formulated at a time when *glasnost* had made it possible for East-West dialogue to make more meaningful pronouncements on fundamental human rights issues, the Vienna Concluding Document contains a remarkable list of specific requirements needed to avoid encroachments on religious freedom that had been all too commonplace. These principles thus serve as a useful summary of concrete religious liberty norms that have won acceptance within Europe, including the former Soviet bloc, and in the United States and Canada in the Helsinki process.[77] My aim here is merely to summarize the principles that have been agreed to, because these constitute a set of widely supported norms that deserve acceptance throughout the world. Reflecting as they do sensitivity to recurrent twentieth century problems, these principles constitute an invaluable deposit of experience upon which to build in the future.

Principles 16 and 17 are worth quoting in full:

16. In order to ensure the freedom of the individual to profess and practice religion or belief the participating States will, inter alia,

16a take effective measures to prevent and eliminate discrimination against individuals or communities, on the grounds of religion or belief in the recognition, exercise and enjoyment of human rights and fundamental freedoms in all fields of civil, political, economic, social and cultural life, and ensure the effective equality between believers and non-believers;

16b foster a climate of mutual tolerance and respect between believers of different communities as well as between believers and non-believers;

---

[77] CSCE commitments in the Helsinki Process, by their terms, do not constitute formal legal commitments in the same way that formal treaty obligations such as the Civil and Political Covenant or the European Convention do. They are nonetheless politically binding. See Arie Bloed, "Two Decades of the CSCE Process: From Confrontation to Co-operation, An Introduction," in *The Conference on Security and Co-operation in Europe: Analysis and Basic Documents, 1972-1993*, Arie Bloed, ed. (Dordrecht, 1993).

16c grant upon their request to communities of believers, practicing or prepared to practice their faith within the constitutional framework of their states, recognition of the status provided for them in their respective countries;

16d respect the right of religious communities to

establish and maintain freely accessible places of worship or assembly,

organize themselves according to their own hierarchical and institutional structure,

select, appoint and replace their personnel in accordance with their respective requirements and standards as well as with any freely accepted arrangement between them and their State,

solicit and receive voluntary financial and other contributions;

16e engage in consultations with religious faiths, institutions and organizations in order to achieve a better understanding of the requirements of religious freedom;

16f respect the right of everyone to give and receive religious education in the language of his choice, individually or in association with others;

16g in this context respect, *inter alia*, the liberty of parents to ensure the religious and moral education of their children in conformity with their own convictions;

16h allow the training of religious personnel in appropriate institutions;

16i respect the right of individual believers and communities of believers to acquire, possess, and use sacred books, religious publications in the language of their choice and other articles and materials related to the practice of religion or belief;

16j allow religious faiths, institutions and organizations to produce and import and disseminate religious publications and materials;

16k favorably consider the interest of religious communities in participating in public dialogue, inter alia, through mass media.

17. The participating States recognize that the exercise of the above mentioned rights relating to the freedom of religion or belief may be subject only to such limitations as are provided by law and are consistent with their obligations under international law and with their international commitments. They will ensure in their laws and regulations and in their application the full and effective implementation of the freedom of thought, conscience, religion or belief.

Several of the foregoing provisions deserve comment. Principle 16a is particularly important to smaller religious denominations. Both individual members of such religious communities and such communities as a whole need assurance that they will not suffer discrimination in comparison with other believers or non-believers.

Principle 16c addresses the vital practical issue of granting juridical status to religious organizations and groups. This was a major practical problem faced by religious groups under pre-1989 regimes. If the spirit of

Principle 16c is to be respected, it is important that recognition procedures should not constitute a bureaucratic obstacle and the procedures should be flexible to accommodate organizational differences of differing denominations. Note that Article 16c of the Vienna Concluding Document draws no distinction between "domestic" and "foreign" communities of believers, and that States are to grant, "upon their request" (presumably without imposing significant constraints) "recognition of the status provided for them" (i.e., for communities of believers) "in their respective countries." A major practical implication of this principle is that legislation governing the acquisition of legal personality or corporate status for religious organizations should be designed to facilitate and not to obstruct or disparage the innate rights of such organizations to religious freedom. Bluntly stated, *denial of legal recognition and entity status is denial of religious liberty.*[78] Without legal personality, religious organizations cannot acquire property or other physical materials required for public manifestation of religion or belief. Thus, denial of juristic personality to a religious group may be permitted only where this is necessary to protect some overriding state interest that can be attained in no less restrictive way.

There is no indication that anything but equal status for all religious communities is contemplated by Principle 16c. Of course, taking a facilitative posture toward religious organizations does not require a state to allow a group to evade legitimate requirements and laws necessary in any democratic society simply by claiming religious status. The preferred approach that has emerged in the West is to establish procedures that facilitate recognition of religious groups at the stage of acquiring juristic personality (regardless whether it has foreign ties). In effect, at that stage there is a presumption that a religious organization is innocent and deserving of religious liberty protections until the contrary is proven. Problems of abuse or unlawful conduct can be dealt with better and more justly later, when and if they occur. More rigorous review at a later stage may be appropriate in connection with granting tax exempt status or other governmental benefits (where these are allowed), but all religious organizations should be entitled to some relatively simple form of entity status that will allow them to rent or purchase facilities, enter into contracts, and otherwise engage in actions that are required as a practical matter in modern legal systems to make religious worship and practice not only possible but convenient. If problems or abuses do occur, these can be dealt with through normal civil and criminal penalties or through

[78] See note 56, *supra*.

terminating financial benefits such as tax exempt status. Denial of entity status at an earlier stage is an inappropriate type of prior restraint.

Principle 16d is particularly vital, because it addresses issues of a religious community's right to autonomy and self-determination. This principle has several features. Obviously, if religious liberty is to extend beyond the freedom of the hearth, it is critical for religious organizations to be allowed to build, lease, or own edifices appropriate to their mode of worship and their religious (and social) practice. (As stressed above, a religious community and way of life often involves more than worship alone.) This means that land use regulations should not be manipulated to effectively bar places of worship from geographical communities.[79] It also means that religious groups should be granted sufficient legal personality to be able to acquire or at least possess facilities appropriate to their needs, as emphasized by Principle 16c.

Freedom to organize according to a tradition's own hierarchical, connectional, congregational, non-hierarchical or other institutional structure is extremely important to most religious communities. Ecclesiology constitutes a central doctrinal issue for many religious communities that is itself a matter of conscience. State interference in these areas strikes at the heart of exercise of religious beliefs regarding the structuring of religious communities. Former communist regimes often required that religious organizations organize in a "democratic" way that was in fact inconsistent with the organizational principles of the religion in question. (Similar constraints still apply in China.[80]) Laws dealing with the legal structures available for religious communities to organize their affairs should be sensitive to the needs of diverse religious groups in this area.[81]

The mode of selection of church personnel is also a sensitive doctrinal issue for many religious groups. Unless the church in question consents, the state should have no say in appointment or discipline of individuals holding church office. It is also important to remember that appropriate exemptions need to be made in a country's labor legislation to allow re-

---

[79] For an overview of pertinent land use issues in the United States, see Laurie Reynolds, "Zoning the Church," *Boston University Law Review* 64 (1984): 767. Legislation protecting historical landmarks has also caused significant burdens on religious freedom in recent years. See Angela C. Carmella, "Landmark Preservation of Church Property," *Catholic Lawyer* 34 (1991): 41; id., "Houses of Worship and Religious Liberty: Constitutional Limits to Landmark Preservation and Architectural Review," *Villanova Law Review* 36 (1991): 401.

[80] See generally Human Rights Watch/Asia, *Freedom of Religion in China* (New York, 1992).

[81] Cases involving church property disputes or contested church disciplinary proceedings have presented these issues most dramatically in the United States. See, e.g., *Presbyterian Church v. Hull Church,* 393 U.S. 40 (1969); *Jones v. Wolf,* 443 U.S. 595 (1979). For a commentary on case law since 1979, see Patty Gerstenblith, "Civil Court Resolution of Property Disputes Among Religious Organizations," *American University Law Review* 39 (1990): 513.

ligious organizations to give preferential treatment to their own members. Laws that ban religious discrimination by normal employers lead to undesirable consequences when a religious employer is involved. It would be bizarre, for example, to require a Protestant congregation to hire a Roman Catholic priest or a Jewish rabbi as its minister, even though the latter are otherwise well qualified. A Baptist clergyman may feel uncomfortable hiring a Mormon secretary. In general, religious organizations have strong religious freedom interests in giving employment preferences to their own believers. At every level, this affects the autonomy of the religious group in structuring its affairs, carrying out its mission, and shaping its communal life and practices.[82]

Churches, like other organizations, need funds to operate. Regulations dealing with solicitation should not be structured in ways that discriminate against some groups in comparison with others.[83] While secular fraud may be regulated in this as in other contexts, churches should be granted greater flexibility in how they use and report on their funds than other not-for-profit organizations to avoid inappropriate intervention in matters of religious belief.[84]

Principle 16e contemplates that the State will "engage in consultations with religious faiths, institutions and organizations in order to achieve a better understanding of the requirements of religious freedom." Many of the violations of religious liberty that arise in the category of unintentional infringement can be resolved by reasonable dialogue. Not all sources of tension can be resolved in this way, but many sources of annoyance and distrust can be eliminated through this practical technique.

Principles 16f-16h relate to religious education and training, always one of the most sensitive areas in any church-state model. Principle 16f provides that the State will "respect the right of everyone to give and receive religious education in the language of his choice, individually or in

[82] The importance of preferential hiring and linking employment to religious beliefs as an issue of religious autonomy issue was recognized in *Corporation of the Presiding Bishop v. Amos*, 483 U.S. 327 (1987). For an excellent article dealing with issues religious autonomy in the labor area in the United States, see Douglas Laycock, "Toward a General Theory of the Religion Clauses: The Case of Church Labor Relations and the Right to Church Autonomy," *Columbia Law Review* 81 (1981): 1373-1417.

[83] *Larson v. Valente*, 456 U.S. 228 (1982).

[84] Newer not-for-profit corporation laws in the United States recognize the greater flexibility warranted for religious corporations, in deference to principles of religious freedom. See, e.g., Cal. Corp. Code §§ 9110-9690 (Deering 1979 & Supp. 1993)(California Religious Corporations Act); Revised Model Nonprofit Corp. Act §§ 1.40(30), 1.80, 2.02(a)(2)(iii) (1987) (defining "religious corporation," listing the constitutional protections enjoyed by religious corporations, and requiring the articles of incorporation to state whether a corporation fits the definition of "religious corporation").

association with others." Generally, significant interdenominational tensions can be reduced if religious education is left to family and church, without intermeddling by the state. Certainly in those contexts, it is important to be able to provide religious education at all age levels, both at home and in religious buildings that are leased, purchased, or built by religious organizations. To the extent public facilities are made available for religious instruction, this should be done on a non-discriminatory basis.[85]

Principle 16g's requirement that parents (or legal guardians) should have the right to guide the religious education of their children is also recognized in Article 12(4) of the American Convention of Human Rights. Some countries permit religious instruction designed to cooperate with parental and church efforts, but the public sector simply cannot replace what family and church can do on their own. General curriculum requirements in an educational system should not be allowed to run roughshod over conscientious beliefs and practices. Modern educational systems have great flexibility in attaining their objectives, and there are few educational aims that are so compelling that they justify violating sincere conscientious claims.

Principles 16i and 16j call for the protection of the acquisition, possession, production, importing, and dissemination of religious literature and other materials by churches as organizations and by members or others interested in learning about such organizations and their teachings. Access to religious literature and materials was a critical problem under many communist regimes, and limitations in this area can have an extremely deleterious effect on a religious community. Locke was no doubt correct that the civil magistrate cannot coerce an individual to accept a particular belief, but a regime clearly can prevent people from having access to information upon which to base their beliefs. This is a particularly important problem for relatively small denominations, because otherwise members may feel isolated and may be unable to deepen their faith and receive the full benefit of association with their religious community. Legislation here should recognize that many items may fit in these categories beyond the traditional forms of religious literature such as books,

---

[85] The equal access debate has attracted extensive discussion in the United States. See, e.g., Frank Calabrese, "Equal Access Upheld as the *Lemon* Test Sours," *De Paul Law Review* 39 (1990): 1281-1318; Richard F. Duncan, "Religious Civil Rights in Public High Schools: The Supreme Court Speaks on Equal Access," *Indiana Law Review* 24 (1991): 111-133; Steven Green, "The Misnomer of Equality under the Equal Access Act," *Vermont Law Review* 14 (1990): 369-400; Frank R. Jimenez, "Beyond *Mergens*: Ensuring Equality of Religious Speech under the Equal Access Act," *Yale Law Journal* 100 (1991): 2149-68; Nadine Strossen, "A Constitutional Analysis of the Equal Access Act's Standards Governing Public School Student Meetings," *Harvard Journal on Legislation* 24 (1987): 117-190.

magazines, and other publications. Ability to use film, video recordings, and other media (and the equipment necessary to display them) may be as important in a contemporary context as ability to have access to more standard publications. In addition, it is important that the references in Principles 16i and 16j to "other articles and materials related to the practice of religion or belief" and to "religious publications and materials" be understood to apply not only to literature and publications (in whatever media) but to physical items, such as religious objects or items of clothing used in worship services or in daily practice of religion.

The right to disseminate information about a religious belief system should be understood to embrace the right to share one's religious views with individuals of another faith. In the United States, it has long been axiomatic that both freedom of religion and freedom of speech protect evangelizing activities.[86] This is quite understandable because in many religious traditions, carrying the message of one's belief system to others is an integral part of religious observance. At the international level, this has been a more controversial issue, particularly in Islamic cultures. It now seems well settled, however, that the key international covenants at a minimum protect the right of individuals to change or abandon their religious beliefs.[87] Moreover, the European Court of Human Rights has recently held that a Greek law criminalizing proselytizing violated the right to religious freedom, at least as applied to a Jehovah's Witness engaged in conventional door-to-door missionary efforts.[88] The case did not rule out the possibility that there might be extreme cases where proselytism involving fraud or coercion might be subject to regulation, but it clearly protected traditional missionary activity.

Conclusion and Recommendations

Different countries with different traditions are particularly likely to have differing institutions in the sensitive area of religious liberty. The model developed in this chapter provides a helpful framework for comparing such differing institutions. While the model is flexible enough to suggest that a considerable range of church-state configurations may be consistent with genuine religious liberty, it does suggest some normative conclusions. Greater religious liberty is likely under regimes that provide equal treatment for individuals and religious communities. On the religious freedom gradient, history has demonstrated that a "rule of law"

---

[86] See, e.g., *Murdock v. Pennsylvania*, 319 U.S. 105 (1943); *Cantwell v. Connecticut*, 310 U.S. 296 (1940).

[87] Human Rights Committee, General Comment No. 22(48), ¶5.

[88] *Kokkinakis v. Greece*, 260 Eur. Ct. H.R. (ser. A) at 4 (1993).

constraint on permissible limitations on manifestations of religious freedom is not adequate. One of the most important features of religious liberty—one that makes it a fundamental and inalienable right—is that it is prior, "both in order of time and in degree of obligation, to the claims of Civil Society."[89] A state which assumes that any law it passes, even if the law is general and facially neutral, fails to understand how fundamental religious liberty is.

While institutions of religious liberty inevitably take on differences of coloring and detail in light of local traditions and culture, there is now sufficient historical experience with religious liberty to be able to identify certain principles that deserve universal acknowledgment. At a minimum, these include not only the religious liberty principles enunciated in the major international human rights conventions but also those spelled out in the Vienna Concluding Document and the 1981 United Nations Declaration on the Elimination of All Forms of Intolerance and of Discrimination Based on Religion or Belief. Practical steps should be taken to identify constitutional and statutory provisions that do not measure up to these principles as a minimum international standard. Steps should also be taken to endorse these principles more broadly. Securing the formal recognition and actual achievement of all of these principles would constitute major progress in the field of religious liberty.

---

[89] James Madison, "Memorial and Remonstrance Against Religious Assessments," reprinted in *The Mind of the Founder: Sources of the Political Thought of James Madison*, Marvin Meyers, ed., rev. ed. (Hanover, NH, 1981). The Memorial and Remonstrance is also reprinted as an appendix to *Everson v. Board of Education*, 330 U.S. 1, 63 (1947).

Studying "Religious Human Rights": Methodological Foundations

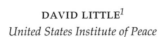

DAVID LITTLE[1]
United States Institute of Peace

Although it will be necessary in due course to express some reservations about the term "religious human rights," it is still possible to embrace the broad purposes of this volume. It appears that the purposes are, first, to clarify the history, grounds, character, scope, and efforts at implementation of legal means, guaranteed under existing international human rights instruments, for protecting legitimate interests, as well as prohibiting special biases, that are associated with holding religious and similar beliefs. A second purpose is to examine the responses and the evaluations of various religious communities and traditions regarding these same legal means.

Presumably, a chapter on the "Methodological Foundations of Religious Human Rights" ought to lay out and clarify the basic terms and some considerations regarding causality and explanation appropriate to studying both these concerns. I shall try to do that, at least in a preliminary way, but only after insisting upon two provisos.

First, a methodology is obviously affected by the interests and objectives of the investigator. All one can do—especially regarding something as inchoate and uncertain as the study of religious human rights—is to select *one* perspective, and then endeavor to lay out and clarify the basic terms as well as certain considerations regarding causality and explanation that are involved in approaching the subject from that perspective.

[1] A shorter and modified version of this paper will appear in *Nationalism and Ethnic Politics* 1 (2) (March/April, 1995). I wish to express my gratitude to my associate, Scott W. Hibbard, for assistance in summarizing the results of our work on Sudan and Tibet. I would also like to thank John Torpey, Program Officer at the Institute, for helping me rethink some of my opinions concerning the idea of nationalism, and for making some useful suggestions for revision. The opinions expressed in this paper are the author's own, and do not necessarily reflect the view of the United States Institute of Peace.

J.D. van der Vyver and J. Witte, Jr. (eds.), Religious Human Rights in Global Perspective, 45-77.

Second, any pretensions to providing a methodology for *the* study of religious human rights would seem to be woefully misguided, not only because things at this stage are so inchoate and uncertain, but also because the subject is so complicated. Investigating the "history, grounds, character, scope, and efforts at implementation" of existing legal means for protecting religious interests and prohibiting religious bias is obviously a highly complex activity. And complexities increase when the variety of considerations involved in examining "the responses and the evaluations of various religious communities and traditions regarding these same legal means" is figured in. Again, it is possible to pursue but one small part of this huge area of study, making clear, of course, why and how that part is to be examined.

Despite the difficulties, it is useful, I believe, to induce people to reflect on and share some methodological considerations regarding these matters. While no one effort will completely satisfy all students of the subject, it can prompt others to clarify their own approaches, and it can help to raise to common consciousness some of the underlying perplexities and deficiencies at our present level of understanding.

The particular perspective that will serve as the basis, largely, for the methodological reflections contained in this paper is developed in a series of reports being published under the auspices of the United States Institute of Peace (USIP), where I am employed. When completed, the series will consist of studies of seven countries or regions—Ukraine, Sri Lanka, Lebanon, Sudan, Nigeria, Tibet,[2] and Israel—studies organized under the general title, "Religion, Nationalism, and Intolerance." These particular cases were selected out of many possible examples of religiously-related ethnic conflict because of the cultural, religious, political, and geographical diversity they represent. Reports on Ukraine, Sri Lanka, and Tibet[3] have already been published, and the study on Sudan[4] is nearing completion. I call attention to these products, since I shall be drawing on some of the findings as I go along, though I should also acknowledge that the work of the Religion and Human Rights Project, and

[2] Tibet is at present regarded by the Chinese government, and by the large majority of the international community, as an "autonomous region" rather than as an independent state or country.

[3] David Little, *Ukraine: The Legacy of Intolerance* (Washington, 1991); id., *Sri Lanka: The Invention of Enmity* (Washington, 1994); David Little and Scott W. Hibbard, *Sino-Tibetan Co-Existence: Creating Space for Tibetan Self-Direction* (Washington, 1994).

[4] David Little and Scott W. Hibbard, "Sudan: Plural Society in Distress" (in preparation). Two other studies in the series, one on Lebanon to be written by John Kelsay and one on Nigeria, to be written by Rosalind Hackett, are in the early stages of preparation. A study of Israel is contemplated, and, finally, there will be a summary volume reviewing the general findings of the case studies.

the World Report on Freedom of Religion, Conscience, and Belief, with which I have been associated, has provided helpful background.

The focus of the USIP Religion, Nationalism, and Intolerance series (Intolerance Project) is the set of norms the editors of this volume, and its companion, have in mind when they speak of "religious human rights." They are of two sorts. First, there are the articles enshrined in the international instruments that protect legitimate religious interests, such as freedom of belief and conscience, as well as the freedom to manifest belief in "teaching, practice, worship, and observance."[5] Second, there are the articles that prohibit discrimination based on religious belief or affiliation.[6]

The human rights to free exercise and to freedom from discrimination are usefully elaborated in the first two articles of the UN Declaration on the Elimination of All Forms of Intolerance and Discrimination Based on Religion or Belief (the Declaration Against Intolerance).[7] The remaining six articles of that declaration further specify the protections and prohibitions that follow from these two fundamental rights.[8] Because the Declaration against Intolerance represents the most elaborate formulation of "religious human rights," it constitutes the primary reference point for the Intolerance Project.

The Declaration against Intolerance defines the rights of free exercise and freedom from discrimination as follows:

> Article 1.
>
> 1. Everyone shall have the right to freedom of thought, conscience and religion. This right shall include freedom to have a religion or whatever belief of [one's] choice, and freedom, either individually or in community with others, and in public or private, to manifest [one's] religion or belief in worship, observance, practice, and teaching.
>
> 2. No one shall be subject to coercion which would impair [one's] freedom to have a religion or belief of [one's] choice.

---

5 Article 18 of both the Universal Declaration of Human Rights, and the International Covenant on Civil and Political Rights.

6 Article 2 of the Universal Declaration and the Covenant on Civil and Political Rights are the general provisions against discrimination, and Article 7 of the Universal Declaration and Article 26 of the Covenant on Civil and Political Rights guarantee equal protection of the law. There are similar articles in all other major international human rights instruments. See further discussion in Natan Lerner's chapter herein.

7 Resolution Adopted by the General Assembly on November 25, 1981 [on the Report of the Third Committee (A/36/684)] 36/54).

8 The remaining articles deal, among other things, with the obligations of states to enforce religious human rights, as well as with rights to religious education, and they enumerate some of the types of protected religious activity.

3. Freedom to manifest one's religion or beliefs may be subject only to such limitations as are prescribed by law and are necessary to protect public safety, order, health or morals or the fundamental rights and freedoms of others.

Article 2.

1. No one shall be subject to discrimination by any State, institution, or group of persons or person on the grounds of religion or belief.

2. For the purposes of the present Declaration, the expression "intolerance and discrimination based on religion or belief" means any distinction, exclusion, restriction or preference based on religion or belief and having as its purpose or as its effect nullification or impairment of the recognition, enjoyment or exercise of human rights and fundamental freedoms on an equal basis.

The distinction between what we shall call "the right of free exercise" (Article 1) and "the right of nondiscrimination" (Article 2) is a commendable way of classifying "religious human rights." Not only does the distinction rely on the authoritative wording of the international instruments. More importantly, it reliably sorts out two of the most fundamental interests religious people have: being able to affirm, express, and manifest their convictions, and being able to avoid unfair discrimination or bias on account of religion. As such, the categories are preferable to alternative classifications, including dividing "religious human rights" into "active" and "passive" categories.[9]

---

[9] In "The State of Religious Human Rights in the World: A Comparative Religious and Legal Study," *Preliminary Documents of Religious Human Rights Project* 1 (1993): 5-6, John Witte, Jr. uses the terms "active" and "passive rights" to provide a rather different classification from the one contained in the Declaration against Intolerance. However, Witte's classification has two important shortcomings. His categorization is a bit confusing, and, furthermore, it is not clear, once the categories are straightened out, whether it is illuminating, after all, to classify one set of rights as "active" and the other as "passive."

Witte describes "passive religious rights" as entailing "freedom of conscience for the individual and freedom of association for religious groups. . . ," and then describes "active religious rights" as requiring that "individuals be allowed to exercise their religious beliefs privately and groups be allowed to engage in private worship" (5-6). But it is not clear why freedom of association for religious groups is classified as passive, since such a freedom would appear to imply the (active) right to "engage in private worship," as well as in other forms of religious expression. The same point can be made about freedom of conscience. Freedom of conscience could of course be called "a right to be left alone" (a passive right); but it is normally understood to include the freedom actively to express conscience, and even (within limits) to act on conscience. Accordingly, it would appear to be an "active" right.

But, as I say, even if we straightened these things out, the very classification remains ambiguous, since leaving people free to undertake what they feel bound by conscience or religious or similar commitment to do has both passive and active aspects to it.

The general idea of the USIP Intolerance Project is to examine and elaborate upon, by means of case study, the twin premises of the declaration: that "the disregard and infringement . . . of the right to freedom of thought, conscience, religion, or whatever belief, have brought, directly or indirectly, wars and great suffering to [human]kind," and, conversely, that respect for and encouragement of "freedom of religion and belief should . . . contribute to the attainment of the goals of world peace, social justice and friendship among peoples. . . ."[10]

More precisely, the Intolerance Project has two basic and related objectives. The first is to establish the degree to which forms of intolerance that violate existing human rights standards contribute to conflict, as well as how efforts to modify or eliminate those violations contribute to peace. The second is to clarify the sources or causes of tolerance and intolerance, including, in particular, the role of religion and similar beliefs.

There are *conceptual* and *theoretical* problems raised by the Intolerance Project and the approach it takes. The remainder of this paper will be an exposition of and a commentary on those problems.

Conceptual Problems

"Religious Human Rights." It is true that human rights are conventionally categorized according to whether they are "political," "civil," "economic," etc. Since certain human rights obviously pertain to religious matters, why not employ the term "religious human rights" as the editors of this volume and its companion do?

The difficulty is that the Declaration and the relevant provisions in the other instruments clearly intend to include under their protection

---

The same applies to other parts of Witte's description of "passive rights." He includes the right of individuals "to accept, reject, or change religious belief without coercion by the state or other individuals." However, to describe that right as purely passive obscures the active aspect that is implied in allowing people to affirm, reject, or change beliefs.

The same, again, goes for Witte's other examples of passive rights, such as the right "of all peaceable religious institutions [to] be able to organize and perpetuate themselves, without special burdens imposed by the state or other individuals," as well as the rights requiring that "the state accommodate the religious beliefs and practices of individuals and institutions and exempt them from generally applicable laws and policies which compel them to act in violation of their religious convictions." Special consideration for conscientious objectors and immunities from oath-swearing, working on holy days and so on would be illustrations. In all these examples, the state (or another party) is bound to refrain from unfairly interfering with or encumbering a religious person or group (passive right) so that the religious person or group can speak and act in accord with conscience (active right).

It appears to me, therefore, that the distinction drawn from the Declaration against Intolerance is a more useful and less confusing, not to mention more authoritative, way of classifying the range of rights the conference designers wish to address.

10 Preamble to the Declaration against Intolerance.

thoughts and beliefs that are explicitly *not* religious, and that may even be anti-religious.[11] Since allowance is made for protecting such non-religious thoughts and beliefs, it is confusing to refer to the relevant provisions as "religious human rights."

More inclusive terms would seem to be needed. I propose to substitute *"rights of free thought and fundamental belief"* for "religious human rights." The words, "fundamental belief," appear to encompass convictions of conscience as well as convictions based on fundamental (or primary) belief—religious or not—that are implied by the references in the human rights documents to "freedom of conscience and religion or belief." The words, "free thought," are added separately because authoritative interpretation of the documents suggests a crucial distinction between freedom of thought and freedom of fundamental belief. The distinction is this: While even trivial thoughts and beliefs are generally protected against interference or unfair discrimination by the "freedom of thought" provision, fundamental beliefs related to conscience or to commitments of a religious or similar sort occupy *a specially privileged status.* Unlike just any thought or belief, fundamental beliefs may serve, under prescribed conditions, as the basis for legal exemptions and immunities, as, for example, in the case of conscientious objection.[12]

---

[11] See Elizabeth Odio Benito, "Study of the Current Dimensions of the Problems of Intolerance and Discrimination on Grounds of Religion or Belief," UN Doc. E/CN.4/Sub.2/1987/26: 26: "As a result of lengthy discussions in various international bodies, it is now generally accepted that 'religion or belief' includes theistic, non-theistic, and atheistic belief." See also General Comment Adopted by the Human Rights Committee under Article 40, Paragraph 4, of the International Covenant on Civil and Political Rights, UN Doc. CCPR/c/21/Rev. 1/Add. 4, September 27, 1993: 1:

> Article 18 [of the Covenant on Civil and Political Rights] protects theistic, non-theistic and atheistic beliefs, as well as the right not to profess any religion or belief. Article 18 is not limited in its application to traditional religions or to religions and beliefs with institutional characteristics or practices analogous to those of traditional religions. The Committee therefore views with concern any tendency to discriminate against any religion or belief for any reasons, including the fact they are newly established, or represent minorities that may be the subject of hostility by a predominant religious community.

[12] The Human Rights Committee's General Comment interprets "the right to freedom of thought, conscience and religion (which includes the freedom to hold beliefs)" to mean *"freedom of thoughts on all matters,* personal conviction and the commitment to religion or belief" (Ibid., 1; emphasis added). It appears that "the right to free thought" applies to every conceivable kind of thought on any subject an individual might have. By contrast, the notions of "personal conviction" and "commitment to religion or belief" suggest a much more restricted set of beliefs; i.e., those beliefs of which one is strongly persuaded and that occupy an especially important place in one's life ("convictions"), or those beliefs to which one is solemnly bound or pledged that have a primary status in the life of the believer ("commitments"), namely, those that have a "religious" or "religious-like" status.

An instructive model of the idea of "religious-like" status is suggested by *United States v. Seeger,* 380 U.S. 163 (1965), a decision of the United States Supreme Court. In deciding a case

This point about the specially privileged status of fundamental beliefs, in turn, provides a persuasive rejoinder to the common assertion that there is, in fact, nothing at all unusual about protections accorded to conscience or to religious and similar beliefs, and that guarantees of the freedom of thought, conscience, and religion or belief are sufficiently provided for by the ordinary protections of freedom of opinion[13] and freedom of association.[14] While it is not clear (to me) that special protection of freedom of thought is required above and beyond the protection of freedom of opinion,[15] it is quite clear that the convictions of conscience and the commitments to religion and similar belief which we are designating as "fundamental belief" are not, according to a plausible interpretation of the documents, adequately covered by the provisions for freedom of opinion and freedom of association. The human rights documents appear to make unique allowance for the deeply seated human disposition to hold, express, and manifest or act upon conscientious con-

---

regarding conscientious objectors not traditionally religious, the court extended the protections afforded religious believers under the First Amendment of the United States Constitution to those who, though not themselves religious in the normal sense, resembled religious believers in significant ways. They are individuals whose belief, being "sincere and meaningful[,] occupies a place in the life of its possessor parallel to that filled by the orthodox belief in God." Since "belief" is consistently linked to "religion" in the relevant provisions of the human rights documents, it is not unreasonable to interpret it in accord with the "Seeger model." It is, then, this limited set of special beliefs I am designating as "fundamental" or "primary" (in the sense of "that which stands first in order, rank, or importance").

One other reference in the Human Rights Committee's General Comment lends weight to this interpretation. In paragraph 11, the Committee discusses claims in favor of a right to conscientious objection as implied in Article 18 of the Covenant on Civil and Political Rights. "The Covenant," says the Committee, "does not explicitly refer to a right of conscientious objection, but the Committee believes that such a right can be derived from article 18, inasmuch as the obligation to use lethal force may seriously conflict with *the freedom of conscience and the right to manifest one's religion or belief*" (Ibid., 4, emphasis added). There is mention here only of what we are calling "fundamental belief" (conscientious conviction and commitment to religion or belief), and no mention of freedom of thought. See the section on "Scope and Limitations of Conscientious Objection," in "Freedom of Conscience" (Seminar Organized by the Council of Europe and the F.M. Asbeck Centre for Human Rights Studies of the University of Leiden, Leiden, Netherlands, November, 1992; Strasbourg, 1993), 74-143.

The distinction between "freedom of thought" and "freedom of fundamental belief" offered in the text would therefore appear to provide an answer to the question: "In international law, is belief in God, the denial of God, and the holding of trivial beliefs [e.g., the advantages of one kind of popcorn over another] on an equal plane as regards a claim to protection." Kevin Boyle, "Freedom of Conscience in International Law," in "Freedom of Conscience," 41. In keeping with the distinction drawn in the text, it would seem that all beliefs are *not* equal.

[13] Article 19, Covenant on Civil and Political Rights.

[14] Article 22, Covenant on Civil and Political Rights.

[15] Section 2 of Article 19 specifies the right to freedom of expression, and includes the right "to *seek, receive and impart information and ideas* of all kinds. . . ." (emphasis added). This provision would, I think, reasonably cover "freedom of thoughts on all matters," in the words of the Human Rights Committee, though that is perhaps open to further reflection.

victions and religious or similar commitments. By being considered as a possible basis for extraordinary exemptions and immunities, fundamental beliefs represent *an exceptional limitation* on the law. Far from being "neutral" or "indifferent" in the sense of having no interest in religion and similar beliefs, human rights law is in fact *deferent* to such concerns.[16] The term "religious human rights" was undoubtedly intended to protect this point, and the point must not be compromised, even if the term is discarded.

"Intolerance and Discrimination Based on Religion or Belief." Our term "fundamental belief" is, as we suggest, meant to cover what the documents signify by the phrase, "religion or belief." In other words, "fundamental belief" means primary belief of a religious or non-religious sort,[17] as well, of course, as belief based on conscience.

For working purposes, "belief" may be taken to mean "a state of mind disposed to regard a proposition or set of propositions as true,"[18] a definition that includes the idea of "believing in" someone or something often associated with fundamental belief. One reason why conflicts of belief, of the sort anticipated by the human rights instruments, are so stressful and so contentious is precisely because they are conflicts over fundamental truth.

---

[16] Human rights law would appear to be at once deferent and impartial with respect to fundamental belief. Words like "neutrality" and "indifference," which are frequently invoked to describe the desirable relation between law and fundamental belief, convey well enough the impartiality of the law, but do not adequately convey its spirit of deference. "Indifference" and "neutrality" are synonyms, and there is an important ambiguity about the meaning of both terms. "Indifferent" can mean "impartial," "fair," or "just," or it can mean "unconcerned," "unmoved," "apathetic," or "insensible," and the same is true of "neutral." Thus, when the words "indifferent" or "neutral" are applied to the law—carrying with them, as they do, the second as well as the first set of meanings—it is reasonable to infer that the law is "unmoved by" and "has no interest in" the existence of fundamental belief. Unfortunately, that implication provides some basis for the popular conviction, harbored by religious conservatives and others, that human rights law is actually hostile toward religion and similar beliefs. Since human rights law is, on the contrary, manifestly deferential to fundamental belief, words like "indifferent" and "neutral," which can legitimately be understood to convey a different impression, should be abandoned.

[17] What counts as a "fundamental belief" and what distinguishes a "religious" from a "non-religious" belief is, as everyone knows, a complicated and controversial subject. I have nothing very fresh to say in this regard. One reason is that worrying about these definitions has not proved to be an urgent concern of the Intolerance Project. That is because in places like Sri Lanka or Sudan, there is no great perplexity over whether something commonly recognizable as "religion" is involved, as well as whether the beliefs in question are "fundamental" or not. In places like Ukraine and Tibet, where the difference between "religious" and "non-religious" fundamental beliefs is salient, the parties themselves oblige by readily volunteering all the necessary distinctions.

I do not suggest that terminological questions are not, for some purposes, very important. It is just that in our work (thankfully!) these definitions are not especially in dispute.

[18] See Little, *Sri Lanka: The Invention of Enmity*, xxiv.

A familiar complaint holds that the emphasis on "belief" in the documents is too restrictive to encompass many important aspects of religious commitment. It is too "cerebral," too cognitive, and does not sufficiently allow for the implicitness or tacitness of much religious participation, let alone account for the more symbolic, expressive and performative side of religious life.[19]

What the complaint overlooks is the special set of circumstances envisioned by the human rights documents. These are circumstances in which religions (or other forms of fundamental belief) *are explicitly in conflict* with one another, or with public authorities or other parties. However tacit or unreflective religious participation may be under normal or conventional conditions, circumstances of threat and strife have a way of bringing preferences and commitments to the level of consciousness and into the form of articulated beliefs. There is nothing surprising about that. It happens because one group gets accused of standing for something that is regarded as objectionable, and is often penalized because of it. In defending itself, the group is moved to "spell out" or define cognitively its fundamental convictions—to state its "beliefs," partly to clear up confusion and combat false accusation, and partly to identify itself to opponents or outsiders in the way it wishes to be identified. In a word, the emphasis on belief is a function of the general conditions of religious conflict. For the purposes of the human rights documents, that emphasis does not depend upon the character of a given religious tradition.[20]

The Declaration against Intolerance is not particularly clear about the distinction and connection between intolerance and discrimination. Sometimes the terms are differentiated, sometimes not.[21] Interpretation is

---

[19] See comments by David R. Blumenthal in Daniel G. Ashburn, "The State of Religious Human Rights in the World: Preliminary Consultation," *Preliminary Documents of Religious Human Rights Project* 2 (1993): 38-39: "I'm puzzled by the terms, religion and belief. . . . I think the problem is going to be how to include Buddhists and how to include even your average run-of-the-mill Christian, who doesn't really have beliefs which are explicit—and many of them are not even implicit. If that's not true about Christians, it's certainly going to be true . . . about Jews. . . . If we were to . . . ask them what makes them Jewish, belief would be the last thing that comes out. . . . There are many things that make a group or a community cohere, which have to do with social dynamics of community, that have to do with ritualized behavior to define membership in community. I would want to see us move towards these larger anthropological definitions of community, although I don't know how we're going to do away with the words, religion and belief."

[20] It seems obvious that it is a common characteristic of religions (and other human groups as well) that they formulate and sharpen their "beliefs" precisely as the result of either external or internal conflict. I do not deny that some religions elevate and feature the cognitive aspects of religious commitment more than others. I only hold that "belief" will inevitably become a crucial part of religious life for groups who are under attack.

[21] See Little, *Sri Lanka: The Invention of Enmity*, xxii-xxiii.

clearly called for. The Intolerance Project takes the following position. It concedes the important conceptual distinction in ordinary usage between "intolerance," suggesting attitudes of extreme hostility, and probably the direct expression of those attitudes, and "discrimination," suggesting actions that are unfairly biased. However, unless it is analytically necessary to apply the distinction, the Project normally understands intolerance to include discrimination (as well as "persecution"), as in the title, "Intolerance Project."

The ideas of tolerance and intolerance are sometimes thought to be outmoded and therefore of little use. They recall pre-modern circumstances, it is said, in which a majority was considered tolerant if it extended a minority minimal freedoms by sufferance, not equal freedom by right; and it was considered intolerant if it did not do even that. While the historical connotations are real enough, they need not determine our contemporary use of the terms. What is required now is simply a bit of conceptual reform in the direction of equal freedom for advocates of all forms of fundamental belief. As a matter of fact, such an ideal is exactly what the Declaration against Intolerance and related human rights norms are beginning to articulate. Accordingly, attitudes and behavior that conform to human rights norms insuring equal rights of free exercise and nondiscrimination are "tolerant"; those that violate them are "intolerant."[22]

There is an important, if little noted, ambiguity lurking in the words, "based on religion or belief." Certain individuals or groups might become the *recipients* or *targets* of intolerance because of the fundamental beliefs they hold, as in the case of the Baha'is in Iran, or the Jehovah's Witnesses in several countries. That is one kind of intolerance based on religion or belief.

Second, a given community or government might select certain individuals or groups for intolerant treatment because of the fundamental beliefs the community or government holds, as in the biased treatment of the Tamil minority by the Sinhala Buddhist majority government at certain points in recent Sri Lankan history. That is another kind of intolerance based on religion or belief, in which fundamental belief becomes a *warrant* or justification for intolerance.

The point to be emphasized is that these two forms of belief and intolerance—target and warrant—are analytically distinct, and are not nec-

---

[22] Article 20(2) of the Covenant on Civil and Political Rights addresses, as the declaration does not, the problem of "hate speech": "Any advocacy of national, racial or religious hatred that constitutes incitement to discrimination, hostility or violence shall be prohibited by law." This provision would undoubtedly need to be taken into consideration in defining "intolerance," though there are familiar difficulties in properly restricting the reach of "hate-speech" protections so they do not subvert the protections of free speech.

essarily correlative or symmetrical. While it is hard to imagine perpetrators of intolerance acting without justification that is based on fundamental belief, it is easy to imagine victims of intolerance whose selection is based not on their religion or belief, but on purely ascribed characteristics, such as gender, skin color, birthplace, etc.[23]

This distinction between the two forms of belief and intolerance turns out to be of the greatest analytical importance in the Intolerance Project. In the case of Sri Lanka, for example, members of the Tamil minority, who are mainly Hindus, are not, as a rule, discriminated against because of their religious beliefs, but rather because they are ethnically different from the Sinhala Buddhist majority. At the same time, the Sinhala majority has explicitly and extensively invoked Buddhism as a warrant for Sinhala ethnic and cultural preeminence—an attitude that has, from time to time, unmistakably contributed to discriminatory practices against the Tamils, and has therefore intensified conflict between the two groups.[24]

The Logic of Nondiscrimination. According to the right of nondiscrimination, every person is entitled to basic rights and freedoms, including the equal protection of the law, "without distinction of any kind, such as race, color, sex, language, *religion*,[25] political or other opinion, national or social origin, property, birth, or other status."[26] More particularly: "No one shall be subject to discrimination by any State, group of persons or person on the grounds of religion or other beliefs."[27]

It follows that human rights would have to be considered *religiously impartial*,[28] *at least in the sense of excluding religious identity as a condition of citizenship.* Just as race, gender, color, etc. may not limit the legal and other protections and responsibilities of citizenship, so no form of religious reference or appeal, such as expressed allegiance to certain doctrines, texts, practices, or authorities, may serve as a condition for ascribing, withholding, or modifying civil rights and privileges. The General Comment adopted by the Human Rights Committee is quite ex-

---

23 This comment represents a certain clarification of my discussion of this matter in Little, *Sri Lanka: The Invention of Enmity*, esp. xxvii, and Little, *Ukraine: The Legacy of Intolerance*, esp. cc.

24 See, e.g., Little, *Sri Lanka: The Invention of Enmity*, esp. the Conclusion.

25 Emphasis added.

26 Articles 2 and 26 of the Covenant on Civil and Political Rights (cf. Articles 2 and 7 of the Universal Declaration).

27 Article 2 of the Declaration against Intolerance.

28 This term was suggested by my associate Scott W. Hibbard. It is preferable to "religiously neutral" or "religiously indifferent" for reasons given in note 16 above. It is also preferable to the word "secular," which is sometimes employed in this context, because of the objectionable connotations that term has come to acquire. Personally, I am not ready to surrender the term "secular" as appropriate here, but it will have to be carefully defined and defended to avoid misunderstanding. That will be undertaken elsewhere.

plicit about this in addressing the subject of state or official religion or ideology:

> The fact that a religion is recognized as a State religion or that it is established as official or traditional or that its followers comprise the majority of the population, shall not result in any impairment of the enjoyment of any of the rights under the Covenant, including articles 18 [freedom of thought, conscience and religion or belief] and 27 [minority rights], nor any discrimination against adherents of other religions or non-believers. In particular, certain measures discriminating against the latter, such as measures restricting eligibility for government service to members of the predominant religion or giving economic privileges to them or imposing special restrictions on the practice of other faiths, are not in accordance with the prohibition of discrimination based on religion or belief and the guarantee of equal protection under article 26.[29]
>
> If a set of beliefs is treated as official ideology in constitutions, statutes, proclamations of the ruling parties, etc., or in actual practice, this shall not result in any impairment of the freedoms under article 18 or any other rights recognized under the Covenant nor in any discrimination against persons who do not accept the official ideology or who oppose it.[30]

Incidentally, the legislative history of the Universal Declaration of Human Rights underscores the religious impartiality of human rights. The drafters—as the result, to be sure, of considerable controversy—deliberately refrained from including references to a deity or to the immortal destiny[31] of human beings.[32] That decision is consonant with the

---

[29] General Comment Adopted by the Human Rights Committee, para. 9, p. 4.

[30] Ibid., para. 10., p. 5.

[31] See John P. Humphrey, *Human Rights and the United Nations: A Great Adventure* (Dobbs Ferry, NY, 1984), 67: "Later, when the preamble [to the Declaration] was being discussed, Father Beufort of the Netherlands moved that it mention the divine origin and immortal destiny of man[!]. In support of his amendment he used the extraordinary argument that nonbelievers could simply ignore the words. Mrs. Kalinowska of Poland quite properly pointed out that it would be extremely dangerous to admit the possibility that any part of the Declaration could be ignored. . . . [W]hen it became clear to Father Beufort that his amendment would not be supported by the majority, he withdrew it. The result was that the Universal Declaration of Human Rights [does not mention] God. . . ."

[32] It is important to note that a concern for "gender impartiality" was also a very significant part of the drafting exercise, something signalled in article 1 of the declaration by the use of "all human beings" rather than "all men." As in the case of religious impartiality, it would seem that concern with gender impartiality is implied by the logic of nondiscrimination. See Joseph P. Lash, *Eleanor: The Years Alone* (New York, 1972), 70:

> Unexpectedly, a prodigious amount of time was spent on the first article of the Declaration. That article, modeled on the American Declaration of Independence, read, "All men are created equal." That would never do, protested Mrs. Hansa Mehta of India. "All men might be in-

requirements of nondiscrimination. Having excluded religious appeals as a basis for the civil enjoyment of human rights, it would be inconsistent to introduce particular religious references as the preferred basis for affirming human rights in the preamble of the Declaration.[33]

Furthermore, since the rights and obligations enunciated in the instruments are by definition "human," they must be assumed both to be available to and incumbent upon everyone, regardless of race, color, language, religion, etc.[34] That means belief of a certain religious or similar

---

> terpreted to exclude women. In vain did Mrs. Roosevelt argue that the women of the United States had never felt they were cut out of the Declaration of Independence because it said "all men." The women felt strongly. It became a minor *cause celebré* in the Commission on the Status of Women, which voted unanimously to ask the Commission on Human Rights to substitute "all people" for "all men." Mrs. Roosevelt did not resist. While she had not objected to being assigned to the Social, Humanitarian and Cultural Commission (III) in the beginning, she had come to resent the automatic assumption on the part of the men that women were not to be trusted with political issues. Many of the women in the United Nations had reached the top in countries where women had very little recognition. They were afraid of the phrase, "all men": "Oh, no," they protested, "if it says 'all men,' when we go home it will be all men." So it was finally changed to "all human beings," and subsequent articles became "Everyone" or "No one." Occasionally, in the body of an article a lonely "his" was allowed to remain because that seemed a little more elegant than saying "his and hers."

[33] This point does not suggest that religions are precluded from providing whatever theological justifications for human rights they may favor, but it does suggest two qualifications in that regard: (1) that such justifications remain "unofficial" from the point of view of the human rights documents (because of the point about "religious impartiality"); and (2) that in order to be consistent with the basic "logic" of human rights, theological justifications will need to find a way to embrace the "religious impartiality" point. In other words, religious grounds will have to be found for the proposition that no one religion has a right to special *public* advantages that seriously compromise anyone's rights of free exercise and nondiscrimination. (See below for a discussion of the significance of the "public/private" distinction.)

[34] I have elsewhere advanced the following general definition of human rights: "Given that a 'right' *simplicter* is an entitlement to demand a certain performance or forbearance on pain of sanction for noncompliance; that a moral right is a right regarded as authoritative in that it takes precedence over other action and is legitimate in part for considering the welfare of others; and that a legal right is warranted and enforced within a legal system, a human right, then, is understood as having the following five characteristics, according to the prevailing 'human rights vocabulary.' (1) It is a moral right advanced as a legal right. It should . . . [in the words of the Universal Declaration] 'be protected by the rule of law,' thus constituting a standard for the conduct of government and the administration of force. (2) It is regarded as protecting something of indispensable human importance. (3) It is ascribed 'naturally,' which is to say it is not earned or achieved, nor is it disallowed by virtue of race, creed, ethnic origin, or gender. (4) Some human rights can be forfeited or suspended under prescribed conditions (under public emergency, for example), but several primary or basic human rights are considered indefeasible under any circumstances. (5) It is universally claimable by (or on behalf of) all people against all (appropriately situated) others, or by (or on behalf of) certain generic categories of people, such as "women" or "children." Those who are appropriately subject to such claims are said to have 'correlative human duties'. David Little,

kind cannot be required as a qualification for benefiting from human rights or for being expected to live up to them. In short, the religious impartiality of human rights, carefully specified in this way, would appear to be part of the logic of the principle of nondiscrimination, a principle that is constitutive of the whole idea of human rights.[35]

Applying the distinction between "public" and "private" spheres of behavior to questions of fundamental belief also appears to be required by the principle of nondiscrimination,[36] though, again, the distinction must be carefully understood. If religion or belief may not be employed to control what an individual in the role of citizen may or may not do or enjoy, then religious belief and expression will have to be "private," *at least in the sense of being effectively, or for practical purposes, under the direct personal control of each citizen, and only indirectly under the control of the public authorities.*[37]

"The Nature and Basis of Human Rights," in Gene Outka and John P. Reeder, Jr., eds., *Prospects for a Common Morality* (Princeton, NJ, 1993), 82-83.

[35] Paul Sieghart, *The International Law of Human Rights* (Oxford, 1983), 75: "The principle of non-discrimination is fundamental to the concept of human rights. The primary characteristic which distinguishes 'human' rights from other rights is their universality: according to classical theory, they are said to 'inhere' in every human being by virtue of [one's] humanity alone. *It must necessarily follow that no particular feature or characteristic attaching to any individual, and which distinguishes [one] from others, can affect [one's] entitlement to . . . human rights, whether in degree or in kind*, except where the instruments specifically provide for this for a clear and cogent reason. . . ." (emphasis added).

It should be emphasized that non-discrimination, along with several other primary rights, like freedom from torture, arbitrary life-taking, enslavement, and retroactive laws, as well as freedom of thought, conscience, and religion or belief, and two other protections, is considered to be "non-derogable" (unsuspendable or unabridgeable) by the Covenant on Civil and Political Rights. That means that discrimination, along with the other non-derogable rights, may never permissibly be practiced, even in extreme conditions, such as emergency or armed conflict. See article 4(1) and (2) of the Covenant.) The list of non-derogable rights is somewhat different from two regional human rights instruments, the European Convention on Human Rights (article 15, which excludes nondiscrimination!), and the American Convention on Human Rights (article 27, which includes it).

[36] See Martin E. Marty and R. Scott Appleby, "Conclusion," in id., *Fundamentalisms and the State* (Chicago, 1993), 621, and John H. Garvey, "Introduction," in ibid., 13ff. Garvey writes: "There is a certain way of thinking about law and politics that is characteristic of modern industrial nations, and that religious fundamentalist movements invariably reject. I will call this habit of thought the public/private distinction. *Its central premise is that social life can be divided into public and private realms. The function of government is to regulate behavior in the public sphere according to secular rules.* Within the private sphere people are free to do as they like, in religious and other matters. Religious fundamentalists reject this method of political organization. They see the public/private distinction as artificial; they believe in particular that religion is inseparable from law and politics." Ibid., 13.

[37] The word "private" has a variety of meanings, not all of which are relevant to this distinction. The central idea here, as in the term "private property," is of "having sovereignty" vis-à-vis the public authority. The notion of a "specially privileged status" for fundamental belief, mentioned above, illuminates the meaning of "private sovereignty."

This proposition requires elaboration, especially in the light of concessions made in the Human Rights Committee's General Comment to the idea of a state religion or ideology. While the adoption of a state or official religion or ideology is not, according to the Comment, prohibited, it is explicitly and highly qualified by the rights of free exercise and nondiscrimination. So long as it can be demonstrated that these rights are in no way violated, then a state may adopt a religion or ideology as official. Since, however, the consistent and scrupulous implementation of these rights requires religious impartiality on the part of the state, at least in regard to excluding religious identity as a condition of citizenship, religious beliefs and activities must, in practice, be left to the direct private control of individual citizens, and not to direct public control.[38]

According to the rights of free exercise and nondiscrimination, as we have seen, the state may not interfere with fundamental beliefs or use them as a basis for discriminatory treatment in respect to the privileges and responsibilities of citizenship. In this precise but important sense, the "private/public" distinction must "effectively, or for practical purposes" be honored, whether official rhetoric honors it or not. That is true, I suggest, because of the logic of nondiscrimination.[39]

There is an additional complexity about the private/public distinction that ought to be mentioned. Some human rights considered binding in the public sphere may, up to a point, be abridged in the private sphere. Whereas religious confession, for example, would not be accepted as a basis for discriminating in public employment or education, it is, obviously, a permissible basis for deciding the eligibility of the members of religious communities. Similarly, religious communities are allowed to discriminate on the basis of gender in selecting their own authorities, although such forms of discrimination would not be permitted in choosing public officials. To be sure, the abridgment of rights in the private sphere is not unlimited. Religious bodies would not be permitted to violate, in

---

"Private" in this context does not necessarily mean "secret" or "removed from public view." A person's religious beliefs might be secret, but they might also be expressed in public, and still be private in the relevant sense. "Private opinions" are by no means necessarily secret opinions. Moreover, "private control" does not mean that every detail of one's religious life must be personally determined and administered. Individuals may well submit to a given religious authority, and not forfeit their "direct personal control," so long as the act of submission is voluntary, and the religious authority has no public or legal power to compel submission. Finally, just as with private property, private control, in this context, does not imply unlimited control. Religious utterance and practice is always restricted by some human rights standards as well as by "compelling state interests."

[38] The same, of course, goes for ideological belief. It is cumbersome to keep saying it.

[39] If it could be demonstrated that even the use of official rhetoric in favor of a state religion, in given circumstances, impaired "the enjoyment of any of the rights under the Covenant," then such use would, accordingly, have to be adjudged a violation of human rights.

the name of their basic convictions, certain "primary" rights, such as the prohibitions against slavery, torture, and arbitrary life-taking.[40] But beyond that, considerable latitude is conceded, precisely in the name of honoring "freedom of conscience and religion or belief."

Human rights instruments do, of course, permit certain forms of indirect control on the part of the state. Public authorities are permitted to regulate practices ("manifestations") based on fundamental belief, though, it is important to note, they may not regulate the beliefs themselves. Public regulation is so permitted insofar as given religious practices, for example, are held to violate "the fundamental rights and freedoms" of others, or to violate "public safety, order, health, or morals."[41] These latter so-called "limitations" on the rights of fundamental belief are rather elastic and open-ended, and provide, as they stand, a potential threat to human rights guarantees because they can so easily be used as a pretext for reintroducing unwarranted forms of interference and discrimination "based on religion or belief."

Fortunately, the Human Rights Committee Comment offers some help in confining the opportunities for abuse:

> Limitations may be applied only for those purposes for which they were prescribed and must be directly related and proportionate to the specific need on which they are predicated. Restrictions [on the rights of fundamental belief] may not be imposed for discriminatory purposes or applied in a discriminatory manner. The Committee observes that the concept of morals derives from many social, philosophical and religious traditions; consequently, *limitations on the freedom to manifest a religion or belief for the purpose of protecting morals must be based on principles not deriving exclusively from a single tradition.*[42]

This important "pluralistic" restriction on the public limitation of human rights would presumably create a significant obstacle against violating the rights of fundamental belief in the name of one particular state religion or ideology.

---

40 See note 35 above. It is interesting that although nondiscrimination may be thought of as one of the non-derogable rights for purposes of limiting state action under emergencies (article 4(1), Covenant on Civil and Political Rights), it, unlike the other non-derogables, may be partially suspended in the private sphere. This difference perhaps accounts for the fact that nondiscrimination is not included in 4(2), with the other non-derogable rights, but is mentioned by itself in 4(1).

41 Article 1.3, Declaration against Intolerance; Article. 18.3, International Covenant on Civil and Political Rights.

42 Comment Adopted by the Human Rights Committee, para. 8, p. 3 (emphasis added).

Theoretical Problems

As mentioned, the Intolerance Project has two basic and related objectives: One is to establish the degree to which forms of intolerance that violate existing human rights standards, contribute to conflict, as well as how efforts to modify or eliminate those violations contribute to peace. The second is to clarify the sources or causes of tolerance and intolerance, including in particular the role of religion and similar beliefs.

Having sorted out the meaning of "tolerance" and "intolerance" (including "discrimination" and "nondiscrimination") in regard to the relevant human rights standards, it is not difficult, in respect to the first objective, to establish that violations of the rights of free exercise and nondiscrimination intensify conflict in divided multiethnic societies, nor to project with reasonable confidence that the observance and implementation of those norms will serve to reduce conflict.

In the cases of Sudan and Tibet—cases of severe civil conflict—large numbers of religious believers have been systematically interfered with and frequently persecuted. In Sudan and Tibet, as well as in Sri Lanka—another example of ongoing civil strife—minority populations have been seriously discriminated against because of majority attitudes and beliefs that have tended, respectively, to dominate the governments of those places. At the same time, in all three of these cases, respectable proposals for resolving conflict prominently include references to respect for the rights of free exercise and nondiscrimination. In short, intolerance of one kind or another is quite obviously a significant part of the conflict in these (and many other) cases, and its elimination is widely and reasonably regarded as an important ingredient of peace.

So far, there are no acute theoretical problems. Problems do arise, however, at the point where the two objectives of the Intolerance Project intersect, namely, when the question of *the sources* or *causes* of tolerance and intolerance is raised, including the role of religious and similar beliefs. Here, certain considerations regarding causality and explanation that are involved in the study of "the rights of free thought and fundamental belief" must be clarified.

Belief, Ethnicity, and Nationalism. It is a commonplace that contemporary civil conflicts are frequently "ethnic" or "nationalistic" in character. If there has until recently been a failure among social scientists to appreciate "the emotional depth of ethnonational identity and the mass of sacrifices that have been made in its name,"[43] that failure is at

---

[43] Walker Connor, *Ethnonationalism: The Quest for Understanding* (Princeton, NJ, 1994), 74. See particularly, chapter 2, "Nation-Building or Nation-Destroying?", for a convincing discussion of the neglect of ethnic and nationalist sentiments by social scientists.

present being rectified by extensive and illuminating attention to these subjects.

The Intolerance Project seeks to investigate the implications of these phenomena for the rights of free thought and fundamental belief. Each of the seven cases addressed—Ukraine, Sri Lanka, Sudan, Tibet, Lebanon, Israel, and Nigeria—is confronted with deep ethnic tensions and fervent nationalistic aspirations. The problem is to make clear exactly how ethnicity and nationalism relate to fundamental belief.

The first part of an answer to the sources or causes of intolerance follows from an examination of the meaning of the terms, "ethnicity" and "nationalism." Max Weber's discussion remains among the most penetrating we have.[44] For him, the definitions of "ethnic group" and "nation" are very close, though not quite equivalent. An ethnic group is, at bottom, a "people"[45] that holds *"a subjective belief in their common descent."* Their identity is "presumed," which means that it is "artificially" or "accidentally" associated with a set of characteristics such as physical appearance, customs, common memories, language, religion, etc.[46] "Almost any kind of similarity or contrast of physical type and of habits," says Weber, "can induce the belief that affinity or disaffinity exists between groups that attract or repel each other."[47] This way of putting it underscores the fact that the discourse of ethnicity at once *homogenizes and differentiates.*[48] The very artificially selected ethnic indicators that create "affinities" among insiders simultaneously create "disaffinities" with outsiders.

Likewise, the idea of "nation,"[49] says Weber, "is apt to include the notions of common descent and of an essential, though frequently indefi-

---

[44] Weber's seminal discussion of "ethnic groups," "nationality," and "the nation" is to be found in Max Weber, *Economy and Society: An Outline of Interpretive Sociology* (New York, 1968), 1:385-398 and 2:921-926. Weber's approach to the terms has been kept alive by Walker Connor (see, e.g., Connor, *Ethnonationalism*, 102-104), and fits closely with the dominant emphasis these days among social scientists and historians concerning the partially artificial or "invented" character of ethnic and nationalist identity. Liah Greenfield in *Nationalism: Five Roads to Modernity* (Cambridge, 1992) locates herself in a general way in the Weberian tradition (see ibid., 17-18), but, in fact, she deviates from Weber at crucial points, so far as the study of nationalism goes. See notes 58 and 70 below.

[45] The Greek word, "ethnos," rather open-endedly means "people," "race," or "tribe."

[46] Weber, *Economy and Society*, 1:387, 389 (emphasis added).

[47] Ibid., 1:388.

[48] Katherine Verdery, "Whither 'Nation' and 'Nationalism'?" *Daedalus* 122 (3) (Summer, 1993): 38. I am assuming that Verdery's terms, which she applies here to "nationalism" also apply in a similar way to "ethnicity," even though these ideas, while related, are not the same thing for her.

[49] "The word *nation* comes from the Latin and, when first coined, clearly conveyed the idea of common blood ties. It was derived from the past participle of the verb *nasci*, meaning

nite, homogeneity."[50] The concept also "belongs in the sphere of values,"[51] and is artificially constructed or invented, with the same consolidating and differentiating effects that ethnicity involves. Nations are *self-defining*[52] "peoples" in the way ethnic groups are. In these respects, a nation is like an ethnic group.

Yet, Weber goes on, "the sentiment of ethnic solidarity does not by itself make a 'nation'."[53] There are two distinguishing features. Nations are culturally more self-conscious and assertive, more concerned with "cultural prestige" than ethnic groups. "The significance of a 'nation' is usually anchored in the superiority, or at least the irreplaceability, of the culture values that are to be preserved and developed only through the cultivation of the peculiarity of the group." It is in that sense that nations are typically associated with legends of a "providential mission,"[54] and, no doubt, with an intensified image of themselves as a "chosen people."[55] Second, nations are more self-conscious and assertive politically: They naturally want an "autonomous polity," thereby exercising what they regard as their legitimate right of self-rule:[56]

> Time and again we find that the concept "nation" directs us to political power. Hence, the concept seems to refer . . . to a specific kind of pathos which is linked to the idea of a powerful political community of people who share a common language, or religion, or common customs, or political memories; such a state may already exist or it may be desired. The more power is emphasized, the closer appears to be the link between nation and state.[57]

---

to be born. And hence the Latin noun, *nationem*, connoting *breed* or *race*." Connor, *Ethnonationalism*, 94.

[50] Weber, *Economy and Society*, 2:923.

[51] Ibid., 2:922.

[52] Connor, *Ethnonationalism*, 104.

[53] Weber, *Economy and Society*, 2: 923: "Undoubtedly, even the White Russians in the face of the Great Russians have always had a sentiment of ethnic solidarity, yet even at the present time they would hardly claim to qualify as a separate 'nation.' The Poles of Upper Silesia, until recently, had hardly any feeling of solidarity with the 'Polish Nation.' They felt themselves to be a separate ethnic group in the face of the Germans, but for the rest they were Prussian subjects and nothing else."

[54] Ibid., 2:925.

[55] Weber links the notion of "chosen people" to ethnic groups rather than nations (ibid., 1:391). By speaking of nations as having "an intensified image of themselves as a 'chosen people,'" I am simply extrapolating from Weber's suggestion that nations are ethnic groups that are more self-conscious and assertive.

[56] Ibid., 1:395.

[57] Ibid., 1:397.

A nation is a community which normally tends to produce a state of its own.[58]

These comments about the impulse to create a "nation-state" hint at Weber's understanding of nationalism. In Weber's view, nations in general are naturally disposed toward creating autonomous polities. However, under modern conditions, a nation fulfills its political aspirations either by forming a "modern state" or by reforming an already existing state. A modern state, in turn, is to be understood as a political community that possesses a monopoly of the legitimate use of force over a given territory and its inhabitants,[59] and whose legitimacy rests on "legal-rational" or formal, universalistic (impersonal) norms, rather than on rules associated with "sacred tradition" or other forms of particularistic authority that tend to favor one racial, religious, or kin group over others.[60]

The fact that nationalism is the impulse of a nation to form itself into a modern state explains why nationalism is necessarily a modern phenomenon.[61] The very conditions that made the modern state possible

---

[58] H.H. Gerth and C. Wright Mills, eds., *From Max Weber: Essays in Sociology* (New York, 1958), 176. In contrast to Weber, Liah Greenfield explicitly denies that nationalism necessitates "statehood either as a reality or as an aspiration." See Greenfield, *Nationalism*, 494. But this deviation from Weber's approach is not carefully explicated or defended, and it raises some problems. For one thing, in all of the five cases that Greenfield studies—England, France, Germany, Russia, and the United States—there is a strong impulse toward expressing national consciousness in the form of a state. Is that not something of more than passing importance about these different forms of nationalism?

[59] Ibid., 78. For Weber, this definition distinguishes the modern state from premodern forms of political organization, which were typically much less preoccupied with precise territorial borders, and much less capable of achieving a monopoly of legitimate force.

Weber's emphasis on circumscribed territory as characteristic of the modern state, and, by inference, of the ideals of nationalism, brings up the relation of "nationalism" to "patriotism," since patriotism is conceptually linked to the idea of "fatherland" (*patria*) or "country," which means "governed land" or "political territory." Presumably, "patriotism" denotes *loyalty to the institutions and territory of the state.* Nationalism and patriotism are obviously not equivalent, since an individual—for example, a member of the Basque people—might be torn between the ideals of Basque nationalism (the aspiration of the Basques to perpetuate their own culture and form their own state) and a sense of Spanish patriotism (loyalty to the state institutions and the "fatherland" of Spain). On the other hand, it is surely conceivable that under some circumstances nationalism and patriotism can converge—for example, an individual during the Hitler period might have been devoted to the nationalist ideals and aspirations of the Nazi Party and simultaneously loyal to the institutions and territory of Germany. See Connor, *Ethnonationalism*, chap. 8 ("Beyond Reason: The Nature of the Ethnonational Bond") for an interesting, if somewhat sketchy, discussion of the distinction between nationalism and patriotism.

[60] Weber, *Economy and Society*, 1:33-38; 2: 901-4; 3: 956-1005.

[61] "[T]he word *nationalism* is itself of very recent creation. G. de Bertier de Sauvigny believes it first appeared in literature in 1798 and did not reappear until 1830. Moreover, its absence from lexographies until the late nineteenth and early twentieth centuries suggests that

have affected the idea of national identity in a profound way. Those conditions include the capacity to consolidate and standardize a population into a mass society through new, expansive patterns of commerce, industry, transportation, communication, education, and the like that are associated with the rise of modern capitalism. These developments are themselves accompanied by a new idea of the individual as someone no longer defined primarily by local membership in family, clan, or town, but rather as an "equivalent member" of a potentially vast "imagined community," which is the modern nation.[62]

This idea of equivalent membership, or what Anderson refers to as "a deep, horizontal comradeship"[63] in an extended national community, is, in Weber's mind, directly tied to the formal, impersonal legal and political system that characterizes the modern state. Thus, linked as it is to the modern state, nationalism must cope in one way or another with the universalistic demands of "mass democracy" and "the equal rights of the governed" that are implicit in a legal-rational political system.[64]

At this point, a crucial distinction suggested in Weber's writings and recently elaborated by contemporary scholars needs to be introduced.[65] It is the distinction between "liberal" and "illiberal nationalism," alternatively typified as "civic" versus "ethnic nationalism,"[66] or as "nonaggressive versus aggressive nationalism."[67]

Eric Hobsbawm characterizes the distinction this way:[68] On the one hand, there is the version of nationalism expressed in the French or American revolutions that rested fundamentally on the ideals of citizenship and involved a commitment to common "civic" participation in ac-

---

its use was not extensive until much more recently. Furthermore, all of the examples of its early use convey the idea of identification not with the state, but with the nation as properly understood [as a 'people']. While unable to pinpoint nationalism's subsequent association with the state, it indubitably followed and flowed from the tendency to equate state and nation. It also unquestionably received strong impetus from the great body of literature occasioned by the growth of militant nationalism in Germany and Japan during the 1930s and early 1940s." Connor, *Ethnonationalism*, 98. See Ernest Gellner, *Nations and Nationalism* (Ithaca, NY, 1983) for similar conclusions. For a brief discussion of Weber's view, see *From Max Weber*, 176-179.

[62] Benedict Anderson, *Imagined Communities* (London, 1983), 6-7. Cf. Craig Calhoun, "Nationalism and Ethnicity," *Annual Sociological Review* 19 (1993): 229-233.

[63] Anderson, *Imagined Communities*, 7.

[64] See, e.g., "The Levelling of Social Differences," in Weber, *Economy and Society*, 3: 983-987.

[65] E.J. Hobsbawm, *Nations and Nationalism since 1780* (Cambridge, 1991); Greenfeld, *Nationalism*; Isaiah Berlin, "Two Concepts of Nationalism," *The New York Review* 38 (November 21, 1991: 19-24). Cf. Yael Tamir, *Liberal Nationalism* (Princeton, NJ, 1993).

[66] Greenfeld, *Nationalism*, 11.

[67] Berlin, "Two Concepts of Nationalism," 19.

[68] Hobsbawm, *Nations and Nationalism*, 22.

cord with constitutional norms. This type of nationalism inclines toward Weber's "legal-rational" or formal, universalistic norms and the associated ideas of mass democracy and "the equal rights of the governed" that he identifies with the modern state. What is more, these ideas are obviously compatible with the human rights norms identified earlier. Particularly in the American case, for example, the national ideal is in part a multi-ethnic and nondiscriminatory one, expressed inclusively in terms of a "people of peoples." We shall label this type "liberal nationalism."

On the other hand, there is a different version of nationalism manifested, for example, in the German campaign of the nineteenth and twentieth centuries, for political unification that rested its aspirations for a state upon a belief in "the prior existence of [a] community [that distinguished] itself from foreigners" according to its special history and culture.[69] While German nationalists took some account of the democratic and universalistic norms associated with the modern state, their emphasis upon the priority and preeminence of one particular racial and cultural community over others, particularly during the fascist period, obviously pulled against the legal-rational norms and in the direction of an ethnically discriminatory and preferential political and legal system. This type we designate as "illiberal."

In a Weberian spirit, I stress that, however useful these types may be, they are nevertheless artificial. They indicate "tendencies" and "options" available to nationalists under modern conditions. Numerous intermediate types are no doubt imaginable. We may assume that all cases of nationalism experience pressure in both directions, inclining toward one type of nationalism or the other depending on the circumstances. Indeed, nationalism is properly understood as fundamentally ambivalent as between the liberal and illiberal types, and the individual "story" of each case of nationalism may best be described as a dynamic response to the countervailing tendencies represented by the two types.[70]

For however committed to "civic," "universalistic," "liberal" norms a given form of nationalism may be, nationalism is at bottom, as Weber saw, both an homogenizing and a differentiating mode of discourse. Na-

---

[69] Ibid.

[70] By ignoring the (eventual) interdependence of nationalism and statehood, another deficiency in Greenfield's approach in her *Nationalism* book emerges. She fails to see what Weber's position indicates, namely, the "countervailing tendencies" that underlie the modern commitment to the nation-state. The "civic" imperatives of mass democracy and the "equal rights of the governed," which are formal and universalistic in character, typically pull against the tendency towards particularlism and exclusivity directly associated with the modern state's dedication to defined borders and sharply differentiated notions of national identity. One tendency of the other is no doubt accentuated by the kind of national spirit or sentiments that influences the formation of the state, as in the differences, for example, between the German and the American cases Greenfield describes.

tionalist discourse—even of the liberal sort—drives toward cultural standardization within the nation, which makes it hard to sustain genuinely multi-ethnic and multinational expression.[71] Concomitantly, a modern nation favors clear territorial boundaries that distinguish its citizens from "foreigners" and "aliens." In fact, sovereignty over a sharply circumscribed community of inhabitants and a sharply circumscribed territory is one of the hallmarks of the modern "nation-state." Under certain conditions, the tendency to differentiate between nationals and foreigners can express itself in strongly xenophobic terms, which tends to put a strain on the commitment to legal-rational or "civic" norms.

Moreover, the subjective belief in common descent that is characteristic of liberal nationalism is typically ambivalent with respect to how total its commitment to universalistic norms really is. In the American case, for example, there is a notorious ambiguity in the thought of the "founding fathers," from whom American citizens believe themselves, in a spiritual sense, to be descended.[72] On the one hand, there is a strong and frequently heralded commitment to the universalistic principles of equal rights for all, tolerance and nondiscrimination, and government by the consent of every citizen. On the other hand, there is the familiar and unmistakable evidence of racism and sexism in both the utterances and the laws of the founding period. This deep national schizophrenia—appropriately called "the American dilemma"—obviously underlies many of the major tensions and conflicts that have appeared throughout American history.

By the same token, however "illiberal" a given case of nationalism may be, however committed it may be to the political priority and preeminence of one racial, religious, or linguistic group over other groups in

---

[71] For a highly original and provocative critique of traditional liberal thinking regarding cultural diversity in modern societies, see Will Kymlicka, *Multicultural Citizenship: A Liberal Theory of Minority Rights* (New York, NY, forthcoming). I am grateful to Professor Kymlicka for letting me see the manuscript.

[72] "From my own primary school education, a century or so ago, I recall how we students—many, probably most, of whom were first-, second-, or third-generation Americans from highly diverse national backgrounds—were told we shared a common ancestry. We were programmed to consider Washington, Jefferson, et al. as our common 'founding fathers.' We memorialized Lincoln's reminder in the Gettysburg Address that four score and seven years earlier, it was 'our Fathers [who had] brought forth upon this continent a new nation.' We repetitively sang that very short song—'America'—one of whose seven lines read 'land where my fathers died.'" Connor, *Ethnonationalism*, 207-208. Though Connor is not altogether clear about it, he seems to be giving an example here of the convergence or overlapping of patriotism (loyalty to the institutions and territory of the state) and nationalism (political and cultural assertiveness disposed toward expressing itself in the form of a modern state). In the context of this reference to American beliefs in common descent, he suggests that multiethnic states, like the U.S., often "adopt the idiom of nationalism when attempting to inculcate loyalty to the state." Ibid., 207.

the same society, illiberal nationalism is still, as we saw, a "modern" phenomenon, and in its own way as much a product of the universalizing tendencies of modern economic, political, and cultural life as is liberal nationalism. Even Hitler's Germany possessed a constitution, and sought legitimacy—at least in the early 1930s—through democratic elections and parliamentary procedures.

It is of course true that the Nazi version of a subjective belief in common descent—the myths about racial superiority and so on—were relentlessly illiberal. But that only proves, in a negative way, how potent and inescapable a threat liberal beliefs are perceived to be by proponents of illiberal nationalism. Similarly, contemporary examples of illiberal nationalism in places like Sri Lanka and Sudan give strong evidence of a continuing struggle between the imperatives of constitutional democracy and the deep and abiding pressure for policies of cultural and ethnic preference and discrimination.

Accordingly, Weber's analysis suggests two connections between belief, ethnicity, and nationalism. One is the obvious point that ethnic and nationalist identity rests, after all, upon nothing more than "subjective belief." If, as Weber says, it is finally belief and not "objective factors" that provides the foundations for group identity, then it is clear why the belief held in common would itself become the special, even "sacred," focus of group attention and consciousness, and why considerable effort would be expended in shoring up that belief and in protecting it against threats of pervasive doubt and disaffection. If, as a matter of fact, the feeling of solidarity, the feeling of belongingness that undergirds ethnic and national identity, as well as the spirit of nationalism, expresses, at bottom, a deep emotional attachment,[73] then it is easy to understand why challenges to the fundamental beliefs associated with ethnicity and nationalism would be defended in such an intense and passionate way.

Second, nationalism (and, incipiently, ethnicity) is related to belief insofar as nationalism constitutes a theory of political legitimacy. For Weber, political legitimacy, as an example of social authority, involves a "belief" in the existence of a valid or justified political order.[74] Presuma-

---

[73] Though Connor never quite uses the term "emotional apriori" to describe the need for a feeling of solidarity that appears to underlie ethnic and national identity, he comes close. The term captures his emphasis, clearly in line with Weber's, on the fundamentally affectional or nonrational character of ethnic and national identity. See *Ethnonationalism*, 94.

[74] "All ruling powers, profane and religious, political and apolitical, may be considered as variations of, or approximations to, certain pure types [legal-rational, charismatic and traditional]. These types are constructed by searching for the basis of *legitimacy*, which the ruling power claims." Gerth and Mills, eds., *From Max Weber*, 294. Cf. Weber, *Economy and Society*, 1:31: "Action, especially social action which involves a social relationship, may be guided by the belief [*Vorstellung*] in the existence of a legitimate order." It should be noted, that even though Weber's "affectional"-"charismatic" as well as his "traditional" types of legitimacy

bly, the nationalist, in justifying a claim to state authority, would advance basic national beliefs as worthy of political expression and enforcement.

Now, the implication of this for the study of intolerance is that insofar as all nationalists—liberal and illiberal—are loyal to particular cultural and territorial communities, they will have a certain problem complying consistently with universalistic norms, such as are expressed in international human rights documents.

At the same time, liberal nationalists will do relatively better than the illiberal nationalists accommodating and respecting diverse beliefs, and thus promoting tolerance and peace. That is because liberal nationalism is by definition more committed to protecting the rights of free exercise and nondiscrimination than illiberal nationalism. A multiethnic political setting, where prevailing nationalist beliefs exclude or demean minority populations and their beliefs, is a setting liable for serious conflict, especially where the dominant beliefs are translated into law. In that sense, illiberal forms of ethnicity and nationalism constitute a special source or cause of intolerance.

Religion and Nationalism. While Weber's emphasis on the "artificial" and "accidental" character of beliefs about ethnic and nationalist identity is warranted and important, that emphasis must not be allowed to obscure some special affinities between religion and nationalism, affinities that are also relevant to other forms of fundamental belief.

The point by now should be obvious: If ethnonational groups are at bottom constituted by "a subjective belief in their common descent," a belief that naturally becomes "the special, even 'sacred' focus of group attention," then we have already begun to describe something very close to "religious belief." The connection between religion and myths of human origin is well-known. As the anthropologist Malinowski and others have shown, such myths encourage and support cultural and social self-consciousness by validating and affirming what are believed to be the primordial terms of human identity.

Add to that the strong religious ring of ideas associated with ethnicity and nationalism: a "chosen people" with a "providential mission"; a belief in "the superiority, or at least the irreplaceability, of the [group's peculiar] culture values"; and the right to form an autonomous polity in the name of advancing a holy mission. Hebrew Scripture, whether interpreted by Jews or Christians, the Qur'an, and some significant Buddhist doctrines and texts, for example, all provide the foundation and the in-

---

are considered by him to be nonrational, he does, nevertheless employ "belief" in regard to both; for example, see Gerth and Mills, eds., *From Max Weber*, 295-296.

spiration for enlisting political and military power in the cause of defending and advancing certain sacred values and ways of life.

And these natural affinities make understandable why, as Benedict Anderson and others have argued,[75] the modern nation-state, even in its more liberal forms, readily takes on some sacral attributes and functions. Its memorials for fallen heroes, its ceremonies commemorating past glories and woes, its rhetoric of obligation and sacrifice "for God and country," all give meaning to the suffering and death of those defending the nation, and at the same time provide a certain "transcendent continuity among all members—living, dead, and yet unborn."

Causal Complexities: Some Examples

These observations might lead us to conclude that since religion is so deeply interconnected with ethnic and nationalist identity, religion determines nationalism. But, of course, things are more complicated than that. Weber's general comment about causation in social life is highly pertinent: "If we set out the causal lines [of social behavior], we see them run one moment from the technical to the economic and the political, at the next moment from the political to the religious and then the economic, and so on. Nowhere is there any resting point."[76]

On the one hand, it is the tentative conclusion of the studies so far produced by the Intolerance Project that "fundamental belief" of either a religious or ideological sort plays an important role in shaping the forms of nationalism that exist, for example, in Sri Lanka, Sudan, and Tibet.

The specific role of religion and related cultural factors in the Sri Lankan conflict is clearly significant.[77] While nationalism is a relatively modern invention in Sri Lanka, it nevertheless draws on and puts to use traditional religious warrants. Sinhala Buddhist "revivalists" of the late nineteenth and twentieth centuries have artfully manipulated ancient legends concerning Buddha's alleged associations with Sri Lanka, as well as the patterns of cooperation and mutual support between king and monastery that are part of the island's history. These appeals have done much to mobilize support for Sinhala nationalism among the monks and laity, and to provide the movement with sacred authority. The appropriation by Tamil nationalists of religious and cultural appeals is also important, though the subject has not been as fully investigated as has the Sinhala side.

---

[75] Anderson, *Imagined Communities*, 17-25.

[76] Cited in David Beetham, *Max Weber and the Theory of Modern Politics* (London, 1974), 254.

[77] See Little, *Sri Lanka: The Invention of Enmity.*

What is most menacing about the type of religious and ethnic nationalism that has appeared in Sri Lanka is precisely its more or less systematic incompatibility with the right of nondiscrimination. The eminent Sri Lankan historian, K.M. de Silva, has pointed out that the Sinhala Buddhist revivalists had no time for such norms: "In the Sinhala language, the words for nation, race and people are practically synonymous, and a multiethnic or multicommunal nation or state is incomprehensible to the popular mind. The emphasis on Sri Lanka as the land of the Sinhala Buddhists carried an emotional popular appeal, compared with which the concept of a multiethnic polity was a meaningless abstraction."[78] The same could be said of the more radical forms of Tamil nationalism.

As in the Sri Lanka example, the internal strife that has divided Sudan since its independence in 1956 has deep religious roots. The ascension to power of the National Islamic Front in 1989 reflects both the influence of Islam on the political culture of Sudan and the ability of Islamic conservatives to shape the debate in Sudan, despite the deleterious effects on the country.

Islam has long played a key role in forming the northern Sudanese identity and in providing political legitimacy to opposition parties and governments alike. The Mahdist revolution in the late nineteenth century solidified the link between religion and politics, and defined an identity in northern Sudan that transcended traditional loyalties. The post-independence era saw a continuation of these trends. The withdrawal of British colonial rule after 1956 provided an opportunity for the Muslim majority in the north to establish some form of Islamic rule.[79] Fearing domination by the northerners, the southern Sudanese opposed Islamic rule.

Southern fears are aroused by the prospect of discriminatory treatment imposed on minorities under strict Islamic rule: "The attempt by the north not only to define the identity [of Sudan] as Arab and Islamic, but to structure and stratify the life and role of citizens along those lines" has been an underlying cause of the civil war.[80] While northerners see

---

[78] K.M. de Silva, *Religion, Nationalism, and the State* (Tampa, FL, 1986), 31.

[79] At independence, all but one political party supported some form of Islamic rule. The inspiration for such rule is rooted in the revivalist movements of the nineteenth and twentieth centuries. Reacting to the experience of colonial domination, Islamic reformers have consistently sought to establish a society based on the Qur'an, the traditions of the prophet and Shari'a. Recognizing Muslim society to be in a state of decline—economic, political, and social—and attributing that decline directly to the deviation of the community from the "straight path" of Islam, the logical "cure" is a return to Islam. This entails a reshaping of society in accord with Islamic principles, eliminating any distinction between politics and religion, and, most importantly, the implementation of Islamic law (Shari'a).

[80] Francis Deng, "The Tragedy in Sudan Must End: A Personal Appeal to Compatriots and to Humanity," *Mediterranean Quarterly* 5(1) (Winter, 1994): 47.

themselves as Muslims, southerners—though divided along tribal lines—share a common identity of being non-Muslims. The south's introduction to Islam was associated with an extensive slave trade during the nineteenth century, an era characterized by economic exploitation and military domination. Appeals by northern politicians for an Islamic constitution at the time of independence evoked fears among southerners of a return to this earlier stage of relations.

The actions of the north since independence have done little to alleviate these fears. Some northerners sincerely feel that Sudan can only be united through religious and cultural uniformity, and they have therefore supported efforts to Islamize the south. The military offensives conducted by Major General Ibrahim Abboud in the late 1950s and early 1960s,[81] and the implementation of the Shari'a-based "September laws" under the regime of Colonel Ja'far Muhammad Numairi (which led to a resumption of the civil war after a brief reprieve based upon the Addis Ababa Agreement of 1972) are examples of the recurring attempts to unify Sudan through enforced Islamization. Far from achieving the desired unity, however, the result has been continued civil war.

Religious revivalism, whether in Sri Lanka or Sudan, then, has provided the resources for mobilizing a strong form of illiberal nationalism that has from time to time inspired intolerance and discrimination "based on religion or belief."

The relation between religious belief and ethnonationalism in the case of Tibet is somewhat different. The Tibetan people have for a long time identified strongly with their religious tradition. Buddhism permeated Tibetan culture and society to such an extent that "the history of Tibet . . . is almost the same as the history of the importation of Buddhism into Tibet."[82] The centrality of Tibetan Buddhist identity remained strong in the face of the initial Chinese invasion of Tibet in 1949-50. An aggressive campaign to eradicate Buddhist culture was undertaken largely because "the Chinese authorities viewed religion as the principal obstacle to their control of Tibet."[83] Over 6,000 monasteries were destroyed, approximately 1.2 million Tibetans were killed, many others were forced into exile (including the Dalai Lama), and an influx of Chinese soldiers, administrators, and settlers transformed the region.

---

[81] "Abboud believed that the way to unify the Sudan was to homogenize its people, which, in his view, meant transforming the south into an Islamic society." Ann Mosley Lesch, "The Republic of Sudan," in Ta'eq and Jacqueline S. Ismael, eds., *Politics and Government in the Middle East and North Africa* (Miami, FL, 1991), 365.

[82] Robert Thurman, "Religious Intolerance/Tolerance in the Future of Tibet and China," unpublished paper, 1.

[83] *International Campaign for Tibet, Forbidden Freedoms: Beijing's Control of Religion in Tibet* (Washington, DC, 1990), 7.

The Chinese campaign was inspired by a combination of Maoist ideology and Han Chinese nationalism.[84] Convinced of its mission as the agent of progress and of the liberation of "backward" Tibetans, the Chinese government considered itself justified in controlling and reconstructing Tibetan society. Resistance was based on the Tibetans' "desire to protect their religious and cultural traditions,"[85] and religion came to represent for the Tibetans the principal expression of nationalist sentiment.[86]

In reaction to Chinese nationalism, which is distinctly illiberal, Tibetan nationalism has for the most part taken a nonviolent form and has expressed itself in liberal terms. Tibet's noted leader and principal spokesperson, the Dalai Lama, has repeatedly called for a liberated Tibet dedicated to parliamentary democracy and to the principles of human rights, including the rights of free exercise and nondiscrimination. Indeed, the Dalai Lama has gone so far as to advocate the separation of church and state. Such a system, he says, is duly respectful of the rights of religious and other minorities in a way that has not occurred under Chinese rule, nor for that matter under the traditional pattern of Tibetan government.[87]

---

[84] Interestingly enough, the two were apparently blended in Mao's mind. When he appealed for support from the masses, Mao frequently referred to the Chinese Communist Party, "not as 'the vanguard of the proletariat,' but as 'the vanguard of the Chinese nation and the Chinese people.' The Chinese communists in Mao's propaganda became 'part of the Great Chinese nation, flesh of its flesh and blood of its blood.'" At other times, Mao would appeal to "the family ties deriving from a single common ancestor." Connor, *Ethnonationalism*, 199.

[85] Ibid., 7.

[86] It needs to be noted that efforts by the Chinese authorities to eradicate Buddhist practice greatly diminished traditional Buddhist influence on the subsequent generations who grew up in Communist Tibet with little or no religious teaching. However, in recent years, there has been a revival of Buddhist practice in no small part because it represents for many Tibetans an effective form of dissent.

[87] Lodi G. Gyari, "Religion and the Future of Tibet," presented at the USIP conference, "Tibet: Religion, Conflict, and Cooperation," (September 28, 1993), 3:

> The most recent formal proclamation by His Holiness the Dalai Lama was the "Guidelines for Future Tibet's Policy and the Basic Features of its Constitution" in which His Holiness restates *his decision not to play any role in the future government of Tibet*. For religion, this is a significant development as it clears the way for the head of state to be a *secular leader*. . . . Whereas the Guidelines say that the 'Tibetan polity should be founded on spiritual values," nowhere does it refer to a "Buddhist nation" . . . or say that government would have the duty to safeguard and develop religion. . . ."
>
> On the contrary, the Guidelines provide explanatory language on many areas, but not on religion, envisioning a full separation of church and state....The only mention of religion is found in the section, 'Fundamental Rights,' which simply says *all Tibetan citizens shall be*

But if religion plays an important role in such cases, questions still remain: Why, exactly, has religion taken the shape it has in modern Sri Lanka or Sudan or Tibet, and yet has not taken the same shape elsewhere? Why does religious or ideological belief go together with such a hostile form of nationalism in Sri Lanka or Sudan or among the Han Chinese leadership, and not everywhere? More precisely, why does Buddhism take the shape it does in Sri Lanka or Tibet, and Islam take the shape it does in Sudan? To raise the questions is to suggest that the causal connections are not all in one direction.

In the case of Sri Lanka, the chauvinistic character of Buddhist revivalism itself demands explanation. The basic tenets and doctrines of Buddhism would not seem to affirm ethnic favoritism. Such attitudes apparently resulted from a combination of historical pressures on the Theravada sangha around the fifth and sixth centuries A.D. and certain colonial and other experiences, especially in the nineteenth and early twentieth centuries. These were attitudes of racism and anti-Buddhist intolerance fostered by Christian missionaries and British colonial authorities, a sense of threat among the Sinhala represented by the combined strength of the Tamil communities in Sri Lanka and south India, and the imperatives of modern nationalism, including the intensification of ethnic identity because of political and economic developments.

So far as Sudan goes, it has been difficult for northern political—and military—leaders to move away from the appeal to Islam as the basis for political support, although that emphasis has so alienated the south. Efforts by northern leaders to deal constructively with southern grievances by supporting more moderate and nondiscriminatory polices have produced strong counterreactions among other parts of the Sudanese political elite, frequently stimulating a reversion to religious militancy. In that way a process of "religious-one-upsmanship" characterized political life in the north during successive post-independence governments. This process, coupled with bitter sectarian political divisions, led to the failure of Sudan's experiments in parliamentary rule, further discrediting moderate policies. The instability created by sectarian divisions and by alternating military regimes did little to provide the kind of environment necessary for the peaceful and enduring resolution of north-south differences. The result has been an environment conducive to an interpretation of Islam that is deeply intolerant of diversity.

As for Tibet, we have already mentioned how the Chinese campaign for domination had the effect of intensifying Tibetan allegiance to Buddhism, and strengthening the role of religion in rallying the people to the

---

equal before the law without discrimination on the grounds of religion and other classifications" (emphasis added).

nationalist cause. While much of the explanation for the nonviolent emphasis of Tibetan nationalism undoubtedly rests with the character of the Tibetan Buddhist tradition and, more especially, with the direction and style of leadership provided by the Dalai Lama, it is possible that a realization of the futility of violence against overwhelming Chinese military advantage has also contributed to the commitment to nonviolence. Finally, there can be little doubt that the experience of intolerance and discrimination at the hands of Chinese authorities has importantly influenced the conviction that a future Tibet, once liberated, must be a Tibet reformed in keeping with liberal norms.

Conclusion

The perspective on questions involving the connections among belief, ethnicity, and nationalism adopted in this paper derives from the USIP project on Religion, Nationalism, and Intolerance. As befits the work of an institution dedicated to the study of peace, the project traces the connections between tolerance and peace, or, putting it negatively, between intolerance and conflict. The study concludes, tentatively, that the connection is important: Intolerance, defined essentially as the violation of the human rights of free exercise and nondiscrimination, undermines peace, while respect for those rights undergirds and promotes peace.

When it comes to the more theoretical questions of the sources or causes of intolerance, the project gives special attention to the role of ethnicity and nationalism. Those forms of nationalism, such as are manifest in the policies of the Chinese government toward Tibetans, or in the treatment by the Sudanese government of citizens not in sympathy with its sectarian objectives, or in Sri Lankan policies, now thankfully in retreat, favoring the Sinhala majority over the Tamil minority, are essentially illiberal in character.

Under illiberal forms of nationalism, the requirements of nondiscrimination are systematically disregarded: Civil identity, or citizenship, is deeply conditioned by ethnic, linguistic, religious, ideological, and other indicators. It would be difficult to conclude that this kind of "ethnonationalism" does not directly contribute to antagonism, hostility, and instability, especially in multiethnic, multireligious societies.

We acknowledged that not all nationalism is of the illiberal variety. Though never entirely free of countervailing tendencies, liberal nationalism inclines to support and institutionalize universalistic norms of nondiscrimination and free exercise. It is more in accord with human rights imperatives. The implication is that, on balance, liberal nationalism contributes to the conditions of peace by cultivating ethnic and religious respect and harmony.

One urgent question emerging from the Intolerance Project concerns *why* nationalism takes one form rather than another. Our tentative answer is complicated. One part suggests that "fundamental belief" plays a distinctive role because by its nature nationalism attracts and thrives on "subjective belief" of the most fervent and primary sort. The affiliation between nationalism and religious "revivalism" of a Sudanese or Sri Lankan kind, or between nationalism and an ideology of cultural superiority of the Han Chinese variety, is accordingly, not surprising.

We speculate, based on the evidence produced so far by the Intolerance Project, that the relevant religious or cultural beliefs place their own peculiar stamp on the form and shape of nationalism. There are, one would assume, certain dispositions in Buddhism, Islam, or Christianity, or in the Han Chinese cultural tradition that, under conducive circumstances, can be readily appropriated in the service of an illiberal kind of nationalism.

By the same token, of course, one may just as well speculate that there are contrary dispositions in these and other religious and cultural traditions that, under conducive circumstance, favor liberal nationalism. The example of the influence of Buddhism in the Tibetan case springs to mind. One thing about the Tibetan nationalist movement that is, so far, significantly different from comparable movements in Sudan and Sri Lanka is the reliance, in general, upon nonviolent means. This emphasis upon nonviolence has given special authenticity to another theme of equal importance to the Tibetan cause: the urgency of observing human rights norms as a basis for just and peaceful relations between the Tibetans and the Chinese.

In the same vein, one could also point to certain manifestations within the Ukrainian Christian churches—especially among the Ukrainian Catholics, but also among certain elements within the Russian and Ukrainian Orthodox—of strong support for the rights of free exercise and nondiscrimination.[88] That support is accompanied by a desire to reverse the dominant tradition in Ukraine which, effectively, effaces the distinction between public and private when it comes to religion, and invests direct religious control in hands of public authorities.

So, religion is a significant factor in the emergence and expression of nationalism. It can, it would seem, be a force for tolerance or intolerance, and needs to be so analyzed. At the same time, there is more to the answer than that. The causal factors do not, as Weber said, run all in one di-

---

[88] See Little, *Ukraine: The Legacy of Intolerance*, 25-27, 67-74.

rection. We must be as attentive to the conditioning effects of politics, economics, historical accidents, etc. on religion and culture, as we are to the contribution religion and culture make to the formation of nationalism, and thence to the incidence of tolerance and intolerance.

Religious Human Rights Under The United Nations

NATAN LERNER[1]
Tel-Aviv University

This chapter deals with the approach of the international community to the issue of religious human rights, or human rights related to religion, after the establishment of the United Nations. In the five decades since the San Francisco Conference and the establishment of the UN, a wide spectrum of global and regional instruments intended to protect human rights has been developed, not necessarily with the same emphasis and identical firmness. Religious rights (or human rights related to religion and beliefs) are among the protected rights, but no global obligatory treaty has been adopted in this sensitive area. Nearest to it is the Declaration on the Elimination of All Forms of Intolerance and of Discrimination Based on Religion or Belief, proclaimed in 1981 by the UN General Assembly, the implementation of which has already given rise to considerable work by the UN, although it is not a mandatory instrument. This document and its implementation will be reviewed in detail.

The treatment of religious human rights, as compared to other basic freedoms, has induced specialists and observers to assert that religious rights have been neglected by the world community, probably as a consequence of the basic disagreement on the nature and extent of some religious freedoms. Lobbying in international bodies was thus necessary to ensure the adoption of adequate steps leading to the general enjoyment of religious rights by everyone, on an equal footing with other fundamental rights. These efforts yielded some results.

[1] The author would like to thank the Ninawo Peace Foundation for the support extended to his research on the subject, and Mr. Yehuda Mechaber, of the United Nations Library of the Israeli Ministry for Foreign Affairs, for his help in obtaining access to UN documents.

J.D. van der Vyver and J. Witte, Jr. (eds.), Religious Human Rights in Global Perspective, 79-134.

In the absence of a specific treaty, mandatory provisions regarding religious human rights are those contained in the 1966 Covenant on Civil and Political Rights, on the worldwide scene, and corresponding provisions in respective regional human rights instruments. Many of them reflect customary international law and thus bind not only the states that have ratified such instruments but other states as well. Additional obligatory texts form part of several conventions on specific subject matters; they are thus of a more limited character. Those provisions will be reviewed herein with an eye to reaching some coherent recommendations on how to make further progress in the protection of religious human rights.

Since this is part of a comprehensive and ambitious two-volume work, this chapter will not discuss ideologically the meaning of religion in general, or attempt to propose a viable definition of religious human rights. However, it will be impossible to avoid theoretical references to the question of what religious human rights, or human rights related to religion, are. My approach will be a broad one. I shall include in my discussion the differences between individual and collective rights of persons, the rights of the group, the nature of religious-based congregations or communities, the interaction between freedom of conscience and freedom of expression of religious feelings and their translation into forms of cult, the status of religious sites, religion and criminal law, blasphemy, proselytizing, conversion, limitations and derogations, group libel, and the clash between the protection of religious rights and other freedoms. In most cases, these themes will be dealt with in connection with the positive provisions incorporated into the instruments to be considered, mainly intended to prevent and/or avoid discrimination in religious-related areas, including in particular in education and family law.

I am aware of the relationship between international and municipal protection of human rights. Constitutional law and domestic legislation are, of course, beyond the scope of this chapter, although in some cases it will be necessary to compare certain international provisions with similar ones in the internal sphere. This also applies to possible comparisons between judicial or quasi-judicial decisions in the international arena and concurring or conflicting domestic jurisprudence. Because of their particular role and possible international consequences, some special arrangements made by individual states with churches or religions will be mentioned.

I was confronted with a major methodological dilemma in drafting this chapter. Should one deal separately with the existing instruments, pointing out merits and shortcomings, and so discussing the different substantial issues? Or is it preferable to identify those issues and clarify each of them in the light of adopted (or aborted) provisions in the various instruments? I hope that the methodology followed in these pages will allow the reader to know what international law provides on such issues, what it should have stated in my view, and what substantive problems are, at this stage, not adequately covered by the body of legislation developed by the international community in the half century under review.

I am also aware of the fact that this volume is intended to reach a large audience, and not only a public strictly interested in or acquainted with legal matters. I have tried, therefore, to avoid a legalistic approach and terminology, as well as too many references to sources. I aimed at a balance which I know is difficult to achieve. The result may in any case be useful, since the neglect of religious human rights is also felt in the human rights literature. For example, a recent comprehensive book on *Human Rights: An Agenda for the Next Century* does not devote one of its seventeen chapters to the issue of religion and human rights.[2]

The far-reaching events and changes that have taken place in the last years in international life have not exercised any direct or immediate influence on the legal approach to religious human rights, despite their relevance. Those changes must be kept in mind, however, when we approach this delicate field. Human history has been deeply affected by the role of religion. Civilizations and peoples have felt the impact of the emotional and political implications of religion. War and peace have been their consequence. Present international life cannot escape such an impact. The way in which religion influences these events and changes is of enormous weight. Religion is certainly not marginal to the tragic conflicts of our time involving ethnicity, racism, group hatred, or to aspirations related to self-determination, separation, or segregation. Against the background of those conflicts, the United Nations General Assembly proclaimed 1995 to be "the United Nations Year for Tolerance."

Trends and movements have developed in different parts of the world opposing the universal acceptance of basic rights in the sphere of religion and belief that became—or should be—an international minimum standard from which no derogation of departure is legitimate.

---

[2] Louis Henkin and John Lawrence Hargrove, eds., *Human Rights: An Agenda for the Next Century* (New York, 1994). See also Mark Weston Janis, "Panel on Religion and International Law," *American Society of International Law Proceedings* 82 (1988): 195. Some of the presentations at the panel were included in Mark W. Janis, ed., *The Influence of Religion in the Development of International Law* (Dordrecht/London/Boston, 1991). See, inter alia, J.A.R. Nafziger, "The Functions of Religion in the International Legal System", in ibid., 147. Roger S. Clark points out that the human rights literature "is surprisingly sparse on the issue of religious intolerance." See Roger S. Clark, "The United Nations and Religious Freedom," *New York University Journal of International Law and Politics* 11 (1978): 197.

Having stated the basic principle of the universality of human rights, it is however necessary to acknowledge the legitimacy of some particularities, provided they do not affect the international minimum standard and do not fall into a relativism incompatible with a modern conception of human rights.

Persecution on religious grounds is a grave and present danger, as is seen in current conflicts between believers and non-believers, or between different religions or churches in multi-religious states, or between states with an official or preferred religion and persons and communities not belonging to it. In some cases, the conflict is between a given church or congregation and its own members, and the law is expected to introduce a balance between the opposing rights.

The following pages address what the international community has achieved in the last five decades to introduce some systematic order in this sensitive area, and what challenges remain for it in the new century and millennium. Hopefully, these pages will reflect the fact that the protection of religious human rights during the United Nations era, although limited, does exist. It has to be improved and strengthened, particularly from the viewpoint of implementation.

Modern human rights law avoided philosophical controversies by asserting the rule that the terms "religion" and "belief" mean theistic views of the universe and codes of behavior, as well as atheistic, agnostic, rationalistic, and other convictions where both elements are not contained. That system of law did not produce a consolidated mandatory treaty regarding religious human rights in general. But Article 18 of the Covenant on Civil and Political Rights, and some other provisions in global or regional conventions, are obligatory for the many states that ratified them. Most of the principles proclaimed by the Universal Declaration on Human Rights are seen today as reflecting customary international law and some of them as constituting *jus cogens*, that is, peremptory rules that cannot be derogated except by similar new rules developed by international law.

Against this background, the international community is discussing the convenience and the disadvantages of pressing the issue of a mandatory treaty, that may perhaps provide a low common denominator of protection of religious rights or not obtain an adequate number of ratifications. In the absence of such a treaty, the implementation of presently existing measures to monitor those rights and facilitate the access to international tribunals or quasi-judicial bodies becomes particularly important. As to basic substantive norms, the most outstanding is the 1981 UN Declaration on the Elimination of All Forms of Intolerance and Discrimination Based on Religion or Belief, which provides a comprehensive catalogue of rights respecting religion. Proclamation of the Declaration shows considerable progress in this area, for it is a constructive attempt to harmonize individual, collective, and group freedoms in matters of religion, as well as to provide answers to some of the difficult unsolved problems that have been indicated.

There is need for a renewed interest on the part of all major religions, beliefs, or philosophical trends, as well as on the part of international lawyers and human rights specialists, in the complex and fascinating area of religious human rights. I hope that the following pages may stimulate that interest, in the light of the results, and shortcomings, of half a century of international work in this field.

Religious Rights in the Era of the United Nations

Religious freedom is seen as the first fundamental right that was incorporated into political instruments "long before the idea of systematic protection of civil and political rights was developed," in the words of Karl Partsch. This view is shared by many scholars. John Humphrey writes: "Freedom of religion is indeed the oldest of the international recognized human freedoms and therefore the one with which the international community has had the longest experience." Paul Sieghart shares this view and points out that the movement for "freedom of belief" "precedes every other in the history of the struggle for human rights and fundamental freedoms."[3]

Protection of religious groups by bilateral treaties was well known to international law from the early stages of its development, particularly after the signing of the Peace of Westphalia in 1648, which modified the rule of *cuius regio eius religio* and started to pay attention to religious rights. Thereafter, international human rights law actually began—although timidly and emphasizing tolerance[4] more than rights—to make modest attempts to protect specific religious groups or minorities. This was not surprising, given that religion and religious intolerance were, and still are, one of the main causes of conflict in the history of human-

---

[3] See, respectively, Karl Josef Partsch, "Freedom of Conscience and Expression, and Political Freedoms," in Louis Henkin, ed., *The International Bill of Rights* (New York, 1981), 209; John P. Humphrey, "Political and Related Rights," in Theodor Meron, ed., *Human Rights in International Law* (Oxford, 1985), 176; Paul Sieghart, *The International Law of Human Rights* (New York, 1983).

[4] On the legal meaning of the words "tolerance" and "intolerance," see pages 116-117 below. In its resolution 48/126, of 20 December 1993, on the 1995 Year for Tolerance, the General Assembly described "tolerance" as "the recognition and appreciation of others, the ability to live together with and to listen to others" and as a "sound foundation of any civil society and of peace." Press Release GA/8637, 1994, 382-384.

kind. Treaties concluded since the seventeenth century incorporated clauses protective of religion, sometimes but not always on grounds of reciprocity. States also extended, unilaterally, their diplomatic protection to subjects of countries where religious rights were violated. After the 1815 Congress of Vienna, the protection was expanded to cover minorities not only of a religious nature. Religious rights were in some cases a condition for territorial arrangements or the recognition of states.[5]

Domestic laws and constitutions promulgated after the Protestant Reformation started to incorporate the principle of religious toleration and basic rules on freedom of religion and belief. The 1598 Edict of Nantes and the 1689 Toleration Act in England represented important early stages in this development, which culminated with the French and American revolutions.[6]

The period between World War I and II witnessed an interesting development with regard to religious rights. Article 22 of the Covenant of the League of Nations imposed upon Mandatory States the duty to guarantee freedom of conscience and religion. More specifically, the minority treaties concluded with several countries and the unilateral declarations formulated by certain states in order to ensure the adoption of measures for the protection of national, ethnic, religious, or cultural minorities,[7] contained numerous provisions belonging to the area of religious human rights. In those treaties and unilateral declarations the emphasis was not on the particular nature of the group, but on the fact that such a group existed, had a well individualized identity, and was entitled to have such identity protected, including protection against forced assimilation. In more than one case, protected groups were those with a combination of

---

[5] On these early developments, see Alessandra Luini del Russo, *International Protection of Human Rights* (Washington, 1971); Myres S. McDougal, Harold D. Laswell, and Lung-chu Chen, *Human Rights and World Public Order* (New Haven, 1980), 653-689; Stephen C. Neff, "An Evolving International Legal Norm of Religious Freedom: Problems and Prospects," *California Western International Law Journal* 7 (1977): 543-582. On religious rights and minorities, see Patrick Thornberry, *International Law and the Rights of Minorities* (Oxford, 1991); Natan Lerner, "The Evolution of Minority Rights in International Law", in Catherine Brolmann et al., eds., *Peoples and Minorities in International Law* (Dordrecht/Boston/London, 1993), 77-101.

[6] On religious rights in national law, see Arcot Krishnaswami, *Study of Discrimination in the Matter of Religious Rights and Practices*, United Nations, 1960 (Sales 60, XIV.2), 4.

[7] The literature on the minorities treaties and on the minorities issue is immense and cannot be listed here. Recent works include: Francesco Capotorti, *Study on the Rights of Persons Belonging to Ethnic, Religious and Linguistic Minorities* (New York, 1991), esp. chap. IV; Felix Ermacora, "The Protection of Minorities Before the United Nations", *Recueil des Cours* 182/IV (Alphen, 1983): 247; Natan Lerner, Group *Rights and Discrimination in International Law* (Dordrecht, 1991); Thornberry, *International Law and the Rights of Minorities*; Yoram Dinstein and Mala Tabory, eds., *The Protection of Minorities and Human Rights* (Dordrecht/Boston/London, 1992). On the inter-war experience, J. Robinson et al., *Were the Minorities Treaties a Failure?* (New York, 1943).

ethnic, cultural, and religious characteristics, and religious human rights were only a segment of the legitimate interests covered. It should be mentioned that the minorities system also included implementation measures.[8]

With the collapse of the League of Nations, this system of minority rights protection also collapsed, together with peace and democracy in Europe. It is difficult to assess how the system would have evolved if World War II had not ended it, but it was certainly suspect and in fact discredited when the San Francisco Conference started to build a new international order based on the United Nations. The emphasis was now almost exclusively on individual rights and freedoms. Group rights were ignored. Religious human rights were supposed to be adequately protected by the general rules regarding the rights of the individual, jointly with the principle of non-discrimination. The new approach was that, whenever someone's rights were violated or jeopardized because of a group characteristic—race, religion, color, ethnic or national origin, culture, or language—the necessary remedy would be the result of protecting the rights of the person, on a purely individual basis, mainly by the non-discrimination rule.[9] Still, some peace treaties concluded after World War II contained provisions on religious and other communities.

Although the UN General Assembly emphasized that the minorities issue had to be dealt with, proposals for inclusion of an article on minorities in early human rights documents were rejected. Many states were firmly opposed to any reference to group rights, each for its own reasons, in addition to the general reaction to what was considered the general failure of earlier protections of minorities. The horrors of World War II, including the Nazi genocide of Jews and others, rendered more pressing the need to adopt concrete steps to prevent and suppress discrimination and intolerance against ethnic or religious groups on grounds of theories of superiority. At Dumbarton Oaks and San Francisco, there was support for the Charter clauses on discrimination, but few states were ready to take concrete steps to combat it, and certainly to adopt effective means of implementation.

It was on this basis that the UN Charter and the Universal Declaration on Human Rights were drafted. The two Covenants, on Economic, Social and Cultural Rights and on Political and Civil Rights, adopted in

---

[8] The Permanent Court of International Justice adopted important decisions in this respect. Prominent among them is the Court's Advisory Opinion on the subject of (Greek) Minority Schools in Albania (1935), PCIJ, Ser.A/B, No. 64.

[9] Cf. Marc Bossuyt, *L'interdiction de la discrimination dans le droit international des droits de l'homme* (Brussels, 1976); Warwick McKean, *Equality and Discrimination under International Law* (Oxford, 1983); E.W. Vierdag, *The Concept of Discrimination in International Law* (The Hague, 1973); Lerner, *Group Rights*.

1966, nearly two decades after the Declaration, followed the system of the Declaration with only modest changes, despite the evolution of legal thinking in the interim. The Charter[10] asserts in its Preamble the determination "to practice tolerance" and proclaims, among the purposes of the UN, respect for human rights and for fundamental freedoms for all "without distinction as to race, sex, language, or religion" (Article 1(3)), reiterating this approach in Article 55(c).[11] The Charter does not contain any other reference to religious rights. Proposals submitted by several delegations during the San Francisco Conference to include provisions on religion were unsuccessful.[12]

The Universal Declaration of Human Rights. The Universal Declaration of Human Rights, adopted by General Assembly Resolution 217 A (III) of 10 December 1948,[13] forbids, in Article 2, distinctions of any kind, including religion, in the enjoyment of the rights and freedoms set forth in the Declaration. Article 18, of crucial importance, states:

> Everyone has the right to freedom of thought, conscience and religion; this right includes freedom to change his religion or belief, and freedom, either alone or in community with others and in public or private, to manifest his religion or belief in teaching, practice, worship and observance.

A reference to "religious groups" is included in Article 26, on the right to education. Article 29, on limitations in the exercise of the proclaimed rights, is also relevant to the subject.

Article 18 was of great influence on the respective texts incorporated in the 1966 Covenants, in the regional treaties and in the 1981 Declaration which we shall analyze in detail. As pointed out by Nehemiah Robinson in his classic commentary on the Declaration, Article 18 consists of two parts: the first clause guarantees the right to freedom of thought, conscience, and religion; the second enumerates the specific rights included therein. This second part is not exhaustive. It only contains those rights

---

[10] For text, see Ian Brownlie, ed., *Basic Documents in International Law*, 2d. ed. (Oxford, 1972), 1.

[11] On human rights in the UN Charter, see Hersch Lauterpacht, *International Law and Human Rights* (London, 1950). Philip Alston, "The Commission of Human Rights," in Philip Alston, ed., *The United Nations and Human Rights* (Oxford/New York, 1992), 127 ascribes the unsuccessful efforts to include human rights provisions in the Charter to the expectations for an international Bill of Rights.

[12] Krishnaswami, *Study of Discrimination*, 12. Early UN treaties contained clauses on freedom of religion and on religious education. Such were the 1951 Convention on the Status of Refugees and the 1954 Convention on the Status of Stateless Persons. For their text, as well as for other human rights instruments mentioned in this essay, see *Human Rights: A Compilation of International Instruments* (New York, 1993), Sales No.E.93.XIV.1 (Vol.I, Part 1), 634 and 621 respectively. [This compilation is hereafter referred to as *Human Rights*.]

[13] *Human Rights*, 1.

which the United Nations thought essential to include "because their observance might not be universal at present."[14]

Robinson indicates that freedom of thought is a very broad category, including the right to profess a religion or to profess none—in other words to believe or not to believe. This interpretation is confirmed by the use of the term "belief." Robinson points out that "freedom of thought" includes the other two freedoms, of conscience and religion, explicitly mentioned "in order not to leave any doubts" in the minds of the peoples of the world, as it may be deduced from the *travaux preparatoires*. Freedom of conscience was not seen at that stage as a strictly legal concept, and there was some opposition to its inclusion. The sacred and inviolable character of freedom of thought, in the words of Rene Cassin, was underlined by spokespersons of different legal systems.[15]

The term "belief" has a particular meaning in the Declaration. Its inclusion in Article 18, and similar articles in other instruments, should be interpreted strictly in connection with the term "religion." It does not refer to beliefs of another character—political, cultural, scientific, or economic, all of which are entitled to protection according to law but do not belong to the sphere normally described as religion. The term "belief" was incorporated into the Declaration to protect non-religious convictions, such as atheism or agnosticism, and its meaning was clarified during the discussions on the different instruments dealing with religious rights.

Another difficult problem in the drafting of the Universal Declaration, no less controversial when the Covenants and the 1981 Declaration were drafted, was the recognition of the right to change one's religion, denied by some religions and countries. The clause was opposed but, nevertheless, was adopted by a vote of 27 to 5, with 12 abstentions, apparently writes Robinson "on the understanding that the Declaration must be universal and that this clause did not represent a specific right but was the consequence of freedom of religion and thought." The drafters of the Declaration were aware of the questions involved, such as apostasy,[16] missionary activities, coercion and enticement, proselytism

---

[14] Nehemiah Robinson, *The Universal Declaration of Human Rights* (New York, 1958), 128ff. See also Martin Scheinin, "Article 18," in Asbjorn Aide et al., eds., *The Universal Declaration of Human Rights: A Commentary* (Oslo, 1992), 263; Partsch, "Freedom of Conscience and Expression, and Political Freedoms"; John P. Humphrey, "The Universal Declaration of Human Rights: Its History, Impact and Judicial Character," in B.G. Ramcharan, ed., *Human Rights, Thirty Years after the Universal Declaration* (The Hague, 1979), 21-37.

[15] Scheinin, "Article 18," 266.

[16] Apostasy is still dangerous today. *Time* (July 18, 1994) reports that a person, who was sentenced to death in 1985 in Iran for abandoning Islam and joining a Christian church, was now found dead in Teheran, under mysterious circumstances.

and its limits, the status of new or young religious movements struggling for recognition, and the social dangers inherent in the practices of certain sects using all kind of manipulations to attract adherents.[17]

Article 18 makes a mild concession to group rights. It refers to everyone's right to manifest his religion or belief "alone or in community with others." The words "in community" do not involve a clear reference to religious bodies or institutions, a reference that would not be agreeable with the spirit prevailing in the United Nations at that stage. Still, they do imply that religious rights are not only a strictly individual issue. A right to be exercised "in community with others" must therefore refer to something more than a purely arithmetic addition of individuals.

The critical role of the Universal Declaration in the development of the legal and political philosophy of the second part of the twentieth century is beyond controversy. It is the most important single legal document of our time, and most of its contents constitutes present customary international law. Its impact on domestic law, in the West at least, was powerful.

The Genocide Convention. Against the individualistic approach of the early United Nations years, the Convention on the Prevention and Punishment of the Crime of Genocide, adopted by the General Assembly by resolution 260 A(III) one day before the Universal Declaration and in force since 12 January 1951,[18] should be seen as an exception, born, in part, of the tragic experience of World War II. The United Nations could not ignore the intention behind the crime of genocide, namely the intent to destroy, in whole or in part, a religious or ethnic group as such, whether in time of peace or in time of war.

The prohibition of genocide is seen today as part of *jus cogens*, peremptory norms of general international law in the terms of Article 53 of the 1969 Vienna Convention on the Law of Treaties, from which no derogation is permitted and which can be modified only by a subsequent norm of the same character.

There is abundant literature on genocide since 1944, when the term "genocide" was coined by Raphael Lemkin. It includes the studies pre-

---

[17] The European Court of Human Rights dealt recently with the issue of conversion. In 1993, it decided that the punishment of a member of the Jehovah's Witnesses, condemned in Greece for proselytism, violated Article 9 of the European Convention and basic rights. See, *Kokkinakis v. Greece*, Req. No. 14 307/88 and discussion of the case in the chapter by T. Jeremy Gunn herein. On the issues of conversion and proselytism, Alain Garay, "Liberté religieuse et proselytisme: l'experience Europeene", *Revue trimestrielle des droits de l'homme* 17 (1994): 7-29. See ibid., 137-143 for excerpts from the *Kokkinakis* decision, and ibid., 144-150, observations by Francois Rigaux. See also J.A. Walkate, "The Right of Everyone to Change his Religion or Belief: Some Observations," *Netherlands International Law Review* 30(2) (1983): 146-156.

[18] *Human Rights*, 669.

pared by two Special Rapporteurs appointed by the Sub-Commission on the Prevention of Discrimination and Protection of Minorities.[19] Today, five decades after its adoption, the Convention needs to be updated, and there have been proposals to that effect. On the whole, however, and despite the fact that it does not contain measures of implementation, the Convention should be seen as one of the basic instruments in the protection of human rights and religious groups, starting with the basic right to existence.

For our purpose, Article II of the Convention is essential. This article defines five acts that constitute genocide, provided they are "committed with intent to destroy, in whole or in part, a national, ethnical, racial or religious group, as such." What typifies the crime of genocide is the intent to destroy, in whole or in part, the group. Of course, a group consists of individuals and can only be destroyed by steps taken against those individuals. But the target of the crime is the group, and not every group, but only *national, ethnic, racial or religious groups*. Article II has to be interpreted restrictively, and political and economic groups were explicitly excluded from the Convention. For that reason, the words "as such" are significant. These words were introduced into the text precisely in order to avoid defenses based on the argument that military considerations, and not racial or religious hatred, were the reasons that prompted the genocidal acts.[20]

The Convention deals with the physical destruction of the racial or religious group. The correct decision not to include in the text provisions on "cultural genocide," or "ethnocide," engendered controversy during the preparation of the treaty. Such exclusion also involves measures that could be seen as "religious genocide," such as, for instance, the closing of churches or temples or the prevention of the training of priests, religious leaders, or officials. Such steps are unquestionably denials of fundamental rights, but they are not covered by the Genocide Convention. What is protected is the physical existence of the group, an objective that seems to be, at the time of the writing of these pages, not less urgent than in 1948. Events like those taking place since 1991 in former Yugoslavia, and known under the shocking term of "ethnic cleansing," have been depicted as acts of genocide. Obviously, the attempt to "clean" or "depurgate" some territories from people that do not belong to given

[19] Studies by N. Ruihashyankiko and B. Whitaker, UN doc. E/CN.4/Sub. 2/416 (1978) and E/CN.4/Sub.2/1985/6 and Corr.1, respectively. For basic literature on the subject, see Nehemiah Robinson, *The Genocide Convention* (New York, 1960); Leo Kuper, *Genocide: Its Political Use in the Twentieth Century* (New Haven, 1981); id., *The Prevention of Genocide* (London, 1985); Raphael Lemkin, "Genocide as a Crime in International Law," *American Journal of International Law* 41 (1947): 172.

[20] Robinson, *The Genocide Convention*, 57-65.

ethnic or religious populations always constitutes cultural or religious genocide. Such acts are covered by the 1948 Convention, for they belong to one of the five categories described in Article II of the Convention, namely, acts perpetrated with the intention to annihilate, in whole or in part, a group as such.[21]

From the viewpoint of religious human rights, the adoption of the Genocide Convention in 1948 constituted a very significant departure from the exclusively individualistic approach prevailing in that early period of law-making in the area of human rights. It should therefore be mentioned in the context of an analysis of post-Wold War II legal instruments concerning religious human rights. Unfortunately, it did not become the starting point of an international criminal law system to protect basic human rights.

The Laws of War. The 1949 Conventions on the laws of war, or humanitarian law, contain some specific provisions to protect religious rights. Adopted as a consequence of the lessons of World War II, the four Geneva conventions of 1949, widely ratified, had as a precedent the rules on religious rights in the Hague Regulations.[22] For our purposes, the third and the fourth Conventions are, by their nature, particularly relevant. Common Article 3 prohibits any adverse distinction founded, among other things, on religion or faith, and Article 16 of the Third Convention forbids any adverse distinction between prisoners of war because of, among other things, religious belief. Articles 34 to 37 of the same Convention deal with religious activities, exercise of religious duties, attendance at services, chaplains and ministers of religion, and facilities for the performing of their duties.

In addition to the prohibition of discrimination, the Fourth Convention calls for respect for the religious convictions and practices of the protected persons (Article 27). Article 58 refers to ministers of religion and books and articles required for religious needs. Premises suitable for the holding of religious services should be placed at the disposal of interned persons (Article 86). Article 93 deals with the exercise of religious duties and the activities of ministers of religion.

The clauses on religious rights included in the Geneva Conventions were drafted taking into consideration the experience and advise of ex-

---

21 See Natan Lerner, "Ethnic Cleansing," *Israel Yearbook on Human Rights* 24 (1994): 103-117.

22 For the 1949 humanitarian law Conventions, see International Committee of the Red Cross, *The Geneva Conventions of August 12 1949* (undated). See also the Commentary published by the International Committee under the general editorship of Jean S. Pictet (Geneva, 1958).

perts from various non-governmental organizations interested in the subject, as well as from the Holy See.

The Covenants on Human Rights. The International Covenant on Economic, Social and Cultural Rights (ICESCR) and the International Covenant on Civil and Political Rights (ICCPR) were adopted by the UN General Assembly on 16 December 1966, by resolution 2200 A (XXI). They entered into force, respectively, on 3 January 1976 and 23 March 1976.[23] Despite the time that elapsed between the adoption of the Universal Declaration and that of the Covenants, the 1966 instruments reflect the general orientation and trends that inspired the Declaration. This is important from the viewpoint of our subject, since the evolution of legal thought that permeated, for instance, the approach to ethnic rights in the 1965 Convention on Racial Discrimination did not influence the Covenants, most probably because of the modalities of the drafting process.

The most relevant provisions in the ICCPR are Articles 18, 20, and 27. Article 18 has four paragraphs. The first paragraph follows in general the wording of Article 18 of the Universal Declaration, with some minor changes. The Covenant does not refer to the right to change one's religion or belief but uses milder language, following a compromise: It proclaims that the right of everyone to freedom of thought, conscience, and belief "shall include freedom to have or to adopt a religion or belief of his choice." There is no doubt, however, that the final text recognizes the right to change one's religion or beliefs, to abandon a religion and to adopt a different one. This liberal interpretation is supported by the discussion during the preparation of the Covenant.[24] The issue of change of religion in the 1981 Declaration is discussed below.[25]

Article 18(2) of the ICCPR states that no one shall be subject to coercion which would impair his freedom to have or to adopt a religion or belief of his choice. "Coercion" is not defined but it seems reasonable to interpret this term as meaning not only the use of force or threats but also more subtle forms of illegitimate influence, such as moral pressure or material enticement. The 1981 Declaration elaborated more in detail on the notion of coercion.

---

[23] For the text of both Covenants, see *Human Rights*, 8 and 20, respectively. Among the many works on the Covenants, see generally Henkin, ed., *The International Bill of Rights*; Meron, ed., *Human Rights in International Law*; Alston, ed., *The United Nations and Human Rights*; Dominic McGoldrick, *The Human Rights Committee* (Oxford/New York, 1991). See also the Reports of the Human Rights Committee, published as Official Records of the General Assembly (GAOR), Supplements No. 40.

[24] See, Partsch, "Freedom of Conscience and Expression, and Political Freedoms"; Scheinin, "Article 18"; Walkate, "The Right of Everyone to Change his Religion or Belief."

[25] See pages 115-116 herein.

Article 18(3) deals with limitations,[26] and should be read in conjunction with Article 4 of the Covenant, which includes Article 18 as a whole among the articles that do not permit derogation even in times of public emergency. Article 18(3) should be compared with Article 29(2) and (3) of the Universal Declaration. Article 18(3) permits only limitations on the freedom to manifest one's religion or belief "as are prescribed by law and are necessary to protect public safety, order, health, or morals or the fundamental rights and freedoms of others." National security is not listed, and the text must be interpreted in a restrictive way. In such a delicate sphere as religion, the issue of limitations is of great sensitivity.

Only manifestations of religion, or religious practices, can be restricted. The freedoms of thought and conscience and religious ideas not translated into practices are beyond any restriction. There are virtually no problems regarding the religious practices of the major, well established religions. There have been some difficulties with shehitah, slaughtering of animals according to the Jewish tradition (and similar practices of the Santeria religion),[27] as well as regarding the wearing of turbans, skullcaps, and veils or the growing of beards, and some of these issues have required adjudication. But there are rites, customs, and rules of behavior of some religious groups that may clash with norms related to public order, health, or morals of the general society, as expressed in the legal framework of each country, and in more than one case judicial intervention was necessary. The notion of morality is indisputably the outcome of cultural and historical factors that vary from society to society, and the determination of an international minimum standard in this respect may not be equally acceptable to all religions, civilizations and countries.[28]

The last paragraph of Article 18 deals with the liberty of parents and/or legal guardians to ensure the religious and moral education of their children in conformity with their own convictions. This is again a highly sensitive area. Interaction between religion and education is of great importance and caused difficulties in connection with the UNESCO Convention against Discrimination in Education, the 1981 Declaration,

---

[26] On limitations in the Covenant, Thomas Buergenthal, "To Respect and to Ensure: State Obligations and Permissible Derogations," in Henkin, ed., *The International Bill of Rights,* 72 and Alexandre C. Kiss, "Permissible Limitations on Rights," in ibid., 290.

[27] For a recent U.S. Supreme Court decision on animal sacrifices according to the Santeria rite (*Church of the Lukumi Babalu Aye, Inc. et al. v. City of Hialeah,* 61 U.S.L.W. 4587 (June 8, 1993); see also *Journal of Church and State* 35 (1993): 668-695; on shehitah, 7 U.S.C., 1902(b); Fla. Stat. 828.23 (7)(b) (1991).

[28] See, among others, Donna J. Sullivan, "Gender Equality and Religious Freedom: Toward a Framework for Conflict Resolution," *New York University Journal of International Law and Politics* 24 (1992): 795-856, at 819; Leon Sheleff, "Tribal Rites and Legal Rights," *Israel Yearbook on Human Rights* 18 (1988): 153-172; Aviam Soifer, "Freedom of Association: Indian Tribes, Workers, and Communal Ghosts," *Maryland Law Review* 48 (1989): 350-383.

the Convention on the Rights of the Child, and other international instruments.[29] This is a field of concurring interest both for international and constitutional law, and adjudication at the national and international levels has been frequently necessary. For example, in 1978, the Human Rights Committee dealt with an interesting complaint submitted by the Secretary of the Union of Free Thinkers in Finland against his country on the issue of teaching of history of religion in public schools.[30] The Committee took the view that such instruction, if given in a "neutral and objective way" and respecting the convictions of parents and guardians who do not believe in any religion, does not violate Article 18 of the Covenant.

Incitement and Clash of Rights. Article 20(2) of the ICCPR states: "Any advocacy of national, racial or religious hatred that constitutes incitement to discrimination, hostility or violence shall be prohibited by law." Article 20 does not require intent. Its wording was criticized, and several states entered reservations to it. Professor Partsch, discussing the changes introduced in the different drafts since 1953, states that the final text implies abandoning a previous "balanced compromise" reached in the Commission on Human Rights.[31] The Human Rights Committee, on its part, in its "general comment" on Article 20 made it clear that states parties "are obliged to adopt the necessary legislative measures prohibiting the actions referred to therein." The prohibitions incorporated into Article 20 "are fully compatible with the right of freedom of expression contained in Article XIX, the exercise of which carries with it special duties and responsibilities."[32]

Article 20(2), and similar provisions incorporated in regional treaties and other recent instruments, should be compared with Article 4 of the Convention on Racial Discrimination.[33] This is considered one of the most important provisions of this treaty, imposing clear-cut obligations on states parties to enact anti-incitement legislation, as many have done.[34]

---

29 For the three mentioned instruments, *Human Rights*, 101, 122 and 171, respectively.

30 *Erki Hartikainen v. Finland*, Communication No. 40/1978, Human Rights Committee, Selected Decisions under the Optional Protocol, vol. 1 (1985), UN Sales No. E.84.XIV.2, p. 74 [hereafter Selected Decisions].

31 Partsch, "Freedom of Conscience and Expression, and Political Freedoms," 453-4, n.75.

32 General Comment No.11(19), Annual Report of the Human Rights Committee, 38 GAOR, Supp. 40, A/38/40, Annex VI (1983).

33 For the text of the Convention, see *Human Rights*, 66. For discussion, see pp. 103-106 herein.

34 See José D. Ingles, Positive Measures Designed to Eradicate All Incitement to, or Acts of Racial Discrimination, United Nations (1983) Sales No. E/85.XIV.2. See also Natan Lerner, *The UN Convention on the Elimination of All Forms of Racial Discrimination*, 2d ed. (Alphen aan den Rijn, 1980). For a model national legislation against racial discrimination and incitement,

A clash between rights may be involved, since some states have feared that provisions prohibiting advocacy of racial or religious hatred may jeopardize their legal systems regarding freedom of speech and association.[35] There is a close relationship between this problem and the issue of hate crimes that came up lately in some countries. The United States Supreme Court, for example, recently declared the constitutionality of state legislation on enhancement of punishment for offenses motivated by racial or religious hatred.[36]

Minorities in the Covenant. Article 27 of the Covenant deals with minorities, including religious minorities. Its interpretation has engendered difficulties, and scholars are divided as to whether this article adds anything to the provisions of Article 18. Capotorti and Dinstein favor a liberal interpretation of Article 27, and Dinstein points out that its purpose is to grant "collective human rights to members of a religious minority qua a group." If Article 27 is not to be rendered meaningless, he writes, "it must go beyond the ambit of Article 18."[37] Other authors, such as Sohn, Ermacora, and Tomuschat, consider that Article 27 did not intend to grant any group right and protects only individual persons, and not communities as such.[38] A violation of Article 27 by Canada was claimed in the well-known case of Sandra Lovelace, a native American woman who had lost her status and rights as a native American after having married a non-native. Religion was not the main issue considered in this case, but the Committee emphasized the relevance of Article 27 to the issues of cultural and community rights and the loss of identity.[39]

General Comment of the Human Rights Committee. The body in charge of implementation of the Covenant on Civil and Political Rights has dealt on several occasions with issues related to religious rights. In

---

see UN Doc.A/48/558 (1993). Incitement on religious grounds is not specifically mentioned in this document.

[35] See, "International Colloquium on Racial and Religious Hatred and Group Libel," *Israel Yearbook on Human Rights* 22 (1992), especially Natan Lerner, "Incitement in the Racial Convention: Reach and Shortcomings of Article 4," ibid., 1 and R. Bernhardt, "Human Rights Aspects of Racial and Religious Hatred Under Regional Human Rights Conventions," ibid., 17. See also Kevin Boyle, "Religious Intolerance and the Incitement of Hatred," in Sandra Coliver, ed., *Striking a Balance: Hate Speech, Freedom of Expression and Non-Discrimination* (London, 1992), 61-71. In 1993, the Committee on the Elimination of Racial Discrimination stated that the prohibition of the dissemination of racist ideas is "compatible with the right to freedom of opinion and expression." (General Recommendation XV(42), A/42/18,1993, pp.115-116).

[36] *Wisconsin v. Mitchell*, No. 92-515, U.S.L.W. (June 8, 1993): 61.

[37] Yoram Dinstein, "Freedom of Religion and the Protection of Religious Minorities," in Dinstein and Tabory, eds., *The Protection of Minorities and Human Rights*, 157.

[38] For this discussion, see Lerner, *Group Rights and Discrimination in International Law*, 15.

[39] See Selected Decisions.

1993, the Committee issued a "General Comment" on Article 18, No. 22 (48).[40]

The Committee felt the need to draw the attention of state parties to the fact that the freedoms of thought and conscience are protected equally with the freedom of religion and belief. Article 18 protects theistic, non-theistic, and atheistic beliefs, as well as the right not to profess any religion or belief. The Committee stresses that the terms "beliefs" and "religion" are to be broadly construed, rejecting "any tendency to discriminate against any religion or belief for any reasons, including the fact that they are newly established or represent religious minorities that may be the subject of hostility by a predominant religious community."[41] The Committee obviously intended with this remark to avoid situations in which old, well-established religious groups enjoy a broader legal recognition and protection than those granted to recently established doctrinal associations. Also involved is the right to propagate religious ideas that do not enjoy support of the majority, provided they do not exceed the limits imposed by law. Still, the question may be asked how broadly the term "belief" may be construed beyond its meaning as a rejection of religious convictions of a transcendental and normative character.

The freedoms of thought and conscience, and the freedom to have or adopt a religion or belief of one's choice, are protected unconditionally. No one can be compelled to reveal his thoughts or adherence to a religion or belief. In this respect, the rights proclaimed in Article 18 should be compared to the right to hold opinions without interference recognized by Article 19(1) of the Covenant. This is not the case with the freedom to manifest religion or belief, individually or in community with others, in public or privately; a freedom which encompasses a "broad range of acts," among them ritual and ceremonial acts and practices integral to such acts, including the building of places of worship, the use of ritual formulas and objects, the display of symbols, and the observance of holidays and days of rest, as well as dietary regulations, distinctive clothing or head coverings,[42] rituals associated with certain stages in life, and the

[40] GAOR, 48th Session, Supp. No. 40, A/48/40, Annex VI (1993).

[41] Ibid., paragraph 2.

[42] These issues have engendered interesting judicial decisions in some countries. See Leon Shaskolsky Sheleff, "Rabbi Captain Goldman's Yarmulke, Freedom of Religion and Conscience, and Civil (Military) Disobedience," *Israel Yearbook on Human Rights* 17 (1987): 197-221. In this case, the U.S. Supreme Court decided that an Air Force regulation on the dress code took precedence over religious traditions. *Goldman v. Weinberger*, 475 U.S. 503 (1986). The issue was solved by legislative means. See 10 U.S.C.A. Sect. 744 (1988). See also the well-known Sikh case, *Mandla v. Dowell Lee and another*, 1108 All England Law Reports (1982); *Panesar v. Nestle Co. Ltd.* (1979), 1980 Industrial Case Reports, 144. In France, after contradictory decisions of the Conseil d'Etat, the Ministry of Education, with the support of the teachers' unions, prohibited in public schools the traditional head coverage used by Mus-

use of a particular language. The freedoms to choose religious leaders, priests and teachers, to establish seminaries or religious schools, and to prepare and distribute religious texts and publications belong to the practice and teaching of religion and belief. The Committee considered useful to list the components of the right to manifest religion or belief, following the 1981 Declaration and, before it, the Krishnaswami study (to be analyzed below). The detailed enumeration made by the Committee should not be seen as exhaustive and should be related to the issue of restrictions dealt with in Article 18(3).

Paragraph 5 of the General Comment reminds one that the Covenant bars any "coercion" that would impair the right to replace one's current religion or belief by another one or by atheistic views, namely the right to conversion, which burdened all stages of the drafting of international instruments dealing with religion. In the notion of "coercion," the Committee includes the use or threat of physical force or penal sanctions, restrictions on access to education, medical care, employment, or other rights guaranteed by the Covenant. The same protection is enjoyed by holders of non-religious beliefs.

The Human Rights Committee also clarified the reach of Article 18(4) concerning education. Public school instruction regarding the general history of religions and ethics is permitted if it is given in a neutral and objective way. But public education that includes instruction in a particular religion or belief is inconsistent with the Covenant, unless provision is made for non-discriminatory exemptions or alternatives to satisfy the wishes of parents and guardians. The guarantee of the freedom to teach a religion or belief includes the liberty of parents or guardians to ensure that their children receive a religious and moral education in conformity with their own convictions.

The 1993 General Comment refers to a former General Comment No. 11(19), which determines that states parties are obligated under Article 20 of the ICCPR to enact laws to prohibit advocacy of national, racial, or religious hatred that constitutes incitement to discrimination, hostility, or violence.[43] The Committee so reiterated the view that the prohibition of

---

lim girls. The ban includes all "ostentatious" religious identifications, as distinguished from discrete signs such as small crosses, stars of David, or the name of Allah. The issue was described in newspaper articles as a "national psychodrama." See Robert Sole, "Derrier le foulard islamique," *Le Monde* (September 13, 1994): 1. In Israel, the Supreme Court affirmed a decision of a Christian private school, in Nazareth, to reject a Muslim girl student who insisted on using the traditional veil. Some cases came before the European human rights bodies. In *X. v. United Kingdom* (7992/77) DR 14, 234, the duty of a Sikh motor-cyclist to remove his turban and wear a crash helmet was seen as interfering with his religious freedom but justified for the protection of public health.

43 See above note 31.

incitement to religious hatred is fully compatible with other basic freedoms.

The Committee stressed that Article 18(3) should be interpreted in strict terms: restrictions are not allowed on grounds different from those specified in the paragraph, even if they would be allowed in respect of other rights protected, such as national security. Limitations may be applied only for their specific purposes and must be directly related and proportionate to the specific need on which they are predicated. They should not involve discriminatory purposes or be applied in a discriminatory manner. The freedom from coercion to have or adopt a religion or belief and the liberty of parents and guardians to ensure religious and moral education cannot be restricted. Permissible limitations must be established by law and should be interpreted with a view to protect the rights guaranteed under the Covenant.[44] Legitimate constraints, such as imprisonment, should not affect religious rights, as far as possible.

In the same paragraph, the Committee deals with the delicate notion of morals, a concept that derives from many social, philosophical, and religious traditions. When the freedom to manifest a religion or belief has the purpose of protecting morals, it must be based on principles not deriving exclusively from a single tradition.

The fact that a religion is recognized as a state religion, or is considered as official or traditional, or is the religion of the majority of the population, should not result in any impairment of the enjoyment of any of the rights under the Covenant, or in discrimination against adherents of other religions or non-believers, and privileges for the members of the predominant religion should be regarded as discriminatory. The Committee expects state members to report on measures taken in this area and on the rights of religious minorities under Article 27. They should also provide information regarding practices punishable as blasphemy. Blasphemy is an issue not dealt with in existing international human rights instruments. Domestic legislation on blasphemy had caused controversy.[45]

---

[44] See above note 40, para. 8.

[45] Ibid., para 9-10. The issue of blasphemy, an offence in some legislations (Britain, Egypt, and Iran, for instance), caused public controversy as a result of the publication of Salman Rushdie's *The Satanic Verses*, in 1988, in Great Britain. The author was condemned to death by the Khomeini regime in 1989. Restrictions on publications considered blasphemous against the Church of England were declared compatible with Article 10(2) of the European Convention on Human Rights by the European Commission on Human Rights. (*Gay News v. U.K.*, 5 EHRR 123 (1983). Recently, the Bangladesh government has brought criminal charges against the writer Taslim Nasreem for blasphemy, and the Ambassador of that country in Washington referred to the possibility of a death sentence. *Washington Post* (July 15, 1994). On blasphemy, generally, see Leonard W. Levy, *Blasphemy, Verbal Offense Against the Sacred, from Moses to Salman Rushdie* (New York, 1993). See also the chapters by Peter Cumper and Said

Paragraph 11 of this important General Comment deals with conscientious objection, a right which is not explicitly mentioned in the Covenant. The Committee believes that such a right can be derived from Article 18, "inasmuch as the use of lethal force may seriously conflict with the freedom of conscience and the right to manifest one's religion or belief."[46] There shall be no discrimination against conscientious objectors on the ground that they have failed to perform military service. The question of conscientious objection exceeds in some cases the area of religion. Pacifism may certainly be considered a belief, but it may belong to an area of convictions of a different, non-religious, nature. "Conscientious" and "religious" may or may not necessarily mean the same thing, as United States and European case law makes clear.[47]

I have dealt in length with the Committee's General Comment because of its intrinsic importance, the authority of the members of the Committee, and its possible influence on the interpretation of religious rights as incorporated in other modern instruments.[48] It is to be hoped that the text may also be taken into consideration with regard to domestic legislation and judicial interpretation. It is worthwhile to stress its relevance to documents such as the Krishnaswami study and principles and the 1981 Declaration.

Implementation. The Covenant on Civil and Political Rights is the only global human rights treaty dealing with religion that contains measures of implementation. As of 30 July 1993, the closing date of the 48th session of the Human Rights Committee, 122 States had ratified or acceded to the Covenant, and 72 states had become parties to the Optional Protocol on individual communications. The periodic reports submitted by states parties and the individual complaints or communications—not many in relation to religious rights—permitted the

---

Arjomand herein, and by Donna Arzt in the companion volume to this one, John Witte, Jr. and Johan van der Vyver, eds., *Religious Human Rights in Global Perspective: Religious Perspectives* (The Hague/Boston/London, 1995).

[46] See above note 40, para. 11.

[47] See generally Chaim Gans, *Philosophical Anarchism and Political Disobedience* (Cambridge, 1992); Kent Greenawalt, *Conflicts of Law and Morality* (Oxford, 1987); Joseph Raz, *The Authority of Law* (Oxford, 1970). The European Commission on Human Rights dealt with the meaning of conscientious objection (see, among others, the Grandrath case, Yearbook of the ECHR 10,626, 1966). The European Convention on Human Rights refers to conscientious objection in Article 4 and not in connection with religion. The U.S. Supreme Court granted exemptions not only on religious premises. In *Welsh v. United States*, 398 U.S. 333 (1970), for instance, the Supreme Court granted such exemption on secular grounds, acknowledging that this may not have been the intention of the First Amendment relgion clauses.

[48] While the General Comments are "neither scholarly studies nor secondary legislative acts," and are "couched in general terms," "they represent an important body experience in considering matters from the angle of the Covenant." Torkel Opsahl, "The Human Rights Committee," in Alston, ed., *The United Nations and Human Rights*, 415.

body in charge of implementation, the Human Rights Committee, to refer to, and comment on, many human rights issues related to religion. The 1993 General Comment on Article 18 summarizes the principal views of the Committee in this regard.

The yearly Reports of the Committee, issued as General Assembly Official Records (GAOR), Supplements No. 40, contain rich information on religious rights. When examining the periodic state reports, members of the Committee asked relevant questions and required additional information from the representatives of the states on legislation and facts concerning such rights. Just to mention a few recent instances, when the second periodic report of Morocco was discussed, questions were asked regarding procedures relating to the recognition of religious sects, the status of the Baha'i faith, marriages between members of different religious groups, and the meaning of terms such as "religion of the state," "revealed religions," or "heretical sects."[49] During the consideration of the second periodic report of Austria, the issues of conscientious objectors, the status of Jehovah's Witnesses, and criminal law rules concerning blasphemy were scrutinized.[50] Colombia's third periodic report provided information on the modifications of the concordat with the Holy See in order to adjust it to the new Constitution.[51] Other issues discussed include blasphemy in the United Kingdom,[52] apostasy in Sudan,[53] differences in the treatment of churches in Argentina,[54] and restrictions on religious rights in the former USSR.[55] Almost every country that submitted periodic reports was subjected to serious scrutiny.

As to individual complaints or communications, the Human Rights Committee dealt with a relatively small number of cases belonging to the sphere of religious rights, as compared with other rights. Out of more than 500 communications concerning 42 states, many of them declared inadmissible, only a few refer to alleged violations of religious human rights. Most of those relate to conscientious objection, education, and equality among churches.[56]

The Covenant on Economic, Social and Cultural Rights. The Covenant on Economic, Social and Cultural Rights refers to religious rights,

---

49 GAOR, Forty-seventh Session, Supp. No. 40 (A/47/40), 1994, 15-17.

50 Ibid., 24-25.

51 Ibid., 89.

52 GAOR, Forty-sixth Session (A/46/40), Supp. No. 40, 1991, 100.

53 Ibid., 127.

54 GAOR, Forty-fifth Session (A/45/40), Supp. No. 40, 1990, 49.

55 Ibid., 26.

56 United Nations, Selected Decisions of the Human Rights Committee under the Optional Protocol, Vol. 1 and 2, Sales No.E.84.XIV.2 and E.89.XIV.1.

albeit in a more limited way.[57] Article 13(1) deals with the need to ensure "understanding, tolerance and friendship among all . . . religious groups." Paragraph 3 of the same article refers to the liberty of parents to ensure the religious and moral education of their children in conformity with their own convictions. Article 2(2) forbids discrimination of any kind, including religious discrimination.

The implementation system of the ICESCR has not been very effective. Shortly after its implementation in 1976, monitoring was done by special Working Groups. In 1986, a Committee on Economic, Social and Cultural Rights, composed of independent experts, was established, and has been meeting periodically to examine the reports submitted by states parties.[58] This have, as yet, yielded little on religious rights and their abuses.

First Specific Steps: The Krishnaswami Study

It has been rightly asserted that the subject of religious human rights was "shunned and neglected" more than any other similar subject, perhaps as a consequence of the generally acknowledged fact that no topic "has divided mankind more."[59] The Sub-Commission on Prevention of Discrimination and Protection of Minorities decided that one of the first studies ordered by the Sub-Commission should deal with this subject, including a program of action to eradicate religious discrimination. To that end, the Sub-Commission in 1956 appointed a Special Rapporteur, Arcot Krishnaswami from India, who submitted a careful and comprehensive report in 1959.[60]

The study was based on information appearing in 82 country monographs analyzed by the author. Krishnaswami was aware of the difficulties involved with a comprehensive study of religious rights and emphasized that "differential treatment meted out to individuals and groups is not always synonymous with discrimination." Sometimes, discriminatory practices are to be found in countries where efforts have been made to eradicate discrimination.

Conscious of the difficulty to define "religion," Krishnaswami uses the term "religion or belief" as including, in addition to various theistic creeds, such other beliefs as agnosticism, free thought, atheism and rationalism, concepts which he does also not attempt to define, and which

---

[57] For its text, see *Human Rights*, 8.

[58] See, generally, Philip Alston, "The Committee on Economic, Social and Cultural Rights", in Alston, ed., *The United Nations and Human Rights*, 473-508.

[59] McKean, *Equality and Discrimination under International Law*, 121.

[60] See above note 6.

are all notions involving philosophical and ideological issues. After dealing with the nature of the right to freedom of thought, conscience, and religion, its recognition as a legal right and the prohibition of discrimination in its respect, he distinguishes between the freedom to maintain, or to change, religion or belief, and the freedom to manifest religion or belief. It is this second aspect that engenders most legal problems.

Krishnaswami also refers to permissible limitations upon the right and to the individual and collective aspects, as well as public and private aspects, of the freedom to manifest religion or belief, inclusive of those violations by individuals or private groups. While the freedom to maintain or to change a religion or belief admits of no restrictions, the right to manifest them is of course the subject of regulation and even limitations by the state.

Krishnaswami stresses that the followers of most religions and beliefs are members of some form of organization, church, or religious community. Therefore, compulsion to join such bodies, or preventing members from leaving them, may become an infringement of the right to freedom of thought, conscience, and religion. Still, prescribed procedures or formalities to that effect do not necessarily involve such infringement. In any case, as stressed by Article 18 of the Universal Declaration, no one should be subject to coercion in this regard. Sanctions against apostasy are rare today,[61] but some legal systems, adopting as the law of the state the religious law of particular religions, confront difficult problems related to change of religion, which may be generally forbidden or require authorization by religious or state authorities. The teaching and propagation of religion, missionary activities, and improper inducements to change one's religion also in some cases involve delicate legal questions.

As to the freedom to manifest religion or belief, the Special Rapporteur considers that the words "teaching, practice, worship and observance" embrace all possible manifestations. The legitimate limitations must satisfy the criteria established in Article 29 of the Universal Declaration and should not "sacrifice minorities on the altar of the majority" but ensure a greater measure of freedom for society as a whole.[62]

Krishnaswami deals with the individual and collective aspects of freedom to manifest religion or belief and concludes that the collective aspect—whether it implies freedom of assembly, or also the freedom of association and organization—is especially important, particularly from the point of view of state intervention and regulation. All this is, of

---

[61] See above note 16.

[62] See above note 6, at 18.

course, related to the position of minorities within the state, particularly in the case of minorities with religious affinities outside the state.

The Krishnaswami study includes a detailed list of the components of the freedom to manifest religion or belief. There may be some permissible limitations, as in the cases of human sacrifices, self-immolation, mutilation, slavery, prostitution, subversive activities, polygamy, and other practices that may clash with the requirements mentioned in Article 29 of the Universal Declaration. In such cases, domestic legislation may only prevail upon norms adopted in international instruments when the minimum standard rule is not affected. The remaining list of freedoms related to the manifestations of religion or belief includes: worship, processions, pilgrimages, equipment and symbols, funeral arrangements, holidays and days of rest, dietary practices, marriage and divorce, dissemination of religion or belief, and training of personnel. Manifestation of religion or belief also includes the freedom to forgo acts incompatible with prescriptions of a religion or belief, such as oaths, military service, participation in religious ceremonies, confession, and compulsory medical treatment.[63]

Krishnaswami devotes a short chapter to the status of religions in relation to the state, including established churches or state religions, recognition of several religions, and separation of state and religion. Norms on management of religious affairs, the financial relationship between the state and religion, and the duties of public authorities are discussed. This is again an area in which local constitutional law may prevail against international rules, and a number of different relationships between the state and religion can be distinguished, profoundly influenced by the various constitutional systems and cultural traditions.[64]

The study ends with a chapter on trends and conclusions that reflects the situation in the period in which it was prepared. In a final footnote, Krishnaswami comments on the manifestations of anti-semitism and other forms of racial prejudice and religious intolerance which became the immediate cause of further measures adopted by the international community. He ends his report enunciating 16 rules to be approved by

---

[63] Ibid., 35ff.

[64] John Witte, Jr. distinguishes seven principal patterns regarding state and religion: (1) state religions; (2) established churches; (3) state neutrality; (4) state concordats with the Catholic church (there are also a few similar agreements with other religions, as we shall see later); (5) no official religion; (6) separation of church and state; and (7) protection of legally recognized religious groups. John Witte, Jr., "The State of Religious Human Rights in the World: A Comparative Religious and Legal Study," *Preliminary Documents of Religious Human Rights Project* 1 (1993).

the United Nations, followed by Draft Principles on Freedom and Non-Discrimination in the Matter of Religious Rights and Practices.[65]

Many of the Krishnaswami principles have been incorporated in the 1981 Declaration and in the draft convention pending before the United Nations; however, some have not been included in those documents. Beyond any doubt, the Krishnaswami study was an important stage in the United Nations work on religious rights and was the first specific step to correct the neglect of the subject of religion by the international community.

General Anti-Discrimination Instruments

The Declaration and Convention on Racial Discrimination. The racial and religious intolerance that manifested itself at the end of the 1950s, mainly in Europe, were the immediate precedent that induced the United Nations to initiate specific action in those spheres. In a first stage, United Nations organs dealt jointly with the racial and religious issues. Only later, for reasons that will be mentioned, did they decide to take separate steps regarding both major areas of discrimination and prejudice. There is no doubt that it was the so-called "swastika epidemic," mainly expressed in attacks against Jewish institutions and the daubing of swastikas on their buildings, that prompted the preparation of United Nations instruments against racism and religious intolerance. But it was the strong pressure on the part of African and other Third World countries that finally ensured the fast adoption of the instruments on racial discrimination. On the other hand, political motives played a role in the delays and postponement in the adoption of instruments on religious rights.[66]

On 12 December 1960, the General Assembly of the United Nations adopted Resolution 1510 (XV), condemning "all manifestations and practices of racial, religious, and national hatred in the political, economic, social, educational and cultural spheres of the life of society" as violations of the Charter and the Universal Declaration. Similar resolutions were adopted by the Sub-Commission on Prevention of Discrimination and Protection of Minorities in January 1960, the Commission on Human Rights in March 1960, and the Economic and Social Council in July 1961.

---

[65] See above note 6, at 61ff.

[66] For the history of the preparation of the Declaration and Convention on Racial Discrimination and its relevance to the instruments on religious intolerance, see Lerner, *The UN Convention on the Elimination of All Forms of Racial Discrimination*, 1-7.

At the General Assembly, a debate took place on the scope of the steps to be taken. African states favored the preparation of a convention on racial discrimination. Some delegations suggested that only a Declaration be adopted; others advocated an instrument dealing with religious and racial discrimination jointly. Finally, the Third Committee adopted two resolutions, similarly worded, asking for the preparation of separate draft declarations and draft conventions on racial discrimination and religious intolerance. This decision was a compromise prompted by the opposition to a single instrument, mainly on the part of Arab and Communist delegations, in addition to the African insistence in favor of fast legislation concerning racism. (I shall revisit this issue when dealing with the 1981 Declaration.)

The Declaration on the Elimination of All Forms of Racial Discrimination was proclaimed by General Assembly resolution 1904 (XVIII) of 20 November 1963. The Convention was adopted by General Assembly resolution 2106 A (XX) of 21 December 1965, and entered into force on 4 January 1969.[67] It became one of the most widely ratified instruments in the field of human rights.

The Declaration is a relatively short document, and its importance was, of course, superseded by the prompt adoption of the Convention and its universal acceptance. References to religious rights are generally absent from its text, as a consequence of the separation between the two areas. The Preamble, however, reiterates the principles of dignity and equality of all human beings on which the Charter is based; principles which exclude distinctions as to race, sex, language or religion. Article 3 calls for the prevention of discrimination based on race, color, or ethnic origin, especially in some fields, including religion.

The Racial Convention, on the whole, follows the orientation adopted in the Declaration with regard to the religious issue. The Preamble refers to the prohibition of distinctions based on religion. Article 5, on obligations of the states to prohibit racial discrimination and guarantee the right of everyone to equality before the law, notably in the enjoyment of some rights, mentions among them: (d(vii)) the right "to freedom of thought, conscience and religion."

Although not directly related to religious rights protection, the Convention on the Elimination of Racial Discrimination is presently the most important treaty regarding discrimination, in a broad sense, and its provisions are therefore a guide to the rules on discrimination based on other grounds, such as religion. The definition of discrimination in the Convention is useful in the interpretation of what discrimination means

---

[67] For both texts, see *Human Rights*, 61 and 66 respectively.

in general: any distinction, exclusion, restriction, or preference based on race, color, descent, or national or ethnic origin which has the purpose or effect of nullifying or impairing the recognition, enjoyment, or exercise, on an equal footing, of human rights and fundamental freedoms in the political, economic, social, cultural or any other field of public life.

The Convention makes no mention of religion, but the clarification of what discrimination means is, naturally, valid for religious discrimination as well. The provisions of the Convention apply to situations in which ethnicity and religion overlap, as in the case of discrimination against Jews, Arabs, Sikhs, Kurds, Armenians, or other groups where ethnicity and religion cannot be separated. Religion, more than any other factor, was often the principal element in the preservation of the identity, unity, and historical development of ethnic groups, peoples, or nations.

The list of obligations of states regarding measures against discrimination cannot strictly be limited to racial discrimination. The Convention is thus an appropriate guideline for state action also in the fields related to religious prejudice and intolerance. Article 4, on prohibition of racial discrimination, incitement, and hatred—although a controversial provision which gave rise to difficulties during the drafting process—is seen today as expressing the view of the United Nations with regard to the possible clash between rights, emphasizing the need to enact anti-incitement legislation. The Convention goes further than Article 20(2) of the Covenant on Civil and Political Rights, on advocacy of national, racial, or religious hatred. Article 4 of the Convention takes an unequivocal view in the sense that freedom of speech and of association cannot prevail over the right to be free from discrimination and incitement to discrimination or intolerance.[68]

Implementation of the Racial Convention. The Convention on Racial Discrimination is today also the most important instrument for the protection of groups at the international level and, as such, it is highly relevant to the rights of religious communities. It has also exercised considerable influence on domestic legislation. Its organ of implementation, the Committee on the Elimination of Racial Discrimination (CERD), has played a significant role in ensuring the protection of minorities and has adopted a broad approach in interpreting the concept of racial discrimination. The Convention, however, has not been too successful in opening the door for individual petitions or complaints, or for groups seeking remedies against discrimination.[69]

---

[68] See above notes 33 and 34.

[69] See Natan Lerner, "Individual Petitions Under the International Convention on the Elimination of all Forms of Racial Discrimination," in Irwin Cotler and F. Pearl Eliadis, eds., *International Human Rights Law* (Montreal, 1992), 435-455.

As of 20 August 1993, 137 states had ratified the Convention; only 18 states have accepted the optional article on individual complaints. Implementation of the Convention is therefore based on the reporting system. Individual state reports have been thoroughly examined by the members of the CERD, who frequently asked for clarification concerning the application of the Convention. In many cases, the reports and requests for clarification dealt with religious issues. Just to mention some recent examples: In 1993, members of the CERD discussing the conflict in Sudan, expressed concern about the way in which "religious questions sometimes overlapped with ethnic questions." During the same session, the Holy See pointed out the "religious dimension" of many conflicts. The United Kingdom reported on recommendations of the Commission on Racial Equality with a view to incriminating incitement to religious hatred and prohibiting any discrimination based on religion.[70] Issues discussed in former sessions included government policy to induce conversion into the Islamic faith in Bangladesh; anti-Semitic activities in Austria; the situation of the Muslim minority in Greece and similar issues. A Cuban report in 1991 pointed out that religious discrimination had existed in that country, but the possibility was being considered that "one day, persons professing a religion might be admitted as members of the Cuban Communist Party."[71] During many years before the dramatic changes in the Soviet Union and Eastern Europe, the position of the different churches under the Communist regime came under repeated scrutiny by the CERD.

Other Anti-Discrimination Instruments. Human rights are indivisible. Human rights related to religion, and intolerance and discrimination in the field of religion, cannot be dissociated from the need to observe the general principle of equality. Therefore, when dealing with religious human rights as a special category, anti-discriminatory measures adopted in other specific areas cannot be ignored, and coordination is necessary. The impact of the instruments on racial discrimination has already been examined. Discrimination on the ground of gender and in the spheres of education and employment will now be dealt with. Special cases, as those of indigenous populations and migrant workers, will also be succinctly referred to. This chapter will close with a review of the provisions on religion in regional treaties.

Gender and Religion. Equality of women in today's society is affected by the fact that some religions, including the major ones, do not respect, even today, the principle of full equality among men and women.

---

[70] See, A/48/18 (1994), 32, 58, 78, respectively.

[71] See, A/47/18 (1993), at 43, 48-51; A/47/18 (1992), at 35; A/46/18 (1991), at 39-42.

The 1979 Convention on the Elimination of All Forms of Discrimination Against Women[72] had to take notice of the fact that "the most comprehensive challenges mounted by states to the international norms guaranteeing women's rights, and their application, have been couched as defenses of religious liberty."[73] Therefore, conflicts between women's rights and freedom of religion may frequently occur, in particular at a time when the principle of equality on the ground of gender is being advanced more than ever before. The issue is especially complicated in those states which adopt religious law for the governance of family relations and personal status.

The prohibition of discrimination on grounds of sex or gender has been incorporated in all global and regional human rights instruments and is seen today as "a strong candidate for inclusion among the norms of customary international law."[74] It is not only limited to governmental acts but also reaches private behavior. The principle of non-discrimination on grounds of sex may clash with religious rules and practices difficult to uproot in some traditions and sometimes incorporated, through the application of personal status law, into the general state law. Human rights in the field of religion extend their protection to such an incorporation and to individual and group practices based on religious traditions, except when the international minimum standard is affected.

There has been a movement towards adjustment of religious laws to the needs of modern society and, consequently, the principle of equality among the sexes has made progress. This was not the case in some parts of the world, and a regressive trend can even be noted in some countries.[75] The provision in Article 23 of the Women's Convention, on the possibility of conflict with other instruments more conducive to the achievement of equality between men and women, is not likely to prevail over such practices.

Conflict may arise in instances involving more that one protected right. Such may be the clash between parental rights to prefer some sort of religious education that can cause gender distinctions, and the general rules prevailing presently. A hierarchy of human rights does not exist,

---

[72] For the text of the Declaration and Convention on the Elimination of Discrimination against Women, see *Human Rights*, 145 and 150 respectively. On the Convention generally, see Theodor Meron, *Human Rights Law-Making in the United Nations* (Oxford, 1986), 53-82.

[73] Sullivan, "Gender Equality and Religious Freedom," 795. This article contains an extense bibliography on women's rights. On the subject, see also several articles in K.E. and Paul Mahoney, eds., *Human Rights in the Twenty-First Century* (Dordrecht/Boston/London, 1993), 71-117.

[74] Sullivan, "Gender Equality and Religious Freedom," 798.

[75] Ibid., 810ff. and Meron, *Human Rights Law-Making in the United Nations*, 77-79.

except with regard to rights considered *jus cogens* and non-derogable, and certain conflicts between different human rights may be difficult to settle. Sullivan mentions the example of sati, the practice of burning a Hindu widow on her husband's funeral pyre: freedom of religion may be affected by the prohibition of such a practice, but the fundamental right must prevail. International law requires states to prohibit such practices despite their religious inspiration.[76] The social context, the centrality of the conflicting rules in the respective protective systems, the need to ensure a wider measure of freedom for society—all these are considerations to be kept in mind when dealing with such rights conflicts. The most difficult cases may be those of states which have adopted religious law as state law and reject the principle of subordination of domestic law to binding norms of international law. General rules on the incorporation of international law, customary or conventional, are pertinent in this respect.

Frequently, conflicts develop between women's rights and family law based on religious traditions, notably in Muslim countries or countries that have been under Muslim domination or influence. Such conflicts may occur in a wide area of rights, and several state parties to the Convention on Women or to the Covenants have entered reservations in this respect, in some cases objected to by other states. Also in countries with a Catholic tradition, or in the State of Israel, religious rules regarding family law clash with the Convention. Both the Human Rights Committee under the Covenant and the Committee on the Elimination of Discrimination Against Women (CEDAW) have had to deal in several cases with alleged violations of the principle of equality for women in issues concerning family law, patrimonial consequences of that law, and procedural rules.[77] Judicial or quasi-judicial intervention has taken place. For example, in 1984 the European Commission on Human Rights rejected the argument that sanctions against a husband who refuses to grant a divorce should be seen as a violation of religious liberties.[78]

The clash between centuries-old religious traditions and modern international human rights law goes beyond the strict field of gender equality and will be discussed again below. But the growing pressure to ensure equal rights for women attaches special weight to this issue.

Education and Religion: The UNESCO Convention. Religious rights and education are two interrelated areas. The freedom to teach one's religion, to ensure that parents' wishes with regard to religious education

---

[76] Sullivan, "Gender Equality and Religious Freedom," 820.

[77] Ibid, 834. Sullivan deals extensively with clashes between women rights and personal status laws.

[78] *D. v. France*, App. No. 10180/82, 35 E.C.H.R. 199, 202 (1984).

of their children will be respected, the degree of state support—if at all—to schools where religious instruction is imparted, are only some of many complicated problems to be solved in the search of a balance between different human rights. All the instruments on religious human rights contain provisions in this regard. So do the specific treaties regarding education, prominent among them the UNESCO Convention Against Discrimination in Education, adopted on 14 December 1960 and in force since 22 May 1962.[79]

The Convention defines "discrimination" to include distinctions, exclusions, limitations, or preferences based, among other things, on religion, and having the purpose or effect of nullifying or impairing equality of treatment in education (Article 1(1)). Either purpose or effect is enough. Article 2 permits the establishment or maintenance, for religious reasons, of separate educational systems, in keeping with the wishes of the pupils' parents or legal guardians, provided that "participation in such systems or attendance at such institutions is optional" and conforms to "standards laid down or approved by the competent authorities." States should not allow, in any form of assistance granted by the public authorities to educational institutions, "any restrictions or preferences based solely on the ground that pupils belong to a particular group" (Article 3(d)). Education shall promote "understanding, tolerance and friendship among all . . . religious groups" (Article 5.1.(a)). It is essential "to ensure . . . the religious and moral education of the children in conformity with their own convictions"; "no person or group of persons should be compelled to receive religious instruction inconsistent with his or their own conviction" (Article 5.1(b)).

The Convention reflects principles generally accepted by international law. The right to education belongs to the sphere of cultural rights, one of the five categories protected by the 1966 Covenants. The system followed by the Convention concerning religion and education conforms to the norm included in Article 26 of the Universal Declaration and more specifically in Article 13 of the Covenant on Economic, Social and Cultural Rights, which imposes upon state parties the duty to have respect for the liberty of parents or legal guardians "to choose for their children schools, other than those established by the public authorities" and "to ensure the religious and moral education of their children in conformity with their own convictions."

The relationship between educational and religious rights has been the subject of adjudication by municipal courts in numerous cases.[80] At

[79] For its text, see *Human Rights*, 101.

[80] U.S. courts, for instance, have dealt on numerous occasions with the mentioned relationship. For recent summaries of important U.S.decisions concerning religious freedom and

the international level, the European Court of Human Rights reaffirmed, in the *Kjeldsen et al.* case, that parents are primarily responsible for their children's education and that states have "to respect parents' convictions, be they religious or philosophical, throughout the entire education program." In *Angelini v. Sweden*, the European Commission on Human Rights rejected the claim that the Swedish policy of providing all children in public schools with some religious education violates the European Convention.[81]

Mention should also be made here of the provisions of the Declaration and the Convention of the Rights of the Child.[82] These instruments follow, with regard to the relationship between education and religion, the pattern that has been already explained, with emphasis on the need to give primary consideration to the best interest of the child. (I shall return to this subject when dealing with the 1981 Declaration.)

Employment and Religion. The principles of equality and non-discrimination may be violated on grounds of religion in the area of employment and labor. Religious persons may also be prevented from performing freely their religious duties as a consequence of conditions of work. Sometimes, religious convictions may be a reason for non-eligibility for a job; on other occasions, membership in a church or religious congregation may create privileges in the access to employment, a situation that may or not be considered illegal, according to circumstances. There are, in this respect, gray areas. A religious congregation that wishes to hire an educational officer or teacher for one of its schools may obviously limit its search to members of that congregation or persons identified with its creed. But how far does this rule go? Is it applicable to a gardener, or to a doorman? There may be different answers to such and similar questions, in accordance with the place of religion in a particular society. On these questions, international law plays only a limited role by adopting the rule of non-discrimination.

This was the approach of the International Labor Organization, which prepared many treaties in the area of occupation and labor rela-

---

equality and discrimination in education, M. Glenn Albernathy, *Civil Liberties under the Constitution*, 6th ed. (Columbia SC, 1993), 172-220, 345-376; Terry Eastland, ed., *Religious Liberty in the Supreme Court: The Cases that Define the Debate over Church and State* (Washington, 1993).

81 For the European cases, *Kjeldsen, Busk Madsen and Pedersen* (1976), see 23 Judgments and Decisions of the European Court on Human Rights, 25; *Angelini v. Sweden*, European Commission on Human Rights, App. No. 1049/83, 10 E.H.R.R. (1988), 123. See also *Hartikainen et al. v. Finland* (R.9/40) HRC 36, 147. This case was also considered by the Human Rights Committee, above note 30.

82 For the Declaration and the Convention, see *Human Rights*, 171 and 174 respectively. See generally Geraldine van Bueren, *International Law and the Rights of the Child* (Dordrecht/Boston/London, 1993).

tions, widely ratified. The 1944 Declaration Concerning the Aims and Purposes of the ILO, adopted by the International Labor Conference in Philadelphia, proclaimed the principle of equality of all human beings, irrespective of race, creed, or sex. The 1958 Convention (No. 111) Concerning Discrimination in Respect of Employment and Occupation, in force since 1960,[83] prohibits any distinction, exclusion or preference made on the basis of, amongst other things, religion, if it has the effect of nullifying or impairing equality of opportunity or treatment in employment or occupation. The ILO has established quasi-judicial bodies to supervise the implementation of the labor treaties, and such bodies have developed a body of case law, based on the examination of reports submitted and proceedings related to complaints. Among such complaints there are many based on denial of equality because of religion, or on difficulties found by employees in the observance of their religious duties resulting from working conditions, particularly in relation to days of rest and holidays. Judicial intervention has been frequent.[84]

Indigenous Populations. Another ILO treaty that deserves to be mentioned in this context is the 1989 Convention No. 169 concerning Indigenous and Tribal Populations or Peoples, a partial revision of the 1957 Convention on the same subject. The new Convention, obviously group-oriented, recognizes in its Preamble the aspirations of indigenous peoples to maintain and develop their identities and religions. Article 5 aims at ensuring protection of the "religious and spiritual values and practices" of the interested populations, both as individuals and groups.

The United Nations, by General Assembly Resolution 45/164 (1990), proclaimed 1993 as the International Year for the World's Indigenous Peoples, and on that occasion the major problems facing the estimated 300 million indigenous people living in many countries have been highlighted. Those problems include forced assimilation, loss of cultural identity, and restrictions on religious customs considered incompatible with the general legal system. The aspirations of the indigenous populations found some expression in the ILO and UN documents, but certainly

---

[83] For its text, see *Human Rights*, 96.

[84] For the work of the ILO and its struggle against discrimination, see N. Valticos, "The International Labor Organization", in Karl Vasak, ed., *The International Dimensions of Human Rights* (Paris, 1979), 405. As to jurisprudence, see, e.g., the decision of the Court of Justice of the European Communities in *Preis v. Council of the European Communities* (Case 130/75), Common Market Law Reports 2 (1976): 708. The Court stated that if a candidate for a job or a religious organization informs the Community in due time that religious reasons make certain dates impossible for potential employees to undergo an examination "that should be taken into account, if possible." A similar case was decided by the European Commission, in *M. v. Austria* (1993), CD 25, rejecting a complaint against the denegation of an adjournment of a hearing for religious considerations. The Committee took into account the complexity of the case.

not to the entire satisfaction of their spokespersons. A Draft Declaration on Discrimination Against Indigenous Peoples prepared by a working group established by the Sub-Commission on Prevention of Discrimination and Protection for Minorities includes several references to religious rights, or derived from cultural and spiritual traditions. Article 12 refers to religious property; Article 13 to access to religious sites and to the respect and protection of sacred places, including burial sites; Article 31 deals with the right to autonomy in matters of religion. This Draft Declaration is likely to cause controversy.[85]

Migrant Workers. The ILO and the UN also dealt with the problems of migrant workers. The great number of such persons, in Europe and other parts of the world, and their cultural and religious needs required special consideration. The 1990 UN Convention on the Protection of the Rights of Migrant Workers and their Families carries provisions to ensure the religious rights of that particular category of migrants. Article 12 is obviously inspired by Article 18 of the Covenant on Civil and Political Rights.[86]

Regional Protection of Religious Human Rights. Religious human rights are protected by the main regional instruments on human rights in general. Such protection is contained in the 1950 European Convention for the Protection of Human Rights and Fundamental Freedoms (Article 9);[87] the 1969 American Convention on Human Rights (Article 12);[88] the 1975 Final Act of the Helsinki Conference on Security and Co-Operation in Europe (Principle VII), the Concluding Document of the Vienna Meeting, 1989, particularly Principles 16 and 17, the 1990 Document of

---

[85] For the text of the 1989 Convention, see *Human Rights,* 471. For its analysis, see Lerner, *Group Rights and Discrimination in International Law,* 99-114. For the UN draft declarlation, see UN Doc E/CN.4/Sub.2/1994/2 Add.1 and E/CN.4/Sub.2/1994/30 and Corr.1.

[86] For the text of the Convention, see *Human Rights,* 550. For a critical analysis, see Ved. P. Nanda, "The Protection of the Rights of Migrant Workers," *Asian and Pacific Migration Journal* 2 (1993): 161-177.

[87] 213 UNTS, 211. Within the vast literature on the protection of human rights in Europe, see J.E.S. Fawcett, *The Application of the European Convention on Human Rights* (Oxford, 1987); Vincent Berger, *Case Law of the European Court of Human Rights* (Sarasota, 1989); Francis G. Jacobs, *The European Convention on Human Rights* (Oxford, 1975); A.H. Robertson, *Human Rights in Europe* (Manchester, 1977). In a recent collective study, R. St. J. Macdonald, F. Matscher and H. Petzold, eds., *The European System for the Protection of Human Rights* (Dordrecht/Boston/London, 1993), Malcolm M. Shaw deals with "Freedom of Thought, Conscience and Religion," with an updated summary of decisions on religious rights adopted by the European bodies. Ibid., 445-463. A protocol to the European Convention, on the rights of national minorities, including religious rights, is presently under consideration.

[88] For its text, see 9 ILM 1970. On the American system generally, see Thomas Buergenthal, "The Inter-American System for the Protection of Human Rights", in Meron, ed., *Human Rights in International Law,* 439-493; Scott Davidson, *Human Rights* (Buckingham, 1993), 126-151.

the Copenhagen Meeting of the CSCE Conference on the Human Dimension, and the 1990 Paris Charter for a New Europe;[89] and the 1981 African Charter on Human and Peoples Rights (Article 8).[90] In addition to the specific articles dealing with religious rights, other articles prohibiting religious discrimination are equally relevant.

In general, regional instruments follow the norms contained in the Universal Declaration and the Covenants. At the European level in particular, the Human Rights Court and Committee had opportunities to deal with religious rights, in connection with articles 9, 14 and others of the Convention. The European bodies considered issues such as the obligation to use crash-helmets, compulsory membership in a health service, compulsory insurance, religious requirements of prisoners, the status of religious congregations and of a state church, rights of clergy, parental rights, conscientious objection, taxation for religious purposes, the classification of minor religious groups, fundamentalism, and blasphemy, amongst others.

Principles 16 and 17 of the 1989 Vienna Meeting of the Helsinki Process deserve special mention and should be compared with the detailed catalogue of rights listed in the 1981 Declaration. These two principles call for measures to prevent and eliminate discrimination against individuals and communities on grounds of religion or belief and ensure equality between believers and non-believers. They recognize the rights of religious communities to establish places of worship and organize themselves, to appoint personnel, to receive financial contributions, to engage in consultations with other faiths and institutions, and to produce, import, and disseminate religious publications and materials. Everyone is entitled to give and receive religious education in the language of his choice, and the liberty of parents to ensure the religious and moral education of their children in conformity with their own convictions is to be respected. Individuals and communities have the right to acquire and use sacred books and religious publications in the language of their choice and other articles and materials related to the practice of religion of belief. Permitted limitations are only those generally recognized in international law. The 1990 Copenhagen Document and the 1990 Charter of Paris for a New Europe reiterate the right to freedom of thought, conscience, and religion, including the freedom to change one's religion. They also refer to the protection of the religious identity of minorities and condemn persecution on religious grounds.

---

[89] For the CSCE documents, see Council of Europe, *Human Rights in International Law: Basic Texts* (Strasbourg, 1991). For the CSCE work in general, see Arie Bloed, ed., *The Conference on Security and Co-Operation in Europe: Analysis and Basic Documents* (Dordrecht, 1993).

[90] For its text, see 21 ILM 1982, 58. See generally, Davidson, *Human Rights*, 152-162.

Although they are not mandatory treaties, these instruments of the CSCE carry great moral and political weight and a clear expectation of observance, given the composition of the group of states represented and the nature of the process that led to their unanimous adoption. Indeed, the CSCE "has adopted some of the most advanced religious liberty norms that have yet emerged at the international level," embodied in Principles 16 and 17.[91] Special mention should be made of the broad approach to the rights of religious communities, expressed in Article 16(d).

The United Nations Declaration on Intolerance and Discrimination Based on Religion or Belief

The Declaration on the Elimination of All Forms of Intolerance and Discrimination Based on Religion or Belief was proclaimed by the General Assembly of the United Nations by resolution 36/55 of 25 November 1981. It is presently the most important international instrument regarding religious rights and prohibition of intolerance or discrimination based on religion or belief.[92] I have already pointed out that the Declaration, as well as the draft convention still pending before the United Nations, have their origin in the outburst of anti-Semitic incidents that occurred in several places in 1959 and 1960—the so-called "swastika epidemics," in which many saw the danger of a revival of nazism.

I have also described the United Nations activity that followed those attacks and the resolutions adopted by the different UN organs, culminating in the General Assembly resolutions 1780 and 1781 (XVII) of 8 December 1962, asking for the preparation of "twin" but separate declarations and conventions on racial and religious manifestations of discrimination and intolerance. The separation between the two subjects was the result of the strong interest of Third World countries in the adoption of a document on racism and their relative indifference to the religious subject, as well as of the influence of international politics, the Cold War, the Arab-Israeli conflict, and the issue of anti-Semitism in the Soviet Union.[93] Theoretical considerations were also invoked, and some

---

[91] See W. Cole Durham, Jr., Pieter van Dijk, Lauren B. Homer, and John Witte, Jr., "The Future of Religious Liberty in Russia: Report of the De Burght Conference on Pending Russian Legislation Restricting Religious Liberty," *Emory International Law Review 8* (1994): 1, 20-25.

[92] For the text, see *Human Rights*, 122. For an analysis of the Declaration, see Lerner, *Group Rights and Discrimination in International Law*, 75-96; Donna J. Sullivan, "Advancing the Freedom of Religion or Belief Through the UN Declaration on the Elimination of Religious Intolerance and Discrimination," *American Journal of International Law* 82 (1988): 487-520.

[93] Lerner, *Group Rights and Discrimination in International Law*, 46. For the reasons of the difference of treatment by the UN of the religious issue as compared to other human rights,

delegates took the view that there was a difference between religious sentiments, even when they meant hostility towards others, on the one hand, and prejudice, hatred, or discrimination against people of a different race or color, on the other hand. In any case, the result was a speedy preparation of the instruments on race, and a very slow process regarding religious discrimination and intolerance.

In 1965, the General Assembly requested the relevant UN bodies to complete the preparation of a declaration and a convention on the subject. Some work was done, but in 1972 the General Assembly decided to accord priority to the draft declaration. This meant in practice postponing indefinitely the adoption of a mandatory treaty, despite the fact that a draft, which will be summarized below, had already been elaborated.

Further work was very slow and consisted mainly in the activities of a working-group appointed by the Commission on Human Rights. In was only in March 1981, after tenacious efforts, that the Commission on Human Rights completed a draft, adopted by a vote of 33 to 0, with 5 abstentions. At the Third Committee of the General Assembly, the vote in favor was 45 to 0, again with 5 abstentions, in both cases of the representatives of the then Communist members of those bodies. Finally, the General Assembly adopted the draft, without a vote, after two decades of procrastination. The decision was preceded by intensive lobbying and pressure on the part of non-governmental organizations interested in religious human rights, supported by several governments. Until the very last moment, amendments were submitted, and complicated consultations and negotiations took place, showing the complexity and sensitivity of the issue.

One of the major problems surrounding the drafting of the Declaration was the meaning of the term "religion." Communist spokespersons argued that the use of the word "religion" did not explicitly extend the principle of tolerance to "atheistic beliefs." They claimed that it was necessary to ensure full equality of treatment between believers and non-believers and that the proposed text was one-sided. On the other hand, Western delegates, in particular the United States representative, took the view that the Declaration was intended to protect religious human rights, while the rights of persons without a religion, such as "materialists, atheists or agnostics," could find adequate protection in the text. The face-saving solution, rather simplistic, was to insert in the Preamble and in Article 1(1) the word "whatever" before the word "belief."

Another difficult issue was the matter of change of religion or conversion. This issue, as pointed out earlier, already created difficulties

---

see also Antonio Cassese, "The General Assembly: Historical Perspective 1945-1989," in Alston, ed., *The United Nations and Human Rights*, 37.

during the preparation of the Universal Declaration and the Covenants. In this regard, the main opposition came from the Muslim delegations. The Iranian spokesperson rejected the provision contained in this respect in Article 18(2) of the Covenant on Civil and Political Rights. Indonesia limited its demands to establish a clear distinction between conversion resulting from persuasion and that which was the consequence of coercion. The matter was settled by way of a double compromise. Explicit references to the right to change one's religion were deleted from the text, both in the Preamble and in Article 1, so departing from the wording used in the Universal Declaration and in the Covenant. The result was a weakened text but, in order to make the change acceptable to the West and to avoid jeopardizing the progress achieved in two decades of protracted and difficult negotiations, a new Article 8 was added. It states that nothing in the Declaration "shall be construed as restricting or derogating from any right defined in the Universal Declaration of Human Rights and the International Covenants on Human Rights." States that did not ratify the Covenants may, after this compromise, claim that the right to change one's religion, although included among the clauses of the Universal Declaration, cannot be afforded the status of customary international law. On the other hand, there was a great desire to see the draft adopted, and, therefore, there was readiness to look for a compromise on this matter, provided it was clear that the right to conversion, although not mentioned explicitly, was not derogated or restricted in the new declaration.

Provisions of the Declaration. The difficulties in the drafting of the Declaration could already be seen in the discussion on its title. Originally, it was intended to be a "Declaration on the Elimination of All Forms of Religious Intolerance," but in 1973 a change was made, following an amendment proposed by Morocco in the Third Committee, in order to adjust the title of the draft declaration to that of the draft convention and to the wording of the Universal Declaration. The two added words "discrimination" and "belief" are meaningful.

"Discrimination," the term used in all the anti-discrimination treaties and declarations, has a clear legal meaning. This is not the case with the word "intolerance," which is rather vague and lacks exact legal meaning. It has been used to describe emotional, psychological, philosophical, and religious attitudes that may prompt acts of discrimination or other violations of religious freedoms, as well as manifestations of hate and persecutions against persons or groups of a different religion or belief.[94]

---

[94] *Webster's New International Dictionary of the English Language*, 2d ed. (New York, 1952) defines "intolerance" as the refusal to allow others the enjoyment of their opinion, chosen modes of worship and the like, and as equivalent to illiberality and bigotry. Elizabeth Odio

However, the wording of definitional article 2(2) of the Declaration indicates that the terms "discrimination" and "intolerance" are actually employed as equivalents. This is not the only case of inadequate drafting in the Declaration. The long preparation process, the many amendments, and the search for compromises may explain such shortcomings.

The addition of the word "belief" was intended to meet the objections of those who wanted to protect the rights of non-believers, such as rationalists, free-thinkers, atheists, agnostics, and supporters of other philosophical attitudes that exclude faith in the traditional sense of this term. There were also proposals to include explicit references to the right to conduct anti-religious propaganda, but the issue was not pressed.

In addition to the change of title, many modifications were also introduced in the drafts of the Preamble, not only of a semantic nature but frequently implying matters of principle and substance that caused much controversy. In these discussions again, the use of the terms "religion" and "belief" occupied a central place. In reply to the demands of those who tried to protect non-believers, it was maintained that the original purpose of the document was to ensure equality among the different religions and protect religious rights. The philosophical substance of religion was completely different from convictions of persons who do not adhere to any transcendental and normative religion, it was argued. Such persons, in addition, are protected by the general freedoms prevailing in a democratic society, while religious persons may require special protection for their worship activities. There was general agreement that coercion against non-believers must always be prohibited.

The question of conversion was frequently raised in this context and related to missionary activities. A clash of rights is possible between the right to teach and propagate a religion and the dangers of coercion and enticement. The right to leave a religious community, doubtful under some legal systems, is involved as well. Political matters were also introduced in the debates on the text.

The final text did not include provisions on incitement. Such provisions did exist in the preliminary drafts prepared by the Sub-Commission and the Commission on Human Rights. The pending draft convention contains a clause to that effect.

The Protected Rights. Articles 1 and 6 of the Declaration contain a catalog of rights that seem to be the universally agreed minimum stan-

---

Benito, *Study of the Current Dimensions of the Problems of Intolerance and Discrimination Based on Religion or Belief* (UN Doc. E/CN.4/Sub.2/1987/26,3) states that manifestations of intolerance go in many cases much further than discrimination "and involve the stirring up of hatred against, or even the persecution of, individuals or groups of a different religion or belief." It is beyond the scope of this article to deal with the philosophical and general juridical meaning of the notions of "tolerance" and "intolerance." See sources cited above in note 4.

dard in the area of religious human rights. Article 1 follows the model of Articles 18 of the Universal Declaration and of the Covenant on Civil and Political Rights, except for the clause on change of religion as amended in the Third Committee, and with the saving provision included in Article 8 of the Declaration. Consequently, authoritative interpretations of the Covenant are applicable to the Declaration.[95]

The Declaration uses in Article 1 the term "everyone" and therefore it should be seen as protecting nationals and aliens, permanent and non-permanent residents.[96] Paragraph 1 proclaims three fundamental freedoms: of thought, conscience, and religion, including "whatever belief" of one's choice. The external manifestations of religion—worship, observance, practice, and teaching—are guaranteed in terms identical to those of the Covenant and should be interpreted in conjunction with the rights listed in Article 6 of the Declaration.

Coercion "which would impair" freedom of religion is prohibited in Article 1(2). But freedom to "manifest" one's religion or belief may, in some cases listed in Article 1(3), be limited, if prescribed by law and necessary to protect public safety, order, health or morals, or the fundamental rights of others, as understood in free societies. Serious difficulties may develop when religious rights clash with the notion of "morals" as interpreted in some countries. General principles incorporated into human rights law with regard to limitations are thus applicable with regard to the Declaration.[97] It should be kept in mind that Article 18 of the ICCPR, according to Article 4 of the Covenant, proclaims one of the rights from which no derogation in time of public emergency is permitted.

The concrete list of freedoms included in the recognition of the rights to freedom of thought, religion, or belief is contained in Article 6. This is a detailed enunciation of rights belonging to the accepted minimum standard. Some rights are missing, but on the whole the list is comprehensive though not exhaustive. It contains the following freedoms: (a) to worship or assemble in connection with a religion or belief, and to establish and maintain places for these purposes; (b) to establish and maintain

---

[95] See, among others, Partsch, "Freedom of Conscience and Expression, and Political Freedoms," 209; Reports of the Human Rights Committee and its authoritative General Comment on Article 18 of the Covenant, summarized above in note 40 and accompanying text.

[96] See Odio Benito, *Study of the Current Dimensions of the Problems of Intolerance and Discrimination Based on Religion or Belief*, 37.

[97] On several occasions, the Human Rights Committee and the European Court on Human Rights dealt with the scope of permissible limitations. The European Court clarified the notion of "morals" in *Handyside v. UK*, 24 European Court of Human Rights (Ser. A) (1976).

appropriate charitable or humanitarian institutions; (c) to make, acquire, and use to an adequate extent the necessary articles and materials related to the rites or customs of a religion or belief; (d) to write, publish, and disseminate relevant publications in these areas; (e) to teach a religion or belief in places suitable for these purposes; (f) to solicit and receive voluntary financial and other contributions from individuals and institutions; (g) to train, appoint, elect or designate by succession appropriate leaders called for by the requirements and standards of any religion or belief; (h) to observe days of rest and to celebrate holy days and ceremonies in accordance with the precepts of one's religion or belief; (i) to establish and maintain communications with individuals and communities in matters of religion and belief at the national and international levels. All these rights are, of course, subject to the limitations, mentioned in Article 1(3). Some of them are closely connected with the constitutional system of the country and the nature of the church-state relationship.

The list of Article 6 left out some rights that the Sub-Commission on the Prevention of Discrimination and Protection of Minorities included in its early drafts. Those include the right to establish federations, completing the right mentioned in Article 6(b); to teach and to learn the sacred language of each religion, not automatically included in Article 6(e), and to bring teachers from abroad; to receive state aid when the state controls the means of production and distribution, a right of importance for religions involving dietary prescriptions; to obtain religious materials and objects; to make pilgrimages to religious sites, inside the country or abroad; the right not to undergo a religious marriage ceremony which is not in conformity with one's convictions, and the right to a burial ceremony in accordance with the religion of the deceased person. The Sub-Commission's draft also included provisions on the legal status of cemeteries, the issue of religious oaths, and discrimination by the state when granting subsidies or in taxation. Some of the missing rights are listed in the pending draft convention. Article 6 should be compared with the already mentioned Articles 16 and 17 of the Concluding Document of the 1989 Vienna meeting of the Conference on Security and Co-Operation in Europe, which includes a few of the omitted provisions.[98]

The original text prepared by the Sub-Commission was strongly indebted to the Krishnaswami principles. The final text was the result of amendments, compromises, and concessions incorporated in the long drafting process. Political considerations played a role. Non-governmental organizations conducted intensive lobbying. Among the most complicated issues, religious education and the preservation of

---

[98] See above note 88.

some rites and customs—the issue of blood transfusions, opposed by some religions, for example—engendered lengthy discussions.

It is important to stress that Article 6 of the Declaration deals with individual rights, collective rights of the persons, and rights that can only be exercised by the group as such. In this regard, it involves progress as compared to previous instruments. Only groups can establish and maintain places of worship and institutions, or appoint religious leaders, or establish federations. The Declaration thus contemplates the needs of religious communities or congregations—needs that are not satisfied by the instruments that follow the orientation of the early years of the UN, based exclusively on individual rights.

Prohibition of Discrimination and Intolerance. Articles 2 and 3 of the Declaration deal with intolerance and discrimination on grounds of religion or belief. They show the influence of the Declaration and Convention on Racial Discrimination and involve difficulties, particularly in relation to the way in which the terms "discrimination" and "intolerance" are employed. It has already been pointed out that, while "discrimination" has a precise meaning in international and human rights law, this in not the case with "intolerance." Article 2(1) refers to "discrimination" only; Article 2(2) mentions "intolerance and discrimination." The term "intolerance" is not used at all in Article 3 or in Article 4(1), dealing with measures to be taken by states. Article 4(2) distinguishes between the need to prohibit discrimination and to combat intolerance, a distinction that may be the result of the differentiation between both forms of behavior. As to the meaning of both words in the Declaration, again the Racial Convention served as the model for the definition in Article 2(2): Intolerance and discrimination based on religion or belief "means any distinction, exclusion, restriction or preference based on religion or belief and having as its purpose or as its effect nullification or impairment of the recognition, enjoyment or exercise of human rights and fundamental freedoms on an equal basis." Religious discrimination and intolerance are not limited to "public life," as in the case of the Convention on Racial Discrimination.

The text is deficient, particularly since Article 2(1) prohibits discrimination not only by the state but also by institutions, groups of persons, or persons. As Krishnaswami reminds us, however, not every preference based on religion or belief can be considered discriminatory, and thus prohibited. An example may be a concordat between a state with a predominantly Catholic population and the Holy See, according to which some preferences are granted to the Vatican as compared to other religious institutions. Many states declare as public holidays the days sacred to the majority of the population, and this would not be discrimination if observance of the minorities' holy days is duly protected, as far as possible.[99] More difficult is the case of states that permit only members of a given religion to accede to some public positions or dignities, for instance to become the president of the state. Some states have an established church or even a state religion. When do such situations become discriminatory?[100] What is important is that no impairment should attach to any person or group in the enjoyment of fundamental freedoms. Otherwise, preferences may in some cases constitute discrimination, and in others not. Social facts and realities, and above all common sense, play a role in this respect.

The prohibition of discrimination by institutions or persons also creates problems. Matters such as the hiring of personnel by religious institutions, dressing habits or observance of some particular customs by persons of one specific religion, may require interpretation. The granting of privileges to members of one religion in given circumstances does not necessarily curtail the basic human rights of others and would therefore not contradict the Declaration.

Another issue concerns the many possibilities of clashes between the recognition of religious rights and norms in other fields. A common example is the need for coordination between religious rights and the prohibition of discrimination based on gender—an issue which has demanded frequent adjudication and to which reference was already made.[101]

In order to guarantee the observance of the rights proclaimed in the Declaration, state action is necessary. According to Article 4 of the Declaration, all states shall take effective measures to prevent and eliminate discrimination on grounds of religion or belief in all fields of civil, economic, political, social, and cultural life, enacting or rescinding where necessary legislation to that effect (para. 1). States should also take all appropriate steps to combat intolerance on the grounds of religion or belief.

The problems involved in the imprecise use of the terms "discrimination" and "intolerance" have already been mentioned. Al-

---

[99] Difficulties arose in the case of elections taking place on days which are holy for some religious minorities in the country, that prohibit work and traveling on such days. Flexibility and good will are necessary in such situations, which may be difficult to foresee.

[100] Krishnaswami points out that an identical formal relationship between the state and religion may result in discrimination in some cases, but not in others. See Krishnaswami, *Study of Discrimination*, 46. Odio Benito, on the other hand, maintains that the establishment of a religion or belief by the State amounts to preferences and privileges that may be discriminatory. *Study of the Current Dimensions of the Problems of Intolerance and Discrimination Based on Religion or Belief*, 21.

[101] Courts of several countries had to decide cases of restrictions in employment for males or females, for religious reasons.

though the meaning of the verb "to combat" is not explained, this may involve an obligation to adopt measures in the area of criminal law against organizations preaching, or inciting others to practice, religious intolerance. Special Rapporteur Elizabeth Odio Benito recommended the adoption of penal laws to that effect by states that have not already done so.[102] This may be contrary to the policies of some countries, strongly reluctant to penalize incitement to racial or religious hatred and thereby limiting freedoms of speech and association.

Article 7 refers to national legislation that should allow everyone to avail himself or herself of the enunciated rights and freedoms in practice. This article was criticized for its poor wording and loose character.

One of the most controversial provisions was the one contained in Article 5, on the rights of the child. It has been frequently mentioned that there is a close relationship between religion and education, and the role of parents and the aspirations of all religions and ideologies to influence the mind of the child at all stages of the formative process may cause serious problems. Article 5 is a long article. It does not clarify who would qualify as a child. It recognizes the rights of parents or legal guardians to organize life within the family in accordance with their religion or belief, and every child should have access to education in matters of religion or belief in accordance with the wishes of his or her parents or legal guardians. The best interest of the child—a requirement that appears in the Declaration and Convention on the Rights of the Child[103] but is not mentioned in the Covenant—should be the guiding principle.

The proviso of the "best interest of the child" is intended to limit the freedom of action of parents or legal guardians. The Declaration does not deal with the many questions likely to be raised in case of clashes between the wishes of the parents (or between both of them) and the best interest of the child. Moreover, in totalitarian or ideological states with an official philosophy, the best interest of the child may be interpreted very differently by the educational authorities and the parents of the child. Limitations on parental authority have frequently required adjudication at the domestic and international levels.[104]

The child should be protected against religious discrimination. The practices of a religion or belief in which a child is brought up should not be injurious to his physical or mental health or to his full development

---

102 Odio Benito, *Study of the Current Dimensions of the Problems of Intolerance and Discrimination Based on Religion or Belief*, 25.

103 Cited above note 82.

104 Domestic jurisprudence on the role of religion in education is enormous and cannot be cited here. For a sampling of European decisions, see above note 80 and the chapter by T. Jeremy Gunn included herein. For American jurisprudence see above note 80 and the chapter by John Witte, Jr. and M. Christian Green included herein.

(Article 5(5)). The limitations mentioned in Article 1(3) of the Declaration, namely public safety, order, health, or morals or the fundamental rights and freedoms of others, should be taken into account.

Evaluation of the Declaration. On the whole, the Declaration was an important breakthrough in the struggle to extend international rights protection to religion. Of course, a Declaration is not a treaty and is not binding. However, it carries with it the weight of a UN solemn statement, giving expression to the trends prevailing in the international community at a given moment. It does have certain legal effect, and it implies an expectation of obedience by members of the international community to the extent that it may be seen as stating rules of customary international law.[105]

As to the contents of the Declaration, the catalog of rights contained in it is most helpful, although not complete. Compromise on several difficult issues has been necessary, and Article 8 made possible the acceptance of the Declaration by all, by referring to the Universal Declaration. Wording is unsatisfactory in several articles, evincing the protracted negotiations and numerous amendments. But, in the final analysis, the Declaration unquestionably shows progress in a sensitive area of human rights that, in comparison with other rights, had been neglected.

The Necessity or Possibility of a Convention. Does the Declaration make a convention unnecessary? I have already mentioned this dilemma, and the answer may be inconclusive, particularly if the result is a treaty with a weaker text regarding substantive rights respecting religion. Interested non-governmental organizations have advocated the adoption of a convention. A similar stand was taken by the Special Rapporteurs, the Sub-Commission on the Prevention of Discrimination and Protection of Minorities, and a 1984 Seminar on the Encouragement of Understanding, Tolerance and Respect in Matters Relating to Freedom of Religion or Belief.[106] The General Assembly of the United Nations, which deals every year with the "elimination of all forms of religious intolerance," has recently not taken up the matter of a convention. In its last resolution before this writing, 48/128, adopted on 20 December 1993, the Assembly urged states to take measures to combat hatred, intolerance, and acts of violence, including those motivated by religious extremism. The General Assembly also welcomed steps to implement the Declaration, and re-

[105] See Stephen Schwebel, "The Effect of Resolutions of the UN General Assembly on Customary International Law," *American Society of International Law, Proceedings of the 73rd Annual Meeting* (1979): 301. Odio Benito, *Study of the Current Dimensions of the Problems of Intolerance and Discrimination Based on Religion or Belief*, 49 refers to concrete "obligations of conduct" for states and individuals.

[106] On the seminar, see Report by Kevin Boyle, UN Doc.ST/HR/Ser.A/16 (1984), particularly para. 102 (q), on the possibility of a convention.

quested the Commission on Human Rights to continue its consideration of measures to implement the Declaration. There is no reference at all to the question of a convention.[107] Also the 1993 Vienna Conference on Human Rights remained silent on this question.[108]

Theo van Boven, in a working paper prepared at the request of the Sub-Commission on Prevention of Discrimination and Protection of Minorities, takes a cautious view on the question of a convention. He recommends that, prior to the drafting of such an instrument, "solid preparatory work" should be done.[109] Yoram Dinstein stresses the "singular contribution" that a convention could make to the promotion of freedom of religion. He is, however, aware of the fact that the prospects are unfavorable, and that there is "very little enthusiasm" for a new implementation mechanism.[110]

The draft convention presently pending, as elaborated by the Commission on Human Rights,[111] has a preamble and twelve articles adopted by the Commission, some additional articles proposed, and a preliminary draft on additional measures of implementation prepared by the Sub-Commission. The draft reflects the orientation prevailing when it was discussed simultaneously with the draft Declaration. The major differences between the substantive articles of the Declaration and those of the draft convention are the result of the amendments in the late stages of the preparation of the Declaration. The draft convention lists some rights not mentioned in the 1981 Declaration. For example, draft Article IX follows the pattern of Article 4 of the Racial Convention and is likely to result in controversy, if work on the draft convention continues at all. The measures of implementation are similar to those incorporated into other anti-discrimination instruments, based mainly on a reporting system and the possibility of individual petitions if the respective state party has declared that it recognizes the competence of a committee to be established.

---

[107] UN Press Release GA/8637, 20 January 1994, 384. At its 49th session, the General Assembly adopted (on 23 December 1994, resolution 49/188) a similar approach. See U.N. Press Release GA/3860, 31 January 1995, 313. Formerly, in its resolution 41/20 of 4 December 1986, the General Assembly stated that "standard setting should proceed with adequate preparation."

[108] For the Vienna Declaration and Programme of Action, see 32 I.L.M. 1661 (1993).

[109] E/CN.4/Sub.2/1989/32. Van Boven mentions suggestions to frame a new binding instrument in the form of a protocol to the ICCPR, in which case the Human Rights Committee would become the implementation machinery. He also points out the practical difficulties for the establishment of a new treaty body. Ibid., 27. See also Theo van Boven, "Advances and Obstacles in Building Understanding and Respect Between People of Diverse Religions and Beliefs," *Human Rights Quarterly* 13 (1991): 437-449, an adapted version of the Arcot Krishnaswami Lecture at a conference of experts on ways to promote the 1981 Declaration, Project Tandem, New Delhi, 1991.

[110] Dinstein and Tabory, eds., *The Protection of Minorities and Human Rights*, 179.

[111] UN Doc. A/7930 (1970).

Since renewal of work on a convention seems doubtful, it may be adequate to examine alternative ways and procedures to monitor the extent to which the 1981 Declaration is implemented. Non-governmental organizations may join efforts to do their own monitoring. Of course, the Human Rights Committee has a duty to perform in connection with the relevant articles of the Covenant. It has been suggested that working groups be established in this regard in accordance with other existing bodies to the same effect, although no formal proposals have been advanced in this regard. In any case, the principles listed in the Declaration should provide governments with guidance to adjust their own legislation in accordance with the international minimum standard.

Implementation of the Declaration. Both the Commission on Human Rights and the Sub-Commission on Prevention of Discrimination and Protection of Minorities appointed Special Rapporteurs to conduct studies and submit reports related to the implementation of the Declaration. The Special Rapporteur of the Commission, Angelo Vidal d'Almeida Ribeiro, was appointed in 1986 and submitted seven reports.[112] A new Special Rapporteur, Abdelfattah Amor, was appointed in 1993. The Special Rapporteur of the Sub-Commission, Elizabeth Odio Benito, was appointed in 1983, and her task was to undertake a comprehensive study of the current dimensions of the problems of intolerance on grounds of religion or belief, using the Declaration as terms of reference, updating in that way the Krishnaswami study.[113]

The contents of the reports submitted by both Special Rapporteurs provides a broad and illuminating picture of the world situation regarding religious rights. Both Special Rapporteurs circulated questionnaires among states and based their reports on the received replies and communications. In addition, they analyzed the present state of affairs, commented on issues reflected in the individual communications, reached conclusions, and formulated recommendations. They also took a clearly affirmative stand on the question whether a convention in this area was necessary and convenient.

Odio Benito concludes in her study that the term "intolerance and discrimination based on religion or belief" encompasses not only discrimination proper, but also acts that stir up hatred against, or persecution of, persons or groups. She stresses the identity of meaning of the Universal Declaration, the Covenant, and the 1981 Declaration as to the right to change one's religion, or to remain without any at all. Full reali-

---

112 For the seven reports, E/CN.4/1987/35, 1988/45, 1989/44, 1990/46, 1991/56, 1992/52 and 1993/62 and Corr.1 and Add.1.

113 Odio Benito, *Study of the Current Dimensions of the Problems of Intolerance and Discrimination Based on Religion or Belief.*

zation of all other human rights is closely linked to freedom of thought, conscience, religion, and belief. Frequently, violations of religious rights involve violation of many other basic rights, including the right to life. A listing of such violations, region by region, is included in the study, which also examines the different church-state relationships, on the basis of information provided by a number of states. The author of the study does not draw a firm conclusion as to whether, and to what extent, any of the existing constitutional arrangements, gives rise, per se or in practice, to religious intolerance. She does, however, point out that, on the whole, the existing situation falls below the standards in the 1981 Declaration.

Odio Benito recommends—in agreement with the conclusions reached in this respect by the 1984 United Nations Seminar on the encouragement of understanding, tolerance and respect in matters related to freedom of religion or belief—that the international community should continue its work to adopt a convention soon. She also suggests that several studies should be prepared on subjects including discrimination against women within churches and within religions, discrimination against centuries-old religions which do not belong to the group of "major religions," and the emergence of new religions and practices of sects.

Pending the adoption of a convention containing implementation measures, it should be considered as essential to set up an information system permitting bodies dealing with human rights to scrutinize the situation in this area, resorting perhaps to arrangements that ECOSOC can make under Article 64 of the Charter.

The former Special Rapporteur of the Commission on Human Rights, Angelo Vidal d'Almeida Ribeiro, included in his seven detailed and documented reports allegations transmitted to the respective governments concerning situations which might depart from the provisions of the Declaration, as well as the comments formulated in that regard by the affected governments. The Special Rapporteur aimed to identify problems and factors which might be an impediment to the implementation of the Declaration generally and collected information on specific situations. He circulated questionnaires to the governments and established a dialogue with them on the basis of their replies. He also directly approached those governments against which allegations have been made. The reports also drew on non-governmental sources, including, naturally, religious groups and organizations.

The cases dealt with refer to persons of various religions under different legal and political systems, in most regions of the world. The Special Rapporteur points out that the majority of allegations relate to the right to have the religion or belief of one's choice, the right to change one's religion, worship in public and in private, holidays and particular ceremonies and, generally, the right not to be subjected to discrimination on grounds like those mentioned. Violations of the provisions of the Declaration have had a negative bearing on other fundamental freedoms and rights. Violence has been frequently alleged, in some cases in a massive way, as recently in Bosnia.

The Special Rapporteur took note of some positive developments, stressing the importance of inter-faith dialogue. D'Almeida Ribeiro clearly favors the preparation of a binding instrument, in the light of the recommendations submitted by Theo van Boven to the Sub-Commission on Prevention of Discrimination and Protection of Minorities, in the special working paper to which reference was already made.[114]

New Relevant Developments

Modern human rights law had to acknowledge the importance of collective and group rights, overcoming the reluctance shown by the international community in the early years after the creation of the United Nations to go beyond the area of individual basic rights and the principle of non-discrimination. We shall now refer to recent documents expressing that acknowledgment, some of a general character and some dealing with particular human groups, to the extent in which they are relevant to rights in the sphere of religion and beliefs.

The 1993 World Conference. We begin with a reference to the outcome of the World Conference on Human Rights, held in Vienna in June 1993, under the auspices of the United Nations and attended by a large number of participants, representing states and international organizations. Many non-governmental organizations, including religious ones, met immediately before and simultaneously with the main conference, the results of which are a subject of controversy. The Vienna Declaration and Programme of Action[115] devotes one single paragraph to the issue. In Part II B.1 (Racism, racial discrimination, xenophobia and other forms of intolerance) the World Conference calls upon all governments to take all appropriate measures in compliance with their international obligations and with due regard to their respective legal systems to counter intolerance and related violence based on religion or belief, including practices of discrimination against women and including the desecration of religious sites, recognizing that every individual has the right to freedom of thought, conscience, expression, and religion. The Conference also invites

[114] See above note 109.

[115] See above note 107.

all states to put into practice the provisions of the Declaration on the Elimination of all Forms of Intolerance and Discrimination Based on Religion or Belief.

This is certainly not a far-reaching text. It must have disappointed those who expected a renewed call in favor of the preparation of a binding instrument. It contains no reference to the institutional rights and status of religious communities as such. The reference to the 1981 Declaration is very mildly worded. Of course, one should be aware of the character of the Vienna Conference and the difficulties that any attempt to add substance to the paragraph devoted to religion would most probably have encountered in such a large meeting of member states.

Minorities. The Declaration of the 1993 Vienna Conference is even less ambitious than the Declaration on the Rights of Persons Belonging to National or Ethnic, Religious and Linguistic Minorities, adopted by the United Nations General Assembly on 18 December 1992.[116] This document, although unmistakably inspired by Article 27 of the ICCPR and definitely not group-oriented, nonetheless made concessions to the need to contemplate the rights of religious, ethnic or cultural groups as such. It mentions the 1981 Declaration in its Preamble. Article 1 asks states to "protect" the identity, including the religious identity, of minorities, and to "encourage" conditions for the promotion of that identity. To protect the identity of a religious or cultural minority means recognizing the existence of a collective entity with its own rights, beyond the individual and collective rights of individuals, covered by Article 27 of the Covenant. The encouragement by states of conditions for the promotion of the identity of the group is important, although the notion of "identity" is not defined.

Article 4 confirms that persons should be able to express their characteristics and to develop their culture, language, religion, traditions, and customs, except where specific practices violate national law or are contrary to international standards. By Article 2, persons belonging to minorities shall enjoy the right to profess and practise their own religion and to participate effectively in the cultural, religious . . . and public life." They are entitled to establish and maintain their own associations and, "without any discrimination, free and peaceful contacts" with other members of their group, as well as contacts across frontiers with citizens of other states to whom they are related by, among other things, religious ties.

---

[116] For its text, see *Human Rights,* 140. For a commentary on the Declaration, see Natan Lerner, "The 1992 UN Declaration on Minorities," *Israel Yearbook on Human Rights* 23 (1993): 111-128.

The Declaration on Minorities is essentially a compromise and implies some progress as compared to Article 27 of the Covenant and the trend it expresses. It seems reasonable to suggest that the 1981 Declaration may have exercised influence in this respect.

On November 10, 1994, the Committee of Ministers of the Council of Europe adopted a Framework Convention for the Protection of National Minorities. Article 8 recognizes the right of "every person belonging to a national minority" to manifest his or her religion and to "establish religious institutions, organizations and associations."[117]

Other recent documents are more outspoken regarding rights of special groups. Such is the text elaborated by the CSCE Meeting of Experts on National Minorities that took place in Geneva in July 1991 and which has some advanced provisions. It includes clauses on self-administration, by national minorities, in areas or aspects concerning their identity, where territorial autonomy does not apply. This is of obvious importance for religious groups not concentrated in specific areas. The report also calls upon states to adopt laws prohibiting acts that constitute incitement to violence based on, among other things, "religious discrimination, hostility or hatred, including anti-semitism."[118]

Bilateral agreements. A passing reference to special arrangements made between several states and religious groups is necessary to complete the picture of the status of religious rights. Such arrangements have been concluded by Italy, Spain,[119] Bolivia, Colombia,[120] and Israel with religious institutions or communities of religious origin. In 1994, an agreement between the Holy See and the State of Israel, conducive to the establishment of diplomatic relations, contains provisions on religious

---

[117] For the Framework Convention and Explanatory Report, see the undated publication of Directorate of Information of the Council of Europe, Strasbourg.

[118] For the text, see I.L.M. 1692 (1991).

[119] Spain replaced the Concordat signed with the Holy See in 1953 by several agreements, presently in effect, in addition to the "Basic Agreement" concluded in 1976. Spain also signed agreements, in 1992, with the Federation of Evangelical Religious Institutions, the Federation of Jewish Communities and the Islamic Commission, all of Spain. For the texts, see, Ministeriio de Justicia, "Libertad Religiosa (Normas Reguladoras)" (Madrid, 1988); Laws 24/1992, 25/1992 and 26/1992, approving those agreements, respectively, BOE 272 (1992), 38209ff. For the Agreements with the Holy See, Ministerio de Relaciones Exteriores, "Acuerdos entre España y la Santa Sede" (1976-1979).

[120] The Concordat between Colombia and the Holy See was modified "to bring it into line with the 1991 Constitution," which grants "full religious freedom" to all churches and sects (statement by the representative of Colombia to the Human Rights Committee, April 1992, GAOR, 47th Session, Supp. No. 40 (A/47/40), 89). Some privileges of the Roman Catholic Church concerning family and education caused constitutional problems.

rights.[121] In the absence of a general treaty on religious rights, these special arrangements, despite their specific and limited character, may perform a useful role in the solution of problems related to the position of the respective religious communities.

Universality vs. "Cultural Relativism." Almost half a century after the adoption of the Universal Declaration of Human Rights, discussion has intensified on the issue of universality versus particularism, namely the extent to which what is called "cultural relativism" may legitimately modify the rule of a minimum standard valid for all.[122] The matter was the subject of controversy at the 1993 Vienna Conference on Human Rights, which reaffirmed "the universal nature" of human rights and freedoms as being "beyond question."[123] A different view was taken by Asian states at the World Conference Preparatory Meeting in Bangkok in April 1993. Recognizing "that while human rights are universal in nature," national and regional particularities and various historical, cultural, and religious backgrounds "must be borne in mind."[124] This was stated in a different manner by the Mediterranean Center for Human Rights, which included among its aims the taking into account of "socio-cultural, linguistic and religious differences in order to reinforce the universality of human rights."[125]

Today, it is obviously necessary to acknowledge the fact that cultural and religious traditions differ as to their understanding of what basic rights are. There are conflicts among rights, and religious rights, among others, are a case in point, as Philip Alston and several authors in this volume and its companion indicate.[126] But this cannot imply the rejection of the universal applicability of human rights law as an aim, or the denial of the need of a minimum international standard.

---

121 The "Fundamental Agreement between the Holy See and the State of Israel" was signed on 30 December 1993 and ratified by the Israeli Government on 20 February 1994. For its text, Justice 1 (1994): 18-20.

122 See Jack Donnelly, "Cultural Relativism and Universal Human Rights," *Human Rights Quarterly* 6 (1984): 400; Fernando R. Teson, "International Human Rights and Cultural Relativism," in Richard Claude and Burns H. Weston, eds., *Human Rights in the World Community*, 2d ed. (Philadelphia, 1992), 42-51; Abdullah Ahmed An-Naim, ed., *Human Rights in Cross-Cultural Perspectives: A Quest for Consensus* (Philadelphia, 1992). *Human Rights Quarterly* 16(2) (May, 1994) carries several articles on the subject.

123 See above note 108, para 1.

124 Doc. IOR 41/WU 02/93, cited by Philip Alston, "The UN's Human Rights Record: From San Francisco to Vienna and Beyond," *Human Rights Quarterly* 16 (1994): 374.

125 Centre Mediterraneen des Droits de l'Homme, *de l'Homme et Solidarites Mediterranees* (Montpellier, 1994).

126 Alston, "The UN's Human Rights Record," 383.

Not all who are described as "cultural relativists" advance identical views or positions.[127] Neither do all the supporters of a universal minimum standard agree as to the nature and degree of differentiation to be legitimately contemplated when universal rules are applied to, or incorporated into, the diverse legal systems. The discussion exceeds the strict area of human rights related to religion, but religion plays a major role in this controversy. A "constructive approach" is recommended by Abdullahi Ahmed An-Na'im, who suggests neither to "underestimate the challenge of cultural relativism to the universality of human rights nor concede too much to its claims."[128]

Conclusions

Based on the foregoing, the following conclusions can be reached:

First, United Nations instruments dealing with religious human rights do not define the term "religion." This is the result of a general trend to avoid ideological or philosophical definitions that may cause controversy and make it more difficult to reach agreement between states in such a delicate area of human behavior. It is, however, indisputable that, in United Nations law and in modern human rights law, the term "religion," usually followed by the word "belief," means theistic convictions, involving a transcendental view of the universe and a normative code of behavior, as well as atheistic, agnostic, rationalistic, and other views in which both elements may be absent.

Second, the United Nations system for the protection of religious human rights does not presently include any specific obligatory treaty regarding religious human rights. Article 18 of the Covenant on Civil and Political Rights, and provisions related to religious issues in the Covenant and in treaties prepared by the United Nations and other international bodies, are, of course, mandatory for those states that ratified such instruments. A significant number of those provisions are seen today as reflecting customary international law, and some, such as the prohibition of discrimination on religious grounds or the outlawing of genocide against religious groups, belong to the restricted category of *jus cogens*. Freedom of religion is one of the fundamental rights that cannot be derogated in states of emergency. The General Comment on Article 18 formulated by the Human Rights Committee constitutes an authoritative source for the interpretation of the Covenant clauses.

---

[127] Reza Afshari, "An Essay on Islamic Cultural Relativism in the Discourse of Human Rights," *Human Rights Quarterly* 16 (1994): 235-276, at 247-248.

[128] An-Naim, ed., *Human Rights in Cross-Cultural Perspectives*, 3.

Third, the discussion on the need and/or convenience of a mandatory treaty on religious rights and freedoms is inconclusive. The main argument in favor of a convention is, of course, the general desire to grant religious rights a protection similar to that extended to other basic rights. The example of the widely-ratified Convention on Racial Discrimination, incorporating a relatively effective system of monitoring and implementation, is pointed out as justifying the treaty-oriented approach. Arguments against a treaty, neither new nor exclusive to the sphere of religion, are the risk of having to compromise on a very low common denominator of protection and the possible reluctance, on the part of some states, to ratify an instrument that may clash with long-established systems of law, mainly in the area of family law, personal status, and conversion.

Given this inconclusive debate over a mandatory instrument, the existence of a monitoring system, in the form of reports or studies by special rapporteurs appointed by UN organs, provides a modest degree of protection of religious rights, naturally not equivalent to conventional obligations assumed by states. There have been proposals, mainly from non-governmental organizations, aimed at improving that system. These include suggestions to establish national bodies to monitor religious rights, in the spirit of the 1981 Declaration, the submission of periodic reports from member States to ECOSOC, and similar measures not implying a mandatory treaty.

Fourth, the 1981 Declaration on the Elimination of All Forms of Intolerance and Discrimination Based on Religion or Belief was a powerful step forward in the search of a system of protection of religious human rights. The Declaration, which incorporated many though not all of the principles enunciated in the seminal 1959 study by Arcot Krishnaswami, includes a comprehensive and detailed catalog of rights related to freedom of conscience, religion, and belief, and their exercise in practice. The Declaration progresses beyond the purely individualistic approach of the Covenants and is nearer to some recent instruments that acknowledge the group dimension of religious human rights. Such rights cannot be adequately protected, unless the rights of religious organizations, communities, or congregations as such are recognized and ensured beyond the purely individualistic freedoms. This may be of great importance for collectivities or communities of a religious origin in which the religious element may appear combined with ethnic and cultural characteristics.

Fifth, in recent years, conventional arrangements between several states and major churches, religions, or religiously-oriented communities, granted recognition to such groups and their specific rights. There may be some advantages in this case-by-case approach, in view of the difficulties that still exist in the area of minority rights and the reluctance of many states to accept such rights.

Sixth, there are some particularly complicated problems that continue to arouse controversy. Examples of such problems include matters of conversion, opting-out from some religions or recognized religious communities, blasphemy, rights of women and children, and conscientious objection (which is a matter not always of a religious nature). A major controversy—not exclusively affecting religious rights—relates to the question of striking a balance between the prohibition of incitement against religious groups, as enunciated in Article 20 of the ICCPR, and the freedoms of speech or association. There have been different answers to this question, depending on the constitutional system of the respective countries. The precedent of the Racial Convention and trends presently prevailing in connection with religious rights seem to indicate a growing understanding of the need to protect substantive social values against abuses of the freedoms of speech and association.

Seventh, another controversy, intensified recently, involves the issue of universality versus "cultural relativism," namely the prevalence of some traditional forms of living and religious customs that may differ from what is described as a Western approach to human rights. It seems legitimate to respect some particular forms of group behavior, also in the field of religion, provided the international minimum standard is not adversely affected.

Eighth, while these pages are being drafted, tragic events affecting the life and welfare of millions of persons are taking place, involving population sectors defined by religion as well as ethnic identity. The need to ensure the protection of religious, ethnic, or cultural groups, irrespective of the nature of the group, was acknowledged by the judiciary of several countries. The shocking practices of "ethnic cleansing" in the former Yugoslavia and Rwanda added urgency to the recognition of that need.

Ninth, the protection of religious and other groups may require a serious intensification of the efforts to adopt and enforce some rules of international criminal law. The Genocide Convention is a principal example of positive international norms to that effect, but unfortunately it does not contain implementation measures. The establishment of an international tribunal to deal with the crimes committed against sectors of the population of the former Yugoslavia, be it crimes against humanitarian law or human rights violations, is a mild positive step, despite its limited mandate. But a more general approach in this respect seems to be necessary.

Tenth, the protection of religious human rights during the United Nations era is thus quite limited. Provisions of a positive character do exist and have exercised a considerable influence on domestic legislation. The claim that they are not enough, particularly at times of high international and intra-national tension, seems however to be supported by current events. Religious human rights deserve more than to remain a neglected chapter in the universal endeavors to ensure observance of and respect for human rights.

The Role of Secular Non-Governmental Organizations in the Cultivation and Understanding of Religious Human Rights

MICHAEL ROAN
Project Tandem, Inc.

The role played by the non-governmental organizations in the endeavor to achieve human rights has been and will continue to be of immense importance: without their support the Universal Declaration of Human Rights could hardly have come into being; without their continued efforts the rights proclaimed therein will never be respected. —Lyman Cromwell White[1]

The role of non-governmental organizations ("NGOs") in the development of human rights has been widely lauded, and in many areas widely documented. This chapter focuses on a field of NGO activism in human rights that has not attracted significant attention from commentators—the right to freedom of thought, conscience, religion, or belief.[2] Through the persistence of NGOs, this right developed from a brief phrase in the United Nations Charter (the "Charter") to a right enunciated and enshrined in the 1981 Declaration on the Elimination of All Forms of Intolerance and of Discrimination Based on Religion or Belief the ("1981 Declaration"). Yet this right is violated on a global scale, and religious tensions are an increasingly salient factor in internal and international conflicts. In this context of on-going unrest, assessing the

[1] Lyman Cromwell White, *International Non-Governmental Organizations: Their Purposes, Methods, and Accomplishments* (New York, 1968), 262.

[2] While this paper will hereinafter use the phrase "freedom of religion or belief," it is simply shorthand for the "freedom of thought, conscience and religion" enshrined in Article 18 of the Universal Declaration and the freedom of "religion or belief" guaranteed in the 1981 declaration.

J.D. van der Vyver and J. Witte, Jr. (eds.), Religious Human Rights in Global Perspective, 135-159.

activities and effectiveness of secular NGOs in protecting and promoting the right to freedom of religion or belief takes on an added urgency.

This study consists of four parts. Part I traces the development of the right to freedom of religion or belief at the United Nations. Part II discusses the unique role of NGOs in the protection and promotion of human rights, including their interaction with the U.N. Part III describes secular NGO activism in the promotion and protection of the right to freedom of religion or belief. Part IV provides recommendations and an overall assessment of secular NGO activism in this field.

The Right to Freedom of Thought, Conscience, Religion or Belief[3]

The right to freedom of religion was first articulated in Article 1 of the U.N. Charter of 1945, which encourages "respect for human rights and fundamental freedoms for all without distinction as to race, sex, language, or religion." In Articles 55 and 56 of the Charter, all Member States pledge to take joint and separate action in cooperation with the U.N. for the achievement of these purposes. The 1948 Universal Declaration of Human Rights ("Universal Declaration")[4] pronounced in Article 18:

> Everyone has the right to freedom of thought, conscience and religion; this right includes the freedom to change his religion or belief, and freedom whether alone or in community with others and in public or in private, to manifest his religion or belief in teaching, practice, worship, and observance.[5]

Charles Habib Malik, as Chairman of the Third Committee on Social, Cultural and Humanitarian Affairs, helped to scrutinize the draft of the Universal Declaration before it was submitted to the General Assembly for adoption. He recalled attaching special significance to Article 18: "[I]n no text did I take as much anxious interest as in this text on freedom of thought, conscience and religion. What constitutes the humanity of man more than anything else is this inward freedom, which should therefore be inviolable."[6]

---

[3] For more detailed discussion of the evolution of the rights to religious freedom at international law, see Natan Lerner's chapter included herein.

[4] Universal Declaration of Human Rights, G.A. Res. 217 A (III), December 10, 1948.

[5] Ibid.

[6] Charles Habib Malik, *Reflections on the Origin of the Universal Declaration of Human Rights*, in O. Frederick Nolde ed., *Free and Equal: Human Rights in Ecumenical Perspective* (London, 1968), 10.

As with all U.N. instruments relating to freedom of religion, Article 18 of the Universal Declaration represented a compromise. One of its crowning achievements was the inclusion of the terms "thought" and "conscience" which quietly embraced atheists and non-believers.[7] The most divisive phrase, however, was "freedom to change one's religion." Representatives of Islamic countries exerted considerable pressure to omit this phrase.[8] Although the phrase was adopted in the Universal Declaration, it was altered in Article 18 of the International Covenant on Civil and Political Rights ("Covenant").[9] The Covenant only speaks of the "freedom to have or to adopt a religion or conviction," reflecting a strengthening of Islamic influence at the U.N.[10]

In 1981, the Declaration on the Elimination of all Forms of Intolerance and of Discrimination Based on Religion or Belief was adopted by consensus—the culmination of 25 years of efforts at the U.N. to achieve more comprehensive protection for religious freedoms.[11] Already in 1956, the Sub-Commission on Prevention of Discrimination and Protection of Minorities appointed Arcot Krishnaswami as Special Rapporteur to prepare a study of discrimination in religious rights and practices. Upon review of the Special Rapporteur's final report, the Sub-Commission prepared a series of draft principles on religious freedom.[12] Two years later, the General Assembly requested the United Nation's Economic and Social Council to prepare a draft declaration and a draft convention on religious intolerance.[13]

Ten years into the process, the General Assembly decided to give priority to preparation of the Declaration over a convention considering that, unlike a convention, a declaration is not a legally binding instrument, and member states might be more likely to adopt it. Because religion is a sensitive topic at the U.N., even the process of drafting a declaration consumed nearly 20 years. In 1974, a working group was

---

[7] Sidney Liskofsky, "The UN Declaration on the Elimination of Religious Intolerance and Discrimination: Historical and Legal Perspectives," in James E. Wood, Jr., ed., *Religion and the State: Essays in Honor of Leo Pfeffer* (Waco, TX, 1985), 441, 457.

[8] The inclusion of this phrase might well be attributed to Sir Zafrulla Khan from Pakistan. He testified before the General Assembly at the final debate on the Declaration that there could be no doubt that the Qur'an yielded to other faiths the free right of conversion and declared support for the article as it stood. See Nolde, *Free and Equal*, 47.

[9] International Covenant on Civil and Political Rights, G.A. Res. 2200A (XXI), December 16, 1966, 21 U.N. GAOR Supp. (No. 16) at 52, U.N. Document A/6316 (1966).

[10] Liskofsky, "The U.N. Declaration," 457.

[11] GA Res. 36/55, 36 UN GAOR Supp. (No. 51) at 171, UN Doc. A/36/51 (1981).

[12] A. Krishnaswami, *Study of Discrimination in the Matter of Religious Rights and Practices*, UN Doc. /CN.4/Sub.2/200/Rev.1, UN Sales No. 60.XIV.2 (1960), and draft principles prepared by the Sub-Commission.

[13] G.A. Res. 1781, 17 UN GAOR Supp. (No.17) at 33, U.N. Doc. A/5217 (1962).

formed to facilitate the process of drafting a declaration. This body functioned, albeit sporadically, until adoption of the Declaration in 1981.

The 1981 Declaration provides specific content to the basic rights of freedom of religion or belief. One commentator has noted that, "although [the 1981 Declaration] lacks the nature of an international agreement, it is regarded throughout the world as articulating the fundamental rights of freedom of religion and belief."[14] The 1981 Declaration is a primary instrument for underscoring the fundamental nature of this right and for communicating to member states the importance of the international norms enunciated in the document.

While it has been common at the U.N. for a convention to soon follow a proclaimed declaration, the divisive nature of religion at the U.N. has delayed—perhaps permanently—this process. However, other measures have been initiated to implement the 1981 Declaration. First, in 1984, the U.N. convened a two week seminar in Geneva on the Encouragement of Understanding, Tolerance, and Respect in Matters Relating to Freedom of Religion or Belief.[15] The seminar, attended by 60 member-states and 40 NGOs, issued a document in which 17 recommendations were made for implementing the 1981 Declaration.[16] Second, the Sub-Commission, in 1985, appointed Professor Elizabeth Odio Benito of Costa Rica as Special Rapporteur to report on dimensions of the problem of intolerance based on religion or belief.[17] Third, the Commission on Human Rights appointed Mr. Angelo Vidal d'Almeida Ribeiro of Portugal as Special Rapporteur to monitor "incidents and governmental actions in all parts of the world which are inconsistent with the provisions of the [1981 Declaration]."[18] The Special Rapporteur's mandate also extends to recommendations for remedial measures including facilitation of dialogue between governments and religious communities.[19] In 1993, Mr. Abdelfattha Amor replaced Mr. Ribeiro as Special Rapporteur. Fourth, Theo van Boven, a member of the Sub-Commission, submitted a Working Paper to the Sub-Commission in 1989, entitled "Compilation of Provisions Relevant to the Elimination of Intolerance and Discrimination Based on Religion or Belief."[20]

---

[14] Donna Sullivan, "Advancing the Freedom of Religion or Belief Through the UN Declaration on the Elimination of Religious Intolerance and Discrimination," *American Journal of International Law* 82 (1988): 487, 488.

[15] UN Doc. ST/HR/SER.A/16 (1984).

[16] Ibid.

[17] Sub-Commission Res. 1983/31, UN Doc. E/CN.4/Sub.2/1983/43, at 98.

[18] Commission on Human Rights Res. 1986/20, UN Doc. E/CN.4/1986/65.

[19] Ibid.

[20] U.N. doc. E/CN.4/Sub.2/1989/32.

The 1981 Declaration cannot, however, be implemented by U.N. bodies alone. Effective implementation also requires efforts by NGOs. "Whatever the ultimate significance of the [1981] Declaration, it will have little impact unless religious and other national and international groups promote it through education and advocacy programs. If it is allowed to gather dust on library shelves, it will be nothing more than a footnote for scholars and students, but if it is used thoughtfully and effectively, it can be made to advance the cause of those who still must struggle to achieve their basic right to freedom of religion and conscience."[21] Fortunately, NGOs have not allowed the 1981 Declaration simply to gather dust. Because of their unique characteristics, NGOs play a vital role in the development of the right to freedom of religion or belief, continuing "to advance the cause" of those still struggling to achieve this right.

The Unique Role of NGOs in the Protection and Promotion of Human Rights

Background. Prior to World War II, only a handful of NGOs were engaged in the protection or promotion of human rights. Among the most notable were the London-based Anti-Slavery Society for Human Rights (established in 1838), the Geneva-based International Committee of the Red Cross (1863), and the French-based League for Human Rights (1902).[22] Since World War II, NGOs have proliferated; more than 5,000 NGOs were in attendance at the 1993 United Nations World Conference on Human Rights.[23] A majority of these NGOs emerged onto the human rights scene within the last 20 years. Initially, they were largely Western-based. Recently, a number of NGOs from throughout the world has also arrived on the human rights scene, although the major human rights groups (in terms of mandate, membership and influence at the U.N.) continue to be found in the West.

NGOs and IGOs. An NGO was defined in 1950 by the United Nation's Economic and Social Council as follows: "Any international organization which is not established by intergovernmental agreement shall be considered as a nongovernmental organization."[24] NGOs differ from intergovernmental organizations (IGOs), which are organizations

---

[21] Liskofsky, "The U.N. Declaration," 478.

[22] Laurie S. Wiseberg and Harry M. Scoble, "Recent Trends in the Expanding Universe of Nongovernmental Organizations Dedicated to the Protection of Human Rights," V. Nanda, ed., *Global Human Rights* (Washington, 1981).

[23] "Forum stresses Universality and Indivisibility of human rights," *Agence France Presse* (June 12, 1993).

[24] U.N. ECOSOC Resolution 288(X), February 27, 1950.

established by intergovernmental agreements or treaties and governed by international law. NGOs are voluntarily created organizations, governed by applicable domestic law. Although active internationally, they are not accorded the status of international legal persons, and are not restricted to mandates established by treaty. The actions of NGOs are entirely determined by their membership, and delimited by domestic law. For example, Amnesty International (an NGO) has modified its mandate a number of times in response to human rights situations requiring immediate attention.

NGOs are able to be respond creatively to human rights issues, because they often lack the entrenched bureaucracies characteristic of IGOs. Most NGOs have boards of directors willing and able to respond to human rights situations with versatile approaches. Most importantly, because they are usually not indebted to any government, they are free to act without fear of governmental retribution. In contrast, IGOs are created by governments and rely on governments for their very existence. Whatever action an IGO takes will generally be in conformity with the political will of a governmental authority.

General Characteristics and Activities of NGOs. NGOs cover the globe. They are local, national, subnational, or transnational bodies. Their memberships are generally composed of private individuals ranging from organizations with a single member to Amnesty International with more than one million members world-wide. Their mandates range from local concerns to global concerns. Some NGOs have highly specialized purposes; for example, Article 19, headquartered in London, is organized exclusively to protect and promote the freedom of expression as articulated in Article 19 of the Universal Declaration of Human Rights. Others have broader or more general aims. Human Rights Watch, for example, protects and promotes all internationally recognized human rights world-wide, and acts as an umbrella organization for its six affiliated bodies—Africa Watch, Americas Watch, Asia Watch, Helsinki Watch, Middle East Watch, and the Fund for Free Expression.[25] Alternatively, the International League for Human Rights, another NGO with a comprehensive mandate, has an international secretariat located in New York which cooperates with some 35 affiliates in 26 countries, including the National Council of Civil Liberties in the United Kingdom, the American Civil Liberties Union, the Jamaica Council for Human Rights, and the Bangladesh Human Rights Society.[26]

---

[25] *Human Rights Watch World Report* (New York, 1993).

[26] *The International League for Human Rights Annual Report* (1983).

Article 71 of the U.N. Charter provides the source for the legal status of NGOs at the U.N.[27] It directs the Economic and Social Council[28] to "make suitable arrangements for consultation with NGO's which are concerned with matters within its competence." The Council formally established that status by passing ECOSOC Resolution 1296 (XLIV) on May 23, 1968. Resolution 1296 established three levels of consultative status: NGOs granted consultative status under Category I and II are entitled to observe all public meetings held by the Commission and Sub-Commission, participate in U.N. conferences, and submit statements as official U.N. documents. Those in Category I are also permitted to make oral interventions and propose agenda items for consideration at Council meetings and the subsidiary committees. Category III NGOs are permitted only to submit written statements.

Part III of Resolution 1296, entitled "Principles Governing the Nature of the Consultative Arrangements," underscores the distinction between participation without vote in the deliberations of the Council and arrangements for consultation with NGOs. It states:

> Under Articles 69 and 70, participation is provided for only in the case of States not members of the Council, and of specialized agencies. Article 71, applying to NGOs, provides for suitable arrangements for consultation. This distinction, deliberately made in the Charter is fundamental and the arrangements for consultation should not accord the NGOs the same rights of participation as are accorded States not members of the Council and to the specialized agencies brought into relationship with the United Nations.[29]

Part III makes clear that the participatory rights granted NGOs are for the purpose of securing expert information or advice from NGOs which have special competence in their respective areas of expertise.[30]

Currently, 938 NGOs are affiliated with the U.N. Economic and Social Council. To receive consultative status, an NGO must apply to the U.N. Committee on NGOs.[31] The Council requires that: "[NGOs] be of a

---

[27] ECOSOC Red. 1296 (XLIV), 44 U.N. ESCOR (Supp. No. 1) at 22, U.N. Document E/4548 (1968), May 23, 1968.

[28] ECOSOC is one of the principal organs of the U.N. relating to matters of economic, social and humanitarian concerns. It is comprised of 54 member states, each serving a term of three years.

[29] ECOSOC Res. 1296 (XLIV), 44 U.N. ESCOR (Supp. No. 1) at 22, U.N. Document E/4548 (1968), May 23, 1968.

[30] Ibid.

[31] The Council Committee on Non-Governmental Organizations was established by ECOSOC Resolution 1099 (XL) of 4 March 1966 and Rule 82 of the rules of procedure of ECOSOC. This body meets every two years and is composed of 19 member states elected to serve two-year terms.

representative character and of recognized international standing; [the NGO] shall represent a substantial proportion, and express the views of major sections of the population or of the organized persons within the particular field of its competence, covering, where possible, a substantial number of countries in different regions of the world."[32] Generally, the organizations that have sought consultative status and acquired international standing at the U.N. are Western-based NGOs with headquarters in North America or Western Europe.[33] By requiring an NGO to achieve some measure of international recognition before obtaining consultative status, local or national NGOs may be effectively prevented from obtaining affiliation with the U.N. Often the deference given internationally-recognized organizations is in response to the observation that the information these groups provide has proven to be reliable and credible. Although local and national NGOs may not possess a formal affiliation with the United Nations, often they gain access to the U.N. bodies through associations with the major human rights organizations. These groups will gather information from the local and national NGOs, consult on issues within their specific mandates, and allow representatives from these groups to present information to the United Nations on their behalf. Often it is the major NGOs, such as Amnesty International and Human Rights Watch, that set the human rights agenda at the U.N. by calling attention to particular human rights violations. To avoid a largely Western perspective, grassroots NGOs must play an increasingly active role in deciding what issues major human rights organizations address at the U.N.[34]

NGO Interaction With the U.N. Human Rights Machinery. NGOs contribute to U.N. bodies that are either created under the authority of the U.N. Charter or established under human rights treaties.[35] In the

[32] ECOSOC resolution 1296 (XLIV), para. 4. The term "recognized international standing" is determined on an ad hoc basis, however, paragraph 17 in Part III of this resolution underscores that the interests of NGOs should not be restricted to a single state, group of states, or interests of a particular group of people.

[33] Wiseberg and Scoble, "Recent Trends," 27.

[34] Ibid.

[35] The principal Charter-based bodies with a human rights role are the Security Council, General Assembly, the Economic and Social Council, the Commission on Human Rights, the Sub-Commission on Prevention of Discrimination and Protection of Minorities, the Commission on the Status of Women, and the Commission on Crime Prevention and Criminal Justice. The principal treaty-based bodies are the Human Rights Committee (HRC), the Committee on the Elimination of All Forms of Racial Discrimination (CERD), the Committee on Economic, Social and Cultural Rights (CESCR), the Committee Against Torture (CAT), the Committee on the Rights of the Child (CRC), and the Committee on the Elimination of Discrimination Against Women (CEDAW). See Minnesota Advocates for Human Rights and the International Service for Human Rights, *The U.N. Commission on Human Rights, Its Sub-Commission, and Related Procedures: An Orientation Manual* (Minneapolis, 1993).

protection and promotion of the right to freedom of religion, NGOs primarily interact with four Charter-based bodies, the General Assembly, the Economic and Social Council, the Commission on Human Rights and its Sub-Commission on Prevention of Discrimination and Protection of Minorities ("Subcommission"). NGOs also interact with two treaty-based bodies, the Human Rights Committee and the Committee on the Elimination of All Forms of Racial Discrimination. The Human Rights Committee's function is to review the compliance of governments with the International Covenant on Civil and Political Rights and its Optional Protocol. NGOs are not accorded a formal status with the Human Rights Commission.

Of these bodies, the Commission on Human Rights, the Sub-Commission on Prevention of Discrimination and Protection of Minorities, and the aforementioned Special Rapporteurs on religious intolerance are often the most accessible forums for NGOs.[36] ECOSOC Resolution 1235 (XLII) authorizes this Commission and Sub-Commission "to examine information relevant to gross violations of human rights and fundamental freedoms," to prepare thorough studies and investigations of situations that reveal "a consistent pattern" of human rights violations and report to the Economic and Social Council with accompanying resolutions, including drafts of new human rights standards."[37] Because IGOs generally lack fact-finding capabilities, the NGOs elevate the quality of deliberations at the Sub-Commission and Commission by providing nearly all of the information on human rights violations considered by these bodies. Experienced NGO delegates may also be consulted by Commission and Sub-Commission representatives regarding the drafting of new human rights standards and resolutions, often playing a substantial role in this process.[38] Additionally, because the information provided by NGOs to the Commission emphasizes patterns of violations, NGO contributions are often determinative of Commission decisions in establishing Special Rapporteurs on specific types of human rights violations. In general, the mandates of these bodies are to seek and receive information, prepare studies or reports, and visit countries. The mandate of the Special Rapporteur on religious intolerance permits seeking and receiving information from NGOs with consultative status or simply any relevant national or international NGO.

---

[36] Ibid.

[37] Under ECOSOC Resolution 1296, para. 23, 44 U.N. ESCOR, Supp. (No.1), at 22 U.N. Doc. E./4548 (1968), NGOs in Consultative Status Category 1 may suggest items for the agenda of ECOSOC, the Commission and the Sub-Commission. According to Rule 75 of U.N. Doc. E/4767 (1970).

[38] "Commentaries: UN Sub-Commission on Discrimination and Minorities," *ICJ Review* 41 (1988): 26.

It is a widely held opinion that NGOs are indispensable to the work of U.N. "rapporteurs," who monitor compliance with U.N. instruments. The Special Rapporteur on torture, Professor P.H. Kooijmans, for example, described the NGOs' information as "the life-line to their province of action."[39] Indeed, Professor Kooijmans states that, in individual cases acted on by mandataries, nearly all the information is provided by NGOs.[40] Because the mandataries lack the staff or resources to ascertain the credibility of this information, the Special Rapporteur generally welcomes only information from sources known to be reliable.

It is no accident that nearly 1,000 NGOs currently hold consultative status, for NGO participation at the U.N. is vital, if not indispensable. As Nitin Deasai, U.N. Under-Secretary-General for Policy Coordination and Sustainable Development, noted: "NGOs have increasingly assumed the role of promoters of new ideas; they have alerted the international community to emerging issues, and they have developed expertise and talent which, in increasing numbers of areas, have become vital to the work of the United Nations."[41] Currently, less than one-percent of the U.N.'s total budget is allocated to U.N. human rights work. The U.N. human rights machinery simply lacks resources to obtain credible information on human rights violations. Without the fact-finding capabilities of NGOs, the U.N. would not be able to utilize its one enforcement mechanism—the mobilization of shame. Mrs. Stamatopoulou, chief of the New York Office of the U.N. Center for Human Rights says that "shame" is the U.N.'s chief weapon, and an effective one. "Countries that are violators know they will be talked about. It's extraordinary how hard many of them will lobby to make sure that their names will not be mentioned. . . . There is a constant pressure on them."[42]

In addition to contributing information and expertise, NGOs enhance the global constituency of the U.N. NGO consultative status opened a "recognized channel through which an international point of view of 'We the peoples' could be brought to bear on the formulation of economic, so-

---

[39] P.H. Kooijmans, "The Non-Governmental Organizations and the Monitoring Activities of the United Nations in the Field of Human Rights," in id., *The Role of Non-Governmental Organizations in the Promotion and Protection of Human Rights* (New York, 1990), 15.

[40] Ibid., 18. See also Nigel S. Rodley, "United Nations Non-Treaty Procedures for Dealing with Human Rights Violations," in H. Hannum, ed., *Guide to International Human Rights Practice* (Washington, 1992), 71.

[41] Jaya Dayal, "United Nations: U.N. Wary of NGO Glut," *Inter Press Service* (February 19, 1994).

[42] Lucia Mouat, "U.N. Raises Stronger Arm Against Nations Violating Human Rights," *Christian Science Monitor* (May 23, 1990): 1.

cial, and human rights policies and programs of the U.N."[43] For example, where a member nation is unresponsive to its citizens' demands for human rights, an NGO may serve as the conduit through which their unheeded interests are raised. Indeed, one of the principles guiding U.N. decisions on arrangements for consultative status is to "enable organizations which represent important elements of public opinion in a large number of countries to express their views."[44]

NGOs are unique bodies at the U.N. because their independence offers certain advantages over U.N. mechanisms to promote and protect human rights. "In most circumstances," David Weissbrodt writes, "nongovernmental organizations are more independent of political forces and thus are able to identify and criticize human rights violations wherever they may occur. NGOs do not need to wait for the coming into force and active enforcement of international development acceptable implementation procedures in the UN Human Rights Commission or other international governmental organizations."[45] In general, NGOs strive to remain independent of governmental controls—such as financing—in order to provide information to U.N. bodies that appears to be and is non-partisan and non-ideological. In the field of human rights, it is imperative that an NGO be perceived as independent of governmental influences. An NGO acting on an international scale should direct its work to a wide variety of countries to reflect a geopolitical and cultural balance. Information regarding governmental funding or influence may irreparably damage the NGO's most valued asset when criticizing a state's human rights record—its credibility. Moreover, independence is crucial to safeguarding the role of an NGO in the U.N. process. Paragraph 36(b) of ECOSOC Resolution 1296 allows for the suspension or termination of consultative status if an NGO engages in "unsubstantiated or politically-motivated acts against the States Members of the United Nations." The seriousness of this provision was underscored when ECOSOC's Committee on Non-Governmental Organizations sent a questionnaire to NGOs inquiring into the financing of NGOs by governments and NGO criticism of governments. One commentator noted that "the exercise was undoubtedly designed to make NGOs more cautious in their criticism."[46]

---

[43] Maya Prasad, "The Role of Non-Governmental Organizations in the New United Nations Procedures for Human Rights Complaints," *Denver Journal of International Law and Policy* 5 (1975): 460.

[44] Resolution 1296 (XLIV) of the Economic and Social Council, 23 May 1968, para. 14.

[45] David Weissbrodt, "The Role of Nongovernmental Organizations in the Implementation of Human Rights," *Texas International Law Journal* 12 (1977): 293, 300 .

[46] Jerome J. Shestack, "Sisyphus Endures: The International Human Rights NGO," *New York Law School Law Review* 24 (1978): 89, 115, referring to U.N. Doc. E/C.2/ST. 224 (1968).

An NGO's established objectivity and international credibility will enable it to combat charges of unsubstantiated or politically motivated criticism.

Tensions Between NGOs and U.N. Member States. The aforementioned questionnaire illustrates the tension between Member States and NGOs at the United Nations. On the one hand, it is the role of NGOs to criticize the human rights records of governments; on the other hand, NGOs must forge alliances with governments to lobby effectively for votes adopting international norms and thematic mechanisms such as Special Rapporteurs.[47] This tension, however, further underscores the value of NGOs. It is the NGOs that highlight the need for international mechanisms by reporting human rights abuses. Without the information, NGOs provide and their lobbying efforts on behalf of enforcement mechanisms, international norms would remain weak. Governments abusing human rights naturally refrain from advocating stronger mechanisms.[48] Additionally, it is rare for governments to criticize another state's record for fear of the same.

Secular NGOs and the Right to Freedom of Religion

In defining the activities of secular NGOs in the protection and promotion of the right to freedom of religion, it may be noted that there are two categories of "secular" NGOs.[49]

The first category includes organizations with a defined ontological or philosophical belief system that provides ultimate answers to ultimate questions on the meaning of human existence. Organizations in this category are extremely varied—Communist Party members in states such as China, Vietnam, and Cuba, various schools of materialism, Western style democratic atheist or "non-believers" groups, or respected secular NGOs such as the International Humanist and Ethical Union (an activist group registered in consultative status with the United Nations). For the most part, such organizations have not been active in the defense of religious freedom, preferring to attribute cause and effect to human effort, not transcendental or supernatural intervention.

The second category includes NGO organizations that do not take a stand or even an interest in answers to ultimate questions. Instead, they have missions that in general ways reflect the need to unite as human

47 See Kooijmans, "The Non-Governmental Organizations," 15.

48 Ibid.

49 For discussion of the work of religious NGOs, see the chapters by J. Bryan Hehir, Irwin Cotler, and Donna Arzt included in the companion to this volume, John Witte, Jr. and Johan van der Vyver, eds., *Religious Human Rights in Global Perspective: Religious Perspectives* (The Hague, 1995).

beings toward making the life we have here as good as possible. These NGOs embody what might be considered a practical humanist approach. Such organizations believe we should get on with the job of human development, not allowing religious, racial, political, or economic divisions to stand in the way.[50] A broad spectrum of organizations such as the International Red Cross or Amnesty International are included in this category, with wide-ranging interests in fields such as refugee work, environmental protection, economic and social development, as well as human rights. While individual members of these organizations may be deeply religious or spiritual, most often such organizations offer mission statements that reflect a secular moral purpose encompassing a vision of human and social cooperation—with strict neutrality as to religion or belief.

NGOs in both categories have important contributions to make in defense of religious freedom; however, they approach the topic of religious human rights from different perspectives with varying degrees of enthusiasm and success. In general, their contributions to the protection and promotion of the right to freedom of religion include (1) efforts to develop human rights norms at the U.N.; (2) lobbying national governments; (3) monitoring, investigating, and reporting on violations of the right to freedom of religion or belief; (4) protecting victims of religious rights abuses; and (5) promoting tolerance, understanding, and respect among people of diverse beliefs. Although these activities overlap and are interdependent, they are useful in providing a framework to assess NGO activism. What follows are examples that demonstrate how secular NGOs have served the field of religious human rights.

Efforts to Develop Human Rights Norms at the U.N. International relations and the treaty-making process are traditionally thought to be the privileged domain of governments as representatives of nation states. NGOs, however, have been active for quite some time in this field. Most notably, the International Red Cross has been instrumental in developing standards of international law—from the 1864 Geneva Convention for Protection of War Victims to the 1977 Protocols additional to the Geneva Conventions of 1949. The necessity for NGOs to play a role in standard-setting has been summarized as follows:

> The old style treaty-making process which predominantly serves state and inter-state interests is entering a new phase in international relations—at least in theory—a phase of international cooperation which is supposed to

[50] H.J. Blackham, *Modern Humanism* (Neuchatel, Switzerland, 1964), published for the International Commission for a History of Scientific and Cultural Development of Mankind, with the financial support of UNESCO.

> serve common goals and common interests that are vital to the survival of humankind. After two destructive world wars the U.N. Charter introduced the idea of the internationalization of Human Rights. . . . The International law of human rights is a peoples-oriented law and it is only natural that the shaping of this law should be a process in which representative sectors of society participate. While the orientation of contemporary international law and *a fortiori* of international human rights law is supposed to bend towards serving human and welfare interests, the international law making process follows by and large traditional patterns with a predominant role for states. This is an anomaly and reveals a lack of democratic quality.[51]

Since the inception of the U.N., NGOs have helped to enhance the representative process of standard-setting by influencing the creation and adoption of international human rights norms. Often, NGOs initiated the ideas for standards and norms, and persistently pursued them till they were adopted. NGOs were largely responsible for the drafting of the human rights provisions in the U.N. Charter and the International Bill of Rights, as well as the preeminent status these rights enjoy at the U.N.[52]

Efforts by NGOs to create human rights norms regarding recognition and protection of the freedom of religion or belief at the U.N. began as early as 1945. Forty-two NGOs lobbied to include precise, detailed provisions for the protection of freedom of religion in the U.N. Charter.[53] In the drafting process itself, Article 18 on freedom of religion or belief was written by an NGO.[54]

Besides participating in the drafting of human rights norms, NGOs monitor progress on their implementation. Throughout the protracted and complicated process of drafting a Declaration on the Elimination of all Forms of Intolerance and Discrimination Based on Religion or Belief, it was the NGOs that insisted that action should be continued on this document.[55] On January 29, 1974, for example, 23 international NGOs—a dozen of which were secular—circulated a joint statement to the Commission expressing dismay at the slow pace of the drafting of the Declaration. They urged the member states to assign the Declaration sufficient priority to allow completion of the instrument. They further recommended that a working group be established to facilitate the project. If

---

[51] See Prasad, "The Role of Non-governmental Organizations," 441; John P. Humphrey, "The U.N. Charter and the Universal Declaration of Human Rights," in E. Luard, ed., *The International Protection of Human Rights* (New York, 1967), 41-46.

[52] Roger S. Clark, "The United Nations and Religious Freedom," *New York University Journal of International Law and Policy* 11 (1978): 197, referring to Doc. 723, 1/1/A/19, 6U.N.C.I.O. Docs 705 (1945).

[53] Ibid.

[54] Liskofsky, "The U.N. Declaration," 462.

[55] U.N. doc. E/CN.4/NGO/176/1974

the NGOs had not continued to apply pressure at the U.N., the 1981 Declaration may well have fallen by the wayside.

The mandate of the U.N. Special Rapporteur on Religious Intolerance and Discrimination on Grounds of Religion or Belief is implemented with the crucial information collected from NGOs. Numerous NGOs provide information to the Special Rapporteur. Sadly, only a few of these have been secular NGOs. Amnesty International is the exception; it has submitted whole reports including information of violations of the right to freedom of religion or belief in over twenty countries.[56] This report largely consists of a compilation of information which has already appeared in different Amnesty documents and publications.[57]

Secular NGOs do continue to supply creative ideas towards strengthening existing norms. For example, in light of careful movement towards a convention, the International League for Human Rights ("The League") has suggested that the Commission and the Sub-Commission create a Working Group on Religious Freedom parallel to that of the Sub-Commission's working group on Slavery.[58] The League has proposed that, while lacking the strength of a treaty-based body, a working group would be beneficial because it could be established more quickly at the U.N. than a convention, thus, providing the norms in the 1981 Declaration greater effect by interceding with offending governments.[59]

Some of the most penetrating and thought-provoking discussions on the future of human rights norms in this field took place at the Third Meller Conference on International Law New York University School of Law in May, 1987. The conference brought together key international human rights lawyers, representing universities and law schools, and representatives of religious NGOs, governments, and human rights activists, to discuss the future direction of the 1981 U.N. Declaration. Distinguished lawyers such as Theo van Boven, Roger Clark, Torkel Opsahl, Philip Alston, Thomas Franck, and Theodore Meron agreed that careful study must occur before a Convention is considered. The publication of Donna Sullivan's conference presentation led to a three year international project to draft a Commentary on the articles of the 1981 U.N. Declaration. The proceedings of the Meller Conference have provided appropri-

---

[56] Amnesty International, Religious Intolerance Index: POL O3/03/86, Addendum.

[57] Ibid.

[58] Prepared Statement of Jerome T. Shestack, President of the International League for Human Rights, reprinted in Roger S. Clark, "United Nations Declaration on the Elimination of All Forms of Intolerance and of Discrimination Based on Religion or Belief," *Chitty's Law Journal* 31 (1983): 23, 29 .

[59] Ibid., 27.

ate U.N. bodies with a scholarly examination of what might become future international legal norms for freedom of religion. [60]

Another major effort by secular NGOs to set norms for religious freedom is "A World Report on Freedom of Thought, Conscience and Religion or Belief," being prepared by The University of Essex, Colchester, England, and Project Tandem, Inc. Minneapolis, Minnesota, for release in the fall of 1995. The Report will provide a comparative survey of the law and practice of freedom of religion or belief in at least 50 countries—setting out the evidence of intolerance and discrimination, as well as the efforts to secure greater protections for freedom of religion or belief and increased tolerance and understanding among different religions or beliefs. The Report will provide information to the U.N. that will be instrumental in ending the present lack of information and understanding of freedom of religion or belief as an internationally guaranteed right.

Lobbying National Governments. NGOs apply pressure to domestic governments, most often to ratify existing treaties or to rally support for the drafting of others. American NGOs frequently appear before various legislative committees. This lobbying effort has also been employed on behalf of the right to freedom of religion or belief. For example, at the first World Conference on Religion and Peace held in Kyoto, Japan in 1970, Sean MacBride, Secretary-General of the International Commission of Jurists, encouraged such lobbying by informing several participants that the U.N. was preparing a declaration or convention on religious freedom. He suggested that organizations and individuals represented at the assembly should put pressure on their governments to support this process of enhancing religious freedom.[61] His plea was heard; both religious and secular NGOs around the globe began lobbying their governments on behalf of the 1981 Declaration—with obvious success.

Comparable examples of lobbying for protection of religious freedom can be found in Norway and Russia. The Norwegian chapter of the International Humanist and Ethical Union, proportionately the largest humanist group in the world with 52,000 members, lobbied the Norwegian government to amend Section II of their constitution which requires the monarchy to be a member of the Evangelical Lutheran State Church. This secular NGO wants the state to base its values on fundamental human rights found in the U.N. Universal Declaration of Human Rights, which

[60] Proceedings of The Third Meller Conference on International Law, The U.N. Declaration on the Elimination of All Forms of Intolerance and of Discrimination Based on Religion or Belief: Achievements, Problems and Future Directions, New York University School of Law, May 10-12, 1987.

[61] A. Jack Homer, *WCRP: A History of the World Conference on Religion and Peace* (New York, 1993).

allows all individuals to change their religion or other belief as they so choose.[62] Similarly, in January 1994, a group of international human rights experts, representing both secular and religious organizations, wrote a critique and began lobbying to change a decision by the Russian Parliament to amend the remarkable Law on Freedom of Conscience and Religion passed by the Supreme Soviet of Russia on October 25, 1990.[63] The issue involves the "August 27 Amendment" restricting minority religions from freely organizing and operating in Russia, seemingly giving favor to the majority established religions. This group of human rights experts (which included W. Cole Durham. Jr., a law professor from a law school with a religious tradition, as well as Pieter van Dijk of the secular Netherlands Institute of Human Rights) made a thorough review of the international violations of religious freedom which would occur if the Russian Parliament passed the amendment—using as standards for their review, the General Comment on Article 18, the 1981 U.N. Declaration, the European Convention for the Protection of Human Rights and Fundamental Freedoms, and Principles 16 and 17 of the Vienna Concluding Document to the Conference on Security and Cooperation in Europe (CSCE).

Monitoring, Investigating and Reporting on Violations. NGOs monitor and investigate state compliance with the right to freedom of religion or belief to hold governments accountable for any violations of the right. They undertake in-depth investigations of abuses through fact-finding missions and research conducted at their international centers, and, generally, compile their findings in reports. Such reports are disseminated to their constituency, the media, and the U.N. to draw attention to the violations, and to "shame" governments into compliance with the 1981 Declaration. On rare occasions, reports may be presented solely to the government as a tool to spur negotiations. Such negotiations may include demands for the release of prisoners of conscience, access to victims, or to persuade the state to conform to the norms contained in the 1981 Declaration.

For example, in September, 1993, Amnesty International produced a 28 page report on religious intolerance in Saudi Arabia—a rather rare document for a secular NGO.[64] The report documents the arrest, deten-

---

[62] Glenn Ostling, "Religion, or Philosophy of Life?," *Norway Now* (April, 1994).

[63] W. Cole Durham, Jr., Lauren B. Homer, Pieter van Dijk, and John Witte, Jr., "The Future of Religious Liberty in Russia: Report of the De Burght Conference on Pending Russian Legislation Restricting Religious Liberty," *Emory International Law Review* 8(1) (Spring, 1994): 1.

[64] See Amnesty International, *Guatemala: The Human Rights Record* (New York, 1987). Earlier reports by Amnesty rarely focused on the right to freedom of religion or belief. Vio-

tion, and torture of Christian worshippers and Shi'ite Muslims. It provides an historical background to the problem and the source of the suspect Saudi laws in Shari'a. It makes various recommendations for the Saudi government to implement future protection of human rights within the country, based specially on the 1981 Declaration.[65] More recently, Amnesty issued a report released in July 1994, entitled, "Pakistan: Use and Abuse of the Blasphemy Laws."[66] A review of this study in *The Japan Times* stated that Amnesty was urging Prime Minister Benazir Bhutto to revamp Pakistan's blasphemy laws, saying they were being used to terrorize religious minorities.

Another international secular NGO has been active in producing reports exclusively on the violation of freedom of religion or belief. The International Federation of Human Rights, along with its local affiliate the Vietnam Committee on Human Rights, produced a 29 page report on the repression of Buddhists in Vietnam. The report not only documented the oppression but included the most important documents of religious dissent to have emerged out of Vietnam since April 1975. This effort is a good example of an international NGO with consultative status to the U.N. acting as a conduit through which a local NGO can present its information to the U.N. The report was presented to the 49th session of the Commission on Human Rights.[67]

With the encouragement of Project Tandem, an NGO with the sole mission of promoting the 1981 Declaration, The Minnesota Advocates for Human Rights published a report on "Human Rights in the People's Socialist Republic of Albania," which contained a lengthy section on the right to freedom of religion or belief as enunciated in the 1981 Declaration.[68] To compile this report, the Minnesota Advocates spent two years documenting human rights conditions in Albania. Its requests to conduct on-sight investigations were ignored by the government, so it compiled its information by reviewing Albanian documents and gathering secondary sources (such as videotapes and conducting personal interviews). Albania was selected because of its draconian, anti-religion laws and the lack of international scrutiny of its human rights record. The study ana-

---

lations of this right were often noted in a one to two page discussion within a two-hundred page report. Additionally, the 1981 Declaration was seldom referred to.

[65] Amnesty International, *Saudi Arabia: Religious Intolerance, The Arrest, Detention and Torture of Christian Worshippers and Shi'a Muslims* (September 14, 1993).

[66] *The Japan Times* (July 29, 1994): 7.

[67] The International Federation of Human Rights, *Vietnam: Violations of Religious Freedom and Freedom of Conscience* (February, 1993), a dossier prepared by the Vietnam Committee on Human Rights.

[68] Interview with Barbara Frey, Director of Minnesota Advocates for Human Rights (March 6, 1994).

lyzed the current legal status of religion as well as the current religious practice in Albania.[69]

Various constituencies of Human Rights Watch frequently report on the right to freedom of religion or belief in their publications. The right is typically addressed in three to four pages within a circa 200 page report or in brief newsletters. For example, Africa Watch published a report on South Africa's confrontation with Activist Churches in August 1989, and in 1993 produced two newsletters on official attacks on religious freedom in Ghana and the persecution of the Copts in Sudan. Future projects are planned to discuss the rising ethnic and religious-based conflict in Liberia and the persecution of non-Muslims in Sudan. Human Rights Watch also launched "The Project on Religion and Human Rights" in May, 1994 at a meeting in New York. Although the role of Human Rights Watch will largely focus on analysis and research on the right to religious freedom, it is clear that this Project will heavily influence the coverage of the right to freedom of religion or belief in the reports of the umbrella organizations and in subsequent issues of the Annual Human Rights Watch World Report. In this connection, Human Rights Watch is cooperating with the University of Essex and Project Tandem, Inc., by drafting a 15 page report on discrimination and intolerance in 18 of the 50 countries identified for the World Report on Freedom of Thought, Conscience, Religion or Belief.

Finally, counter-reports in response to the required periodic reports of Member-States to the U.N. Human Rights Committee will take on increasing importance for religious human rights now that the General Comment on Article 18 has been passed. In 1993, the Buraku Liberation Research Institute, Osaka, Japan, published a counter-report to the third Periodic Report to the Human Rights Committee by the Japanese Government, pursuant to the provisions of Article 40-1 (b) of the International Covenant on Civil and Political Rights (ICCPR).[70] This secular NGO has taken an active part in the formation of The Asia-Pacific Human Rights Information Center (ASPHRIC), which will open its doors in August, 1994. The Buraku Research Liberation Institute and eight other Japanese organizations, including the International Movement Against All Forms of Racial Discrimination-Japan Committee (IMADR), hosted a public meeting in Osaka, in July 1994 for country writers in the region working on the University of Essex and Project Tandem World Report.

---

[69] Minnesota Advocates for Human Rights, *Human Rights in the Socialist Republic of Albania* (January, 1990).

[70] Buraku Liberation Research Institute, *Human Rights in Japan from the Perspective of the International Covenant on Civil and Political Rights: Counter-Report to the Third Japanese Government Report* (Osaka City, 1993).

ASPHRIC is the major human rights effort in Japan, and the Osaka Workshop represented a coming together of the secular and religious NGO communities to begin serious research in the region on freedom of religion or belief.

Protecting Victims. Amnesty International protects victims of violations of the right to freedom of religion by sending quarterly newsletters to religious communities encouraging members to send airmail letters or telegrams on behalf of prisoners of conscience who are victims of religious intolerance. Greetings and messages are also sent out to detainees who would otherwise live and die in obscurity. Recently, Amnesty's Canadian section waged a three month letter-writing campaign focusing attention on human rights violations against religious people in Chad, China, Colombia, Greece, Honduras, Iraq, Vietnam, Zaire, and Rwanda. Letter-writing campaigns improve the likelihood of release for prisoners and offer additional protection by illustrating to their captors that the outside world is aware and concerned about their plight. This attention often results in better treatment afforded by their captors.

Amnesty International has also protected victims of religious intolerance by their appeals. In February 1994, for example, seven American Christian missionaries were detained for four days in China under new legislation restricting foreigners from religious activities in the country. They were released by China after Amnesty International intervened on their behalf.[71]

Another form of protection is illustrated by the actions of PEN, a secular NGO composed of writers, scholars, poets, essayists, and novelists. The organization is collecting signatures on petitions to condemn the *fatwa* against Salman Rushdie. These actions are an effort to reawaken public outrage over the death threat and encourage Islamic leaders to repeal the religious decree.[72] More recently, PEN and other secular NGOs have taken up the case of Taslima Nasrin in Bangladesh, who has been accused by her government of defaming the Muslim faith. Fundamentalist Muslims have been demanding the death penalty for her alleged blaspheming the Qur'an.[73] This case is largely a political response by the government to internal pressure within the country and, as of this writing, publicity by NGOs and others to counter such pressure has provided protection.

---

[71] Tony Walker, "China Arrests Missionaries: Protests Follow Crackdown on Foreign Christians," *Financial Times* (February 16, 1994): 6.

[72] Nadine Brozan, "Chronicle," *New York Times* (September 24, 1993): 6.

[73] John F. Burns, "The World, A Writer Hides. Her Country Winces," *New York Times* (July 31, 1994): A3.

Another program in protection for human rights is sponsored by the American Association for the Advancement of Science (AAAS). Since its inception in 1976, the Science and Human Rights Program of AAAS has taken action on behalf of more than 1,000 scientists, engineers, and health professionals in over 70 countries who have been victims of human rights abuses. Many of these cases indirectly involve the religious rights of scientists. Project Tandem has requested the assistance of the AAAS program in Science and Human Rights to identify cases of discrimination and intolerance that impact on freedom of religion or belief for its World Report.

Promoting Tolerance. All the activities discussed in the foregoing contribute to the promotion of the right to freedom of religion or belief, and of toleration. Amnesty's letter-writing campaigns educate and promote the right to freedom of religion or belief by educating the public about global violations of this basic human right and by reminding them of the need for tolerance. Reports and media attention on these issues serve a similar function. Promotion of this issue comes from holding international conferences on freedom of religion or belief, disseminating information on the 1981 Declaration, and teaching the populace about the norms contained therein.

The first conference on this subject, "the Geneva Seminar," was sponsored by the United Nations Secretariat at the Palais des Nations in Geneva in December 1994.[74] One hundred member-states, IGOs, and NGOs were invited to attend. From this two week seminar, a number of recommendations to promote the 1981 U.N. Declaration were made: (1) to establish the possibility of designating national institutions charged with promoting the Declaration; (2) to include programs on freedom of religion or belief in the ongoing activities of cultural and educational institutions; (3) to hold inter-faith dialogues among religious bodies and groups at every level; (4) to encourage the mass media to convince their audiences that religious tolerance is desirable; (5) to provide copies and translation of the Declaration and other relevant human rights instruments; (6) to urge the establishment of action programs by UNESCO, the International Labor Organization, and various IGOs and NGOs; (7) to prepare and to disseminate widely a special U.N. publication setting out the international standards on freedom of religion or belief in as many languages as possible; (8) to encourage studies by the United Nations University and other academic and research institutions on the contemporary manifestations of intolerance and discrimination based on religion or belief; (9) to develop curricula for educating teachers, tutors, and stu-

[74] United Nations G/SO/216/3 (37), ST/HR/SER.A/16, Original: English

dents for schools and institutions of all learning types, religious and secular, on all levels; (10) to encourage NGOs to initiate, develop, publish, and present proposals and projects on issues of freedom of religion or belief; and (11) to utilize the advisory services of the U.N. Centre for Human Rights to promote the Declaration.

These recommendations have borne ample fruit. The Seminar inspired an important anthology *Attitudes of Religions and Ideologies Toward the Outsider* by Leonard Swidler and Iwao Munakata (the Japanese delegate to the seminar). It inspired publication and wide distribution of the 1981 U.N. Declaration, in the six languages of the United Nations. Eight annual reports on the implementation of the 1981 U.N. Declaration have been submitted to the U.N. Commission on Human Rights by the Special Rapporteur . These began in 1987 with Mr. Angelo Vidal d'Almeida Ribeiro and have continued each year through his resignation on 18 February 1993. The newly appointed Special Rapporteur to replace Mr. Ribeiro, Mr. Abdelfattah Amor of Tunisia, submitted his first report to the Commission on 20 January, 1994.[75] These reports follow the seminal report of Arcot Krishnaswami, *Study of Discrimination in the Matter of Religious Rights and Practices* in 1960 and the excellent report by Elizabeth Odio Benito of Costa Rica.[76] Since the Geneva Seminar, religious NGOs proposed that November 25 (the date the 1981 U.N. Declaration passed the General Assembly) be set aside and proclaimed Annual Freedom of Religion or Belief Day in honor of the Declaration—with global celebrations involving the U.N., NGOs, IGOs, governments, churches, and communities. Unfortunately, ten years later, very few of these recommendations to promote freedom of religion or belief have been initiated.

Project Tandem, Inc., was organized in 1985 as an international secular NGO committed to the implementation and promotion of the 1981 U.N. Declaration. The previous year, The World Federation of United Nations Associations (WFUNA) in Geneva, Switzerland played a major role in the development of Project Tandem by allowing the present author to participate in the Geneva Seminar as their delegate. Project Tandem has hosted three international conferences—in Minneapolis, 1986, Warsaw, 1989, and New Delhi, 1991—to promote the 1981 Declaration entitled and dedicated to a single purpose: "Building Understanding and Respect Between People of Diverse Religions or Beliefs." In attendance at each of these conferences were religious leaders, government

---

[75] United Nations Economic and Social Council E/CN.4/1994/79, 20 January, 1994 (the whole series of eight reports are available from the U.N. Documentation office).

[76] Arcot Krisnaswami, United Nations Publication, Sales No. 60.XIV.2. Elizabeth Odio Benito, *Study of the Current Dimensions of the Problems of Intolerance and Discrimination on Grounds of Religion or Belief*, E/CN.4/Sub.2/1978/26.

diplomats, educators, human rights experts, artists, U.N. representatives, and NGO representatives. These diverse participants were encouraged to contribute their time, thought, and resources to implementing the right to freedom of religion or belief. The goal of the conferences was to build an educated constituency within all religions or beliefs who were willing to try to implement the 1981 Declaration within their own traditions, and that constituency seems to be growing. Secular NGO sponsors of these endeavors included the Institute of State Law of the Polish Academy of Sciences, the Norwegian Institute of Human Rights, the Anti-Discrimination Board of New South Wales, the International Service for Human Rights, and the World Federation of United Nations Associations. Both secular and religious NGOs were active in these conferences, thus bringing the two together to form a cooperative movement amongst them for the promotion of the 1981 Declaration.

In 1991 the United Nations Association (UNA) of Sri Lanka in conjunction with World Federation of United Nations Associations organized a meeting in Sri Lanka on ways a local UNA may initiate inter-belief dialogue groups, speak out on specific human rights violations and build understanding and respect between people of diverse religions and beliefs. Various others projects on the subject are being undertaken by The International League for Human Rights, one of the oldest secular human right groups,[77] The Congressional Human Rights Foundation, a secular NGO in Washington, and The International Movement Against All Forms of Discrimination and Racism (IMADR). The four major inter-faith groups in the world—the World Conference on Religion and Peace (WCRP), International Association for Religious Freedom (IARF), Temple of Understanding, and the Association for the Defense of Religious Liberty—which have been mainstays in the promotion of religious freedom, are increasing their efforts in this area by inviting secular NGOs into their events.

Conclusions and Recommendations

Secular NGOs are beginning to pay closer attention to the role of religion in conflicts all over the world. In the past, secular NGOs seldom produced a report or project exclusively on the freedom of religion or belief, a field largely left in the hands of religious NGOs. Secular NGOs tended to be wary of covering human rights abuses associated with religion. Although most, if not all, secular human rights NGOs base their mandates on the Universal Declaration of Human Rights—which in-

[77] Telephone Interview with Charles Norchi, Executive Director of the International League for Human Rights (January 20, 1994).

cludes the right to freedom of religion or belief—they have tended to dismiss the right as being outside their secular mandates. At present, secular NGOs play a varied, and often vital, role in the development, protection, and promotion of religious human rights. They have become increasingly aware of the fundamental right to freedom of religion or belief, and with this awareness have made efforts to establish norms at the U.N. regarding this right as well as contributed to the promotion and protection of these norms outside the U.N. framework. Clearly, the activism of secular NGOs has been a major factor in preventing the 1981 Declaration from simply lying on a shelf gathering dust.

The Preamble to the 1981 Declaration acknowledges that "religion or belief, for anyone who professes either, is one of the fundamental elements in his/her conception of life and that freedom of religion or belief should be fully respected and guaranteed." Given previous attitudes of NGOs towards this fundamental right, the first recommendation for secular NGOs is to take others' basic conceptions of life more seriously (including those secular NGOs with a philosophy that includes answers to ultimate questions). A global ethic of tolerance for religious human rights cannot exist without an equally respectful tolerance of non-religious beliefs. Universal acceptance of the right to all conceptions of life, whether religious, non-religious, or atheist, is the first step in reducing an increasingly violent clash of socio-political norms and values between fundamentalists of all religious persuasions and what in the West is defined as "secular humanism."

In light of this preamble, secular NGOs with practical humanist approaches should examine their mandates, realizing that actions are rarely taken in complete neutrality and that deeply-held conceptions of life, whether religious or atheist, influence decisions on a daily basis. Such an examination might lead to a richer understanding of the responsibilities of those secular NGOs holding neutral roles and a deeper respect for freedom of religion or belief as a fundamental foundation for life.

The field of religious and philosophical human rights is acutely in need of basic research. One commentator has noted that the "literature in the field is thick in reporting but thin in analysis or conceptual thinking."[78] NGOs tend to react whenever there is an emergency, rather than contemplating means of prevention or early detection of human rights abuses. Many NGOs, such as Amnesty International or The Lawyer's Committee For Human Rights, do not stress the immediacy of social analysis or reform; rather their efforts are directed at reporting atrocities and supporting victims. While these efforts are an important tool to mo-

[78] Shestack, Prepared Statement, 118.

bilize "shame" against human rights abusers and provide services to victims, research and analysis should not be ignored. As Professor Theo van Boven put it in his working paper for the U.N. Sub-Commission on Prevention of Discrimination and Protection of Minorities:

> The overall thrust of this paper is the need for solid preparatory work, on the basis of sound research and careful analysis, if it were decided to draft a further binding international instrument on freedom of religion or belief. In the drafting process, the initial input should come from experts, but government opinion should also be duly and adequately taken into account. The drafting process (assuming a binding international legal instrument on freedom of religion or belief is proposed) should be accompanied by consultation and dialogue among interested groups, organizations and movements from across a broad socio-political and religious spectrum. While full attention should be given to the need that a new instrument be consistent with existing standards and raise the level of protection, the issue of implementation merits further thought and reflection in the light of long-term approaches and solutions.[79]

It has been six years since the van Boven study. The thrust of his paper—that the issue of implementation of the 1981 U.N. Declaration merits thought and reflection in light of long-term approaches and solutions—must be taken seriously. Few people and fewer NGOs are calling for a Convention in the immediate future. Given these circumstances, recent interest in funding religious human rights studies and increased media attention to the role of religion in current ethnic and civil disputes give rise to hope that we are beginning to find the will to invest time and effort to implement the spirit of the Declaration. Work already accomplished since the 1984 Geneva seminar needs to be reviewed. Secular and religious NGOs should evaluate what has been done, coordinate their work to avoid previous mistakes and duplication of efforts, and carve out areas of expertise, each building on the knowledge and work of the other.

---

[79] E/CN.4/Sub.2/1989/32/, 11 July, 1989

The Cultivation and Protection of Religious Human Rights: The Role of the Media

JAMES FINN
Freedom Review, *New York*
Puebla Institute, Washington

In the protection and cultivation of human rights, the media play a crucial, though not, as we shall see, uncontroversial role. When we refer to the media today we refer to an array of communication systems that, in their collective strength, are truly staggering. The media comprise many avenues of dissemination: books, newspapers, journals, magazines, proceedings, documents of various kinds, tapes, cassettes, Faxes, satellite dishes, Internet, television and radio, stage, screen, happenings, museums.

One of the first distinctions to be made in discussing the media is that between the message and the messenger. The media, however impressive, remain only the agent. *How* they convey a message can be simple or a near-miracle of human ingenuity, but *what* they convey depends upon who employs them. Their remarkable strengths can be used or abused. Control of the media means control of information. When employed by totalitarian countries or authoritarian dictatorships, they can be used as an instrument of oppression against the citizens of those countries, and as an obscuring veil to hide various abuses from outside observers. In more open societies, they can be used as instruments of disclosure and exploration, an almost necessary part of any effort by an individual or organization to engage seriously in education and advocacy. In considering the media and religious rights here, we shall look at both groups, but it is with this second group of countries that we shall be most concerned.

Today, the media encircle the globe, and can reach into the smallest hamlet as well as the highest offices. They can move with the speed of the

J.D. van der Vyver and J. Witte, Jr. (eds.), Religious Human Rights in Global Perspective, 161-189.

electronic impulse or with what we might term the more stately pace of scholarly publications. They allow what is happening in one part of the world to have an almost simultaneous impact in countries half a world away. The Tiananmen Square massacre in China, for example, provided an additional powerful thrust to the revolutionary impulse in Poland. And various media have revealed to the world the murderous lengths to which the ethno-religious rivalries of a former Yugoslavia have driven the antagonists. They can disdain national boundaries, carrying messages even into countries whose rulers would rather not receive them. As one of the most immediately powerful instruments of the media, television can arouse the public attention of a vast audience and force responses from political and social leaders. It can, as it has, focus attention on human rights abuses in countries as disparate as Iraq, China, Somalia, and Haiti. The media can also add, slowly and incrementally, to a deeper and more sophisticated understanding of human rights.

Yet even as the media increase in scope, variety, technological sophistication, and complexity, they are constrained to perform their traditional tasks: to inform and entertain, to interpret and advocate. (Correspondingly, they are capable of misinforming, of boring, and of inducing complacency and lethargy.) By these means the media help shape our view of the world. They not only provide information, they provide a framework within which that information can be evaluated. More specifically, they help shape our awareness of and response to human rights and to the violation or abuse of those rights.

It has been argued—persuasively, I believe—that religious freedom is the first freedom, the keystone on which all other human rights ultimately depend. In 1978, Pope John Paul II advanced this view very forcefully in a letter to the Secretary General of the United Nations:

> Allow me to call the attention of the Assembly to the importance and the gravity of the problem still today very keenly felt and suffered. I mean the problem of religious freedom which is the basis of all other freedoms and is inseparably tied to them all by reason of that very dignity which is the human person.
>
> True freedom is the salient characteristic of humanity; it is the fount from which human dignity flows. . . .[1]

Other religious leaders have expressed this core idea in other formulations. (This view is allied with the natural law argument that grounds

---

[1] Quoted by James V. Schall, *The Church, the State and Society in the Thought of John Paul II* (Chicago, IL, 1982), 43.

human rights on the worth and dignity of the person, but it goes beyond that view in asserting the transcendental dimension of the person.) But even those who assert that religious freedom is, in philosophical and religious terms, the first freedom must acknowledge that one would not know that on the basis of the public attention given to religious rights compared to that given a number of other human rights.[2] In the world of human rights theorists, activists, and advocates most attention is given to violations based on race, gender, and class; on national, ethnic, and linguistic groupings.

It is a measure of the difficulties that lie in the path of those who take religious rights seriously that The Universal Declaration of Human Rights was completed in 1948, but that it was not until 1981, after decades of determined advocacy, that the UN Commission of Human Rights adopted the Declaration on the Elimination of all Forms of Intolerance and Discrimination Based on Religion or Belief, a document of 1,319 words. That declaration is now a useful instrument and, whatever its legal limitations, remains an international reference point for those who seek to make a case based on religious freedom. Although it does not have the force of binding law, it provides a generous but not exhaustive catalogue of religious rights. By contrast, the final document that emerged from the not altogether successful UN-sponsored World Conference on Human Rights held in Vienna in June of 1993 has only the slightest of references to religious liberty.

As is evident from the extensive range of organizations devoted to human rights—governmental and non-governmental, international, national and local, religious and secular—there are many ways in which to approach the subject. It is probable, however, that most people would associate media attention to human rights with reporting the violation of such rights. It is there that I shall begin. I shall note, first, a variety of publications, primarily religious, that, focus on human rights and then publications, primarily secular, for which human rights are only a small part of their agenda. This overview will allow a consideration of the considerable achievements of religious leaders and agencies. It will also allow, in fact it will necessitate, a look at an unhappier side, one of failure and even dereliction of duties.

---

[2] The concept of "religious human rights" has not reached definitive definition. The meaning of the phrase as used in this paper is that offered by John Witte, Jr. in his "The State of Religious Human Rights in the World: A Religious and Legal Study," *Preliminary Documents of Religious Human Rights Project* 1 (1993).

(Religious) Media and Religious Rights

An exhaustive list of publications that report only on violations of religious rights would itself be a formidable publication. Some idea of their variety may be conveyed, however, by even a highly selective list. Many of the following publications are issued by organizations as one aspect of their overall work, others are independent, with no formal ties to any organization. They are usually very clear about their religious focus, motivation and intent.

One of the most ambitious regular publications is *News Network International* (NNI). Global in its reach, this monthly reports on human rights issues that concern Christians and their institutions. A typical number reported in mid-1994 on events in twenty different countries (eight separate reports on events in China, two each in Ethiopia, Colombia, India, Poland, Iran, and Turkey) and the United Nations. Some of the items reported positive or promising actions taken by governments or other agencies, but most of them involved the violation of religious rights through acts that ran the gamut from murder, kidnapping, and bombings to undue detainment, job discrimination, and harassment. The reports are professional and provide a wide-ranging if dispiriting view of Christians under attack in every continent.

The First Freedom is published by Puebla Institute. The institute defines itself as a human rights group that focuses on freedom of religion. Founded by Roman Catholic laypeople, it "supports religious freedom for all people, of all faiths, in all parts of the world." In addition to this small quarterly, it publishes irregularly reports on violations of religious rights in particular countries. In 1994, for example, it published its sixth annual report on religious persecution in China, documenting by name and situation over 100 cases of Christians deprived of their liberties. Late in 1991, it also released a report of over one hundred pages on Vietnam, detailing the persecution there of Catholics, Evangelical Christians, Buddhists, and adherents of Hoa Hoa Buddhism and Caodism. Officials and agencies of the United States governments have relied on these various reports, which include those on Haiti, Sudan, and Nicaragua.

A number of organizations have published over extended periods of time reports that focus on a particular religion, a particular country, or a specified group of people. For example, The Aurora Foundation in California concentrates on violations of religious liberty in North Vietnam, a country that dropped out of intense international scrutiny after the end of the Vietnam war in 1975. The International Association for the Defense of Religious Liberty, based in Switzerland, publishes a quarterly journal entitled *Conscience and Liberty.* It channels much of its findings to the U.N. Human Rights Commission.

Tygodnik Powszechny, a Catholic newspaper published in Cracow under the long-time, inspired editorship of Jerzy Turowicz, called attention to violations of religious liberty under decades of Communist rule, sometimes resorting to Aesopian language. It continues under conditions of democratic freedom. *The Chronicle of the Catholic Church* in Lithuania was published continuously underground in the USSR for many years, documenting a variety of violations suffered by religious believers. For many years, *Religion in Communist Dominated Areas* (RCDA) presented information found nowhere else about persecution in countries indicated by its title. *Mensaje*, in Chile, reports on religious human rights issues with an emphasis on South America. The Zwemer Institute in California focuses on religious rights in Muslim-dominated areas, and in its publication *Islamic Assemblies* it examines, for example, Muslim views on democratic and theocratic models for national governance. A number of Jewish organizations publish a variety of material on Jewish matters, their special focus often indicated by the title of the organization, The Union of Councils for Soviet Jews and the National Conference on Soviet Jewry, for example. Both the American Jewish Committee and the American Jewish Congress are active advocates for Jews who are subject to harassment and persecution in various countries of the world, publications being one of their very effective tools. The latter organization is also represented in the World Jewish Congress.

As part of their concern with human rights generally, a number of organizations note the conditions of religious liberty and its sometime repression. These include international governmental organizations and a growing number of non-governmental organizations (NGOs). Although most of these are based in Western countries, every continent has a share of organizations that voice support for religious rights and publicize violations. These include well-known organizations such as Amnesty International; the various Watch Committees; the Human Rights Resource office of the World Council of Churches; the International Commission of Jurists; and Freedom House, which every year monitors and ranks every country in the world according to the observance of political rights and civil liberties. The Conference on Security and Cooperation in Europe (CSCE) also issues regular reports on violations of human rights. All of these organizations publish information about human rights that receive considerable attention. The findings of the organizations that have earned a reputation for accuracy and integrity are often picked up and recycled in the major media, print and electronic.

These various publications have varying degrees of influence. They give to generic violations of religious rights a local habitation and a name. They offer the necessary abstractions and statistics. But they also break through the abstractions to illuminate the human measures, often noble and heroic, of those who strive to live a life of faith in harsh and uncongenial conditions. They sometimes help to effect the release of prisoners jailed because of their attempts to proclaim and practice their religion, and to alleviate the sufferings of those still imprisoned. Even when they cannot effect a physical improvement in the lives of oppressed believers, they can help to create or strengthen a sense of solidarity, of community, among believers. They can offer prisoners the comfort of knowing that they are not forgotten. They can sustain the memory of those who have suffered and incorporate them into the history and tradition of their respective faiths.

Beyond these measures, the media can help change harsh and punitive laws. They can call to account governments with entrenched practices detrimental to religious liberty. They can challenge long-standing cultural biases and practices. They can establish ties between believers separated by time and space who can then profit from shared experience.

Employed effectively, the media can help do all this and more. If religious persecution and discrimination are world-wide, so, too, are the various media that deal with them. In open and democratic societies religious rights advocates have large access to different avenues of communication. Even in closed, totalitarian societies, personal testimony and underground writing—often little more than hastily scratched messages—have slipped through constraining forces to shine light in dark and almost impenetrable corners. And through the multiplication factor afforded by the media their messages have reached an audience in the larger outside world.

Although the work of religious advocates is, not unexpectedly, uneven, what they are able to accomplish is impressive. Based on years of working with Freedom House, I would emphasize three aspects of that work. First, in gathering the raw information which it uses to rank each country according to its observance of political rights and civil liberties, Freedom House draws upon its own team of observers, the testimony of others, and the reports of other agencies and publications. An extensive network of trustworthy sources is, therefore, essential to the early stage of the ranking process. Inevitably this process involves different countries, different political and economic systems and different cultures. The possibilities of misunderstanding are manifold.

Second, the key word here is "trustworthy." A serious error or misattribution will be enough to call into question a report that is otherwise accurate and well-balanced. To be effective, especially over an extended period, reports and analyses of human rights abuses must be dependable. There will always be critics, well-intentioned or otherwise, who will be ready to challenge accounts that show groups to which they belong in an unflattering light. Those who use findings of any human rights group to advance the cause of religious liberty must feel confident in the merit and solidity of the material they are using.

Third, leaders of countries are usually sensitive to well-publicized, well-documented reports of human rights abuses in their countries. They may deny that such abuses exist; they may say that the alleged abuses have been corrected; they may attempt to discredit the findings; they may try to explain them away; they may invoke cultural differences and therefore different standards of judging; they may say that the alleged failings are no more than those found in other countries. They may hunker down behind different strategies of denial, but almost never are they totally indifferent to the criticism.

Freedom House has learned to expect, after the publication of our annual survey of political rights and civil liberties, a surge of phone calls, letters, and personal visits from emissaries who wish to challenge our findings about their respective countries. It would be foolish to claim that the ensuing dialogue always bridges the gap or leads to a shared conclusion—or that a particular country readily changes the practices that are criticized. At a minimum, however, the exchange establishes that violations of human rights are being publicly monitored and evaluated. It also introduces the idea of human rights standards that are universal, that transcend different cultures and circumstances.

What applies to Freedom House applies, *mutatis mutandis*, to other organizations that attend to violations of human rights, including those that focus on religious rights. They will be effective to the degree that they communicate to their designated audiences well-documented and persuasive concerns about those rights and their abuses, about the flesh and blood persons whose rights are being violated.

Of Derelictions and Failures

The twentieth century has been termed the bloodiest of centuries, armed conflict and persecution having taken the lives of hundreds of millions of people and imposed cruel suffering on millions more. Many of these people suffered and died because of their religious beliefs, affiliations, and practices. In large part, the vast expansion of human rights activity has developed in response to the abuses. It should be a source of gratification for advocates of human rights that there are so many varied instruments to stem the abuses of human rights.

The record is not without its blemishes, however. Political, ideological, cultural, and religious biases have sometimes flawed otherwise good intentions and good work. In any overview of the media and the uses to which they have been put by religious leaders and organizations, these derelictions cannot be overlooked. The international political landscape has changed remarkably since the end of the last decade and so, too, has the profile of many countries where the most egregious abuses once took place. But the recent past still has much to teach us, and some few snapshots from a time when the Cold War distorted many perceptions will make this abundantly evident. The incidents are sufficiently removed in time so that they may be viewed, possibly, with a greater degree of impartiality than was evident during those years. Further, these responses took place in a political atmosphere that must be appreciated if they are to be properly evaluated. We must make an imaginative effort to recall or to appropriate the temper of the 1960s and 1970s, and even the 1980s, a remarkable period for many regions of the world. Examples are available in plenitude from many countries, but for ease of illustration I will concentrate on a small, self-contained entity—the island of Cuba.

The Cuban revolution that brought Fidel Castro to power in January, 1959 posed serious problems not only to policy makers but to religious communities in Cuba and the United States.[3] The responses of these communities were too varied to categorize easily. They were not all of a piece. However there was, first, a noticeable tendency among many church people in the United States to approach the new Cuban society sympathetically, to look with a benign eye on what was described as the Cuban experiment. Second, as the United States entered the period of the Vietnam war, its overall policies came under very skeptical review. The 1960s and 1970s constituted a period when revolution, as word and concept, was given high approbation, from European countries to North America to Asian countries. (Some people might recall that even President Richard Nixon called himself a revolutionary at that time.) As a consequence a double standard began to develop. What was not acceptable in the United States, censorship, for example, was acceptable, even necessary in a Cuba that could not allow its Revolution to be challenged. What was necessary in the United States, a black power movement, for example, had no place in Cuba, which needed unity not divisiveness.

---

[3] The loss of institutional religious strength during the first decade of the Revolution is indicated by some statistics. In 1960, there were 723 priests in Cuba and 2,225 nuns; in 1970 there were 215 priests and 161 nuns. The Protestant and Jewish communities suffered corresponding losses. However, Jorge I. Dominguez, a noted Cuba scholar, noted: "The government's antireligious policies in the 1960s made only a modest difference—it reduced the number of nominal Catholics, but not of those few who were practicing Catholics. Cuba had already become, and still remains, a largely secular society." Jorge I. Dominguez, *Cuba: Order and Revolution* (Cambridge, MA, 1978), 487.

It was in this political climate that religious commentators began to assess the conditions of the religious communities in Cuba. Late in the 1960s, *The Christian Century*, an influential Protestant journal, printed an overview of the situation in Cuba, focusing primarily on the role of intellectuals and writers. Conscious that Castro had said of intellectuals that "the one thing they cannot do is write against the Revolution" the author says: "True, freedom of expression as capitalist countries understand it does not exist in Cuba. . . . The problem goes deeper than semantics; it lies in the socio-economic basis of one's thinking. The socialist and capitalist conceptions of the world rarely intersect."[4]

Editorially, the journal applied this judgment to the churches in Cuba. On the basis of what they accurately described as meager information about religious affairs in that country, the editors concluded that churchmen there seemed to have reached an accommodation with the regime similar to that reached by the intellectuals. And they surmised that relations between the Catholic Church and the government would remain normal as long as the church confined its activities to ecclesiastical affairs.

At the beginning of the 1970s, an increasing number of United States visitors under religious auspices were admitted into Cuba. They were able to bring back much more information than had previously been available and with it a considerable amount of opinion and interpretation. In a foreword to a 1971 book on religion in Cuba, a noted theologian, Harvey Cox, offered a strong presentiment of the tone of the general commentary that was to come. Because of the United States embargo on Cuba, he wrote:

> We have been kept in ignorance. We have been told about Cuba only what we were supposed to hear. We have been fed stereotypes, horror stories, distortions, rumors, half truths, and just plain lies. This includes most of the news about religious developments and theological ideas in Cuba. Now thanks to the dogged determination of the editors of this book, we can at last read and think for ourselves. We can hear what the Christians of Cuba say, "Viva la libertad."[5]

And he then added what came to seem the obligatory coda to such observations: "In the twentieth-century edition of the Exodus story, we North Americans seem to be the Egyptians, defying the God of justice by

[4] Manuel Maldonado-Denis, "The Situation of Cuba's Intellectuals," *The Christian Century* (January 17, 1968): 80.

[5] Alice Hageman and Philip E. Wheaton, eds., *Religion in Cuba Today: A New Church in a New Society* (New York, 1971), 9.

trying to stamp out movements of human liberation wherever they appear. The news from Cuba not only tells us that this Pharonic policy is morally and religiously wrong, but it also tells us that it is futile." It is on the basis of this understanding that Cox was able to say that the book tells "of the Cuban people's liberation from colonial imprisonment, and it tells how the Christians of Cuba are freeing themselves from the oppressive religious patterns of a previous era."[6]

Other observers, representing many different Christian denominations, spoke and wrote in similar, almost euphoric, tones. In 1975, a member of the Sisters of Providence testified before subcommittees of the United States House Committee on International Relations. Speaking as both a philosopher and cultural anthropologist, she addressed herself particularly to the people of Cuba and institutionalized religion. While the post-Revolution situation is not perfect, she reported, it is "exceedingly better" than what preceded it. The same judgment, she added, can be made of the Church.

Some visitors responded to the challenge put to them by a Cuban doctor: "In Cuba we think we are distributing the loaves and fishes like Christ. Ask yourself as you visit our cities and villages, what would happen if Jesus came here, and what would happen if U.S. investors returned. Then draw your own conclusions about our revolution." Mary Lou Sohur, an administrative assistant of the United States Catholic Conference answered the question with complete confidence. The Revolution could be termed "Christian" because it fulfilled "the Christian mandate to feed the hungry, give shelter to the homeless, cure the sick, and in general to create conditions where all can participate in a more abundant life." But she added that because the Revolution that accomplished these things was Marxist it presented a challenge to the church, which had failed to do them.[7] Commentaries such as these, disseminated through the agencies with which these observers were affiliated, became the ordinary staple of many religious and some secular publications.

Although they were never completely neglected by those who brought back favorable reports about life in Cuba, questions concerning political prisoners were usually raised only to be shunted aside in favor of issues that would more readily yield positive responses. To the extent that Castro's clamp-down on information about political prisoners engendered uncertain and disparate reports, it could only be judged, in his terms, a success. His control of information not only discouraged active investigation by Cubans on the island and the United States citizens who

---

[6] Ibid., 10.

[7] Betty Medsger, "Cuban Church Identity Crisis," *The Washington Post* (January 15, 1972), "Religion Section," 20.

visited them, but it cast a shadow on all reports by exiles, dissidents, and former prisoners, whose accounts were sometimes dismissed as being sensationalized. Throughout the 1960s and early 1970s the voices of religious visitors who left praising the socialist regime provided a chorus that rose high above the relatively few voices that protested the harsh treatment meted out to the thousands and the tens of thousands in Cuban jails—men and women, young and old, literary, political and religious dissidents. Only later were we to learn that, as the Cuban expert Jorge Dominguez wrote, "Cuba's rate of political imprisonment is well above that of other authoritarian Latin American governments."[8]

In the mid-1970s, several events converged to bring more attention to the plight of prisoners in Cuba. The first was the signing of the Helsinki Final Act on 1 August 1975. The second was the initiation of improved relations between the United States and Cuba. The third was the new Carter administration. President Carter said soon after he assumed office in 1977 that the existing ties between Cuba and the United States could be strengthened but the number of political prisoners in Cuba was a stumbling block.

During the next few years, a number of influential individuals and organizations addressed themselves to the question of political prisoners in Cuba, made their own best estimates, called for the release of particular prisoners, and asked for some official response. The estimates ranged from 5,000 to 50,000, testimony to Castro's successful tactics in concealment.[9] Even as information about actual prison conditions began leaking out, visitors were bemused by official pronouncements.

In the late 1970s, a group of prominent religious leaders, influential both within and outside of their respective denominations, accepted an invitation from Cuba's Foreign Ministry. On their return Methodist Bishop James Armstrong reported publicly: "Castro insisted that no person is being held on the basis of political dissent, only because of 'crimes against the revolution,'" and, the bishop appended: "Until some kind of international inspection is permitted many questions will remain unanswered—questions that might well be answered in Cuba's favor."[10] He

---

[8] Dominguez, *Cuba: Order and Revolution*, 253-254.

[9] An array of different estimates and statements about political prisoners made during the 1970s and early 1980s was produced by Comite pro Derechos Humanos en Cuba. Entitled *The Political Prisoners in Cuba* (Madrid, undated), it contains declarations by, among others, Amnesty International, Fidel Castro, The International Rescue Committee, President Jimmy Carter, The New Democracy and Freedom, Hugh Thomas, K.S. Karol, Herbert Mathews, Romulo Betancourt, and the International Commisssion of Jurists.

[10] James Armstrong, "A Conversation with Castro," *The Christian Century* (August 31, 1977): 743.

then proceeded to defend Castro's record on human rights and Cuba's penal system compared with others in South America.[11]

During these years, the impressive number of political prisoners in Cuba included many who were jailed because of their religious beliefs and practices. A full picture of their plight and their grievous suffering emerged only slowly as different bits of testimony were added each to each. In the mid-1970s, Theodore Jacquenay, an American investigative reporter, was asked by Cubans on the island why the Organization of American States (OAS) investigated political prisoners in Chile but not in Cuba. And he was given, surreptitiously, a message smuggled out of La Cabana prison: "No arbitrariness or vileness of Castro and his system can surprise me . . . but there is something that I cannot understand. Why isn't this denounced, loud and clear, day after day, in the streets of Caracas, in the universities of Mexico, in the pulpits of churches in Scotland, on French television, in the Canadian press, in the U.N.?"[12] A later message, dated December 1979, was smuggled out of Combinado del Este prison in Havana. The rhetoric is highly religious, the accusations very direct: "1. Believers in cuban prisons to believers in other Satanic Marxist prisons. 2. Dear Brothers, 3. Greetings in the name of our king and Lord—Jesus Christ—the Alpha and Omega. Like Peter, we do not think it strange concerning the fiery trial which is upon us, but with you we rejoice. Our fellowship with Him, Head of the same precious body, is fellowship with you, as we enter together the bitter-sweet sufferings which bring glory to His name. I Peter 4:12-14. 4. As we hunger in Havana, we pray for you hungering in Moscow. 5. As we are beaten on the Isle of Pine, we pray for you beaten in Riga. 6. As we were naked in La Cabana, we pray for the sisters who were naked in Siberia. 7. As we were sick in Boniato, we pray for you sick in Bucharest. 8. As we now sit in prison in Matanzas, Las Villas, Sandino, we praise the same Jesus who visits you in Sofia, Prague and Berlin. Matthew 25: 34-40." And to show that they hear of visiting dignitaries they go on: "Sadly, some of our foreign brothers say that we have religious freedom, but their eyes are blinded during their guided visits—the blind leading the blind. . . ." This letter, which

---

11 The names of those with whom Bishop Armstrong traveled are listed in "A Report from Cuba," United Methodist Church, Dakotas Area (June, 1977). They were Alan McCoy, O.F.M., President of the Conference of Major Superiors of Men, U.S.A.; B. Davie Napier, President, Pacific School of Religion, Berkelely, California; Joy Napier, Ecumenical Peace Institute, Berkeley, California; Russell Dilley, Administrative Assistant to the Bishop, Aberdeen, South Dakota; Sydney Brown, Union Theological Seminary and Project Work, New York City; Robert McAfee Brown, Professor of Ecumenics, Union Theological Seminary, New York City. Individually and collectively their views were influential.

12 Theodore Jacqueney, "The Yellow Uniforms of Cuba," *Worldview* (New York, January, 1977): 4-9.

continues, is carefully signed by twelve people, and after their signatures are printed their names, occupations, and sometimes religious affiliation.[13]

The sudden emigration of 120,000 Cubans to the United States in 1980—the Mariel migration—also brought additional information about conditions in Cuba, including conditions about its prisons. Human rights organizations issued regular reports on violations in Cuba. In 1983, Americas Watch was highly critical and noted that human rights groups are not permitted to conduct inquiries. In the same year, Amnesty International referred by name to religious prisoners of conscience, observing that a number of Jehovah's Witnesses had been sentenced to eight years of imprisonment for religious activities. The Seventh Report (1983) of the Inter-American Commission on Human Rights stated that there was a continuing history of deliberately severe and degrading treatment of prisoners, including beatings, solitary confinement for prolonged periods, deprivation of food and water, extreme crowding, withholding of medicine, enclosure in hermetically sealed cells subject to extreme heat and cold.[14] U.S. Ambassador Richard Schifter reported to the UN's Social, Humanitarian and Cultural Committee that for 25 years Cuba has been one of the most repressive totalitarian police states in the world, and he offered graphic personal testimony of a prisoner who had been subjected to electro-shock "treatment."[15]

In June of 1984, several former Cuban prisoners and representatives of Amnesty International and Americas Watch testified before a congressional human rights subcommittee. Soon after that Presidential candidate Jesse Jackson met with Castro in Havana and attended with him a Martin Luther King memorial service at which there were about 300 representatives from churches in Cuba, the Caribbean and the United States. One report provided a rationale for the conference:

> Recognizing the influence on public opinion and politics in the U.S. by religious leaders, pro-Cuban Central American solidarity networks are reported to be seeking support from black ministers following a week-long conference of leaders of black religious, civil rights and activist groups in Havana.

---

[13] The letter continues: "We also have wolves in religious sheep's clothing who go visiting other countries deceiving the flock. Our children are placed in State atheist boarding schools. Matthew 10:22 We are not allowed to print bibles or hymn books. We are considered maniacs by the courts. Hebrew 11:36."

[14] *The Situation of Human Rights in Cuba: Seventh Report, Organization of American States* (Washington, DC, October, 1983), Doc. 29, rev 1.

[15] "Human Rights Violations in Cuba," United States Department of State, Bureau of Public Affairs (Washington, DC, December 7, 1984).

> Throughout the conference, the Cubans and their supporters applied the language of religious and spiritual liberation to armed struggles for state power by "national liberation movements." They attempted to convince ministers, pastors and lay activists that commitment to spiritual liberation meant also that they were "morally" bound to support totalitarian political movements intolerant of religious loyalties.
>
> The conference was held June 22-28, 1984, in the Methodist Church at 23rd and K Streets, in the Velado district of Havana.[16]

Jackson's appearance was one of the high points of the conference. He returned to the United States with many of the 22 American prisoners and 26 Cuban political prisoners whose release he had successfully negotiated. All of the prisoners were grateful for the intervention that led to their release, but they were skeptical of Castro's motives and, most important, they brought out with them detailed information about the wretched and debilitating conditions in which they had been forced to live for many years.

Their overlapping testimony confirmed the most horrifying descriptions of what took place in the prisons of Castro's Cuba. The testimony of Armando Valladares, who was released separately about the same time, is remarkable for a number of reasons. He had gained a world-wide reputation because of poetry he had smuggled out of the prisons. This helped gain his release after he had served 22 years of his sentence. Still bearing the scars of his own torture, he told in detail of seeing others tortured and killed; of political prisoners being executed by firing squads while crying out "Long live Christ the King"; of such prisoners being gagged after 1963; of a Protestant minister being beaten cruelly after being caught reading a Bible; of prisoners preparing to be executed refused permission to see a priest: of young boys led off to execution for opposing the regime—peacefully.[17]

All of these actions, it must be emphasized, were taking place as many religious visitors to the island were describing it in glowing terms. For our purposes, it is important to note Valladares's comment on such visitors. In an attempt to demoralize prisoners with religious beliefs, he said, the authorities would publicize every statement in support of Castro made by representatives of American churches, every favorable article written by a clergyman, every admiring tribute made by religious visitors, every comparison of Marxist accomplishment with Christian

---

16 "Cuba Courts the Black Churches," *Information Digest* (New York, August 3, 1984): 240.

17 "Inside Castro's Prisons," *Time* (August 15, 1983): 20-22.

failure. "That was worse for the Christian political prisoners than the beatings or the hunger. While we waited for the solidarity embrace from our brothers in Christ, incomprehensibly to us, those who were embraced were our tormentors." Nevertheless, he added, he could not hate his tormentors "because if man gives up his moral and religious values, or if he allows himself to be carried away by a desire to hate or for revenge, his existence loses all meaning."[18]

It may be well to add that such findings and judgments were made not only by human rights activists, former prisoners, government spokesmen, or ideological opponents of Cuba. Anticipating the twenty-fifth anniversary of the Cuban Revolution, the *Village Voice,* a radical-liberal New York weekly, published a cover story on the revolution's course to date.[19] Asserting that United States policies toward Cuba have been stupid and immoral, the writer nevertheless concludes that "Cuba is now a fully totalitarian state. . . . The Castro regime actually suppresses opposition and ideological deviation with a ruthlessness unmatched anywhere in Eastern Europe, including the Soviet Union. . . . I believe that those of us who once supported the revolution as a humanist alternative have a special obligation to say something regarding their plight. Unfortunately, too many people on the left refuse to acknowledge the victims, preferring still to celebrate the jailers."

One might expect that after such revelations and judgments, which received considerable publicity, religious visitors to Cuba might have been both more circumspect and more searching in their observations. Some were, but not enough to shift the general temper of their responses. In 1985, a dozen theological educators from seminaries across the country paid a ten-day visit to Cuba. One of these theologians was Rosemary Ruether, a well-known Catholic scholar, writer, lecturer, and teacher. She returned to report that freedom of religion is guaranteed by law in Cuba and that "the relationship between the churches and the revolution has been traumatic in the past twenty five years. But this has more to do with the failures of Christianity there than with the revolution."[20]

More recently, in February of 1993, Ambassador Richard Schifter, then the U.S. representative to the UN Human Rights Commission in Geneva, gave a statement to the Commission on the subject of religious intolerance. In Cuba, he said, "state security agents have outraged the Catholic bishops by infiltrating church services and making their arrests

[18] Ibid.

[19] Sol Stern," Cuba and Repression: Castro's Victims," *The Village Voice* 28 (49) (New York, December 6, 1983): 1ff.

[20] Rosemary Ruether, "Some Well-Guarded Secrets About the Churches in Cuba," *National Catholic Reporter* (August 30, 1985): 14-15.

during the worship service. Cuba also either bans outright or severely restricts religious schools, seminaries, church-run health clinics, the observance of religious holy days and religious media. Those protesting these restrictions have been harassed."[21] Such actions by the state were long observable to those who elected to observe them.

The religious visitors to Cuba had their counterparts, visitors to other countries that knew religious persecution. I will here add only a few more examples, some of which have been well-reported.

Billy Graham is a renowned evangelist whose international reputation commands major media attention. When he returned from a six-day visit to Moscow in early May, 1982, he expressed surprise at the critical reception that awaited him in the United States. He had, after all, carried his gospel message into the very heart of the Communist empire, engaging in one of the most remarkable crusades of his long ministry. He had prepared for the trip carefully, attended in Moscow a religious peace conference with participants from many countries and many denominations, consulted with high dignitaries of state and church, preached to many thousands of people who had crowded the churches, commanded considerable attention in the Soviet press, and had brought back good news of the religious vitality he had encountered. Why then the negative reaction?

For those who followed his trip as it was covered in the American press, the answer was at hand. Graham was reported to have dismissed references to food shortages in the Soviet Union, saying that "The meals I have had here are among the best I have ever eaten. In the United States you have to be a millionaire to have caviar, but I have had caviar with almost every meal."[22] This remark, recalling the inanities of foreign visitors who, in the 1930s, could find no evidence of hunger during that famine-ridden period, made it seem as if Graham had slipped into a time-warp. More important, however, was the picture presented by his reported comments on religious life in the Soviet Union. It differed sharply from the perceptions of informed observers and the reports of emigres.

In response to a question, Graham said that he had seen no evidence of religious repression, and that on a Saturday night he had gone "to three Orthodox Churches that were jammed to the rafters. You would

---

[21] Richard Schifter, 49th Session of the U.N. Commission on Human Rights, Item 22, (February 18, 1993).

[22] John F. Burns, *New York Times* (May 13, 1982): A1. The trip was covered extensively by the *New York Times, Washington Post, Los Angeles Times,* and many other newspapers inside and outside of the United States, and was reported on daily by the wire services of the Associated Press (AP) and United Press International (UPI) during the visit of May 7 to May 13.

never get that in [Graham's home town] Charlotte, North Carolina." Asked about the report of a woman who was arrested for unfurling during one of his services a banner calling attention to religious prisoners of conscience, Graham replied that he had not seen her. Furthermore, "I have had people coming to my services in the United States and causing disturbances and they have been taken out by the police." Pressed to evaluate religious freedom in the Soviet Union, he refused, disclaiming sufficient knowledge to make such a judgment. But he made a startling comparison between the Church of England and organized religion in Russia, implying that the latter was more free. And he did judge that both the United States and the USSR were "searching for peace, and I would not want to put one above the other."[23] When Graham returned to the States, he attempted to put these and other comments into a context in which they took on different coloration and meaning, but for many of his auditors the attempt was less than successful. Particularly for those who were interested in religious liberties in the Soviet Union, the gap between his reading and their perception of what he had accomplished in the Soviet Union was considerable.

Between Graham's experience and that of a 266-member religious delegation that subsequently visited the Soviet Union there is an eerie resemblance. In June, 1984, under the auspices of the National Council of Churches (NCC), this delegation of American Christians visited religious communities of the Soviet Union. They could not expect the major media attention given to Billy Graham, but they had at their disposal their own wide network of media outlets. Having to their general satisfaction largely accomplished their declared purposes, they were taken aback at the flurry of critical reaction that attended their return.

According to spokesmen for the NCC committee, the delegation had extensive preparation for their part in "the most ambitious project undertaken by the NCC and the churches in the Soviet Union."[24] The leaders of the delegation were selected because they were knowledgeable about the Soviet Union and Soviet Christians. All of the participants were deeply interested in "peace issues" and were eager to be bridge builders. Once in the Soviet Union, they spread out to visit churches in different parts of the country. In the Soviet press the American visitors were said to support world peace and praise religious freedom in the Soviet Union.

The accumulated experience of this large group was then mediated to the press through their leaders. As reported in news stories across the United States, they found "vital religious communities" wherever they

---

[23] UPI, Moscow, May 12, 1982.

[24] Press Release, National Council of Churches (May 22, 1984).

had gone. They praised the status of religion in the Soviet Union and criticized the United States for its role in the arms race. Asked whether church leaders in the USSR could speak out independently for disarmament as could religious leaders in the United States, they said they believed the Soviet government and the Soviet people joined in their desire for peace. When asked about demonstrators who, during a service in a Moscow church, had unfurled banners protesting religious persecution, one member of the group said he was disturbed to have religious services "interrupted by any kind of group."[25] The leader of the group, V. Bruce Rigdon, added that he believed the protestors were free and he understood "that in the United States a situation like this would have been handled by the police."[26]

About those who had suffered and were suffering for their faith, they offered scant information. This in spite of the fact that, according to a 1984 Helsinki Watch report, most of the dissenters who have died under unexplained circumstances in the Soviet Union in the previous five years have been religious activists, and that in the same year The International League for Human Rights in New York reported the persecution of unregistered religious associations and groups of the faithful. In the same year the Council of Evangelical Baptist Churches published *And Ye Visited Me*, a prisoner directory of the Evangelical Christian Baptists in the Soviet Union. Such reports were only one bit of evidence of the intense persecution religious believers were undergoing in the Soviet Union at that time. Many of those who followed in the press the reports of the NCC delegation and their often glowing statements about what they were encountering in the Soviet Union found their rare mention of religious prisoners of conscience almost incomprehensible.

The members of the NCC-sponsored group held news conferences in Moscow on June 20, 1984 and in New York on June 22. They subsequently found sympathetic audiences, but they also encountered a continuing rain of criticism. They responded in additional press conferences and in a number of individual interviews and articles. One of the most spirited defenses was offered by a leading member of the group, Alan Geyer, executive director of the NCC's Center for Theology and Public Policy in Washington. "Do not doubt that the print and electronic media of the Soviet Union are captive to the official policies of a closed authori-

---

[25] Quoted by Joshua Muravchik, *This World* 9 (Washington, DC, Fall, 1984): 31.

[26] *The American Bulletin, Czechoslovak National Council of America* (Cicero, IL, September, 1984): 3. A brief first-person account of why one person participated in the demonstration with the banners was published in "Silent Testimony of the Persecuted Church," *International Representation for the Council of Evangelical Baptist Churches of the Soviet Union, Inc.* (November, 1984): 4.

tarian society. . . . But the media of the United States, whether captive to policies, profits or plain ignorance, are too often unworthy of the trust of an 'open' and 'free' society." He then took to task for biased reporting the *New York Times*, the *Los Angeles Times*, the *Washington Post*, the *Wall Street Journal*, and *Time* magazine, two WNBC-TV editorials, and James Rudin of the American Jewish Committee. And referring to one of the issues that had stirred controversy he wrote: "There is another dimension of the peace vs. human rights agendas that any religious or political delegation to the USSR must think through carefully: It is the question of *wisdom* in how to relate the two agendas. If human rights is used as an ideological bludgeon to promote the arms race, both justice and peace are the losers."[27]

A fuller account of this and other visits to the Soviet Union under the sponsorship of the NCC would not substantially alter the overall pattern. And the pattern that emerges is very similar to that of the World Council of Churches (WCC) in its dealings with political and religious leaders of the Soviet Union during the 1970s and 1980s, a pattern that has been described as that of undue accommodation. This was also the essence of the charge that some critics brought against the NCC's use of one of the most powerful of the media.

The Church of the Russians is the title of a "religious special" broadcast by the National Broadcasting Company, Inc. (NBC) in association with the NCC. The two-part film, focused on the Russian Orthodox Church, was shown on July 17 and July 24, 1983. The Reverend Michael Bourdeaux, founder and director of Keston College and an acknowledged authority on religion in the Soviet Union, said he saw it belatedly. He described it thus:

> It was beautiful, it was glossy, it was stunning in representing the visual and even the spiritual beauty of an age-old faith, apparently untouched by 67 years of propaganda. It was also, even if not intentionally, a piece of highly damaging propaganda, all the worse for being presented by a scholar who has built himself a reputation and by being promoted by America's foremost television network.

> The film presents those aspects of the life of the Russian Orthodox which the camera saw. It does not claim to have raised awkward questions or to have investigated the inner tensions re-

[27] "The NCC Takes Another Beating," *Christianity and Crisis* (New York, October 1, 1984): 349-352, and in a letter to *The New Republic* (Washington, DC, August 26, 1985): 6. Both the NCC and the WCC were defended by William Thompson, Stated Clerk of the Presbyterian Church, USA, in *U.S. New and World Report* (October, 31, 1983): 55-56.

> sulting from state control. It is nowhere stated, for example, that Russian Orthodox believers are in prison for their religious activities or that thousands of towns and village are without churches.[28]

Bourdeaux then quotes Peter Reddaway, an expert scholar on the Soviet Union, who wrote to Grant Tinker, Chairman of NBC thus:

> The whole concept of the documentary is fatally flawed. It is, quite simply, impossible "to examine the life of the Russian Orthodox Church . . . and allow its leaders and members to speak for themselves," without devoting at least a part of the programs to the harassment, discrimination and persecution to which the Church and its members are, in certain respects, subjected. By omitting all this, Rev. Bruce Rigdon was precisely preventing many worthy members of the Church from "speaking for themselves." The moral and educational effects of the documentary can only have been profoundly damaging. First, large sections of the Russian Church were, to be frank, betrayed. And, second, the American public at large was severely misled by a large dose of propaganda in what purported to be an objective programme.[29]

Neither Bourdeaux nor Reddaway regarded as serious the standard response from the Director of Audience Services at NBC. She denied that the film was inaccurate or misleading, asserted that it was praised in the press and had won the "Religion in Media Angel Award," and urged Mr. Reddaway to evaluate it again when it was repeated on June 24 and July 1. Further exchanges followed, but no conclusive resolution was reached.

By what standards are we to analyze and evaluate the merits and failures of those religious visitors who tried to inform their fellow believers and the larger outside world about the Cuban experiment, about religion in the USSR? If we were to restrict our focus to the single issue of religious rights and their violation, we would be forced to say that, with notable exceptions, religious visitors to Cuba performed poorly. They did not overcome, and often made no attempt to overcome, the obstacles they government put in their way. They did not disclose—and sometimes refused to accept—information about the bad treatment meted out to prisoners of conscience.

But it would be unfair to focus only on the issue of religious rights, since the visitors themselves did not. Often, for a variety of reasons, they wished to bring the good news of the revolution back to their constitu-

---

[28] "The Church of the Russians," Keston News Service No. 204 (Keston College, July 19, 1994), 1.

[29] Ibid.

ents. And that good news was often put in terms of social issues: of health, education, food, housing, work, transportation, and the equitable sharing or resources. It was accepted, sometimes explicitly, more often implicitly, that these accomplishments were purchased at the cost of diminished political freedom and the partial dissolution of traditional structures and practices, specifically including those of religion.

It was highly appropriate, therefore, that these religious visitors stress that North Americans should not exploit the issue of political prisoners, or religious violations generally, in order to dismiss what they judged to be real social gains. But it was also appropriate, indeed morally obligatory, to ensure that their accounts were accurate and not, as they often were, primarily restatements of what they received from the regime and its sympathizers. And although it is undeniably true that real social gains of any country should not be dismissed or minimized because political rights are abused, even impressive social accomplishments should not be allowed to disguise the ugly reality of the inhuman treatment of prisoners of conscience.

It is also undeniably true that the declared purposes of Billy Graham and the NCC delegation were admirable: to spread the gospel message, to meet with co-religionists, to work for peace, to become bridge builders. But it is not admirable to attempt, even successfully, to do such things at the cost of the truth. And insofar as the picture of religious life in the Soviet Union that emerged from their observations was partial, incomplete, innocent of the human cost on which it rested—that picture was a distortion, a disservice to the truth. It remains, in that measure, unworthy of those who would bring religious witness to social issues. And it abuses rather than develops the marvelous strengths of the media, which transmitted faithfully that distorted picture.

The major news media, not always sensitive to nuances of religious issues, are frequently alert to differences or clashes within or between religious communities. They responded, therefore, when the then-fledgling organization, The Institute on Religion and Democracy tendered collegial criticism of the National Council of Churches and World Council of Churches for not being themselves more critical of the persecution suffered by religious believers in Eastern Europe and the Soviet Union. (At that time the WCC was a 36-year-old umbrella organization whose 300 Protestant and Orthodox denominations had more than 400 million members. A year earlier the WCC had rejected a bid to criticize strongly the incursion of Soviet troops into Afghanistan after Russian Orthodox Archbishop Kiril of Leningrad told the Sixth General Assembly of the WCC meeting in Vancouver that such criticism would imperil the Orthodox loyalty to the ecumenical movement.)

This criticism inspired articles in *Reader's Digest* and a "60 Minutes" special on CBS, which focused much widespread and unfavorable attention on some activities of these organizations. One of the strongest criticism's of the NCC came from a then-Lutheran minister, Richard John Neuhaus: "So we have religious leaders who go to countries which are massively repressive regimes in which Christians are jailed and being tortured . . . to consort with the persecutors of the church of Christ. This is evil. This is wrong. This discredits the church as social witness."[30]

This attention was not well received by either the NCC or the WCC at the time, but quite recently leaders of both organizations have acknowledged that they did not speak out clearly enough about the violation of religious human rights in some Communist countries. For example, the Rev. Laszlo Tokes, who helped ignite the revolt against the long-time dictator of Rumania, said church authorities "under the label of ecumenism successfully represented the direct interest of an inhuman, ungodly and oppressive regime—all at the expense of believers." In response, the general secretary of the WCC, Emilio Castro, acknowledged that the organization "didn't speak strongly, that is clear. That is the price we thought we needed to pay in order to help the human rights situation inside Rumania."[31] And, more forthrightly, the Reverend Joan Brown Campbell, General Secretary of the National Council of Churches, in an article in the *Washington Post,* wrote: "We did not understand the depth of the suffering of Christians under communism. And we failed to really cry out against the Communist oppression." She also added that she gave credit to those who did speak out against Communist oppression during the Cold War but received no response from the NCC.[32]

Such acknowledgments take on even greater force with the release of once-secret files. James H. Billington, a noted historian of Russia, wrote in mid-1994 the following:

> [T]he Russian Church was brutalized anew by Khruschev, who shut half of the remaining churches and most of its surviving seminaries between 1959 and 1962. The survivors were forced into a firmer support of Soviet political positions in the World Council of Churches. Recently released archival materials show that there were links between the KGB and many members of the ruling synod of the Church during the last quarter-century of communism. . . . The former metropolitan Filaret of Kiev (code name "Antonov") was a particularly compliant state servant. . . .

---

30 Kerry Ptacek, "Waging Words," *Action* (Wheaton, IL, September/October, 1983): 8.

31 "The WCC: Repentance?" *Religion and Democracy* (Washington, DC, May, 1990): 6.

32 Quoted by Diane Knippers in UPI radio commentaries, December 1993.

> The Church made a pact with power under late communism that rendered it a partial handmaiden in the continued persecution of believers.[33]

The battles of the Cold War are now in the past, open to cooler examination than they often received during that fevered period. But the present period presents conflicts no less fierce, no less difficult to cope with, on both theoretical and practical levels. For example, Sudan, the largest country in Africa, has been plagued with conflict between its majority Islamic Arabs and black Christians; reports of Burundi's violence have largely disappeared from Western media, but the violence itself has not; China's record of religious persecution remains deplorable; in the name of cultural differences, a number of Asian countries, including China, attempt to relativize human rights—and thereby justify some kinds of persecution. And there continue to be strong tensions between those who would elevate human rights as an element in foreign policies and those who would subordinate them to other considerations. Each of these issues deserves and requires the best efforts of those who are advocates of human rights. And they are not less complex or demanding than the issues once presented by Cuba and the USSR.

The Major Media and Religious Interest

To promote religious rights is to protect them. The media that human rights advocates have at their disposal are, as we noted, impressive. But those who wish to promote religious rights most effectively must also carry their story beyond their own media. In the United States that means turning to the major media, print and electronic, often referred to as the secular media. At a minimum this includes the *New York Times*, the *Washington Post*, the *Wall Street Journal*, the *Los Angeles Times*, *U.S. News and World Report*, *Time*, *Newsweek*, the three major TV networks, and Public Broadcasting System. But it also includes the many more newspapers, journals, and local TV programs across the country, whose writers, editors, and programmers will often be more empathetic to religious issues than the media elite in the East.

These media will necessarily report on and reflect what takes place within a culture—with all its informing values—of which they are a part. Since the people of the United States have been described as an incorrigibly religious people, with various indices to support that description, one might expect the media to reflect that fact. Alas, between the expectation and the reality falls the shadow—the shadow of secular indifference. Al-

---

33 "The Case for Orthodoxy," *The New Republic* (May 30, 1994): 25.

though more people attend religious services over the weekend than attend sports events, the proverbial visitor from Mars would not guess this from the media attention accorded to these two different spheres of human interest. Those who wish to see that religion and its attendant rights receive due attention in these media find their task an arduous one. The relation of religion and the secular media has a checkered history. We move here in murky waters, frequently roiled by contention, contradiction, confrontation, and simple misunderstanding. Some intimation of the difficulties faced by those who would see religion treated equitably, and competently in the mainstream media will be conveyed by a random variety of indicators.

In a book entitled *The Media Elite* (1986) the authors made the following observations:

> A distinctive characteristic of the media elite is its secular outlook. Exactly half eschew any religious affiliation. Another 14 percent are Jewish, and almost one in four (23 percent) was raised in a Jewish household. Only one in five identify as Protestant, and one in eight as Catholic. Very few are regular churchgoers. Only 8 percent go to church or synagogues weekly, and 86 percent seldom or never attend religious services.[34]

From this study the authors concluded, as a fact not a judgment, that the media elite perceived the matters they dealt with from a particular perspective, within a worldview that diminished the importance of religion. A number of media people disputed this conclusion and one study, *Bridging the Gap: Religion and the News Media*, challenged it directly. Nevertheless, the authors of the second study wrote as follows:

> Millions of Americans are attuned to spiritual matters. . . . For most people, faith is a spiritual melody that gives meaning and definition to life. . . . Yet many journalists are tone deaf. To them religion in all its complexity is either a disturbing cacophony of sound or innocuous background music easily tuned out.[35]

And again:

> To the extent that the news media unthinkingly reflect secularized culture and discount the validity of committed beliefs contrary to secular culture, coverage of religion and religious

---

[34] Stanley Rothman and Linda S. Lichter, *The Media Elite*, (New York, 1986).

[35] John Dart and Jimmy Allen, *Bridging the Gap: Religion and the News Media* (Nashville, n.d.)

> influences sinks below journalism's own standard of fairness and insightful perspective.[36]

A number of the journals and newspapers studied do have as religion news editors professionals who are highly educated and religiously sophisticated. But they work within a journalistic world in which they are a minority. It was one of these editors, Peter Steinfels of the *New York Times,* who pointed out what a secular worldview can mean. "Religion," he wrote, "remains the missing dimension of statecraft," and that "[i]t is not surprising that the index of Mr. Kissinger's new book, *Diplomacy,* a massive realist study of modern world politics, contains no entry for religion or Christianity, Judaism or Islam. Nor does it contain any entry for . . . Pope John II."[37]

The distinguished editor of a leading political journal, Owen Harries, surmised in the early 1990s that religion was destined to play only a small role in world affairs.

In his new history, *Russia Under the Bolsheviks,* Richard Pipes notes:

> In histories of the Russian Revolution, religion receives little if any attention. W.H. Chamberlain devotes to this subject fewer than five pages in a book of nearly one thousand. Other scholars (for instance, Sheila Fitzpatrick and Leonard Shapiro) ignore it altogether. . . . And yet, even if historians are secular, the people with whom they deal were in the overwhelming majority religious: in this respect, the inhabitants of what became the Soviet Union—Christians, Jews, and Muslims alike—may be said to have lived in the Middle Ages. . . . Their lives revolved around the ceremonies of the religious calendar, because these not only glorified their hard and humdrum existences but gave even the humblest of them a sense of dignity in the eyes of God, for whom all human beings are equal. . . . Next to the economic hardships, no action of Lenin's government brought greater suffering to the population at large, the so-called "masses," than the profanation of its religious beliefs, the closing of the houses of worship, and the mistreatment of the clergy.[38]

A survey of "Islam and the West" in an American edition of *The Economist* opens with the dazzling statement that "The idea, Islam, ignores the frontier that most people draw between man's inner life and his public actions, between religion and politics. . . . [I]t may . . . prove to be

---

[36] Ibid., 17.

[37] Peter Steinfels, *The New York Times* (July 15, 1994).

[38] Quoted by Hilton Kramer, "Angry History: Richard Pipes on the Bolshevik Revolution," *The New Criterion* 12(9) (May, 1994): 8.

the force that persuades other people to rediscover a connection between day-to-day life and a moral order."[39] This pseudo-observation is dazzling in its apparent incomprehension that Christianity and Judaism are historical this-world religions, that they do not sever a person's inner life from his public actions, and that both have a keen interest in the development of society, in the political order, in which their adherents must work out their salvation.

In an editorial comment on studies of the relation between religion and the media, *Commonweal*, a lay Catholic weekly stated:

> Sometimes the media show bias by omission. . . . Sometimes there are problems of cultural ignorance: *Commonweal* occasionally fields inquiries from junior staff members of newspapers or, more likely, TV shows that reveal a level of illiteracy about Catholicism and about religion that would make the devil weep. And sometimes journalists are simply dense, as in the familiar dismissal, occasionally subtle, often blatant, of Catholic opposition to abortion as rising purely out of misogyny and medievalism.[40]

In a mid-1994 edition of *World Perspectives*, Paul Marshall observed:

> The contents of the new Harvard Law School *Guide to Human Rights* lists rights to housing and food, the rights of refugees, children's rights, women rights, rights pertaining to sexual orientation, labor rights, development rights, human rights and the environment, but nothing at all on religion.
>
> The guide lists categories, bibliographies, newsletters, information services and activist organizations, but ignores the myriad of religious bodies involved in religious rights. Apparently the compilers think that religion is of marginal concern. This omission trivializes the plight of hundreds of millions of believers around the world who suffer for their faith....
>
> The role of religion is key to addressing conflict, persecution, political order and economic development. It is germane to almost every human rights question. . . . Harvard usually prides itself on

---

[39] "A Survey of Islam" *The Economist* (New York, August 6, 1994): 3.

[40] "Thin-skinned," *Commonweal* 118 (10) (May 17, 1991): 309.

setting trends. In this case a Western, secular myopia leads it askew.[41]

The Media Research Center, which regularly monitors television programming, conducted a two-part study of the television networks' news and prime time television treatment of religion in 1993. Among their primary findings are the following:

> Television news coverage of religion and controversies showed a pattern of anti-religious bias of omission and commission, including coverage of clerical sex abuse, the "religious right" and polls claiming traditional values are unpopular among the religious. Most tragically, the networks did 25 news stories on the unfounded allegations of sexual abuse against Joseph Cardinal Bernardin, based only on a 17-year-old "repressed memory."
>
> News reports on religion are numerically insignificant. Out of 18,000 stories on evening news shows, only 211 focused on religion; on morning news stories, only 197 out of 23,000 covered religion; and magazine show segments, including the Sunday morning talk shows, numbered only 18.
>
> Only 116 treatments of religion on prime television were located—a small number given that well over 1,000 hours of original entertainment programming are broadcast annually.
>
> Devoutly religious characters on prime time's dramas and sitcoms were more likely to become victims of Hollywood's anti-religious prejudice, particularly if they were Catholic. By 68 to 18 percent, the laity—not just casual churchgoers, but those who were shown as taking their faith seriously—were depicted negatively. Negative portrayals of the clergy dominated, 59 to 15 percent.[42]

Peter Steinfels is both observer and practitioner in the world of religion and the media. A veteran journalist, he is currently a religion editor of the *New York Times*. He has, over the years, also observed and written about how religious news and opinion are mediated to the public. In a keynote address to a conference devoted to this subject, he said that in the journalistic world it is generally recognized that the news media's presentation of religion is less than satisfactory. He then offered what he

---

[41] Paul Marshall, "Ignoring Religion Distorts All Human Rights," *World Perspectives* (Santa Ana, CA, July 6, 1994).

[42] "Faith in a Box: Television and Religion," *Media Research Center* (Alexandria, VA, March 24, 1994).

said are three standard explanations for this shortcoming: "First, ideology: journalists are ideologically opposed to religion or unusually influenced by negative stereotypes of most faiths and believers. Second, the three "i's": ignorance, incompetence, insufficient resources. Third, the framework of journalism itself, the working definitions of news and the practical conditions under which it is carried out."[43]

With care and nuance, Steinfels then examines these three alleged causes, noting that religion reporters whom he himself respects highly differ from him on important aspects of disputed findings. Then, acknowledging that "I cannot really quantify these matters, and of course the reality actually varies from one form of media to another and from one outlet to another within each form,"[44] he assigns responsibility roughly equally among the three named causes for the shortcomings of reporting on religious matters.

These scattered references should make crystal clear that advocates of religious human rights must be prepared to encounter in the secular news media less outright hostility or opposition than blank incomprehension. (One should not, however, discount the element of hostility completely, as the reporting on Cable News Network (CNN) has made clear more than once.) There are always exceptions to the general rule; some media personnel are themselves both informed believers and highly professional journalists, and their work is of high quality, but they too must work in a cultural world permeated by a miasma of religious indifference. Religious rights advocates must learn how to operate in this world, explaining where necessary what religious human rights are and in what various ways they can and are being violated. In a country like the United States, in which commentators often confuse the relation between religion and society with that between church and state, this is not an easy undertaking. Other countries and cultures, of course, present their own particular complicating problems and procedures. In each case the abilities of human rights advocates will be sorely tested.

Summary and Conclusions

Those who have enlisted in the struggle to protect religious freedom and persons who are persecuted in its name have given themselves to issues of the greatest seriousness. Their task is enormous. The obstacles they must encounter and the temptations they must turn aside are correspondingly great. The allure of apparently desirable political and eco-

---

[43] Peter Steinfels, "War of the World Views: Religion and the Media," Keynote address for a *Commonweal* Forum, New York, October 25, 1994 (unpublished ms.).

[44] Ibid.

nomic goals has always threatened to challenge, to assimilate, to subordinate the religious message. Yesterday, those temptations existed in now familiar forms; tomorrow, they will appear in new guises no less tempting.

Under these conditions, the media are part of the problem, but they are also a necessary part of the resolution. They must be regarded as a powerful, neutral ally that must be attended with a watchful eye.

The Impact of Religious Rules on Public Life in Germany

MARTIN HECKEL
Eberhard-Karls-Universität, Tübingen

From Unity to Plurality and Separation

The age of Constantine is over. The former unity of church and state has been dissolved.[1] After one and a half millennia, where there has been much closeness as to their respective aims, powers, institutions and criteria for membership, church and state have separated and developed into independent bodies, each with its own legal system. We can see this development all over Europe, America, Israel, and most Third World countries, save in places where the archaic system of Islamic fundamentalism prevails. In Germany, neither the Constitution of 1919 (the constitution of the Weimar Republic) nor the Constitution of 1949 (the *Grundgesetz*) have by any means brought about a revival of the "Christian Occident" and its unity of church and state. Rather, they have abolished the last remnants of what was called the "Christian State" and of the privileges of the Roman Catholic and the main Protestant churches. Ever since then the fundamental principles of German law on church and state have been separation, secularity of the state, freedom of religion,

[1] See Martin Heckel, *Gesammelte Schriften. Staat, Kirche, Recht, Geschichte*, 2 vols. (Tübingen, 1989); id. *Staat, Kirche, Kunst. Rechtsfragen kirchlicher Kulturdenkmäler* (Tübingen, 1968); id., *Korrollarien zur Säkularisierung* (Heidelberg, 1981); id., *Die theologischen Fakultäten im weltlichen Verfassungsstaat* (Tübingen, 1986); id., *Organisationsstrukturen der Theologie an der Universität* (Berlin, 1987). For a general survey and orientation in church-state law, see E. Friesenhahn & U. Scheuner (Hrsg.), *Handbuch des Staatskirchenrechts der Bundesrepublik Deutschland*, 2 vols. (Berlin, 1974-1975) (a new edition is being prepared by J. Listl and D. Pirson); J. Isensee and P. Kirchhof (Hrsg.), *Handbuch des Staatsrechts der Bundesrepublik Deutschland: Vol VI. Freiheitsrechte* (Heidelberg, 1989), esp. 369-434, 471-633.

J.D. van der Vyver and J. Witte, Jr. (eds.), Religious Human Rights in Global Perspective, 191-204.

and equal rights for all religions and religious communities within a pluralistic system.

Gone are all reminiscences of the introduction of Christianity as the exclusive state religion by Theodosius the Great in 380, of Byzantine Caesaropapism and the Roman Church State, of the imperial ecclesiastical law in the Holy Roman Germanic Empire, of Protestant church establishment with the monarch as *summus episcopus*, of the Roman Catholic idea of unity expressed during the Counter-Reformation, of the Holy Alliance of 1815 and of the guarantee of persistence of Christian state institutions in the Prussian constitution of 1850. All this is history now. No political party, including the so-called Christian parties, has ever tried to undo this. Christianity is given no precedence, let alone predominance, over other religions. Having broken with a millennium-old tradition, German law is *liberal in principle* and tries to avoid the constraints of anti-religious radicalism. Accordingly, the fundamental problems of modern legislation on church and state appear on many occasions.

Church and State: Differing and Competing

The relations between the state and religious communities in general, and with respect to present-day cultural and social policies, are complicated by many factors. I would like to mention five such complicating factors.

First, the secular state, on the one hand, and the religious communities based on transcendental beliefs, on the other, do not seem to be commensurable. The outer differences and inner divergences between these two institutions are rather deep. The *aim and function* of the secular law is to secure outward peace and earthly welfare, whereas the law of the churches serves the preaching of the word of God and supports the *Diakonie* (the organized charitable services of the church). The *legitimacy* of government is based in almost all states of the world today on the constituent power of the people. Already the early formulas of sovereignty proclaimed during the sixteenth- and seventeenth-century wars of religion were directed against ecclesiastical claims to supremacy. Religious communities, however, are based upon divine law and revelation. The *organizational structure* of the state is characterized by democratic elections, sovereignty of the people, separation of powers, rule of law, and responsible government. The organization of religious communities, however, depends on how they understand ministry, hierarchy, the *potestas jurisdictionis* and *ordinis*, the sacraments, the priesthood and pastorate, and the concept of congregations and synods. The secular and neutral law of the state is concerned with the *exterior regulation* of cultural and social issues without considering the theological question of "truth." Within the church, however, the law has always to be measured against its duty to the truth of divine revelation and to the preaching of the word of God. This means that all institutions and activities of the church are dependent on and limited by the confession of faith. Today's secular state, on the one hand, and religious communities defined by their different confessions of faith, on the other hand, appear to be deeply incommensurable, heterogeneous, and quite often incompatible.

Second, it is now widely acknowledged that the legal orders of both church and state are *not dependent* on each other, but are *basically self-coherent*. The secular state—in spite of the very general invocation of God in the preamble of the German constitution—does not derive its legitimacy from any normative theological assumption or even ecclesiastical authorization. Moreover, the law on church and state has been enacted unilaterally; it has not been negotiated with the churches. The legal power of the churches, however, is founded on a theological basis alone. This power has been simply "acknowledged" by the German state in its 1919 and 1949 constitutions, not "given," as would be the case in giving power or autonomy to local municipal law.[2] The spiritual and sacramental aspects of ecclesiastical law transcend the competencies and the tasks of the secular state. Church and state thus meet as independent entities, in ways however which are much more complex than those addressed by public international law.

Third, the legal powers of both church and state *compete* and thus create conflicts and problems of loyalty. These powers do not meet at their outer limits as the frontiers of states do, but they meet and overlap within the same human being *("idem civis et christianus")*, on the same territory (both secular and ecclesiastical), concerning the same social and cultural subject matters for which both church and state feel responsible and claim a right to legislate. Since faith and works, the commandments of God and the obedience of men, serving God and serving one's neighbor cannot be separated, a liberal constitutional order grants much freedom to religion, so that people can practice their individual and corporate religious concepts of life.[3]

Fourth, the *difference* between ecclesiastical and secular *values* also creates problems. The state as the "homeplace of all citizens"—in the words of the Federal Constitutional Court[4]— has a duty to legislate ac-

---

[2] Article 140 *Grundgesetz*, with Article 137, III *Weimar Reich Constitution*.

[3] Judgment of October 16, 1968, Bundesverfassungsgericht (German Constitutional Court) [BVerfG], W. Ger., 24 Entscheidungen des Bundesverfassungsgerichts [BVerfGE] 236 [246-252].

[4] Judgment of December 14, 1965, BVerfG, W. Ger. 19 BVerfGE 206 [216].

cording to the principles of liberty and equality without subjugating its citizens and institutions to the ideological or religious standards of some particular part of the population. In addition, the state must refrain from aligning its law with the views of a predominant *Weltanschauungspartei* or of a particular religious community. The state is, rather, obliged to adhere to the principles of non-identification,[5] of neutrality in religious and ideological matters,[6] and of parity.[7] These principles have to be upheld in all areas of the law, including the law of church and state.

Religious communities, on the other hand, have their own specific concepts of divine right and natural right, especially of the Mosaic Decalogue and the Sermon on the Mount, of creation and redemption. They have their own specific concepts of what the state should do, what the secular law should be like, what is entailed by liberty and service to God and to one's neighbor. They have their own system of religious ethics that applies to all branches of politics including culture, social allowances, economy, defense, domestic and foreign affairs. Certainly, the main Christian churches have accepted the secularity of the state and the responsibility of the "secular" for its own sphere. The claim of the medieval Christian church to world government has long been abandoned. But in the church's teaching, even this secular sphere much be aligned with and limited by theological explanations of the world as the good creation of God, on the one hand, and as a sinful world to be contained by secular power according to the commandments of God, on the other.

Fifth, it can be seen from the foregoing that *tensions* between church and state and their respective legal orders are inevitable. In matters of education, matrimonial and penal laws (think of the problem of abor-

---

[5] Judgment of March 31, 1971, BVerfG, W. Ger. 30 BVerfGE 415 [422]; Judgment of July 17, 1973, BVerfG, W. Ger. 35 BVerfGE 366 [375]; Judgment of December 17, 1975, BVerfG, W. Ger. 41 BVerfGE 29 [52]; Judgment of October 16, 1979, BVerfG, W. Ger. 52 BVerfGE 223 [237].

[6] Judgment of February 17, 1965, BVerfG, W. Ger. 18 BVerfGE 385 [386]; Judgment of April 28, 1965, BVerfG, W. Ger. 19 BVerfGE 1 [8]; Judgment of December 14, 1965, BVerfG, W. Ger. 19 BVerfGE 206 [216]; Judgment of October 16, 1968, BVerfG, W. Ger. 24 BVerfGE 236 [246]; Judgment of March 31, 1971, BVerfG, W. Ger. 30 BVerfGE 415 [422]; Judgment of October 19, 1971, BVerfG, W. Ger. 32 BVerfGE 98 [106]; Judgment of April 11, 1972, BVerfG, W. Ger. 33 BVerfGE 23 [28]; Judgment of July 17, 1973, BVerfG, W. Ger. 35 BVerfGE 366 [375]; Judgment of September 21, 1976, BVerfG, W. Ger. 42 BVerfGE 312 [330].

[7] Judgment of November 8, 1960, BVerfG, W. Ger. 12 BVerfGE 1 [4]; Judgment of February 17, 1965, BVerfG, W. Ger. 18 BVerfGE 385 [386]; Judgment of April 28, 1965, BVerfG, W. Ger. 19 BVerfGE 1 [8]; Judgment of October 4, 1965, BVerfG, W. Ger. 19 BVerfGE 129 [131]; Judgment of December 14, 1965, BVerfG, W. Ger. 19 BVerfGE 206 [216]; Judgment of October 16, 1968, BVerfG, W. Ger. 24 BVerfGE 236 [246]; Judgment of March 31, 1971, BVerfG, W. Ger. 30 BVerfGE 415 [422]; Judgment of October 19, 1971, BVerfG, W. Ger. 32 BVerfGE 98 [106]; Judgment of April 11, 1972, BVerfG, W. Ger. 33 BVerfGE 23 [28]; Judgment of July 17, 1973, BVerfG, W. Ger. 35 BVerfGE 366 [375]; Judgment of July 20, 1962, Bundesverwaltungsgericht [BVerwG], W. Ger., 14 Entscheidungen des Bundesverwaltungsgerichts [BVerwGE] 318 [322].

tion), this fact together with the different roles of the individual person leads into mostly latent, but sometimes open conflicts. The introduction of civil marriage and the enactment of the so-called liberal statutes of the *Kulturkampf* followed by the pope's declaration that they are null and void illustrate the tensions of church-state law, even more so the open suppression of religion by Nazi and communist dictatorships, which remain painful episodes.

The difference in the values and normative systems of church and state brings about a conflict of loyalties within people that have both religious and secular obligations. A good example of this conflict is that concerning the compulsory social security system that makes all members contribute financially to the killing of every third unborn human being. Even more frequent and acute than the conflict between secular duties and religious convictions is the conflict between secular liberty and religious duties. It was the state-guaranteed freedom of religion that was supposed to enable the individual to free himself from the bonds of religion and the laws of the church—by granting freedom of apostasy to the dissident and the freethinker, by destroying the religious pressure of the established church and so permitting the citizen, by virtue of secular law, to break the commandments of God and to ignore His offer of grace.

It is true that after the Second World War both the Roman Catholic Church and the main Protestant churches have come to accept democracy without reservation, abandoning fully their former support for Christian monarchies. It is also true that the modern state unreservedly acknowledges the independence and freedom of the churches and their legal orders within the framework of liberal, religion-supporting laws and within the boundaries set out in the constitution. But all this does not neutralize the fundamental differences between church and state and the tensions created thereby. They still have to be bridged or at least made tolerable by a liberal system of arrangements, skillfully worked out by critical minds.

Limits and Possibilities of Modern Church-State Law

The pluralism of religious communities—the *division of society* into different ways of thinking and believing—is the basic theological and sociological datum for all secular legislation on church and state today. The last effort to reunify religion in Germany was made by Charles V after the victory over the Smalcaldian League in 1547 by means of the Augsburg Interim. When in the *Paulskirche* Parliament of 1848 the

Bavarian *Kultusminister*[8] von Beisler suggested to unify the Roman Catholic and the Protestant Churches by a decree of the National Assembly, his proposal was ridiculed and swept aside by Ignaz von Döllinger's fulminating reply. Ever since the religious wars of the sixteenth and seventeenth centuries ended, the state has had to ensure the coexistence of different denominations, their outer, worldly peace and liberty. Religious denominations have not been able to obtain inner, spiritual peace among themselves (by reconciliation and peace with God) nor true, ecumenical freedom (out of true faith in the unity of the true church of Christ).

In a constitutional order, where there is separation of church and state, where religion is free and where independence is guaranteed to all religious communities[9] the state does *not* possess a *right to reform the Church* (*"ius reformandi"*) any more, neither in the sense of an atheistic state ideology, nor in the sense of a Roman Catholic, Protestant, or "ecumenical" denomination of whatever future kind. This prohibits the state from trying to fuse Protestant and Catholic religious education in schools or faculties of theology, teachers' education, care of souls in prisons and the military. That some would-be "progressive" claims cannot acknowledge this fact was made clear when the "ecumenical" faculty of theology in Frankfurt am Main had to be closed.[10]

The state has completely withdrawn from the theological battlefield of "truth"—the era of the "Christian State" has definitely ended. The modern state limits itself to Pilate's question. This should not be understood as cynical or as imposing non-religiosity on society, but rather as a means to take it seriously as a question and to leave it to the citizens and religious communities who may then find answers according to their religious views.

As a consequence, the modern law on church and state has been confined to a mere worldly *framework*; its interpretation is done without traditional reference to the main Christian churches. Given that the state aims to protect outer peace and freedom, it can never grasp, let alone solve, the burning problems of theology. Whenever the state supports religious communities, this is not done because of their theological "truth," nor because of the claim for absoluteness still held by some churches, as was the case when there was an established church. Rather, the state supports religious communities because of their wide-spread activities in the fields of care for the sick and elderly, education and cultural life, which therefore do not need public funding. Thus, whereas the state is strictly banned from discriminating between religious communities on

8 Minister for Culture, Education and Church Affairs.

9 See Articles 4 and 140 *Grundgesetz*, with Article 137 I, III *Weimar Reich Constitution*.

10 See Heckel, *Organisationsstrukturen der Theologie*, 13-89, esp. 35-45.

grounds of theological or ideological criteria,[11] there is no such prohibition as to treat or support them differently according to their secular performance.[12]

This constitutional principle precludes a *twofold danger*. On the one hand, liberal legislation on church and state as a free and open framework protects religion and religious communities from being *abused* by the state—as occurred in caesaropapism, in the Nazi church scheme called *"Deutsche Christen,"* or in the reign of communist "priests of peace." On the other hand, this principle defends religious communities against being disregarded and even *eliminated* from public life and the legal system in general—as is advocated in the anti-religious programs of radical separation set forth by atheistic ideologies born of the French Revolution.

This constitutional principle of pluralism is not free from difficulty, however. The *meta-juridical aporias* of the pluralistic law on church and state are very often ignored or consciously put aside. However, unless they are addressed, no legitimate, workable, and acceptable solution will be found. A number of points must be mentioned:

First, most religions' *claims of absoluteness* are incompatible with and opposed to their integration into any secular concept of competition such as the free marketplace of opinions or trade which are common in modern constitutional orders. "I am the LORD, thy God, thou shalt have no other gods before me," the Decalogue commands. For centuries, this First Commandment of the Decalogue has been the most distinguished purpose of the state and the cornerstone of the law on church and state. Is not this Commandment—from a Christian point of view—constantly and openly violated by constitutions that allow persons to dethrone the LORD God and to replace him with thousands of idols?

Second, the *truth* of divine revelation in the view of the religious communities and the close ties of their law to their respective confession of faith seems to contradict overtly the secular law on church and state that treats all denominations *equally*. Already the Holy Roman Empire left the question of "truth" undecided, *suspending* canonical jurisdiction after the Reformation.[13] Likewise, the modern state refrains from any Christian confession in its constitution and institutions.

---

11 See Articles 3 III, 4, 140 *Grundgesetz*, with Article 137 I, III, V, VII, *Weimar Reich Constitution*.

12 Martin Heckel, *Gleichheit oder Privilegien? Der Allgemeine und der besondere Gleichheitssatz im Staatskirchenrecht* (Tübingen, 1993).

13 *Augsburger Religions frieden* (1555), 2 para. 20; *Instrumentum Pacis Osnabrugense* (1648), Art. V para. 48.

Third, the religious assumption that the divine revelation and the true Church are *one and unique*, universal and incomparable, is obviously opposed to the secular law guaranteeing religious plurality, freedom and equality to all religions and making these features the basis of material and immaterial support.

Fourth, since the modern law on church and state tends to *generalize*, one might ask whether it can ever treat in a fair and just way all religious communities, despite their differences in doctrine, institutions, law and vitality.

Fifth, modern legislation in religious matters *abstracts* from the intrinsic spiritual nature of the ecclesiastical law of all churches and religious communities, regardless of their size and denomination. This makes the secular law appear superficial, pale, and hollow. How can it perceive and appreciate the deeper meanings and heterogeneous aspects of religious phenomena?

Sixth, the *transcendental nature* of the concepts of God and the transcendental foundation of the churches seem not to fit into the immanent framework of any modern constitutional order and to call into question the priority of secular law on spiritual commandments and powers.

Separation and Coordination of Church and State

Unlike communist countries, as well as France and the United States of America, Germany has developed a system of separation of church and state which is moderate and *pro-religious.* The constitution provides: "There is no established church."[14] But the demands to eliminate radically all religious elements from constitutional law, to prohibit all forms of institutional links between church and state, and to organize the churches as associations governed by private law, were rejected both in 1919 and 1949. The right to self-determination[15] enables the religious communities to have a hierarchical or episcopal constitution and to base membership on sacraments such as baptism, without being bound to the law of private associations (which could not be applied in accordance with the divine law and the hierarchical structure of the Roman Catholic Church). The German Federation as well as the *Länder* guarantee several institutional links between state and religious communities on the constitutional level. These include faculties of theology, religious education in schools, the organization of religious communities as public law corporations, church taxes, compensation for the secularization of real es-

[14] Article 140 *Grundgesetz*, with Article 137 I Weimar Reich Constitution.

[15] Article 140 *Grundgesetz*, with Article 137 III Weimar Reich Constitution.

tate, protection of monuments, church holidays, and care of souls in prisons and the military.

The German constitutional concept of separation has not been developed as a *means of conflict*, but rather as an instrument of cooperation.[16] Separation brings about emancipation. It frees the churches from state dominance. It frees the state from denominational tutelage. It frees the individual person from the bonds of confessionalism and of church establishment. Historically as well as dogmatically, separation constitutes a guarantee complimentary to religious freedom in both its "negative" and "positive" form, leaving the decision for or against religion to the individual person. Indeed, separation of church and state can be seen as the religious part of the overall and more general program of separation of state and society, of state and economics, of state and culture, as it was designed in theory by the political liberalism in the nineteenth century.

The *concept* of separation protects the churches from being incorporated into the organizational structure of the state. It keeps the state from accepting a religious confession as its own. It prohibits secular control of confessions of faith and prevents any ecclesiastical moulding of the state constitution. Separation thus leads to a division of ecclesiastical and secular administration according to their respective tasks, aims, and responsibilities. Public offices and civil rights become independent from religious confessions. Religious privileges and discrimination are banned.[17] Matrimonial and family law must be neutral in religious matters. Everybody has the unconditional right to leave the church.

The German constitution, however, does not prescribe a radical separation of church and state.[18] The prohibition of church establishment brings about an urgent need for the secular state to find ways of *coordinating and cooperating* with religious communities whenever facing religious matters in the areas of "common interest," since the modern state, unlike the former Christian state, lacks the competence to decide religious questions. No attempt to *eliminate* religion by means of discrimination may take place, because any such attempt would violate the constitution.[19] It follows, for instance, that theology has to remain part of the university, that sacred monuments must not be left to dilapidation, that religious education is available in public schools. Nevertheless, the state is bound to abstain from *falsifying* religious phenomena—by turning theology into atheistic philosophy of religion, religious education into general moral education or sacred monuments into a church museum as

---

[16] See Judgment of September 21, 1976, BVerfG, W. Ger. 42 BVerfGE 312 [330].

[17] See Articles 3 III, 140 *Grundgesetz*, with Article 136 I-IV Weimar Reich Constitution.

[18] See Article 140 *Grundgesetz*, with Article 137 I Weimar Reich Constitution.

[19] Specifically, it would violate Article 3 III and Article 4 I, II, *Grundgesetz*.

it used to be done in the Soviet Union. Wherever the state encounters religious phenomena, the views of the religious communities have to be respected, since the state lacks all religious competence. This is what was taught by the *Kulturkampf* between Bismarck and the Roman Catholic Church and the *Kirchenkampf* under the Nazi regime to our law on church and state.

New Links Between Church and State

There is a development contrary to the separation of church and state. The *ancient ties* between the Christian state and the churches have been severed since 1919, ending the state's traditional influence upon ecclesiastical legislation, appointments of church offices, and other instruments of state supervision and approval of the church. But the modern state has *overcome* the *traditional liberal* program of strict separation of state and society. We find state activity, whether by means of legislation, planning, or subsidies, in increasing areas of cultural and social life, including church activities such as Roman Catholic or Protestant hospitals, kindergartens, retirement and nursing homes, monuments of art, among other things. This resulted in a great number of *new links* between church and state, a multitude of new *"common issues"* where church and state interact in new and intense ways. Accordingly, the traditional liberal model of separation of state and society has finally proved to be outdated, in its religious aspects as well as in all others. The concept of separation of church and state, consequently, has been substantially modified.

"Separation of church and state" can no longer be understood and realized in the traditional liberal way of drawing outer boundaries between the so-called secular and so-called ecclesiastical spheres. Rather, church and state must adopt a precise and inward *sharing of competencies and responsibilities*: whenever "common issues" are concerned, the state has to confine itself to the secular and the church to the spiritual aspects of those issues. This self-restraint makes it necessary for both church and state to cooperate and coordinate their activities.

This concept is reflected in numerous statutory provisions that expressly take account of ecclesiastical principles and decisions. For instance, the appointment of a professor of theology or of a religion teacher will be done with due respect for the dogma and ethical rules of the church concerned; the same can be said as to the curriculum of religious instruction at schools, the protection of sacred monuments or questions of church membership raised by the church tax system (where the state recognizes merely ecclesiastical criteria such as baptism as decisive). The organization of hospitals or the secular planning and building laws and regulations will not neglect the spiritual needs of religious orders and sacred architecture.

Accordingly, the concept of separation of church and state has not become obsolete in these new fields of social and cultural interaction. Rather, it is newly realized in a precise separation of competences in the context of coordination and cooperation. This seems to be the only way to prevent the state from interfering with the churches' spiritual independence and, at the same time, to prevent the churches from intruding into the sphere of state authority, which, according to German constitutional law, is to be governed by the sovereignty of the people and not of the churches.[20]

The Secularization of Church-State Law

The modern law on church and state is the result of a long process of *secularization*. "Secularization" means that spiritual issues become worldly, thus transformed or even alienated from their origins, and that secular forces loosen, dissolve or even annihilate the bonds of and to faith and church. These two aspects of secularization are interwoven in many different ways and deeply influenced the history of ideas as well as constitutional and legal history. Secularization was brought about both by revolutionary changes, like the French Revolution of 1789 or the *Reichsdeputations hauptschluss* of 1803 and by a continuous process of change and transition in legal philosophy and practice.

In the course of transition from church establishment to the modern pluralistic system, all notions and terms of church-state law have been entirely deprived of their former theological and denominational meanings. The German constitution uses the term "religion" in an unspecific, general way, outlining a *framework* in which all sorts of religious beliefs and practices may fit, even atheism and anti-religious philosophies.[21] For purposes of the modern law on church and state, all theological and ecclesiastical notions like "faith," "confession," "liberty," "religious practice," "office," and "ecclesiastical property" have long lost their theological meanings of the one "true" faith and the one "true" confession.

Furthermore, the constitution does not refer to "the Church," but speaks simply of "religious communities"[22] and grants to all of them the

---

[20] Article 20 II 1 *Grundgesetz*.

[21] Articles 4 and 140 *Grundgesetz*, with Article 137 *Weimar Reich Constitution*. See Judgment of November 8, 1960, BVerfG, W. Ger. 12 BVerfGE 1 [3]; Judgment of February 5, 1991, BVerfG, W. Ger. 83 BVerfGE 341 [355-362].

[22] Article 140 *Grundgesetz*, with Article 137 I Weimar Reich Constitution.

same rights of establishment, self-determination, and the like. All of them are offered the status of corporations of public law, provided they meet some minimum sociological requirements. All are entitled to provide religious education in public schools and religious care in prisons and in the army. Basically, the same can be said of faculties of theology and the protection of sacred monuments in virtue of the principle of non-discrimination.[23]

This schematic *generalization* guarantees *equality and liberty* to all religions, bans all kinds of privileges or discriminatory practices, and prevents the secular law from being "re-confessionalized." All religious communities are treated equally, are subject to the same secular legislation,[24] and, whenever public funds are given to them, this is done according to secular, cultural, and sociological criteria, rather than theological or denominational considerations. As the Constitutional Court has held: "The state must not evaluate the belief or unbelief of its citizens,"[25] the state "does not claim any competence for decisions in religious matters"[26] or for any secular definition of any confession of faith of any religious community.[27]

Although the law on church and state has been deprived of its former religious character, this is not aimed to *eliminate* religions, as is the case in an ideology-based atheistic state. It serves rather as an instrument to ensure free religious life—but now for all religious communities. The modern state, secular and neutral in religious matters, refrains from answering the theological question of "truth," not because this question is irrelevant, but in order to leave such questions up to the citizen and the religious communities. Their search for "truth" is protected by the fundamental right of freedom of religion, which applies as a worldly framework to every individual and to every religion. By confining itself to immanent matters, the law on church and state is open to things transcendent.

Furthermore, the fact that the state *denies exclusivity* to any specific religion by granting equal rights to all religions should not be seen as a disparagement of the religious message itself. After all, it is exactly this freedom that enables all religions to claim their message to be absolute. But the state as the "homeplace of all citizens" has to guarantee freedom

---

[23] See Article 3 III *Grundgesetz*.

[24] See Article 140 *Grundgesetz*, with Article 137 I, III *Weimar Reich Constitution*.

[25] Judgment of November 8, 1960, BVerfG, W. Ger. 12 BVerfGE 1 [4]; Judgment of April 11, 1972, BVerfG, W. Ger. 33 BVerfGE 23 [29].

[26] Judgment of September 21, 1976, BVerfG, W. Ger. 42 BVerfGE 312 [330].

[27] Judgment of December 17, 1975, BVerfG, W. Ger. 41 BVerfGE 65 [84 f.]; Judgment of October 16, 1979, BVerfG, W. Ger. 52 BVerfGE 223 [237].

of belief and religious practice to all citizens and also has to protect their liberty and equality from being threatened or jeopardized by other religious communities. If the law on church and state allows the religious communities freely to preach their respective claims of absoluteness, it must at the same time make sure that they will not be in a position to exercise any undue influence on non-members.[28] In short, this relativity of the modern secular law on church and state promotes the claims to absoluteness of religious communities.

The Legal Importance of the Views of Religious Communities

The modern law on church and state can be described as a secular framework which is constantly *referring* to the religious communities to fill this frame with their respective religious contents. Thus, whereas the worldly framework is always the same, the religious contents differ. This has two consequences.

First, in the absence of any state religion, the state is confined to ensure that the aforementioned legal framework will be observed by all. This, however, is not only a right, but also a *duty* of the state. The state has to prevent the notion of "religious community" from being abused by dubious commercial enterprises calling themselves "religions" in order to escape the narrow limits of commercial, social, and competition law.[29] The state therefore must determine whether an organization or association is a religious community. The legal framework has to be constructed and *applied equally* to all persons and religious communities.[30] The notions of "faith," "confession," "religious practice," and "religious community" defined in the German Constitution,[31] therefore turn out to have only a very general and vague meaning, much like encyclopedia definitions that can be applied to many religious phenomena. This, however, is a necessary precondition to any secular and non-discriminatory legislation on church and state.

Second, it is not for the state but for the individuals and the religious communities to fill the secular legal framework with religious contents.[32]

---

[28] Judgment of December 14, 1965, BVerfG, W. Ger. 19 BVerfGE 206 [216]; Judgment of December 14, 1965, BVerfG, W. Ger. 19 BVerfGE 226 [235-242]; Judgment of December 14, 1965, BVerfG, W. Ger. 19 BVerfGE 242 [247].

[29] Judgment of February 5, 1991, BVerfG, W. Ger. 83 BVerfGE 341 [353].

[30] Judgment of October 16, 1968, BVerfG, W. Ger. 24 BVerfGE 236 [247 f.]; Judgment of February 5, 1991, BVerfG, W. Ger. 83 BVerfGE 341 [353].

[31] Articles 4 and 140 *Grundgesetz.*

[32] Judgment of October 16, 1968, BVerfG, W. Ger. 24 BVerfGE 236 [247]; Judgment of October 11, 1977, BVerfG, W. Ger. 46 BVerfGE 73 [85, 95]; Judgment of February 5, 1991, BVerfG, W. Ger. 83 BVerfGE 341 [356].

The state is bound by *their respective definitions* and understandings of their "belief," "confession," and "religious practice." The state is bound by what they regard as "their affairs" in matters of dogma and liturgy, *Diakonie* and responsibility for the world, what they define as sacraments and offices, and what they by consecration and dedication define to be ecclesiastical property. Hence, there is not only the possibility but also the need that the secular framework of the law on church and state is filled with religious content. Secularization in the modern state thus only means *secularization of the legal framework* but not of the religious contents.

In all areas of the law on church and state—including the faculties of theology, religious instruction in schools, religious training for school teachers, protection of sacral monuments, church taxes, cemeteries, welfare, holiday regulations or religious care in prisons and in the army—we find the same basic structure: the state sets up a uniform, general, and secular legal framework confining itself to the cultural and social aspects of the subject-matter concerned. The religious communities, though, rule and administer independently and variously the specifically religious aspects of the subject matter concerned.

The difference in the nature of the state, on the one hand, and the religious communities, on the other, their competition and interaction in many areas of life and society results in a very complex relationship. The secular character of the law on church and state protects the transcendent aspects of religious life. Modern legislation has freed itself from granting exclusivity to some privileged churches or denominations. And yet, in spite of this secularization, the worldly framework of the law is filled with theological content, by virtue of the state allowing all religious communities to define their faith and "their affairs" according to the way they perceive themselves. This will be respected by the state, especially as far as "common issues" are concerned, and each institution's competences and responsibilities will be carefully distinguished.

Religious Liberty in the United Kingdom

PETER CUMPER
The Nottingham Trent University

In one of his famous radio broadcasts during the Second World War, Winston Churchill commented that "religion has been a rock in the life and character of the British people upon which they have built their hopes and cast their cares."[1] Half a century later, the veracity of this statement is questionable. According to a recent British Social Attitudes Survey, only 16% of Britain's population regularly attend religious services, unlike 43% of Americans, and 78% of Irish citizens.[2] Similarly, the British are less likely to believe in God,[3] life after death,[4] heaven,[5] hell,[6] miracles[7] and the infallibility of the Bible,[8] than their contemporaries in the United States and Ireland. So even if there ever was a "golden age" of British religious zeal, it would appear to have faded.[9]

While the United Kingdom's traditional Christian denominations struggle to fill empty pews, British people can seek spiritual nourishment from a variety of new sources. The homogeneous Christian nation in which Churchill lived is now a remnant of history. The Britain which approaches the millennium is a cosmopolitan, multi-faith society. It has

[1] Prime Minister Winston Churchill, Broadcast on *BBC Radio*, March 21, 1943.

[2] *London Guardian* (November 18, 1992): 9.

[3] In Britain (GB), 69% of people believe in God, compared to 94% in the United States (USA) and 95% in the Irish Republic (Eire). Ibid.

[4] 55% (GB), 78% (USA), 80% (Eire).

[5] 54% (GB), 86% (USA), 87% (Eire).

[6] 28% (GB), 71% (USA), 53% (Eire).

[7] 45% (GB), 73% (USA), 73% (Eire).

[8] 44% (GB), 83% (USA), 78% (Eire).

[9] It may be unwise to attach too much significance to these figures. After all, "Religious statistics must . . . be viewed with caution. They tell us how many people belong to the Churches, but they do not tell us how many of them go to Church. Still less are they able to point to the strength of religion, or the place held by religious beliefs in people's hearts and minds." A.F. Sillitoe, *Britain in Figures* (Harmondsworth, 1973), 13.

J.D. van der Vyver and J. Witte, Jr. (eds.), Religious Human Rights in Global Perspective, 205-241.

been estimated that in the United Kingdom, there is currently a *community* membership of 39.0 million Christians; 0.3 million Hindus; 0.3 million Jews; 1.2 million Muslims; 0.5 million Sikhs; and 0.3 million adherents of other faiths.[10] Notwithstanding the influence of the Established Anglican Church, each of these faiths is ostensibly guaranteed religious liberty. In Britain, all religions are guaranteed freedom of worship and the right to manifest publicly their beliefs. Yet it has not always been the case. In a land which has enjoyed a reasonably stable democratic heritage, one might have assumed that the principle of religious tolerance would have had a long history in the United Kingdom. Surprisingly, this is not so. It was only in the middle of the nineteenth century that freedom of worship came to be legally guaranteed for all faiths and denominations.

The History of Religious Liberty in the United Kingdom

Early Developments. Toleration of religious difference was largely unheard of during the Middle Ages. Religious minorities had few, if any, rights or privileges. In 1290, Edward I banished all Jews from England,[11] while non-conformity with the Catholic faith was an offence under canon law.[12] The ecclesiastical authorities had considerable power, and writs for the burning of heretics were issued by the common law courts.[13] Even with the Protestant Reformation in the sixteenth century, prosecutions for heresy were common,[14] and heresy remained a capital offense until 1679.

The Protestant Reformation was a catalyst for inter-faith conflict in the British Isles. Increasingly, the Church came to be seen as an integral part of the state. The English historian W.S. Holdsworth notes that during the Tudor period, the interests of the church and state were synonymous, with the church expected to "help the state to maintain its authority and the state . . . help the church to punish non-conformists and infidels."[15] As Thomas Hobbes once wrote, the prevailing view was that "the true religion and the laws of God's kingdom are the same." This correlation of church and state interests was echoed by a British judge, Lord Sumner, as late as 1917, when he noted: "[O]urs is, and always has been,

---

[10] Peter Brierley and David Longley, eds., *United Kingdom Christian Handbook* (London, 1992/1993). It would appear that there is an active membership of 7.23 million Christians; .14 million Hindus; .11 million Jews; .99 million Muslims; .39 million Sikhs; and 1.86 million adherents of other faiths. *Social Trends* (London, 1992), 22:191.

[11] See H.S.Q. Henriques, *The Jews and the English Law* (Oxford, 1908).

[12] W.K. Jordan, *The Development of Religious Toleration in England* (Oxford, 1908), 2 vols.

[13] W.S. Holdsworth, *A History of English Law* (London, 1938), 13:402.

[14] Jordan, *The Development of Religious Toleration in England*, 1:172.

[15] Holdsworth, *A History of English Law*, 13:402.

a Christian state. The English family is built on Christian ideals, and if the national religion is not Christian, there is none."[16] Yet Lord Sumner drew an important distinction between attitudes in this and earlier centuries. He pointed out that criticism of Christianity cannot be equated with subversion, observing that in the twentieth century, "reasonable men do not apprehend the dissolution or downfall of society because religion is publicly assailed by methods not scandalous."[17]

The latter part of Sumner's statement is certainly true today. Four hundred years ago, however, things were radically different. At that time, toleration of religious diversity was unknown. It was believed that religious dissent threatened to undermine society and that minority faiths constituted a threat to the very existence of the state. Such fears led to a series of statutes. Legal penalties imposed on Roman Catholics included the Test Acts, while the rights of Protestant dissenters were restricted by the Clarendon Code. The net effect of this legislation was that all holders of municipal office had to receive the sacrament of the Church of England, the celebration of mass became a crime, unofficial religious meetings of more than five people were made illegal, and all Members of Parliament and teachers were forced to swear an oath accepting the King as the Head of the English Church.[18] Thus the law was used as the tool for controlling religious unorthodoxy.

Restrictions on Roman Catholics. The Recusancy legislation, penalizing "recusants" (those who refused to attend Church of England services) obviously affected dissenting Protestants, "but the legislation was clearly aimed at Catholics."[19] In 1548, legislation was enacted stipulating that only the Anglican Book of Common Prayer could be used in church services.[20] Two years later, failure to attend Anglican services was made a crime. An Act in 1551 required that each Sunday, everyone "shall diligently and faithfully, (having no lawful or reasonable excuse to be absent), endeavor themselves to report to their Parish Church or Chapel."[21] The Act of Uniformity of 1559 imposed a range of punishments on those who failed to attend Anglican services. Fines of 12 pence were levied on recusants who missed a Sunday or holy day,[22] while an absence of a month could lead to a fine of 20 pounds, forfeiture of all possessions, and

16 *Bowman v Secular Society* [1917] AC 406 House of Lords.

17 Ibid., 473.

18 See Reid Mortensen, "Establishment and Toleration: The British Pattern of Secularism," *University of Queensland Law Journal* 17(2) (1993): 187.

19 Ibid.

20 2 & 3 Edw. 6 c 1.

21 5 & 6 Edw. 6 c 2.

22 S 14, 3 Jac. 1 c 4.

two-thirds of all lands.[23] An Act of 1592 even provided that failure to attend church without lawful excuse could lead to imprisonment, exile, or death.[24]

This legislation, which ensured a high rate of church attendance, was supplemented by measures which interfered with the educational, professional, and civic privileges of Roman Catholics. Recusant school teachers were ineligible for employment,[25] and it was even an offense for Roman Catholic parents to send their children to school on the continent of Europe.[26] A recusant was forbidden to practice law or medicine, to enter public life, or to hold a public office.[27] Most menacingly, it was a capital offence to convert others, or oneself be a convert to Catholicism.[28]

Other penalties imposed on Catholics included the Test Acts. Under the First Test Act of 1673, employees and officers of the Crown had to swear an oath of allegiance set out in the Recusancy Act of 1606, take the Anglican Eucharist, and declare that they rejected the doctrine of transubstantiation.[29] These tests have been criticized as "absurd and odious,"[30] but in 1678, in response to public fears of Catholicism, Parliament passed the Second Test Act. This effectively banned Roman Catholics from sitting in either the House of Commons or the House of Lords. Members of Parliament were required to deny the doctrine of transubstantiation and to reject the deity of Mary.[31] Even James, the Duke of York, then heir to the throne who had converted to Catholicism in 1668, only avoided being penalized by a majority of 2 votes in the House of Commons.[32]

James's 1685 succession to the throne as James II of England and James VI of Scotland is a crucial date in English history. It precipitated the crisis which ultimately led to the *Glorious Revolution*. Eager to repeal the restrictions on his fellow Roman Catholics, James sought to use the Royal Prerogative powers to dispense with the operation of the First Test Act of 1673.[33] Furthermore, in an effort to forge an alliance between Roman Catholics and Protestant dissenters, James issued an edict guaranteeing the free exercise of religion. His gamble failed. The Indulgence

---

[23] 25 ch. 2 c 2.

[24] S 1, 35 Eliz. 1, c 1.

[25] S 5, 23 Eliz, 1 c l.

[26] S 5, 27 Eliz. 1 c 1.

[27] SS 6 and 7, 3 Jac.1 c 5.

[28] S1, 23 Eliz. 1 c 1.

[29] 25 ch. 2 c 2.

[30] T.B. Macaulay, *The History of England* (Harmondsworth, 1979), 457.

[31] 30 ch.2 c 1.

[32] J.P. Kenyon, *The Stuart Constitution 1603-1688* (Cambridge, 1966), 452.

[33] *Godden v Hales* [1686] 2 Show K.B. 475.

which James ordered to be read in all parish churches in 1688 provoked the wrath of the Anglican clergy. Most significantly it also failed to win him non-conformist Protestant support. Dissenting Protestants were deeply suspicious of James's pro-Catholic sympathies. Their refusal to align themselves with the Stuart king and their support of the Established Church were key factors in William and Mary's replacing of James on the throne in 1688. The Toleration Act, which was immediately enacted, was in large part designed to reward Protestant dissenters for their loyalty. A corollary of this was that Catholics would be forced to wait another fourteen years before they could enjoy complete freedom of worship.

Restrictions on Protestant Dissenters. As noted, Protestant dissenters were also affected by the Recusancy Legislation. It was the Clarendon Code, however, a term used for a series of Acts passed between 1661-1670, which was the main vehicle used for controlling Protestant dissent. This included the Corporation Act of 1661,[34] which prohibited from public office anyone who refused to take the Eucharist in accordance with the rites of the Church of England within one year of election. Similarly, restrictions were placed on freedom of assembly. The Conventicle Act of 1664 made it an offense to attend a non-Anglican religious gathering of five persons or more.[35] The Act imposed a fine of 100 pounds, or transportation for seven years, on a third conviction. The following year, under the Five Mile Act, dissenting preachers were forbidden from coming within five miles of a town or parish without swearing that it was unlawful to bear arms against the King.[36] Dissenters were also prohibited from teaching or preaching in schools and in public meetings, a ban which led to the City of London's prosecution of the Quaker, William Penn.[37]

In the 1670s and 1680s, such restrictions on Protestant non-conformists were eased. Hostility was diverted away from Protestant dissenters to Roman Catholics, particularly after the Popish Plot of 1678 aroused public fears of Catholic sedition. Reflective of this change of mood were the Parliamentary debates on a Toleration Bill, which was later the framework for the Toleration Act of 1689.[38] It has been claimed that "the very origins of the secular state in the English speaking world lie in the success Protestant dissenters had in their struggle for religious

---

34 13 Ch. 22 st 2 c 1.

35 16 Ch. 2 c 4.

36 17 Ch.2 c 2.

37 *R v Penn & Mead* (1670) 6 St. Tr. 951.

38 1 Will and Mar. c 18.

freedom."[39] The immediate consequences of the Toleration Act were less radical and more modest.

The Toleration Act 1689 and Subsequent Reforms. The grandiose title of the 1689 Toleration Act is misleading. The Act only applied to Protestant non-conformists who believed in the Trinity.[40] Their meetings for worship were legalized, so long as they were not held behind locked doors[41] and their places of worship were formally registered.[42] The influence of the Established Church remained considerable, and Protestant non-conformists turned to the courts to enforce the Act. In *Green v Pope*,[43] for example, dissenters were forced to obtain an order of mandamus after the Bishop of Chester's registrar failed to license their meeting place. Yet, English judges were initially reluctant to interpret the Act generously,[44] and it was not until the middle of the eighteenth century that even the limited freedoms of the Toleration Act were fully realized.[45]

The 1689 Act is significant in that it established the principle of exemption from a legal penalty on grounds of belief.[46] The Act failed to protect Catholics, however.[47] On the contrary, contemporary events and the *Glorious Revolution* of 1688, which brought William and Mary to the throne, culminated in Catholicism being viewed as synonymous with treason.[48] Anti-Catholic measures remained in place after passage of the Toleration Act.[49] The Recusancy legislation was only repealed by the Catholic Relief Acts of 1778 and 1791, and it was not until 1832 that other penalties against Catholics were removed.[50] Similar legislation was

---

39 Mortensen, "Establishment and Toleration," 192.

40 See E.N. Williams, *A Documentary History of England* (Harmondsworth, 1965), vol. 2, chap. 7.

41 Toleration Act 1689, section 5.

42 Ibid., s 19.

43 (1696) 1 Ld. Raym. 127.

44 See Lord Harcourt LC in *AG v Eades* (1713) 2 Ves Sen 274N.

45 See the opinions of Lord Mansfield, C.J. and Foster, J. in *R v Barker* (1762) 3 Burr. 1265.

46 A. Bradney, *Religions, Rights and Laws* (Leicester, 1993), 6.

47 Toleration Act, 1689, s 17. The 1689 Act benefitted Presbyterians, Baptists, and Quakers. In 1792, these rights were extended to Lutherans by *R v Hube* [1792 Peake 179]. However Catholicism and Unitarianism remained illegal.

48 See Holdsworth, *A History of English Law,* 6:201-2.

49 Catholics were still forbidden form working as teachers, could only hold land in limited cases, and continued to be liable to pay penalties for not attending Church of England services.

50 Roman Catholic Charities Act 1832. This followed on from the Roman Catholic Emancipation Act 1829, which increased the rights of Catholics to worship. Thus Catholics could vote, own property, sit in Parliament, and were relieved from the requirement of taking special oaths. The Religious Disabilities Act 1846 removed most remaining restrictions on non-conformists and Roman Catholics.

passed in the mid-nineteenth century granting Unitarians[51] and Jews[52] freedom of worship, while in 1855 certain curbs on religious services with more than twenty people were lifted.[53] Today, Roman Catholics enjoy complete freedom of worship, but the British Constitution's historical antipathy to Catholicism has resulted in some curious anomalies. Catholic priests are still ineligible to sit in the House of Commons,[54] while Catholic bishops (unlike 26 of their Anglican contemporaries), have no right to sit in the House of Lords. It was only in 1974 that the office of Lord Chancellor was formally opened to a Roman Catholic.[55] The Sovereign is still prohibited from marrying a Roman Catholic.[56] These and other minor restrictions on Roman Catholics[57] once prompted the most senior Roman Catholic cleric in England, Cardinal Basil Hume, to comment: "I'd quite cheerfully remain a second class citizen; it doesn't worry me."[58] It is unlikely that Hume's nonchalance is shared by many of his fellow Catholics, particularly those in Northern Ireland.

The Present Position. Religious liberty evolved slowly in the United Kingdom.[59] Today its legal basis is still a series of seventeenth and eighteenth century statutes. This piecemeal process is in part due to the absence of a written constitution in the United Kingdom. Unlike the United States, where the "free exercise" of religion is enshrined in the First Amendment to the Constitution,[60] the United Kingdom lacks any law which positively asserts a general right to the free exercise of religion.

---

[51] Unitarians Relief Act 1813. See also *R v Waddington* (1823) 1B&C 26 1St. Tr (NS) 1339, and *Shore v Wilson* (1839-42) 9 CL&F 355.

[52] The Jewish Relief Act 1845 enabled Jews to hold public office.

[53] Liberty of Religious Worship Act 1855.

[54] House of Commons (Clergy Disqualification) Act 1801 and the Roman Catholic Relief Act 1829, s 9. It should also be noted that clergy who have been Episcopally ordained in the Church of England and the Church of Ireland are also disqualified from sitting and voting in the House of Commons. However under the Clerical Disabilities Act 1870, an Anglican clergyman may relinquish the rights and privileges of his office and become eligible for the Commons.

[55] Lord Chancellor (Tenure of Office and Discharge of Ecclesiastical Functions) Act 1974. The Lord Chancellor's duties are multifarious. He is the head of the judiciary, a Cabinet Minister, and speaker of the House of Lords. See R.F.V. Heuston, *Lives of the Lord Chancellors 1885-1940* (Oxford, 1987), introduction.

[56] The Act of Settlement 1701 s 2.

[57] See E.G. Moore *An Introduction to English Canon Law* (Oxford, 1967), 161-2.

[58] "Charles and the Church," *The Sydney Morning Herald* (June 28, 1994).

[59] For the history of religious liberty in Scotland see W.L. Mathieson, *Politics and Religion: A Study in Scottish History From the Reformation to the Revolution* (Glasgow, 1902).

[60] See Arlin M. Adams and Charles J. Emmerich, *A Nation Dedicated to Religious Liberty: The Constitutional Heritage of the Religion Clauses* (Philadelphia, 1990) and Gregg Ivers *Lowering the Wall: Religion and the Supreme Court in the 1980s* (New York, 1991). It has been claimed that it was the "English traditions of dissent which directly influenced, more than any other source, the American struggle for religious liberty and the separation of church and state."

Of course, the United Kingdom is a party to international treaties which contain guarantees of freedom of religion, most notably the 1950 European Convention on Human Rights (ECHR),[61] and the 1966 International Covenant on Civil and Political Rights (ICCPR).[62] These documents require contracting states to guarantee freedom of "thought, conscience and religion," including the freedom to change or adopt religion or belief, as well as an individual's freedom "either alone or in conformity with others and in public or private, to manifest his religion or belief in worship, teaching, practice or observance."[63] Both treaties, however, permit signatories to impose legal limitations upon the manifestation of religion, to the extent that these are required for public safety, for the protection of public order, health, or morals, or for the protection of the rights and freedoms of others.[64] The ECHR and the ICCPR have only "treaty" status in British law.[65] The House of Lords, the United Kingdom's highest court, has held that a treaty cannot alter British law, unless it has been incorporated into British law by an Act of Parliament.[66] Neither the ECHR nor the ICCPR have been so incorporated.[67]

Notwithstanding several unsuccessful attempts to pass such an Act, the ECHR Act and the ICCPR are influential in the United Kingdom. First, both the ECHR and the ICCPR can be used by the courts as an aid

---

James E. Wood, Jr., "Editorial: Church and State in England," *Journal of Church and State* 9 (3) (1967): 305, 307.

[61] The ECHR was signed on 4 November 1950, and entered into force in September 1953. The United Kingdom signed and ratified the ECHR in 1965. See generally R. Beddard, *Human Rights and Europe* (Cambridge, 1993).

[62] The ICCPR was adopted in 1966 and entered into force in 1976. See M. Nowak, *UN Covenant on Civil and Political Rights: CCPR Commentary* (Kehl a Rhein, 1993).

[63] Article 9(1) ECHR and Article 18(1) ICCPR.

[64] Article 9(2) ECHR and Article 18(3) ICCPR.

[65] See the judgment of Sir Robert Phillimore in *The Parliament Belge* (1878-9) 4 P.D. 129.

[66] *J H Rayner (Mincing Lane) Ltd v Department of Trade and Industry* [1989] 3 WLR 969. Lord Oliver considered it "axiomatic that municipal courts have not and cannot have the competence to adjudicate upon or enforce the rights arising out of transactions entered into by independent states by themselves on the plane of international law" and concluded that a treaty is "outside the purview of the court". Ibid., 1001H and 1002E.

[67] In *R v Sec of State, ex parte Brind* [1991] 2 WLR 558, Lord Ackner declared: "The [European] Convention which is contained in an international treaty to which the United Kingdom is a party has not been incorporated into English domestic law." In 1978 a select committee of the House of Lords was divided as to whether the United Kingdom should have a new Bill of Rights. However it was unanimous that if a new Bill was desirable, it should be enacted in the form of incorporating the ECHR into British Law: *HL 176 (1977-78)* The Institute for Public Policy Research, (Constitution Paper No.1: *A British Bill of Rights*, London, 1990) has drafted its own Bill of Rights, which builds upon both the ECHR and the ICCPR. The case for the incorporation of the ICCPR into British law is put in D. Harris and S. Joseph, eds., *The International Covenant on Civil and Political Rights and the United Kingdom* (Oxford, 1995), chap. 1.

to statutory interpretation. The presumption that Parliament intends to legislate consistently with the United Kingdom's treaty obligations means that the provisions of an unincorporated treaty are applicable to resolve ambiguity in any subsequent legislation.[68] Second, opinions of the ECHR's and ICCPR's chief organs of implementation, the European Court of Human Rights[69] and the United Nations Human Rights Committee[70] are politically persuasive. Although neither treaty is legally binding in the United Kingdom, it would be naive to underestimate their political influence. Certainly, minority faiths, suspicious of the secular nature of contemporary British society and the traditional influence of the Established Church, have availed themselves (albeit so far largely unsuccessfully) of these international remedies.[71] Thus it would appear that, in the absence of a United Kingdom Bill of Rights, these international standards will increasingly be relied upon by those who claim that British law fails to take cognizance of their faith.[72]

The Constitutional Position of the Church of England[73]

Establishment. It has been suggested that "the relationship between the state and religion in modern secular states is regulated by two principles: the separation of the state and religion, and the freedom of religion."[74] A case in point is the United States. It reflects both principles. The principle of freedom of religion is satisfied by the First Amendment's prohibition that "Congress shall make no law respecting an establishment of religion, or prohibiting the free exercise thereof." This has been

---

68 Bills seeking to incorporate the ECHR into British law have been passed in the House of Lords, but rejected by the House of Commons: see HL Bill 54 (1980-81); HL Deb, 5 December 1980 col 533; 3 February 1981, col 1102; HC Deb, 8 May 1981, col 419. Also see HC Bill 73 (1983-84), and HC Bill 39 (1990-91).

69 Lord Ackner in *R v Sec of State, ex parte Brind* [1991] 2 WLR 588 ("It is well settled that the European Convention may be deployed for the purpose of the resolution of an ambiguity in English primary or subordinate legislation"). See also *Derbyshire CC v Times Newspapers Ltd.*, [1992] 1 QB 770, where the English Court of Appeal relied heavily on Article 10 of the ECHR to decide that a local authority could not sue in libel.

70 See Harris and Joseph, eds., *The International Covenant on Civil and Political Rights and the United Kingdom*, chap. 1.

71 On the ECHR see, e.g., *Choudhury v U K*, (1991) 12 HRLJ 172. No such similar cases have been brought under the ICCPR, since the United Kingdom has refused to extend the right of petition to individual applicants. Harris and Joseph, eds., *The International Covenant on Civil and Political Rights and the United Kingdom*, chap. 1.

72 See e.g. *The Need for Reform*, Memorandum submitted by U K Action Committee on Islamic Affairs (UKACIA) to the Home Secretary (April 1993), 17.

73 On the Church of Scotland, see T.B. Smith, *A Short Commentary on the Church of Scotland* (Edinburgh, 1962).

74 W. Sadurski, *Moral Pluralism and Legal Neutrality* (Dordrecht/Boston, 1990), 167.

interpreted as meaning that "no person can be punished for entertaining or professing religious beliefs or disbeliefs, for church attendance."[75] The principle of separation of the state and religion is met by the constitutional prohibition of the establishment of religion by law. As Justice Black observed, the Establishment Clause "means at least this: neither a State nor the Federal Government can set up a church."[76] Thus, in the United States the "clause against the establishment of religion by law was intended to erect a wall of separation between church and state."[77] By contrast, in the United Kingdom only the principle of freedom of religion is satisfied; there is no separation of religion and the state.[78]

Religious liberty is certainly a quintessential element of life in contemporary Britain. Individuals enjoy freedom of worship, while members of religious groups may construct, manage, and register their own religious buildings,[79] celebrate their own religious festivals, worship freely in prison,[80] and swear their distinctive oaths in judicial proceedings.[81] *The London Times* has observed that "among those things which are held to be self-evident in British society is the principle that there should be no coercion in matters of religion."[82] Thus it is ironic that the only person who is not free to change his or her religion is the monarch. The Sovereign is the Head of the Church of England.[83] As "Supreme Governor"[84] of the Established Church, the sovereign must be a communicant of the Church of England, must pledge to uphold the Protestant succession to the throne, and is forbidden from marrying a Roman Catholic.[85] Therefore in 1978 the Queen's cousin, Prince Michael of Kent, publicly renounced his claim to the throne after marrying a Roman Catholic. Around this time,

---

75 Leo Pfeffer, *Church, State and Freedom* (Boston, 1967), 149.

76 *Everson v Board of Education,* 330 U.S. 1, 15 (1947).

77 Pfeffer, *Church, State and Freedom,* 149.

78 The United Kingdom is not the only European state to have officially established or supported a Church. Andorra, Denmark, Finland, Greece, Iceland, Liechtenstein, Monaco, Norway, San Marino, and Sweden are other examples.

79 Places of Worship Registration Act 1855.

80 See S.J. Robilliard, "Religion in Prison," *New Law Journal* 130 (1980): 800.

81 The Oaths Act 1979 s 1(3).

82 *The London Times* (August 14, 1984): 13.

83 "We acknowledge that the Queen's most excellent Majesty, acting according to the laws of the realm, is the highest power under God in this kingdom, and has supreme authority over all persons in all causes, as well ecclesiastical as civil." *The Canons of the Church of England* (Convocations of Canterbury and York, 1964, 1969), Canon A7.

84 The Act of Supremacy 1534 conferred on Henry VIII the title of "the only supreme head in earth of the Church of England." That was later repealed by Queen Mary, but Elizabeth I's Act of Supremacy 1559 declared her "the only supreme governor of this realm . . . as well in all spiritual or ecclesiastical or causes as temporal."

85 Bill of Rights, 1688, Section 1; Act of Settlement 1700, Sections 2 and 3; Accession Declaration Act 1910, Section 1.

there was press speculation that then unmarried Prince Charles was romantically involved with a Roman Catholic Princess from Luxembourg. The resulting public interest prompted the Government to announce that it had no plans to remove the Catholic ban by amending Section 2 of the Act of Settlement of 1700.[86]

Recent reports would appear to indicate that Prince Charles is less than enthusiastic about being bound by these religious shackles of office. Under the Coronation Oath Act of 1688, the Monarch promises to maintain "the Protestant reformed religion established by law."[87] Yet, Charles has described as "absurd"[88] the rule that the monarch may not marry a Catholic and maintains that "the Catholic subjects of the sovereign are as important as Protestants, not to mention the Islamic, Hindu and Zoroastrian."[89] Thus, Prince Charles has admitted that he sees his future constitutional role as a "Defender of Faith."[90] This is markedly different from "Defender of *the* Faith," the term originally bestowed on Henry VIII by Pope Leo X and, since 1544, officially used to define the Monarch's responsibilities.

Defender of Faith. Prince Charles' evident desire to reach out to non-Christian faiths is to be applauded. After all, as Robertson sardonically comments, "it is difficult to understand why Prince Charles would be unfit to mount the throne were he to become a Methodist or had his wife taken communion with priests rather than tabloid journalists."[91] Nevertheless, Charles's proposals, in the wake of his admission to adultery, have incurred the wrath of some Christian leaders. Predictably, most radical evangelical Protestants were outraged. The Grand Secretary of the Orange Lodge of Scotland complained that "there is no place for Charles imposing his worldly religious beliefs or disbeliefs on the United Kingdom."[92] Similarly the Reverend Ian Paisley, a member of Parliament and Head of the Fundamentalist Free Presbyterian Church, warned that his loyalty to the Crown was conditioned on the Sovereign being prepared "to maintain in the United Kingdom the Protestant Reformed religion."[93] Of greater concern to Charles will have been the reaction from within the ranks of the Anglican community. Most senior Anglican clergy have re-

---

86 989 HC DEB 29 July 1980, written answers col 607.

87 Coronation Oath Act 1688 (1 Will.& Mar., c. 6). Under the Coronation Oath, the Monarch also promises to "maintain and preserve inviolably the settlement of the Church of England, and the doctrine, worship, discipline and government thereof in England."

88 *The London Daily Mirror* (June 27, 1994): 4.

89 Ibid.

90 *The Christian Science Monitor* (July 6 1994): 3.

91 G. Robertson, *Freedom, the Individual and the Law*, 7th ed. (Harmondsworth, 1993), 490.

92 *The Christian Science Monitor* (July 6, 1994): 3.

93 *The London Evening Standard* (July 12, 1994): 11.

acted cautiously. Dr John Habgood, the Archbishop of York and the second most senior figure in the Church of England, warned that changing the coronation oath to "Defender of Faith" would create a myriad of problems: "[I]t would be a difficult and dangerous thing to start tampering with because in the process of picking out some threads you do not know what else will unravel."[94] Implicit in Habgood's warning is the fear that reform may stir up Republican sentiment. Since Parliament's approval is necessary for such a change of title, advocates of disestablishment might seize this as an opportunity to undermine the church-state relationship. Press reports would appear to suggest that these fears were also shared by the Archbishop of Canterbury.[95]

Perhaps surprised that his comments had generated such controversy, Prince Charles acted quickly to restore calm. Charles immediately contacted the Archbishops of Canterbury and York to reassure them that his remarks should not be construed as implying support for disestablishment.[96] Seemingly satisfied by Charles's assurances, the Archbishop of York responded by condemning "misleading speculation" in the press.[97] Instead, Habgood now welcomed Charles's "remarks about the importance of faith in an increasingly secular society."[98] But what of Charles's original remarks? Will a future King Charles take the title of "Defender *of* Faith" rather than that of "Defender *of the* Faith"? And might the Archbishop of Canterbury or other senior Anglican clergy oppose such a course of action? Answers to these questions remain unclear. What can be ascertained is that the Church of England's two Archbishops approve of Charles's sensitivity to non-Christian faiths. They have praised the Prince for his "concern for all subjects"[99] and have indicated that they would welcome the involvement of minority faiths in Charles's future coronation service.[100] This is an interesting scenario. Traditionally the Sovereign is only crowned by the Archbishop of Canterbury.[101] The sight of Muslim, Hindu, Sikh, Jewish, and Buddhist leaders participating in the coronation of the next sovereign is likely to be opposed by tradi-

---

94 "Do Not Loosen Church-State Ties Warns Bishop," *Reuters, Ltd. (Lexis ed.)* (July 1, 1994).

95 *The Christian Science Monitor* (July 6, 1994): 3.

96 *The London Times* (July 11, 1994): 1.

97 "Charles Reassures Leaders on Church's Role," *Reuters Limited (Lexis ed.)* (July 10, 1994).

98 Ibid.

99 Ibid.

100 *The London Daily Mail* (July 11, 1994): 7.

101 The Coronation customarily takes place in Westminster Abbey some months after accession and is conducted by the Archbishop of Canterbury, assisted by the Archbishop of York.

tional Anglicans. It could have enormous symbolic influence, however, and would be an official recognition that Britain is a multi-faith society.

Privileges of the Church of England. The Church of England's status means that it enjoys certain privileges denied to other faiths. The Church of England is uniquely entitled to organize national events such as coronations and war remembrance services. Of course, this can lead to tension between church and state. In 1982, in a service commemorating the recapture of the Falkland Islands from Argentina, the Archbishop of Canterbury, Robert Runcie, incurred the wrath of Prime Minister Margaret Thatcher when he prayed for both British and Argentine victims of the conflict.[102] Archbishop Runcie was accused by some of meddling in politics. Ironically, however, perhaps the most significant privilege enjoyed by the Church of England is the presence of the twenty-six most senior Anglican Bishops in the House of Lords (Parliament's Upper Chamber). These twenty-six "Lords Spiritual" are free to debate and vote on all issues discussed in the House,[103] so their influence is not merely confined to ecclesiastical matters.[104] Unlike other faiths and denominations, only the Church of England has seats reserved in Parliament for its representatives. Yet establishment comes at a price.

In 1950, a former Archbishop of Canterbury wrote: "[E]xcept possibly in the early days, the Church of England never has had complete freedom." In the Middle Ages, the Church was controlled by "the Pope and the Crown; later by the Crown; and eventually by Parliament."[105] The Anglican Church is currently subject to "external" control, in so far as *Measures*[106] passed by the Church's General Synod (its main law-making body) require the approval of Parliament,[107] while ecclesiastical *Canons*[108]

---

[102] On the Falklands conflict, see A.R. Coll and A.C. Arend, *The Falklands War* (London, 1985).

[103] It would appear that since the 26 Lords Spiritual are full members of the House of Lords, they are excluded from voting in the election of members of the House of Commons. "Voting Bishops," *Public Law* (Autumn, 1983): 393.

[104] During the 1988-1989 session, the House of Lords bishops cast a total of 37 votes, 23 anti-government and 14 pro-government. Today Bishops tend to remain aloof from partisan political controversy. However they "tend to see it as being their duty to scrutinize matters under debate in the light of the Christian faith, forming and expressing the Christian conscience on some of the major problems of the day." D. Shell and D. Beamish, *The House of Commons at Work* (Oxford, 1993), 58.

[105] Cyril Garbett, quoted in Wood, "Editorial: Church and State in England," 315.

[106] "A measure is a law, above a Church matter, that applies to the entire Church and will also, where necessary, bind others as well, because it has the force of an Act of Parliament and may even repeal or amend an Act dealing with an ecclesiastical matter." See John Robilliard, *Religion and the Law* (Manchester, 1984) (citing Halsbury, para 399).

[107] Church of England (Assembly) Powers Act 1919.

[108] A canon is "essentially a power to make rules for the clergy, and in spiritual matters only." Quoted in Robilliard, *Religion and the Law*, 9. However canons must not be contrary or

must receive royal assent before they can become law.[109] Forms of worship within the Church of England require Parliamentary authorization. The Church's Prayer Book was given statutory force by the Act of Uniformity of 1558, and subsequent changes to the Prayer Book were authorized by Parliament in 1662 and 1872. Most controversially, in 1928 the House of Commons rejected the Church's proposals for changes to the Prayer Book,[110] while in 1989 the Commons initially rejected a measure which would make divorced men who have remarried, eligible for the priesthood.[111] Finally, Parliament's approval was recently necessary for the ordination of women priests.[112] Thus it has been claimed that "no change in important church law can be made without the sanction of Parliament."[113]

Perhaps the most significant power exercised by the state is that Archbishops and Bishops of the Church of England must be appointed by the Crown on the advice of the Prime Minister.[114] Usually the Prime Minister will "rubber stamp" the preferred candidate of the Church of England's Crown Appointment Commission. However, in 1981 Prime Minister Thatcher nominated Dr. Leonard, a "conservative" and the second choice candidate, to act as the Bishop of London. This provoked considerable controversy, and Sir John Robilliard comments "that there is no constitutional convention that the state must accept the first choice of the Church."[115]

This anomaly—that a Prime Minister who may not even be a Christian should have the power to veto the appointment of archbishops and bishops in the church—has been highlighted by advocates of disestablishment.[116] For example, Anglican Bishop Colin Buchanan describes the state's involvement in the promotion of clergy and church law as "obnoxious."[117] The campaign for the formal separation of church and

---

repugnant to the Royal Prerogative or the customs, laws, or statutes of the realm: Submission of Clergy Act 1533, ss 1 and 3.

109 Synodical Government Measure, 1969, s 1.

110 See Alec Vidler, *The Church in an Age of Revolution* (Harmondsworth, 1961), 163-168.

111 157 HC Deb 17 July 1989 col 174. The House of Commons later approved this Measure: 167 HC Deb 20 February 1990 col 882.

112 The first women were ordained in the Church of England in March 1994. It has been estimated that 215 of the approximately 11,000 Anglican clergy left the Church in protest. The Church of England now has some 1,000 women priests. *The London Times* (November 5, 1994).

113 Robilliard, *Religion and the Law*, 91.

114 The Appointment of Bishops Act 1533, s 3.

115 Robilliard, *Religion and the Law*, 91.

116 See *The London Guardian* (May 20, 1991): 18.

117 "Britain's Church-Crown Ties up for Review," *Reuters World Service (Lexis ed.)* (July 7, 1994).

state, however, is not a recent phenomenon. It can even be traced back to the seventeenth century. Already in 1613 Leonard Busher suggested that: "Kings and Magistrates are to rule temporal affairs by the swords of their temporal kingdoms, and bishops and ministers are to rule spiritual affairs by the Word and Spirit of God, the sword of Christ's spiritual kingdom, and not to intermeddle one with another authority, office and function."[118] The case for disestablishment was even made by a former Archbishop of Canterbury—before he took office. The then Reverend Michael Ramsay, in explaining his preference for disestablishment commented: "I wish . . . that the Church would become worthy of it—would become so annoying to the state that it had disestablishment forced upon it."[119] However the present Archbishop of Canterbury, Dr. George Carey, has vigorously defended the existing constitutional structure, arguing that the formal separation of church and state would seriously damage the nation's spiritual and moral values, and undermine its national institutions.[120]

Religion and Charitable Status

Charitable Trusts. A privilege which the Church of England enjoys alongside other religions is that of charitable status. In *IRC v Pemsel,* Lord MacNaughton considered that "charity" consists of four elements, one of which was "the advancement of religion."[121] The English law of charities claims to be neutral on matters of religion.[122] It was a decision in 1862 which established this principle.[123] The Court of Appeal accepted that a trust for the promotion of the works of Joanna Southcott was a valid charitable trust. Southcott claimed that she had been made pregnant by the Holy Spirit and at the age of sixty-five she would give birth to the

---

118 Leonard Busher, *Religious Peace or a Plea for Liberty of Conscience,* quoted in Wood, "Editorial: Church and State in England," 308.

119 Ibid. See also N.J. Richards, "Disestablishment of the Anglican Church in England in the Late Nineteenth Century: Reasons for Failure," *Journal of Church and State* 19 (1988): 193-211.

120 *The London Observer* (April 4, 1993): 7.

121 *IRC v Pemsel* [1891] AC 531 at 583, HL. Lord MacNaughton's test was later qualified in *Scottish Burial Reform and Cremation Society Ltd v Glasgow Corporation* [1968] AC 138, where Lord Wilberforce pointed out that there may be charities which do not fall under any of the four headings.

122 For the position in Scotland where a special category of charitable trusts has not traditionally been recognized, see K. Norrie and E. Scobbie, *Introduction to Scots Law of Trusts* (London, 1991), 30-31.

123 *Thornton v Howe* [1862] 31 Beav 14.

second messiah.[124] At her death she left a box, which she claimed would solve all of the world's problems, if opened in the presence of twenty-four bishops. The then Master of the Rolls, Sir John Romilly, described Southcott as a "foolish, ignorant woman."[125] However, he pointed out that "the Court of Chancery makes no distinction between one sort of religion and another," nor "any particular distinction between one sect and another."[126] More recently Plowman, J. relied on this decision when he held that a trust to publish the writings of a retired builder could be accorded charitable status, despite evidence that they were of no intrinsic value and merely repeated the teaching of the author's sect.[127]

The main advantage of according a religion charitable status in the United Kingdom is tax relief.[128] Charities receive favorable tax treatment as well as other financial and trust law privileges.[129] This principle can even be traced back to the Old Testament[130] and has long been recognized in the United Kingdom.[131] The granting of tax exemption to religions, however, has been accompanied by detailed discussion of what actually constitutes a religion, and whether a religious trust is for the benefit of the public.[132] In 1980, Dillon, J. distinguished religion from ethics: he suggested that "religion is concerned with man's relations with God, and ethics are concerned with man's relations with man."[133] For Dillon, "ethical principles" were beliefs in the excellence of truth, love, and beauty, but not belief in anything supernatural, while the essential attributes of religion were faith and worship: faith in a god and worship of that god.[134] The consequence of this was that the South Place Ethical Society, a humanist society in the Platonic tradition established for the study of "ethical principles," could not be regarded as charitable on religious grounds.

---

124 James K. Hopkins, *A Women to Deliver Her People: Joanna Southcott and English Millennarianism in an Era of Revolution* (Austin, TX, 1982).

125 *Thornton v Howe* [1862] 31 Beav 14, 18.

126 Ibid.

127 *In Re Watson* 1973 1WLR 1472. For a comment on this case see J.C. Brady, "Public Benefit and Religious Trusts: Fact or Fiction," *Northern Ireland Legal Quarterly* 25 (1974): 174.

128 See G. Moffat and M. Chesterman, *Trusts Law: Text and Materials* (London, 1988), 643-645.

129 See S. Bright, "Charity and Trusts for the Public Benefit—Time for a Re-Think?" *Conveyancer and Property Lawyer* (January/February, 1989): 29-31.

130 See Ezra 7:24.

131 See Leo Pfeffer, *Religious Freedom* (Skokie, IL, 1988), 39.

132 See Moffat and Chesterman, *Trusts Law*, 643.

133 *Re South Place Ethical Society: Barralet v Attorney-General* [1980] 3 All ER 981.

134 Ibid., 1073.

New Religions. The transformation of Britain into a multi-faith society has exposed the shortcomings of the rule that groups that have no theistic content to their beliefs should be refused charitable status. In 1970, Lord Denning noted that there may be many exceptions to the traditional test,[135] while a decade later Dillon, J. suggested that Buddhism might be exempt from the requirement that a religion must be theistic.[136] Presumably Dillon's comments would cover other long established non-theistic religions such as Jainism. Thus British law would appear to draw no distinction between monotheistic and polytheistic religions. Charitable trusts have been registered for the advancement of the Church of England, Catholic,[137] Baptist,[138] Quaker,[139] Exclusive Brethren,[140] Jewish,[141] Sikh, Islamic, Buddhist, and Hindu religions.[142] Newly established religions, however, would appear to create special problems.[143] The Unification Church ("The Moonies") has been accorded charitable status,[144] but not the Church of Scientology. In *R v Registrar General ex p Segerdal,*[145] the Court of Appeal refused to designate a chapel of the Church of Scientology as a "place of meeting for religious worship," under the Places of Worship Registration Act of 1855. Lord Denning suggested that religious worship involves the veneration of God or a Supreme Being, and since this was absent in the Church of Scientology, Scientology was "more a philosophy of the existence of man rather than a religion."[146]

The Church of Scientology. The Church of Scientology has attracted considerable controversy in the United Kingdom. Until 1980, foreign members of the Church were forbidden from entering this country, and its creed has even been judicially described as "dangerous material,"[147] and "pernicious nonsense."[148] Although British courts have long claimed

135 *R v Registrar General ex parte Segerdal* [1979] 2QB 697, at 707.

136 *Re South Place Ethical Society,* at 1573.

137 *Bradshaw v Tasker* (1834) 2 Myl. & K. 221.

138 *Re Strickland's W.T.* [1936] 3 All E.R. 1027.

139 *Re Manser* [1905] 1 Ch. 68.

140 *Holmes v Att-General., The London Times* (February 12, 1981): 8.

141 *Neville Estates Ltd. v Madden* [1962] Ch. 832.

142 See (1989) Cm. 694, para 2. 19.

143 See H. Picarda, "New Religions as Charities," *New Law Journal* (April 23, 1981): 436.

144 See *[1982] Charity Commissioners Annual Report* paras. 36-38. In 1988 the Attorney General brought, but later withdrew, a High Court action to deprive them of charitable status. *Hansard* (February 3, 1988): 977.

145 [1970] 2 Q.B. 697.

146 Ibid., 707.

147 *Hubbard v Vosper* [1972] 2 Q.B. 84, 96 (per Lord Denning).

148 *Church of Scientology v Kaufman* [1973] R.P.C. 635, 658 (per Goff J).

to be neutral with regard to the content of different religions,[149] there appears to be a general agreement that Scientology is not eligible for charitable status.[150]

This is not the view of comparable countries.[151] The Australian High Court, for example, has held that "regardless of whether the practices of Scientology are harmful or objectionable, Scientology must, for all relevant purposes, be accepted as a religion in Victoria."[152] Explaining this decision, Mason, A.C.J. and Brennan, J. observed that "charlatanism is a necessary price of religious freedom."[153] Similarly, the United States Supreme Court has adopted a non-theistic view of religion, allowing exemption from conscription on the ground of the religious conviction of one who holds a "sincere and meaningful belief, which occupies in the life of its possessor a place parallel to that filled by the God of those admittedly qualifying for the exemption on the grounds of religion."[154]

By contrast, in the United Kingdom it has been claimed that some new faiths are "so fanciful or freakish that public benefit can justly be said to be lacking, and charitable status should not be accorded to them."[155] This view echoes that of the government-commissioned Goodman Committee which recommended that organizations detrimental to the moral welfare of the community should be excluded from charitable status.[156] However the Goodman Committee offered no guidelines as to the moral criteria by which religions should be assessed. Thus, the value judgments inherent in such decisions are difficult to make. Surely, there is a danger that newly established religions may be denied charitable status on irrational grounds. As Murphy, J. stated: "[A]dministrators and judges must resist the temptation to hold that groups or institutions are not religions because claimed religious beliefs or practices seem absurd, fraudulent, evil or novel."[157]

---

[149] See *Thornton v Howe* (1862) 31 Beav 14.

[150] See D. Hayton, ed., *Hayton and Marshall: Cases and Commentary on the Law of Trusts*, 9th ed. (London, 1991), 329.

[151] *Church of the New Faith v Comr for Payroll Tax* (1983) 57, AJLR 785. The Australian test has also been applied in New Zealand: *Centrepoint Community Growth Trust v I.R.C.* [1985] 1 NZLR 673.

[152] Per Wilson and Deane JJ in *Church of the New Faith v Pay Roll Tax Commissioners* (1983) 57 AJLR 785, at 808.

[153] Ibid., 791.

[154] *United States v. Seeger*, 380 U.S. 163, 176 (1965) (per Clark, J.)

[155] A.J. Oakley, *Parker and Mellows, The Modern Law of Trusts*, 6th ed. (London, 1994), 319.

[156] Charity Law and Voluntary Organisations, *The Goodman Report* (Bedford, 1976), 24.

[157] *Church of the New Faith*, 796.

Britain should adopt the United States and Australian tests, and formally recognize as "religious" the wide variety of world faiths which are presently in existence in the United Kingdom. Certainly, the British courts have drawn rigid distinctions between religious and non-religious beliefs.[158] This often means that religious bodies enjoy charitable benefits denied to non-religious groups. Thus, the present tax exemption rules can be criticized in that they may result in less favorable treatment to non-religious bodies (such as humanist societies) and new religions and more favorable treatment for long established religious groups.[159] The current system seems unlikely to change. Bradney, in a damning indictment of the law of charity, claims that it "provides yet another illustration of the mixture of bias and muddle which characterizes British law's attitude towards religions."[160]

Blasphemy

History of the Offense. In addition to the privilege of establishment, the Church of England is protected by the law of blasphemy.[161] Blasphemy is particularly difficult to define. A matter is blasphemous if it denies the truth of Christian doctrine[162] or the Bible[163] and uses words which are "scurrilous, abusive or offensive to vilify the Christian religion."[164] The offence was created by the courts in 1676.[165] In *R v Taylor*, Hale, C.J. directed the jury that calling religion a cheat as the defendant had done was an attack on Christianity, the state religion; that "to reproach the Christian religion is to speak in subversion of the law."[166] Previously, such attacks on Christianity would have been dealt with in the

---

158 The Australian High Court has even described the British definition of religion as "too narrow." Ibid., 790.

159 For example, organizations such as Amnesty International, the Defence Aid Fund (South Africa), the National Council for Civil Liberties and the Disablement Income Group, are not entitled to charitable status, while groups such as the Spiritual Regeneration Movement of Great Britain, Voice of Methodism (against Union with the Church of England), Reading Temperance Society and the British Society of Dowsers, are charities: see Bright, "Charity and Trusts for the Public Benefit," 33.

160 Bradney, *Religions, Rights and Laws*, 132.

161 There have been no recorded cases of blasphemy in Scotland since the 1840s. Similarly the scope of the offence in Wales is uncertain, as a result of the disestablishment of the Welsh Church in 1920. *Law Commission Working Paper*, No. 79, 32.

162 *R v Taylor* (1676) 1 Vent. 293.

163 *R v Hetherington* (1841) 9 St. Tr (NS) 563.

164 *Criminal Law: Offences against Religion and Public Worship*, Law Commission Report No. 145 (1985).

165 *R v Taylor* (1676) 1 Vent. 293, 86 ER 189.

166 Ibid.

ecclesiastical courts. However, the common law courts came to assert jurisdiction over the subject, since blasphemy as a crime was concerned with the protection of the state rather than religion per se. [167]

In the twentieth century, blasphemy has been generally viewed as an offense to protect Anglicans from the vilification of their faith. This aim of protecting religious sensibility led the Court of Appeal in 1922 to hold as blasphemous a publication which described Jesus entering Jerusalem, "like a circus clown on the back of two donkeys."[168] However, such cases have been rare. Between 1922 and 1978 there were no prosecutions for blasphemy, prompting Lord Denning to describe the offence as "a dead letter."[169] The offense was resurrected in 1979, however.[170] In *R v Lemon,* a jury considered that the publication of a poem in Gay News by a professor of English literature that linked homosexual practices with the life and crucifixion of Christ was a blasphemous libel. The House of Lords, by a 3-2 vote, confirmed the trial judge's ruling that the publisher's intentions were irrelevant and that there was no need for the prosecution to prove any risk of a breach of the peace.[171] Thus Professor Kirkup's proclaimed motive of celebrating the universality of God's love was irrelevant: blasphemy was a crime of strict liability.[172]

The Crime of Blasphemy. In *R v Lemon,*[173] the House of Lords did not recognize any defence of publication in the public interest. It seems unlikely, however, that prosecutions for blasphemy would be brought against publications with any literary or artistic value. The Gay News case was exceptional, in that it was a prosecution instigated by a private individual without official support. Neither Monty Python's "Life of Brian" nor Martin Scorsese's "The Last Temptation of Christ" were considered to have the necessary elements of vilification or scurrility to be banned as blasphemous. Nevertheless, the mere existence of a blasphemy law is guaranteed to encourage some Christians to call for such films to be banned. For example, the retired trial judge in *R v Lemon* has claimed

---

[167] As late as 1979 Lord Scarman noted that the crime of blasphemy "belongs to a group of criminal offences designed to safeguard the internal tranquility of the kingdom:" *R v Lemon* [1979] AC 617 at 658-659.

[168] *R v Gott* 1922 16 Cr. App. R. 87.

[169] A. Denning, *Freedom Under Law* (London, 1949), 46.

[170] *Whitehouse v Lemon* [1979] AC 617.

[171] Ibid.

[172] On blasphemy and blasphemous libel see J. Spencer, "Blasphemy: The Law Commission's Working Paper," *Criminal Law Review* (1981): 810; G. Robertson, "Blasphemy: The Law Commission's Working Paper," *Public Law* (1981): 295; St. J. Robilliard, "Report of Committees. Offences Against Religion and Public Worship," *Modern Law Review* 44 (1981): 556.

[173] *Whitehouse v Lemon* [1979] AC 617.

that the distributors of the Scorsese film should be prosecuted.[174] Uncertainty surrounding the scope of the law of blasphemy has also prompted the British Board of Film Classification (BBFC) to take such matters seriously. In 1989, a video entitled "Visions of Ecstasy," concerning Saint Teresa, was refused a certificate by the BBFC on the ground that it was blasphemous.[175] The United Kingdom Law Commission has even formally recognized that the ambit of the law of blasphemy is so wide that it is impossible to predict in advance whether a particular publication will constitute an offense.[176]

Blasphemy and Minority Faiths. The Law Commission has also expressed reservations that the present law on blasphemy protects only Anglican beliefs.[177] In 1991, a group of Muslims unsuccessfully sought to invoke the law of blasphemy against Salman Rushdie and the publishers of his book *The Satanic Verses*. The Divisional Court rejected their argument on the basis that the law of blasphemy only extends to Christianity and the Established Church.[178] By way of explanation, Watkins, L.J. referred to the findings of the Law Commission that "at most other denominations are protected only to the extent that their fundamental beliefs are those which are held in common with the Established Church."[179] The Court accepted that this was "a gross anomaly"[180] arising from "the chains of history,"[181] but pointed out that it was the "proper function" of Parliament and not the Courts to change the law. [182] Thus the Church of England is uniquely covered by the law of blasphemy.

It has been suggested that the law of blasphemy in the United Kingdom breaches Article 14 of the European Convention on Human

---

174 See G. Robertson and A. Nicol, *Media Law*, 3d ed. (London, 1992), 162.

175 See R. Stone, *Textbook on Civil Liberties* (London, 1994), 216.

176 Law Commission, Working Paper No. 79: Offences Against Religion and Public Worship, 1981

177 Ibid. See also Criminal Law: Offences Against Religion and Public Worship, Law Commission Report No. 145 (1985).

178 *R v Metropolitan Stipendiary Magistrate, ex parte Choudhury*, [1991] 1 All ER 306.

179 Ibid., 317.

180 Ibid. (Watkins, L.J., quoting AG Sir John Simon in 1914).

181 Ibid.

182 Bradney points out the anomaly that ten days before this judgment, the House of Lords in *R v R* [1991] 4 All ER 481, had overturned the 100 year old marital rape exemption for husbands, even though Parliament had refused to abolish that rule as recently as 1976. Bradney, *Religions, Rights and Laws*, 96.

Rights,[183] in so far as it discriminates against non-Christians.[184] However Muslim applicants failed in their petitions to have the European Commission on Human Rights ban Rushdie's *The Satanic Verses.*[185] It would appear that a stronger argument could be brought under the equivalent non-discrimination clause of the International Covenant on Civil and Political Rights.[186] This has been noted by individual members of the Human Rights Committee. Mr. Sadi of Jordan has complained that the blasphemy law in the United Kingdom is "not extensive enough" and should be "modified"[187] and that since it covers only Christianity it is "clearly in contravention of the letter and spirit of the Covenant."[188] The United Kingdom, however, has maintained that there are no plans to reform this law, since there is no consensus between those who would abolish the offense of blasphemy and those who would extend it to cover all other faiths.[189] Human Rights Committee member Mr. Mavrommatis of Cyprus has suggested that abolition of the law of blasphemy is the "most acceptable approach."[190] This has also been advocated by the United Kingdom Law Commission,[191] a member of the House of Lords,[192] a number of academic writers,[193] and even the Archbishop of Canterbury.[194] Yet, any such attempt would likely be opposed vigorously. It would cause particular concern to those Muslim groups which are presently campaigning for the law on blasphemy to be extended to cover all major religions.[195]

---

183 "The enjoyment of the rights and freedoms set forth in this Convention shall be secured without discrimination on any ground such as sex, race, color, language, *religion*, political or other opinion. . . ." ECHR, Art. 14 (emphasis added).

184 See S. Poulter, "Towards Legislative Reform of the Blasphemy and Racial Hatred Laws," *Public Law* (1991): 375.

185 *Choudhury v U K*, reprinted in *Human Rights Law Journal* 12 (1991): 172.

186 "[T]he law shall prohibit any discrimination and guarantee all persons equal and effective protection against discrimination on any ground such as race, color, sex, language, *religion*, political or other opinion. . . ." ICCPR, Art. 26 (emphasis added).

187 CCPR/C/SR 1050, 10.

188 Ibid.

189 HC Deb, 27 June 1989, col 395.

190 CCPR/C/SR 1050, 4.

191 *The Law Commission Report*, No 145 (1985).

192 See debate in HL Debs vol 555, No. 1604, 16 June 1994, cols. 1891-1909, amendment to the Criminal Justice Public Order Bill proposed and eventually withdrawn by Lord Lester of Herne Hill.

193 See S. Lee, *The Cost of Free Speech* (London, 1990), 76; A. Bradney, "Taking Sides: Religion, Law and Politics," *New Law Journal* (March 26, 1993): 443; Poulter, "Towards Legislative Reform of the Blasphemy and Racial Hatred Laws," 375.

194 Robertson and Nicol, *Media Law*, 163.

195 See *The Runnymede Bulletin* (March, 1992): 3.

The British government acknowledges that blasphemy is a "difficult area."[196] The problems created are considerable. Its complexity is illustrated by the fact that even a distinguished former judge, Lord Scarman, appears to have publicly changed his mind, from earlier advocating an extension of the blasphemy law[197] to now calling for its repeal.[198] Nevertheless, the "gross anomaly" remains: the law of blasphemy at present only protects Christians, presenting *prima facie* discrimination against non-Christian faiths. It is difficult to see how the preferential treatment, accorded to the Church of England in the area of blasphemy, can be considered reasonable and objective in contemporary multi-faith Britain.

Restrictions on Freedom of Religion

Cultural Factors. Freedom of religion is a relative, not an absolute, right. As with most human rights, the right to manifest one's faith usually has to be weighed against other factors such as social harmony. In the United Kingdom, it is often members of minority faith groups who are most directly affected by necessary restrictions on freedom of religion. The observance of minority faith customs, rituals, and rules of dress is a area of particular controversy. On one occasion, a Sikh woman aspiring to train as a nurse was refused permission to wear *shalwar* (trousers) with her uniform, as her religious dress code mandated. Initially this decision was endorsed by an Employment Appeal Tribunal.[199] However the relevant Health Authority[200] and the General Nursing Council[201] later relaxed the uniform requirements for minority faith nurses. In another case, a Muslim woman successfully challenged a policy which prohibited her wearing trousers rather than a skirt, while at work in a shop.[202]

Where strict uniform requirements are imposed as a condition of employment, however, problems of religious freedom arise. Minority faith employees have often been denied the right to wear clothes which are associated with their own religious traditions. A number of these cases have involved Sikhs. Sikhism requires that its male adherents wear long

---

196 See The United Kingdom's Third Human Rights Report submitted under the ICCPR. ICCPR/C/58 Add.6, p.58.

197 *Whitehouse v Lemon* [1979] AC 617 at 658.

198 See S.J.D. Green, "Beyond the Satanic Verses," *Encounter* (June, 1990): 15.

199 *Kingston and Richmond Area Health Authority v Kaur* [1981], IRLR 337.

200 *The London Times* (June 26, 1981): 3.

201 Nurses and Enrolled Nurses (Amendment) Rules Approval Instrument 1981, SI 1981/1532.

202 *Malik v British Home Stores*, COIT 987/12.

hair, a beard, a steel bracelet, and a turban.[203] Yet, in *Panesar v Nestle Co. Ltd.*[204] the Court of Appeal held that a rule forbidding the wearing of beards in the respondent's chocolate factory was justifiable on hygiene grounds. Lord Denning cited Article 9(2) of the ECHR[205] and specifically referred to the restrictions which are "necessary in a democratic society" for the protection of public health.[206] It has also been held that considerations of health and hygiene justify a "no beards" rule in a confectionery factory,[207] a bakery,[208] a meat factory,[209] and an ice-cream manufacturing factory.[210]

Health and Safety Restrictions. The requirement that a Sikh employed in the maintenance of railway carriages remove his turban and wear a safety helmet[211] is consistent with international law.[212] There is even some evidence to suggest that the law of the United Kingdom accords Sikhs greater freedom than some international human rights instruments. For example, the European Commission on Human Rights has held that the protection of public health justifies the compulsory wearing of crash helmets.[213] In 1976, however, Parliament specifically exempted turbaned Sikhs from the statutory requirement that all motorcyclists must wear crash helmets.[214] A similar exception is provided for turbaned Sikhs working in the construction industry.[215] Finally, the Criminal Justice Act of 1988, which contains provisions designed to penalize those who carry knives in public places, deals with the Sikh *kirpan* (ceremonial dagger), by means of a specific exemption for those carrying sharply pointed articles for "religious reasons."[216]

---

203 See A. James, *Sikh Children in Britain* (Oxford, 1974), 47-52.

204 [1980] ICR 144.

205 "Freedom to manifest one's religion or beliefs shall be subject only to such limitations as are prescribed by law and are necessary in a democratic society in the interests of public safety, for the protection of public order, health or morals, or for the protection of the rights and freedoms of others." ECHR Art 9(2).

206 Ibid., 147.

207 *Singh v Rowntree Mackintosh Ltd* [1979] IRLR 199.

208 *Kabal Singh v RHM Bakeries (Southern) Ltd* 1.8.78, EAT 818/77.

209 *Gill v The Walls Meat Company Ltd* 9.6.77 COIT 11961/77/B.

210 *Singh v Lyons Maid Ltd* [1975] IRLR 328.

211 *Singh v British Rail Engineering Ltd* [1986] ICR 22. This decision was recently approved in *SS Dhanjal v British Steel General Steels,* (Case No 50740/91), December 16, 1993.

212 See *Singh Bhinder v Canada,* UN Human Rights Committee Application No. 208/1986.

213 *Application No. 7992/77 DR 14, 234.*

214 Motor-Cycle Crash Helmets (Religious Exemption) Act 1976.

215 Employment Act 1989, s 11.

216 See s 139(5)(b).

There are a number of other restrictions relating to the protection of public health or safety. It has been suggested that conditions may be placed on the wearing of Sikh steel bangles, since they may cause accidents and get caught up in fast-moving machinery.[217] Similarly, the categorization of marijuana as a controlled drug under the Misuse of Drugs Act of 1971 may be justified (albeit controversially) as a measure necessary for the protection of public health.[218] The Rastafarian's motive for using marijuana *("ganja")* is irrelevant,[219] as is the motive of the Jehovah's Witness who physically prevents his or her child from receiving a blood transfusion. Should the child consequently die, the Jehovah's Witness parent would be guilty of manslaughter.[220] Thus the physical welfare and the "best interests" of the child over-ride the religious preference of the parent. Endorsed by the 1989 *UN Convention on the Rights of the Child*,[221] this principle also applies to female circumcision. Commonly practised in parts of Africa for religious and cultural reasons, female circumcision is prohibited in the United Kingdom,[222] as is the ritual tattooing[223] and scarification of children.[224] Of course, these restrictions can be justified not merely on health or safety grounds, but as necessary to protect the "fundamental rights and freedoms of others."[225] Specific examples of the need to protect the freedom of others include curbs on the rights of Hindus and Sikhs to scatter human ashes in British rivers,[226] public order conditions imposed on the right of the Hare Krishna sect to march through busy town centers,[227] and the prohibition of the electrical amplification of the Muslim "call to prayer," so as to avoid disturbing local non-Muslims.[228]

---

217 See James, *Sikh Children in Britain*, 51.

218 See. e.g. T. DuQuesne, "Cannabis and the Rule of Law," *Lancet II* (1981): 581; M. Rose, "Cannabis and the Rule of Law," *Lancet II* (1984): 138-139.

219 Rastafarians cite Biblical passages such as Genesis 1:11-12 to support their assertion that the use of marijuana is necessary for the proper exercise of their faith.

220 Manslaughter is homicide without malice aforethought. See Homicide Act 1957, s 3. To withhold medical treatment from a child may be manslaughter whatever the religious views of the parents. *R v Senior [1899] 1 Q.B. 283.* See also Robertson, *Freedom, The Individual and the Law*, 493.

221 "In all actions concerning children . . . the best interests of the child shall be a primary consideration." Art. 3(1). See also, Art. 19(1): "State parties shall take ... measures to protect the child from all forms of physical or mental violence, injury or abuse."

222 The Prohibition of Female Circumcision Act 1985.

223 The Tattooing of Minors Act 1969 s 2.

224 *R v Adesanya, The London Times* (July 16, 1974): 6.

225 Article 18(3) of the International Covenant on Civil and Political Rights uses this phrase .

226 See S. Poulter, *Asian Traditions and English Law* (Trentham, 1990), 125.

227 The Highways Act 1980, s 137.

228 See Poulter, *Asian Traditions and English Law*, 116.

Controversial Restrictions. In Britain, most major Christian festivals are public holidays. Minority faiths enjoy no such privileges for their holy days and festivals.[229] Often their religious festivals fall within the working week. Where a member of a minority faith fails to comply with a condition of employment because of a religious observance, they can be fairly dismissed, with no judicial relief. For example, in *Ahmad v ILEA*,[230] a teacher, who was a practicing Muslim, required an extra 75 minutes after his Friday lunch break to attend the nearest mosque for prayers. After his colleagues objected that this disrupted work in the school, his employers, the Inner London Education Authority, offered him a four and a half day weekly contract. Ahmad refused and left claiming unfair dismissal. On appeal, the Court of Appeal, by a 2-1 majority, held that this dismissal was fair.[231] Ahmad could not claim the right to rewrite his contract of employment. A later attempt to petition the European Commission on Human Rights to hear the case was also unsuccessful.[232] The floodgate fears that hundreds of minority faith teachers might disrupt the teaching week by taking work off to pray obviously influenced both the Court of Appeal and the European Commission. The rationale for this decision is harsh but may be objectively tenable.

The same may not be said about the case of *Dawkins v Crown Suppliers (PSA) Ltd*.[233] Dawkins, a Rastafarian, applied for a job as a van driver with the Crown Suppliers (PSA). At an interview Dawkins was informed that PSA drivers were required to have short hair, so he would have to cut his "dreadlocks." Dawkins indicated that he was unwilling to do so, and was refused employment. An Industrial Tribunal found that the PSA had been guilty of both direct and indirect racial discrimination. This decision was reversed by an Employment Appeal Tribunal. The case then went to the Court of Appeal, which held that because Rastafarians shared no long history, group descent, or common language, they were in effect only a religious sect. Moreover, since Rastafarians were not a racial group within section 3(1) of the Race Relations Act 1976, the appeal failed.[234] Although Dawkins' motives were not entirely clear, it appears reasonable to assume that, like many other Rastafarians, his dreadlocks were a mani-

---

[229] See *Religious Observance at Work* (1991), 439; Industrial Relations Legal Information Bulletin 4.

[230] *Ahmad v ILEA* [1978] 1 All ER 574.

[231] Ibid. Lords Denning and Orr dismissed Ahmad's appeal. Lord Scarman dissented.

[232] *Ahmad v U K* (1982) 4 EHRR 126.

[233] [1993] IRLR 284, CA.

[234] For a comment on this case see N. Parpworth, "Defining Ethnic Origins," *New Law Journal* (April 30, 1993): 610-612.

festation of his Rastafarian beliefs.[235] Consequently, the requirement that a Rastafarian must cut his hair to work as a van driver is hard to justify. Unlike cases such as *Singh v Lyons Maid Ltd*,[236] where a Sikh male working in an ice cream factory was required to remain clean shaven for health reasons, there is no objective rationale for the PSA policy. Since this restriction on the manifestation of Dawkins' religious belief cannot be justified on the grounds of health, safety, public order, morals, or the rights of others, it would also seem to violate international human rights law.[237] An appeal from the Dawkins case is (at the time of this writing) pending before the House of Lords, though it has been suggested that it is unlikely that the Lords will overturn the Court of Appeal's ruling.[238]

Religious Discrimination. The *Dawkins* case adds weight to the argument that legislation should be introduced expressly to protect the rights of religious minorities in Britain.[239] Discrimination on religious grounds is forbidden by all major human rights treaties,[240] including those to which the United Kingdom is a signatory. Thus it is ironic that the United Kingdom has failed to enact legislation which would expressly protect the rights of religious minorities. The *Dawkins* case highlights this anomaly. Since Rastafarians cannot be considered a "race," Dawkins could not argue that he was a victim of indirect discrimination under the Race Relations Act 1976. Indirect discrimination occurs where a condition or requirement is applied and the proportion of a particular racial group who are justifiably able to comply with it is "considerably smaller" than those of individuals of a different racial group who are able to comply with it.[241]

This argument of indirect racial discrimination was successfully advanced by a Sikh boy who was denied admission to his school on the ground that he wished to wear a turban.[242] The school's head teacher ob-

---

235 On Rastafarian beliefs, see E. Cashmore, *The Rastafarians*, Report No 64 (The Minority Rights Group, Oxford)

236 *1975 Industrial Relations Law Reports*, 338.

237 "Freedom to manifest one's religion or beliefs may be subject only to such limitations as are prescribed by law and are necessary to protect public safety, order, health, or morals or the fundamental rights and freedoms of others." *International Covenant on Civil and Political Rights*, Article 18(3).

238 E.O.R. No. 49 May/June 1993 p.38.

239 This has been proposed by the Commission for Racial Equality, as well as a number of Muslim groups. See *The Need For Reform*, UKACIA Memorandum submitted to the Home Secretary, April 1993, 12.

240 See. e.g., *European Convention on Human Rights*, Art. 14 and *International Covenant on Civil and Political Rights*, Art. 26.

241 Race Relations Act 1976, s1(1)(b). See also Robilliard, "Discrimination and Indirect Discrimination: The Religious Dimension," *New Community* (1980): 261.

242 *Mandla v Dowell Lee* [1983] 2 AC 548.

jected on the ground that the turban contravened the school's rules on pupils' dress. The House of Lords, however, ruled that Sikhs are an "ethnic" as well as a religious group and are thus protected by the 1976 Act. Lord Fraser identified two characteristics which had to be possessed by any community if it was to qualify as an ethnic group under the Race Relations Act: first, a long shared history of which the group is conscious, as distinguishing it from other groups; and, second, a cultural tradition of its own, including family and social customs, a common geographical origin, descent from common ancestors, a common language, a common literature, and a common religion.[243]

Applying these criteria, all Sikhs (including converts) constitute an "ethnic group." The courts consider that Jews are an "ethnic group,"[244] but it would appear that Muslims fail this test.[245] The only explanation for this is that the Muslim community in Britain originates from a number of different countries and lacks the same degree of group cohesion as the Sikh or Jewish communities. The absurdities of this rule are apparent. A Kuwaiti Muslim living in the United Kingdom is protected against discrimination, insofar as his "ethnic origin" brings him within the confines of the Race Relations Act 1976. A white indigenous British convert to Islam, however, is not guaranteed such a right. Thus a "No Muslims" or "No Hindus" sign is only unlawful if indirect racial discrimination can be shown.[246]

Northern Ireland is the only region of the United Kingdom where religious discrimination is prohibited by law. The Fair Employment (NI) Act of 1976 made discrimination on religious or political grounds unlawful in both the public and private spheres of employment, and established machinery to promote equality of opportunity. A Fair Employment Agency (FEA) has responsibility to receive and investigate complaints of discrimination. Despite the frequent FEA investigations and the improvements of the Fair Employment (NI) Act of 1989 and Fair Employment (Amendment) (NI) Order of 1991, the problem of religious discrimination continues in Northern Ireland.[247] The influential independent research organization, The Policy Studies Institute, has questioned the effectiveness of the Fair Employment legislation in eliminating

---

[243] Ibid.

[244] See *Simon v Brimham Associates* [1987] IRLR 307 and *Seide v Gillette Industries* [1980] IRLR 427.

[245] *Nyazi v Rymans* (E.A.T., 10 May 1988 unreported.)

[246] See S.H. Bailey, D.J. Harris, and B.L. Jones, *Civil Liberties: Cases and Materials,* 3d ed. (London, 1991), 586.

[247] See C. McCrudden, "The Evolution of the Fair Employment (NI) Act 1989 in Parliament" in R.J. Cormack and R.D. Osborne, *Discrimination and Public Policy in Northern Ireland* (Oxford, 1991).

inequality of opportunity between Protestants and Roman Catholics.[248] Religion remains a major determinant of male unemployment, with Catholic male unemployment two and a half times that of Protestant male unemployment.[249] This has continued despite a decade of legislation, and over 10,000 job changes per year.[250] In putting forward their demands for a permanent end to hostilities in the North of Ireland, the Irish Republican Army has called for the ending of job discrimination against Catholics and the ending of "sectarian bias" of economic investment against Catholic areas.[251] One would anticipate that should peace finally be secured, the Catholic regions of Northern Ireland, which have often been devastated by "The Troubles," will enjoy economic revitalization.[252]

The anomaly that religious discrimination is prohibited in Northern Ireland but not in the rest of the United Kingdom is striking. In *Mandla v Dowell Lee*, Lord Templeman suggested that one explanation might be that religious discrimination is less of a problem on the British "mainland" than in Ulster.[253] Historically, this may be so, but such an explanation risks ignoring the current problems of Britain's religious minorities. As long ago as 1976, the omission of religion from the Race Relations Act was criticized by a House of Commons Select Committee.[254] The United Kingdom would do well to follow the examples of the United States and Canada[255] and enact legislation outlawing religious discrimination.[256]

Religion in the Classroom

The Principle of Parental Choice. The 1948 Universal Declaration of Human Rights decrees that "parents have a prior right to choose the kind

---

248 D.J. Smith and G. Chambers, *Inequality in Northern Ireland* (London, 1991).

249 See *The New York Times* (September 1, 1994): 3.

250 DED, *Equality of Opportunity in Employment in Northern Ireland: Future Strategy Options: A Consultative Paper* (1986), para. 2.20.

251 *The London Guardian* (June 1, 1994): 5.

252 "With agreement, co-operation to the mutual benefit of all living in Ireland could develop without impediment, attaining its full potential for stimulating economic growth and prosperity." United Kingdom Government Document, *Frameworks for the Future* (1995), para. 57, page 37.

253 [1983] 2 WLR 620, at 631.

254 *H.C. Select Committee* "A" 29th April 1976, col. 84.

255 For example Ontario, Nova Scotia, and the Northwest Territories. See I.A. Hunter, R. St. MacDonald, and J.P. Humphrey, eds., *The Practice of Freedom: Canadian Essays on Human Rights and Fundamental Freedoms* (Toronto, 1979), 85.

256 See Poulter, "Towards Legislative Reform of The Blasphemy And Racial Hatred Laws," 375 where a model for reforming the law is provided.

of education that shall be given to their children."[257] This principle has also been recognized under British law. Section 76 of the Education Act of 1944 provides that children are to be educated in accordance with the wishes of their parents, so far as that is compatible with the provision of efficient instruction and the avoidance of unreasonable public expenditure. The right of parents to choose an education for their children within the public sector was reaffirmed by section 6 of the Education Act of 1980.

This principle of parental choice in the education of their children is far from absolute. The House of Lords has held that a state-funded Roman Catholic school may discriminate in favor of Catholics and refuse to admit non-Catholic or non-Christian children on the basis that it is already over-subscribed.[258] In that case, two Asian parents (a Muslim and a Hindu) tried unsuccessfully to send their daughters to a Catholic girl school. Keen to protect traditional Asian values, some Asian parents consider that boys and girls must be trained for different roles in life, with girls educated primarily for marriage and motherhood.[259] Yet for many Muslims, opposition to co-education is based not merely on the preservation of cultural norms, but on religious grounds. Part of the Islamic doctrine of *purdah* (seclusion) prescribes the separation of the sexes from puberty onwards.[260] Accordingly, Muslims have long been firm advocates of single-sex schooling.[261] This preference illustrates the gulf between Islamic and Western attitudes towards education. Unlike Western education which aims to foster the intellect of the rationally autonomous individual, Islamic education seeks to equip a child "in preparation for this life and the *Akhirah* (the life after death)."[262] For Muslims, Islam should be the basis of a child's education, and it is claimed that the separation of religion and secular learning in British schools accounts for Britain's "low moral values."[263] Thus of all Britain's religious minorities,

---

[257] Article 26(3).

[258] *Choudhury v Governors of Bishop Challoner Roman Catholic Comprehensive School* [1992] 3 All ER 277.

[259] Cmnd 9453 *Education for All.* The Report of the Committee of Inquiry into the Education of Children from Ethnic Minority Groups (HMSO, London).

[260] See M. Iqbal, "Education and Islam in Britain—A Muslim View," *New Community* (1976-1977): 397; also H. Papanek, "Purdah in Pakistan: Seclusion and Modern Occupation for Women," *Journal of Marriage and the Family* 33 (August, 1971): 517.

[261] See M. Anwar, "Young Muslims in Britain: Their Educational Needs and Policy Implications", in M.W. Khan, ed., *Education and Society in the Muslim World* (London, 1981), 100-121.

[262] G. Sarwar, *British Muslims and Schools* (London, 1994), 2.

[263] G. Sarwar, *Muslims and Education in the United Kingdom* (London, 1983).

Muslims are the most vociferous in the campaign for their own state-funded schools.

Religious Schools. In Britain there are approximately 4,500 voluntary aided (that is, state-funded) religious schools.[264] Ninety-nine per cent of these schools are controlled by the Roman Catholic and Anglican churches.[265] "Voluntary aided" status has yet to be granted to a single Muslim school, and when two of the twenty-eight independently-funded Muslim schools applied to the Department for Education for state funding, their requests were rejected. The explanation provided was that there were surplus places in neighboring schools, in accordance with the principle that new state-funded schools may not be established in areas where existing schools already have vacancies.[266] Since many Asians live in inner city areas where schools often have surplus places, it has been claimed that this policy unfairly discriminates against Muslims.[267] Certainly Muslims themselves are in no doubt that the prospect of a state-funded Islamic school is "too much for the establishment to bear."[268] The Chairman of the Islamic Schools Trust protests this "grossest of injustices,"[269] and the leader of the Muslim Parliament warns that "on this issue, we are just about reaching the end of our tether."[270] Thus, Muslim leaders have pledged that they will invoke the European Convention on Human Rights[271] to rectify an anomaly which even a former Conservative Government Education Minister has described as "totally unjust."[272] However, they have only a slim chance of successfully relying on the principle of parental choice under the European Convention and the International Covenant on Civil and Political Rights.[273] Article 18(4) of the

---

[264] Under this scheme the state is responsible for a school's running costs and 85% of capital expenses. School governors exercise control over the curriculum and may appoint teachers without being responsible for their salaries. See *The Education Act 1944*, ss 15-17.

[265] There are also a few Jewish and Methodist voluntary aided schools.

[266] See, e.g., *R v Secretary of State for Education, ex parte Yusuf Islam, The Times Law Report* (May 22, 1992): 260. The Department for Education is presently considering a request for voluntary aided status from a girls' school in Bradford, Yorkshire. *Times Educational Supplement* (May 6, 1994): 5.

[267] This view has been expressed by Jack Straw, the former Labour Party Education spokesman in *The Times Educational Supplement* (January 31, 1991): 5.

[268] Sarwar, *British Muslims and Schools*, 29.

[269] *Islamia* 22 (November, 1993): 1.

[270] *The London Times* (January 6, 1992): 1.

[271] *Islamia* 22 (November, 1993): 1.

[272] Sir Rhodes Boyson, in ibid.

[273] The ECHR guarantees that "the State shall respect the right of parents to ensure such education and teaching [as is] in conformity with their own religious and philosophical convictions." Article 2 of the 1st Protocol. The ICCPR stipulates that states should "undertake to have respect for the liberty of parents and, when applicable, legal guardians to ensure the re-

International Covenant does not require states to subsidize private schools.[274] Similarly, the European Court of Human Rights has said that there is no obligation on the state to "establish at their own expense or to subsidize education of any particular type."[275] Of course, international human rights law prevents a state from prohibiting the establishment of private religious schools,[276] but this is not a problem in the United Kingdom where religious minorities remain free to set up their own schools. And the British requirement that such schools conform to minimum educational standards conforms with international law.[277]

In refusing to grant Muslims and other faiths their own state-funded schools, the British Government has been accused of "blatant religious discrimination."[278] Even *The London Times* denounced this policy as "being perversely obtuse or explicitly prejudiced."[279] It would appear that this inconsistency of state funding for some but not for others constitutes discrimination. In the absence of British legislation prohibiting religious discrimination, however, minority faiths must once more resort to international human rights standards. The non-discriminatory provision of Article 26 of the International Covenant on Civil and Political Rights would appear to be particularly significant. In interpreting this provision, the Human Rights Committee has suggested that "the fact that a religion is recognized as a state religion . . . shall not result in . . . any discrimination against adherents of other religions . . . such as . . . giving economic privileges [to] . . . members of the predominant religion."[280] Thus, it seems that Britain's failure to grant voluntary aided status to minority faith schools, is arguably inconsistent with the letter, and certainly the *spirit*, of Article 26. Since this Covenant has not been incorporated into British law, however, it has only persuasive, not legal, value. Unable to rely on legislation expressly prohibiting religious discrimination, minority faiths lack an effective domestic legal remedy. As the Deputy Leader of the Muslim Parliament lamented, "state funding seems to be a

---

ligious and moral education of their children in conformity with their own convictions." Article 18(4).

[274] This is the view of Human Rights Committee member, Ms. Higgins, CCPR/C/SR.1209 p.5.

[275] *The Belgium Linguistic Case Series* A No.6, Judgment 23.7.68, 33.

[276] Nowak, *UN Covenant on Civil and Political Rights: CCPR Commentary*, 310.

[277] See *International Covenant on Economic, Social and Cultural Rights*, Article 13.

[278] Michael Barber, a leader of the National Union of Teachers, in *The Times Educational Supplement* (September 25, 1992): 2.

[279] *The London Times* (August 20, 1993): 19.

[280] The *General Comment* of the ICCPR's Human Rights Committee on Art. 18, para 9.

right for Jews, but not for us, and I don't believe we will see any change in that attitude."[281]

Collective Worship in Schools. In the United Kingdom, parents have considerable influence as to what is taught in the classroom. Section 6 of the Education Reform Act of 1988 provides that state-funded schools must ensure that all children attend a daily act of collective worship. In "county" schools (which educate 75% of pupils in England and Wales),[282] this worship must be "wholly or mainly of a broadly Christian character" reflecting "the broad tradition of Christian belief without being distinctive of any particular Christian denomination."[283] Pupils cannot be compelled to attend Christian school assemblies. Where a majority of children at a school are of a religion other than Christianity, the head teacher may apply to the local Standing Advisory Council on Religious Education for a ruling that Christian worship is inappropriate for some or all of the pupils in the school.[284] If granted, the head teacher must arrange "alternative" daily worship, and all approved worship, whether "alternative" or not, must be provided free of charge.[285] Of course, the notion of collective worship itself may be anathema to some parents. In such circumstances parents enjoy the right to withdraw their children from religious assemblies.[286] According to the Department for Education, this right should be "freely exercisable" and "is not for debate."[287]

Religious Education. As with collective worship, parents have a legal right to withdraw their children from religious education lessons.[288] Religious education is taught in state-funded schools according to a locally agreed syllabus. Since the Education Reform Act of 1988, new syllabuses must "reflect the fact that the religious traditions in Great Britain are in the main Christian whilst taking account of the teaching and practices of other principle religions represented in Great Britain."[289] Legislation also requires that every school must review its agreed syllabus for religious

---

[281] *The London Times* (June 13, 1994): 9.

[282] County schools are maintained wholly by Local Education Authorities (LEAs), who employ staff to work in them and own their premises. *The Education Act 1944*, s 9(2). Since voluntary aided schools must be conducted in accordance with their trust deeds, the act of worship in them may be denominational. Ibid., s 17(4).

[283] *The Education Reform Act 1988*, ss 7(1) and 7(2).

[284] Ibid., ss 11 (1)(b) and 12(1). The SACRE's function is to advise the LEA on religious worship and religious education in county schools. *The Education Reform Act 1988* s 11(1)(a).

[285] See N. Harris, *The Law Relating to Schools* (Fourmat, 1990), 215.

[286] The Education Act 1944 s 25. This right of withdrawal was reenacted in the *Education Reform Act 1988*, s 9(3).

[287] *DFE Draft Circular on Religious Education and Collective Worship*, 11th October 1993, paras. 75 and 79.

[288] *The Education Act 1944*, s 25(4).

[289] *The Education Reform Act 1988*, s 8(3).

education after five years.[290] Such syllabuses must achieve a complicated balancing act; they are expected to confirm Christianity as the dominant faith in religion yet also take account of the wishes of the local community.[291] Problems arise in areas where non-Christians form the majority of school pupils.[292] So far, even the production of two model syllabuses by the School Curriculum and Assessment Authority (SCAA) has failed to break the deadlock. According to the SCAA proposals, schools are expected to teach the basic tenets of five religions (Islam, Judaism, Sikhism, Hinduism, and Buddhism), while devoting most of their time in religious education to the study of Christianity.[293] Former Secretary of State for Education John Patten was confident that these proposals "could represent a turning point in the spiritual life of this country."[294] His optimism is not shared by evangelical Christians[295] and representatives of minority faiths,[296] who have criticized the SCAA's recommendations for failing to accord enough time for the study of their beliefs in the classroom.

In the past, allegations were made that minority faith children were pressured into attending Christian assemblies and religious education lessons.[297] Any such coercion is, of course, illegal, and the Department for Education has recently affirmed that where parents seek to withdraw their children from religious education lessons or collective worship "the school must comply."[298] The practical problems which this often causes for schools are considerable and have led the Archbishop of York to claim that this legislation is unworkable.[299] In theory minority faith children who opt out of religious education may either be assigned alternative work, or may receive religious lessons from a teacher of their own faith, on the condition that it imposes no financial burden on the school.[300] In the area of religious education, therefore, British law appears to comply with international law guidelines, since there is no evidence of

---

[290] *The Education Act 1993*, s 256.

[291] *DFE Draft Circular on Religious Education and Collective Worship*, 11 October 1993, para. 34.

[292] This point is made by Ibrahim Hewitt, Assistant Director, The Muslim Educational Trust, in a letter to *The London Times* (January 29, 1994): 17.

[293] *The London Times* (January 26, 1994): 6.

[294] *The London Guardian* (February 1, 1994): 7.

[295] *The London Times* (January 26, 1994): 6.

[296] *The London Guardian* (January 25, 1994), 8.

[297] See G.R. Barrell, *Teachers and the Law*, 5th ed. (London, 1975), 249.

[298] *DFE Draft Circular on Religious Education and Collective Worship*, 11th October 1993, para 73(2).

[299] *The Times Educational Supplement* (January 13, 1995): 10.

[300] *The Education Act 1944*, s 26.

proselytism and religious education should be taught in a "neutral and objective way."[301]

Conclusions

Contemporary advocates of the Establishment usually justify their position on four grounds. First, the establishment of the Church of England reminds the state's rulers that they may ultimately be accountable to a higher, divine power. Second, the established Church has a responsibility to the state which independent churches can easily avoid. Third, the ties between the Church of England and state should be preserved, since they are of historic value. Fourth, the established Church is worth protecting because of the unique role it plays in the unwritten British Constitution.

The first submission is, sadly, quite fanciful. Temporal control mechanisms, such as Parliamentary question time,[302] select committees,[303] and judicial review,[304] appear to be greater checks on those exercising power than any personal conviction that they are running God's kingdom on earth. Similarly, it is questionable whether the Church of England should owe a special responsibility to the state.[305] Such a proposition seems doubtful, both theologically[306] and morally. It certainly appears incongruous with the image of a Messiah who was born in a cattle-shed, drove the money-changers out of the Temple, and incurred the wrath of the religious hierarchy!

The third argument has more to commend it. The notion is that establishment is "the legacy of a long history in which the church has generated a nation"[307] and that to sever the Church's link with the state would in some way be a repudiation of Britain's heritage. It is undeniable

---

[301] The UN Human Rights Committee applied this test in *Hartikainen v Finland* (40/1978). A similar approach was adopted by the European Court of Human Rights in *Kjeldsen, Madsen and Petersen v Denmark*, Series A No 23 .

[302] See *Select Committee on Procedure: Question Time* (1969-70; H.C.198). See also P. Howarth, *Questions in the House* (London, 1956).

[303] See G. Drewry, "Select Committees and Back Bench Power", in G. Drewry, *The Changing Constitution*, 2d ed., J. Jowell and D. Oliver, eds. (Oxford, 1989), 141.

[304] See J.F. McEldowney, "Judicial Review," in *Public Law* (London, 1994), chap. 15.

[305] It should not be forgotten that a non-established religion is still subject to state control. For example, the disestablished Church of Wales is subject to its instrument of disestablishment, The Welsh Church Act 1914. See also the Churches (Scotland) Act, 1905, (5 Edw VII, c.12). Thus a Free Church is only free in so far as the state is prepared to leave it alone, while an Established Church is controlled only in so far as the state so decides.

[306] The Church claims to be the body of Christ (1 Corinthians 12:27), and is charged to complete the mission of Jesus (John 4:34.)

[307] Edward Carpender quoted in Wood, "Editorial: Church and State in England," 314.

that the Church of England has had a profound influence on the evolution of modern Britain. Important historical events such as the English Civil War,[308] the Glorious Revolution,[309] and the Conflict in Northern Ireland,[310] cannot be fully understood without some rudimentary knowledge of the Christian faith. However, if the Anglican Church's contribution over time to the nation is a reason for retaining an established Church, one should not disregard the historical inequities perpetuated by the Church in the name of Christ. The toleration of slavery, the subjection of women, and the persecution of Roman Catholics, dissenters, and Jews are as much a part of the Church of England's history as the "glories" which some tend to emphasize. Therefore, the fourth argument for the Church-State link, the constitutional significance of the Anglican Church, would appear to be the most persuasive.

The Archbishop of York has warned that any loosening of the links between church and state might ultimately cause the entire British constitution to disintegrate.[311] While such a dramatic scenario is unlikely, there is no doubt that the disestablishment of the Church of England would have a significant impact on the unwritten British constitution. Constitutional questions would remain as to who would replace the Bishops in the House and who would crown the Sovereign. Without a written constitution to provide guidance, the British Courts would probably be reluctant to arbitrate such disputes. Politicians would invariably make decisions, which might exacerbate latent divisions in the Anglican Church. As the Bishop of London recently observed: "Establishment is a deftly woven tapestry. Once you start to pull out this thread and that thread, the question is how much remains. Does not the whole thing unravel?"[312] Thus, the constitutional problems which disestablishment would invariably create are in themselves an argument for maintaining the status quo.

The Church of England has a special status in the United Kingdom. Yet, what of minority faiths? The Archbishop of Canterbury has claimed that "the establishment of the Church of England gives a religious dimension to the public culture. The loss of that dimension would damage the interests of *other* faiths as well as the Christian churches."[313] This statement is surely questionable. Notwithstanding the proclaimed neu-

---

308 See generally Kenyon, *The Stuart Constitution*.

309 See J. Miller, *The Glorious Revolution* (London, 1983).

310 See K. Boyle, T. Hadden, and P. Hillyard: *Law and State: The Case of Northern Ireland* (London, 1975).

311 *The London Times* (July 8, 1994): 4.

312 Ibid.

313 *The London Observer* (April 4, 1993): 7.

trality of the law in matters of religion,[314] the Anglican church enjoys a legislative influence and a protection from vilification denied to other faiths. Working life in the United Kingdom provides for Sunday attendance at Christian churches, while most public holidays and festivals are based on the Christian calendar. A Christian is likely to find it easier to practice his or her faith than a non-Christian. Members of minority faiths have been dismissed for taking time off work to pray or to celebrate their religious festivals.[315] This Christian bias is clearly a product of history, but seems increasingly difficult to justify in a multi-faith democracy approaching the millennium.

A leading member of the Muslim Education Forum has complained that "part of the British establishment hoodwinks itself into thinking that this is a white, Anglo-Saxon Christian country. . . . It will be a long term battle to remove the inequalities."[316] For a country that cherishes its stable constitutional heritage, Britain has been surprisingly reluctant to legislate against religious discrimination. Of course, it would be naive to imagine that a United Kingdom Religious Discrimination Act, modelled on the Racial Discrimination Legislation and Sex Discrimination statutes, would provide some kind of panacea. The success of such legislation would depend on its interpretation by the judiciary, as well as on social and cultural factors. Legislation outlawing religious discrimination in Northern Ireland has only been of limited effect.[317] However, it would reassure minority faiths that the state values them as equal citizens. Until this happens, suspicions of injustice will linger and many will perceive Britain as a land where "all faiths are equal, but some are more equal than others."[318]

---

[314] In *Neville Estates v Madden* [1961] 3 All ER 769 at 781, Cross, J. commented that "between different religions the law stands neutral."

[315] See Religious Observance at Work, (1991) 439 *Industrial Relations Legal Information Bulletin*, 4.

[316] Moeen Yaseen, *The London Guardian* (March 23, 1993): 6.

[317] See D.J. Smith and G. Chambers, *Inequality in Northern Ireland* (London, 1991).

[318] Cf. George Orwell, *Animal Farm* (London, 1951), chap. 10 ("All animals are equal, but some animals are more equal than others.").

The Main Problems of Religious Freedom in Eastern Europe

TAMÁS FÖLDESI
Eötvös Loránd University, Budapest

The Past

Any author trying to analyze the problems related to the freedom of religion in Eastern Europe is confronted with an especially difficult task. Eastern Europe is comprised of many states in a relatively small geographical area (and their number has further increased since 1989, with the dissolution of the Soviet Union and Yugoslavia). Though these countries have certain features in common, they are very different. There are both winners and losers of World War II among them. The majority of these states embrace heterogeneous nationalities and religions. The borders of most of these states were established only after World War I, and there have been many ethnic conflicts, often coupled with conflicts between the churches and religions. Although Christianity generally dominates in this region (Muslims and Jews are an insignificant minority), individual countries embrace significantly different forms of Christianity. Those more to the East, including Ukraine, Rumania, Bulgaria and Serbia, are predominantly Eastern Orthodox. In Poland, Slovakia, Hungary, Croatia, and Slovenia, the Catholic religion is predominant. In the Czech Republic and the former German Democratic Republic, Protestantism is strong, and the number of Protestant believers is also high in portions of Hungary, Western Rumania, and Slovakia.

Despite the large-scale ethnic and religious heterogeneity of the region, however, there is something else, besides geographic proximity, that unites the countries of this region. Until recently, each country belonged to the Soviet bloc for at least four decades. Consequently, the en-

J.D. van der Vyver and J. Witte, Jr. (eds.), Religious Human Rights in Global Perspective, 243-262.

tire region inherited from the Communist era certain common attitudes and actions respecting human rights and religious freedom.

In order to address the problems related to religious freedom in Eastern Europe today, I must discuss briefly the concept and practice concerning human rights in the former Communist countries.[1] The totalitarian system of those countries—no matter whether it amounted to a soft or a hard dictatorship—was incompatible with the majority of political and civil rights recognized in international law, for these countries had a one-party system. For example, the rights to organize or to free expression could not be realized. It made no difference that, as members of the United Nations, the Communist countries formally recognized the importance of human rights and embarked on efforts to implement certain economic, social, and cultural rights. Since political and civil rights played a subordinate role, less than they deserved, a specific dichotomy developed between the proclaimed principles and the actual practice of these countries. This rendered profoundly hypocritical their political leaders' testimony to human rights principles.

A similar attitude characterized the *concept of religious freedom* in these Communist countries. This state of affairs was fundamentally influenced by the Communist Parties' Marxist thinking about the present and future of religion, especially respecting the role of the church in society. In this regard, there were basic differences between the evaluations of the social roles that political parties and that churches were expected to play. On the one hand, the ruling idea was that in socialism the Communist Party could have no rivals. No genuine opposition party, including a religious group, was allowed to be organized, operate, or propagate their ideas. Moreover, the prevailing conservative line of Marxism considered religion to be a dead end which, instead of helping people to experience real liberation as offered by the revolutionary parties, offered no more than an illusory solution. Thus religion was always dismissed, in Marx's phrase, as "the opium of the people." On the other hand, the Communist Party did tolerate religion and the churches, albeit only temporarily, and the limitations imposed upon religious freedom were thus different in nature from those imposed upon political liberties. According to Marxism, religion throughout its history has helped to meet certain social demands. Religion constitutes a specific reflection of the idea that human beings are defenseless first against nature and later against social conditions. That is why persons turn to heavenly powers to overcome their misery. Since socialism is, as yet, unable to solve certain basic social

---

[1] Tamáas Földesi, "Reflections on Human Rights: An Eastern European Perspective," *Israel Law Review* (1989): 27-28.

problems, some people still need religious consolation. For that reason alone, religion must be tolerated.

Churches and religions were thus considered to be *necessary evils* in communist society. Since they were ultimately undesirable rivals to the Communist Party, however, restrictions on their activities were absolutely necessary, desirable, and deliberate.[2] It was just one short step from this concept to the view that religion is an *unnecessary evil*, that it will not die out with the ceasing of the social needs, and that already now it must be eliminated. This step was indeed taken by Albania in the early 1970s (although here, too, the lesson of history was repeated that attempts to eradicate religion by violence only creates martyrs and consolidates a religion's illegal survival).

Viewing religion as a "necessary evil," socialist countries developed similar strategies for the maintenance of religions and churches, on the one hand, and the restriction of their operation and influence, on the other. The most important strategy was the conscious effort to achieve and perpetuate the increasing *inequality of opportunities* of religious and secular ideologies, with Marxism being the main competitor among the ideologies. One field where this was clearly demonstrated was in higher education. Many hours of the school week were devoted to compulsory instruction in Marxism (with the explanation that this was the "only scientific ideology"). No opportunity was given for the propagation of religious ideas (which was based on the philosophy that religious views represented false ideas and, like pseudo-science, had no place in university curricula). Similarly, in primary and secondary schools, all subjects, especially the humanities, were taught in the spirit of Marxism, and any teacher who was outspoken about his own religious conviction during teaching was resented. In the media, too, Marxism was the dominant ideology; religious ideas were given very little or no place in programs. Publication of church literature was severely restricted. In some countries, such as the former Soviet Union, the Bible was a rarity and could hardly be obtained legally.

Religiously-based prejudice also culminated in inequality of opportunities in all the socialist countries. The schools were nationalized in the late 1940s (in the Soviet Union that happened earlier), and few if any church schools were left. In most countries, the religious orders were dissolved, and religious communities were declared illegal. Social activities provided by the church were also either eliminated or drastically restricted. As a consequence, nuns were not allowed to care for patients,

---

[2] Z. Rooter, "The Position of Believers in Socialist Countries," *Occasional Papers on Religion in Eastern Europe* (June, 1989): 5-7; Tamás Földesi, "Gedanken über die Gewissens und Religionsfreiheit," *Kirchiche Zeitgeschichte* (1990): 80-83.

and chaplains were barred from providing consolation to prisoners. Army chaplaincies were terminated, rendering national military service all the more burdensome. These measures were particularly inhumane since, because of their commitment, nuns had provided the best health care and chaplains had provided soldiers with the best means of coping with the pressures of service and provided prisoners with the greatest incentives to rehabilitate. At the same time, churches lost their traditional autonomy in every socialist country. State church offices were installed to control the financial and ideological activities of the church and to influence, even at times to direct, clerical appointments.

This general policy toward religion and the church was more or less characteristic of all the socialist countries, although the level of antireligious sentiment varied over time in the different countries.[3] Within this general framework, however, there were fundamental differences between "hard" and "soft" dictatorships. The situation of religion and the church was much more intolerable in the hard dictatorships. The leaders of the church were often persecuted and prosecuted in sham judicial trials. Religious believers were regarded as second class citizens, whose position and advancement in the social hierarchy were very negatively influenced by their religious association. Indeed, in the hardline Stalinist era, Jezhov and Berija carried out a full-fledged genocide against religious believers.[4] An organic part of the socialist countries' policy towards the church and religions was to try to corrupt certain church leaders and to win them over to support the regime. This strategy was particularly successful in some Eastern and Balkan states, for example in the Soviet Union, Rumania, and partially in Bulgaria. Moreover, in Rumania and Bulgaria, a further encumbrance was the elimination of certain churches or the amalgamation of one church with another. In the Soviet Union and Rumania, the Greek Catholic church ceased to exist for decades, or was incorporated into the Orthodox church.[5]

Under such conditions, the position of the leaders of the different churches became extremely difficult. On the one hand, they had to ensure the survival of their church and religion, and to promote the faith of the believers. On the other hand, they had to fulfill their clerical duties, which under such circumstances necessarily required a certain degree of cooperation with the Communist system. At the same time, they had to

---

[3] Otto Luchterhand, "The Human Rights and Freedom of Religion and Soviet Law," in Leonard W. Swidler, ed., *Religious Liberty and Human Rights* (Philadelphia, 1986), 93-94; Roter, "The Position of Believers," 14.

[4] A. Bessmertnij-Anzimirov, "Freedom of Faith: Internal Norms and Stalinist Legislation," *Occasional Papers on Religion in Eastern Europe* (June, 1989): 18.

[5] In several countries, most notably the Soviet Union, most of the church buildings were closed down or used for some other purpose.

preserve their relative independence from that system. Throughout the reign of socialism, but especially after its collapse, heated debates arose over what measure of church cooperation with the state was acceptable, and when such cooperation would amount to voluntary renunciation of basic church and religious interests.

These longstanding limitations on religious freedom did not yield the result which the Communist system had hoped to achieve. The majority of the society in most of these countries did not accept prevailing restrictions on their religious liberties. Moreover, given the Communist system's lack of political and economic legitimacy, people became increasingly skeptical of Marxist teaching, including its teaching on religion. Socialist society did not become atheist. Surveys carried out after 1989 show that in the socialist era only a very small proportion of the community was consciously atheist. (There was increased secularization, however, for a substantial number of people now do not belong to any religion despite the fact that they claim to believe in God or be agnostic.) Consequently, in the soft dictatorships, well before 1989—in fact already in the late 1970s and during the 1980s—critical voices demanded to place church and religious policy on a new footing, with a view to reducing or eliminating limitations on religious freedom. Poland was an exception, because there the Catholic church preserved its influence to such an extent that its word and activities fundamentally influenced the position of Polish society; opposition forces to a large extent found a haven in the church. In other countries, it was believed that, since the church also played a positive role, cooperation with the church would be necessary to solve social and other problems. A dialogue was organized to pinpoint common moral and other values. All of this contributed to the erosion of the Communist system and the preparation for a new era of religious freedom.

The Present

In 1989, the socialist system suffered a domino-like collapse in the countries of Eastern Europe, followed two years later by the collapse of the Soviet Union. It mattered little in what form the revolution took place—whether it was like "velvet," as in Czechoslovakia, or peaceful, as in Hungary, or armed, as in Rumania. The end result was the realization of a *pluralist democracy* in which multi-party parliamentary democracy was achieved through basically free elections. This new democracy dramatically changed the relationship between state and law. While law in the previous system functioned as a means of power, the new regimes set out to create a law-guided state along the lines of the European notion of the "rule of law." This new democracy also brought fundamental changes in the relations between the state and individual citizens. While in the previous society people were subordinated to state power and served its totalitarian goals—their rights being regarded as nothing more than a gift from the paternalistic state—the new society was to be formed in the spirit of civic society whose legal system is based on human rights, including fundamental political and civil rights. Without such fundamental rights, such as the right to organize or assemble or the freedom of expression, there could be no pluralistic democracy.

This political transformation of Eastern Europe dramatically changed the status of human rights. Human rights were afforded a central place in the new (or basically transformed) constitutions of the Eastern European nations. Consistent with standards of the United Nations and the European Convention on Human Rights, the rights to move from one place to another or to petition the state were included in constitutional bills of rights. Human rights were not merely recognized hypocritically, as mere words, but acquired true legal relevance. This new acceptance of human rights was typical of those East European countries which—even if not free from contradictions—consistently embarked on the road of democracy. There are, of course, exceptions to this in the warring countries, and those parts of a country where human rights were subordinated to nationalist endeavors and securing victory in prevailing conflicts.

It should be pointed out that this revival of human rights in Eastern Europe is still incomplete. The full realization of human rights norms will be a *long process* which had and still has to be carried out under very difficult conditions. The new political regimes must transform their economies by changing the economic system of centralized regulation that had largely failed to a social market economy. At the same time, they must transform their entire political and legal system. This has raised several basic problems. Let me mention just one:

In most countries, democratic transformation caused a drop in the living standards and conditions of a significant part of the people, and this has brought about significant social tensions. In human rights terms, it means that economic and social rights have been realized to a lesser extent than before. Unemployment, for example, has increased significantly. Progress is not so clear cut in other areas either. Despite the new pluralism, in more than one country political parties in power have tried to bring the electronic media under their control in order to realize their political interests. However, this has not changed the general state of affairs that fundamental, positive changes concerning human rights have taken place in Eastern Europe.

Changes in the political system also brought greater *religious liberty* to Eastern Europe. The new political regimes regarded the restriction of religious liberties, introduced by the socialist state, to be incompatible with democracy. The limitations on religious freedom were thus immediately, or gradually, eliminated, and general constitutional protections for religion were introduced. At the same time, since the restrictions of religious freedom also had been legally formalized under the Communist regime—such as the closing down of the religious orders, the nationalization of schools, the establishment of the State Office for Church Affairs, and the regulation of religious organizations—many Eastern European countries considered it necessary to supplement these constitutional protections with separate statutes on religious freedom, in accordance with the human rights documents of the United Nations and the European Convention on Human Rights.

Two laws passed by the Hungarian Parliament in 1990 and 1991 typify the legislative patterns of other East European countries. Act IV of the 1990 law on the *Freedom of Religion and Conscience* explicitly rejects the concept of the negative social role of the church and religion proclaimed by Marxism for the previous 40 years. The churches in Hungary, the introduction to the article proclaims, are "outstandingly important factors of society bearing values and creating community which play a basic role in culture, education, and teaching and in the development of social, health and national awareness." Consequently, the Republic of Hungary not only tolerates but protects by law and promotes the operation of the church. The law provides that churches may be involved in any activities that are not exclusively state functions, and it lists the spheres where church activity is especially desirable. It discusses specifically the activities of church officials in prisons and hospitals. All this makes it possible for the church to reestablish federations and organizations. Here, the legal limitations are only those which are included in the general regulations concerning the establishment of associations. (It is worth mentioning that the operation of religious orders was regulated a year earlier in another law, Act XVII of 1989.)

Section 16 of the 1990 Act also responded to the former situation in providing that no organization can be established to supervise the church. This is a basic legal guarantee of church autonomy. While the previous regime failed to provide any legal guarantee for citizens in cases where their religious freedom was violated, Act IV of 1990 states clearly that those who limit the practice of religion with force or threat can be punished with imprisonment of up to three years.

The creation and implementation of Act IV of 1990 provided the legal conditions for the restoration of religious freedom in Hungary. But, since in the previous period, the church was deprived of its economic basis, assets, and schools, it was necessary to make a separate law to regulate the material conditions that are needed for the free, unrestricted church to carry out its ministries and activities. That goal was served by Act XXXII of 1991 on the *Settlement of the Ownership of Church Assets*. The law recognizes that the church suffered various legal violations in the past which have to be remedied. It focuses on the objective conditions for the operation of the church and the need to ensure its assets. The law does not provide for simple and immediate restitution of church property confiscated in the previous four decades. Such property was, after all, not infrequently put to commendable uses, such as university housing and student hostels, and its immediate return could create social tensions. (Indeed, to date, no large landed property, previously owned by the church, has been returned, either in Hungary or in any of the other East European countries.) Instead, the law lays down that buildings previously owned by the church must be returned within ten years—in kind or by providing sufficient resources to construct a replacement building. In Hungary, and elsewhere in the region, the old State Church Office which restricted the church has been replaced by committees that do not control the church but manage the relationship between state and church. These committees are headed by state secretaries in Hungary, and one of their duties has been to settle issues concerning the conditions and date of the return of former church properties, in collaboration with church and the local public administrations.

The Hungarian example shows how complicated the return of church property can be. Following the political change, a Christian-national, conservative government was in power from 1990 to 1994. It officials emphasized the return of church property. Despite this, according to 1993 data, a mere 2.5% of real estate—only 150 properties out of the total of 6,000 assets requested—have been restored. While in 1948, 60% of the elementary schools were owned by the church, the figure today is still only 2%.[6]

The situation is not much better in the other East European countries. In Bulgaria, for example, three years after the political change, a law on the return of church property is in place, but the regulations on the implementation of that law have not yet been issued. The Czech Republic and Slovakia have no law on the subject at all. The return of Greek Catholic church buildings proceeds in a similarly slow fashion in Russia and Rumania. A typical situation can be found in Rumania: in the ab-

[6] J. András's comments in *Egyházpolitika Magyarországon [Church Policy in Hungary]* 4-5 (Távlatok, 1993): 555-556.

sence of church buildings, most of the Greek Catholic services are held outdoors.[7]

The situation is better in instances where church buildings do not have to be returned by one church to another (to the Greek Catholic church in the previous example), but where it is the duty of the state to return the assets nationalized in the years of religious persecution. This process accelerated after 1989. In Russia, for example, in 1990, the State Church Office, which was then still in place, decided to return about 1,000 church buildings; at the time, this was considered to be a great achievement. According to surveys carried out in 1991, 4,500 church buildings had been returned, and those primarily to the Greek Orthodox church.[8]

While the return of church buildings is welcome, this is just one part of the preconditions for the free exercise of religious freedom. In almost every East European country (with the exception of Poland, perhaps), there is a severe shortage of priests. It is fully understandable that if religious freedom is severely limited and the church and religion are presented as negative social institutions, then the popularity of a career in the church would decline, since becoming a priest would entail special sacrifices. An interesting development is that in some Baltic countries, the number of people taking up priestly careers has declined because in the past some people used this opportunity only to avoid compulsory military service. In Bulgaria, priests were not trained inside the country but abroad.

There is a shortage not just of priests but also of ordained religious teachers in Eastern Europe. The schools returned to church ownership need well-trained teachers, but despite the restoration of the church orders there are not enough ordained religious teachers at hand. Efforts are being made to remedy this situation by including religious teachers in education who are not priests or ministers but are committed to the church. At the same time, the number of university students who are preparing to become ordained religious teachers has increased.

Although the creation of genuine constitutional and statutory freedom of religion in Eastern Europe has changed the relationship of church and state and eliminated most state controls, patronage, and interference with the church, there are still many vestiges of the old order. For example, in May, 1992, the Bulgarian government announced "a war" against the Bulgarian Orthodox church and as a result, it immediately dismissed

[7] P. Török, *Közép és Keleteurópai, Egyházi Körkép 1992 [Central and Eastern European Church Overview]* 4-5 (Távlatok, 1993): 563.

[8] B. Filippov. "The Role of the Church in Restoring a "Civil Society" in USSR," *Occasional Papers on Religion in Eastern Europe* (January, 1992): 3-4.

the lawfully-elected Patriarch and dissolved the Holy Synod. Simultaneously, the office for church affairs installed a pseudo-synod and appointed four metropolitans to replace the Patriarch. This measure was justified as being part of the so-called "decommunization" of Bulgaria. The real reason, however, was that the Bulgarian Orthodox Church was internally divided, and contestants for the throne sought to attain their goal through such political means. Naturally, the question remains to what extent the Patriarch could preserve the Orthodox church under socialism and to what extent he cooperated with socialist government. But a democratic state doubtless does not have the right to interfere with the church is this manner. Debates as to clerical appointments and discipline have to be settled in an autonomous way within the church, without state involvement.[9]

Some Theoretical Problems of Religious Freedom

According to human rights literature, at least two basic conditions are needed for the full realization of the freedom of religion: (1) the *separation of state and church*; and (2) the so-called *ideological neutrality* of the state.

The consistent separation of state and church is an American invention. The First Amendment to the United States Constitution, ratified in 1791, contained the basic idea that the state had to ensure the free exercise of religion and, at the same time, the state was not allowed to set up a church. State and church were to be separated. This idea was not born in a secular country, but in a society that is religious to this day, and where it was considered to be useful and reasonable for the interest of both the state and church to remain separate. The basis of the principle lies in the fact that the state and the various churches *fulfil different social functions*, which, if conjoined, would harm both of them. Hugo Black of the United States Supreme Court is of the view that unification of the state and church would lead to the destruction of the state and the degradation of the church.[10] H. Woben similarly writes in his work on church law that "the state and church are two independent entities, realities that cannot be deducted from one another."[11]

But since the state and the churches exist in the same society, under given historical conditions, it is natural that, though basically separated, certain relationships have remained between them. For churches operate in many spheres of society that can be controlled by the state. As a conse-

[9] S. Raitzin, "Schism in the Bulgarian Orthodox Church," *Religion in Eastern Europe* (February, 1993), 19-20.

[10] *Everson v. Bd. of Education*, 330 U.S. 1 (1947).

[11] H. Woben, *Grundproblemen der Staatkirchenrechts* (Zürich, 1978), 19.

quence, the question arises what conditions must be satisfied for upholding the principle and practice of consistent separation of state and church? Generally, the answer to this question is that the state is neutral toward religion, confining religion to the sphere of free choice and autonomy.[12] The state may not guarantee priority or disadvantage to any of the religions.[13]

According to German constitutional law, neutrality means that the state does not identify itself with any of the churches, refrains from interfering in the activities of the churches, and does not ensure privileges for any of them.[14] Many concrete problems, however, may emerge in practice from the legislation of an individual country, especially whether the principle of the neutrality of the state is meticulously observed. The United States Supreme Court has developed the so-called *Lemon* test of 1971, to determine whether a law was made in the spirit of neutrality. A challenged law or policy must meet three requirements to satisfy the constitution: (1) the legislation should have a secular goal; (2) it should not provide advantages to any of the religions, nor should it ban any of its activities; and (3) there should be no entanglement between the state and the church.[15] Many authors argue that such ideological neutrality of the state does not mean indifference toward religion. Similarly, when interpreting religious liberty in Germany, they stress that the state cannot treat churches in a more disadvantageous manner than any other institutions that receive state support, such as sport federations.[16]

If we compare these definitions of neutrality, then it soon becomes clear that they are principally negative in their formulation; each definition speaks of what the state should not do to remain neutral. On this basis, an attitude of the state can also be imagined that maintains no connections of any kind with the churches. This attitude would mean that the state permits these organizations to exist as they can according to their own resources, no matter how their social role is evaluated. I think such an attitude would be acceptable as a special interpretation of neutrality, but it certainly cannot be regarded as the only possible interpretation. In this attitude, neutrality means indifference.

---

[12] Terry Eastland, ed., *Lowering the Wall: Religion and the Supreme Court in the 1980s* (New York, 1991), vii.

[13] N. Blum, *Die Gedanken Gewissens und Religionsfreiheit nach Artikel 9. der europäischen Menschen Rechts Konzepzion* (Berlin, 1990), 56. See further discussion in the chapter by John Witte, Jr. and M. Christian Green included herein.

[14] Balázs Schanda, *Religious Freedom in Hungarian Law* (Ph.D. Diss., Budapest, 1988), 20. See further discussion in the chapter by Martin Heckel included here.

[15] T. Orlin, "Religious Pluralism and Freedom of Religion," in *The Strength of Diversity* (Dordrecht 1992), 107.

[16] Balázs Schanda, *Religious Freedom*, 20.

A democratic state, however, would behave inappropriately if it were indifferent to religion. Religious neutrality is different from the type of neutrality which is expected of a neutral country in times of war. In war, neutrality indeed signifies the idea that the given state should keep itself at a distance from the warring sides; it should not help or support either side. But the relationship between churches and secular state organizations is not one of war. It is no violation of religious liberty for the democratic state to uphold the positive role of churches and religions in society. For this reason, the positive recognition of the church laid down in the introduction to the Act IV of the 1990 Hungarian law is, in my view, in full compliance with the principle of religious liberty. It would only become dubious if the same law would treat non-religious organizations differently, for that would amount to discrimination.

A democratic state may also, consistent with the principle of neutrality, provide certain forms of support to churches. A democratic state has many duties in which it can correctly rely on the activities of the churches as partners. Culture, education, and health care, for example, are areas in which, in Europe at least, the prevailing structures have long relied and will continue to rely on both state and church support. From the state's perspective, they are, in the language of the *Lemon* test, secular functions, and the state can support churches that are helping to discharge them. Such support is compatible with the principle of state neutrality, however, only if the state does not differentiate among the different churches in furnishing its support. If support is given, it must be given indiscriminately to all churches.

The question frequently arises whether a democratic state, consistent with the principle of neutrality and religious freedom, may withhold or withdraw support from so-called "socially destructive churches," those that detract from the public morality accepted by the vast majority of the population. The Hungarian Parliament, for example, passed a resolution in 1993 proclaiming that Act IV of 1990 should be amended to that effect. At the same time, support was withdrawn from four small churches that were viewed as "destructive." This policy seems to be consistent with prevailing international law of human rights, including the European Convention on Human Rights. While liberty of conscience is absolutely protected in international law, religious activities may be restricted to protect public order, security, health, or morality. The 1993 draft law of Hungary, it is therefore argued, should not be regarded as a limitation, but as an enhancement of religious liberty. The withdrawal of support from "destructive" churches is first of all based on the idea that their activities contradict public morality. Some other countries have concurred in this view. For instance, in 1960, the Constitutional Court of the German Federal Republic stated in connection with a concrete case that those religions may be defended and supported which throughout their history have embraced a common and general morality.[17] The practice of other European countries, however, shows that *religious liberty is generally not limited with reference to public morality.* It would be different, of course, if the activities of the church or its followers were to violate the law. Laws are limits on human rights, including the right of religious liberty.

There is ample theoretical justification for this general European practice. Van Dijk and van 't Hoof, for example, state in their work on the European Convention on Human Rights that, in fact, the "public morality" clause cannot be used to limit religious freedom, because public morality constitutes a too ambiguous and historically relative criterion.[18] Indeed, the history of most world religions shows that at their emergence, they proclaimed moral principles that were significantly different from the more or less generally accepted morality of the age. Think, for example, of the emergence, first of Christianity, later of Protestantism in Europe. Gábor Kardos takes a position similar to that of van Dijk and van 't Hoof. He points out that paragraph 9 of the European Convention of Human Rights, which deals with religious freedom, fails to provide guidelines as to (1) what would constitute a public morality; and (2) what the conditions of incorporating religious communities ought to be for purposes of their official, state registration.[19]

From all this, it can be concluded that religious liberty mandates that if the state does provide support for churches, it ought not to exclude certain churches from such support.

Equality and Inequality of Opportunities

Another recurrent theoretical problem is whether religious liberty requires a *relative equality of opportunities for religion, and, if so, to what extent.* Does equality of status demand equality of opportunity for religion? How, and by what method, may inequalities that had existed earlier, be eliminated?

In theory, at least *two models* can be imagined in this regard. The first model states that since, symbolically speaking, the pendulum swung against religion in the past forty years, then in order to eliminate the ensuing inequalities (harms) that religion had to suffer, the pendulum must

---

[17] Ibid., 24.

[18] P. van Dijk and G. van 't Hoof, *Theory and Practice of the European Convention of Human Rights* (Boston, 1990), 402.

[19] Gábor Kardos, "Remarks Concerning the Draft Law No.9473 of the Hungarian Republic" (unpublished manuscript), 6.

now swing back in favor of religion. "Compensation" can be realized only if the churches, currently and in the near future, gain significantly greater support than the materialistic ideology had permitted. One concrete manifestation of this idea was the effort to introduce *compulsory religious education* because only that would help to remedy what had been missed in the past decades, and in this way the balance would be restored. The other model—once again speaking symbolically—does not agree with the idea that the pendulum should now swing in the other direction; the pendulum should stop and remain in the middle.

The problem persists as to how to ensure an equality of opportunities for churches, given, among other things, their confiscated assets, the nationalization of their schools, and their reduced intellectual capacities over the past forty years. Speaking metaphorically, the "badly buttoned vest" could be corrected by unbuttoning it and then rebuttoning it in the proper way.

But when assessing the desirable equality of opportunities another interesting factor also has to be taken into account. With the political change in Eastern Europe, religious ideas now have no organized antireligious rival. The change of system perhaps most radically transformed the relationship between religious ideas and Marxism by eliminating the compulsory teaching of Marxism—not only at the university level, but everywhere. At present, Marxism has lost its organized form and in actual fact it is no longer a real rival of religion—at least, if one disregards what goes on in people's minds.

This must be stressed because some churches—believing that "those who are not with us, are against us"—view the state as the rival of the church, even in cases where the state is neutral toward religion. These churches, in particular, view state schools as rivals of church schools, for they identify the present, ideologically-neutral state school with the former, ideologically-committed one. In an article in the Catholic weekly *New Man*, entitled "It Should not be Neutral Under any Circumstances," the author writes:

> In connection with the school at Sari [a small Hungarian village], we heard the term "ideologically neutral" on many occasions. This term, in fact, is the definition of the former communist, atheist school. For this reason, it is necessary to warn that if a neutral school is demanded in the future, those who demand it, want to maintain the communist, atheist educational establishment. This, in itself, would not be a problem if there is need for it, but it should be called by its name and no one should make it appear as if the

Catholic school would represent some kind of extreme in contrast to the gentle, innocent, "objective" school."[20]

Although, I disagree with this line of reasoning, it does have an element of truth in it. With the elimination of Marxism, church school teaching now has only one rival, and that is what is taught in the state schools. Though state schools have abandoned their anti-church and anti-religious stance, they now have a pluralistic approach that introduces different ideologies without supporting any one of them. This attitude differs from the spirit of the church schools, which is monistic and committed to one definite ideology. So here, indeed, a certain tension prevails, which can cause problems for state-school teachers who are committed to a particular religion but who are also required to uphold the pluralistic ideology of the state institution.

Moreover, although the previous political system failed to convert most people to atheist ideology, its disproportionate and distorted educational structure left very little scope to the genuine teachings and history of churches and religions. Basic changes would thus be necessary to create an equality of opportunities for religion. For this reason, it is psychologically understandable that individual churches have done their utmost to enhance themselves, to spread information about their faith and history, and thus gradually to close the gaps in popular understanding of religion.

It follows from all of this that realization of religious liberty in the broadest possible sense would require the extensive dissemination of knowledge about religious alternatives, especially in public educational institutions. It would also require of the state to furnish church institutions with sufficient support to rehabilitate them and to ensure their proper functioning. This is true even though religion and the churches no longer confront an organized anti-religious competitor. (It is paradoxical that the previous political regime, too, was compelled to provide state support for the churches that were rather detached from some of their needs, in order to avoid plunging church activities into an impossible situation.)

At the same time, providing state support for the churches is not an ideal solution for achieving religious freedom, particularly if this support is necessary, not just because the churches are poor for historical reasons but also because they fulfill public functions which the state ought to support even if such functions are not carried out by church institutions. State support, even if it takes the form of historical compensation, inevitably creates unequal relations between the state and the churches. A les-

---

[20] *Uj Ember* (September 12, 1993).

son drawn from history is that ever since patronage of the arts has existed, artists who receive money—either from the state or from private individuals—have been compelled to make concessions in return for such financial help. And even if the relationship between the state and the church is basically different from that which pertains to artists, the possibility remains in principle that the state could impose certain demands and conditions on its support for the churches. There is a certain inevitable contradiction between state support for religion and church autonomy.

At present, there is no ideal solution to achieving religious liberty in Eastern Europe. Both policies of state support and of state withholding of support for churches have their drawbacks. For this reason, individual countries have proceeded, at least implicitly, on the basis of the principle of choosing "the lesser evil." Taking historical circumstances into account, several countries have adopted "no aid" policies; others have preferred to provide aid. It is instructive for Eastern European nations that, at least in the United States and Europe, these two models are not considered mutually exclusive. States that have adopted the principle of no support have also made concessions in the opposite direction; state that do provide support have sought to balance their support with the need to protect autonomy of the churches.

Two Models Concerning Religious Freedom and State Support in Europe

Two models on religious freedom and state support for religion prevail in Europe.

The first model has been developed in Germany and with some modifications in other European countries as well. In Germany, the churches receive state support for their operations as compensation for expropriated church assets. However, the activities of the churches are not primarily dependent on state support but on the donations of their members and church taxes, which the state collects for large churches. This church tax practice, however, is frowned upon by many who argue that the state thereby unjustifiably discriminates against smaller churches as well as against those who do not belong to churches. I agree with this reasoning, even if one bears in mind that any person has the right to leave the church and thus exempt himself from paying the church tax. In Germany, support for the church also includes compulsory religious education in state schools. Religious teachers are members of the state school staff. The mark of religious education is included on school diplomas. Prayer is also allowed at school. Also, on certain occasions, for example when declaring one's personal income or when being admitted to the hospital, a person is also asked to state his or her religious affiliation.

The second model, illustrated by Hungarian practice, is basically different. Religious education is not compulsory in Hungary. It is prohibited by law to ask anyone about his or her religious affiliation. Religious teachers are not members of state school staffs. Prayer in the school is not permitted. Church taxes cannot be collected the same way as state taxes are collected.

One may ask whether either of these measures is in harmony with religious freedom? As far as the first component of that question is concerned, the practice of the European Human Rights Committee and Court provides some guidance. Surprisingly, these organizations of the Council of Europe do not regard the practice in Germany and some other countries to be a violation of religious liberty, because these policies are subject to inherent limitations. Religious education is not compulsory in Germany in the same way as it was in Hungary and neighboring countries before World War II. Parents have the religious right to ask for their children to be excused from religious education, and children above the age of 14 may do so on their own behalf. Similarly, anyone may refuse to state his or her religious affiliations or to participate in public prayer.

The Council of Europe's interpretation of the viability of German practice has both positive and negative sides. On the one hand, there indeed is a fundamental difference between those regulations that render strictly compulsory one's participation in religious education, and those that allow one to be exempt from such participation, thereby providing an important degree of freedom. This freedom can be lawfully interpreted as the minimum of religious liberty, and in this context the interpretation of the Council of Europe is acceptable, especially given the historical circumstances of Germany.

At the same time, it would be incorrect to view the German model as a prototype of religious freedom. The German model follows the minimal demands of religious liberty, but this model can be rightfully criticized from the point of view of equal opportunities. The practice of compulsory religious education expresses a social value judgment that the average German citizen would want his or her child to participate in compulsory religious education and prayer. But it is not at all clear that parents with the opposite attitude would not be viewed, at least informally, as deviant and deserving of significant disadvantages. Realistically, this may lead to the violation of religious freedom, because many parents might very well encourage their children to participate in religious education so as to avoid being excluded from the community and being subjected to other disadvantages. In this way, these parents are compelled to be guided by considerations other than their convictions and to yield to informal social pressure. In my view, this contradicts certain requirements of religious freedom, for religious liberty indispensably involves respect for the conviction of those who do not identify with the views of the majority or with the dominant religion, but subscribe to minority religions.

Just as German practice satisfies standards of religious liberty, so too does the Hungarian practice, which is fundamentally different. The differences between these two systems can be explained, in part, on the basis of the historical experience of Hungary (and of other East European countries) during the socialist era of excessive state controls. Hungarian people have a quite different attitude toward compulsory religious education. I do not have German data, but the results of Hungarian surveys are available. In 1991, only 16%, and in 1992, only 18%, of the Hungarian people agreed that religious education should be compulsory for every child. The vast majority—in 1991, 78%, and in 1992, 73.5%—disagreed with compulsory religious education.[21] (It is insignificant that the ratios are slightly different.) But, even if an overwhelming majority of the people would opt for compulsory religious education, its introduction should be carefully considered. The absence of compulsory religious education would not be disadvantageous for religious parents and their children, because it would not limit the possibility of the children to participate in religious education, and at the same time it would not cause harm to children of parents with other convictions. I fully agree with E. Jackson who argues that one's right to life, freedom, religion, and assembly and other basic rights should not be subordinated to any kind of voting and should not depend on the result of any referendum. I do not doubt that during compulsory religious education, pupils would learn valuable information that would also shape their convictions, but I think if religion and religious conviction belong to the sphere of liberties, then it is not correct to give priority to any particular ideology. Similar arguments could be offered to show why the Hungarian solution is more acceptable from the point of view of religious freedom, where the state is not burdened with the duty of involvement in collecting church taxes and why it is correct not to ask anyone in Hungary about his or her religious affiliation.

---

[21] *Educatio* 1 (1992): 74.

Positive and Negative Aspects of Religious Freedom

Like any other freedom, religious freedom is at first sight a negative freedom. It expresses the conviction that the citizen need not belong to a church or religion, or conversely that no one is compelled to identify with certain ideologies, ideas, or convictions. But religious freedom clearly entails more than this negative element. It means that in the overwhelming majority of cases, people choose to belong to certain churches and to identify with certain religions, or conversely to maintain a secular stance. In this regard, religious freedom differs from political freedom. With regard to political freedom, a significant part of the people, maybe the majority of them, may distance themselves from political parties and even politics altogether. The positive side of religious freedom is that genuinely belonging to a church and truly identifying with a religion develops many distinct values in a person. Viewed negatively, it is no coincidence that criminals, drug users, and those who feel no responsibility towards society and who are socially insensitive are often not deeply religious. However, those features characterize not only the deeply religious people but also the majority of the humanistic, non-believers. It follows from this that a positive aspect of religious freedom should be the dialogue between the churches, not only ecumenical dialogue but dialogue with persons of other faiths, and with no faith, to realize the values which exist on both sides to the benefit of the individual and society.

It is regrettable that since the political transformation of Eastern Europe, such religious dialogues rarely take place. In my opinion, prejudice has a lot to do with this, for dialogue has long been associated with "communist making"—a practice that the communists urged, which is now no longer necessary. I do not agree with this line of reasoning. In the past few decades, so much prejudice, distrust, and misunderstanding has accumulated. Divergence should be replaced with convergence, isolation with openness.

This picture works well in East European countries living in peace. Unfortunately, however, there are countries living in a state of war with each other. In these countries, the positive form of religious freedom raises even more topical questions. One of the fundamental features of the wars in Eastern Europe—I have in mind the former Yugoslavia and, further, the conflicts in the successor states of the former Soviet Union—is that their concern with religion has become predominant. The war between the Serbs and the Posing in Bosnia is at the same time a struggle between the Eastern Orthodox Serbs and the Muslim Posing. What position should the churches take where the countries are engaged in a war with each other, where national and religious minorities are not tolerated by the dominant religious or ethnic faction?

Since religious and ethnic identities are closely related, the ethnic conflicts are generally religious conflicts at the same time, and for this reason, the churches of warring countries are basically confronted with two alternatives.[22] One alternative is that the dominant church is expected to identify itself with the nationalistic endeavors, in fact to give its blessing to the arms. This is a great temptation because, otherwise the churches could be regarded as irrelevant and people would turn away from them. A second alternative, however, is that the churches of the warring sides unite against the war, in defence of peace, to save the lives of their own members and those of other churches. Furthermore, they oppose nationalism, which is good since every church, in essence, is universal.

Mirror Vol is correct when he states that under such conditions, "being different," "otherwise," is, theologically, a positive value. Instead of using slogans of ending oppression and implementing liberation, the theology of fraternity and remittal should be addressed. Sometimes, this is extremely difficult when the other side had been engaged in actions of cruelty and ethnic cleansing, but there is no other way open to a Christian church, or indeed a Muslim mosque, if it wants to keep its religious identity and adherence to its basic religious ideals.[23]

If we examine the history of the thus far unfinished wars from this point of view, then it has to be acknowledged that the churches of the warring sides have tried more than once to come to terms with one other, but their efforts have not been sufficient or consistent in propagating remittal and Christian love. This failure might well be one of the causes of the ongoing wars, especially in the former Yugoslavia whose end is not yet in sight.

---

[22] Paul Mojzes, "War between Religions," *Religion in Eastern Europe* (February 1993): I-II.

[23] M. Volf, "Exclusion and Embrace: Theological Reflections in the Wake of Ethnic Cleansing," *Religion in Eastern Europe* (December, 1993): 6-7.

Religious Human Rights in Post-Communist Balkan Countries

PAUL MOJZES
Rosemont College

The purpose of this chapter is to provide an overview of the changes that took place after the Great Transformation[1] in several of the formerly Communist countries of the Balkan Peninsula in the area of religious human rights. The analysis builds upon a book-length study of this topic entitled *Religious Liberty in Eastern Europe and the USSR: Before and After the Great Transformation*[2] which I completed in late 1991.[3]

[1] The term "Great Transformation" connotes the transition from the Communist to the Post-Communist socio-political arrangement. Generally it is considered that the Great Transformation took place between 1989 and 1991, but the process started earlier (1980, the Solidarity Era in Poland may be taken as an early sign and 1985 with Gorbachev's perestroika as a definite boost to the process) and that it still continues at this time, since it is not at all clear what "Post-Communism" actually means.

[2] Paul Mojzes, *Religious Liberty in Eastern Europe and the USSR: Before and After the Great Transformation* (Boulder, CO, 1992, distributed by Columbia University Press).

[3] See also, among other writings, Stella Alexander, *Church and State in Yugoslavia since 1945* (Cambridge, 1979); Trevor Beeson, *Discretion and Valour* (Glasgow, 1974); Janice Broun, *Conscience and Captivity: Religion in Eastern Europe* (Washington, 1988); Barbara A. Frey and Carl E.S. Söderberg, *Human Rights in The Socialist Republic of Albania* (Minneapolis, 1990); Ingeborg Gabriel, *Minderheiten und nationale Frage* (Vienna, 1993); Barbara Jelavich, *History of the Balkans: Twentieth Century* (Cambridge, 1983), vol. 2; Paul Mojzes and Gerald Shenk, "Protestantism in Bulgaria an Yugoslavia Since 1945," in Sabrina Petra Ramet, ed., *Protestantism and Politics in Eastern Europe and Russia* (Durham, NC, 1992), 209-236; Paul Mojzes, "Religious Liberty in Yugoslavia: A Study in Ambiguity," in Leonard W. Swidler, ed., *Religious Liberty and Human Rights in Nations and in Religions* (Philadelphia, 1986), 23-42; id., "Religious Liberty: Definitions and Theoretical Framework," in Leonard W. Swidler, ed., *Human Rights: Christians, Marxists and Others in Dialogue* (New York, 1991), 173-198; id., *Yugoslavian Inferno: Ethnoreligious Warfare in the Balkans* (New York, 1994); Marko Orsolic, "Religious Freedom as a Civil Right," in Swidler, ed., *Human Rights*, 209-218; Spas Raikin, "The Bulgarian Orthodox Church," in Pedro Ramet, ed., *Eastern Christianity and Politics in the Twentieth Century* (Durham, NC, 1988), 160-182; Pedro Ramet, "Catholicism in Yugoslavia," in Pedro Ramet, ed., *Catholicism and Politics in Communist Society* (Durham, NC, 1990); id., *Religion and Nationalism in Soviet and Eastern European Politics* (Durham, NC, 1988); Robert Lee Wolff, *The Balkans in Our Time* (Cambridge, MA, 1956). Among periodicals, see *Glaube in der*

J.D. van der Vyver and J. Witte, Jr. (eds.), Religious Human Rights in Global Perspective, 263-284.

In that book, I formulated a typology of social arrangements based on criteria of religious liberty which may be helpfully carried over into this work and will be summarized here. That framework will then be applied to the successor states of the former Yugoslavia, namely Slovenia, Croatia, Bosnia and Herzegovina, Yugoslavia (Serbia and Montenegro), and Macedonia, as well as to neighboring Bulgaria and Albania. Greece and Rumania rightfully belong in the study of Balkan states, but in order to reduce the scope of the study, they will not be covered here. The author also wishes to alert the readers that the situation in all of the Balkan countries is extraordinarily fluid at this time and that in order to write a more authoritative study one would have to spend a considerable time on location exploring the situation in these countries, which he was able to do only in a limited fashion.[4] Written studies on the concrete situation in the specific countries are quite rare; most of them are news releases.

Background Information

It has been said that Yugoslavia is the despair of tidy minds, and that is even truer in respect to the entire Balkan Peninsula. Since the present configuration of Balkan countries, a process unfinished as yet, is being established in the twentieth century, a brief review of that process will be offered.

With the decline and dissolution of the two dominant empires—the Ottoman Turkish, and the Hapsburg Austrian—throughout the nineteenth and early twentieth century, the local nationalities were awakened by rising nationalism throughout Europe. Most of them had their own independent states in the medieval period, and now they started fighting for the establishment of their own nation-states. With the peace treaties after World War I there emerged the independent countries of Rumania, Bulgaria, Greece, and Albania, while Serbia, Montenegro, Croatia, Slovenia, Macedonia, and Bosnia and Herzegovina were united into a multinational state which was eventually named Kingdom of Yugoslavia (South Slavia). Aspirations to achieve the alleged medieval greatness by these new states was and continues to this day to be a curse, since nearly all of them lust for the same territory on which their ethnic members are hopelessly intermingled. During World War II, states which claimed to

---

2. *Welt* (monthly, Zollikon, Switzerland); *Religion in Communist Dominated Areas* (monthly, New York, NY); *Religion in Eastern Europe* (formerly *Occasional Papers on Religion in Eastern Europe*) (bi-monthly, Rosemont College, Pennsylvania); *Religion, State and Society* (formerly *Religion in Communist Lands Quarterly*) (Keston Research, Oxford, England).

4 Except for shorter visits to Serbia, Macedonia, Croatia, and Slovenia in 1993.

have been dispossessed through the peace treaties (Germany, Austria, Italy, Hungary, and Bulgaria) profited from Hitler's aggression and redrew the borders. Yugoslavia was thus eliminated from the map between 1941 and 1945 only to reappear as the "new," federal republic of Yugoslavia. All Balkan countries except for Greece fell under Communist control and into the Soviet sphere of influence. Yugoslavia extricated itself from the Soviet bloc in 1948, Albania in 1961, while the others remained in the bloc until 1989. Yugoslavia under Josip Broz-Tito became a revisionist socialist country, very much open to the West and even more so to the Third World, while Albania remained Stalinist-Maoist, and Bulgaria and Rumania were ruled by rigid dictatorial regimes, the first slavishly dependent on Russia and the second an international maverick but domestically a Ceausescu family despotism.

Upon the death of Tito in 1980, the tensions between the republics of the Yugoslav federation increased until full-fledged ethnic nationalist chauvinism became prevalent in the second half of the 1980s. The sequel of this conflict is now well-known: In 1991 several wars broke out, first a very short one in Slovenia, then one in Croatia where an uneasy cease-fire now prevails after the Serbs took nearly a third of the territory, and then finally, in 1992, a horrendous war broke out in Bosnia and Herzegovina that has not ended at the time of this writing. With the collapse of the federation, the Serbs undertook the task of gathering all Serbs into one country, officially still called Yugoslavia but in fact a "Greater Serbia." They did so under the slogan of "ethnic cleansing," namely attempting to oust all non-Serbs from the territories which they occupied; thus the war in the former Yugoslavia assumed genocidal dimensions.

Politically, the Balkans (except for Greece) are former Communist countries that have entered into post-Communism allegedly seeking democracy and free market economies, but in fact having neither the tradition nor the stability to have anything but economic chaos and political authoritarianism. With the economic catastrophe, the population is now starting to look with some nostalgia to the more economically secure socialist period, but since Communist internationalism is irretrievable, there is a great chance of a sharp turn to the right to a nationalist socialism or fascism. During the Communist period, both law and media were used as tools in the class struggle and monopolized by the state. Thus there was no independent judiciary, no state of laws, no public dissent. This legacy will be hard to break; the new governments find quite irresistible the temptation to use the laws and the media in order to stay in power. Yet, slowly, there is an emergence of greater media openness, of better laws, of inklings of a more independent judiciary, but one suspects that the path to an open society will be long and arduous. The increasing nationalist hatred produced by war and proximity to war will make the process even harder if not impossible.

The Theoretical Framework

Four distinct types of arrangements regarding religious human rights have developed historically on European soil.

Type A: Ecclesiastic Absolutism. This type could also be called Absolutist Sacral, because of the exclusive power vested in a single religious option, or Preferential/Discriminatory, because one religious institution is given preferential treatment while others are discriminated against. For conciseness, however, the term Ecclesiastic Absolutism seems best. Ecclesiastic Absolutism means that only one religious organization is supported by the state. The government provides preferential treatment and extends freedom only to those who fully comply with the beliefs and practices of that "state church," but denies or sharply curtails freedoms to all those who do not believe or believe differently. This type seemed to be, when I constructed it in 1990, by and large a model of the past; yet in Eastern Europe, it was not so long ago that certain national churches were in a distinctly privileged position (one might call it an intimate relationship between church and state), while other churches and atheists suffered various degrees of unfreedom.

Type B: Religious Toleration. Another name for this model might be Preferentially Religious, because religion as such is preferred and supported by the state. This means that, theoretically, the state is separated from the religious organizations, which are treated equally before the law; yet the state remains benign toward all religions. In reality, such states give practical preferences to the stronger, historically dominant churches and discriminate against non-believers, either legally or by various manipulations of public opinion. The amount of religious liberty is much greater in Type B than in Type A, and hence this is a definite advance in the right direction.

Type C: Secularistic Absolutism. A different name for this model could be Obstructionist, because it hinders all religious expressions and favors a single secularist worldview. Religion as such is rejected by the state. Seemingly diametrically opposed to Type A, all religions suffer various degrees of restrictions, while non-believers, especially militant atheists, often receive privileges. Not infrequently, this alleged atheist state promotes the adoration of the state, its leadership, and its ideology which renders it a secular religion, thus making it actually a very close kin to Type A.[5] Type C arises as a result of dissatisfaction with Type A, but the exclusivist mentality remains the same. According to the Italian scholar, Giovanni Codevilla, such a state "refuses to recognize that there can exist a difference between a nation and its official ideology and acts with force to create an absolute *religious (spiritual)* unity within the state."[6] In Type C, religious liberties are drastically reduced, although in some formal ways all such states constitutionally declare the same freedoms as states of Type B. Drastic limitations are imposed on existing religions, because the Communist party advances an ideology that invades the realm of religion by defining itself as the center of truth for the realization in time and space of a universal *salus societatis*, both exclusive and definitive. Indeed, among other goals, it assigns itself the task of seeing to the disappearance of religion, because it finds in Marxism-Leninism, taken as a comprehensive or pseudo-religious doctrine, the justification for its existence. In other words, the Soviet State places itself in a position vis-à-vis the party and Marxism-Leninism equivalent to that of the European Absolutist state vis-à-vis the universal Church and religion. It finds precisely here the entity which justifies its own sovereignty.

The famous Serbian novelist and social analyst Dobrica Cosic, a former Communist, points out correctly that Bolshevism and/or Stalinism is/are political religions.[7] Those who say that the religious policy of Bolshevism was primarily pragmatic need to explain why such severe repression and total alienation of the religious population followed after Bolshevism prevailed and when the religious population could have been turned into allies. The pre-revolutionary rhetoric of Lenin and of all Communist parties conceding religious liberties mislead many people into thinking that only pragmatic considerations brought about the conflict between Communists and religious believers and institutions. Actually Lenin's Bolshevik approach was temporary. The attack on all religions was related to the distinctly religious belief of the Bolshevik/Stalinist type Communists that Marxism-Leninism *alone* gives the full understanding of the world and can promote human happiness.[8]

The Communist revolutions established Secularistic Absolutism (Type C) in all countries where they were successful. This meant a sudden and dramatic loss of liberties for those who were privileged or at

---

[5] A very strong case is made, especially in regard to the religious nature of Soviet Communism, by Giovanni Codevilla, "The Limits of Religious Freedom in the USSR," in Dennis J. Dunn, ed., *Religion and Communist Society* (Berkeley, CA, 1983), 67-84, esp. 68-74.

[6] Ibid., 69.

[7] Dorica Cosic, "Zbiva se civilizacijska revolucija" [A Civilizational Revolution is Taking Place], *NIN* 2045 (March 11, 1990): 60.

[8] John Anderson, "Legislative and Administrative Control of Religious Bodies," in Eugene B. Shirley, Jr. and Michael Rowe, eds. *Candle in the Wind* (Washington, DC, 1989), 68.

least equally tolerated before the revolution. Momentarily, as a matter of tactics, the state in Type C may improve the conditions of those religious groups that were being repressed in previous societies in order to manifest publicly that it is not discriminating against religion but only restricting abuses of formerly privileged churches. But both Marxist theory and practice show that such accommodations can only be temporary, since no religion is seen as beneficent for the population. In later developments of Type C, there are evident some vestiges of Type A and B, as well as a tendency to tolerate some features of Type B or Type D.

Type D: Pluralistic Liberty. Other possible names for this type could be Free Non-interventionist or Unhindered Libertarian, Enabling, or Tolerant Secular, but Pluralistic Liberty connotes the full exercise of freedom in a context of a variety of truth claims. The state is really indifferent and neutral toward religion or non-religion. This type is a human possibility, but it is difficult to achieve fully. Yet, this model has been and is being experienced, at least in rudimentary form, in some areas of the world. In such a state, religious organizations and the government are truly separated with no intention on the part of either to dictate or mix into the domain of the other. There are evidences that features of this Type D are gradually appearing in various modern societies.

There is a close linkage between Types A and C, on the one hand, and Types B and D, on the other. In their pure form, Type A and C are both intolerant toward all except those whom the state decides to favor. Type C was more problematic in the period from 1945 to 1990, because Type A was all but non-existent in modern Western societies (not so in the Islamic world), while Type C came into existence in the twentieth century when the totalitarian and manipulative power of the state has reached unprecedented scope. Hence the inquisitorial practices and religious wars which characterized Type A seem to pale into insignificance when Type C makes its brutal appearance.

Type B and Type D are very close in principle. Both not only proclaim but respect at least a *de facto* separation of church and state (certain Western European societies still contain *de jure* preferential treatment of certain churches but in real life make no efforts to suppress atheism or the work of other religious organizations). It is the practice of Type B that sometimes handicaps non-believers or adherents of new or minority religions. Yet, there is a dynamic in societies of the B Type, which aims at extending in practice the freedoms granted in principle and therefore Type B can gradually become Type D.

One of the major questions posed during the Great Transformation was whether it is possible to move from Type C to Type D. Perhaps a more vigorous dialogue between proponents of Type B and Type C may stimulate the transition of both into Type D. One possible scenario would be that the memory of a Type A with its absolute, total, monolithic claims, has two options in development. One is to develop gradually into a Type B, pluralistic democratic society, or into Type C, which is the reactive counterpart of Type A, seeking to develop a secularist, atheist totalitarian claim/society, by dismantling religious institutions and persecuting religion. This society likewise seemed in 1990 to be destined to develop into a Type B or a Type D society, which is pluralistic. The necessity of that development was due, I thought, to the historically evident inability (except perhaps in Albania) to suppress religion effectively, so that there is practical pluralism even during periods of oppression. Such oppression is capable of giving way to toleration and then perhaps to genuine pluralism of religious and secular worldviews and practices within a society. What did not seem likely in 1990, but which appears to be a trend in 1994, is for *Type C to show strong tendencies to revert to Type A,* which seemed to me at the time as a historical anachronism. But the post-socialist societies in the Balkans show a situation in which there are currently *mixtures of Type A and Type B* and the results are tensions that come with the coexistence of incompatible models within the same society.

Thus the stages would be as follows: (1) Type A: Monopoly of a religion society; (2) Type B: Social preference for religions, and religious toleration with religious views being at an advantage and atheism at a disadvantage; (3) Type C: Near-monopoly of state atheism, with a decisive disadvantage for religion; and (4) Type D: Pluralism and freedom for all views and practices, except those most patently destructive.

General Trends After the Great Transformation

One of the characteristics of the Great Transformation was the rehabilitation and renascence of religion in all former Communist countries. It is not surprising that this happened last in Albania (in 1990), since there religious human rights had been most radically curtailed, to the point of constitutionally denying the right to the existence of religion and in practice carrying out this policy with utter consistency and ruthlessness. In other countries, where religious liberties were at least constitutionally guaranteed though in reality both legally and practically hampered to various degrees, the changes came both earlier and with greater ease.

The basic characteristic of the vastly improved situation in regard to religious liberty is that, with the exception of Albania, it was not manifested primarily by massive change in legislation but by a radical improvement in the behavior of governmental agencies toward religious communities and individuals. The general legal provisions regarding religious liberty did not need to be changed, because they already adequately expressed the principles of freedom of religion and conscience. The government officials started neglecting those legal provisions that were instituted during the Communist regime to hinder and restrict the functioning of religious communities. Thus, the religious communities and individuals experienced a sudden sense of freedom and a corresponding ability, yea an opportunity and even a mandate, to break out into the limelight. The media started evaluating religion positively and provided opportunities for religious groups to be present at various public functions. Religious leaders and members were interviewed and given the opportunity to condemn past repressions and indicate their hope for the reestablishment of their rights—and some of them even sought privileges. Politicians pledged their support to religious communities and were eager for picture opportunities with clergy and at worship. Studies about Communist religious oppression were published. Religious buildings that had been confiscated began to be returned to their previous legal owners; old buildings were renovated and new buildings were built. Religious activists of various sorts began to advance the cause of their faith in various ways. Religious education again became possible. All in all, a radical improvement for nearly all religious communities was being experienced. This was the point at which there seemed so much hope that Type C would transform itself into Type D or at least Type B society.

But it turned out that these expectations or predictions were premature. The patterns of Type A had been too deeply infused into the traditionalist social matrix of most Eastern European societies, especially the Balkans, so that the lessons that *could* have been learned by the captivity of all religions under Communism were quickly forgotten by most. The general instinct of the Great Transformation was not to look forward but backward and sideways, that is, not to build new social relations but to revert either to the pre-Communist patterns of the respective societies or to emulate what certain other non-Communist societies were doing.

Concretely, this means that the traditional ethnoreligious identification in the respective societies established itself with, in some cases, a fury and vengeance and, in others, with less fanfare but equally resolutely. The historically dominant religion or church of a region sought the restoration of all of its lost privileges from the Type A era and, considering other religious communities as rivals, sought to influence state authorities to limit the rights of other religious communities and of nonbelievers. Sometimes government officials also urged the reestablishment of said privileges and/or restrictions, as they themselves favor such ethnoreligious identification. Whatever ecumenical relationships may have existed during the Communist period—and these were not pronounced in the Balkans—vanished among mutual recriminations of proselytism and repression by the respective players. Thus, currently one can observe an area-wide struggle between the dominant church or religion that wishes to restrict the activities of rival denominations and the numerous old and new religious groups that are threatened by the prospect of monopoly (or establishment) by the dominant national church (religion).

The constitutions of the new states uniformly accepted the principle of freedom of religion and conscience, but the separation of church and state was not so enthusiastically endorsed. Thus, for instance, the 1991 Constitution of Macedonia, which can be taken as illustrative, proclaims in paragraph 19: "Freedom of religion is guaranteed. Free and public expression of faith, individual and communal, are guaranteed. The Macedonian Orthodox Church, other confessional communities and religious groups are separated from the state and are equal before the law. The Macedonian Orthodox Church, other confessional communities and religious groups are free to organize religious schools and other social and charitable institutions in accordance with the law." Paragraph 16 provides: "Freedom of conviction, conscience, thought, and public expression of thought are guaranteed." Paragraph 54 provides: "Limitation of freedoms and rights cannot be discriminatory on the basis of gender, race, skin color, language, religion, national or social origin, economic or public circumstances. Limitation on freedoms and rights cannot pertain to the right to life . . . as well as freedom of conviction, conscience, and public expression of thought and religion."[9]

The fundamental problem in regard to equal application of religious human rights is the equation of ethnicity and religion in all of the states except Albania—and even there, the majority of the population identifies itself with Islam, to the detriment of Orthodoxy and Catholicism which are minority religions. There is a widely held conviction that the dominant historic religion or church is so closely determinative of nationhood that somehow all members of the nation belong collectively to that religion; those who consciously change religion are de-nationalized, and those who do not practice religion are potentially still members of the national church. Hence activities of the minority religions as they affect even unchurched or non-religious people are seen to be to the detriment of the dominant religion. The dominant religion sees itself as having been so greatly harmed by Communist efforts of atheization among its traditional members that it is felt that any inroads (such as conversions) made by other religious groups are unethical acts of pilfering. Many representa-

---

[9] *Ustav na Republika Makedonija* (Skopje, 1991), translated from Macedonian by the author.

tives of dominant churches do not fully understand the concept of religious liberty; perhaps not surprisingly, because historically they have not experienced such arrangements since they knew only of privileged and oppressive conditions. Thus, they now seek to restrain members of smaller religious groups by setting legal obstacles in their way, for example, requiring registration by the government which can be denied arbitrarily, or requiring the permission of the priest of the dominant church for another denomination to enter a village in order to carry out evangelization, or denying permissions for the purchase and or rebuilding of worship centers, or requirements that heads of religious groups must be citizens of the country, and so forth. The minority churches, on the other hand, have a memory of oppression which often creates a negative reflexive reaction to any consideration of size and are sometimes uncreatively seeking a mechanical leveling of all religious communities. Thus, the opportunity is lost for any creative grappling with the situation as it emerged after the Great Transformation, and instead security is sought in reverting to past patterns.

The war (or more accurately wars) that have broken out since 1991 have affected the situation most drastically. Though these conflicts are not explicitly religious wars, they are ethnoreligious due to the very close identification between ethnic and religious affiliation; practically speaking, there is a union or merger between ethnic and religious identification, and since these seem to be predominantly wars over territory that should be held by certain ethnic groups the phenomenon of "ethnic cleansing" occurred. "Ethnic cleansing" is an antiseptic word behind which are hidden both planned and spontaneous policies of exterminating ethnicities other than one's own in order to change an ethnically mixed population into an ethnically compact, uniform one. This is done by murder, torture, rape, arson, pillage, and forcible eviction of "undesirable" ethnic groups and a deliberate raising of the level of horror and fear so as to discourage any future thought of returning to this land and resettling it. Even the memory of past habitation of the persecuted ethnic groups is sought to be erased, and this is done by destroying—even wiping out all trace of religious and cultural monuments. All that is sacred to an ethnic group is demolished, such as churches, mosques, shrines, cemeteries, historical landmarks, memorials, and other symbols of the "alien" faith. All kinds of clergy—priests, imams, hodjas, pastors, and others—are murdered or expelled, and the pastoral care of their respective group is impeded. The holding of religious services is obstructed in every conceivable way. In such a situation, religious human rights along with all other human rights, including the right to life(!), are for all practical purposes obliterated. The existence of laws on paper and the guarantees which leaders issue are simply irrelevant, because the purpose of waging these wars, while ostensibly defensive in nature to provide for the continued existence of an ethnic group, usually means the desire to remove the other ethnic groups. The continued coexistence of these groups living in a mixed society is no longer envisioned by the political leaders or by most of the population which is at war with each other.

Specific Trends After the Great Transformation

The foregoing section provided an overview of the situation in general through the Balkans. What follows is some specific information, country-by-country, going from northwest to southeast.

Slovenia. Slovenia was the first state of the former Yugoslavia to secede from the federation. After a short war of about 10 to 14 days in duration, the federal army and government agreed to Slovenia's independence and sovereignty. Since that time, Slovenia has developed under relatively advantageous circumstances and is closest to achieving a Western European model of religious and political liberty.

The great struggle in Slovenia is about the overall concept of the state. One group wishes to promote a secular, Western European style democratic arrangement which would guarantee separation of church and state and equality to all religions. The other promotes a central European concept in which the Roman Catholic Church of Slovenia would have special responsibilities and privileges. The responsibility of that Church would be to provide for the spiritual and ethical needs of the Slovenian nation by promoting a unique Slovenian post-Communist model, which would neither be a liberal democracy nor a fascist or Communist dictatorship but a state in which Catholicism would imbue the entire nation with collective responsibility and avoid the extremes of liberty that so easily lead to excessive individualism.

The greatest single legal issue is the question of returning properties that had been expropriated from the Church during the Communist period. A mixed Catholic-government Commission has been established to discuss how much, which, and in what time frame properties should be returned. One view is that only those properties that are of direct use to the Church's religious, charitable, social, and educational work ought to be returned but not arable land and woods. Janez Juhant, a Catholic professor of theology at the Ljubljana Theological School, argues that without the return of particular woods the Church will not be able to have the income necessary to run its educational, social, charitable, and religious work. He maintains that the Church is capable of being a responsible economic agent and would capably administer the land which would be returned. Churches other than the Catholic are not involved in this process, nor are they consulted, as they did not have large possessions.

Another question is religious education in the schools. The Roman Catholic Church desires for Slovenia to pattern itself again after the Austrian or German model of conducting religious education in schools. They variously wish to see optional, or preferably required, classes teaching religion and morals to all children except those who are exempt at the request of their parents, with the government paying for this education as it would for all other mandatory classes. Children of non-Catholics would presumably receive similar instruction from the pastors of their religious communities also subsidized by the state. People of a more secular orientation favor introduction of religious studies (but not catechetics) for which the university would train specially certified teachers who would teach about religion rather than give religious instruction. Some scholars, like Niko Tos, have carried out careful studies of public opinion in Slovenia, pointing out that the Slovenian population has a more Western European rather than Middle European attitude toward the Church, an argument which goes hand-in-hand with the more secularly oriented arguments in these discussions. Minority churches and religions are concerned that their children and the children of atheists are going to feel discriminated against in the school system, or else that they will be proselytized by the Catholic teachers.

Croatia. Croatia resembles Slovenia as being a predominantly Catholic country which was for centuries part of the Austro-Hungarian empire. But the situation in Croatia is infinitely more complex than it is in Slovenia. For one thing, about 10-15% of the population of the republic of Croatia, as it functioned within the Yugoslavian federation, was Serbian, which means Orthodox. Second, after the outbreak of the war in Bosnia and Herzegovina, an enormous number of not only Catholic Croats but also Muslims took up residence as refugees in Croatia. Third, Croatia is in a state of war and between one fourth to one third of its pre-war borders are now in the hands of Serbs who have proclaimed a Serbian Republic of Krajina, as yet totally unrecognized internationally, yet *de facto* totally out of Croatian control. From 1991 to 1992, a fierce war raged in Croatia which yielded about 10,000 dead and enormous numbers of wounded, refugees, and material and economic damage.

One of the several reasons for the war was a perception of the Serbian population (strongly fanned by the Milosevic regime in Serbia) that an independent Croatia will not respect the cultural and religious rights of Serbs. While the Communist constitution of Croatia proclaimed that both Croats and Serbs are the constitutive nations of Croatia, the new Croatian constitution proclaims that only Croats are the constitutive nation of Croatia and that Serbs are relegated to a minority status which only after the commencement of the war received assurances that their rights were going to be respected but by that time it was too late. Another important factor in the war in Croatia as well as the one in Bosnia and Herzegovina was the memory of the slaughters of Serbs by Croats during World War II when Croatia was a Nazi puppet regime. As a prelude to the war there was some pressure and even violence against Orthodox Churches and priests, and some of them fled to Serbia (according to some they did so in order to provoke Serbian aggression).

Today, it is hard to speak of true religious liberty within the entire territory of Croatia. Certainly in the Serb-occupied parts of Croatia there is freedom only for the Serbian Orthodox while others have their religious rights sharply curtailed and are at the whim of the local commanders of the rebel army and paramilitary extremists. Large number of Croats felt constrained to move out of their homes, and many of their churches were destroyed.

In the Croat areas, the situation is to a degree reversed. The Serbian Orthodox claim that many of their churches were destroyed and that their clergy are afraid to live under Croat government control. It will take a long time to sort out the various claims and counter-claims, but it is clear that both populations seeing that the war does have a religious dimension have projected great hatred toward each other and that under these conditions one can hardly speak of the normal development of religious human rights. Joint statements by the heads of the two churches have helped some, but it is clear that many Catholics will justify their destruction of an Orthodox Church by saying that they have done it in retaliation for the Serb Orthodox destruction of a Catholic Church. Since the situation in Croatia is currently neither war nor peace, under a flimsy Vance-Owen agreement and UNPROFOR troops, there is no great hope for improvement of the situation in the near future, especially when one takes into account the desire of Croats to reclaim their lost territories while the Serbs want the exact opposite, namely the annexation of these lands to Serbia.

Otherwise the major church-state issues are similar to Slovenia, namely the question of the return of former church properties and religious education in schools. The Catholic Church has succeeded to obtain the approval of the Croatian *Sabor* to include religious education apparently showing no concern as to what such a measure does to children of non-Catholics. The Serbian Orthodox Church has expressed deep concern about this measure, but has on its own part succeed to pass legislation in Serb-held territories of Croatia for Orthodox religious education in schools, having no concern for the views of the non-Orthodox.

Since the vast majority of the leadership and clergy of both the Catholic and Orthodox Churches support their respective war efforts, it will take a long time before vested clergy can even walk in peace on the streets without possibly being subject to abuse and harassment. During times of Croat-Muslim hostility, the Croatian press heaped abuse on Muslims, and some Muslim refugees experienced the harassment of Croat ethnofascist gangs—an experience parallel to what Serb ethnofascist gangs carry out in Serb-held territories.

Bosnia and Herzegovina. Currently Bosnia and Herzegovina is hell, and in hell there are no religious human rights. The basic narrative about the war in Bosnia and Herzegovina is well enough known. It was a war that the Yugoslav Army started along with Serb extremist aggression and which later on assumed characteristics of both a civil and religious war. The original tragedy was that when the multi-party political system was permitted, Croats rushed to join the Croatian Democratic Community in which Croat people pledged their loyalty to Croatia, the Party of Democratic Action gathered among its ranks only Muslims, and the Serbian Democratic Party expressed its sense of unity with Serbia rather than with the other Bosnian people—thus all three constitutive people of multiethnic and multi-religious Bosnia and Herzegovina expressed allegiances which necessarily led to the break-up of the country. The most vicious war on European soil after World War II ensued, with the estimated dead being about 250,000 and half the population (two out of four million) becoming refugees—not to speak of the horrors of torture, rape, concentration camps, and other travesties.

The government in Sarajevo (which was democratically elected by Muslims and Croats and some Serbs but where the majority of Serbs boycotted the referendum and the election and are unwilling to recognize the legitimacy of that government) officially proclaimed itself as the government of a unitary Bosnia with laws that would presumably protect the freedom of all. But it is nonsensical to talk about freedom amidst "ethnic cleansing." Serbian extremists executed the first and most of such "ethnic cleansing," but Croat and Muslim extremists have shown that they too are adequate to the task and have retaliated with some "cleansing" of their own. The hatred and recriminations, as well as the killing, goes on fluctuating up and down. There are estimations that 1,000 mosques, over 300 Roman Catholic and over 300 Serbian Orthodox church buildings were destroyed. There are Serb-held cities in which all visible traces of Muslim religious presence has been erased. Forcible expulsions of people still continue and the fate of many Muslim and Christian religious leaders has been tragic.

Only a lasting cease-fire or, better yet, a U.N. protectorate with attempts to build a civil society and with local efforts to develop a multireligious society by means of tolerance and respect could turn the situation around, but it might be too late for that. The ultimate partition of Bosnia and Herzegovina seems more in the offing than the restoration of a multinational and multicultural and multireligious society.

Yugoslavia. Rump Yugoslavia consists of Serbia and Montenegro with some aspirations of the annexation of the Bosnian Serb areas and Serb-held territories in Croatia to make up what some would regard "Great Serbia." The population is predominantly Serb Orthodox, except in the two formerly autonomous regions whose autonomy was stripped by the Belgrade government in 1988, namely Vojvodina to the north which has a large number of ethnic and religious groups, and Kosovo to the southwest in which the Albanians (who are predominantly Muslims) make up a 9:1 majority over against the Serbs. In the Sandzak part of Serbia there are also numerous Muslims.

In Montenegro there is currently a great politico-religious debate whether the inhabitants of the territory are Serbs or Montenegrins and whether the Orthodox Church of Montenegro should simply remain as part of the Serbian orthodox Church or whether a Montenegrin autocephalous or at least autonomous church ought to be established. Currently, there is a church schism along those lines.

The problem of the truncated Yugoslavia is that it is a national socialist, or fascist, dictatorship which is in reality at war in Croatia and Bosnia and Herzegovina, despite assurances to the contrary by the government of Slobodan Milosevic.

Initially, the Serbian Orthodox Church gave full support to the Serb nationalist government of Milosevic, but since 1992 and 1993, the leadership of the Serbian Orthodox Church has increasingly distanced itself from Milosevic. The Serbian Orthodox Church has been offered a special status as the church of the Serbian nation and has been given media and other support. Both the government and the Serbian Orthodox Church have shown disdain and fear of other churches whose activities are attacked either as schismatic or sectarian/heretical. The leadership of the Serbian Orthodox Church has defended the actions of the Serbs in the wars that accompanied the decomposition of Yugoslavia and blamed other ethnoreligious communities for the war. Generally, the church blessed the war effort and defended Serbs against accusations of barbarity. The government expects the Serbian Orthodox Church to provide concrete alliances with other Orthodox nations, such as the Russian,

Greek, and Rumanian, as well as representation in the World Council of Churches.

Yugoslavia has not changed much of its socialist legislation in regard to churches; even the secretariat for religious affairs continues to exist, though it is now headed by a person quite partial to the Serbian Orthodox Church. In general (the exception will be noted below) the churches have been given simply much more leeway by the police. The Serbian Orthodox Church became very visible, and its programs are frequently on television and radio and in the press. But its leadership has complained that, unlike the "legislatures" of Knin Krajina and Bosnian Serb "Republic," the *Skupstina* (Congress) of Yugoslavia has not approved even optional religious education in schools.

The most serious problem is the *de facto* persecutions of minority churches and the Muslim community in Vojvodina and Kosovo. The authorities condone and perhaps even encourage violence and harassment of non-Orthodox believers.

Vojvodina. Having lost its autonomous status on account of the *coup d'etat* carried out by Milosevic's "Antibureaucratic Revolution," Vojvodina no longer has its own separate legislation and court system or executive branch of government. The same applies to Kosovo. Hence legally the entire republic of Serbia operates on the entire territory of Serbia with the same system of laws. But the situation in Vojvodina is drastically different from Serbia proper, because of Vojvodina's multinational, multireligious, and multicultural societal makeup. Until 1990 these diverse communities lived alongside one another with minimal frictions, though there were some tensions, for instance between the Serb and Hungarian population.

After the outbreak of the war much changed. The change was not so much in official policy as it was in unofficial harassment by Serb thugs of other religions and ethnic groups and the unavailability or slow response on the part of the authorities to prevent or punish such behavior. Concrete cases include the persistent defacement with obscene graffiti of the Catholic Cathedral in Novi Sad and somewhat less drastic scriblings on the Lutheran church, then reports by a Catholic priest of numerous intimidations of non-Orthodox people by shooting into church buildings during worship as well as at other times, verbal insults of believers, and the takeover of non-Orthodox church buildings by the Orthodox Church without any negotiations. A Lutheran pastor reported threats in Stara Pazova against the Slovak Lutheran Church which ignorant bullies mistook for a Croat church and wrote graffiti such as "For every dead Serb a thousand Croats," until he posted a large sign pointing out that the church is Slovak. Then Serb politicians in Stara Pazova would say at political rallies, "our Slovaks are smart people; they won't wait for us to expel them." Large numbers of Hungarians, many of whom had been completely pro-Yugoslav, were forced to migrate to Hungary because of intimidation—just as Slovaks migrated to Slovakia. The newspapers would usually avoid identifying ethnoreligiously-motivated crimes by picturing them as simple crimes. Thus, a group of young Serbs killed a Muslim in Backa Palanka, wounded his mother, and chased away his brothers simply on account of their ethnoreligious identity, yet the police on purpose arrested an obviously innocent youth so as to mask the identity of the real killer(s) while prohibiting the newspapers from publishing the real story. These are but a few cases I chanced upon during my short visit in August 1993. No one knows the true extent of persecutions either authorized or tolerated by the regime.

Kosovo. The situation in Kosovo is far worse than in Vojvodina. It might be the place with the worst repression of human rights, aside from Bosnia and Herzegovina. Both the Albanian group (predominantly Muslims with a small Catholic minority) and the Serbian and Montenegrin group (Orthodox) complain that their religious rights are being violated by the other. Initially, Serbs complained of the desecration of holy places, including monasteries and cemeteries, the rape of their women, including nuns, and the physical threats which caused major migration of Serbs from Kosovo to the point where the ratio which they claim was once 1:1 became a ratio of 9:1 in favor of the Albanians. The Albanians, on the other hand, lodge complaints of systematic and structural persecution which from time to time increases to martial law proportions, with Albanians losing their right for an education in their language, right to employment, physical beatings, and so forth. In recent years, the Albanians boycotted all elections and created an underground government and educational system requesting the status of a separate republic for Kosovo. One may say that conditions of apartheid exist in Kosovo, with the Serbs now in sole possession of authority, which is to say that human rights in general and not only religious human rights are basically denied. Serbs have threatened genocide if Albanians were to rebel; Serbs have also claimed that Albanians carried out genocide, claiming that the Serbs have been all but driven out of the seat of their medieval kingdom and from their holy places.

While there are exaggerations in the claims of both sides about the degree of victimization, it is true that both sides have suffered, and it is also true that for the time being the Albanians suffer far more repression than the one Serbs say they are responding to.

Macedonia. At the center of age-old furor regarding its true identity, namely whether Macedonians are Western Bulgarian, northern Greeks, southern Serbs, or simply Macedonians, Macedonia became an independent and sovereign state in 1992. The international recognition came slowly, and neighboring Greece still withholds recognition and placed an embargo upon Macedonia. The population is predominantly of Slavic stock and Orthodox in faith. In a schism which started in the late 1950s the Macedonian Orthodox Church, despite grievous objections of the Serbian Orthodox Church, proclaimed itself autonomous and is currently seeking autocephaly, which as yet is canonically denied to them by all Orthodox Churches in the world. Obviously the Macedonians regard this as a repressive act, especially since the Serbian Orthodox Church constantly threatens church sanctions and even appoints Serbian clergy to Macedonian cities, thereby creating a dual jurisdiction generally forbidden by Orthodox canon law. The final resolution of this conflict is unforeseeable, but it is likely to get more bitter as time goes on.

The constitution of Macedonia, quoted above, separates church and state, though it specifically mentions by name only the Macedonian Orthodox Church. There are influential legislators who favor the Greek model of church-state relations whereby the Macedonian Orthodox Church would become the state church and not only the national church, and where the relationship between the government and the church hierarchy would be very close, including the financing of the Church by the state.

The major problem for the Macedonians is the large number of Albanians (mostly Muslims) who live within the borders of the state. The estimates are that some 25% to 40% of the population is Albanian and that demographics dictate an increase in that percentage, much to the consternation of the Macedonians. The tension between the two communities is great and plays itself out not only in the Macedonian parliament in which two Albanian parties play a significant role but in some acts of violence between the two communities. In the spring of 1994, two mosques in Veles were burned down under suspicion of arson.

Bulgaria. Bulgaria was long one of the most loyal satellites of the Soviet Union and faithfully replicated the Soviet repressive measures against religion. The churches were persecuted, dominated, and controlled. Particularly severe was the treatment of Protestants and Muslims, while the Bulgarian Orthodox Church was massively regimented and manipulated by the Communist government.

In the post-Communist era, there was at first a great relaxation of persecutions, and for a while it seemed that it would become a model of tolerance. But this was not to be of lasting duration. First of all, a great schism occurred in the Bulgarian Orthodox Church where four bishops declared that the last patriarchal selection under Communism was so interfered with by the government as to make it canonically invalid. The problem was that among the rebelling bishops were two of the most servile during the Communist period. An extremely complicated situation occurred during which time members of the two branches forcibly occupied churches and church offices, fought physically, and asked the government to help their respective sides.[10] Thus the government office for religious affairs continued to function and to play a supervisory role over the religious activities, thus limiting religious human rights.

While the severe oppression of Bulgarian Muslims have ceased, there are still complaints that the Muslim minority is being discriminated against. The Protestants and Catholics were at first beneficiaries of some returned property and the possibilities to reopen their international ties, to publish, and in general to increase their activities. However, by 1994, due to the complaints and pressure by the Bulgarian Orthodox Church, a number of restrictive decrees and laws were issued as well as local bureaucratic noncompliance with permissions secured in Sofia indicated that their freedoms are being limited. Drafts of laws were designed to limit or even curtail missionary or evangelizing activity by Protestants; though ostensibly directed against the "new sects," in reality all Protestant denominations were lumped together for restraints upon their activities. The Association of Bulgarian Jurists for Human Rights have testified that the government discriminates against Protestant churches and new religions.[11] The government is thus giving preferential treatment to the Bulgarian Orthodox Church.

Albania. Historically, there had been no other state in the world in which the persecution of religion was as thoroughgoing as in Albania—in fact, religion was prohibited by the 1967 Constitution of Albania. Albania was also the very last country of Eastern Europe to abandon the Stalinist or Bolshevik model. Only in 1991 have they rejected Communism and entered into the post-Communist phase. Religious freedoms were at first very gradually permitted, but finally the constitutional principles were changed and religious freedom guaranteed.

Albanians, who were traditionally 70% Muslims, 20% Orthodox, and 10% Catholic, boast of a tradition of mutual tolerance prior to the Communist period, and claims are made that the same tolerance is currently being practiced. After the dismantling of the Communist dictatorship, the new Albanian government proclaimed complete freedom of religion. At

---

[10] Spas T. Raikin, "Schism in the Bulgarian Orthodox Church," *Religion in Eastern Europe* 13(1) (February, 1993): 19-25; Janice Broun, "The Bulgarian Orthodox Church Schism," *Religion in Eastern Europe* 13(3) (June, 1993): 1-5.

[11] "Evangelische Kirchen diskriminiert," in *Glaube in der 2. Welt* 22(2) (February, 1994): 5-6; "Religionsgesetz im Visier," *Glaube in der 2. Welt* 22(6) (June, 1994): 5.

the same time, the three major religious groups started the difficult process of reconstructing, practically from scratch, because there had been few serving religious leaders who were not incarcerated in camps and prisons for practically a lifetime. The Albanian immigrant communities were of considerable help, for some of the immigrants could now return to assist with the process of rebuilding. The Albanian Orthodox hierarchy was so devastated that it actually took the elevation to the episcopacy of a Greek, a professor of theology from Athens, Dr. Anastasios Yannoulatos, to head the Orthodox Church. Protestants, who had been practically absent from the Albanian scene, came in fair numbers, some to proselytize, others to assist with educational, medical, and other institutions. They were permitted to create an alliance named the "Evangelical Brotherhood" (or Albanian Encouragement Project), and they received permission from the Albanian government to carry out their work.

However, before too long, trouble appeared for at least some of the religious communities. Objections were raised that the head of the Orthodox Church was a Greek ethnic; since there were political and emigration tensions between Greece and Albania there were demands that Archbishop Yannoulatos be asked to leave and that he be replaced by an Albanian national (there were as yet no Albanian nationals qualified for that office).[12] There was some insistence that a law be passed that all religious communities must be headed by an Albanian. The Roman Catholic hierarchy addressed a letter to the government in which they expressed their general satisfaction with the state of religious liberty, but they complained that middle level bureaucrats still placed great obstacles to the return of formerly confiscated property and to the issuing of proper permits for the repair of damaged buildings. They also complained that in some schools which were financed by the Catholic Church there was discrimination against Catholics in teaching and administrative positions which were being monopolized by Muslims despite a fairly large number of Catholic children enrolled in the school.[13]

A Secretariat for Religious Affairs was set up emulating the former Communist states, but it was closely related to the Muslim, Orthodox, and Catholic communities. Several attempts were made in 1992 and 1993 to draft laws regulating religions, each of which had the tendency of showing preference for the three major religious communities, but none was passed due to some interventions of groups concerned with religious liberties. The inclination of the drafters was to declare Albania a secular state with religions being declared equal before the law and with guar-

---

[12] "Kirchliches Oberhaupt umstritten," *Glaube in der 2. Welt* 22(6) (June, 1994): 3.

[13] "The Current State of Religion in Albania," *Albanian Catholic Bulletin* 15 (1994): 24-25.

antees of freedom of conscience, thought, and religion, and the requirement that all religions be harmonious with one another and that their leaders be Albanians by birth. The proposal that new religious groups be permitted only with the approval of the existing religious groups was shelved.[14] Some Catholics complained that Muslims were receiving preferential treatment by the government. Catholic bishops felt that the declaration that Albania is a secular state could give rise to totalitarian impulses and felt that it might be in conflict with the democratic principles enunciated in the Constitutional Law passed on April 29, 1992. Thus, while the situation in Albania improved dramatically for those who wished to practice their religious convictions, there were still obstacles in the road to complete religious human rights.

Prospects for the Future

Although in many respects the limitations upon the work of most religious communities in the Balkan states were lifted, a true separation of church and state seems to be undesirable from the perspective both of some church leaders and activists of the dominant national church as well as political leaders. The impulse is to introduce legislation that would place obstacles upon the work of various religious groups—almost always minorities—and attempts are made to restrain and perhaps even to eliminate them from the scene. Tremendously powerful forces are at work in all Balkan states to revert to an historical arrangement where the dominant religious community is privileged by the state while some of the other religious communities are hindered in their work.

The Communist experience has left ambiguous results. On the one hand, there is the universal experience of all religious communities of having been persecuted, restricted, traumatized, and thwarted in their normal progression, and none of them wants to go back to that period. A large segment of the population that was secularized and atheized is showing signs of resurgent religious interest, and many of them have joined churches or mosques. The war in the former Yugoslavia has explicit ethnoreligious dimensions, as I have shown in my recent book, *Yugoslavia Inferno: Ethnoreligious Warfare in the Balkans*, and this means that people are directed toward religion both by the pain of their tragic losses and by the deliberate policies of the politicians. On the other hand, there are many people, in particular among those officials who have remained in place from the Communist period, who are suspicious of re-

[14] Janice Broun, "The Implementation of Religious Freedom in Albania," *Albanian Catholic Bulletin* 15 (1994): 26-27.

ligion and have no appreciation for it except as perhaps in their desire for a cynical abuse of religious sentiments of the masses.

The general aspiration to overcome the legacy of Communist totalitarianism promises to yield laws that are going to expand religious human rights for the vast majority of the population of each country. The return to privilege of the historic churches of each nation, however, threatens that restrictions for minority churches, particularly those labelled as "sects," will be implemented. It goes without saying that in areas where the war rages, those whose ethnicity is threatened will also be greatly jeopardized religiously, with the distinct possibility of entire religious communities not only being persecuted but literally expelled or destroyed. Even historical remnants of their religious monuments are being obliterated. The building of religious tolerance in such areas will be nigh impossible for the foreseeable future. All in all, it is not easy to be optimistic in regard to the establishment of genuine religious human rights throughout the Balkans. It will take massive international pressure and assistance along with cooperation of those segments of the local population who do have a genuine desire for mutual respect and tolerance for any progress to be made which may outlast the momentary political exigencies. A process seems to be underway to homogenize areas of the Balkans along historic religious lines, namely Eastern Orthodox, Roman Catholic, and Islamic, pitting them against each other as of old. Under conditions of such hostility prospects, for full blown exercise of religious human rights do not appear to be bright.

Religious Rights in Russia at a Time of Tumultuous Transition: A Historical Theory

HAROLD J. BERMAN
Emory University

"Human" rights are rights in a global context, rights that are universal. "Religious" human rights are universal rights of persons to hold religious beliefs and to manifest and propagate those beliefs. But in attaching the word "rights" to "religious" and "human," we are speaking not only universally and globally but also locally. "Rights" are claims that are meant to be enforced, and enforcement is necessarily local. It is therefore important, in discussing religious human rights, to view them not only in a global, or universal, perspective but also in the perspective of the positive laws, the moral theories, and the historical experience, of the different places, the different countries, where those rights are claimed. Through such a comparative approach we confront the question whether rights to hold and propagate religious beliefs, declared to be applicable always and everywhere, should be, and must be, in their application, adapted and even modified in the light of the particular circumstances of particular cultures.

My task in this chapter is to interpret the meaning of religious human rights in the context of a great country—Russia—which is undergoing an unprecedented historical experience of tumultuous and even catastrophic transition from one type of political system to another, from one type of economic system to another, and from one type of belief system to another. It is entirely *in*appropriate, in my view, to apply to Russia today the broad provisions on religious freedom of the international human rights covenants *without* taking into consideration Russia's present situation viewed in the light of Russia's historical experience. Rights may properly be declared in universal terms, but their application in specific

J.D. van der Vyver and J. Witte, Jr. (eds.), Religious Human Rights in Global Perspective, 285-304.

cases must always take into account the specific circumstances of those cases.

I have referred to positive laws, moral theories, and historical experience. These are three different sources of Law. It is often supposed that the only source of Law (Law with a capital "L": in Latin *jus*, in French *droit*, in German *Recht*, in Russian *pravo*)—that the only source of Law in that large sense—are laws (with a small "l": *leges, lois, Gesetze, zakony*), that is, norms laid down by lawmaking authorities, including, in the international sphere, laws agreed to by sovereign states. This positivist theory of law is opposed by adherents of a theory of natural law, who maintain that the ultimate source of law is not the will of the lawmaker but reason and conscience, which are inherent in human nature itself, and that positive laws that violate reason and conscience have no validity. A major topic of this volume is the relationship between the positive laws prevailing in particular countries affecting freedom of religious belief, on the one hand, and, on the other hand, the natural law of human rights reflected—but only reflected—in international human rights covenants and agreements.

But there is a third theory of law, now generally forgotten by professional legal philosophers but still very much alive in the legal practice of most countries, namely, the historical theory: that history, historical experience, our memories of the past and our anticipations of the future, our living traditions, are not merely data, not merely objective facts, but also have a normative character and may be legally authoritative. We are creatures of will, political animals; we are also creatures of reason and conscience, moral animals; but we are also creatures of memory and imagination, creatures of time, of past and future; we are historical animals. Our historical traditions are a source of law, in the sense that we turn to them not only in making new law but also in determining what the old law, the pre-existing positive law, means; moreover, we also interpret and apply moral laws, "natural laws," in the light of our interpretation of our past experience. In the Anglo-American legal tradition, this historical theory of law is embodied in the dynamic doctrine of precedent.[1]

One may put this very simply. We can justify a legal action on three different grounds, each of which has a certain validity: on the ground that we have been authoritatively told to do it; alternatively, on the ground that it is right; or third, on the ground that that is the way we

---

[1] See Harold J. Berman, "Toward an Integrative Jurisprudence: Politics, Morality, History," *California Law Review* 76 (1988): 779, reprinted in Harold J. Berman, *Faith and Order: The Reconciliation of Law and Religion* (Atlanta, 1993), 289. See also Harold J. Berman, "Law and Logos," *DePaul Law Review* 44 (1994): 143, 151-166.

have done it before, that is what our collective experience has taught us to do in such a situation. If all three grounds lead to the same action or conclusion, then that action or conclusion will have maximum acceptability. If what we have been told to do by a statute enacted by the supreme political authority is unjust, that is, violates a moral law, we are in difficulty; yet we may be able to resolve a conflict between politics and morality, between order and justice, by resort to historical experience, including not only our experience of the past but also our anticipation of the future. We may say that past precedents—or future needs viewed in the light of past precedents—require a decision in favor of one or the other of the conflicting political and moral concerns. Indeed, in some circumstances we may be bound by our historical situation to do what might *otherwise* be contrary *both* to a political theory of law *and* to a moral theory of law.

I should like to apply a historical theory to the developing law of religious rights in Russia. I shall present, first, a brief summary of religious rights in Russia prior to the Communist Revolution of 1917, then an analysis of Soviet law and practice with respect to religion in the period prior to the reforms of the late 1980s and early 1990s, followed by a report of those reforms. I shall conclude with a discussion of recent efforts by the Russian Orthodox Church to secure the adoption of legislation providing for state support of so-called traditional confessions of the Russian Federation, imposing restrictions on foreign religious organizations, and prohibiting foreign missionary activity entirely.

The Pre-Soviet Period

Prior to the Bolshevik Revolution of November 1917, the Russian Orthodox Church was the established church of the Russian Empire, and the Tsar was its head. The Empire itself, however, embraced many different ethnic and religious cultures, each of which was allowed to have a degree of autonomy. Finland, ceded by Sweden in the early eighteenth century, was largely Protestant, as were the Baltic provinces of Latvia and Estonia. Poland, ceded by the Congress of Vienna in the early nineteenth century, was largely Roman Catholic, as was the Baltic province of Lithuania. The Central Asian regions, originally inherited from the Mongols and finally subdued in the nineteenth century, were largely Muslim. A large number of ethnic Germans, originally invited by Catherine the Great to settle in the Volga region of Russia on condition that they not intermarry with Russians, remained Lutheran. The vast majority of the five-and-a-half million Russian Jews were required to live in the Pale of Settlement stretching from Riga to Odessa and from Polish Silesia to

Kiev. Ethnic Russians, who constituted most of the Empire's population, and who governed all its territories, were largely Russian Orthodox, but a substantial minority adhered to the schismatic Church of the Old Believers and a smaller number adhered to sectarian churches (Dukhobors, Molokane, Stundists). Other ethnic-territorial Orthodox churches within the Empire included the autocephalous Georgian Orthodox Church and Armenian Orthodox Church. Although in the early twentieth century some ethnic Russians became converts to Roman Catholicism and to foreign Protestant sects (such as the Baptists), and although there were some converts to Russian Orthodoxy among Jews and other ethnic minorities, nevertheless the religious map of the Empire coincided to a considerable extent with the ethnic map. It was, indeed, a tenet of Russian Orthodox theology that religious affiliation is closely connected with ethnicity and, to a lesser extent, with territory—with blood and with soil.

Only in the early twentieth century, and especially after the 1905 Revolution, both the supremacy of Russian Orthodoxy and the subordination of the Russian Orthodox Church to the Tsar began slowly to be challenged. In 1905 a Law on Tolerance, issued by the Tsar, granted Russians the right to depart from Orthodoxy, the right of parents who departed from Orthodoxy to raise their children in a new religion, the right of persons previously considered Orthodox against their will not to be so classified, and the right of people raising abandoned children to baptize them according to their own faith. The Law also gave new rights to Old Believers and Christian sectarians, including the right to have houses of worship, the right to property, and the right to organize their own elementary schools that would provide religious instruction. Also important in the 1905 Law on Toleration were provisions extending to adherents of foreign Christian denominations the right to build churches and prayer houses and to provide religious education for children.[2] These provisions reduced substantially the effect of earlier prohibitions against missionary activity by foreigners.[3]

Developments after 1905 also led to slightly greater freedom of the Russian Orthodox Church from control by the Tsar and by the Holy

---

[2] Ob ukreplenii nachal' veroterpimosti [On the Establishment of the Principle of Religious Tolerance], Polnoe Sobranie Zakonov Rossiiskoi Imperii, 3d series, vol. 25, no. 26126 (1905), arts. I (4), II, IX.

[3] An 1896 law provided that "only the ruling Orthodox Church has the right to persuade followers of other Christian confessions and other faiths to accept its teachings concerning faith." Persons of other Christian confessions and faiths were declared to be subject to criminal punishments if they "encroached upon the convictions of conscience of those not belonging to their religion." Svod' uchrezhdenii i ustavov' upravleniia dukhovnykh' del' inostrannykh' ispovedanii khristianskikh' i inovernekh' [Collection of Institutions and Statutes of Administration of the Spiritual Affairs of Foreign Confessions of Christians and Other Believers], Svod Zakonov Rossiiskoi Imperii, vol. XI, part 1, ed., 1986, art. IV.

Synod, a lay body created in 1721 by Peter the Great to govern the Church. In the first two decades of the twentieth century, there was a movement within the Church to restore the Moscow Patriarchate which Peter had abolished in 1700. After the abdication of the Tsar in February 1917 and the establishment of the Provisional Government, the first All-Russian Church Council was called. It was convened, however, only in August 1917; on November 5, it elected a Patriarch;[4] two days, later Lenin and his Bolshevik Party seized power and proclaimed the establishment of an atheist state.

The Soviet Period, 1917-1987

Soviet atheism was derived in part from Marxist theory, but for Marx atheism had been primarily a philosophical tenet, an inference drawn from his theory of historical materialism, whereas for Lenin and his Russian followers atheism was a militant faith, a revolt against God, with deep roots in Russian anarchism. Lenin could have repeated what the nineteenth-century Russian revolutionary Bakunin had said: "If God really existed, he would have to be destroyed." Leninist atheism was not only something to be believed but also something to be believed *in*, something to be practised in one's daily life. It rested on the passionate conviction—of which Lenin, not Marx, was the great apostle, and which was more Russian than Western—that humanity is master of its own destiny and by its own power can construct a paradise on earth. For the Russian Communist Party, which Lenin created, atheism represented man's power to do by himself, by his own intellect and will, through collective action, what Russian Christianity had taught that only God can do, namely, create a universal peace in human hearts.

For seventy years, from the Bolshevik Revolution to the closing years of the Gorbachev regime, militant atheism was the official religion, one might say, of the Soviet Union, and the Communist Party was, in effect, the established church. It was an avowed task of the Soviet state, led by the Communist Party, to root out from the minds and hearts of the Soviet people all belief systems other than Marxism-Leninism. This was surely the most massive and the most powerful assault on traditional religious faith that was ever launched in the history of mankind.[5]

---

[4] See Timothy Ware, *The Orthodox Church* (Baltimore, 1969), 137-138.

[5] For sources of data presented in the following paragraphs concerning Soviet restrictions of religious freedom, see Michael Bourdeaux, *Gorbachev, Glasnost, and the Gospel* (London, 1990); Ware, *The Orthodox Church;* Paul Anderson, *People, Church, and State in Modern Russia* (New York, 1944); Harold J. Berman, "Christianity and Democracy in Soviet Russia," in id., *Faith and Order*, 397.

The policy of the Soviet government toward religion was laid down in the first law on the subject in January, 1918, called "On the Separation of the Church from the State and of the School from the Church." To American ears, the title sounds harmless enough, but when the Soviets said "separation" they really meant it! In principle, the state would give not the slightest support whatsoever to the Church, and the Church was forbidden to engage in activities which were within the sphere of responsibilities of the state. This had a special meaning in a socialist system of the Soviet type, in which State and Party swallowed up civil society. Churches, mosques, and synagogues were deprived of almost all activities except the conduct of worship services. Moreover, schools were not merely to avoid the teaching of religion; they were actively to promote the teaching of atheism.

These doctrines were spelled out in a 1929 law that remained the basic legislation on the subject until the Gorbachev reforms of the late 1980s. There was freedom of religious worship, but churches were forbidden to give any material aid to their members or charity of any kind, or to hold any special meetings for children, youth, or women, or general meetings for religious study, recreation, or any similar purpose, or to open libraries or to keep any books other than those necessary for the performance of worship services. The formula of the 1929 law was repeated in the 1936 Constitution and again in the 1977 Constitution: freedom of religious worship and freedom of atheist propaganda—meaning (1) no freedom of religious teaching outside of the worship service itself, plus (2) a vigorous campaign in the schools, in the press, and in special meetings organized by atheist agitators, to convince people of the folly of religious beliefs.

Moreover, since the Party was avowedly atheist, and Party membership was a prerequisite for most offices, open religious believers were generally deprived of any possibility of advancement in most secular professional careers.

The 1960 Criminal Code of the Russian Republic imposed a fine for violating laws of separation of the church from the state and of the school from the church, and, for repeated violations, deprivation of freedom up to three years (Article 142). Such violations included organizing religious assemblies and processions, organizing religious instruction for minors, and preparing written materials calling for such activities. Other types of religious activities were subject to more severe sanctions: thus leaders and active participants in religious groups that caused damage to the health of citizens or violated personal rights, or that tried to persuade citizens not to participate in social activities or to perform duties of citizenship, or that drew minors into such group, were punishable by deprivation of freedom up to five years (Article 227). This provision was directed primarily against Evangelical Baptists, Jehovah's Witnesses, Pentecostals, and other sects.

These articles of the Criminal Code were enacted as part of the severe anti-religious campaign launched under Khrushchev in the early 1960s, when an estimated 10,000 Russian Orthodox churches—half the total number—were closed, together with five of the eight institutions for training priests, and the independence of the priesthood was curtailed both nationally and locally. Similar attacks were made against the other religious communities. The anti-religious campaign ended with Brezhnev's accession to power in 1964; nevertheless, the rights of believers that were taken away in the Khrushchev period were not restored. The closed churches, monasteries, and seminaries remained closed. Parents who baptized their children had to register, and could then be subjected to harassment. Practical impediments were placed in the way of church weddings. Sermons were strictly controlled.

Notwithstanding this massive effort to suppress traditional religious belief, or perhaps partly because of it, there was, in fact, a strengthening of Christian faith. Christianity not only survived the assault upon it but was purged and purified by it. Despite Soviet official claims to the contrary, and despite the superficial impressions of Western tourists, religion did not die out in Soviet Russia. And it was not only the aged who clung to religious faith. It is possible, and even likely, that among the Russian half of the Soviet population a majority of the adults were Christian. Indeed, in the 1970s and 1980s there was a substantial turn to Christianity among students and other young people. In the 1970s Soviet writers themselves estimated the number of believers at twenty percent of the total Soviet population—about 50 million. Competent non-Soviet observers said forty percent or more.

These were only guesses, since there were no published statistics. Also, there was no satisfactory definition of a "believer" (which is the word generally used in Russia for one who believes in God). I remember asking a Moscow taxi driver, who was pointing out churches to me as we drove along, whether he was a believer. He said, "No." I then asked him, "Do you ever go to church?" He answered, "No." I asked "Never?" He replied, "Well, sometimes when things get very hard I go." The evidence is strong, even without statistics, that, as a lay leader of the Russian Church said to me in Moscow in 1962, "Our people is a believing people, despite Communism."

What I have been describing so far is the elemental confrontation of two fundamental faiths, Christianity and atheism, a confrontation that existed in the Soviet Union for seventy years. One was a faith in man's power to raise himself, by his own collective will and by disciplined obedience to the Communist Party leadership, to a political order of power and wealth, and ultimately to a utopian social order of universal peace and brotherhood. The other was a faith in God's merciful forgiveness of human weakness and selfishness and in his offer of redemption from suffering and death to all who follow the example of Jesus Christ. Both these faiths showed an extraordinary capacity to survive in the Soviet Union, despite frequent betrayal by their adherents.

In 1989 Alexy II, Patriarch of Moscow and Russia, defended the hierarchy of the Russian Orthodox Church against the charge of subservience to Communism in the past, saying that the only alternative would have been to expose their flock to the danger of destruction. "The Church," he said, "with its many millions of members, cannot descend into the catacombs in a totalitarian state. We sinned. But . . . [f]or the sake of the people, for the sake of preventing [many] millions of people from departing this life for good." In order to save those who have remained faithful, he said, "the hierarchs of the Church took a sin upon their souls, the sin of silence, the sin of nontruth. And we have always done penance before God for this."[6]

He then added something which is significant for an understanding of Russian Orthodox Christianity today. "Our refusal to take the Church down into the catacombs," he said, "bore an even more intense spiritual fruit. We members of the Russian Orthodox Church did not cultivate in ourselves hate and a thirst for revenge. I fear that a catacombs psychology would have driven us precisely to this."

It should be added that although the Russian Orthodox Church—and other religious bodies in Russia—sinned, perhaps *had* to sin, in their submission to the Soviet State and Communist Party, nevertheless, in proclaiming in their worship services the existence of God they constituted for seventy years the one and only voice of public dissent from a fundamental tenet of Marxist-Leninist doctrine.

The Russian Orthodox Church also represented a continuity with the prerevolutionary Russian past. The liturgy, with its Church Slavonic prayers and chants, its ikons and candles, its Moussorgsky and Tschaikovsky masses, and, above all, its invocation of a higher world of angels and saints, represented a Russian vision which transcended the secular utopia of Communism. I recall hearing a sermon in Leningrad, at the height of the Khrushchev anti-religious campaign, in which the priest read from the Bible the story of Joseph's interpretation of Pharaoh's dream of the seven sleek and fat cows eaten up by the seven lean and

---

[6] See Berman, *Faith and Order*, 397.

ugly cows, and the seven full and ripe ears of corn swallowed up by the seven meager and scorched ears. The priest told the congregation—2000 devout parishioners at a weekly Wednesday evening service: "The Russian Church is now living through the seven lean years, but we have all the riches of the past to sustain us." I thought then of the statement of a Soviet admiral stationed in England during World War II, told to me at the time by a British emigré from Russia who had been acting as interpreter in high-level discussions between Soviet and British naval commanders: "Do not forget," the Soviet admiral said privately to the interpreter, "that the true Russia is the Russia of St. Sergius and Dostoevsky."

The Reforms Since 1988

The Gorbachev political reforms of the late 1980s, including the introduction of genuine freedom of speech and the end of the one-party system, were accompanied by a movement to restore freedom of religion. In 1988, the Soviet state itself celebrated the 1000th anniversary of the introduction of Christianity into Russia. In December, 1988 President Gorbachev, in an important speech to the General Assembly of the United Nations, promised that new Soviet legislation on freedom of conscience would meet "the highest [international legal] standards."[7] In 1989, the new popularly elected USSR Congress of People's Deputies included clergy among its members as well as lay persons previously persecuted for religious activities. After widespread discussion, new laws on freedom of religion and the rights of religious organizations were enacted in 1990 both in the USSR and in the Russian Republic (RSFSR).

The USSR law of October 1, 1990, entitled "On Freedom of Conscience and [on] Religious Organizations,"[8] declared in Chapter I ("General Provisions") that "every citizen . . . shall have the right, individually or in conjunction with others, to profess any religion or not to profess any, and to express and disseminate convictions associated with his relationship to religion" (Art. 3); that the exercise of such freedom shall be subject only to restrictions "that are compatible with the interna-

---

[7] "The Gorbachev Visit; Excerpts From Speech to U.N. on Major Soviet Military Cuts," *New York Times*, December 8, 1988, at A16.

[8] O svobode sovesti i religioznykh organizatsiiakh [On Freedom of Conscience and [on] Religious Organizations], PRAVDA, October 9, 1990 [hereinafter 1990 USSR Law]. An English translation appears in *Journal of Church and State* 33 (1991): 191-201. In the Russian text, the first word of the law, "O," meaning "on" or "concerning," only appears once, but because "Religious Organizations" in the Russian appears in the prepositional case an additional "on" should be included in the English translation to avoid the erroneous implication that the law concerns freedom, rather than regulation, of religious organizations.

tional commitments of the USSR" (Art. 4); that "all religions and denominations shall be equal before the law" (Art. 5); that there shall be "separation of church (religious organizations) from the state" but that "clergy of religious organizations shall have the right to participate in political life on an equal footing with all citizens" and "the state shall facilitate the establishment of relations of mutual toleration and respect between citizens who profess a religion and those who do not profess one" (Art. 5); and that "religious organizations whose charters (or statutes) are registered in accordance with established procedure shall have the right . . . to create educational institutions and groups for the religious education of children and adults. . . ." (Art. 15).

These provisions constituted a complete repudiation of fundamental tenets of Leninist theory and a complete reversal of more than seventy years of Soviet policy. In Chapter II of the law, however, entitled "Religious Organizations," some state controls were preserved. Although citizens were permitted freely, and without informing state agencies, to form "religious societies"—apparently meaning congregations—"for the joint profession of faith and the satisfaction of other religious needs," other types of religious organizations, including religious centers and administrations as well as monasteries, brotherhoods, missions, and educational institutions founded by such centers and administrations, were required to submit their charters for registration by the Soviet executive committee—in effect, the government—in the locality in which they were situated (Art. 14). Such charters were to contain detailed information concerning the nature and structure of the religious organization, its property, its powers, special features of its activity, and related matters (Art. 12). Registration gave the religious organization the character of a legal entity, with capacity to own property and to enter into contracts (Art. 13). A decision by the Soviet executive committee to refuse to register the religious organization, or a failure to register it within one month, could be appealed to the courts (Art. 15). Nothing was said in the 1990 law, however, about the grounds on which the courts were to reverse such a decision.

State supervision was also to be exercised, under the USSR law, by a USSR state agency for religious affairs, to be formed by the USSR Council of Ministers. Similar agencies were to be formed in the various republics of the USSR. The USSR agency was to be "a center for information, consultation, and expert review," and its stated purposes were entirely benign; nevertheless, its powers were not defined, and its denomination as "USSR state agency for religious affairs" was an ominous reminder of the former USSR Council for Religious Affairs, which for decades had enforced the harsh anti-religious legislation of the pre-Gorbachev era.

The 1990 USSR law concluded with the provision that "[i]f an international treaty to which the USSR is a party establishes rules other than those contained in legislation on freedom of conscience and on religious organizations, the rules of the international treaty shall apply." Since the USSR was a party to the International Covenant on Civil and Political Rights, this provision was an important step toward realization of the goal set by President Gorbachev in his 1988 speech to the United Nations. The 1990 law did not go so far, however, as to provide for conformity with international agreements of the USSR that fell short of being treaties. Perhaps the most important such agreement is the so-called Concluding Document of the Vienna Follow-Up Meeting of the participants in the 1975 Helsinki Final Act.[9] That Document, signed in January, 1989, represented a consensus of the signatories concerning the meaning of freedom of religion in international law. It went far beyond pre-existing international treaties in specifying religious rights. The head of the Soviet delegation to the Vienna Meeting later stated that "the Vienna agreements were not imposed on us from the outside; they were the goals that the USSR has itself set, they are what our society required."[10] It is possible that an oblique reference to the Vienna Concluding Document is made in the provision of Article 4 of the USSR law, quoted above, that only such restrictions on freedom of conscience shall be permitted as are "compatible with the international *commitments* of the USSR" (italics added).

The RSFSR law, enacted on October 25, 1990, which at the time of this writing (December 1994) was still in effect in the Russian Federation, repeats many of the provisions of the USSR law but goes considerably farther in its protection of religious freedom. In contrast to the USSR law, it is entitled "On Freedom of Religion," a phrase that is broader than "freedom of conscience," implying freedom to give expression to one's religious beliefs through the activities of religious organizations.[11] This is borne out in Article 1 of the RSFSR law, which states that the purpose of

---

9 Concluding Document of the Vienna Follow-Up Meeting, reprinted by U.S. Comm. on Security and Cooperation in Europe (Jan. 1989).

10 Quoted in Harold J. Berman, Erwin N. Griswold, Frank C. Newman, "Draft USSR Law on Freedom of Conscience, with Commentary," *Harvard Human Rights Journal* 3 (1990): 137, 138, an article-by-article critique of the draft 1990 USSR Law. The critique was presented to Soviet specialists involved in the legislative process, but seemed to affect only slightly the final version of the 1990 USSR Law. However, many of its recommendations were included in the 1990 Law of the RSFSR on Freedom of Religion.

11 O svobode veroispovedanii [On Freedom of Religion], Vedomosti RSFSR, Issue No. 21, Item No. 267-1, at 240 (1990) [hereinafter RSFSR Law]. The Russian word "veroispovedanie," translated here as "religion," means literally "profession of faith," whereas the Russian word "sovest," meaning "conscience," refers to the inner belief rather than the outer profession of the belief.

the law is to secure "observance . . . of the principles of freedom of conscience . . . as well as realization of the right of citizens to exercise that freedom." Also the RSFSR law states in the Preamble that freedom of religion is an "inalienable right of citizens of the RSFSR guaranteed by the Constitution of the RSFSR and by international obligations of the Russian Federation," and that "[t]he present law proceeds from principles contained in international agreements and conventions providing that freedom to have religious or atheist convictions and to engage in actions corresponding to such convictions is subject only to limitations established by Law and necessary for the security of the rights and freedoms of other persons." The use of the word "agreements" instead of "treaties" was undoubtedly intended to include the Vienna Concluding Document, which also stresses not only the right to hold religious convictions but also the right to engage in actions corresponding to such convictions.

The Russian law also goes beyond the USSR law in providing explicitly that not only citizens but also foreigners and stateless persons "may exercise the right to freedom of religion individually as well as jointly through creation of appropriate social associations" (Art. 4).

Under the RSFSR law, such associations are only required to register their charters if they wish to have the rights of a legal person. Moreover, in contrast to the registration requirements of the USSR law, the charter is to be registered not by the local Soviet executive committee but by the Russian Ministry of Justice, which may refuse to register the charter "only if its contents contradict the requirements of the present Law and other legislative acts of the RSFSR."[12] As under the USSR law, the refusal to register the charter of a religious association may be appealed to a court; however, in contrast to the USSR law, the RSFSR law does not leave the decision to the discretion of the court but requires the court to decide on the basis of "the present Law and other legislative acts of the RSFSR." It should be noted, however, that the Russian conception of

---

[12] RSFSR Law at Art. 20. As of September 1, 1993 a total of 9,489 religious associations were registered under the RSFSR Law. Of that number, the following religious denominations were most numerous: Russian Orthodox Church (5,019), Old Believers (121), Russian Orthodox Free Church (64), Muslim (2,639), Roman Catholic (90), Buddhist (59), Jewish (48), Lutheran (86), Evangelical Christian Baptist (490), Evangelical Christians (49), Pentecostal (165), Seventh Day Adventist (130), Charismatic (73), Hare Krishna (68), Christian Nondenominational associations (137). In addition there were 21 Methodist associations, 41 Presbyterian, 47 Jehobah's Witnesses, 3 Mormon, and 1 Unification Church (Moonie). The types of associations registered include religious centers, congregations, monasteries, convents, religious educational centers, nursing centers, and missions. A. I. Kudriatsev and A. O. Protopopov, eds., Zakonodatel'stvo Rossiiskoi Federatsii o svobode Sovesti, Veroispovedaniia i Religioznykh Ob'edineniiakh [Legislation of the Russian Federation on Freedom of Conscience, Religion, and [on] Religious Organizations] (1994), 100-103. This publication was financed by Law and Liberty Trust, located in Annandale, Virginia.

"legislative acts" is a broad one, including regulations of administrative bodies, and only in recent years has such delegated legislative power begun to come under strict scrutiny to make sure that it is exercised in conformity with statutory law.

The Vetoed Law of August 1993

The 1990 USSR Law on Freedom of Conscience and on Religious Organizations expired on December 8, 1991, with the expiration of the Soviet Union, leaving in force the 1990 RSFSR Law on Freedom of Religion. In July, 1993, however, the Russian Parliament ("Supreme Soviet") passed a new comprehensive law entitled "On the Introduction of Changes and Additions to the RSFSR Law on Freedom of Religion."[13] That law was returned to the Chairman of the Supreme Soviet by President Yeltsin, unsigned.[14] It was re-enacted by the Supreme Soviet, with minor changes, in August 1993, but again vetoed, in effect, since it was not signed by the President prior to his dissolution of the Parliament in September 1993. At the time of this writing, new drafts of a law on religion are under consideration for presentation to the new Russian Parliament, now called the State Duma, which was elected in December 1993.

Although the vetoed law of August 1993, like the July law, was called "A Law on Changes and Additions to the [1990] RSFSR Law On Freedom of Religion," and was often referred to in English and American publications as an "Amendment" to the 1990 law, it was, in fact, an entirely new version of that law, repeating many of its provisions but subtracting some and adding others.[15] The main additions were provisions granting special rights to "traditional confessions" (Art. 8) and sharply restricting the rights of foreign religious associations (Arts. 10, 13, 16, and 21). The main subtractions were the omission of articles providing for the equality of all religious associations before the law and granting equal rights to foreign religious associations. I shall confine my comments on the vetoed law to those additions and subtractions, although it has been justifiably criticized for many of its other provisions as well.[16]

---

13 David Filipov & Pyotr Zhuravlyov, "Parliament Puts Limits on Foreign Churches," *Moscow Times*, July 15, 1993, at 1.

14 Yeltsin's letter to Chairman Khasbulatov sharply criticized the law, emphasizing that it violated both the Russian constitutional and international treatises to which Russia adheres. It was especially critical of provisions that discriminated against nontraditional confessions. See W. Cole Durham, Lauren B. Homer, Pieter van Dijk, John Witte, Jr., "The Future of Religious Liberty in Russia," *Emory International Law Review* 8 (1994): 1, 10-11.

15 The vetoed 1993 law is translated and analyzed in ibid.

16 Ibid.

On July 14, 1993, as the Russian Supreme Soviet was to vote on the first version of the new law, Patriarch Alexy distributed a letter to the chairman and the deputies, urging them, "on behalf of the Russian Orthodox Church, to which the majority of Russians belong," to adopt the bill. "It is gratifying," he wrote, "that the new version of the law makes the church a social power that stands above political discords and is one of the guarantees of the all-national union. . . ." The Patriarch praised the bill for "bring[ing] order to the activity of the representatives of foreign religious organizations in Russia." "Standing firmly," he wrote, "for the stability of spiritual freedom for every individual and for the right to choose one's religion or ideology and to change one's choice, we Russian Orthodox believers are convinced that this choice must not be imposed upon us from the outside, especially by exploiting the difficult economic situation of our people or through harsh pressures on human beings," "The state," he added, "whose tasks is to protect the freedom of its own citizens," should be "more scrupulous in its support of non-traditional religious groups, many of which act in direct violation of the law and create totalitarian structures which entirely paralyze the will of the people involved in them. So it is very important that the new version of the law contains norms which allow a balanced approach to the registration of non-traditional religious organizations."[17]

Article 10 of the 1990 law, which provided in the strongest terms for equal treatment of all religions and all religious associations, was removed in the August 1993 version, and a new paragraph was inserted in Article 8 requiring the state to "render support" to "the traditional confessions of the Russian Federation." These were defined as "those religious organizations whose activity preserves and develops the historical traditions and customs, national-cultural originality, art, and other cultural heritage of the peoples of the Russian federation." Which denominations would constitute "traditional confessions" was not indicated. Apparently the cultural heritage not only of ethnic Russians, represented by the Orthodox and Old Believers, but also of other "peoples of the Russian Federation" was to receive state support—perhaps that of Roman Catholic Poles and Ukrainians, Lutheran Volga Germans, and other Christian confessions that were included in the 1905 Law on Toleration.[18] Presumably, Muslims and Orthodox Jews were also covered by the concept of "traditional confessions of the Russian Federation." It is not clear whether denominations that only entered later into the Russian heritage, many of which suffered severe repression under the Soviet regime, such

---

[17] Copies of Patriarch Alexy's letter were circulated by its critics to interested persons abroad. A copy is on file with the author. It is brief, and its entire substance is recited here.

[18] See supra note 2.

as Baptists, Pentecostals, and Jehovah's Witnesses, were also meant to be included. Certainly the more recent missionary arrivals from abroad were not to be so favored.

Indeed, foreign missionary activity was expressly prohibited by Article 21 of the August 1993 version, and invitations to foreign citizens and stateless persons for "professional religious work" were subject to approval by state agencies only after strict scrutiny.[19] Moreover, foreign religious organizations whose charters were not registered before October 25, 1990 (the date of enactment of the 1990 law) were required to wait up to twelve months while their applications for such registration were being considered—during which time they could not function as legal entities (Art. 16). This would have meant that many existing foreign religious organizations in Russia would have had to discontinue their property, contract, and other civil-law relationships and activities, at least temporarily.

Foreigners and stateless persons were still permitted, under the aborted 1993 law, to form religious groups and to conduct worship and other religious activities, but they were to inform in advance the agencies of internal affairs of the measures to be taken in these regards, and it was provided further that "agencies of justice and of internal affairs shall have the right to demand from [the organizers of such groups] information concerning the particulars of their religious activity and to control their observance of legislation" (Art. 12).

If the August, 1993 law were to be re-enacted by the new State Duma, elected on December 12, 1993, it would certainly conflict with the provisions of the new Russian Constitution, adopted on the same date by popular referendum. Article 14 of the 1993 Constitution provides: "The Russian Federation shall be a secular state. . . . All religious associations shall be separate from the state and shall be equal before the law." Article 15 declares that "international treaties of the Russian Federation shall be a part of its legal system," and that "[i]f an international treaty of the Russian Federation establishes rules other than those established by a law [of the Russian Federation], the rules of the international treaty shall be applied." Article 19 provides that "[a]ny form of restriction of civil rights on the basis of . . . religious affiliation shall be prohibited." Article 28 provides: "Every person shall be guaranteed freedom of conscience and freedom of religion, including the right to profess individually or jointly with others any religion or to profess none, to freely choose, hold,

---

19 "Professional religious work" is defined in Article 14 as "activity conducted specifically for the purpose of meeting religious needs of believers, which includes making contracts, holding a position in a religious organization, and carrying out decision-making functions over believers."

and propagate religious and other beliefs, and to act in accordance with them." Article 46 provides that "[e]very person shall be entitled, in accordance with international treaties of the Russian Federation, to apply to inter-governmental bodies involved in the protection of human rights and freedoms if all available internal means of legal protection have been exhausted." Article 55 provides that "[t]he enumeration in the Constitution of the Russian Federation of fundamental rights and freedoms shall not be interpreted as a denial or diminution of other generally recognized human and civil rights and freedoms."

In light of these provisions of the Russian Constitution, it seems quite unlikely that the State Duma would submit for Presidential signature a law which expressly permits government support of "traditional" but not of "non-traditional" religious confessions and which substantially restricts foreign missionary activity. If such a law were signed by the President, one would hope that the Russian Constitutional Court would declare it invalid. It is important, nevertheless, to understand the motives that underlay the rejected law, for those motives will continue to exert a strong influence on future legislation affecting religious rights and on future practice in implementation of such legislation.

A Historical Interpretation of the Position Taken by the Moscow Patriarchate

A law must reflect not only the political will of those who drafted it and those who adopted it, and not only the moral values that are expressed in it, but also the historical experience of the society whose law it is—its past and its future. Even a constitution adopted by popular referendum must be interpreted in the light of such historical experience.[20] Indeed, if the historical experience of a people with respect to a matter is sufficiently important that it constitutes a foundation of the constitution itself, then it may even justify departure from the ordinary meaning of the words of particular constitutional norms. Such a historical argument receives some support in the Russian Constitution itself, Article 55 of which provides that "[h]uman and civil rights and freedoms may be restricted by federal law only to the extent necessary for upholding the foundations of the constitutional system, morality, or the health, [and] rights and lawful interests of other persons, or for ensuring the defense of the country and state security."

---

[20] It was reported that of those eligible (106 million), 54.8% voted on December 12, 1993. Of those that voted, 58.4% (32.9 million) voted in favor of the Constitution. See "Election Results Updated (but Still Not Final)," *Current Digest of the Post-Soviet Press* 45:51 (1993): 7.

It was undoubtedly such a historical argument—that the constitutional system itself is founded on the religious heritage of the Russian people—that the Moscow Patriarchate wished to invoke in the summer of 1993 in urging the Supreme Soviet to pass the "new version" of the 1990 RSFSR Law on Freedom of Religion. Although the argument is flawed, as will be shown in the following discussion, it must be taken seriously if religious peace is to be established between foreign missionaries in Russia and the Russian Orthodox Church as well as between the Russian Orthodox Church and other Russian churches that are striving, each in its own way, to restore spiritual health to the tormented Russian soul.

It is particularly important that foreigners come to understand the religious basis for the opposition not only of the Moscow Patriarchate, but also of many lay Russian Orthodox believers, to the influx of foreign missionaries, chiefly but not exclusively American, who flocked into Russia in the early 1990s, and who in 1993 mobilized widespread support abroad for their vigorous protests against Russian Orthodox efforts to restrict their activities. Regardless of the law, it is important for foreigners to understand the historical roots of the Russian conception of the Russian Orthodox Church as the Church of the Russian People.

"Are you a believer?" I once asked a Muscovite. He replied, "I'm Russian, I'm Orthodox."

During a visit to Moscow in September, 1994, I had the opportunity to ask questions about this ethnic dimension of Russian Christianity in a two-hour interview with a representative of the Moscow Patriarchate. In defending the aborted 1993 legislation, he said that the Lutherans should be free to give religious leadership to the German population of Russia, the Roman Catholics to the Polish population of Russia, the Jews to the Jews, the Muslims to the Turks in Russia, and so forth—but the Russians (and this is difficult to say in English, because in Russian there are two words for "Russians," one for citizens of Russia, *rossiane*, regardless of their nationality, and the other for ethnic Russians, *russkie*), the ethnic Russians, the *russkie*, he said, belong chiefly to Russian Orthodoxy.

It is difficult for Western Christians to accept, or even to understand, the belief in ethnic Christian churches. In the Western Christian tradition, now embodied in secular constitutional law in most countries and adopted by the human rights covenants, religious freedom is conceived primarily in terms of the religious faith of the individual believer, including his right to manifest that faith in collective bodies which are conceived to be voluntary associations. The most vivid example of a collective faith of an ethnic culture is the Judaic faith of the Hebrew people. An ethnic Jew may not be religious, but Judaism is considered by most Jews, whether or not they are religious, to be the religious faith of the Jewish people, *am Yisroel*, the Jewish *Volk*, the Jewish *narod*.

It is, above all, this conception of the common Christian faith of the people, the *narod*, of Russian nationality that is the principal source of opposition to the influx of foreign evangelical missionaries. It is not the purpose of the vast majority of these missionaries to draw Russians away from Russian Orthodoxy, and for the most part they have attracted Russians who formerly were atheist or agnostic. When I made this point to the representative of the Moscow Patriarchate with whom I spoke in 1994, he replied: "It is true that after more than 75 years of Marxist-Leninist education and Communist Party pressure, a great many Russians are ignorant of Russian Orthodoxy or indifferent to it. But their roots are Orthodox. It is our task to return them to Orthodoxy."

I noted that in the religious worship services conducted by foreign Christian evangelical missionaries in Russia there is, as far as I have observed, nothing antagonistic to Russian Orthodoxy. They bring the Bible, and especially the New Testament, to Russians previously ignorant of it. Their sermons usually reflect a simple belief in Christian faith, hope, and love, and a doctrine of salvation that is somewhat different from the Russian Orthodox doctrine but not incompatible with it. He replied: "That is fine, but it would be better if at the end of the sermon your preachers would tell the Russians in the congregation that they can also find these same truths in their own Russian Orthodox Church."

But the objection to foreign missionaries goes deeper. The historical argument of the Patriarchate is directed not only to the past but also to the present and future. Russia is now experiencing a severe spiritual crisis, which, in the view not only of the Moscow Patriarchate but of many Russian people, whether or not they are believers, is being aggravated by the foreign evangelical missionaries. My informant in the Moscow Patriarchate expressed this point in the following way:

"The changes now taking place in Russia," he said, "including especially the economic reforms, require a new post-Soviet psychology among the people. For three generations the people has been brought up on a simple monolithic ideology that is now repudiated. The belief in Soviet superiority is gone. The belief in progress toward a bright future is gone. The people feels lost.

"The foreign evangelical missionaries," he continued, "know that there is a spiritual crisis but they do not understand it. In fact, they are offering to the people another simple solution. Like the Communists, they offer salvation in return for a commitment which requires little effort. 'Just believe, and you will be saved.' This reinforces the old psychology, in which simple slogans were offered in return for immediate minimum rewards but great rewards in the future. Russian Orthodoxy is more complex and more difficult. It teaches not rewards but sacrifice. It teaches the positive value of suffering. Its spiritual demands are great."

My interlocutor went on to a different aspect of the same theme of spiritual crisis. "In the past," he said, "whenever there has been a spiritual crisis of this intensity, the people has turned to the Russian Church. That was true at the time of the Napoleonic Wars. It was true in the First World War. It was true even under Stalin in the Second World War. Now we are in a comparable crisis. Moreover, both the extreme nationalists on the right and the radical democrats on the left can be reconciled on this point, namely, that to meet our spiritual crisis it is important that a strong role be played not only by the Russian Orthodox Church but also by other traditional Russian confessions, confessions that have been tested by repression for seventy-five years and that have forged a fraternal relationship with each other."

I responded that many think the Russian Orthodox Church is simply afraid of competition. "Not at all," he replied. "But Russia needs time to recover her health before they descend on us. The Russian Orthodox Church is like a very sick person that is only beginning to recover her health."

"Moreover," he added, "we lack both the material and the human resources needed to compete on an equal basis. The foreign missionaries are pouring huge sums of money into evangelization, paying for billboard advertisements and for television programs featuring American preachers and hiring huge stadiums for spreading their message." Also in human resources, the Russian Church, he said, is lacking in people who are trained to attract outsiders. "For 75 years we were permitted to talk only to the faithful in our congregations. We are only beginning now to educate clergy in how to speak to non-believers."

And then, of course, there are the dangers attendant on the influx of such cults as the Moonies, the Hare Krishnas, and many quite wild and even suicidal cults, who are doing great harm in attracting and brainwashing young people. "In the United States," he said, "you can tolerate and assimilate these groups. You have had 200 years of democracy. We are only beginning our democracy. Today your pluralism would destroy us."

"The August law," my informant said, "was a reaction against the premature invasion of Western missionaries. Of course we do not want to violate international law or our own constitution or principles of human rights. But we hope that those legal and moral norms can be adapted to enable us to meet the acute spiritual crisis that now confronts us."

Conclusion

I have tried to add to the conventional legal analysis of attempts by the Russian Orthodox Church to restrict foreign missionaries and to obtain state support for traditional confessions in Russia a different perspective, based upon a historical jurisprudence. Positivists will say that it is irrelevant. Natural-law theorists will say that it is immaterial. It is true, both will say, that there is a doctrine in the law of human rights called "measure of appreciation," under which special historical circumstances may be held to justify departures from the norms of human rights covenants and treaties; but the exclusion of foreign missionaries goes well beyond what has been brought under the rubric of "measure of appreciation."

I do not contend that historical considerations, or cultural considerations, are always decisive in the interpretation of broad constitutional doctrines—only that sometimes they *may be* decisive. And in a society like the Russian society today, undergoing, on the one hand, a revolutionary enlargement of human rights, including religious human rights, and, on the other hand, tumultuous political, economic, and spiritual changes—at such a time in such a society the arguments of the Moscow Patriarchate deserve to be carefully and sympathetically considered, if only to overcome them.

I conclude with a suggestion that is also more compatible with a historical theory of law than with either a positivist theory or a natural-law theory: that in the present situation in Russia, the resolution of inter-church, inter-denominational conflicts such as the ones I have been discussing should be undertaken not at the level of legislation but at the level of dialogue and negotiation among all the conflicting groups. There is a strong but almost untranslatable word for this in the tradition of Russian Orthodoxy: *sobornost'*, conciliarity, collectivity, or perhaps, if I may coin a new word, "communification," a bringing of diverse groups together into community through the power of speech, the power of prayer. Surely all the parties could ask for divine guidance in reconciling their differences.

Adjudicating Rights of Conscience Under the European Convention on Human Rights

T. JEREMY GUNN
National Committee for Public Education and Religious Liberty

It was not until 1993 that the European Court of Human Rights first found that a government had violated an individual's freedom of conscience. In *Kokkinakis v. Greece*, the European Court decided that the Greek government's conviction of an elderly Jehovah's Witness for illegal proselytizing "amounts to an interference with the exercise of Mr. Kokkinakis's right to 'freedom to manifest [his] religion or belief'."[1] This, the Court held, breached Article 9 of the European Convention on Human Rights and Fundamental Freedoms.[2] Although the European Commission of Human Rights, the body that initially receives, evaluates, and refers cases to the Court, previously had decided more than 45 reported

[1] *Kokkinakis v. Greece*, 260-A Eur. Ct. H.R. (ser. A) 18, ¶36 (1993). For the text of Article 9, see note 14 and accompanying text. For the convenience of the reader, the full case citation for European Court and European Commission cases will be provided each time they occur with the exception of the *Kokkinakis* case (above) and the *Darby Case*, 187 Eur. Ct. H.R. (ser. A) (1990).

[2] The European Convention on Human Rights and Fundamental Freedoms ("Convention") was concluded in Rome in 1950 by fifteen signatory governments that were members of the Council of Europe. Eur. Treaty Series, No. 5. The Convention entered into force in 1953.

The Council of Europe (and its Court of Human Rights) should not be confused with the European Union. The Council of Europe and the European Union are separate entities. The Council of Europe, which was founded in 1949, has more than thirty members, including several formerly communist countries in Eastern Europe. The Council of Europe and its human rights institutions are located in Strasbourg, France. The European Union is the latest incarnation of what began as the European Coal and Steel Community (1951), the European Economic Community (1957), and the European Community (1967). The high court of the European Union, the European Court of Justice, sits in Luxembourg. This paper is concerned solely with the Council of Europe, its Convention on Human Rights and Fundamental Freedoms, and its judicial organs.

J.D. van der Vyver and J. Witte, Jr. (eds.), Religious Human Rights in Global Perspective, 305-330.

cases involving rights of conscience under Article 9, it was not until *Kokkinakis* that the Court itself squarely addressed Article 9 issues.[3] Even though the Court concluded that the conviction of Minos Kokkinakis had breached Article 9, the approach taken by the Court in reaching that decision, the narrowness of the vote (six to three), and the dissenters' harsh attacks on the Court's opinion, all provide substantial grounds for fearing that rights of conscience are, at best, only tenuously protected under the human rights regime that the European Convention created. Indeed, the *Kokkinakis* decision can be seen as a failure of the Court to take the right of conscience seriously.

Background

The suggestion that the European system does not provide adequate protection for rights of conscience surely ought to come as a surprise. After all, the human rights regime of the Council of Europe is generally regarded as the most progressive international institutions working for the protection of human rights. A former President of the Inter-American Court of Human Rights, Professor Thomas Buergenthal, praised the European "human rights system established by the Convention [for being] not only the oldest but also the most advanced and effective of those currently in existence."[4]

Not only is the European system the most advanced international human rights body, the rights encompassed within freedom of conscience and religion are themselves among the oldest rights that international covenants recognize. Since at least the thirteenth century,

---

[3] Historically, the European Convention has had two principal adjudicative bodies: the European Court of Human Rights ("Court") and the European Commission of Human Rights ("Commission"). The Commission effectively has served as a court of first instance that filters "admissible" from "inadmissible" applications for the Court. For a more detailed explanation of the roles and procedures of the Court, the Commission, and the Council of Ministers, see Ralph Beddard, *Human Rights in Europe*, 3d ed. (Cambridge, 1993); P. Van Dijk and G.J.H. Van Hoof, *Theory and Practice of the European Convention on Human Rights*, 2d ed. (Deventer, 1990); J.E.S. Fawcett, *The Application of the European Convention on Human Rights* (Oxford, 1987); R. St. J. Macdonald, et al., eds., *The European System for the Protection of Human Rights* (The Hague, 1993); Vincent Berger, *Jurisprudence de la Cour européenne des droits de l'homme*, 3d ed. (Paris, 1991).

On May 11, 1994, 27 of the 28 States Parties to the European Convention signed Protocol No. 11, which, when ratified, will restructure the Court and eliminate the Commission. See Andrew Drzemczewski and Jens Meyer-Ladewig, "Principal Characteristics of the New ECHR Control Mechanism, as Established by Protocol No. 11, Signed on 11 May 1994," *Human Rights Law Journal* 15 (1994): 81.

[4] Thomas Buergenthal, *International Human Rights* (St. Paul, 1988), 84.

European governments have, albeit inconsistently, protected at least some religious believers from discrimination in foreign realms.[5]

The preparatory sessions of the European Convention included some discussion suggesting that the delegates believed that rights of conscience were of particular significance. The delegate from religiously-torn Ireland told the Preparatory Commission in 1949 that "Civil and religious freedom are but two of the fundamental rights of man. . . . If the Council of Europe achieves no other end than the guarantee of those two rights, it will have justified its existence."[6] This tribute to religious freedom as a fundamental right under the European system, anticipated at its birth, was reiterated most recently in the *Kokkinakis* decision:

> As enshrined in Article 9, freedom of thought, conscience and religion is one of the foundations of a "democratic society" within the meaning of the Convention. It is, in its religious dimension, one of the most vital elements that go[es] to make up the identity of believers and their conception of life, but it is also a precious asset for atheists, agnostics, sceptics and the unconcerned.[7]

Any failure by the European system to take the right of conscience seriously is not, therefore, due to a lack of merit of the European system generally nor to a failure to acknowledge the importance of rights of conscience.

As the European Convention approaches its fiftieth anniversary and as the United Nations and UNESCO celebrate the World Year for Tolerance in 1995, it is appropriate to examine the decisions of the Court and Commission in the area of rights of conscience.[8] Unfortunately, the substance of the Court's decisions often does not equal its rhetoric. The

---

[5] See generally C.A. Macartney, *National States and National Minorities* (New York, 1934), 157-175; András B. Baka, "The European Convention on Human Rights and the Protection of Minorities Under International Law," *Connecticut Journal of International Law* 8 (1993): 227; Patrick Thornberry, *International Law and the Rights of Minorities* (Oxford, 1991), 25-37; Carol Weisbrod, "Minorities and Diversities: The 'Remarkable Experiment' of the League of Nations," *Connecticut Journal of International Law* 8 (1993): 359; Hurst Hannum, "Contemporary Developments in the International Protection of the Rights of Minorities," *Notre Dame Law Review* 66 (1991): 1431, esp. 1431-34.

[6] Statement of Mr. Everett, [Council of Europe], 1 *Collected Edition of the 'Travaux Préparatoires'* (The Hague, 1975), 103-04.

[7] *Kokkinakis*, 17, ¶ 31.

[8] Some recent publications that discuss without seriously questioning the European system's protection of rights of conscience include Malcolm N. Shaw, "Freedom of Thought, Conscience and Religion," in Macdonald, et al., *The European System for the Protection of Human Rights*, 445-463; [Council of Europe], *Freedom of Conscience* (The Hague, 1993); Christian Skakkebaek, *Article 9 of the European Convention on Human Rights* (Strasbourg, 1992).

European court[9] has too often treated rights of conscience as an awkward inconvenience to be tolerated rather than as a matter of fundamental importance.

Rights of Conscience Under the European Convention

The Language of Article 9. The European Convention of Human Rights and Fundamental Freedoms contains several provisions that touch upon rights of conscience, including freedom of expression,[10] freedom of association,[11] rights relating to nondiscrimination,[12] and parental rights pertaining to the religious education of children.[13] Within the Convention the single most important provision guaranteeing rights of conscience is Article 9.

> 1. Everyone has the right to freedom of thought, conscience and religion; this right includes freedom to change his religion or belief and freedom, either alone or in community with others and in public or in private, to manifest his religion or belief, in worship, teaching, practice and observance.
>
> 2. Freedom to manifest one's religion or beliefs shall be subject only to such limitations as are prescribed by law and are necessary in a democratic society in the interests of public safety, for the protection of public order, health or morals, or for the protection of the rights and freedoms of others.[14]

The first section describes "freedom of thought, conscience and religion" as a right belonging to everyone. The text was drawn almost verbatim from Article 18 of the Universal Declaration of Human Rights ("Universal Declaration").[15] The protections extend beyond those nar-

---

[9] In order to avoid cumbersome terminology, and in anticipation of a restructured Court (see footnote 3 above), I will use the generic term "European court" to encompass both the Court and the Commission.

[10] "Everyone has the right to freedom of expression. This right shall include freedom to hold opinions and to receive and impart information and ideas without interference by public authority and regardless of frontiers. . . ." European Convention, Article 10.

[11] "Everyone has the right to freedom of peaceful assembly and to freedom of association with others. . . ." European Convention, Article 11.

[12] "The enjoyment of the rights and freedoms set forth in this Convention shall be secured without discrimination on any ground such as sex, race, colour, language, religion, political or other opinion, national or social origin, association with a national minority, property, birth or other status." European Convention, Article 14.

[13] "[T]he State shall respect the right of parents to ensure such education and teaching in conformity with their own religious and philosophical convictions." European Convention, First Protocol, Article 2.

[14] European Convention, Article 9.

[15] "Everyone has the right to freedom of thought, conscience and religion; this right includes freedom to change his religion or belief, and freedom, either alone or in community

rowly pertaining to religious rights by including rights of conscience and thought.[16] While the first section of Article 9 identifies the rights of conscience that the Convention guarantees, the second section specifies the circumstances under which governments may limit the freedom to manifest those rights.[17] Although the Universal Declaration did not include a comparable limitation on the right to manifest one's beliefs, such limitations were commonplace in other human rights instruments of the post-World War II period.[18]

Reflecting this two-part construction of Article 9, the European Court and Commission now follow a two-step analysis of petitions. The court first determines whether a governmental action restricts a right of conscience under Article 9(1). If no identifiable right of conscience is restricted, the application is dismissed. If, however, the court identifies a restriction, the court then determines whether the restriction is permitted under Article 9(2). The considerations underlying these two steps will be discussed in turn.

Cases Arising Under Article 9. Since its inception in 1955, the Commission has registered more than 20,000 applications, the vast majority of

---

with others and in public or private, to manifest his religion or belief in teaching, practice, worship and observance." Universal Declaration, Article 18. The delegates to the preparatory sessions of the European Convention used the Universal Declaration as a working draft. See *Collected Edition of the 'Travaux Préparatoires' of the European Convention on Human Rights*, 4:52.

The American Declaration on the Rights and Duties of Man ("American Declaration"), which was adopted shortly before the Universal Declaration, provided that: "Every person has the right freely to profess a religious faith, and to manifest and practice it both in public and in private." American Declaration, Article III.

[16] The European Convention protects the rights of conscience of atheists and agnostics. See *Kokkinakis*, 17, ¶ 31 (quoted above). This protection of the rights of conscience of "nonbelievers" continues a trend that started in the Universal Declaration and that was recently enshrined in the 1981 U.N. Declaration of the Rights of Religion, Conscience and Belief and in the "General Comment [on Article 18] Adopted by the Human Rights Committee Under Article 40, Paragraph 4, of the International Covenant on Civil and Political Rights," September 27, 1993.

[17] Like Article 9, Articles 7, 8, 10, and 11 similarly identify guaranteed rights in their first sections and describe permissible governmental limitations on those rights in their second sections.

[18] American Convention on Human Rights, Article 12 (3): "Freedom to manifest one's religion and beliefs may be subject only to the limitations prescribed by law that are necessary to protect public safety, order, health, or morals, or the rights or freedoms of others." International Covenant on Civil and Political Rights, Article 18(3): "Freedom to manifest one's religion or beliefs may be subject only to such limitations as are prescribed by law and are necessary to protect public safety, order, health, or morals or the fundamental rights and freedoms of others." United Nations Declaration on the Elimination of All Forms of Intolerance and Discrimination Based on Religion or Belief, Article 1(3): "Freedom to manifest one's religion or beliefs may be subject only to such limitations as are prescribed by law and are necessary to protect public safety, order, health or morals or the fundamental rights and freedoms of others."

which individuals and groups submit.[19] Although it cannot readily be known what percentage of these cases raised rights of conscience claims, the Commission ultimately published decisions in approximately 45 cases where an applicant squarely raised an Article 9 challenge. In only five of these 45 cases the Commission declared that the applications were admissible—that is, subject to further proceedings.[20] Of these five admissible cases, the Commission subsequently held that three of them ultimately did not warrant a finding of an Article 9 violation. In the first, *Karnell and Hardt v. Sweden,* the Commission successfully negotiated a settlement between the parties that negated any need for further proceedings.[21] In the second, *Grandrath v. Federal Republic of Germany,* the Commission concluded that there had been no violation of Article 9 nor any other portion of the Convention.[22] In the last of these three, *Hoffmann v. Austria,* the Commission found an Article 8 (rather than Article 9) violation, and referred the case to the Court (which also found only an Article 8 violation).[23]

Thus, of the approximately 45 reported cases raising Article 9 claims, only two resulted in final Commission decisions that Article 9 had been violated: *Darby v. Sweden* and *Kokkinakis v. Greece*. The Court subsequently agreed with the Commission that *Darby* and *Kokkinakis* presented violations, although the *Darby* decision ultimately was based upon grounds other than Article 9. Therefore, of the reported cases raising Article 9 issues, the Court has, to date, decided only one on the basis of Article 9: *Kokkinakis v. Greece.*

It is easy to agree with the result reached in *Kokkinakis*: the conviction of an elderly Jehovah's Witness for proselytizing breached the Convention. A close reading of *Kokkinakis,* however, reveals serious problems in the Court's reasoning that are, unfortunately, reflected in most of the European court's Article 9 cases. Although each case ultimately must be treated on its own terms and facts, a summary examination of the results

---

19 Council of Europe, *The Council of Europe and Human Rights* (Strasbourg, 1993), 5.

20 *Karnell and Hardt v. Sweden,* App. No. 4733/71, 14 Y.B. Eur. Conv. on H.R. 676 (Eur. Comm'n) (1971); *Darby Case* (see footnote 1 above); *Kokkinakis v. Greece; Hoffmann v. Austria,* 255-C Eur. Ct. H.R. 68 (ser. A) (1993) (Eur. Comm'n); *Grandrath v. Federal Republic of Germany,* App. No. 2299/64, 10 Y.B. Eur. Conv. on H.R. 626 (Comm. Ministers) (1967).

21 *Karnell and Hardt v. Sweden,* App. No. 4733/71, 14 Y.B. Eur. Conv. on H.R. 676 (Eur. Comm'n) (1971). Sweden agreed to amend its law to provide an exemption for Lutheran-Evangelicals from a compulsory religious-education law.

22 *Grandrath v. Federal Republic of Germany,* App. No. 2299/64, 10 Y.B. Eur. Conv. on H.R. 626 (Comm. Ministers) (1967) (Jehovah's Witness clergy required to perform alternate service although Catholic and Protestant clergy were not). In this case, the Committee of Ministers agreed with the Commission and found that there had been no violation. *Grandrath v. Federal Republic of Germany,* 10 Y.B. Eur. Conv. on H.R. 626 (1967).

23 *Hoffmann v. Austria,* 255-C Eur. Ct. H.R. (ser. A) (1993).

of the European system's jurisprudence reveals a consistent pattern of rejecting Article 9 claims. The Commission has, for example, declared every application brought by a conscientious objector to be inadmissible. This is true for those protesting military conscription and military policy,[24] those contesting the terms of non-military compulsory service,[25] those contesting compulsory insurance taxes,[26] and those objecting to corporal punishment by state schools.[27] Excepting *Kokkinakis* and *Hoffmann*, the European Commission always denied applications from religions that could be called "new," "minority," or "nontraditional."[28]

A poignant example that reveals an institutional bias in favor of traditional religions involves two different petitions that challenged a Swedish law requiring religious education to be taught at public schools. In both suits the applicants alleged that the religious education law favored the established Swedish Lutheran Church. In the first case, the Commission admitted the application filed by the dissenting Evangelical Lutheran Church, and then began negotiations with the Swedish government to resolve the conflict. The negotiations resulted in a successful compromise that gave the Evangelical Lutherans an exemption from the

---

24 *Arrowsmith v. the United Kingdom*, App. No. 7050/75, 19 Eur. Comm'n H.R. Dec. & Rep. 5 (1980) (pacifist protest); *C. v. United Kingdom*, App. No. 10358/83, 37 Eur. Comm'n H.R. Dec. & Rep. 142 (1983) (Quaker war tax); *Grandmaison and Fritz v. France*, App. Nos. 11567/85 and 11568/85, 53 Eur. Comm'n H.R. Dec. & Rep. 150 (1987) (war protest); *N. v. Sweden*, App. No. 10410/83, 40 Eur. Comm'n H.R. Dec. & Rep. 203 (1984) (nonaffiliated pacifist exemption); *X. v. Austria*, App. No. 5591/72, 43 Collection Decisions of Eur. Comm'n H.R. 161 (1973) (Catholic exemption).

25 *Conscientious Objectors v. Denmark*, App. No. 7565/76, 9 Eur. Comm'n H.R. Dec. & Rep. 117 (1977) (pay equality); *Grandrath v. Federal Republic of Germany*, App. No. 2299/64, 10 Y.B. Eur. Conv. on H.R. 626 (Comm. Ministers) (1967) (requirement for Jehovah's Witness official); *X. v. the Federal Republic of Germany*, App. No. 7705/76, 9 Eur. Comm'n H.R. Dec. & Rep. 196 (1977) (Jehovah's Witness).

26 *Reformed Church of X. v. Netherlands*, App. No. 1497/62, 5 Y.B. Eur. Conv. on H.R. 286 (Eur. Comm'n) (1962) (old age insurance); *X. v. Netherlands*, App. No. 2065/63, 8 Y.B. Eur. Conv. on H.R. 266 (Eur. Comm'n) (1965) (old age insurance); *X. v. the Netherlands*, App. No. 2988/66, 10 Y.B. Eur. Conv. H.R. 472 (1967) (automobile insurance).

27 *Campbell and Cosans v. United Kingdom*, 48 Eur. Ct. H.R. (ser. A) (1982).

28 *Angelini v. Sweden*, App. No. 10941/83, 51 Eur. Comm'n H.R. Dec. & Rep. 41 (1987) (Atheist); *X. v. United Kingdom*, App. No. 5442/72, 1 Eur. Comm'n H.R. Dec. & Rep. 41 (1974) (Buddhist); *Church of Scientology and 128 Members v. Sweden*, App. No. 8282/78, 21 Eur. Comm'n H.R. Dec. & Rep. 109 (1980) (Church of Scientology); *Grandrath v. Federal Republic of Germany*, App. No. 2299/64, 10 Y.B. Eur. Conv. on H.R. 626 (Comm. Ministers) (1967) (Jehovah's Witness); *X. v. Federal Republic of Germany*, App. No. 7705/76, 9 Eur. Comm'n H.R. Dec. & Rep. 196 (1977) (Jehovah's Witness); *Chappell v. United Kingdom*, App. No. 12587/86, 53 Eur. Comm'n H.R. Dec. & Rep. 241 (1987) (Druids); *X. v. United Kingdom*, App. No. 7992/77, 14 Eur. Comm'n H.R. Dec. & Rep. 234 (1979) (Sikh, although British law was subsequently changed); *X. v. United Kingdom*, App. No. 8231/78, 28 Eur. Comm'n H.R. Dec. & Rep. 5 (1982) (Sikh); *Ahmad v. United Kingdom*, App. No. 8160/78, 4 Eur. H.R. Rep. 126 (1981) (Eur. Comm'n) (Muslim); *X. v. United Kingdom*, App. No. 7291/75, 11 Eur. Comm'n H.R. Dec. & Rep. 55 (1977) (Wicca).

requirement of attending state religious education.[29] When an atheist filed a claim for an exemption from the same law, however, the Commission declared the application to be "manifestly ill-founded."[30]

The Commission similarly denied a modest request by a Muslim supernumerary teacher to have a 45-minute extension of his lunch hour to attend Friday prayers.[31] Every case involving religious rights of prisoners was declared inadmissible.[32] The European court does not favor challenges to established state churches, even when those churches have been given the legal power to levy and collect religious taxes.[33] As the Commission said in *Darby*, a "State Church system cannot in itself be considered to violate Article 9 of the Convention. In fact, such a system exists in several Contracting States and existed there already when the Convention was drafted and when they became parties to it."[34]

These troubling results do not prove that the European court is insensitive to rights of conscience. Obviously, not every prisoner's claim has merit, and all applications by adherents to minority religions should not be routinely admitted. These summary results nevertheless provide grounds for the concern that the European court is not sufficiently attentive to rights of conscience.

The Scope of Rights Protected Under Article 9(1). In order to understand the full meaning of Article 9, it is necessary to understand the scope of the rights protected under 9(1) before turning to the limitations on those rights permitted under 9(2). Although the European court has referred to the guarantee of rights of conscience as "one of the founda-

---

29 *Karnell and Hardt v. Sweden*, App. No. 4733/71, 14 Y.B. Eur. Conv. on H.R. 676 (Eur. Comm'n) (1971).

30 *Angelini v. Sweden*, App. No. 10941/83, 51 Eur. Comm'n H.R. Dec. & Rep. 41, 49, 51 (1987).

31 *Ahmad v. United Kingdom*, App. No. 8160/78, 4 Eur. H.R. Rep. 126 (1981) (Eur. Comm'n).

32 *Huber v. Austria*, App. No. 4517/70, 14 Y.B. Eur. Conv. on H.R. 548 (Eur. Comm'n) (1970); *Vereniging Rechtswinkels Utrecht v. Netherlands*, App. No. 11308/84, 46 Eur. Comm'n H.R. Dec. & Rep. 200 (1986); *X. v. Austria*, App. No. 1753/63, 8 Y.B. Eur. Conv. on H.R. 174 (Eur. Comm'n) (1965); *X. v. Federal Republic of Germany*, App. No. 2413/63, 23 Collection of Decisions Eur. Comm'n H.R. 1 (1967); *X. v. United Kingdom*, App. No. 8231/78, 28 Eur. Comm'n H.R. Dec. & Rep. 5 (1982); *X. v. United Kingdom*, App. No. 7291/75, 11 Eur. Comm'n H.R. Dec. & Rep. 55 (1977); *X. v. United Kingdom*, App. No. 6886/75, 5 Eur. Comm'n H.R. Dec. & Rep. 100 (1976); *X. v. United Kingdom*, App. No. 5947/72, 5 Eur. Comm'n H.R. Dec. & Rep. 8 (1976); *X. v. United Kingdom*, App. No. 5442/72, 1 Eur. Comm'n H.R. Dec. & Rep. 41 (1974).

33 *E. & G.R. v. Austria*, App. No. 9781/82, 37 Eur. Comm'n H.R. Dec. & Rep. 42 (1984); *Gottesmann v. Switzerland*, App. No. 10616/83, 40 Eur. Comm'n H.R. Dec. & Rep. 284 (1984); *Darby Case* (the Commission, but not the Court, held that the taxing power of the Finnish Lutheran Church should be restricted as applied to nonmembers of the faith).

34 *Darby Case*, 17, ¶45 (Eur. Comm.).

tions of a 'democratic society'," [35] it has for the most part suggested that the guarantee be a narrow one. This narrow right encompasses only beliefs and expressions of those beliefs. It has thus held that Article 9(1) rights include only "the sphere of personal beliefs and religious creeds [that] is sometimes referred to as the *forum internum*" as well as those "acts intimately linked" to the *forum internum*.[36] If one concedes that modern European governments are unlikely to punish citizens solely for holding unfavored beliefs, the only contribution Article 9(1) makes to human rights in this narrow reading of the Article, is its providing some protection for acts that are necessarily and closely tied to expressions of those religious beliefs.

The Commission has long adhered to this interpretation of Article 9(1). For example, the Commission consistently finds that acts of conscientious objection do not come within the scope of Article 9(1). This is true for conscientious objection to military service,[37] to alternative service,[38] to paying taxes used for military purposes,[39] to paying for compulsory insurance,[40] to compulsory voting laws,[41] or even to making tax payments to churches.[42] In such cases the Commission did not believe it necessary

---

[35] *Kokkinakis*, 17, ¶31.

[36] *C. v. United Kingdom*, App. No. 10358/83, 37 Eur. Comm'n H.R. Dec. & Rep. 142, 147 (1983) (Quaker's refusal to pay taxes for military spending not encompassed within Article 9(1)).

[37] *Arrowsmith v. United Kingdom*, App. No. 7050/75, 19 Eur. Comm'n H.R. Dec. & Rep. 5 (1980); *N. v. Sweden*, App. No. 10410/83, 40 Eur. Comm'n H.R. Dec. & Rep. 203, 207 (1984) (finding that nonaffiliated pacifist's "complaint falls into the realm of at least Article 9," but fails to find violation of 9(1)); *X. v. Austria*, App. No. 5591/72, 43 Collection of Decisions of Eur. Comm'n H.R. 161 (1973) (dec. of April 2, 1973).

[38] *Grandrath v. Federal Republic of Germany*, App. No. 2299/64, 8 Y.B. Eur. Conv. on H.R. 324, 336 (Eur. Comm'n) (1965), 10 Y.B. Eur. Conv. on H.R. 626, 630 (Comm. Ministers) (1967) (adopting decision of Commission); *Johansen v. Norway*, App. No. 10600/83, 44 Eur. Comm'n H.R. Dec. & Rep. 155, 162 (1985); *X. v. Federal Republic of Germany*, App. No. 7705/76, 9 Eur. Comm'n H.R. Dec. & Rep. 196 (1977).

[39] *C. v. United Kingdom*, App. No. 10358/83, 37 Eur. Comm'n H.R. Dec. & Rep. 142 (1983).

[40] *Reformed Church of X. v. Netherlands*, App. No. 1497/62, 5 Y.B. Eur. Conv. on H.R. 286, 288 (Eur. Comm'n) (1962) ("Article 9 does not oblige the legislature to make special rules for conscientious objectors"); *X. v. Netherlands*, App. No. 2065/63, 8 Y.B. Eur. Conv. on H.R. 266, 270 (Eur. Comm'n) (1965).

[41] *X. v. Austria*, App. No. 1753/63, 8 Y.B. Eur. Conv. on H.R. 174 (Eur. Comm'n) (1965); *X. v. Austria*, App. No. 1718/62, 8 Y.B. Eur. Conv. on H.R. 168 (Eur. Comm'n) (1965).

[42] The Commission found no Article 9(1) issue with respect to whether a church could require, at law, a church member to pay taxes to support the church. *E. & G.R. v. Austria*, App. No. 9781/82, 37 Eur. Comm'n H.R. Dec. & Rep. 42 (1984); *Gottesmann v. Switzerland*, App. No. 10616/83, 40 Eur. Comm'n H.R. Dec. & Rep. 284, 289 (1984) ("the obligation to pay a tax by virtue of membership of a given church is not an interference with everyone's right to freedom of religion [inasmuch as] such an obligation does not affect the freedom to change or manifest one's religion.")

to determine whether the conscientious objectors were sincere or whether their governments might have had a legitimate basis for compelling the objectors to act against their will. The Commission simply found that no Article 9(1) right was implicated.

The Commission's famous 1978 decision, *Arrowsmith v. United Kingdom*, similarly reveals the narrow scope of Article 9(1).[43] Pat Arrowsmith, whom the Commission acknowledged was "undisputedly a convinced pacifist,"[44] was convicted under Britain's rarely enforced "Incitement to Disaffection Act of 1934." She had been found guilty for distributing antimilitary leaflets to British troops who were about to be sent to Northern Ireland. Arrowsmith's leaflets contained several arguments opposing military service in Northern Ireland, including some arguments that were not strictly pacifist. Although the Commission agreed that Arrowsmith's pacifism "falls within the ambit of the right to freedom of thought and conscience," it nevertheless concluded that not every act motivated by a religious belief is covered by Article 9(1).[45] Rather than acknowledging that Arrowsmith's beliefs and actions were within the scope of Article 9(1), and then deciding whether the government could proscribe such conduct under 9(2), the Commission held that there was no cognizable claim under 9(1). This, the Commission held, was because "the leaflets did not express pacifist views. [Therefore] the applicant, by distributing the leaflets, did not manifest her belief in the sense of Article 9.1."[46] The Commission thereby narrowed the scope of Article 9 by driving the wedge not between acceptable and unacceptable forms of expression, but between religious beliefs and the actions that express those beliefs.

In the same vein, the Commission decided in 1981 that a public school teacher, who was Muslim, did not have a claim under Article 9(1) when the school refused to accommodate his wish to attend Friday prayers.[47] The Commission held that the right to conscience was not violated *because* the teacher himself had originally made the decision to apply for and accept the teaching position. The Commission held that it obviously was not "necessary" to attend prayers in a situation where the petitioner had voluntarily accepted the teaching position and where he remained

---

43 *Arrowsmith v. United Kingdom*, App. No. 7050/75, 19 Eur. Comm'n H.R. Dec. & Rep. 5 (1980).

44 Ibid., 19, ¶ 68.

45 Ibid., 19, ¶¶ 69, 71.

46 Ibid., 20, ¶ 75. A less compelling variation of the *Arrowsmith* problem is found in *Grandmaison and Fritz v. France*, App. Nos. 11567/85 and 11568/85, 53 Eur. Comm'n H.R. Dec. & Rep. 150 (1987). The petitioners in *Grandmaison*, soldiers who distributed antimilitary literature, were neither pacifists nor urging soldiers not to fight.

47 *Ahmad v. United Kingdom*, App. No. 8160/78, 4 Eur. H.R. Rep. 126 (1981) (Eur. Comm'n).

"free to resign" from his position.[48] "[I]f the requirements imposed upon a person [employed] by the church should be in conflict with his convictions he should be free to leave his office, and the Commission regards this as an ultimate guarantee of his right to freedom of thought, conscience and religion."[49] The Commission thereby assumes that an employee's right of conscience is not infringed in the workplace so long as the option of resigning remains open.

In several cases where the Commission might reasonably have found an Article 9(1) violation, it avoided making any such findings by suspending judgment on Article 9(1) and turning immediately to Article 9(2). For example, when the British government prohibited Druids from worshiping at Stonehenge, the Commission assumed, for the sake of argument, that Article 9(1) had been violated and then decided that the government had a sufficient basis under Article 9(2) for limiting midsummer solstice ceremonies.[50]

There is, however, some modest basis for optimism that the Commission and Court may expand the narrow scope of Article 9 rights. They recently have shown signs of somewhat more generous interpretations of rights of conscience. Neither had any difficulty finding that the religious proselytizing by a Jehovah's Witness in *Kokkinakis* was within the scope of Article 9(1).[51] Although the *Kokkinakis* decision only modestly extends

---

[48] By such an analysis, the Commission is implicitly stating that the "fundamental rights" of the European Convention are subject to a simple contractual waiver and that governments need not respect the fundamental rights of their employees, provided that the applicants are informed of the restrictions in advance and that the employees are free to resign. The Commission in *Ahmad* also analyzed Article 9(2) issues, where it similarly found no violation of the Convention.

[49] *Karlsson v. Sweden*, App. No. 12356/86, 57 Eur. Comm'n H.R. Dec. & Rep. 172, 175 (1988). See also *Knudsen v. Norway*, App. No. 11045/84, 42 Eur. Comm'n H.R. Dec. & Rep. 247 (1985) (clergyman); *X. v. Federal Republic of Germany*, App. No. 8741/79, 24 Eur. Comm'n H.R. Dec. & Rep. 137, 138 (1981) (wishes or beliefs do not translate into right to carry out such beliefs). These cases remind one of the famous passage from Anatole France: "The law, in its magnificent equality, forbids both the rich and the poor from sleeping under bridges, from begging in the streets, and from stealing bread." Anatole France, *Le Lys rouge* (1894) (trans. by author).

[50] *Chappell v. United Kingdom*, App. No. 12587/86, 53 Eur. Comm'n H.R. Dec. & Rep. 241 (1987). In other cases the Commission similarly decided Article 9(2) cases without having first decided whether there was an Article 9(1) infringement. *X. v. Netherlands*, App. No. 2988/66, 10 Y.B. Eur. Conv. H.R. 472, 476 (1967) (objection to compulsory insurance); *X. and Y. v. Netherlands*, App. No. 6753/74, 2 Eur. Comm'n H.R. Dec. & Rep. 118, 120 (1974) (compulsion of testimony from witness); *X. v. United Kingdom*, App. No. 7992/77, 14 Eur. Comm'n H.R. Dec. & Rep. 234 (1978) (Sikh's objection to motorcycle helmet law).

[51] The Commission unanimously referred to the Greek prohibition on proselytizing as "a permanent threat weighing particularly heavily on every citizen who is not of Greek Orthodox faith .... [A]cts and practices which are nothing more than the elementary exercise of the freedom to manifest one's religion is incompatible with the spirit of tolerance which should exist in a democratic society." *Kokkinakis*, 46, ¶ 53 (decision of Commission).

Article 9(1), it nevertheless moves in a different direction from *Arrowsmith* and *Chappell*.

Other suggestive evidence of a liberalizing trend comes from the *Darby Case*. Dr. Peter Darby, a naturalized citizen of Finland, worked in Sweden but retained residences in both countries.[52] Dr. Darby sought judicial relief from a Swedish law that required him to pay taxes in support of the established Lutheran Church of Sweden. Although his arguments were unsuccessful in the Swedish courts, both the Commission and the Court agreed with Dr. Darby, albeit for different reasons.[53]

The Lutheran Church of Sweden is the legally established church in Sweden. Under longstanding Swedish law, the local parish councils of the established church set the church tax rate and impose that tax on parish residents.[54] Although the church tax is collected simultaneously with other municipal taxes, the parishes levy it separately. The proceeds from the parish-imposed tax are distributed directly to the parish churches.[55] In addition to using the tax proceeds to advance their sectarian activities, the parishes also provide some "secular" services for the state, including maintenance of birth records and administering nondenominational cemeteries.[56] Sweden estimated, and Darby did not contest, that approximately 30% of the church tax is used for these secular purposes.[57]

Before 1951, all Swedish taxpayers were obligated to pay the church tax, regardless of their religious affiliation. In that year, however, Sweden

---

[52] During the relevant period, Dr. Darby changed residences as well as employment. Sweden also enacted some changes in its tax laws. Although these changes affected the specific relief sought by Dr. Darby, they are not material for the analysis considered here. For a description of these changes and the proceedings in the Swedish courts, see *Darby Case*, 7-9, ¶¶ 8-16.

[53] Darby argued that the Church Tax law violated his right of freedom of conscience under Article 9 of the Convention as well as his right to equal treatment in the enjoyment of his possessions under Article 14 (in conjunction with Article 1 of Protocol 1). Darby also alleged a violation of Article 9 in conjunction with Article 14. The European Commission concluded that the Swedish Church Tax, as applied to Dr. Darby, violated Article 9 of the Convention. The Court, however, did not reach the issue of the applicability of Article 9, but decided instead that it was "more natural to examine the case under Article 14," and that the tax, as applied to Darby, violated Article 14 in conjunction with Article 1 of Protocol 1. Ibid., 12, ¶ 28.

Sweden taxed Dr. Darby as a nonresident for all purposes other than the Church Tax. Although Sweden exempts residents who are not members of the established Church law from the Church Tax, nonresidents are required to pay. The exemption disparity between residents and nonresidents formed a significant part of the Court's Protocol 1 analysis. Ibid., 12-13, ¶¶ 28-34.

[54] Ibid., 10, ¶ 21.

[55] Ibid., 18, ¶ 48 (Eur. Comm'n).

[56] Ibid., 10, ¶ 22.

[57] Ibid.

enacted a Dissenters Tax Act that partially exempted non-members of the Lutheran Church of Sweden from liability for the church tax. Non-members thereafter paid only the 30% portion of the church tax used for secular purposes.[58] The Dissenters Tax Act, however, did not exempt non-Lutheran taxpayers who, like Dr. Darby, were only part-time residents of Sweden. As a result, the law required Dr. Darby to pay the entire church tax.[59]

Dr. Darby made two principal arguments to the Commission and the Court. First, he argued that the requirement to pay the church tax violated his rights of conscience under Article 9. Second, he argued that the Dissenters Tax Act improperly discriminated on the basis of national origin between full-time and part-time residents of Sweden. The European Commission accepted Dr. Darby's Article 9 claim without reaching any other issue. The Court, however, concluded that the tax improperly discriminated on the basis of national origin, but did not reach the Article 9 issue raised in the application. (The following discussion will consider only the opinion of the European Commission.)

In response to Darby's claim that the church tax violated his religious freedom, the Swedish government set forth, according to the Commission, essentially three defenses. First, Dr. Darby's conscience was not violated, because he could have become a Swedish citizen and thereby obtain the Dissenter's Tax Act exemption. Second, the amount of the tax was insignificant. Third, the State must remain free to allocate taxes for purposes to which individuals might object.[60]

The Commission narrowed its own focus to one issue: "whether the applicant's obligation to pay a church tax to a church of which he is not a member is compatible with his right to freedom of religion protected by Article 9 of the Convention."[61] In rejecting Sweden's observation that Dr. Darby could have obtained Swedish citizenship—and thereby obtain an exemption—the Commission responded that "[i]t cannot be accepted that an individual should be forced to move from his home and take up residence in the State concerned before he could enjoy the right to have his freedom of religion respected by that State."[62] This argument cuts against

58 Ibid., 10, ¶¶ 21-22. In accepting the validity of the 30-70% breakdown, neither the Court nor the Commission considered whether all parishes actually appropriate 30% of their tax revenue to their state functions.

59 Under the terms of a convention between Finland and Sweden, Darby was obligated to pay taxes on his worldwide income under the Swedish Municipal Tax Act of 1928, as amended. Ibid., 9-10, ¶¶ 17-20. As a part-time resident of the country, Darby received tax deductions except for the Church Tax. Ibid., 7, ¶¶ 7-8.

60 Ibid., 17, ¶ 42.

61 Ibid., 18, ¶ 49.

62 Ibid., 19, ¶ 52.

the reasoning in *Ahmad v. United Kingdom, Karlsson v. Sweden,* and *Knudsen v. Norway*—cases implying that religious rights are not infringed when the petitioner retains the choice of altering his circumstances. In response to Sweden's second argument—the insignificance of the amount of the church tax—the Commission held that "the right to freedom of religion does not lend itself to an assessment in financial terms."[63] The size of the church tax is thus an irrelevant consideration in determining whether the rights of religious conscience have been infringed.[64] Finally, the Commission rejected Sweden's argument that individuals cannot properly object on the grounds of conscience to the state's appropriations of tax funds. The Commission agreed that individuals cannot refuse to pay taxes into a general fund simply because they conscientiously object to a particular allocation made from the general fund. Thus, a pacifist will not succeed in objecting to payment of the percentage of taxes used to support the military.[65] Unlike at least one previous application, the payments to the Swedish church in *Darby* did not come from a general tax fund, but were raised separately and segregated by the church and for the church. "As regards general taxes," the Court held, "there is no direct link between the individual taxpayer and the State's contribution to the religious activities."[66] The Commission concluded, by a vote of ten to three, that Article 9 required Sweden to exempt Dr. Darby, a nonmember of the state church, from paying the Church Tax.

Although the *Darby Case* offers some hope for a more expansive Article 9 jurisprudence, this hope should be tempered by the fact that none of the Commission's early decisions has been specifically repudiated. Moreover, the Court, unlike the Commission, was sharply divided in *Kokkinakis* and the Court noticeably decided *Darby* on grounds different from those of the Commission.

Kokkinakis and Article 9 Limitations on the Freedom to Manifest Beliefs

Kokkinakis is the Court's only decision that offers a detailed discussion of the limitations that a state may impose on the rights of conscience under the Convention. Although the Court's decision vindicated the

---

63 Ibid., 19, ¶ 55.

64 Unfortunately, the Commission offered no further elaboration of this potentially significant point.

65 The Commission cited *C. v. United Kingdom,* App. No. 10358/83, 37 Eur. Comm'n H.R. Dec. & Rep. 142 (1983), where it had rejected a Quaker's Article 9 claim for a war-tax exemption. The Commission found that the government's appropriation for armaments came from a general fund and it could not be tied to the objector's tax payments.

66 Ibid., 20, ¶ 56.

claim of Mr. Kokkinakis, the Court's opinion unfortunately exemplifies the fragility of the guarantee of rights of conscience in the European system.

The Facts of the Case. On March 2, 1986, Minos Kokkinakis and his wife Elissavet, an elderly Jehovah's Witness couple, called at the Kyriakaki home in Sitia, Crete. Georgia Kyriakaki, the wife of the cantor of a local Greek Orthodox congregation, answered the door and invited the Kokkinakises to come in. Mr. Kokkinakis spoke to Mrs. Kyriakaki for some ten to fifteen minutes. During the visit he told her about some of his religious convictions, quoted from and interpreted the Bible, and explained to her his belief in pacifism. Mrs. Kyriakaki later said that she did not understand everything that Mr. Kokkinakis told her and that the visit did not affect her religious convictions.[67]

Upon learning of the visit, Cantor Kyriakaki promptly informed the police about the circumstances of the visit and asked that the Kokkinakises be prosecuted under the Greek anti-proselytism law. The police immediately arrested and jailed Mr. and Mrs. Kokkinakis overnight. Three weeks later, on March 20, a Greek court convicted them of having violated the anti-proselytism law. The court sentenced the couple to jail terms of four months, fined them 10,000 drachmas, and ordered the confiscation and destruction of four of their booklets.[68]

Both Greek constitutional and Greek criminal law prohibit religious proselytism. The 1975 Greek Constitution, like the 1911 Constitution before it, establishes the Greek Orthodox Church as the "dominant religion" of the state.[69] Ironically, the Greek Constitution prohibits

---

67 *Kokkinakis*, 8, 9-10, ¶¶ 7, 10.

68 Ibid., 9, ¶ 9.

69 See Greek Const. (1975), Article 3 (as translated in *Kokkinakis*, 11, ¶ 13):

> 1. The dominant religion in Greece is that of the Christian Eastern Orthodox Church. The Greek Orthodox Church, which recognises as its head Our Lord Jesus Christ, is indissolubly united, doctrinally, with the great Church of Constantinople and with any other Christian Church in communion with it (omodoxi), immutably observing, like the other Churches, the holy apostolic and synodical canons and the holy traditions. It is autocephalous and is administered by the Holy Synod, composed of all the bishops in office, and by the standing Holy Synod, which is an emanation of it constituted as laid down in the Charter of the Church and in accordance with the provisions of the Patriarchal Tome of 29 June 1850 and the Synodical Act of 4 September 1928.
>
> 2. The ecclesiastical regime in certain regions of the State shall not be deemed contrary to the provisions of the foregoing paragraph.
>
> 3. The text of the Holy Scriptures is unalterable. No official translation into any other form of language may be made without the prior consent of the autocephalous Greek Church and the Great Christian Church at Constantinople.

proselytizing in the same section that otherwise guarantees religious freedom for all Greek citizens.[70] The relevant criminal statute dates from the Metaxas dictatorship, which first promulgated the ban in 1938.[71] By coincidence, the first Jehovah's Witness to be prosecuted and convicted under the anti-proselytism law in 1938 was the same Minos Kokkinakis whose later conviction reached the European Court in 1993. The government amended the 1938 law one year later into the form in which it was used to prosecute the Kokkinakis family in 1986. The amended law provided that:

> 1. Anyone engaging in proselytism shall be liable to imprisonment and a fine of between 1,000 and 50,000 drachmas; he shall, moreover, be subject to police supervision for a period of between six months and one year to be fixed by the court when convicting the offender.
>
> The term of imprisonment may not be commuted to a fine.
>
> 2. By "proselytism" is meant, in particular, any direct or indirect attempt to intrude on the religious beliefs of a person of a different religious persuasion (*eterodoxos*), with the aim of undermining those beliefs, either by any kind of inducement or promise of an inducement or moral support or material assistance, or by fraudulent means or by taking advantage of his inexperience, trust, need, low intellect or naïvety.
>
> 3. The commission of such an offence in a school or other educational establishment or a philanthropic institution shall constitute a particularly aggravating circumstance.[72]

The Jehovah's Witnesses and others unsuccessfully challenged the anti-proselytism law several times before the *Kokkinakis* case reached the European Court.[73] Between 1938 and 1986, the government arrested Kokkinakis himself more than sixty times for proselytizing and jailed

---

[70] Ibid., Article 13, ¶¶ 1 and 2 (as translated in *Kokkinakis*, 11, ¶ 13) provides:

> 1. Freedom of conscience in religious matters is inviolable. The enjoyment of personal and political rights shall not depend on an individual's religious beliefs.
>
> 2. There shall be freedom to practise any known religion; individuals shall be free to perform their rites of worship without hindrance and under the protection of the law. The performance of rites of worship must not prejudice public order or public morals. Proselytism is prohibited.

[71] Law No. 1363/1938, § 4.

[72] Law no. 1672/1939, § 2 (as translated in Kokkinakis, 12, ¶ 16).

[73] *Kokkinakis*, 13-14, ¶¶ 17-21.

him for more than five and one-half years for his proselytizing activities.[74]

The Kokkinakises appealed their sentences. The Crete Court of Appeal quashed Mrs. Kokkinakis's conviction because there was insufficient evidence that she had attempted to proselytize Mrs. Kyriakaki and reduced the fine and sentence imposed on her husband.[75] Mr. Kokkinakis's appeal to the Greek Court of Cassation was, however, dismissed.[76] Dissenters in both the Crete Court of Appeal and the Court of Cassation unsuccessfully argued that the conviction of Mr. Kokkinakis should have been quashed due to insufficient proof of one of the elements of the crime: that he had taken advantage of the victim's "inexperience, trust, need, low intellect or naivety," as the law requires.[77]

The Court's Reasoning in Kokkinakis. Having exhausted his remedies under Greek law, Mr. Kokkinakis applied for relief to the European Commission for Human Rights in 1988. After initially deciding that Mr. Kokkinakis's application was admissible, the fourteen-member Commission unanimously found that his rights under Article 9 of the Convention had been violated.[78] Four years after Kokkinakis first registered his application, the Commission referred the case to the Court. A nine-judge Chamber of the European Court of Human Rights then heard the case and agreed with the Commission that the anti-proselytism law, as applied to Mr. Kokkinakis, impermissibly interfered with his freedom to manifest his beliefs.[79] Unlike the unanimous decision of the Commission, however, the Court split by a vote of six to three on the question whether the case raised an Article 9 question. After offering him this narrow victory, the Court awarded Mr. Kokkinakis 400,000 drachmas for his nonpecuniary damages and 2,789,500 drachmas for costs and expenses.[80]

The Court's opinion begins with a lengthy recapitulation of the arguments made by the Greek government and by Mr. Kokkinakis. With

---

[74] Ibid., 8, ¶ 6.

[75] Ibid., 9, ¶ 10.

[76] Ibid., 10, ¶ 12.

[77] Ibid., 9-10, ¶¶ 10, 12.

[78] The Commission also decided that Greece had not violated Article 7 (offenses must be clearly defined at law). In its admissibility decision, the Commission also found that claims based on Article 5 (no deprivation of liberty without due process) and Article 6 (fair hearing within reasonable time and presumption of innocence) were "manifestly ill-founded." Ibid., 15-16, ¶ 26.

[79] The Court also decided that there had been no violation of Article 7 (by a vote of eight to one), and that it was unnecessary to consider the argument that Article 9 should be analyzed in conjunction with either Article 10 or Article 14 (unanimously). Ibid., 24.

[80] Ibid. In mid-1993, when *Kokkinakis* was decided, the drachma to dollar ratio was approximately 235 to 1, meaning that Mr. Kokkinakis received an award of approximately $1,700 dollars for non-pecuniary damages and $12,000 for costs and expenses.

little analysis and without citation to any case, the Court concludes that the conviction ran afoul of Article 9(1) and that it "amounts to an interference with the exercise of Mr. Kokkinakis's right to 'freedom to manifest [his] religion or belief'."[81] Although it seems correct as a matter of fact and of law that Mr. Kokkinakis's freedom to manifest his religion had been impaired, it is not entirely obvious why the Court reached its decision in such a conclusory manner, particularly in light of the *Arrowsmith*, *Karlsson*, and *Knudsen* decisions discussed above.[82]

Having found that Greece restricted Mr. Kokkinakis's rights under Article 9(1), the Court followed a standard three-part inquiry to determine whether Article 9(2) permitted the limitations.[83] First, the Court decides whether the activity for which the applicant was punished is in fact *"prescribed by law"* (meaning that the law must provide sufficient notice that the activity is prohibited);[84] second, the Court determines whether the government had a *"legitimate aim"* in restricting the activity; and finally, the Court decides whether the restriction is of a type that is *"necessary in a democratic society."* In *Kokkinakis*, the Court and the Commission agreed on the outcome of each of these three steps. Both decided in favor of the Greek government on the first and second steps, but ultimately concluded that the Greek government's restriction on Mr. Kokkinakis's right to manifest his religion was not "necessary in a democratic society." The Court's analysis with respect to each of these three steps suggests, unfortunately, that the Court was moving toward a predetermined result rather than examining carefully the arguments before it. An examination of the Court's reasoning in these three steps shows that it

---

81 Ibid., 18, ¶ 36.

82 Earlier decisions from the European Commission would not have taken such a step without first considering whether Kokkinakis's proselytizing was a religiously motivated action (which might not have been protected because it was in the *forum externum*) or a manifestation of a belief (which may have been protected as within the *forum internum*). See, e.g., *X. v. Federal Republic of Germany*, App. No. 8741/79, 24 Eur. Comm'n H.R. Dec. & Rep. 137 (1981) (wishes or beliefs do not translate into right to carry out such beliefs). Similarly, in *Arrowsmith*, the Commission upheld the conviction of a pacifist whose religious beliefs prompted her to distribute prohibited literature because the literature did not itself express her religious beliefs. "[W]hen the actions of individuals do not actually express the belief concerned they cannot be considered to be as such protected by Article 9.1, even when they are motivated or influenced by it." *Arrowsmith v. the United Kingdom*, App. No. 7050/75, 19 Eur. Comm'n H.R. Dec. & Rep. 5, 20 (1978).

83 See *Kokkinakis*, 18-21, ¶¶ 36-49 (Court); *Kokkinakis*, 47-50, ¶¶ 57-74 (Commission). The Court earlier outlined this three-step inquiry in the *(Case of) Müller and Others*, 133 Eur. Ct. H.R. 20-23, ¶¶ 29-37 (ser. A) (1988), an Article 10(2) freedom of expression case involving obscenity.

84 For use of the somewhat misleading term "prescribed by law," see *Kokkinakis*, 18-20, ¶¶ 37-41 (Court); *Kokkinakis*, 47, ¶¶ 57-60 (Commission); *(Case of) Müller and Others*, 133 Eur. Ct. H.R. 23-25, ¶¶ 38-45 (ser. A) (1988).

made no effort to understand or interpret the scope of the fundamental right to manifest a belief. Rather, the Court sought an acceptable compromise for a politically difficult problem.

Kokkinakis argued that his actions could not have been *"prescribed by law"* because the statute under which he was convicted was so vague that it failed to identify the "'objective substance' of the offence of proselytism."[85] In rejecting the vagueness argument, the Court held that "the wording of many statutes is not absolutely precise. The need to avoid excessive rigidity and to keep pace with changing circumstances means that many laws are inevitably couched in terms which, to a greater or lesser extent, are vague."[86] The Court was satisfied that several earlier decisions from Greek courts had sufficiently defined the offense of proselytism so as to insulate the statute from Kokkinakis's vagueness attack.[87]

The Court's rejection of the vagueness challenge to the anti-proselytism law is disturbing first with respect to a vagueness problem affecting the statute as a whole, and second with respect to a specific problem in the *Kokkinakis* case. First, there is evidence that the law is not enforced against members of the Greek Orthodox faith. The Court's most pronounced supporter of the law, who himself is Greek, admitted that the Greek "Government's representative was not able to give concrete examples concerning other religions [having been prosecuted], but that is not surprising since the Orthodox religion is the religion of nearly the whole population and sects are going to fish for followers in the best-stocked waters."[88] This implies that the law is applied in Greece to allow prosecutorial decisions based upon an individual's religious *status*, not his or her *actions*. Moreover, one could assume that members of the Greek Orthodox faith frequently respond to the proselytizing acts of others by quoting scripture and introducing arguments of their own. Yet these counterarguments do not result in the arrest of Greek Orthodox adherents for attempting to proselytize others. When the anti-proselytism law in reality is used only against adherents of disfavored religions, then the law is impermissibly vague.

Second, the Court initially ignored the specific vagueness problem that was at the heart of the dissenting opinions in the Greek courts. The dissenters believed that Kokkinakis's prosecutors failed to prove an essential element of the crime of proselytism: that the "victim" was a per-

---

85 *Kokkinakis*, 19, ¶ 38.

86 Ibid., 19, ¶ 40.

87 Ibid.

88 *Kokkinakis*, 31-32 (Valticos, J. dissenting).

son of "inexperience, trust, need, low intellect or naivety."[89] The Court seems to acknowledge that there apparently was no evidence offered at trial that Mrs. Kyriakaki was actually inexperienced or of low intellect. If the statute on its face proscribes only proselytizing certain vulnerable persons (as the Court suggests),[90] and if prosecutors in Greece are not actually required to prove that element of the offense, then the law fails to give proper notice of what actually is prohibited.[91]

Under Article 9(2), a government may limit manifestations of belief only "in the interests of public safety, for the protection of public order, health or morals, or for the protection of the rights and freedoms of others." The Court summarizes this provision as requiring governments to have a *"legitimate aim"* when restricting manifestations of belief. In *Kokkinakis*, the Court found that the Greek government had a legitimate aim, which was "the protection of the rights and freedoms of others. . . ."[92] The Court offered no elaboration of this conclusion.

This summary conclusion approving the government's aim is perhaps the single most disturbing portion of the Court's entire opinion. It suggests that the requirement of a law having a "legitimate aim" is in fact a meaningless requirement. By the Court's reasoning, a statute prohibiting the "peaceful assembly" that Article 11 guarantees could be justified by the government's "legitimate aim" of reducing communicable diseases. Similarly, a statute prohibiting the "freedom of expression" that Article 10 guarantees could be justified by the government's "legitimate aim" of reducing social discord. Thus, with respect to the "legitimate aim" requirement, the Court effectively holds that a government satisfies its burden by offering *any* justification that can be tied, however remotely, to the "protection of the rights and freedoms of others."

Although having decided for Greece with respect to the first two requirements under Article 9(2), the Court ultimately decided that the Kokkinakis conviction was not *necessary in a democratic society* and that Greece had thus breached the Convention. The specific rationale is, however, troubling. The explanation that the Court offers is as follows: "the Greek courts . . . did not sufficiently specify in what way the accused had attempted to convince his neighbour by improper means. None of the facts they set out warrants that finding. That being so, it has not been shown that the applicant's conviction was justified in the circumstances of the case by a pressing social need. The contested measure therefore

[89] Law no. 1672/1939 ¶ 2(2).

[90] *Kokkinakis*, 20, ¶ 44.

[91] See, e.g., *Consistency of Certain Danzig Legislative Decrees with the Constitution of the Free City*, 1935 P.C.I.J. (ser. A/B) No. 65 at 51-53 (Dec. 4).

[92] *Kokkinakis*, 20, ¶ 44.

does not appear to have been proportionate to the legitimate aim pursued or, consequently, 'necessary in a democratic society . . . for the protection of the rights and freedoms of others'."[93]

Although this holding was sufficient to vindicate Kokkinakis, it nevertheless has disturbing ramifications. Unlike the Court's decisions with respect to the first two steps ("prescribed by law" and "legitimate aim"), the Court did not consider the anti-proselytism statute as a whole, but focused exclusively on the single conviction of Mr. Kokkinakis. It was not as if the anti-proselytism law had been applied in an unusual way against Mr. Kokkinakis who, after all, had been arrested more than sixty times and convicted more than eight times under the same statute.[94] The Court itself acknowledged this widespread use of the Greek law, but nevertheless treated the *Kokkinakis* conviction as if it were something unusual. The Court refused to criticize the law that had been repeatedly used to incarcerate minority believers.

Thus the Court did not question the legitimacy of the Greek anti-proselytism law as a whole. Its opinion implies that Mr. Kokkinakis could have been properly arrested, prosecuted, convicted, fined, and jailed for his fifteen-minute conversation with Mrs. Kyriakaki—a conversation that she acknowledged had no effect on her religious beliefs.

The Kokkinakis Decision Exemplifies The European Court's Failure to Take Rights of Conscience Seriously

The *Kokkinakis* decision exemplifies the failure of the European Court to take seriously rights of conscience in its jurisprudence. In effect, the Court does not value rights of conscience and belief as "fundamental freedoms which are the foundation of justice and peace in the world. . . ."[95] Rather than recognizing rights of conscience as fundamental and foundational, as the Convention explicitly states, the European court provides a wide latitude to governments to restrain manifestations of those beliefs. By the terms of the Convention, the European court should have treated rights of conscience as being truly fundamental. Three interrelated weaknesses of the court's decisions can now be seen: first, failure to require governments to impose less restrictive burdens on manifestations of conscience; second, deference to state-established religions; and third, bias against nontraditional religions.

Less Restrictive Alternatives. Governments must be able to impose some limitations on the ability of citizens to manifest their beliefs. The

93 Ibid., 21, ¶ 49.

94 *Kokkinakis*, 8, ¶ 6.

95 European Convention, preamble.

question is not whether there should be limits, but how and where those limits should be drawn. In a series of cases in the United States during the 1930s and 1940s, many of which involved Jehovah's Witnesses, American courts analyzed conflicts between governmental regulations imposed for ostensibly legitimate purposes, and the rights of citizens to exercise and manifest their religious beliefs. In the most famous of the cases, the 1940 decision *Cantwell v. Connecticut,* the United States Supreme Court held, unanimously, that the free exercise of religion is embraced by the "fundamental concept of liberty embodied in [the Fourteenth] Amendment."[96] Although recognizing that "the State of Connecticut has an obvious interest in the preservation and protection of peace and good order,"[97] the Court overturned the conviction of a Jehovah's Witness. The Court held that the statute was not "narrowly drawn to define and punish specific conduct," but was vague and subject to prosecutorial discretion.[98] In *Kokkinakis,* the European court, like the United States Supreme Court, should have analyzed the law by reference to the fundamental right that the government had limited. Whenever a government limits the exercise of a fundamental right, it should do so in a way that restricts the exercise of that right in the most narrow way possible consistent with the government's compelling interests.

The European court has not followed this "less restrictive" approach, giving instead wide latitude to governments to restrict the exercise of fundamental rights. In *Ahmad v. United Kingdom,* where a public school teacher who was Muslim requested an additional 45-minute lunch break on Fridays to attend prayers, the Commission decided only that the school had a legitimate reason for denying the request.[99] The Commission did not even ask whether the school could accommodate the request without compromising the needs of students and of other faculty. The Commission summarily concluded that because Mr. Ahmad had applied for and accepted the teaching position, the rights guaranteed by the European Convention were not implicated. Similarly, the assertion of an atheist schoolgirl and her mother did not persuade the Commission that Sweden's compulsory religious education law violated any rights of conscience.[100] Rather than considering whether there were less restrictive means for satisfying the state's interest without hindering the student's

---

96 *Cantwell v. Connecticut,* 310 U.S. 296, 303 (1940).

97 Ibid., 307.

98 Ibid., 311.

99 *Ahmad v. United Kingdom,* App. No. 8160/78, 4 Eur. H.R. Rep. 126 (1981) (Eur. Comm'n).

100 *Angelini v. Sweden,* App. No. 10941/83, 51 Eur. Comm'n H.R. Dec. & Rep. 41 (1986).

right of conscience, the Commission simply accepted the government's stated interest.

The Commission also accepted without question the British government's rationale for excluding Druids from religious celebrations at Stonehenge during the midsummer solstice.[101] Even though the Commission was informed that Stonehenge was originally deeded to the British Government by a Druid on the condition that it be left open to the public, and even though there was abundant evidence that the Druids had themselves caused no disruptions at the site, the Commission again deferred to the government's prohibition of all worship at Stonehenge. Under a "less restrictive" analysis, the British government would have been required to show that there was no other reasonable alternative available.

Similarly, where the Swedish government enjoined the Church of Scientology from advertising a religious implement called an E-Meter, the Commission deferred to Sweden's argument that the case involved only the simple issue of impermissible false advertising.[102] Whether the E-Meter is a mechanical gimmick or is a sophisticated piece of equipment that provides spiritual information is not the question. For a court or a government to presume that it knows the answer to that question, and to impose restrictions accordingly, is to ignore rights of conscience. Following the *Cantwell* analysis, the appropriate approach would be to determine whether the government has a less restrictive means of protecting the marketplace against fraud than by blatantly prohibiting a form of religious advertising.

Impermissible Bias Against Non-Mainstream Religions. The E-Meter case, *X. and Church of Scientology v. Sweden,* suggests not only the European court's unwillingness to look for less restrictive alternatives to laws that affect fundamental rights, but also a bias against non-mainstream religions. In permitting the injunction against advertising the E-Meter, the Commission identified a "distinction . . . between advertisements which are merely 'informational' or 'descriptive' in character and commercial advertisements offering objects for sale. Once an advertisement enters into the latter sphere, although it may concern religious objects central to a particular need, statements of religious content represent, in the Commission's view, more the manifestation of a desire to market goods for profit than the manifestation of a belief in practice."[103]

---

[101] *Chappell v. United Kingdom,* App. No. 12587/86, 53 Eur. Comm'n H.R. Dec. & Rep. 241, 246-47 (1987).

[102] *X. and Church of Scientology v. Sweden,* App. No. 7805/77, 16 Eur. Comm'n H.R. Dec. & Rep. 68 (1979). This case alternatively is named *Church of Scientology and Another v. Sweden* and *Pastor X. and Church of Scientology v. Sweden*.

[103] *X. and Church of Scientology v. Sweden,* 22 [1979] Y.B. Eur. Conv. on H.R. 244, 250.

This rationale would apply equally to an injunction banning bookstores from praising the virtues of the Bible. But the Commission does not consider the very important fact that such rationales are not used to prohibit conventional religions from promoting their religious texts and icons. Rather than conducting any meaningful inquiry into whether governments are targeting particular religions for discriminatory treatment, the European court accepts uncritically the same biases as the governments whose actions should be under careful scrutiny.

The Court even demonstrated a bias towards non-Christian religion in the *Kokkinakis* case. When analyzing whether the ban on proselytizing was "justified in principle," the Court decided, *sua sponte*, that it needed to differentiate between proper and improper proselytizing, a distinction that did not appear in the Greek Constitution or statute. The Court, surprisingly, held that "a distinction has to be made between bearing *Christian* witness and improper proselytism. . . ."[104] Whether intended or not, the European court of Human Rights has thus separated acceptable *Christian* witness from other forms of proselytizing that are unacceptable. The dissenters in *Kokkinakis* were even less constrained in their disdain for the Jehovah's Witness faith. In an opinion that would be unimaginable by a judge in the United States in the 1990s, Judge Valticos's dissent was vituperative:

> Let us look now at the facts of the case. On the one hand, we have a militant Jehovah's Witness, a hardbitten adept of proselytism, a specialist in conversion, a martyr of the criminal courts whose earlier convictions have served only to harden him in his militancy, and, on the other hand, the ideal victim, a naive woman, the wife of a cantor in the Orthodox Church (if he manages to convert her, what a triumph!). He swoops on her, trumpets that he has good news for her (the play on words is obvious, but no doubt not to her), manages to get himself let in and, as an experienced commercial traveller and cunning purveyor of a faith he wants to spread, expounds to her his intellectual wares cunningly wrapped up in a mantle of universal peace and radiant happiness.[105]

A judge on the highest court of human rights thus displays bald-faced prejudice against a religion with which he differs. As was described above, members of minority religions seldom prevail before the European Court.[106] But even in the two rare cases where they did prevail (*Kokkinakis* and *Hoffmann*), the animus of some judges is clear.

---

[104] *Kokkinakis*, 21, ¶ 48 (emphasis added).

[105] Ibid., 31 (Valticos, J. dissenting).

[106] See footnote 28.

Impermissible Bias in Favor of Established Religions. The European court's bias against non-mainstream religions is also suggested by its deference to state-established religions. Several European countries, of course, have constitutions, statutes, and practices that overtly favor established churches.[107] When analyzing the laws and practices that benefit these favored religions, the European Court and Commission are highly deferential to such laws and are generally unwilling to consider or to analyze the impact of such laws on the rights of conscience. The European Commission explicitly held that state establishments do not, in and of themselves, raise Article 9 issues. "A State Church system cannot in itself be considered to violate Article 9 of the Convention. In fact, such a system exists in several Contracting States and existed there already when the Convention was drafted and when they became parties to it."[108]

The deference accorded to state establishments of religion was demonstrated most obviously where both the Court and the Commission concluded that state laws empowering churches to levy taxes do not raise an Article 9 issue. In *Darby*, the Court did not object to the Swedish church's levy of a state-supported tax. In *E. & G.R. v. Austria*, the Commission agreed that the Roman Catholic church could impose state-enforceable religious taxes on Roman Catholics.[109] In *Gottesmann v. Switzerland*, the Commission agreed that the Swiss government could require citizens to pay religious back-taxes to the Roman Catholic church despite an applicant's claim that he had long since abandoned his beliefs in Catholicism.[110] The Commission agreed that the state was entitled, under the circumstances, to make the decision whether the former Catholic had sufficiently manifested his lack of belief in Catholicism.

Conclusions

Judge L. E. Pettiti wrote a concurring opinion in *Kokkinakis* that argued that the Greek statute criminalizing proselytism violated Article 9 on its face. For Judge Pettiti, there was no need to examine the particular circumstances of the case or to explain how the Greek courts could prop-

---

[107] Several European states operate variations on state religious establishments: the United Kingdom (the Church of England and the Church of Scotland); Denmark (Lutheranism); Greece (Greek Orthodox Church); Sweden (Church of Sweden); Norway (Lutheranism); Finland (Lutheran Orthodox Church of Finland); Malta (Roman Catholicism); and Bulgaria (Bulgarian Orthodox Church).

[108] *Darby Case*, 17, ¶ 45 (Eur. Comm'n).

[109] *E. & G.R. v. Austria*, App. No. 9781/82, 37 Eur. Comm'n H.R. Dec. & Rep. 42, 44-45 (1984).

[110] *Gottesmann v. Switzerland*, App. No. 10616/83, 40 Eur. Comm'n H.R. Dec. & Rep. 284 (1984).

erly have convicted Minos Kokkinakis under the same statute and under the same facts.[111] Judge Pettiti was correct. A law that purports to forbid people from expressing their religious beliefs cannot be reconciled with a principled reading of Article 9. The fact that Judge Pettiti's opinion was a solitary concurrence rather than the opinion of the Court speaks loudly of the failure of the European court to take rights of conscience seriously.

[111] *Kokkinakis*, 25-28 (Pettiti, J., concurring). No other member of the Court joined Judge Pettiti's concurrence, although Judges De Meyer and Martens wrote separate concurrences that suggest that do not differ pronouncedly from Judge Pettiti.

Religious Human Rights and the Principle of Legal Pluralism in the Middle East

SAID AMIR ARJOMAND
State University of New York at Stony Brook

Before approaching this—or indeed any—topic in the constitutional and public law of the contemporary Middle East, it is essential to discard a prejudicial and ahistorical dichotomy between the presumptively premodern Islamic law and the Western-inspired law of the modern Middle Eastern nation-states. Although this dichotomy is widely held by contemporary Muslims and non-Muslims alike, it is fundamentally misleading. The basic fallacy implicit in it is that modern constitutional law replaced the Islamic law or the Shari'a(t). In historical reality, modern constitutional law replaced not the Shari'a but the public law of the Muslim monarchies, especially those of the three early modern Muslim empires: the Ottoman empire in Eastern Europe, the Near East and North Africa; the Safavid—and later Qajar—empires in Iran; and the Mughal empire in India.

In *Law and Revolution*, Harold J. Berman deplores the systematic neglect of legal pluralism in the Western tradition which he attributes to the monistic, state-centered legal historiography and the conception of law fostered by the rise of the modern nation-states. To remedy this neglect, Berman urges, among other things, the "study of non-Western legal systems and traditions, of the meeting of Western and non-Western law, and of the development of a common legal language for mankind."[1] To move in this direction while approaching the issue of religious human rights, it is essential to discard the fallacious juxtaposition of modern versus Islamic law, and to adopt instead a historical perspective that acknowl-

[1] Harold J. Berman, *Law and Revolution: The Formation of the Western Legal Tradition* (Cambridge, MA, 1983), 45.

J.D. van der Vyver and J. Witte, Jr. (eds.), Religious Human Rights in Global Perspective, 331-347.

edges the elements of pluralism in the legal history of the Islamic Middle East.

Islam and Public Law

Let me first describe the widespread fallacy concerning Islam and public law that derives much of its current force from a curious convergence of Orientalism and fundamentalism. Only by correcting it will I be able to approach the issue of religious human rights in a new light. Here, the Muslims of India, who are the inventors of modern Islamic fundamentalism, played an important role. After the partition of India in 1947, the citizens of the new Pakistan embarked on the establishment of a constitutional state based on Islam. (The fundamentalists, led by Mawlana 'Abu'l-a'la' Mawdudi, called it an "ideological state.") But to do so, they turned *not* to the constitutional history of the Moghal empire or of any other Muslim state, but rather juxtaposed Western constitutional blueprints to the scriptural sources of Islam. The result was the declaration of God's sovereignty in the 1956 Constitution of the Islamic Republic of Pakistan. About the time of this "comic" transfer of political sovereignty to God (to use the late Fazlur Rahman's words[2]), H.A.R. Gibb, first at Oxford and then at Harvard, was training the generation of scholars who have dominated the study of Islamic political thought in the Anglo-Saxon world. Handicapped by the neglect of public law in the pathbreaking studies of Islamic law by Goldziher and Schacht,[3] the Gibbonians focused on a set of eleventh-century texts in "political theory," giving little systematic attention to their cultural and historical context. Gibb took this set of books by Sunni jurists, which to *him* were the most Islamic, as a description of the Islamic "constitutional organization."[4] The Gibbonian Orientalists thus presented a picture of Islamic political theory that was quite similar to that of the Muslim fundamentalists in Pakistan and elsewhere. What Gibb wrote in 1970 and his student Lambton cited in 1981, could easily have been written by Mawdudi in Pakistan:

---

2 Fazlur Rahman, "Islam and the Constitutional Problem of Pakistan," *Studia Islamica* 32 (1970): 277.

3 In his magisterial Introduction to *Islamic Law* (Oxford 1964), 112, Joseph Schacht dismisses constitutional law because of its intimate connection "with the political history of Islamic states rather than with the history of Islamic law." This is a very curious statement against such common Orientalist assertions as "Islam is a political religion," or "Church and State are one in Islam."

4 H.A.R. Gibb, "Constitutional Organization," in M. Khadduri and H.R. Liebesny, eds., *Law in the Middle East* (Washington, 1955), 3-27.

> The community exists to bear witness to God amid the darkness of this world, and the function of its government is essentially to act as the executive of the Law [meaning the sacred law, the Shari'a].[5]

In 1979, Khomeini's Islamic revolution stole the limelight from the Islamic ideology of Mawdudi and the Islamic political theory of the Gibbonians alike; and in 1988, Khomeini issued the startling ruling that "governmental commandments" take precedence over the primary commandments of the sacred law, including prayer, fasting, and pilgrimage to Mecca.[6] Khomeini's ruling looks like a refutation of Gibb. But we cannot take any comfort in this. Both these statements are as confused and confusing as they are categorical.

I submit that the best way to clear the welter of confusion is by gaining a clearer sense of the constitutional history of the Islamic world. It is a striking fact that there is no constitutional history of the Islamic Middle East. (Imagine where the constitutional debates in Britain would be if there were no Maitland or Pollock,[7] and the debaters were still constantly touting the Bible.) We must begin our considerations from a solid historical standpoint by asking a preliminary question: What *was* the public law of the Muslim lands before the advent of modern constitutionalism?

Contrary to Gibb's assertion and Mawdudi's plea, the function of government was not essentially to act as the executive of the sacred law (Shari'a) but to maintain order and rule with *justice* among the Muslim and non-Muslim subjects *(re'aya)* so that they could abide by the sacred law according to the religion and/or Muslim legal school *(madhhab)* of their choice. Contrary to Gibb and Mawdudi, in the constitutional history of the Islamic Middle East, the *umma*, or community of believers was *never* the political community.[8] The political community of the Ottoman and Moghal empires contained as many or more non-Muslim as Muslim subjects (and the Safavid empire as many Sunnis as Shi'ites). So much so,

---

5 H.A.R. Gibb, "The Heritage of Islam in the Modern World," *International Journal of Middle East Studies* 1 (1970): 11, cited in A.K.S. Lambton, *State and Government in Medieval Islam* (Oxford, 1981), xiv.

6 See Said A. Arjomand, "Shi'ite Jurisprudence and Constitution-Making in the Islamic Republic of Iran," in Martin E. Marty and Scott R. Appleby, eds., *Fundamentalisms and the State: Remaking Polities, Economies, and Militance* (Chicago, 1993), 88-109.

7 F.W. Maitland, *The Constitutional History of England* (Cambridge, 1908); F. Pollock & F.W. Maitland, *The History of English Law* (Cambridge, 1895), 2 vols.

8 See my *Constitutional History of the Islamic Middle East* (forthcoming with the University of California Press).

that the European travellers in the Ottoman empire mistook the term "subjects" *"(re'aya)"* to mean Christians.[9]

The public law of medieval and early modern Islam recognized a basic duality of temporal and religious laws. The divine or sacred law was the Shari'a. Temporal, public law consisted of the *kanun*, used frequently in the singular and the plural, and the norms of statecraft were the *siyasa(t)*. Furthermore, there was a distinct element of pluralism—or rather dualism—*within* the norms of *siyasa* or statecraft itself. There was, on the one hand, the Indo-Persian norms of the Mirrors for Princes, and, on the other, the Greek political science—the *siyasat al-madaniyya* or *siyasat-e mudun*. An Aristotelian political science, however, which was so successfully appropriated for Western medieval Christianity by Thomas Aquinas, never developed within the Islamic tradition, despite gropings in that direction by Aquinas's brilliant contemporary, Nasir al-Din al-Tusi.

Unlike the militant secularists and Islamists of the last seven decades, the first constitution-makers of the Middle East recognized the fundamental dualism of temporal and religious law in the system of public law. For them, the transfer of legislative power—the right to make public laws *(kavanin)*—from the monarch to the people was conceptually non-problematic, and did *not* involve Islam. It would not have occurred to the Ottoman advocates of a constitution or Fundamental Law *(kanun-e esasi)*, in the nineteenth century, and their Iranian followers at the beginning of the twentieth, to identify legislative power as other than that of making public law—*kanun*. This is evident in the terminology of the Ottoman and Iranian Fundamental Laws.[10] Of the contemporary Middle Eastern and North African constitutions, the Morrocan Constitution of 1992 remains true to the traditional dualism of the Muslim monarchies in emphasizing the king's role as the guarantor of both the temporal and the religious legal orders.[11]

It took the arrogance of Ataturk's militant secularists to use the term *"teshri'iyye"* for the Shari'a, for the Legislative Power, thereby confusing by appropriation the people's newly acquired right to make public laws with the divine inspiration of the Shari'a. In historical truth, however,

---

[9] This mistake in turn greatly exercises Arnold Toynbee's theoretical imagination. See E. Kedourie, *The Chatham House Version and Other Middle Eastern Studies* (Hanover and London, 1984), 363.

[10] Incidentally, the term used for "constitution" in Arabic and Urdu is *"dastur,"* an old Persian administrative term that gained currency in Arabic about the same time as the Greek term *"kanun."*

[11] Ann E. Mayer, "Moroccans—Citizens or Subjects? A People at Crossroads," *Journal of International Law and Politics* 26(1) (1993): 63-105; id., "The 1992 Saudi Arabian and Moroccan Constitutions: A Comparative Assessment" (unpublished manuscript presented at the Scahcht Conference 1994), 26.

what in principle was being transferred to the people—at least in 1876 and 1906-1907—was not any divine prerogative but the monarch's right to make public laws.

This does not mean there was no conflict. Legal pluralism inevitably invites conflict among laws and heterogeneous legal principles. The legal history of the medieval and early modern Middle East is replete with examples of conflict between public law and the Shari'a. The same is true of modern constitutionalism in the Middle East. Clashes between the jurisdiction of the state laws and the Shari'a surface in a basic form in the constitutional debates in Iran in 1907-1908, and since then in Pakistan and elsewhere. These points of incompatibility have been meticulously catalogued by Abdullahi An-Na'im.[12] We must acknowledge the inevitability of such conflicts—as did the medieval and early modern Muslim jurists—while reminding ourselves that a chief purpose of all constitutional law is the reconciliation of heterogeneous and often contradictory principles. One obvious lesson to be drawn from this legal history is that where the conflicts between the Shari'a and public law were resolved by the abeyance of the Shari'a, as in the case with the penal code of the Shari'a, the historical precedent should be followed. But this is not our subject.

I shall focus more specifically on conflicts arising between the two systems of public law and the Shari'a concerning religious human rights. Three areas can be singled out: (1) the inequality of Muslims and the *dhimmis* (the protected "Peoples of the Book"[13]) according to the Shari'a; (2) the rights of Muslim religious minorities and religious minorities that are offshoots of Islam; and (3) apostasy and religious freedom of the individual. The last two issues are obviously related.

Muslims and Dhimmis

The history of modern constitutionalism in the Middle East opens with the granting of equal rights to all Ottoman subjects irrespective of their religion by the imperial decrees of 1839 and 1856. Prior to that period, the status of Muslim and non-Muslim subjects of the Ottoman Sultan was unequal. Both groups, however, were beneficiaries of the legal pluralism of the Ottoman Empire. Depending on the composition of the

---

[12] Abdullahi Ahmed An-Na'im, *Toward an Islamic Reformation* (Syracuse, 1990), chap. 4.

[13] In the Middle Ages, the notion was extended beyond the Jews and the Christians originally designated by the term, to cover the Hindus in northern India, and the "Sabaeans," adherents of Graeco-Roman and other unclassifiable religion, in Mesopotamia. See Roy P. Mottahedeh, "Toward an Islamic Theology of Toleration," in Tore Lindholm and Kari Vogt, eds., *Islamic Reform and Human Rights: Challenges and Rejoinders* (Copenhagen, Lund, Oslo, Abo/Turku, 1993), 26. The same status of a tolerated religion was extended to the Zoroastrians in Iran.

population, Jews, Christians, and the four official Sunni Muslim schools of law had their own courts, and subjects were free to choose the court to which they wished to appeal. It was not at all unusual for Christian subjects to resort to the Muslim courts if they so wished.[14] Furthermore, both Muslim and non-Muslim subjects had the right to complain to the Sultan in cases of miscarriage of justice and violation of the public law by administrators or judges.[15] It is an unfortunate fact that the equal rights were granted to the non-Muslim subjects under the pressure from the European Powers which acted as their protectors. Cevdet Pasha, the great Ottoman statesman and legal reformer who created the first modern Shari'a-based Ottoman code, recorded the popular reaction to the Sultan's decree of 1856 as follows:

> Many Muslims started complaining, saying: "Today, we lost our sacred rights as a religious community, [rights] which had been won by the blood of our fathers and forefathers. . . . Today is a day of mourning and despair for the Muslims." For the minority subjects [instead], this was a day of joy.[16]

A half a century later, however, the demand for the equality of the rights of all citizens was written into the constitutional law of the Middle East as a result of popular pressure during the constitutional revolutions on 1906 in Iran and 1908 in the Ottoman empire. The Shi'ite religious leaders who had supported the constitutionalists in Iran obtained significant concessions during the constitutional debates of 1907.[17] On this important issue, however, the conflict between the Shari'a and the new constitutional law was resolved in favor of the latter. The religious leaders vehemently opposed the principle of equality of all citizens before the law (Article 8 of the Supplementary Fundamental Law of 1907), which they correctly perceived as contradictory to the provisions of the Shari'a. Even Mirza Hosayn Na'ini, the religious jurist who wrote a tract to justify constitutional government in Shi'ite terms, would restrict the principle of

---

14 R.C. Jennings, "Zhimmis (Non-Muslims") in the Early Seventeenth-Century Ottoman Judicial Records; The Shari'a Court of Anatolian Kayseri," *Journal of the Economic and Social History of the Orient* 21(3) (1978): 250-252; id., "Kadi, Court and Procedure in Seventeenth-Century Kayseri," *Studia Islamica* 48 (1978); F.M. Gocek and M.D. Baer, "Social Boundaries of Ottoman Women's Experience in Eighteenth-Century Galata Court Records," in M. Zilfi, ed., *Women in the Ottoman Empire* (Bloomington, IN, 1995).

15 Haim Gerber, *State, Society, and Law in Islam: Ottoman Law in Comparative Perspective* (Albany, NY, 1994), 154-173.

16 Ahmed Cevdet Pasa, *Tezakir* (Ankara, 1986), 67-68, cited in F.M. Gocek, "Ethnic Segmentation, Western Education, and Political Outcomes: Nineteenth-Century Ottoman Society," *Poetics Today* 14(3) (1993): 517.

17 See S.A. Arjomand, "Religion and Constitutionalism in Western History and Modern Iran and Pakistan," in id., *The Political Dimensions of Religion* (Albany, NY, 1993), 77-82.

equality before the law to man-made laws *(kavanin mawzu'a)*. But in the end, the Shi'ite religious leaders had to give in, reportedly because of both personal threats of violence and the restlessness of the Armenian minority.[18] The legal implications of Article 8 were far-reaching. By declaring all citizens equal before the law, it established public law, the state law, as the general law of the land, and overrode the typical legal particularism of the Shari'a concerning the legally autonomous Muslim and non-Muslim religious minorities.

The Pakistani constitutions of 1956 and 1962 recognized the principle of equality before the law but without eliminating legal pluralism completely. There were good reasons for considering the provisions of the Shari'a concerning the *dhimmis* inapplicable to the public law of Pakistan. Commenting on the first address of the Founder of Pakistan to the Constituent Assembly on August 11, 1947, Chauduri Muhammad 'Ali, who had served as Prime Minister in the 1950s, stressed the point that "Pakistan came into being not by conquest but as the result of a negotiated agreement between the representatives of the Hindu and Muslim communities" and therefore the "life, property, and religious beliefs" of all citizens were guaranteed full and equal protection by the state.[19] In 1972, a former Chief Justice of Pakistan, S.A. Rahman, similarly stated that the relationship between the Muslim and non-Muslim citizens of Pakistan was a contractual one, and the provisions of the Shari'a concerning the dhimmis did not apply to the latter whose "position is assimilable to that of *mu'ahids*—the beneficiaries of a binding pact."[20] Traditional Islamic legal pluralism, however, received some acknowledgement by the fact that the Muslim citizens could follow the personal law of the Shari'a according to any legal school *(madhhab)* they belonged to. The constitution of 1973 finally ended this element of pluralism in personal law for the Muslim citizens of Pakistan *de jure*.[21]

The principle of equality before the law is generally accorded explicit recognition in other Middle Eastern constitutions, including those which grant Islam a special place, such as the Moroccan constitution of 1992. In the Islamic Republic of Iran, the provision of the equality of all citizens before the law was carried over from Article 8 of the old constitution into Article 20 of the new constitution, but was qualified "with due observance of the Islamic standards." The fact that "the Islamic standards" are

---

[18] A.-H. Hairi, *Shi'ism and Constitutionalism in Iran* (Leiden, 1977), 225, 232-233.

[19] Chauduri Muhammad 'Ali, *The Emergence of Pakistan*, cited in S.A. Rahman, *Punishment of Apostasy in Islam* (Lahore, 1978), 169.

[20] Ibid., 2-3.

[21] Fazlur Rahman, "Islam and the New Constitution of Pakistan," in J.H. Korson, ed., *Contemporary Problems of Pakistan* (Leiden, 1974), 40.

not made explicit in this provision is significant. There is no reference to the provisions of the Shari'a regarding the inferior status of the *dhimmis* any more than to its provisions regarding slavery. The *principle*[22] of the equality of citizens irrespective of religion in the public law of the Middle East can thus be said to have withstood the impact of Islamic fundamentalism, even in the theocratic constitution of Iran.

The Rights of Religious Minorities

It is otherwise with the rights of Muslim religious minorities, and with the right to religious freedom, including apostasy.

During the first decade of Ottoman reforms *(tanzimat),* the issue of the proselytization of Muslims into a new faith surfaced in Ottoman Iraq with the spread of the Babi millenarian movement among the Shi'ites. In January 1845, the Ottoman governor of the province of Baghdad assembled a special court consisting of twenty Sunni and twelve Shi'ite jurists to try a missionary cleric, Molla 'Ali Bastami, who was active on behalf of the Bab who claimed to be the Mahdi and the Expected Imam of the Shi'ites returning from Occultation on the thousandth anniversary of his birth. As Bastami was a subject of Iran, the Iranian Consul was also present at the trial. According to the report of the trial sent by Najib Pasha, the governor of Baghdad, to the Sublime Prote, Bastami denied knowledge of the contents of the book of the Bab found in his possession, and refused to disclose the name of its author. No disagreement between the Sunni and the Shi'ite jurists is mentioned in the report. However, the Sunni jurists, headed by the Mufti of Baghdad, found the accused guilty of apostasy and recommended the death penalty while the Shi'ite jurists proved more protective of a stray member of their community and implied, by the careful wording of their opinions, that they did not find him deserving of death. Thirty individual rulings *(fatwas)* by the Sunni and Shi'ite jurists of the special court were appended to the report.[23] It is interesting to note that the two most prominent Shi'ite jurists *(mujtahids)* in the group had been "most unwilling" to attend the trial in Baghdad. The senior one, Shaykh Hasan Kashif al-Ghita', is reported by the Shi'ite sources to have argued that the heretical teachings were not Bastami's own and "the book [of the Bab in his possession] by itself could not be regarded as a firm piece of evidence."[24] The culprit was dispatched with

---

[22] The practice and extralegal persecutions are another matter.

[23] M. Momen, "The Trial of Mulla 'Ali Bastami: A Combined Sunni-Shi'i Fatwa against the Bab," *Iran* 20 (1982): 113-143.

[24] A. Amanat, *Resurrection and Renewal. The Making of the Babi Movement in Iran, 1844-1850* (Ithaca and London, 1989), 226, 232-233. This opinion is not recorded in the summary

the governor's report and the thirty verdicts to the Sultan who condemned him to hard labor at the galleys. The Ottoman government later agreed to extradite Bastami to Iran, but the unfortunate Babi missionary expired under hard labor before the extradition order could be carried out.[25]

The Babi millenarianism, being an offshoot of Shi'ism, was a far greater threat to the Shah of Iran than to the Ottoman Sultan, and the Bab's trials for apostasy in Iran are the more instructive. It was not the Shi'ite hierocracy in general, but some of its members belonging to the rival mystical-millenarian Shaykhi movement that produced *fatwas* enjoining the Bab's execution on grounds of apostasy. However, while there was no threat to the monarchy and public order, the government did not feel obliged to take any action. In July 1848, the government convened a special court of examination in the presence of the Crown Prince in Tabriz. The leading *mujtahid* of the city did not attend, instead sending a note that states the Bab's heresy was evident. The Bab was interrogated by other clerics, including the Crown Prince's tutor. According to the report of the trial to the Shah by the presiding official, Amir Aslan Khan, when the hearing was concluded, the Shaykh al-Islam of Tabriz (who had been pressing for the Bab's execution but had not been invited to the interrogation) was summoned and had the Bab bastinadoed, thereupon the latter repented and was returned to prison awaiting further royal orders.[26] It was only after the outbreak of a series of serious millenarian uprisings that the government solicited a set of three new *fatwas*—one of which was given reluctantly and only because of the Bab's firm refusal to recant —and executed the Bab by a firing squad in July 1850.[27]

We may conclude from these cases of prosecution of the Babis for apostasy that, at the time of the onset of legal modernization in the Middle East, the authoritative interpretation of the Islamic law of apostasy, which had originated with the rebellion of the Arab tribes against the Islamic state after the death of the Prophet,[28] still remained closely tied to the disturbance of the political order. The Shari'a's law of apostasy did not find its way into the constitutional law of the Middle East in the first half of the twentieth century; these constitutions remained silent on the

---

report of the trial by the Ottoman governor. The Shi'ite sources, furthermore, disagree as to whether the charge against Bastami was apostasy *(irtidad)* or unlawful innovation *(bid'a)*.

25 Ibid., 235-237.

26 E.G. Browne, *Materials for the Study of the Babi Religion* (Cambridge, 1918), 248-255.

27 Amanat, *Resurrection and Renewal*, 387-94.

28 See the early treatise by the great jurist, Shaybani (d. 805), edited and translated into English by M. Khadduri as *The Islamic Law of Nations* (Baltimore, 1966), 47-48, 215-227. See D. Little, J. Kelsay and A.A. Sachedina, eds., *Human Rights and Conflicts of Culture: Western and Islamic Perspectives on Religious Liberty* (South Carolina, 1988), Appendix 1 by Sachedain.

heretical offshoots of Islam. It was only in the early 1950s and in the midst of agitation for an Islamic constitution in Pakistan that the Pakistani *'ulama* (clerics) and Islamic activists began to demand the ouster of the Foreign Minister, Zafarullah Khan, who was an Ahmadi, and the exclusion of the Ahmadis from the Islamic community and public office. The Ahmadis were the followers of Mirza Ghulam Ahmad of Qadiyan, who had claimed prophethood as a successor to Muhammad in the nineteenth century, a generation or so after the Bab. The anti-Ahmadi agitation led to the serious Punjab riots of 1953. At that point it backfired and, owing to the change of government and the impact of the so-called Munir Report by the Chief Justice Muhammad Munir of the Supreme Court, resulted in the dilution of the Islamic provisions in the Pakistani constitution of 1956.[29] It was in 1974, and under the socialist government of Zulfikar 'Ali Bhutto, whose constitution of 1973 (still in effect) contains the most liberal provisions of religious freedom in the Middle East or in the world,[30] that the impact of Islamic fundamentalism was translated into a constitutional amendment defining the Ahmadis as non-Muslims. This opened the way for the persecution of the Ahmadis which was greatly intensified after President Zia al-Haqq's 1984 Ordinance on un-Islamic activities which lent considerable momentum to a series of laws that have become known as "blasphemy laws." These laws have been enforced by the Shari'at benches (introduced in 1978) and the Federal Shari'at Court (set up in May 1980). Ordinance no. XX of April 26, 1984 made the Ahmadis liable to prosecution for engaging in activities associated with Islam.[31] Amendments to the penal code in the same year prohibited the Ahmadis from preaching, naming themselves Muslim, calling their places of worship mosques, and "outraging the feelings of the Muslims" by any words or deeds.[32] Over a hundred Ahmadis have been arrested under these laws, often on the strength of the testimony of a single witness, and some 2,000 cases brought against them for outraging the feelings of the Muslims by praying, making the call to prayer *(adhan)*, or simply pretending to be Muslims. It may be noted that Mawlana 'Abdu'ssattar Niyazi, who had been condemned to death for inciting mobs to violence against the Ahmadis in 1953, served as the Minister for

---

[29] See S.V.R. Nasr, *The Vanguard of the Islamic Revolution* (Berkeley, CA, 1994), chap. 6.

[30] The 1973 Pakistani constitution compares most favorably to those of other nations as regards provisions for religious freedom and forbidding of discrimination. See Elizabeth Odio-Benito, *Elimination of All Forms of Intolerance and Discrimination Based on Religion or Belief* (New York, 1989).

[31] See Y. Friedmann, *Prophecy Continuous* (Berkeley, CA, 1989), Appendix C, 192-94, for the text of the Ordinance.

[32] Human Rights Watch, Asia, *Persecuted Minorities and Writers in Pakinstan* (Washington, 1993), 3.

Religious Affairs under the loose Islamic coalition government from 1990 to 1993.[33] In July 1993, the Supreme Court of Pakistan upheld the Ordinance of 1984 and dismissed an Ahmadi appeal to declare it unconstitutional. Among reasons given for the majority opinion was that the Ahmadis are not forbidden to coin their own religious terminology, and have no reason to appropriate the terminology of Islam.[34]

In Iran, the members of the Baha'i faith—the successor movement to the nineteenth century Babi sect which underwent considerable transformation and spread beyond Iran as a universalist religion—have been treated as apostates, often without any regard to legal formalities as in the persecution of the Ahmadis in Pakistan. During the decade after the Islamic revolution, some 200 Baha'is were executed with or without trial, at times with unnecessary cruelty and savagery. In 1992, there were two executions.[35] Meanwhile, tremendous pressure has been put on the Baha'is to reconvert to Shi'ite Islam under ordinary administrative law. In Saudi Arabia, where Islam is taken to mean the regime's Wahhabi faith and the Basic Law of 1992 declares the Shari'a fully in force, the Shi'ite minority has been persecuted as heretics, and in September 1992, a young Shi'ite was beheaded for apostasy and blasphemy.[36]

Religious Liberty and Apostacy

Islamic fundamentalism has had its strongest influence on the legal culture and public law regarding religious liberty and apostacy. To understand this fundamentalist influence, we need to return briefly to the historical context of the dual legal tradition in medieval and early modern Islam.

In medieval Islam, there *was* a fundamentalist thrust to obliterate this dual legal tradition of public law and Shari'a, which took the form of the (mainly Hanbalite) theories of the *siyasat al-shar'iyya*. These theories urged a synthesis of the *siyasa* (statecraft) and the Shari'a, and a subjugation of the former to the latter. Such monistic theories were usually advocated as a program of action in a crisis. The most notable of these by Ibn Taymiyya (d. 1328)[37] was put forward in the context of the triple threat of the Mongols, Shi'ites, and Christians. The monistic *siyasat al-shar'iyya* was

---

33 See Nasr, *The Vanguard of the Islamic Revolution*, 137-141 for Niyazi's role in the anti-Ahmadi riots in the 1952-53.

34 *The Supreme Court [of Pakistan] Monthly Report*, 26/3 (1993): 1718-1780.

35 Baha'i International Community, *The Baha'i Question. Iran's Secret Blueprint for the Destruction of a Religious Community* (1993), 44-47.

36 Ann E. Mayer, "Universal versus Islamic Human Rights: A Clash of Cultures or a Clash of Constructs?" *Michigan Journal of International Law* 15(2) (1994): 358.

37 H. Laoust, *Le traité de droit publique d'Ibn Taymiya* (Beirut, 1948).

pious, programmatic, and arguably utopian. It was never the public law of any Muslim realm. Historically, it was always counterbalanced by purely secular norms of statecraft in the *siyasat* literature of Persian, pre-Islamic origin. With the subversion of modern constitutionalism by ideology and the emergence of an Islamic ideology as an alternative to secular ideologies, the *siyasat al-shar'iyya,* in the form of an "Islamic state," in charge of the execution of the Shari'a, has become the panacea of Islamic fundamentalists.[38] This reactive Islamic monism is, needless to say, aggressively intolerant and expansionist, and would in no way allow for religious liberty, not to mention apostasy. The crucial point to make is that the concentration of power and the unified legal system of the modern nation-state with its rejection of legal pluralism—at least in the European civil-law version adopted by most countries in the Middle East and North Africa but with the notable exception of Pakistan—opens possibilities for a monistic Islamic system that never existed before.

On January 18, 1985, the date subsequently chosen for the annual celebration of Arab Human Rights by the Middle Eastern rights organizations, the Islamic reformist Mahmud Mohammad Taha was hanged for apostasy by the order of the Sudanese President Numeiri, and on March 22, 1991, the Sudanese government enacted Dr. Hassan al-Turabi's new Islamic penal code, based on the Shari'a, that included the death penalty for apostasy for "any Muslim who advocates the rejection of the Islamic beliefs or announces his own rejection of Islam by word or act."[39] Similarly, one of the Pakistani blasphemy laws, a 1987 amendment, "makes the death penalty mandatory for anyone convicted of blasphemy involving the name of the Prophet Mohammad."[40] Several cases have been brought against Muslims, Christians, and Ahmadis; death sentences have been passed, and some of the accused have been murdered with impunity.[41]

The most celebrated case of apostasy generated by the impact of Islamic fundamentalism concerns Salman Rushdie.[42] In a particularly low

---

[38] The literature on Islamic fundamentalism has grown enormously in recent years. Some of the more important works are cited in an analytical discussion of the topic against the background of medieval Hanbalism and Ibn Taymiyya in S.A. Arjomand, "Unity and Diversity in Islamic Fundamentalism," in Martin E. Marty & Scott E. Appleby, eds., *Fundamentalisms Comprehended* (Chicago, 1995), 179-198.

[39] Ann Elizabeth Mayer, "The Fundamentalist Impact in Iran, Pakistan and the Sudan," in Marty & Appleby, eds., *Fundamentalisms and the State,* 141.

[40] Human Rights Watch, *Persecuted Minorities* (Washington, 1993), 3.

[41] Ibid., 11-22.

[42] It should be noted that the condemnation of Salman Rushdie is not limited to the Islamic fundamentalists. Among condemnations of Rushdie by Muslim modernist intellectuals, Ali Mazrui's interpretation of the case is noteworthy. Bracketing the Shari'a's law of apostasy, together with the death penalty, Mazrui finds Rushdie primarily guilty of "treason: po-

point of the Iranian post-revolutionary politics, after Rushdie's *Satanic Verses* had been banned in India, South Africa, Bangladesh, Sudan, Sri Lanka and Pakistan, and after the outbreak of violent protests in India, Pakistan, and Britain, Ayatollah Ruhollah Khomeini broadcast the following *fatwa* on Teheran radio on February 14, 1989:

> I inform the proud Muslim people of the world that the author of *The Satanic Verses* book which is against Islam, the Prophet and the Koran, *and all involved in its publication who were aware of its content*, are sentenced to death.

Anyone who carried out this sentence would be "a martyr and go directly to heaven."[43] The ruling was issued neither impulsively, nor without knowledge of the contents of the book, as is often asserted.[44] Nevertheless, its crudely political quality stands in sharp contrast to the legal subtlety and judicious moderation of Kashif al-Ghita's ruling against the Babi missionary accused of apostasy in the mid-nineteenth century.[45] It has no legal reasoning and no concern for due process. Instead, as indicated by the italics, it issues a blanket extension of the death sentence from the alleged apostate or blasphemer (neither charge is explicitly stated) to the publishers and disseminators of his work. The next day, a cleric in charge of one of Iran's independent foundations put a bounty of $1 million on Rushdie's head,[46] a move without legal precedent. On the first anniversary of the issue of the *fatwa*, after Khomeini's death, the Head of the Judiciary of the Islamic Republic of Iran, Ayatollah Muhammad Yazdi, with the endorsement of Ayatollah 'Ali Khamane'i, Khomeini's successor as the Leader of the Islamic Republic, stated: "Through a legal and judicious eye we announce explicitly that this verdict is a binding and irrevocable one and not a religious judgement alone."[47]

Nevertheless, the whole Rushdie matter has been treated as a political, rather than a legal affair. For instance, in a move that is clearly contrary to the separation of the legislative and judicial powers in the

---

litical and cultural" on the grounds that "Rushdie subordinates the real anguish of Muslim believers to the titillation of his Western readers." A.A. Mazrui, *The Satanic Verses or a Satanic Novel?* (Greenpoint, NY, 1989), 4, 28.

43 Middle East Watch, *Guardians of Thought: Limits of Freedom of Expression in Iran* (New York, 1993), 85 (emphasis added).

44 Khomeini ordered the book to be translated into Persian after being approached by Indo-Pakistani Muslims, and I am told the translation was circulated among the top echelon of the officials of the Islamic Republic of Iran.

45 See page 338 above.

46 The bounty was doubled in March 1991 and raised yet again by an unspecified amount in February 1993. Middle East Watch, *Guardians of Thought*, 89.

47 Ibid., 88.

Constitution of the Islamic Republic of Iran (Article 57), two thirds of the Majlis deputies endorsed the death sentence against Rushdie in February 1993. No wonder the editors of the semi-official daily, *Jomhuri-ye Islami* had no qualms about taking the sacred law into their own hands and stretching it, beyond all plausibility, by extending the death penalty to the fifty Iranian writers abroad who had signed a declaration in defense of Rushdie's right to freedom of expression in 1992, and by extending the same lethal compliment, in February 1993, to Aziz Nesin, the famous Turkish writer who had announced that *The Satanic Verses* would be published in translation in Turkey. Guilt by association has also made its way into the administrative law of the Islamic Republic of Iran. In March 1992, Ayatollah Ahmad Jannati, a member of the Council of Guardians, declared the work of the fifty signatories to the defense of Rushdie banned; and in November 1992, the Ministry of Culture and Islamic Guidance specifically banned the works of two of the signatories, citing their support for Rushdie and Article 6.9 of the Press Law of 1985 which allows for the abrogation of the freedom of the press "in the instances where the meaning and principles of Islam . . . are damaged."[48]

Notwithstanding these instances of fundamentalism, particularly the Rushdie affair, the increasing integration of the Middle Eastern states into the international system has exposed them to the strong contrary human rights demands of international law. This exposure has introduced a new element of legal pluralism and generated ambivalent reactions throughout the Middle East.

Whereas in the first half of the twentieth century the international legal culture witnessed the amplification of "civil" and "political" rights by "social" rights, its second half is marked by the ongoing "human rights revolution." This revolution has a strong international—indeed transcendental—dimension. On the one hand, most Middle Eastern countries have acceded to international human rights instruments, and all have paid at least lip service to human rights. The Preamble to the new Constitution of Morocco (1992), for instance, reaffirms the Kingdom's "attachment to human rights as they are universally recognized." Even Saudi Arabia's Basic Law of 1992 pays lip service to this. Article 26 declares the protection of human rights *(huquq al-insan)* in accordance with the Shari'a to be a function of the state.[49]

The impact of the human rights revolution on the legal culture of Middle Eastern societies has also been considerable. In 1972, S.A. Rahman, a former Chief Justice of Pakistan, wrote a treatise on *Punish-*

---

[48] Ibid., 89-93.

[49] Mayer, "Saudi Arabian and Moroccan Constitutions," 15, 21.

ment of Apostasy in Islam which is a remarkable instance of *ijtihad* (independent legal endeavor) in modernist Islamic jurisprudence. Noting that traditional Islamic jurists generally acknowledge that the Qur'an did not prescribe a punishment but nevertheless, in principle, upheld the death penalty for apostasy, Rahman reports that their legal rationale for this punishment varied considerably, and together with it, the procedural and positive legal norms that different jurists derived from agreed upon premises. The opinions of the authoritative Islamic jurists varied on the critical question of repentence that in principle nullifies the punishment for apostasy. The opinion ranged across the whole spectrum from the eighth-century jurists al-Nakha'i and Sufiyan al-Thauri, who ruled that no limitation could be imposed on the time allowed for repentance—which was taken to mean that the opportunity to repent should be available throughout the lifetime of the apostate who could therefore *never* be executed—to Ibn Taymiyya's ruling that the call for repentance before sentencing was not obligatory because the call of the faith had already reached the apostate. Following the methodology of Islamic legal science, Rahman thus reaches the conclusion that the Qur'an postpones the punishment for apostasy to the Hereafter, and the contemporary public law should do likewise.[50]

More recently, an increasing number of both non-governmental human rights organizations and vocal intellectuals have argued for basic human rights in the Middle East, and particularly have upheld Rushdie's right to the freedom of expression.[51] Others have insisted that religious liberty and freedom of conscience are clearly deducible from the text of the Qur'an. Theirs is by no means a weak position. It is the case that a large number of Qur'anic verses state that "there is no compulsion in religion" (Qur'an 2.256),[52] establish freedom of conscience and religion, and strongly imply a form of "natural religion" among mankind which entails religious liberty.[53]

On the other hand, the transnational Islamic resurgence has caused the rejection of the assertion of the universality of human rights, and has

---

[50] Rahman, *Punishment for Apostasy*, esp. 118, 127, 161-165.

[51] Mayer, "Universal versus Islamic Human Rights," 364-379.

[52] There can be no doubt that this principle had the force of law. For instance, on December 10, 1610/Shawwal 14, 1019, the Shari'a Court of Ottoman Kayseri ruled that a man who had been 15 years old at the time his mother had converted "cannot be forced to Islam." Jennings, "Zhimmis (Non-Muslims") in the Early Seventeenth-Century Ottoman Judicial Records," 245.

[53] See, e.g., Mohammed Talbi, "Religious Liberty: A Muslim Perspective," in Leonard W. Swidler, ed., *Religious Liberty and Human Rights* (Philadelphia, 1986), 175-187; Little, Keslay, and Sachedina, *Human Rights and Conflicts of Culture*. Mottahedeh, "Toward an Islamic Theology of Toleration, 32-34 makes the case for the presumption of "natural religion".

generated an official "Islamic alternative." This Islamic alternative is embodied in the 1990 Cairo Declaration on Human Rights in Islam. As is to be expected in an imitative document, much of the legal terminology of the international human rights conventions is swallowed while quite a number of rights are in substance nullified. The Cairo Declaration offers no guarantee of religious freedom. It prohibits any form of compulsion or exploitation of poverty and ignorance to convert anyone to atheism or a religion other than Islam (Article 10). Article 22 of the Declaration bars "the exploitation or misuse of information 'in such a way as may violate sanctities and the dignity of Prophets, undermine moral and ethical values or disintegrate, corrupt, or harm society or weaken its faith'."[54] It is interesting to note that, in flat contradiction to the historical experience and the public law of virtually all signatory countries, Article 19 of the Cairo Declaration provides that "[t]here shall be no crime or punishment except as provided for in the Shari'ah." Article 25 further declares the Shari'a to be the only source for explanation and clarification of the articles of the Declaration.[55] While endorsing the Cairo Declaration, the Islamic Conference of Foreign Ministers in April 1993 also confirmed "the existence of different constitutional and legal systems among [the] Member States and various international or regional human rights instruments to which they are parties."[56]

With this acknowledgement, we can conclude our discussion of religious human rights from the perspective of legal pluralism. One cannot have legal pluralism without conflict of laws. Membership in the international community makes the legal systems of the contemporary Middle East permeable to principles of international law, and introduces an element of legal pluralism. A process of osmosis is set in motion, not through the implementation of international law—we all know how woefully inadequate the mechanisms for such implementation are—but rather through the eventual absorption of international legal phraseology

---

[54] Mayer, "Universal versus Islamic Human Rights," 336.

[55] Ibid., 327-350 for a general analysis of the Cairo Declaration.

[56] Ibid., 350. This amounts to a very significant qualification of the categorical recognition of the Shari'a in the Cairo Declaration as most Middle Eastern countries are signatories to several such international instruments. Iran, for instance, is among the signatories to the International Covenant on Civil and Political Rights.

into the constitutional laws of the Middle Eastern countries. Owing to this osmosis, the seeds for future change remain firmly planted in the actual and potential contradictions between the national and international laws, and especially legal cultures.

Religious Human Rights in the State of Israel

ASHER MAOZ
Tel Aviv University [1]

The Israeli approach to religious human rights is inherently eclectic. It combines traditional and new theories, communal and individual rights, freedoms from religion and religious coercion, freedoms of religion from state intervention, and equality among religions and differential treatment of them. These eclectic principles are rooted in historical, theological, political and national grounds. Perhaps the most significant factor contributing to the complexity of religious human rights in the State of Israel is that this part of the world—the Holy Land—is the birthplace of monotheism. The Holy Land has been the subject of several "holy wars." It occupies a central place in the theology of many religions, including the three main monotheistic religions, and each religion has its own view of the relationship of state and religion, which views sometimes come into conflict. Moreover, the principles and practices of previous regimes that governed the Holy Land still work their influence, even though today Israel is predominantly Jewish in culture and religion.

Religious Demography and Structure of Israel

The population of the State of Israel at the end of 1974 consisted of 5,473,100 people, 81.15% (4,441,300) of whom were Jewish. The population at the end of 1993 stood about the same (5,327,600), with 81.37% Jewish, 14.1% Muslim, 2.85% Christian, and 1.68% Druze and others.[2]

[1] I would like to extend my gratitude to the many individuals and institutions who furnished vital information for the preparation of this chapter. I would also like to thank my research assistant Tal Arbel.

[2] These figures are provided in the Central Bureau of Statistics. It is easy to get data on religious affiliations of Israeli subjects, since under the provisions of the Population Registry Act of 1965, the religious affiliation of each subject is noted.

J.D. van der Vyver and J. Witte, Jr. (eds.), Religious Human Rights in Global Perspective, 349-389.

Jews. The Jewish religious population in Israel is overwhelmingly Orthodox. Although a Conservative congregation of German Jews has worshipped in Jerusalem since 1937, the non-Orthodox streams are fairly new in Israel. They were generally founded by recent immigrants from Anglo-Saxon countries, mainly from the United States, and by Israelis who have been exposed to their practices when spending prolonged periods of time there. Though non-Orthodox groups are spreading in Israel, their numbers are still fairly small. Possibly, the social functions performed by these groups abroad are either not viewed as relevant by most Israelis or regarded as functions to being taken care of by other institutions in Israel.

Even many Israelis who are non-observant still identify Judaism with Orthodoxy.[3] The Orthodox stream is divided into the National Religious and the Haredi Ultra-Orthodox. The latter is subdivided into dozens of sects, each concentrating around a rabbi. In general, the difference between the National Religious movement and the Ultra-Orthodox is expressed in their attitude towards the State of Israel. The National Religious Movement is Zionist in its concepts, intermingles with the non-religious population, and fully participates in national projects. The Ultra Orthodox groups tend to live a segregated life and are non-Zionist, even anti-Zionist, in their philosophy; the most extreme of these groups do not even recognize the legitimacy of the State of Israel and shun its authorities and institutions. However, both the National Religious and the Ultra Orthodox movements (save for the most extreme Haredi sects) take an active part in Israel's political life. They are represented, through their own political parties, in its House of Representatives, the Knesset, and participate in its coalition governments.

There are various estimates of the number of religious Jews living in Israel.[4] Whatever the exact number, only a minority observes the precepts of Jewish religion, the Halakha, in daily life. Nevertheless, it is wrong to regard Israeli society as secular. In a recent comprehensive study con-

---

[3] See Ephraim Tabory, "Religious Rights as a Social Problem in Israel," *Israel Yearbook on Human Rights* 11 (1981): 256, 262.

[4] In the recent 1992 elections to the Knesset, the religious parties scored 345,177 votes out of 2,615,159 valid ballots (13.2%) and are represented by 16 out of 120 members of the Knesset. However, it to futile to base an estimate of the proportion of religious people within Israeli society upon religious representation in Parliament. Not only are the elections to the Knesset boycotted by the extreme Orthodox, but many religious Jews vote also for non-religious, parties. It is equally futile to base this estimate on school enrollment, for "traditional," and even religious, parents sometimes send their children to non-religious schools, and non-religious parents send their children to religious schools in order to get a "Jewish" education.

ducted among the Jewish adult population in Israel,[5] only 24% of the respondents regarded themselves as "totally non-observant," and only 7% described themselves as "anti religious." Moreover, when asked about observance of specific precepts of religion, even the figure of 24% seems high. For example, over 70% of those who regarded themselves as "totally non-observant" still viewed the celebration of the bar-mitzvah as "important" or "very important," and half of them favored its celebration in synagogue. Again, 70% of those same respondents regarded religious circumcision as "important" or "very important," and 56% percent of them thought similarly with regard to wedding ceremonies being performed by a rabbi. Indeed, 4% of the "totally non-observants" nevertheless regarded themselves as "traditional." A survey conducted on the eve of Yom Kippur in 1995 reveals a similar attitude—79% percent of the Jewish adult population declared its intention to fast on the Day of Atonement.[6]

There are several possible explanations for this seeming contradiction of religious identification and affiliation, on the one hand, and persistent religious observance and practice, on the other. An important factor is the national character of the Jewish religion. To be part of the Jewish people is, implicitly, to be part of the Jewish religion. The identification with religion is not restricted to the Jewish population. Indeed religious adherance is most common.

Karaites. The Karaites ("people of the Scriptus") are a Jewish sect that departed from the mainstream of Judaism ("Rabbinical Judaism") in the eighth century C.E. They observe only the Commandments of the Torah, and disregard post-Biblical Halakha. They are a small group, with estimates as high as 25,000 people, though judging by statistics of marriage and divorce, the correct number seems to be about half that amount. The Karaites have their own synagogues and religious institutions. They are Jewish, although rabbis of Askenazi (European) origin will not marry them to Jews, while rabbis of Sephardi (Oriental) origin tend to be more lenient on the matter. This difference in treatment may be historically based: the Jews in Egypt enjoyed a good relationship with the Karaites, while their brethren in Eastern Europe disconnected themselves from the Jews. The Karaite religious leadership also opposes intermarriage with "Rabbinical Jews."

Samaritans. The origin of the Samaritans is somewhat obscure. They follow numerous Jewish customs in their religious practice, yet they are not regarded as Jewish. Today there are about 600 Samarites, half living

---

[5] Shlomit Levy et al., *Beliefs, Observance and Social Interaction among Israeli Jews* (Jerusalem, 1993) (Hebrew)

[6] Per a poll conducted by Dahaf Institute with a possible 4% error.

in the Israeli township of Holon, and half in Nablus in Samaria, near the holiest site of their religion, Mt. Grizim. They are led by priests headed by the elder priest, called the Great Priest.

Muslims.[7] Most of the Muslims in Israel adhere to the Sunnite rite. Out of the four schools of faith within Sunnite Islam, the Shafi'i mazhab is most common among rural Muslims, the Hanafi mazhab is prominent in urban areas. The Shar'ia religious courts of the Muslims follow the Hanafi mazhab school. Most Muslims in Israel are Arabs, though the Circassian community, which is of Caucasus origin, are also Muslims of the Sunnite rite. Unlike Arab Muslims, members of the Circassian community are enlisted in the Israeli army as are the Bedouins as well as the Druze who are not Muslims. Another non-Arabic sect is the Ahmedans, of Punjab origin, with some 300 adherents in Israel. Their Middle Eastern center is in Haifa. They engage in missionary work, but they oppose religious coercion and the spread of Islam through "holy war" (*jihad*). Many of the Muslims in Israel live in villages. There are also Arab towns with large Muslim populations. There are a few mixed Jewish-Arabic townships. The Muslims live within a traditional community and are characterized by strong religious feelings, which might have been strengthened by nationalistic motivations. They have not been immune to the recent fundamentalism tides in the Muslim world. A political religious movement called "The Islamic Movement" has been created, which combines religious fundamentalism with nationalistic ideology. The movement has gained strength, and encouraged by its success, the leadership of the movement is considering standing for elections to the Knesset.

Christians.[8] In spite of their relatively small number, Christians in Israel are divided into some 35 different churches and denominations. This variety of churches should be of no surprise, given the central role of the Holy Land in Christianity and the vast number of holy Christian sites in Israel. The largest churches are Greek Catholic and Greek Orthodox, each comprising nearly one third of the Christian population. Another large community is the Roman Catholic Church. The Maronite Church has considerably fewer followers. Other churches have a rather small number of followers, in some cases no more than a few dozen members. The Chaldean Church, for example, is headed by a clergyman, himself a for-

---

[7] See Odi Stendel, *The Minorities in Israel: Trends in the Development of the Arab and Druze Communities 1948-1973* (Jerusalem, 1973); id., *The Arab in Israel: Between Hammer and Anvil* (Jerusalem, 1992) (Hebrew); Aharon Layish, ed., *The Arabs in Israel: Continuity and Change* (Jerusalem, 1981) (Hebrew).

[8] See Saul A. Colbi, *Christianity in the Holy Land* (Tel Aviv, 1969); id., *Christian Churches in Israel* (Jerusalem, 1969); A. Roy Eckardt, ed., *Christianity in Israel* (New York, 1971).

mer Presbyterian, who has virtually no community. Besides the locally established churches, there are representatives of several overseas churches. The number of Christians and of Christian churches has grown substantially since the 1967 War and the unification of Jerusalem under Israeli rule. Most of the Christians in Israel are Arabs.

Today, Catholic Churches, collectively, claim the largest number of Christians in Israel. These include the Latin Church with some 20,000 followers, six Unitarian Catholic Churches, the Greek Catholic Church, which considers itself descendent of the first Christians in the Holy Land, with some 45,000 members, the Maronites with 2,000 members, and four other Catholic churches. The Greek Orthodox church is the largest among the Orthodox churches with some 45,000 members. Other Orthodox churches include the Russian Orthodox Church. Prior to 1967, this Orthodox Church was associated solely with Russian Mission representing the Russian Orthodox Patriarchate of Moscow (the "Red Russian Church"); after the 1967 War, the new occupied territories brought into Israel churches and convents associated with the Russian Church in exile situated in New York (the "White Russian Church"). The Rumanian Orthodox Church is also represented through the Rumanian Orthodox Mission. Israel also is home to the Monophysite Churches. These are pre-Chalcedonian churches, which emerged in the fifth century after the theological split within the Western Church regarding Christ's nature. They comprise four churches: the Armenian (Orthodox or Gregorian) Church with over 2,000 believers; the Coptic Church and the Syrian-Jacobite (Orthodox) Church with about 1,000 followers each, and the Ethiopian Church with about 100 members. Alongside these are more than 20 Protestant Churches, of more recent origin, including the Church of England, Lutheran Church, Scottish Presbyterian Church, Society of Friends, Baptists, Pentecostals, Seventh Day Adventists, and Mennonites—all claiming some 4,000 members. Given their late arrival to Israel, they are not in possession of holy places. In 1959 the Israel-American Institute of Biblical Studies was founded as a seminar for Protestant clergy.

The Druze.[9] The Druze community stems from the Isma'alia, an extreme sect of Shi'ite Muslims, yet they are not Muslim. The basics of the Druze faith are secret and are not known even within the community. The Druze do not accept converts. Most of the Druze are concentrated in Syria (350,000), in Lebanon (300,000), and in Israel (90,000) where they constitute 1.7% of its population. They live mainly in villages, in five of which they constitute the whole population. Following the death of the veteran leader of the Druze community in Israel, Sheikh Amin Tarif,

---

[9] See Stendel, *The Minorities in Israel*; id., *The Arab in Israel*; Layish, ed., *The Arabs in Israel*.

heated disputes broke out regarding the nomination of a new leadership. These disputes suggest that they are attempts to liberalize and modernize the Druze community.

The Baha'i Faith. Like the Druze, the Baha'i faith originated in Islam, but disconnected itself from it. The international headquarters of the community is situated in Haifa where the religious leadership convenes. In Israel, there are some 300 Baha'is, most of them foreign citizens who serve in the community's institutions.

Legal Status and Organization of Religious Communities[10]

The policy of the State of Israel towards religion and its relationship to the state must be understood in its historical context. The basic structure of church-state relations was established during the Ottoman era, which preceded the British occupation of Palestine. During that period, Islam was the established religion of the Empire. Muslim religious law, the Shari'a, was applied by Muslim religious courts, particularly in the area of family law. Muslim law drew a distinction between "heathens" and the Jewish and Christian religions that were based on the Sacred Book (the Kitabaia). While heathens were severely restricted, the Turkish Sultan adopted a "millet" system for "religions of the book," which afforded them organizational autonomy and jurisdiction in matters of personal status. Jewish and Christian communities were not automatically recognized; they were required to procure a special charter from the Sultan; this charter would define the legal status of the community[11] and the jurisdiction of the courts.

This Ottoman structure of church-state relations was largely preserved by the British. The Palestine Order in Council of 1922, as amended, granted eleven religious communities autonomy in matters of personal law and communal jurisdiction—Muslims, Jews, and nine Christian Churches.[12] Interestingly, in spite of the power conferred upon them, the Palestinian Government did not grant recognition to the Anglican Church, nor to any other religious communities during the Mandate era. (The Israeli Government, by contrast, extended its recognition to the Druze, evangelical Episcopal, and Baha'i communities.) The Palestine Order in Council assured these communities full autonomy in their in-

---

10 See Edoardo Vitta, *The Conflict of Laws in Matters of Personal Status in Palestine* (Tel-Aviv, 1947).

11 Frederic M. Goadby, *International and Inter-Religious Private Law in Palestine* (Jerusalem, 1926).

12 These are the Eastern Orthodox, Roman Catholic, Gregorian Armenian, Armenian Catholic, Syrian Catholic, Chaldean Uniate, Greek Catholic Melkite, Maronite, and Syrian Orthodox.

ternal affairs, subject to any future enactments. Recognized communities were given exclusive jurisdiction over their internal constitution and their administration of religious endowments foundations (*wakfs*). Muslim religious courts no longer served as state courts, though they continued to enjoy broader jurisdiction than Jewish and Christian courts.

In practice, the Palestinian Government dealt differently with each of the recognized religious communities. All Christian communities were organized on an internal basis, and were largely left alone.[13] The Jewish community was more closely regulated by the High Commissioner, which allowed the rabbinical court to operate only over persons who had voluntarily subjected themselves to its jurisdiction by registering in the register of the Jewish Community. On the other hand, Muslim as well as Christian religious courts exercised jurisdiction over all members of their communities. By special order, the Supreme Muslim Council was formed in 1921 and was in charge of the religious affairs of the Muslim community as well as over administration of Muslim *wakfs*. When irregularities occurred in the election of the members of the Council, the High Commission came to appoint members to the Council, and the administration of *wakf* funds was placed in the hands of a specially appointed committee.

Upon its establishment in 1948, the State of Israel adopted this Mandatory law, save for modifications resulting from the establishment of the State.[14] The entire traditional system of personal law and religious jurisdiction was retained. The most important change related to the Jewish community. Rabbinical courts now operated not only over those who voluntarily accepted their jurisdiction, but over all who belonged to the Jewish people.[15] In 1957, the Druze community was recognized; under a 1962 statute, the same jurisdictional principle relating to rabbinical courts applied to their religious courts.[16] At present, all religious courts have exclusive jurisdiction over members of their respective communities in matters of marriage and divorce. In other matters of personal status, some courts enjoy exclusive jurisdiction, while others exercise concurrent jurisdiction with the civil courts. Moreover, the Knesset has removed several matters from the application of personal law and has applied civil law to them. It is interesting to note that, although Israel is a Jewish state,

---

[13] With the exception of the Greek Orthodox community, which was regulated by Ottoman Imperial regulations dating back to 1875 as well as further Mandatory ordinances. All of these ordinances were abolished in 1936.

[14] See section 11 of the Law and Administration Ordinance, 1948.

[15] Another significant modification included the imposition of Rabbinical jurisdiction on permanent residency as an alternative to citizenship as was the case under Mandatory law

[16] Druze Religious Courts Law, 1962

the Muslim religious court retained its status, which is still wider than that of the Rabbinical or the Christian courts.

While there were no major changes in the traditional jurisdiction of religious communities, substantial changes took place in the organization and administration of the Muslim and the Jewish communities. As for Muslims, the communal organization inherited from the Mandate era collapsed in 1948 when members of the Supreme Muslim Council and of the special committee for administration of *wakfs* as well as the Qadis of the religious courts fled the country during the war of independence. The Knesset thereafter abolished the Council, and no new members were appointed to the special committee which, as a result, also dissolved. In their place, the Knesset appointed committees of trustees in the five towns with substantial *wakf* assets. The Custodian of Absentee Property, who is in charge of this property, is vested with full ownership of the *wakf* assets and must either transfer them to those committees who must use their profits for the benefit of the Muslim population or use the profits himself for that purpose. The Minister of Religious Affairs has recently expressed his intention to re-establish a religious Muslim Council comprised of Muslim clergymen recommended by Muslim heads of local councils and by the minister.

The Minister of Religious Affairs has recently promulgated regulations for the internal organization of the Druze community. According to these regulations, a religious Druze council will be established consisting of thirty Druze clergymen, twelve members recommended heads of Druze local councils, and twelve members appointed by the Minister following his consultation with Druze clergymen and leaders. The Council will represent the Druze community in all religious matters, will engage in religious instruction and the development of religious sites and places of worship as well as religious communal centers, and will decide on principle religious non-judicial matters.

By establishing the Druze religious council as well as the Muslim religious Council, the institutional structure of both communities will become, in principle, similar to the institutional structure of the Jewish Community, though on a more centralized basis. Judges of the rabbinical as well as the Muslim and Druze religious courts are appointed by the President of the State, upon the recommendation of nomination committees similar to the committee for the selection of Civil Court judges. The committees are headed by the Minister of Religious Affairs and most of their members are appointed by bodies other than the relevant religious community. Only religious courts are under the responsibility of the Minister of Religious Affairs. No statute governs procedures, administration or appointment of judges to Christian religious courts. Such matters are left to the discretion of each Christian community.

The law sets the structure of Jewish religious institutions. The legal structure and authority of the Chief Rabbinate is set in the Chief Rabbinate Law of 1980. Another statute provides for the establishment of Jewish Religious Councils and defines their powers.[17] The form of electing the Chief Rabbis of the State, the Council of the Chief Rabbinate, the Religious Councils, and City Rabbis is provided for by statutory law. The electing bodies consist of members suggested by the Ministry of Religious Affairs, the local council and the local Rabbinate. Moreover, according to a Israeli Supreme Court ruling, candidates for these religious councils do not need to conform to Halakhic requirements since the councils govern matters such as marriage for the entire Jewish community, not merely for religious Jews.

Israel as a Jewish State[18]

Israel was established as a Jewish state. The Declaration of the Establishment of the State of Israel (the "Declaration of Independence") specifically states that Israel will be "a Jewish state in Eretz Israel." This comports with the Balfour Declaration of 1917 and the Resolution of the League of Nations of 1922 calling for the establishment of "a national home for the Jewish people" in Palestine as well as the U.N. General Assembly Resolution of 1947 (the "Patrition Resolution") concerning the establishment of independent Arab and Jewish states in Palestine. Though, initially, the Declaration of Independence had no constitutional status, it has always expressed "the aspirations of the people and their basic credo"[19] and served as a vital instrument in interpreting Israel's laws and in introducing extra-legal principles. In 1994, this Declaration was raised to a constitutional level, when two of Israel's Basic Laws, which eventually will form its constitution, were amended and declared that "[h]uman rights in Israel . . . will be safeguarded in the spirit of the principles contained in the Declaration of Independence." Moreover, these Basic Laws, the only ones dealing with human rights, specifically provide that "the values of the State of Israel as a Jewish and Democratic State" are the basis of human rights in Israel. Moreover, in accordance

---

[17] See Jewish Religious Services Law (Consolidated Version, 1971). See Asher Maoz. "Constitutional Law," in Itzhac Zamir, ed. *Introduction to Israeli Law* (Jerusalem, 1995).

[18] See David Kretzmer, "Constitutional Law," in Amos Shapira, ed., *Introduction to Israeli Law* (Amsterdam, 1995), 39.

[19] *Yardor v. Knesset Central Election Committee* (1965) 19(3) Piskey Din (Law Reports of the Supreme Court of Israel) 365 (Hebrew).

with Basic Law, the Knesset and the Political Parties Law, 1992 enjoins any group whose aims or actions negate the existence of the Israel as "the State of the Jewish People" from registering as a political party and running for the Knesset.

The Jewishness of the State of Israel is reflected in its legislation. The best example is the Law of Return, which confers upon every Jew the right to emigrate to Israel. Such an emigrant (*oleh*) receives automatic Israeli citizenship. The law further recognizes the central role of Zionist institutions in the immigration of Jews to Israel and in Jewish settlement in Israel. Moreover, "principles of freedom, equity and peace of Israel's heritage" serve as a source of positive law in Israel.[20] The Jewish character of the State is further reflected in its national days of rest and festivals and in State education. The national flag, the State emblem, and the anthem are all packed with Jewish symbols.

The Jewishness of the State of Israel is a matter of sharp controversy, with positions on the question ranging from the strictly religious to the highly democratic. It is obvious, however, that when declaring Israel to be a Jewish state, the Knesset certainly did not have in mind a Halakhic state. After all, the Zionist movement, which led to the establishment of the State, emerged as a reaction to traditional life in the Diaspora. When speaking of Jewish values, the Knesset has in mind the national values of Judaism. But these national values cannot be separated from their religious origin. Judaism is a national religion. National and religious components of Judaism are inseparable. A Jewish State divorced of religion is an impossibility.[21] It is no coincidence that the Zionist Movement chose the traditional prayer shawl as its flag just as it seems only natural that the founders of the State chose the seven branched candelabra of the Second Temple as the State emblem.

Nothing in Israeli law, however, confers upon the Jewish religion the status of a State religion. There are no provisions for the preferable treatment of the Jewish religion as such. It is of significance, in this regard, that the separation between state and religion, between state business and religious matters, is alien not only to Judaism but also to Islam, the second largest religion in Israel. The Jewishness of the State of Israel does not contradict its democratic nature. Israel has, from the start, been both a Jewish state and a democratic state, dedicated to equality and basic freedoms. This synthesis of the national, religious, and democratic natures of the State pose some difficulties. Yet, as the Supreme Court has

[20] See The Foundation of Law Act, 1980

[21] See Asher Maoz, "State and Religion in Israel," in Menachem Mor ed., *International Perspectives of Church and State* (Omaha, 1993), 239.

repeatedly put it,[22] these values are not necessarily contradictory, and every effort must be made to enable their co-existence.[23]

Israel, therefore, does not fit easily into any common category of religion-state relations. It is most accurately classified as a multi-religious state, where various religions are recognized, yet none enjoys the status of official state religion.

Freedom of Religion and Freedom From Religion[24]

The Declaration of Independence proclaims that the State of Israel "will guarantee freedom of religion and conscience, of language, education and culture." It further undertakes to "safeguard the Holy Places of all religions." Since these principles were incorporated in the recent Basic Laws, they should be regarded as enjoying entrenched constitutional status.

Israeli Penal Law includes a whole section dealing with offences against religious and traditional feelings. It imposes a penalty of three years imprisonment on a person who disturbs religious worship or assaults a worshipper. A similar sanction is imposed for trespassing on a place of worship with the intent to hurt religious people or to revile their religion. One year imprisonment is imposed on a person who publishes, or voices in a public place, words calculated to outrage the religious feeling or belief of other persons. Further provisions deal with promotion of ill will between different sections of the population, seditious publications, and racial incitement. A group that incites racism may not be registered as a political party and is deprived of the right to be elected to the

---

[22] See *Neiman v. Chairman of the Central Election Committee to the 12th Knesset* (1988) 42.

[23] See Asher Maoz, "The Values of a Jewish and Democratic state," *Iyunei Mishat* 19 (1994-1995).

[24] See Itzhak Englard, "Law and Religion in Israel", *American Journal of Comparative Law* 35 (1987): 185; id., "Religious Freedom and Jewish Tradition in Modern Israeli Law: A Clash of Ideologies," in Edwin B. Firmage, et al., eds., *Religion and Law: Biblical-Judaic and Islamic Perspectives* (Winona Lake, 1990), 365; Ariel Rosen-Zvi, "Freedom of Religion: The Israeli Experience," *Zeitschrift für auslandische öffentliches Recht und Volkerrecht* 46 (1986): 213; Norman L. Cantor, "Religion and State in Israel and the United States," *Tel-Aviv University Studies in Law* 8 (1988): 185; Maoz, "State and Religion in Israel"; Amnon Rubinstein, "Law and Religion in Israel," *Israel Yearbook on Human Rights* 3 (1973): 223; Shimon Shetreet, "Some Reflections on Freedom of Conscience and Religion in Israel," *Israel Yearbook on Human Rights* 4 (1974): 194, 241; Simha Meron, "Freedom of Religion as Distinct Freedom from Religion in Israel," *Israel Yearbook on Human Rights* 4 (1974): 219; S. Zalman Abramov, *Perpetual Dilemma: Jewish Religion in the Jewish State* (Rutherford, NJ, 1976); Donna E. Arzt, "Religious Freedom in a Religious State: The Case of Israel in Comparative Constitutional Perspective," *Wisconsin International Law Review* 9 (1990): 1; Ruth Lapidoth, et al., "Freedom of Religion in Israel," in Alfredo M. Rabello, ed., *Israeli Reports to the xlv International Congress of Comparative Law* (Jerusalem, 1994).

Knesset. A bill now pending in the Knesset provides that an offence committed out of racist motives is punishable with double sanctions.

Israeli legislation supports the exercise of religious freedoms in a number of ways. Religious education, for example, which fulfills the requirements of compulsory education, is heavily supported by the state. Various regulations enable non-Jewish believers to carry on their religion practices without suffering any disadvantage.

Israeli courts also encourage freedom of religion. The Supreme Court has interpreted the term "freedom of religion" to include freedom of worship and not merely the freedom of belief; thus a public authority that permitted social activities in its halls, must also permit use of the hall for religious worship.[25] During the Gulf War, the Supreme Court made it clear that when supplying gas masks the government should endeavor to supply men who grow beards out of religious conviction with special masks.[26] Many more examples can be cited.

Freedom of religion may be curtailed on the grounds of pressing public interest.[27] One example of such regulation concerns religious conversion. Each individual enjoys the right to change his or her religion. However, since such a change may affect the personal law and family law governing the neophyte, the rights of other members of the neophyte's family are given special protection.[28] Moreover, the religion of a minor may not be changed against the wish of either parent, save with the court's approval. And, while missionary work and proselytizing are legal, using material inducement to conversion constitutes a criminal offense.[29] A second example may be found in the statutory prohibitions against bigamy or polygamy. Even though the polygamy is common among Muslims and to some extent with Jewish newcomers from Arab countries, the Supreme Court upheld the prohibition. The Court was of the opinion that polygamy was a privilege, not a religious precept of Islam.[30] Though the Court's position has been criticized as an infringement of the freedom of religion, it is aimed at protecting the public order. A third example concerns regulation of marriage. The Knesset has declared

---

25 *Peretz v. Head of Local Council of Kfar Shmaryahu*, (1963) 17 Piskey Din 2101

26 See *Miller v. Minister of Defence* (1991) 45(2) Piskey Din 293.

27 In the absence of a written constitution, there is no formal obstacle for the Knesset to infringe this freedom—subject to the entrenched Basic Laws—for whatever reason it may deem fit. The courts, however, will try to interpret such legislation in accordance with civil liberties.

28 See Religious Community (Change) Ordinance, 1927. Thus the unilateral change of one's religion will not affect the validity of his marriage and the applicable law in matters of marriage, divorce, and alimony.

29 See Penal Law Amendment (Enticement to Change Religion), 1977.

30 See *Milchem v. Shari'a Court* (1954) 8 Piskey Din 910.

that the severance of marriage, without a court order, against the wife's wishes constitutes a criminal offence. The Knesset also imposed a minimal marriage age for women, which was substantially higher than was customary among Muslims, especially Bedouins, as well as among several Jewish groups. The Supreme Court declared the banning of women from serving on Jewish Religious Councils illegal, though the banning was based on religious grounds.[31]

Freedom *from* religion, being rooted in guarantees of freedom of conscience, seems to stand on an equal footing with freedom *of* religion. Yet, in the Israeli legal system, the protection of the freedom from religion seems weaker than the protection of freedom of religion. From a Jewish religious point of view, even demanding this freedom may be regarded as illegitimate. Those Ultra Orthodox Jewish groups who do recognize the legitimacy of the State of Israel demand it to be instituted on the law of the Torah. The more liberal Orthodox approach demands the imposition of religious behavior, or at least the prevention of anti-religious behavior, in public. Orthodox Jews have a genuine problem with freedom from religion, since under the Halakha every Jew is responsible not merely for his behavior but also for that of his fellow Jew. Moreover, religious people do not regard the clash between freedom of religion and freedom from religion as a conflict of ideologies, but as a conflict between ideology and convenience.

This latter approach finds support in some decisions of the Supreme Court. Thus when the Rabbinical Court, consistent with Halakha, refused to marry a male of priestly origin (a Cohen) with a divorcee, the Supreme Court recognized the validity of their wedding ceremony, which had been conducted in private. On the other hand, when a secular couple wished to marry in a private ceremony in order to avoid the presence of a rabbi at their wedding, the Supreme Court refused to intervene.[32] Yet the courts, notably the Supreme Court, have sought to soften the effect of religious legislation by giving maximum interpretation to civil liberties. Moreover, the Supreme Court has ruled that no administrative authority may act to further religious interests unless specifically authorized to do so by the legislature. This impediment has been applied also to subordinate legislation. These judicial tactics are of major significance in the protection of civil liberties, especially the freedom from religion.

Religiously-motivated legislation in Israel is not limited to enabling religious people to observe the precepts of religion. It is also intended to impose a religious way of life in the public arena, thereby affecting the

31 *Shakdiel v. Minister of Religious Affairs* (1988) 42 (2) Piskey Din 221, abridged in *Israel Law Review* 24 (1990): 128.

32 *Segev v. Rabbinical Court* (1967) 21 (2) Piskey Din 505.

freedom of the non-observant civil subject. Some writers have attempted to justify this intrusion on the freedom from religion with arguments respecting freedom of religion. Thus, it has been suggested that non-observance of the Shabbat by the public in general will impede the rights of the observant Jew, who will not be able to compete in the marketplace. He will also be deprived of the social and cultural activity of Israeli society if that takes place on Shabbat.[33]

It must be stressed that the beliefs of Ultra Orthodox Jews may require them to attempt to impose religious norms upon the non-observant. Since religious political parties are traditional partners to governmental coalition, this leads to a wide range of religiously-motivated legislation and administrative activities. These initiatives do not necessarily stop at the door of private homes. For example, the Israel Land Administration, which owns some 85% of the land in Israel, used to impose on its lessees a duty to abstain from doing work in their private homes on Shabbat and religious festivals. Only judicial intervention ended this procedure.[34]

The recent Basic Laws provide a source of freedoms for each religion. Particularly the provisions in the Basic Law on Human Dignity and Freedoms are phrased in broad terms that lend themselves to broad interpretation. Sections 2, 4, and 7 of this law specifically protect human dignity, the right to privacy, and personal confidentiality. These guarantees, coupled with the guarantee of freedom of occupation in the other Basic Law provide ample protection for each religion. The identical purpose clause in both Basic Laws, that their purpose is to entrench the values of the State of Israel as a Jewish and a Democratic State, is certainly a provision upon which both freedom of religion and freedom from religion may be based.[35]

Judicial intervention in the area of religious freedoms area took a new phase with the enactment of the Basic Laws. The Supreme Court declared that legislation that would prohibit the import of non-kosher meat would violate the provisions of Basic Law: Freedom of Occupation and is therefore invalid. Judicial intervention is sometimes frustrated by Knesset future legislation as was done in the case of the import of non-kosher meat when the Basic Law itself has been amended, yet in most cases the rul-

---

[33] See Simha Meron, "Freedom of Religion as Distinct from Freedom from Religion," 223.

[34] *Ornan v. Israel Land Administration* (1969) 67 Psakim Mehoziim (Law Reports of the District Courts) 284 (Hebrew).

[35] This possible interpretation is somewhat ironic, since the Knesset has not to date adopted a comprehensive bill of rights, given the firm religious opposition to it. Religious political parties feared that a bill of rights may hamper existing and potential religious legislation on grounds that it violates basic rights of non-believers.

ings are respected. Moreover, the rejection of religiously motivated activities of the administration drastically reduces the volume of state intervention with freedom from religion.

Group Rights and Their Effect on Religious Freedoms

As mentioned, wide religious autonomy is accorded to religious communities in Israel. These communities enjoy special legal status and have jurisdiction, inter alia, in matters of marriage and divorce. This religious autonomy substantially affects the rights of non-observers, for religious law and jurisdiction in family matters apply also to observers and non-observers alike. Marriage in Israel may take place only according to religious law[36]—although the Supreme Court has recently limited the scope of religious law and enlarged the application of civil law in matters connected with marriage.[37] The Supreme Court of Israel has sought to alleviate the hardships of such religious laws for non-observers by recognizing a whole range of alternatives to religious marriages—marriages performed abroad even via proxies, private religious ceremonies celebrated in Israel between spouses who have been rejected by the rabbinate, and even simple *de facto* marriages.[38]

The autonomy granted to the Orthodox Jewish community, in particular, infringes the freedom of non-Orthodox Jews. Jewish religion in Israel is usually identified with Orthodoxy. Thus, for example, an attempt to force the Minister of Religious Affairs to authorize Reform rabbis to perform marriages has failed.[39] Here, too, the Supreme Court has removed some of the worst discrimination. The Court ruled, for example, that a person who underwent conversion "in any Jewish community abroad" will qualify for registration as Jewish under the Population and Registration Law.[40] This decision opened the way for Reform and Conservative converts to immigrate to Israel and register as Jews. The Court also ruled that Reform and Conservative members cannot be disqualified from being appointed to Religious Councils,[41] and ordered a local council

---

[36] It should be pointed out that a nationalist justification has been asserted in support of this practice, viz., to avoid splitting the nation over the issue.

[37] See the recent landmark ruling in *Bavli v. Bavli* (1992), not yet published.

[38] See generally Amnon Rubinstein, "The Right to Marriage," *Israel Yearbook on Human Rights* 3 (1973): 233.

[39] See *Progressive Judaism Movement v. Minister of Religious Affairs* (1989) 43 (2) Pisky Din 661, abridged in *Israel Law Review* 25 (1991): 110.

[40] See *Shas Movement v. Minister of Interior,* 40 (4) Piskey Din 436. See also *Miller v. Minister of Interior,* 1986 40 (40) Pisky Din 436. A petition to recognize the legal affect of reform conversion performed in Israel is pending before the Supreme Court.

[41] See *Hofman v. The City Council of Jerusalem,* not published yet.

to make a public hall available for the Reform community services during the High Holidays.[42] The Court also ordered that state funding be accorded applicable religious institutions of both the Reform and the Conservative movements.[43]

The status of the Karaites, let alone unrecognized religious communities, is even more problematic. As Jews, the Karaites are subject to the jurisdiction of the rabbinical courts. Yet their entire religious conviction is based on the rejection of rabbinical teachings. The Ministry of Religious Affairs sought to solve this situation by appointing a marriage registrar from within the community and by recognizing the validity of divorces performed by the Karaite religious court. Yet, since this court has no binding legal status, it may try divorce suits only if both parties are willing to accept its jurisdiction and even then the legal affect on its rulings is questionable. Even more unsatisfactory is the governance of marriage and divorce in unrecognized religious communities. They have their marriage registrars, yet they do not have their own religious courts, and must instead apply to the courts of recognized communities.

The special legal status conferred upon Jewish religious institutions communities, however, invites intrusions not only on the religious freedom of others, but also on the religious freedom of the Jewish religious community. The price these religious institutions must pay for having a state legal status is the intervention of state authorities into their activities. Christian tribunals, which lack such legal status, have no state interference in appointments to their tribunals; such matters are left to the total discretion of the communities. Rabbinical courts, by contrast, are constituted by law. Therefore secular state institutions have a say in the way religious judges are elected. The same goes for other Jewish religious institutions, such as the Chief Rabbinate and the Religious Councils.

State intervention is not limited to elections of officials to statutory religious bodies. The entire operation and decisions of these bodies are subject to judicial review, mainly by the Supreme Court of Israel. A case in point is *Raskin v. Jerusalem Religious Council and the Chief Rabbis of Jerusalem.*[44] The Chief Rabbinate of Jerusalem granted a kashrut certificate to wedding halls, only if such weddings did not include "immoral performances," such as belly dancing. This condition was not without Halakhic basis; moreover, no court of law in a country committed to freedom of religion would seemingly have intervened in such matter. Yet the Supreme Court of Israel declared the rabbinate's demand illegal and or-

---

42 *Peretz v. Head of Local Council of Kfar Shmaryahu*, 17 Piskey Din 2101.

43 See *Hebrew Union College v. Minister of Religious Affairs*, not published yet.

44 44 (2) Piskey Din 673; abridged in *Israel Law Review* 26 (1992): 77; Jerusalem Post Report, 150. See also Maoz, "State and Religion in Israel," 239.

dered it to grant an unconditional certificate. The court did so, since the rabbinate was acting under the authority conferred upon it in the 1983 Kashrut (Prohibition of Deceit) Law, which provides that "in issuing a kashrut certificate, the rabbi shall have regard to the kashrut laws only."

Such review of the activities of religious institutions—particularly those of the Chief Rabbinate,[45] supposedly the highest religious authority in the state—has raised much criticism among religious Jews. Legally, however, in carrying out functions imposed by law, the Chief Rabbinate simply functions as an administrative agency of the state, and as such is subject to judicial review.[46] It should be noted, moreover, that the Supreme Court demonstrates more readiness to intervene when Jewish religious institutions are involved than when the petitions concern other religious communities.

Religion in the Military

From the time of their establishment, the Israel Defence Forces has insisted that there will be no separate units for religious soldiers.[47] Instead, conditions had to be set in all army units, to enable religious soldiers to serve without affronting their religious commandments. Indeed, one of the first enactments adopted by the Knesset was the Kosher Food for Soldiers Law of 1949. Similar regulations were passed to enable a religious soldier to worship and not to desecrate the Holy Shabbat and Jewish festivals. Such regulations, however, often came at the cost of interfering with non-observer's rights to be free from religion. Thus, on Shabbat no cantines are open in army units, and no driving is permitted. Before the High Holidays, a "spiritual revival project" takes place in all units, and all soldiers are required to listen to lectures by chaplains on "the values of the High holidays."[48] These regulations and practices have been rationalized as being based on the nationalistic nature of Judaism and as being useful to maintain national identification and uniformity within the ranks. The latter rationale is also used to justify the traditional

[45] Itzhak Englard, "Die Stellung des judischen Rabbinats im Rahmen des Staat Israel," *Festschrift zum 70. Geburtstag von Werner Kagi* (Tübingen, 1979), 101. It should be noted moreover that the status of the Chief Rabbinate results from the Law of the Knesset. Unlike Christianity, Judaism does not recognize any hierarchy among Rabbis. The status of each Rabbi is determined by the number of his followers and by their devotion.

[46] See generally Asher Maoz, "The Rabbinate and the Rabbinical Courts Between the Legal Hammer and the Halakhic Anvil," *Shenaton Ha-Mishpat Ha-Ivri* 16-17 (1990-1991): 289 (Hebrew).

[47] There are, however, several Yeshivot (schools of higher Halakhic education) which combine religious studies with active military service.

[48] Until recently, non-military religious believers, such as the Lubavitch missionaries, were allowed to conduct religious ceremonies and to deliver lectures in army camps.

religious rites of funerals; only in recent years has the army honored individual family requests for non-religious funerals.

The Army chaplaincy, which is Orthodox, is a standard military unit headed by the Chief Chaplain at the rank of General, who is also a member of the General Staff. Given this, and the army's almost exclusively Jewish character,[49] it may be said that Orthodox Judaism is the religion of the Israeli Defense Forces. A manual issued by the Chief Chaplaincy, for example, states that it has two aims: to enable soldiers to preserve religion while in service, and "to ensure maintenance of religious, spiritual and moral values, based on the Jewish Torah, by all soldiers and units, as this is the basis for a unified Jewish character for the army, and according to it, it would be feasible to maintain a unified forum in which all Jewish soldiers of whatever religious convictions may live together."

State Funding of Religious Institutions

Religious institutions in Israel enjoy wide state financial support—in the form of both direct funding and tax exemptions. Both forms of state support are not uniform with regard to the various religious communities and lack clear criteria to ensure equal support for all religions. State funding for religious institutions has not developed on a systematic legal basis. It should be noted that, to some extent, discrimination in one area of state funding for religion may be offset by preferential treatment in another. Thus, though Christian churches seem to enjoy less direct state funding, they enjoy tax exemptions to a substantially larger degree than other communities, including Jews and Muslims.

Direct State Funding. Religious institutions are supported by the state. Jewish, Muslim, and Druze religious courts, which are established under state law and constitute state organs, are fully financed by the state as are other courts of law. The judges of these courts are paid salaries on a par with the judges of other states courts of law.

Jewish religious needs are furnished by the Jewish Religious Services Law, 1971, which states that the entire budget of the Religious Councils, as approved by the local council or by the Ministry of Religious Affairs, shall be funded by the government and by the local council. The state also pays the salaries of the Chief Rabbis of the state and of local rabbis who are elected according to law. The Ministry of Religious Affairs provides specific funding for various needs of religious life, such as partici-

---

[49] Minorities who are drafted in the army, such as Druze and Circassians, usually serve in separate units and care is being taken of all their religious needs. Formally, the Chief Rabbinate is in charge of non-Jewish soldiers, but, practically, they are handled by a special staff officer.

pation in the construction of synagogues, cemeteries, and ritual baths, or the supplying of praying books and other ritual articles. The Ministry allocates special funding for religious instruction and education, maintenance of cemeteries, cultivation of ties with Jews in the Diaspora, and care for the religious needs of new immigrants.

Within the Ministry of Religious Affairs, special departments deal with Christian, Muslim, Karaite, Druze, and Samarite communities. This arrangement is apparently designed to enable the Ministry to tailor its services to the distinct needs of each minority communities—though some consider this to be a form of preferential treatment of the Jewish community. Since none of the religious services of these minority religious communities operate according to law, a fact which as shown before has its advantages, their budgets are not fully funded by the state.

The Druze community enjoys full financing of its religious courts as well as state funding for other communal activities. This includes state subsidies for the salaries of clergy, operating expenses, building and maintenance of places of worship.

Muslim religious courts are state courts, and are likewise fully financed by the government. The Ministry of Religious Affairs pays the salaries of some 300 clergy connected with mosques, notably imams and muezzin. The Ministry also allocates funds for Muslim religious services as well as for the construction, renovation, and maintenance of mosques and cemeteries. Another important source of income for the Muslim community is the revenue derived from various *wakfs*, now administered by the Custodian of Absentee Property. Representatives of the Muslim community have criticized this arrangement and demanded that the *wakf's* assets be placed in the control of the Muslim community. They have further criticized the seemingly preferential treatment accorded Christians, whose assets are exempt from the Absentee Property Law. The state has replied that Christian properties, unlike Muslim properties, are exempt since they were in 1948 and are now still registered not in the corporate name of the Church but in the individual names of the Archbishop and clergymen who are not absentees.[50] Moreover, they had an organized church structure within recognized Christian communities, which could administer these properties.[51] This explanation has not satisfied the Muslim Leadership. Present government guidelines indicate that

---

[50] The Greek Catholic community was registered in the name of an archdiocese belonging to Archbishop Hakim, who had left Palestine during the 1948 war and considered technically an absentee. As a result the community's assets were seized by the Custodian. Upon the Archbishops return to Israel, the assets were released.

[51] Aharon Layish, "The Muslim Waqf in Israel," *Asian and African Studies* 2 (1966): 41, 60.

a special committee of Muslims will be established to administer the *wakf* for and within the Muslim communities.

As mentioned, Christian institutions, which are not state institutions, receive little direct funding, but ample tax exemptions. Christian communities do, however, benefit directly from the funding of several important historical sites in Israel. These include the two million dollar renovation of the *Via Delaros* in the old city of Jerusalem—the last journey of Jesus crossing fourteen stations, from his trial until his crucifixion—as well as the construction of a modern facility for baptizing in the Jordan River near the lake of Galilee and the construction of a special road to an isolated monastery in the Judea Desert. The Israeli administration in Judea and Samaria is also participating in the reformation and construction of other Christian holy sites. The Ministry of Religious Affairs announced is intention to prepare festive celebrations for the second millennium of the birth of Jesus.

Besides the direct funding of religious courts and religious services, the State of Israel supports various religious institutions. These allocations were, at earlier times, openly partisan, and not according to legal provisions. The Supreme Court has had to criticize more than one such allocation scheme, leading to reforms and interventions by the State Comptroller. In recent years, such state funding has been more fairly distributed, though Israel still lacks a comprehensive clear scheme of equal distribution of state funding among the various religious communities and the different sects within each community.

In the past, such state funding came from the general budgets of the different ministries, not from designated resources. This practice was challenged in a 1971 petition to the Supreme Court, when organizers of a music festival where church music was to be played were denied financial support by the Ministry of Education.[52] The Ministry stated that it was not its duty to support the performances of church music. The majority of the court, though expressing discontent with the ministry's decision, ruled that courts are not authorized to intervene in the distribution of funds, which are not regulated by law. The minority opinion by Justice Cohn, however, paved the way for later reform. Justice Cohn disqualified the ministry's considerations, although he was sympathetic to its reservations about funding a performance of *St. John's Passion*, which treats the Jews as responsible for Jesus Christ's crucifixion. Such considerations, he said, illegitimately discriminate against the art work of minority religions. Although the law provided no criteria for allocation of funds,

---

[52] *Abu Gosh v. Ministry of Education and Culture* (1971) 25(2) Piskey Din 821, (1972) *Israel Yearbook of Human Rights* 2 (1972): 336.

content-based discrimination was illegitimate, Justice Cohn concluded, and the ministry's decision should be overruled.

Such decisions notwithstanding, Jewish religious institutions generally enjoy substantially more state funding than do other religions, and most of that funding goes to Orthodox institutions. This is not only a function of demography, that is, the vast preponderance of (Orthodox) Jews in Israel. National, historical and political factors have all contributed to this disparity as well. Israel, as the homeland of the Jewish people, has assumed as one of its major tasks the maintenance and development of Jewish culture and tradition, which naturally have religious dimensions. Moreover, following the Holocaust which destroyed the world center of Jewish learning, Israel assumed the task of replacing those centers in Israel, and rebuilding the institutions of learning destroyed in Europe. Israel continually strives to maintain the chain of Torah learning and to establish a Torah center in place of the one destroyed. The state thus allocates substantial financial support to Yeshivoth (Jewish religious academies). This policy has won the approval of the Supreme Court in the 1984 case of *Watad v. Ministry of Finance*. In upholding this policy, the Court stressed "the unique and special place of Torah studying among the Jewish people and the place of Yeshivoth and of the Torah students."[53] Students pursuing traditional study of the Torah were thus worthy of state support. The Court stated, however, that similar allocations should be granted to non-Jewish religious educational institutions, which are parallel to the Yeshivoth when established.

Debates over state funding for religious institutions has brought on several rounds of rulings. In a 1983 Supreme Court case, *Central Tomchei Tmimim v. The State of Israel*, the Lubavich movement argued that a state scheme of funding educational institutions discriminated against the movement.[54] In response, the Knesset made allocations of funds to specific religious institutions. Due to parliamentary sovereignty, the Court could not enjoin this Knesset policy, but it did sharply criticize the practice of allocating funds to favored institutions and without objective criteria. It did not regard the remedial proceedings pending in the Knesset as an obstacle to trying the case, and ordered that thereafter no funds could be allocated without "clear, relevant and equal criteria."

Following the Court's decision, the Attorney General issued directives for governmental support of public institutions. According to the new policy, state money may be allocated to public institutions only in accordance with just and equal criteria. Direct allocation of funds to

---

[53] *Watad v. Ministry of Finance* (1984) 38(3) Piskey Din 113, *Israel Yearbook of Human Rights* 17 (1987): 267.

[54] *Central Tomchei Tmimim v. The State of Israel* (1984) 38 (2) Piskey Din 273.

named institutions on an unequal basis is strictly forbidden. The Foundations of Budget Law was also amended to provide that annual budget laws must specify the state subsidy for each category of public institution, and promulgate in the official Gazette the objective criteria and application procedures used for its distributions. Various ministries have, in response, published detailed criteria for the allocation of State funding on an objective and equal basis. Funding for Jewish institutions, as a consequence, is no longer automatic. For example, a recent application by a religious Zionist institution for grants allocated for Orthodox cultural activities was denied by the Ministry of Religious Affairs, and the applicant's appeal was dismissed by the Supreme Court.[55]

The debate on the issue of state funding for religious institutions is far from closed, however. Not only has it been difficult to set objective guidelines, but state funding has remained subject to constant political pressure and preferences. Orthodox and Ultra-Orthodox movements traditionally take part in Israeli political life and were usually part of its coalition governments. Representatives of these movements sponsor allocations that support their own institutions, and that discriminate against various non-Orthodox groups in Judaism or against unfavored sects within Orthodoxy. Non-Orthodox Jewish groups, in particular, have often not qualified for funding according to the criteria published by the Minister of Religious Affairs. This has led to further litigation before the Supreme Court. In response, the Ministry of Religious Affairs included a category of "support for other Jewish religious institutions," which provides allocations to institutions affiliated with the Reform and the Conservative movements.

Muslim and Druze religious institutions are allocated even fewer funds by the Ministry—even though Muslim groups receive additional distributions from *wakfs.* Recently, high officials within the Ministry have admitted to discrimination against these groups, and special funds have been distributed in an attempt to bridge the gap. The present Government has declared its intention to rectify the funding of these communities, and to treat them equally henceforth. It also made a commitment to integrate the Arab and Druze communities in Israel into areas of state life, to shore up their support for education, welfare, industry, housing and health services in these communities, and to absorb Arabs and Druze holding academic degrees into the civil service. A progress report published recently by a non-political association for the advancement of equality of opportunity shows considerable progress in this area in recent

---

[55] *Ma'ale, Religious Zionist Center v. The Minister of Education and Culture and others* (1992) 46(5) Piskey Din, 590.

years.[56] Thus, the state funding of Muslim religious sites in 1994 exceeded 20 times the funding in 1993. The newly appointed Minister of Religious Affairs published a platform in which he pledges commitment to full equalization of financial support for all religions. This reform includes the establishment of a center for the development of religious services and structures for the Muslim community which will be duly financed and will take care of the existing Muslim holy sites as well as building new mosques and cemeteries. Within this program all existing buildings of the Shari'a Courts will move into new buildings by the end of 1996.

An administration for Muslim religious services will be established which will take care of the entire religious services for Muslims, will administer the Muslim clergy, and will take care of Muslim shrines. Ample independence will be conferred upon this administration which will promote religious services for the Muslim community. Specific care will be taken for the appointment of sufficient Muslim clergymen and in their status and conditions.

This entire policy of state funding of religious organizations is the subject of a special report by the State Comptroller on the Ministry of Religious Affairs.[57] In her report, the State Controller sharply criticized both the criteria and their implementation. Following the report, the incoming Minister of Religious Affairs established a public committee which examined the entire matter and offered its recommendations. The Minister adopted these recommendations, and in July 1995 published new criteria for allocation of funds. Those criteria were formulated on objective considerations to ensure that no preference may be conferred upon certain institutions. Moreover, the new criteria establish a tight inspection mechanism to insure the equal allocation of funds and their spending in accordance with the criteria.

Besides direct funding by the Ministry of Religious Affairs, religious institutions are eligible for funding from bequests made in favor of the State of Israel, according to the Ministry's recommendations. According to the guidelines published by the Ministry, equal criteria will be applied to Jewish and to non-Jewish institutions and projects. Moreover, funding will be made available to assist the pilgrimages of Muslims to Mecca and Christians to the Holy Land. Special funds will be made available for the encouragement of the understanding among Jews, Christians, and Muslims and other religions. The Ministry is also contemplating the establishment of public committees for the advancement of inter-religious understanding and of religious tolerance.

[56] Sikkuy, The Association for the Advancement of Equal Opportunity, Annual Progression Report (1993-94).

[57] State Comptroller, 45th Annual Report (1994), 236-289.

Tax Exemptions. Various tax enactments exempt from taxation those public institutions that engage in social and cultural activities, including non-profit religious institutions. The Municipal Ordinance, 1938, exempts religious communities from urban property tax on buildings owned by them, and used for worship, hospitals, orphanages, religious courts, or clerical housing. The Land Appreciation Tax Law, 1963, exempts from sales tax transfers of real estate without consideration to religious institutions, among others. The Property Tax and Compensation Fund Law, 1961 exempts from income tax religious institutions that yield no income or have all their income devoted to religious purposes. The Income Tax Law, 1985 exempts public institutions with religious objectives from paying income tax. The Value Added Tax Law exempts from taxation non-profit organizations, which in practice includes religious institutions.

Beyond these exemptions, which are available to all religious communities, a number of extra-legal exemptions are granted to Christian communities. These exemptions are in fact a continuation of the capitulation system which operated during the Ottoman era. Shortly after the establishment of the State of Israel, the Israeli Government, via ambassador Fischer, and the French Government, via the Deputy Director of the Ministry of Foreign Affairs, Chouvel, exchanged a series of confidential letters on this subject. This correspondence, now known as the Fischer-Chouvel agreement, exempts from customs and local taxes all goods—religious and other kinds—imported for the use of French and Italian churches, hospitals, hostels, and other affiliated institutions. This agreement also exempts the heads of these churches from customs on their import of vehicles devoted to official use.[58] This special agreement on exemptions applies only to the French and Italian Christian churches. Other Christian churches are either refunded for the customs they pay, or they may ask the Ministry of Religious Affairs to pay their customs directly. Other churches also have narrower exemptions: their goods are exempt from customs, but they are exempt from only 30% of the urban property tax.

There is no legal basis for these exemptions granted to Christian communities. Indeed, they may even be infringements of the law, since only Christians and Bahi'as receive them, not Jews, Muslims, or other re-

[58] The exchange of the Fischer-Chouvel missives is highly classified and reviewing them is not permitted. It should be noted that Israel holds that this exchange of letters is not a binding agreement but rather represents an understanding to negotiate a detailed agreement. Despite its stand, Israel in practice, operates in line with the French version, namely that the exchange of letters constitutes a binding agreement in itself. By and large, the exemption accorded by the Fischer-Chouvel agreement is similar to that provided for foreign embassies in Israel. In 1975 the Government decided to extend these exemptions to all other Christian churches.

ligious groups. This disparity of treatment is all the more striking, since Christian churches refrain from incorporating according to state law, and are thus formally prohibited from all exemptions.

Nonetheless, Article 10 of the Fundamental Agreement between the Holy See and the State of Israel signed last December "reaffirm[s] the right of the Catholic church to property" and provides that a comprehensive agreement will be worked out "on unclear, unsettled and disputed issues concerning property, economic and fiscal matters relating to the Catholic church generally, or to specific Catholic communities or institutions." Such a comprehensive agreement, once reached, will reify these privileges even further, not only for the Catholic Church, but for all Christian churches.

Education and Religion

Jewish State Education.[59] When the State of Israel was established in 1948, four forms of Jewish education were available, each associated with a political movement—liberal, labor, national religious, and Ultra Orthodox non-Zionist respectively. The State Education Law, 1953 sought to transform the education system to the state. It integrated the existing system into two education systems—the religious state education system and the general state education system—a classic example of the non-separation between state and religion in Israel.

The State Education Law provides that both religious and non-religious schools must teach the values of Jewish culture and the loyalty of the Jewish people. Religious state schools may further give religious content to their way of life, curriculum, teachers, and inspectors. A Council of Religious State Education supervises these state religious schools, setting standards for hiring and dismissal of teachers and other staff. Teachers are required to be religiously observant, both in public and private life, in order to be models for their students. Teachers whose beliefs or practices prevent them from communicating religious values to their students cannot be part of state religious education.

Not only the teachers, but also the families of teachers are regulated. The Council of Religious Education requires that spouses of teachers observe the precepts of Orthodox Judaism. It further requires that teachers in the religious education system send their children to state religious schools—not general state schools that teach no specific religious values, nor private orthodox schools that are often non-zionist, sometimes even

[59] See S. Goldstein, "The Teaching of Religion in Government Funded Schools in Israel," *Israel Law Review* 1 (1990): 36-64.

anti-zionist. Failure to abide by these regulations may lead to dismissal of the teacher.

While teachers and other employees in state religious schools must be religiously observant, students need not be. State religious schools may encourage students' families to observe a religious way of life, so as to avoid confusion of the students, but they may not impose these demands on them in activities which are not connected with school life. Non-religious students may thus freely attend religious state schools; indeed, a survey conducted a few years ago indicated that up to 25% of the students in state religious schools do not come from observant families. Even non-religious parents seem to want to give their children the basics of Jewish tradition and religion.

Though non-religious in character, the curriculum of the general state schools includes many subjects relating to Jewish learning. Bible lessons form a major part of their timetable at all levels. In elementary schools, more curricular hours are devoted to Bible studies than to any other subject. The object of teaching Bible in state general schools, however, is to transmit cultural, historical, and aesthetic values rather than to teach specific religious precepts of Orthodox Judaism. Little time is devoted to teaching Halakhic religious literature, which is a subject of great emphasis in the religious schools. The school routine includes daily prayers.

The State Education Law provides parents with ample opportunity to influence the curriculum of state schools. Where three-quarters or more parents request a unique supplementary program, such a program may be approved by the Minister of Education. In some cases, parents have used this right in order to strengthen the religious education of general state schools. By and large, these supplementary religious classes are more in line with Conservative Judaism, thus expanding the types of religious education within the state system.

Non-Jewish Religious Education. While Arab students may choose to attend state schools in Jewish residential areas, a separate Arab State Education System operates in quarters with large Arab populations. The main language of study is Arabic, and Arabic subjects are taught. These are not religious schools, yet they adapt their curriculum and routine to the religion of the student body, be it Muslim or Christian (of whatever sect). The State Education Law provides that in non-Jewish educational institutions the curriculum should be adapted to the special conditions thereof. In accordance with this provision the Minister of Education provided that "State education in the Arab sector in Israel will be based on the values of Arab culture, the yearning for peace between the State of Israel and its neighbors the love of the country common to all citizens of the state loyalty to the State of Israel, while emphasizing the common interests of all the citizens of the state as well as the special character of the Arabs of Israel. . . ."[60]

Recognized Schools. The State Education Law allows for "recognized" schools which are not state schools. The majority are religious schools. They include Ultra-Orthodox Jewish educational institutions, known as the Independent Education System, and the new "El Ha'Ma'ayan" school system, which was established by a political party of oriental Jews. They also include a non-orthodox primary and secondary school in Haifa affiliated with the Reform World Union of Progressive Judaism, many church schools that belong to the Greek Catholic Church, and several new schools of the Latin Patriarch and the Anglican Church are in the process of being granted recognition. Recognized schools are financed by the Ministry of Education though not necessarily at the same level as state schools. There are two exceptions to this rule: the Independent Education System dating back to the period preceding the state schools as well as the El-Ha'Ma'ayan Schools receive state funding equal to state schools. There are also several non-religious schools that receive no state financial support. However, the attendance of children in these schools does satisfy the requirements for Israel's compulsory education law. These schools are autonomous and are not subject to the supervision of the Council of Religious State Education.

Secondary Schools and Schools of Higher Education. Secondary schools are generally maintained by local councils, rather than by the Ministry of Education, yet they enjoy state funding. In non-Jewish sectors, there are high schools operated by local councils as well as private high schools, operated by various churches. In Jewish sectors, Orthodox secondary education includes religious high schools and Yeshivoth. There are national religious and ultra Orthodox Yeshivoth, the latter usually operating as boarding schools in which students devote most of their time to religious studies. Those studying in Yeshivoth in Israel make up the largest number of Yeshiva students in the world. Military service of Yeshiva students is delayed until they conclude their study. This exemption, granted by the Minister of Defence, has been endorsed by the Supreme Court. The Yeshivoth of higher education—termed "Great Yeshivoth"—are budgeted according to the number of students attending them. Their support has risen substantially over the years, and they are now entitled to the same level of state support granted to other institutions of higher education.

In Israel, several institutions are recognized as institutions of higher education. The law confers full autonomy on these institutions in con-

---

[60] See the Arab Citizens of Israel, *Relationships between Jews and Arabs in Israel*, intermediate ed. (Jerusalem, 1984), 86.

ducting their academic and administrative affairs. Yet, they are prohibited from discriminating in the enrollment of students and in the appointment of teachers on racial, sexual, religious, national or social status grounds.

The University of Bar Ilan is the only religious university in Israel, with several branches throughout the country. The student body includes a substantial number of non-religious and non-Jewish students. Graduates of religious high schools are more readily admitted given the university's emphasis on excellence in the study of Judaism. Also, graduates of Great Yeshivoth are admitted preferentially to the Law School of Bar Ilan University, which emphasizes instruction in Jewish law. These preferences have been upheld by the Supreme Court.[61] Religious teachers tend to be preferred, though this is not a stated policy of the university. Though the university has sought to maintain a religious atmosphere on campus, the religious character of the university seems to have declined in recent years.

In addition to the University of Bar Ilan, branches of American religiously-affiliated universities, such as the Hebrew Union College Biblical and Archeological School and the Jewish Theological Seminar, operate in Israel. These institutions are licensed by their home states, not by Israel, and confer their own academic degrees. They are not recognized as institutions of higher education under Israeli law. Moreover, several Islamic colleges and universities operate in the West Bank. Their numbers have increased significantly under Israeli occupation. Since 1983, two Islamic colleges have operated within Israel. One of these has gained recognition by the Ministry of Education and may grant senior teacher's certificates. These colleges engage mainly in religious studies with the goal of preparing graduates for religious and judicial leadership in the Muslim community, a goal which the Ministry of Religious Affairs has supported. These Islamic colleges are currently self-funded, but they have applied for recognition by the Ministry of Education; if recognized, they will also receive state funding. With the peace process and the relationship between Israel and its Arab neighbors strengthening, graduates of the Islamic colleges hope to pursue their studies in Arab countries, and receive higher diplomas in Islamic studies.

Days of Rest and Employment

The issue of observing Shabbat in the public arena constitutes a central part of the religious struggle for the preservation of the Jewish char-

[61] See *Dover v. The Council For Higher Education* (1981) Piskey Din 35(4), 263.

acter of the state. Soon after the establishment of the State of Israel, the provisional council enacted the Days of Rest Ordinance, 1948: "The Shabbat and Jewish festivals . . . shall be the prescribed days of rest in the state of Israel. Non-Jews shall have the right to observe their own Shabbat and festivals as days of rest." In 1951, the Israeli Hours of Work and Rest Law was enacted. It provides that the weekly days of rest include, in the case of Jews, the Shabbat. Non-Jews are given an option to rest on the Shabbat or, alternatively, on Sunday or Friday, whichever day they ordinarily observe as their weekly day of rest. The same rule applies to Jewish and non-Jewish festivals.

These Shabbat regulations were designed to fulfill both social and national religious goals. On the one hand, the prohibition of work on rest days fosters social cohesion and public health. On the other hand, the designation of Shabbat as the weekly day of rest was made with explicit deference to Halakha and the Jewish tradition. In the words of the Supreme Court of Israel: "It is clear that it is no coincidence that . . . the Hours of Work and Rest Law the legislator instructed that the weekly rest day shall include—in the case of a Jew—the Shabbat, a statement which teaches that he saw the issue of keeping Shabbat in that sense as a national asset of the Jewish people that should be observed in the state of Israel."[62] Unlike America's Sunday blue laws, which must be justified on non-religious grounds to survive establishment clause scrutiny, Israeli Sunday laws are explicitly rooted in religious national elements of the days of rest.

Shabbat restrictions are elaborated by city and local councils. The Municipal Corporations Ordinance (New Version) authorizes city councils to regulate the opening and closing of "shops, canteens, and other such places, and of cinemas, theaters and other places of public entertainment. . . ." These Local Councils Ordinance, 1950, authorizes local councils to define the hours and days of rest and to restrict or prohibit the operation of "every service undertaking and public institution." In the past, local councils sometimes even enacted by-laws restricting traffic and closing movies and theaters on days of rest, and during Shabbat. In 1987, however, the Jerusalem Magistrate Court overruled such local by-laws declaring that limitations imposed on religious grounds must be enacted by the Knesset alone. The 1950 Law has since been amended to authorize local councils to regulate the opening and closing of businesses on explicitly religious grounds.

The Hours of Work and Rest Law, 1951, prohibits employing workers on days of rest. No work is permitted on the weekly day of rest, unless

[62] *Simcha Meron v. The Minister of Labour* (1970) 24(1) Piskey Din, 349.

permitted on an individual basis, by the Minister of Labor. The Minister may grant such permissions only if he is content that a full day interruption of work will jeopardize the defence of the state or the security of persons or property, or seriously prejudice the economy or a process of work or the supply of services which, in the opinion of the Minister, are essential to the public or part thereof. In special cases, general permits to work on a day of rest may be granted by the resolution of a special Committee of Ministers composed of the Prime Minister, the Minister of Religious Affairs, and the Minister of Labor. The volume of permits granted is substantially influenced by the political composition of the Government.

The Employment Service Law, 1959, as amended in 1988, provides further that the State Employment Agency, which is in charge of providing manpower, as well as private employment agencies, private employers or employment agencies may not discriminate against candidates on the grounds of their religion, race, nationality, origin, or political views. The Hours of Work and Rest Law provides, moreover, that "a person in need of an employee shall not refuse to accept a person for employment by reason only that on being accepted for employment such person states that in accordance with a prohibition imposed by commandments of his religion observed by him, he does not agree to work on days of rest. . . ." According to this law, only a person who observes the commandments of his religion may refuse to work on the days of rest prescribed by his religion. The Law authorizes an employer to demand such an employee to sign an affidavit attesting to his religious convictions and his observance of the commandments of his religion. He must also attest to his observance of dietary laws and abstention from travelling on the Shabbat. These prohibitions against discrimination on religious grounds do not apply to employers concerning with public security, hotels, or work connected with the maintenance of essential supplies and services.

Despite the efforts to avoid discrimination on religious grounds, several petitions have been filed in court claiming open discrimination against certain religious employees. This litigation has had mixed results. In response, a private bill, entitled "Prohibition of Discrimination in Work, 1994," was submitted to the Knesset. The bill prohibits direct or indirect discrimination on grounds of religion, views, or beliefs (among other grounds) in admission to work, work conditions, promotion, professional qualification or severance pay. The bill imposes on the employer the duty to prove that he did not discriminate on these grounds whenever the worker has proved that he seemingly fulfilled the conditions for admittance to work or for promotion. The bill provides, however, that discrimination which is required by the nature of a specific job is not regarded as prohibited discrimination. If passed into law, current prohibitions against religious discrimination in the workplace will be substantially strengthened.

It seems that more so than many other religious laws in Israel, Shabbat laws have caused divisiveness between the religious and the secular population. The Shabbat laws impose inconveniences on the non-observers such as lack of public transportation on Shabbat.[63] Until recently Israel had a six-day working week, and Shabbat was the only free day for Israelis to pursue their social and recreational activities. Israelis which did not own a car or could not afford a taxi, which does run on Shabbat, had limited options available for their day of rest. Currently, Israel is concluding a transgression to a five-day week, hence this discomfort is eased to some degree.

Holy Places[64]

Some of the most sacred sites of Judaism, Islam, and Christianity are in Israel—the Temple mount, the Western wall, and the Church of the Holy Sepulchre. Where holy sites are sacred to more than one religion, great disputes arise over control and access, disputes which are not always amenable to rational resolution.

Among Christian holy places, there are more than 200 churches and chapels of all Christian denominations in Israel. Until the crusades, from 1099 to 1313, the Greek Orthodox Patriarch held principal control over these and other Christian Holy Places, which other Christians had the right to visit and pray. During the crusades, the Latin Church gained ascendancy. At the time of the Ottoman rule, the Greek Orthodox Churches gradually gained control. At the same time, Western powers applied continuous pressure to obtain more concessions for the Roman Catholic Churches. In the eighteenth century, disputes among Christians regarding the holy places led to international political pressures on the Ottoman ruler, who in response froze the status quo, and defined in detail the rights of Catholic and Eastern (Greek) Orthodox Churches to various Holy Places. This arrangement was confirmed by the Treaty of Vienna in 1858.

At the end of World War I, when General Allenby entered Jerusalem leading the victorious British army, he announced that the British would

---

[63] The National Bus Carrier Egged is not permitted to run on the Shabbat.

[64] See Itzchak Englard, *The Legal Status of the Holy Places of Jersalem: Aspects of Law* (Jerusalem, 1973); Stephen J. Adler, "The Temple Mount in Court," *Biblical Archaeology Review* 5 (1991); Walter Zander,"On Settlement of Disputes About The Christian Holy Places," *Israel Law Review* 3 (1978): 331; Walter Zander, "Jurisdiction and Holiness: Reflections on the Coptic-Ethiopian Case," *Israel Law Review* 17 (1985): 245.

continue this status quo policy of the Treaty of Vienna. The Mandate writ, by virtue of which Britain gained control over Palestine, included an obligation to preserve existing rights and to ensure the requirements of public order and decorum in the holy places. Article 14 of the Mandate writ ordered the appointment of a special commission to study and define the rights and claims of the different religious communities in the holy places. The report of this committee, known as the Cust Report, still governs the area today. The Cust Report defines in detail the rites that may be practiced in each of the holy places by each religion, and the location and permitted times of worship. It relates to traditional places of the crucifixion and the burial of Jesus, which has been an object of Christian pilgrimage since the fourth century. The major area of contention relating to the holy Sepulchre is *Deir el Sultan.* Other problematic holy places in Jerusalem include the Tomb of the Virgin and the Sanctuary of the Ascension, which is holy to both Muslims and Christians. In Bethlehem, disputes have arisen over the Church of the Nativity, the Grotto of the Milk, and the Shepherd's Field.

From 1948 to 1967, when Jordan controlled East Jerusalem, Muslim and Christian holy places were protected, although Christian rights of access to them were limited. In 1953, Jordan passed laws restricting the right of Christian religious communities to own or purchase property near a holy place. In 1964, Jordan further limited Christian rights by prohibiting churches from purchasing real estate anywhere in Jerusalem.

During the Jordanian control over East Jerusalem, synagogues, Yeshivoth and cemeteries were damaged (intentionally) and sometimes destroyed. The most notorious example was the desecration of graves in the Jewish cemetery on the Mount of Olives, and the use of the tombstones for the construction of Jordanian army camps. In this same period, Jews were totally deprived of access to their holy places—in open violation of the cease-fire agreement. Even Israeli Muslims were not permitted to visit their holy places in East Jerusalem.

Following the 1967 war, the holy places in Jerusalem came under Israeli rule, and East Jerusalem was attached to the municipal area of the city of Jerusalem. Since then, Israeli law has guaranteed all residents freedom of religion, including freedom to perform their religious rites, subject to the limitation that they do not disrupt public order. Since this policy was enacted, many historical religious monuments have been discovered and restored by archeological explorations. The Israeli Government has strived to protect the holy places and to maintain public order, while guaranteeing free access and freedom of prayer for all.

Soon after the 1967 War, Israel applied its law, jurisdiction, and administration to East Jerusalem[65] and enacted the Protection of Holy Places Law, 1967. This law provides: "The holy places shall be protected from desecration or any other violation and from anything likely to violate the freedom of access of the members of the different religions to the places sacred to them or their feelings with regard to those places. . . ." The Law declared it a crime to desecrate or otherwise violate a holy place or to impede freedom of access to it. Indeed, it was the need to protect the holy places that served, in part, to justify the Israeli government's application of Israeli Law to East Jerusalem, which practically meant the annexation of it to Israel.

The Basic Law: Jerusalem, 1980 provides that united Jerusalem is the capital of Israel and repeats the provisions of the Protection of Holy Places Law—thus raising the protection of holy places to a constitutional level. The Penal Law, 1977 contains several sections relating to offenses against holy places: A person destroying, damaging, or desecrating a place of worship is liable to three years imprisonment. Trespassing on places of worship is punishable as a crime. The holy places in the West Bank, which are administrated by the Israeli military governor, are protected by an order of the Military Administration.

A 1924 Palestine (Holy places) Order in Council provides that "no cause or matter in connection with the Holy Places or religious buildings or sites in Palestine or the rights or claims relating to different religious communities in Palestine shall be heard or determined by any court in Palestine." The major ground for this legislation is no doubt the awareness of the difficulty in rulings in these matters based on legal tools. For this reason the authority was put in the hands of a non-judicial body. Originally, there was an intention to establish a special committee which would deal with these issues, however such a body has not been constituted. Since Basic Law: Government states that any authority of the State which is not allocated to a specific authority, shall be placed under the power of Government, this duty rests with the government.

The intention of the 1924 legislation was to enable legal and even political considerations to be taken into account. The Order in Council permits however the court to intervene in order to ensure public order and proper conduct in Holy Places. The Supreme Court ruled that it is up to the Courts to determine if the dispute in question involves substantial rights, in which case the matter is not in the authority of the court; if the issue does not relate to substantial rights, it may be tried in court.

---

[65] Asher Maoz, "On the Legal Status of the Golan Heights: Application of Israeli Law or Annexation? Application of Israeli Law to the Golan Heights is Annexation," *Brooklyn Journal of international Law* 20 (1992): 365.

The most renowned (and still unresolved) dispute over holy places is the Coptic-Ethiopian case. This conflict began in the Middle Ages, when the Ethiopians moved to the monastery of *Dier el Sultan*. This monastery is situated east of the Church of the Holy Sepulchre. Eventually, a bitter conflict over the monastery arose between the Ethiopian and Coptic churches—the Ethiopians claiming that they were expelled from the church and deprived of their rights to the monastery, the Copts maintaining that the monastery had always been theirs and that they had admitted the Ethiopians merely as their guests. (It should be noted that the Ethiopian church was derived from the Coptic church.[66]) At the time the status quo policies of the Ottoman Empire Treaty of Vienna were crafted, Copts held control over the area in dispute. The two rival churches sought, several times, to have Turkish and, later, British authorities resolve their dispute. After the Church of the Holy Sepulchre came under the control of Jordan, the Ethiopians presented a petition to a committee established by the government, which found the Ethiopian claim justified. This decision was later, inexplicably, reversed. This was the situation when Israel acquired control over East Jerusalem (and thus the site of the monastery) in 1967.

On Easter night, 1970, while the Coptic monks were praying in the Church of the Holy Sepulchre, the Ethiopians changed the locks of the doors to the passage of *Dier el Sultan* and seized possession. The police refused to intervene, and the Coptic Archbishop submitted a petition to the Supreme Court. The Court considered the Archbishop's claim to be justified in principle.[67] It issued an unqualified *order nisi*, though implementation was postponed in order to enable the Israeli government to deal with the substantive dispute in the manner they deemed fit. Following the Court's ruling, the government appointed a ministerial committee for the purpose of resolving the dispute. After attempting unsuccessfully to negotiate a settlement between the parties, however, the Committee resolved to work towards an atmosphere of peace and trust, in which, ultimately, an agreement might be reached. Unsatisfied with the process, the Coptic Archbishop submitted a second petition to the Supreme Court in 1977.[68] The Court denied the petition and refused to intervene, now arguing that it was up to the Israeli government to act. The Government has still not reached a solution, and apparently the Copts are considering yet another petition to the Supreme Court. The unhappy adventures of *Dier el Sultan* illustrate the intractability of dis-

[66] For a detailed history, see Kirsten Peoplessen, *The History of the Ethiopian Community in the Holy Land From the Time of Emperor Teodorus II till 1974* (Jerusalem, 1983).

[67] *The Coptic Patriarchate v. The Minister of Police* (1971) 25(1) Piskey Din 225.

[68] *The Coptic Patriarchate v. The Government of Israel* (1979) 33(1) Piskey Din, 225

putes over holy places, and the inherent limitations of judicial and governmental officials to resolve them.

Another source of dispute concerns registration of church properties in Israel. Since Christian Churches are not incorporated, there is no systematic means of registering their properties. In many cases, church property is held and registered in the name of its priest; this leads to disputes within the community and makes it difficult to discharge a priest. In addition, there is a long unsettled dispute between the Russian Delegation of the Moscow Patriarchate and the Russian Church in Exile over churches, monasteries, and other assets belonging to the Russian Orthodox Church.

A source of constant tension between Muslims and Jews relates to the Temple Mount, which is revered by both groups as the site where Abraham offered to sacrifice his son, Isaac. This is the Jews' most holy site, where Solomon's Temple and the Second Temple later stood. Muslims consider this their third most holy site, after Mecca and Medina. The disputes regarding the control of the site as well as the freedom to hold religious services there commenced soon after the 1967 war. Muslims claim absolute rights over the site; Jewish activists demand that Israel exercise control of the site, or at least enable Jews to have full access and the right of worship. What renders the dispute even more complicated is that Jewish Halakha prohibits indiscriminate entrance by Jews onto this holiest of sites. Governmental policy has sought a middle way among these competing concerns. Israeli authorities have allowed the *wakf* to continue their administration of the Temple Mount, while denying full right of access and worship to Jews. When Jewish claimants sued to gain greater access, the Supreme Court was ambivalent: it recognized the validity of the Jewish claim, yet abstained from fully implementing it.[69] On the one hand, the Court recognized that all religious groups must have freedom to worship on Temple Mount—not least, Jews for whom the Temple Mount was religiously central. On the other hand, the Court opined that it could not intervene while the matter was in the hands of Government regulators. Subsequent appeals to the Court to intervene were repeatedly denied.[70] The *modus vivendi* eventually introduced by the government, and upheld by the Court,[71] was to grant all individuals access to the Temple Mount to conduct their own silent prayers. However, public prayers by Jews are not permitted, nor are individuals allowed to carry

---

69 *National Circles v. Minister of Police* (1970) 42(2) Piskey Din 141, (1990), *Israel Yearbook on Human Rights* 20 (1990): 376.

70 See *Shtanger v. Government of Israel* (1981) 35(4) Piskey Din, 673.

71 *Kach Movement v. Minister of Religious Affairs* (1993) 47(2) Piskey Din, 1, (1990); *Israel Yearbook on Human Rights* 20 (1990): 376.

with them a prayer book or to wear any religious apparels such as *tfilin* and *talit.* Such acts, the government reasoned, would provoke Muslims into breaches of public order, that might end in tragic results for all parties.[72]

Jews and Muslims have also clashed over non-religious activities on Temple Mount. Jewish groups have claimed that construction work carried out by the *wakf* on Temple Mount results in destruction or damage to ancient sites and artifacts. Israeli authorities, however, chose not to prosecute the *wakf* for these acts, given the relative little damage that had been done. The government's decision was upheld by the Supreme Court on appeal, though the Court ordered the authorities to supervise the site and ensure no such damage occurs in the future.[73] In a similar case, where Jewish parties claimed that Muslim *wakfs* were performing unlicensed construction work on Temple Mount, and desecrating it by allowing Arab youths to hold picnics and ball games there,[74] the Court stated:

> In this petition we are dealing once again with the problem of enforcing Israeli law on the Temple Mount. There is no doubt that the rule of law demands strictness in the enforcing of the law, any law, in all of the area of the state and on all its citizens and inhabitants equally. Nevertheless, the appropriate authorities must exercise their discretion in a manner that will ensure that the enforcement of the law will be made reasonably, bona fide, logically and seriously. When the issues are related to The Temple Mount, with all the emotional, religious and political aspects involved, a special caution is demanded. [75]

Similar disputes between Jews and Muslims have broken out over access to the Cave of the Patriarchs, the place of burial of the patriarchs of both Jews and Muslims. Jewish law imposes no restriction on entrance onto this site. During the Jordanian era, however, secular law denied Jews any entrance. After 1967, Israeli law mandated joint use of the cave for worshippers. This led to constant conflicts between the two communities, for Muslims demanded exclusive rights to the cave. At the tragic height of the conflict, a fanatic Jew committed a massacre of Muslim worshippers. A state Commission of Inquiry was established following the event, and it concluded that the massacre was the result of individual

---

[72] A few years ago, during a Jewish licensed demonstration against this policy, masses of Muslims fortified in the Temple Mount and a deterioration in the situation led to riots and bloodshed.

[73] *Temple Mount Faithful Association v. Attorney General* (1993) 47(5) Piskey Din 122.

[74] *The Temple Mount Association v. The Mayor of Jerusalem* (1993) 47(5) Piskey Din 865.

[75] Ibid.

initiative.[76] Following this event, the military administration introduced total separation between Jewish and Muslim worshippers, and limited their numbers. Jews are also prohibited from entering the cave on Fridays, when the main Muslim services take place.

These disputes over holy sites demonstrate clearly the inherent limitations of any simple human rights solutions to religious conflict in Israel. The decisions that these disputes have generated also demonstrates Israel's sensitivity to the feelings and aspirations of non-Jewish religions and its dedication to respect them, even at the price of frustrating seemingly legitimate Jewish claims.

Future Developments

The future development of religious human rights in Israel will be shaped by at least two related events—the agreement recently signed between the Holy See and the State of Israel and the peace talks with Arab states and the Palestinians.

The fundamental agreement with the Holy See is of historic significance. The agreement marks a dramatic shift from the Church's traditional attitude towards Judaism. From the early dawn of Christianity, the Church regarded the destruction of the Temple and the exile of Jews from the Holy Land as proof of the divinity of Jesus and the abrogation of the Old Covenant in favor of the New. These acts were viewed as divine retaliation against the Jews for their rejection of Jesus. Moreover, the Church regarded itself as a replacement for the Jewish people. Christianity was thus hostile to the Jews throughout the Middle Ages. The Catholic Church, in particular, persecuted the Jews and sought to convert them, forcibly if necessary. Even in the new era, Christianity was not neutral toward Jews.

Particularly tragic was the silence of the Holy See during the atrocities of the Holocaust. It is no wonder that the Church developed a negative attitude towards the Zionist Movement which was seen as a faint attempt to end God's curse of exile.[77] Note, for example, the reply of Pope Pius X to Theodor Herzels' request for the Church's support of the Zionist cause: "We are unable to favor this movement. We cannot prevent the Jews from going to Jerusalem, but we could never sanction it. The Jews have not recognized our Lord, therefore we cannot recognize the Jewish people; and so if you come to Palestine to settle your people there, we will be ready with churches and priests to baptize all of you."

---

[76] *Report of the Investigation Committee Regarding the Massacre at the Cave of the Patriarchate* (Jerusalem, 1994) (Hebrew).

[77] D. Rosen, "Vatican-Israel Relations: The Jewish Perspective," *Justice* 3 (1994): 22.

The establishment of the State of Israel posed both a theological and political problem for the Vatican. On a theological level, this event meant the revival of the "condemned" people of Israel in the Holy Land. On a political level, the event triggered war between Israel and its neighboring Arab states. Global international interests as well as concern for the many Arab Christians in Arab countries forced the church into silence about Israel. Moreover, the Vatican could not simply disregard the holy Christian sites that fell within the jurisdiction of Israel. A special problem was presented by the most holy places in East Jerusalem,[78] which came under Israeli control after 1967. The State of Israeli would have to be dealt with.

The appointment of Pope John XXIII signified a radical change in the attitude of the Church towards the Jews. The document known as the *Nostre aetate*, issued in 1965 by the Second Vatican Council, officially rejected the idea of Jewish responsibility for the death of Jesus. This document enabled the church to accept a Jewish state, and provided the cornerstone for building a new relationship between the two parties. In 1985, the Vatican Commission for Religious Relations with the Jews issued a document stating the importance of the state of Israel for the Jewish people. After the promulgation of this document, the present pope, John Paul II, made several declarations condemning anti-semitism and recognizing the centrality of Israel for the Jews. Moreover, the Middle Eastern peace process, starting with the peace treaty between Egypt and Israel and continuing with peace negotiations with other Arab countries and the PLO, paved the way for the normalization of the relations between the Vatican and the state of Israel.

The current pope has dramatically changed the Holy See's theological stance toward the Jews, spurning the Church's traditional negativism and aloofness. Until recently, his relations with Israel were based on a de facto recognition of Israel; the only visit of a pope to Israel was purely private. Since that visit there was extensive talk of visits by other high clergy to the Holy Land; these never matured, possibly because of the political embarrassment they might cause. Though there were no official visits, there were meetings between representatives of the State of Israel and the Vatican. These eventually led to the signing of the Fundamental Agreement between Israel and the Holy See on December 30th 1993, in Jerusalem and at the Vatican.

This agreement was, in part, a product of the emerging peace process in the Middle East. Most Catholics in Israel and the territories administered by Israel identify themselves as Palestinian; they had opposed any relations between Israel and the Vatican until Palestinian political claims

---

[78] A. Macchi, "Vatican-Israel Relations: The Catholic Perspective," *Justice* 3 (1994): 26.

were satisfied. The peace talks between Israel and the PLO removed this obstacle to Vatican-Israeli relations. Moreover, the Catholic Church had substantial interests in Jerusalem and various holy places in Israel, and its representatives did not wish to be left out of any peace treaties between Israel and the Palestinians and other Arab states.

The agreement between Israel and the Vatican does not deal expressly with the problem of Jerusalem. Earlier, the Holy See had supported the internationalization of Jerusalem, a policy recommended in 1947 by the General Assembly of the United Nations. Since the 1967 war, representatives of the Vatican have abandoned this demand, yet formally this is still its official stand. The Agreement is silent on this contentious issue. Instead, it provides a number of provisions concerning the Church's rights in holy places.[79] Article 5, for example, commits both parties to favoring Christian pilgrimages to the Holy Land. In other articles, both parties agree to maintain the status quo respecting control, access, and use of the Christian holy sites.[80]

The holy places of Jerusalem were subject to additional references in the 1994 Peace Treaty between the state of Israel and the Hashemite Kingdom of Jordan. Article 9 includes a commitment to provide mutual freedom of access to places of religious and historical nature. It further commits Israel to respect Jordan's "special" role in the Muslim holy shrines, which consists of appointing the administration of the Temple Mount and paying their salaries out of the Jordanian Ministry of Religious Endowment, and planning and financing the restoration of the Golden Dome of the Omar Mosque. The same Article has an opaque paragraph stating that "when negotiations on the permanent status will take place, Israel will give high priority to the Jordanian historic role in these shrines. . . ." This language might suggest that Jordan may participate in the negotiations between Israel and the Palestinians, though several commentators have dismissed this suggestion. Other commentators have argued that this provision in the Jordan-Israel treaty is incompatible with the 1993 declaration of principles signed with the PLO, which left the problem of Jerusalem open for future negotiations. Yet Israel has assumed no specific obligations to Jordan in negotiations over the holy places in Jerusalem. At most, Israel has committed itself to adopting a favorable attitude to Jordan's interests.

---

[79] R. Lapidoth, "Jerusalem: The Legal and Political Background," *Justice* 3 (1994): 7.

[80] Despite this provision, in a letter by Israel's Minister of Foreign Affairs presented to his Norwegian counterpart on October 1993, the role of certain Palestinian institutions in East Jerusalem was recognized, including those relating to the Christian and Muslim holy places. The legal status of this document is unclear and is subject to conflicting interpretations. One of the opinions expressed regards the vagueness of the letter as intentional, thus stressing the idea that it is of no binding authority.

The agreement with Jordan has aroused much antagonism from Palestinians as well as criticism from other Arab states, such as Morocco, which claim special interests in Muslim holy places in Jerusalem. Representatives of the Russian Patriarch of Moscow have made similar claims, and have asked to participate in any future negotiations for their final settlement. A research group operating within the Jerusalem Institute for Israeli Studies, which is of no official status, has studied the issue and delivered its finding and recommendations to the Israeli Government.[81] From what has been published about this putative secret report, it seems that the team has mapped all the holy sites in Jerusalem, and found that there are 65 active mosques in East Jerusalem and several cemeteries. The team has also noted that the *wakf* administration is endeavoring to expand the list of Muslim holy places. The team has compiled various historical proposals for resolution of the problem of Jerusalem.

It seems clear that the present Israeli Government will not consider any solution that leaves any part of Jerusalem beyond Israeli sovereignty. The PLO, on the other hand, demands the withdrawal of Israel from all territories occupied by it during the 1967 war, leaving full control over East Jerusalem to the Palestinians. The Hamas, a fundamental Islamic terror movement which enjoys large support within the Palestinian population, have adopted even more radical views. Egypt has expressed its views on the matter in letters attached to the Camp-David agreements with Israel. Egypt supports Palestinian control over East Jerusalem and opposes all steps taken by Israel to change the status of the city. Jordan, on the other hand, wishes to regain control over Muslim shrines in Jerusalem and restore its historic role there.[82]

The holy places are the chief stumbling blocks of the current peace talks between Israel and the Palestinians, and they will be the last item to be negotiated. All parties now have, at least publicly, taken uncompromising stands. If agreement can be reached on all other matters, thereby making real the possibility of peace in the region, these conflicting stands may soften.

---

[81] M. Hirsch, D. Housen-Couriel, supervised by R. Lapidot, *The Jerusalem Question: Proposals for its Resolution.*

[82] The position of Jordan regarding the status of Jerusalem is of great importance in view of the ties which exist today between Jordan and the city and in light of the peace agreement with Israel. Until 1974 Jordan demanded the restoration of its control over East Jerusalem and the West Bank. Following the Arab summit conference at Rabat in 1974, which affirmed the Palestinian right to self determination in the territories occupied by Israel, the Jordanian stand towards Jerusalem modified. Jordanian new policy called for the establishment of a federation between the West Bank and Jordan. At present Jordan expresses its desire to regain control over Moslem shrines in Jerusalem and restore its historic role there.

The word "Jerusalem" *(yerushalayim)* in the Hebrew language comprises two nouns: peace *(shalom)* and wholeness *(shalem)*. Let us hope that its destiny will be one of an undivided city of eternal peace.

Africa's Search For Religious Human Rights Through Returning to Wells of Living Water

JOHN S. POBEE
World Council of Churches, Geneva

Religion: One Major Spring of Human Life

It is my assumption and *first thesis that religion of one sort or another is one of the living springs of human beings, if not the living spring, and thus influences the course of people's lives.* It was George Bernard Shaw who wrote that "religion is a great force—the only real motive force in the world; but what you fellows don't understand is that you must get at a man through his own religion and not through yours."[1] Certainly *homo Africanus homo religiosus radicaliter*, for African cultures have a religious epistemology and ontology. Religion as a carrier of human and liberatory values, has the capacity to inspire people to do what is right rather than worship at the altar of expediency and self-interest. Those values are too long to list here but they include love, justice, decency, human dignity and rights, honesty, decent education, housing, and concern for the poor. The Nigerian writer Akinpelu has expressed traditional African moral values and virtues to include "honesty, integrity, chastity, vivacity, modesty, toleance, truthfulness, self-discipline and brotherliness, honor, humility, patience, industry, self-control and many more from the bag of virtues. . . ."[2]

[1] George Bernard Shaw, *Getting Married. The Play* (1914).

[2] J.A. Akinpelu "Values in Nigerian Society," in id., *New Perspectives in Moral Education* (Lagos, 1983), 36.

J.D. van der Vyver and J. Witte, Jr. (eds.), Religious Human Rights in Global Perspective, 391-415.

Confession of Healthy Cynicism About Rights

I must confess to cynicism about superficial and glib talk of human rights—not only in Africa, but in many other contexts as well. At least three things lead me to such cynicism.

First, originally discussions of rights did not mean rights for everyone, but predominantly rights for the middle class. The upper class had rights already; workers and women were not on the agenda. It required a suffragette movement to put women on the agenda in the nineteenth and twentieth centuries. After the American Civil War, the Thirteenth and Fourteenth Amendments to the United States Constitution were introduced, conferring the rights and duties of citizens, including the right to vote, on newly freed slaves. But the word "male" was introduced into the amendments, thus excluding women from these rights. White women were told to be patient.

Today, however, women still do not enjoy full equality of rights with men. In the 1970s, the United Nations found it necessary to declare the International Decade of the Woman to make the peoples of the world conscious of the rights of women in our own times. At the Nairobi gathering to mark the end of the Decade, a delegate of the World Council of Churches (WCC) said: "[T]he churches had not been sufficiently aware of the Decade; and in many churches, the position of women has not improved in the last ten years."[3] At the time of writing this chapter, the WCC is at the mid-point of the Ecumenical Decade of the Churches in Solidarity with Women, declared at Easter 1988. The WCC by this declaration has challenged the churches to explore critically the matter of "women's full participation in church and community life; women's perspectives on and commitment to justice, peace and the integrity of creation; women doing theology and sharing spirituality."[4] The International Labour Organization continues to struggle to champion the cause of the rights of workers.

The modern concept of human rights has been very much shaped by the Judaeo-Christian tradition, which for long has been the texture of Euro-American and Byzantine cultures. That tradition has become part of the collective consciousness of humanity. That tradition, however, was not exactly conscious of the full spread of cultures on the globe. Its original statements of human rights were thus, dare I say, inherently limited. Today, we are struggling to expand the concept of human rights, and their scope on the ground, in practice. As yet, we have not completely overcome the flaws in the concept of human rights or accord rights to all.

---

[3] Cited in Mercy Oduyoye, *Who will Roll the Stone Away?* (Geneva, 1990), 1.

[4] Ibid., 9.

We need to revisit the contours of the origins of the concept of human rights for the purpose of updating and renewing it for this time and this place. We may not assume that the traditional statements of it are the last word, high sounding as they may be. The directions in which a revisit may proceed, shall be returned to in due course.

A second reason for my cynicism is that much of the discussion of human rights is a case of "putting the cart before the horse." The first question should be the old question: what is humanity? In the Judaeo-Christian tradition the Psalmist asks: "What are human beings that you are mindful of them, Mortals that you care for them?" (Psalm 8:4). The question needs today's answer. Only then can we come to the question of what instruments, vehicles, and rights will carry and secure the integrity, identity, and dignity of that human being.

But here the problem begins, for there is a demonstrable crisis today about what it is to be human. One index of the crisis is the widespread poverty not only in Africa, but even in the so-called countries of the North. That story of widespread poverty represents a culture of hopelessness, stripping peoples, sometimes deliberately, of hope. It represents marginalization, and homelessness, even in places like London, New York, and Rome in the midst of affluence. It represents massive public suffering and the cry of abandonment.[5] Another index of the crisis is the culture of violence. We see this culture in the wars and genocide in Africa and other continents, in the widespread violent crime perpetrated by young teenagers in the United States, in the assault and battering to death of a two-year-old by two ten-year-old boys in Lancashire, England. (This latter story raises a fundamental question about the assumed innocence of the youth. Can a human child still be assumed to be innocent or credited with innocence?) Yet another index is the apparent increase in ugly ethnicity, in racially-motivated acts of violence in Europe (Germany, France, Great Britain, and the former Yugoslavia), in the United States, and in Africa (Republic of South Africa, Burundi, Uganda, and elsewhere). (Later, I shall suggest that religion is sometimes a factor in these acts of violence.). We are together in a crisis concerning what it is to be human, across the nations and regions and continents of the world as well as across religions. *The universality of the crisis in the global village calls for an ecumenical broaching of the subject of what it is to be human today—ecumenical in the sense of global, inter-church, inter-faith, inter-cultural.*

Discussions of human rights all too often begin with recitations of the United Nations Declaration of Human Rights. It is my submission that those freedoms are meaningless unless they are rooted in a profound and

[5] See John S. Pobee, "Mission from Below," *Mission Studies* 10 (1-2) (1993): 159.

healthy sense of what it is to be human. Here again we confront the crisis with regard to anthropology. Semitic-biblical anthropology has been hardly reconstructed meaningfully and articulately since the encounter with modern science and technology. The anthropology implied in science and technology itself has proven unsatisfactory—under the impact of technology and economics a human being is primarily a potential consumer rather than a human being with rights, talents, and potential. The consequence is that many from these backgrounds yearn for the esoteric and transcendental, sometimes, if not often, of a crude nature.

The anthropology implied in Marxism-Leninism seems to have crumbled partly because people who made avowals of Marxism-Leninism lived a lie. As Harold J. Berman has written: "The collapse of Communism was primarily a moral collapse, a spiritual collapse. Soviet socialism preached altruism, social responsibility, and honesty—but it practiced self-seeking, corruption, and deception. A primary reason for that failure . . . was its doctrine of the fundamental goodness, and consequently the self-sufficiency of man and its lack of belief in a transcendent order, personal salvation, and an eternal life. If honesty is only a virtue and not a divine commandment, it lacks the necessary element of sanctity, and it will be discarded when it becomes expedient."[6] Similarly, Her Excellency Mohtarma Benazir Bhutto, Prime Minister of the Islamic Republic of Pakistan, said in her address at the 50th Session of the Commission of Human Rights: "Communism was not defeated by capitalism or by the forces of NATO; it was defeated by humanism. In the words of Czech President Havel, in his essay entitled *The End of the Modern Era*, 'Communism was not defeated by military forces, but by the human spirit, by consciences, by the resistance of man to manipulation. It was defeated by a revolt of human individuality against imprisonment within a uniform ideology'."[7]

Traditional African anthropology has not been immune from the crisis of anthropology—it has not been reconstructed since the assault on it by Christian and Western cultures, touched by such ideologies as social Darwinism, racism, colonialism, imperialism, and Christendom. Indeed, *homo Africanus* has had to go in the image and likeness of the Caucasian, resulting in some identity crisis. We cannot hope to look for the rights of an entity we do not precisely know in its integrity. And so, I come to reiterate my thesis that clarification of a renewed anthropology is a prerequisite for the search for human rights and that clarification must be made

---

[6] Harold J. Berman, "Christianity and Democracy in the Soviet Union," in John Witte, Jr., ed., *Christianity and Democracy in Global Context* (Boulder, CO/San Francisco, 1993), 287, 295.

[7] Speech to the United Nations Human Rights Commission, Winter, 1994.

with ecumenical sensitivity. That anthropological quest is a religious as well as a spiritual quest.

My third reason for cynicism is the discrepancy between the ideal and the reality of human rights. Consider the track record of those who are most vocal on human rights. From the 1940s to 1960s, the British government of the nation which went to war against Germany to protect human dignity and freedom, locked away African leaders whose only alleged "crime" was to ask for political independence for their peoples. Ghana can cite the fate of the "big six."[8] Kenya can cite the story of Jomo Kenyatta. Malawi can cite the story of Kamuzu Hastings Banda. The British tried, so to speak, to deny the Africans the right to govern or misgovern themselves. The reason for this is, in part at any rate, anthropological: the peoples of the tropical regions were deemed infants to be taken in hand by the peoples of the temperate zones.

Similarly, the racism of the Republic of South Africa and Southern Rhodesia (now Zimbabwe), where white minority regimes in the name of preserving "Christian civilization" trampled the majority Blacks under foot, also illustrates the same point. The tragedy is that the very African leaders who won independence turned to beat their own peoples mercilessly.

The government of the United States, the archpriest of human rights at least by rhetoric, was hand-in-glove with oppressive regimes in Chile and El Salvador. In El Salvador, for example, they supported an oppressive rightist regime in the name of fighting communists, even though some of the measures followed by the El Salvador military were atrociously anti-human. Archbishop Romero writes: There was "the increasing danger that is represented by the military and to El Salvador, especially, the new concept of special warfare, which consists of eliminating in a murderous way all the efforts of the popular organizations, using the pretext of communism or terrorism. This kind of war purports to do away not only with the people directly responsible but also with their families, who according to this theory, are totally poisoned by these terrorist concepts and must be eliminated."[9] Similarly, on the African continent, in spite of seemingly right rhetoric, the United States under President Reagan was lukewarm in confronting apartheid in the Republic of South Africa and supported Jonas Savimba of UNITA in a bloody and vicious war in Angola, which took a heavy toll on the lives of Angolans.

---

[8] John S. Pobee, *Kwame Nkrumah and the Church in Ghana 1949-1966* (Accra, 1988), 18ff.; Dennis Austin; *Politics in Ghana 1946-1960* (London, 1964).

[9] Archbishop Oscar Romero, *A Shepherd's Diary*, Irene B Hodgson, trans. (Cincinnati, 1993), 493, 497.

In February 1994, Prime Minister Bhutto of Pakistan and Prime Minister Tunsa Ciller paid a five-hour visit to embattled Sarajevo, the capital of Bosnia. In a joint statement, the two described the "appalling human tragedy" in the heart of a "continent which prides itself on its commitment to human rights and respect for human dignity." To this, Tunsa Ciller added that "values are no good unless we defend them."[10] *There must be congruence and consistency between the rhetoric and the practice of human rights. The importance of credible rhetoric in regard to human rights is a condition for achievement in the area of human rights.*

We cannot remain in our cynicism, however, for a renewed understanding of human rights is a necessary tool for justice, peace, and dignity. The task is, in part at any rate, to state the issue correctly and realistically in the contemporary context. This entails that we return and revisit the living wells of our respective traditions, especially the religious traditions. Since we cannot go straight from old traditions to modern day, we must look anew at the traditions so as to remove blockages and release the liberating power of tradition. *A tested and renewed tradition is the living well from which the stream of human rights will arise and flow.*

Religion in Africa

Religious Pluralism. Africa is the second largest continent. The ancient and the modern stand together on one continent and even in one country, thanks to the experience and encounter with colonialism, Western culture, Christian culture, Islam, and others. For all these external influences, African cultures, with their strong religious component, hold their ground. There is a plurality of peoples, races, cultures, and religions. Present nation-states have been welded out of congeries of tribes and, in some cases, races. Thus the search for human rights in Africa must not proceed with simplistic generalizations, but proceed in a context of pluralism—religious, cultural, ethnic, and racial.

One can discern at least four sets of religious pluralism in Africa. First, in some areas Islam dominates—as in Senegal (91%), Mali (80%), Sudan (73%), and the Gambia (84%). Second, in other areas Christianity dominates—as in Ghana (62%), Kenya (73%), the Uganda (78.3%), Republic of South Africa (79.2%), Namibia (96.3%), and Zimbabwe (58%). Third, in still other areas, traditional religions have an edge on others—as in Burkina Faso (Upper Volta), with traditional religions (44.8%), Muslims (43%), and Christians (12.2%). Fourth, in areas like Nigeria, Christians and Muslims are about equal in numbers. These different scenarios

---

[10] Reported in *Time* (February 7, 1994): 51.

have different dynamics in relationships, which dynamics are also very much determined by non-religious factors such as inherited power structures and misperceptions. For example, sometimes what is denounced as discrimination may well be an attempt to correct injustices done in earlier times, and people, especially the beneficiaries, not wishing to see a change in the *status quo*.

To be fully comprehensive, I would like to add a fifth scenario, where the state declares itself to be atheist, as in the case of Ethiopia under Mengistu Haile Mariam. Though Ethiopia had a long tradition of being a Christian nation, Mengistu installed an administration that was committed to militant atheism and religious intolerance. While I do not hold a brief for Mengistu's misdeeds, he might well have been emboldened to do what he did because the dictatorship of the church under the Emperor Haille Selasie gave him a pretext.

I cite this story to say that our concern for religious human rights must include the rights and behavior of the non-religious. Indeed, the freedom to be non-religious is as important as the freedom to be religious. *Religious human rights includes the freedom to be religious or not to believe, without suspicion, prejudice, or fear of retribution.* The Mengistu story is past history. But the issue of non-religious governments cannot be ignored. In Mozambique, FRELIMO imposed a Marxist-Leninist ideology with the aim of unifying the country. Many a time fears are expressed about the African National Congress government because of its ties with the South African Communist Party. Maybe, we need healing from our pathological fear of communism and the other religions!

The different dynamics revealed in these relationships leads me to another thesis: *a person's freedom of conscience is the key to essential human and religious rights*. By that we understand the freedom to make choices in respect of one's religious commitments. Conscience becomes the sanctuary of personal autonomy, which must be respected: "Freedom of conscience and religion implies freedom not only to adhere to a religious faith, but also to leave the faith, to change one's religious beliefs and practices . . . because God cannot be worshipped under compulsion, and human conscience is by nature destined to search for the truth and that ultimately is God Himself, the Creator of Conscience and the redeemer of men."[11]

Religious Fundamentalism. Today there is heightened concern for religious fundamentalism—not only in Africa. The violence and carnage that happened at New York's Trade Center in 1993 has time and again

[11] Roland Minerath, "Freedom of Religion: A Challenge for Peace in the Teaching of the Catholic Church," in *Freedom of Religion: Hope for Lasting Peace and Unity. Proceedings of the All African Religious Liberty Congress* (Nairobi, September 1991), 47.

been cited as evidence of the negative nature of Islamic fundamentalism. On the African continent, Algeria, Egypt, and the Sudan are tense because of the activities of Islamic Fundamentalists. Afrikaaner nationalism is fed by a certain Reformed Church fundamentalism.

The term "fundamentalism" is often misused, however. Fundamentalism is not the preserve of Islam; there are Christian fundamentalists, too. Moreover, "fundamentalism" is not really a helpful word. As the Nigerian Muslim scholar Oloyede writes:

> Is it offensive of a friend or neighbour, considered rightly or wrongly as dying, to gain consciousness and jump back to life? Non-Muslim writers on Islamic resurgence often make the assumption that the resurgence of Islam is a negative development. It ought to be noted that the Islamic resistance to external onslaught is a duty which Muslims owe to their Creator, and this resistance should be given an attention that is no less than the attention being given to the forces which Islam finds itself resisting. Justice and freedom, in our opinion, are prerequisites for peace and harmony.[12]

Fatima Mear, an Indian South African, Muslim woman and activist, has also written:

> [F]undamentalism means going back to the basics of something, getting back to the essentials of religion. To ascribe all that has gone wrong in Iran and elsewhere to Islamic fundamentalism is to suggest that at heart Islam is a fanatical, disruptive religion. By implication it means that the West is only prepared to accept a form of Islam which adapts to its demands and standards. This is imperialist jingoism. It smacks of talk of colonialism being for the good of the natives! It must be condemned in the strongest possible terms, because it creates a moral milieu within which it becomes acceptable to do almost anything to crush the demon. The dispossession of the Palestinian people, the founding of the exclusivistic Zionist State of Israel and the expectation that Palestinians should accept their violation is a case in point. The average person in the West hears of conflict in Palestine and assumes that the Palestinians are to blame.
>
> The history of colonialism and religious proselytism has turned people of different cultures, religions and races into enemies. The anti-Islamic hysteria concerning Muslim fundamentalism tells us that the ravages of colonial conquest are not yet over."[13]

---

[12] I.O. Oloyede, "A Muslim's Response" in John S. Pobee et al., eds., *Encounter of Religions in African Cultures* (Geneva, 1991), 122.

[13] Cited in Charles Villa-Vicencio, *The Spirit of Hope* (Johannesburg, 1993), 183-184.

This quotation underlines that a good deal of the discussion in terms of fundamentalism is not helpful, for the term itself is laced with prejudice. We need to distinguish religious reactionism or renewal or reawakening, which is the real point of fundamentalism, from the excesses which are not of the *esse* of the faith. We need to negotiate the essential faith from the cultural and other additives and to channel it into creative activity in the search for peace with justice.

However, it is not enough to lament and condemn the excesses of some who claim to be going back to the basics of the religions. *It is necessary to address the issues which turned people to violent actions in the name of a return to fundamentals of the faith. Often they include issues of human dignity.* Bruce Nelan writes:

> [A]lmost every secular Arab state from North Africa to the Persian Gulf confronts a fundamentalist threat. . . . "The Problems in Egypt . . . stem from problems in Egypt. . . ." Egypt is plagued by a pervasive discontent with the country's poverty, unemployment and corruption and widespread conviction that things are not getting better. The slogan "Islam is the solution" is embraced by millions of impoverished Egyptians who have been completely disillusioned by the failures of Arab nationalism and socialism. "The nation's difficulties are multiplied by its unchecked population growth. Young, educated Arabs who have no job prospects, even as taxi drivers have been willing recruits to fundamentalism." These people are coming not only from the slums but also from the middle class.[14]

The governments have not behaved themselves: When the moderate Muslim Brotherhood applied in 1992 to become a political party, the government declined the application.

Similarly in Algeria, the government did not accept the victory of the fundamentalists at the first round Parliamentary elections in 1991. In so doing, the government denied people the freedom to decide whom they wish to govern them and forced the people into underground activity. The story now is the struggle of the populist Islamic Fundamentalist Movement to overthrow an army-backed state which annulled the country's free elections in order to keep the fundamentalists out of power. The struggle has been bloody and costly.[15] In many African countries those associated with Islam often had low status—they were slaves, servants, petty-traders, and the like. It is those indices of marginalization that lie at the root of the violence done in the name of fundamentalism. In any case,

---

[14] Bruce W. Nelan, "Bombs in the Name of Allah" *Time* (August 30, 1993): 23.

[15] Lara Marlowe, "Algeria—No One is Safe" *Time* (February 7, 1994): 38-39; Christopher Dickey and Marcus Mabry, "Powder Keg: Algeria: Islamic Militants Have Launched a New Jihad," *Newsweek* (February 7, 1994) :6-11.

as George Bernard Shaw says in *Major Barbara*: "I can't talk religion to a man with bodily hunger in his eyes."[16] Religious human rights and life in its fullness are inseparable.

Missionary Vocation of Some Religions. Of the religions on the African continent, Christianity and Islam, the two most significant, are avowed missionary religions. The ultimate goal of God's mission through Christ was and is to bring into being a common human community in justice, peace, and wholeness. But all too often, in the name of mission, people have been manipulated, bludgeoned, forced into submission. The responses of the Third World to mission are well known.

In a proper Christian view, "mission" has three dimensions: proclamation (sometimes called evangelism), making disciples, and engagement with the socio-ethical imperative laid out in the values of the kingdom of God. The problem is the model or models that have been chosen to carry out this threefold task. Missions are most effective if two conditions are met. First, missions must be the process of building community of communities guided by the values of God's rule, namely sacrificial love, truth, justice and righteousness, freedom, reconciliation, and peace. *We must pursue a model of missions that, from start to finish, respects and fosters human dignity of all and in community.* Second, every effort should be made to keep the autonomy of the religion apart from secular power. In Algeria, for example, the Islamic Salvation Front (ISF) has sought to turn the country into a theocratic state. That proposition has become particularly attractive, because the one-party socialist government has been synonymous with 30 years of misrule and economic mismanagement. And so, there are some rather tough issues: "[A]t the heart of the deepening crisis lies the conundrum of democracy. When a party calling for Islamic law stands to win a free election, should their wishes be respected if their use of democracy endangers the lives and freedom of opponents."[17] The same question needs to be put to states that have had Christian culture.

African Anthropology. One must look beyond a democratic tempering of the excesses of Islam and Christianity, however, to come to terms with religious human rights in Africa. Earlier on, attention was drawn to the crisis of anthropology everywhere. A major aspect of the pursuit of religious human rights in Africa is helping to secure a healthy anthropology. A sound anthropology should not be prefabricated, for a person's identity is formed by social forces and experiences of one's con-

---

[16] George Bernard Shaw, *Major Barbara*, 1907, Act II.

[17] Marlowe, "Algeria—No One is Safe," 39.

text and by one's response to those factors. But one's response is in turn linked with how God has made us.

As we search for a renewed anthropology as a basis for religious human rights in Africa, I believe the Christian idea of humanity in God's image and likeness and the African idea of *Ubuntu* need to be explored ecumenically. The Christian idea has been much developed. Let me here concentrate on the African contribution. The concept of *Ubuntu* asserts that each person is endowed with inner energy called *seriti* (Tswana), or *Isithunzi* (Xhosa). It is a force or presence in us originating in God. This inner energy is one's dignity or personality. Thus a human being is not only a physical body, trapped in the material reality; a human being also has potential, is thoughtful, is endowed with self-control, is given to justice, and is given to serve the purposes of God in the world. Stanley Mogoba, bishop of the Methodist Church of South Africa comments as follows: "[I]t has to do with realizing one's full potential as a person. This is an affirmation of a way of life that embodies the qualities of decency, honesty, integrity and respect for others. It means that when somebody behaves in an untrustworthy way, that person is in danger of losing his or her humanity. Wherever people are strongly to regain their humanity or to promote the human cause, I believe that God is at work."[18]

There is, however, another dimension to African anthropology. *Homo africanus'* epistemology and ontology is *cognatus sum, ergo sum*[19]— "I have blood relatives, therefore I am." In other words, one is human to the extent that he or she is integrated into a community. Of course, in the ecumenical context, we need to transcend the narrow kinship base of community to a wider concept. In other words, we need also to be freed from contextually imposed presuppositions so as to encounter other races, ideologies, and religions. That is why as we search for a renewed anthropology I would take lessons from the ecumenical emphasis on *Koinonia*. The basic meaning of this Greek word is participation. You are human to the extent that you participate in the whole, sharing the symbols, stories, memories, and practices which weld communities together. This creates a sense of belonging. But one has to watch that participation does not become conformism, opportunism, and absorption into other's values. I am pleading for a broad ecumenical vision and an inclusive understanding of human existence.

Equally important is it to find renewed models of being in community. The family model, which Africans opt for, needs renewal as my comments on *cognatus sum, ergo sum* suggest. I do believe the major re-

---

[18] Ibid.

[19] John S. Pobee, "An African Christian in Search of Democracy," Witte, ed., *Christianity and Democracy in Global Context*, 278.

ligious players in Africa have ideas to help. I have already highlighted the Christian emphasis on *Koinonia*. Helpful as a starting point also will be the Islamic idea of *ahl-al-kitab*, which is the designation of Christianity and Judaism as "Religions of the Book" and therefore, of a common parentage and therefore, protected religions (*dhimmah*). That is, the adherents of those religions are under the protection of God and have full rights to the protection of the Islamic state.

African Case Studies

With that background, I wish now to take some case studies of religious human rights in illustrative African nations.

Nigeria. The modern Federal Republic of Nigeria was created by the British out of a number of protectorates in 1914. It gained political independence in 1960. The Federation falls into three geographical areas. The North is the home of Islamic Hausa (16.8%), Fulani (10.3%), with minorities in Plateau, Benin, Gongola and parts of Kaduna which are Christian and Animist. The West is very much Yoruba (17.8%). The East is largely Ibo (17.5%), who are largely Christian and Animist; it also has some significant minorities —Ijaws and Ogonis who produce about 80% of Nigeria's wealth because of the oil industry. Thus there is a mixture of ethnic numbers, economic power, plural religion.

Since 1922, Nigeria has had seven constitutions: Clifford Constitution (1922), Richards (1946), Macpherson (1951), Lyttleton, (1954), Independence (1960), Republican (1979), and the Untested Constitution of 1989. In spite of all these constitutions, the country has experienced instability not only because of the interference of the military but also because of the more basic issue of welding a nation out of distinct groups. There is a lesson to be learned: Constitutions *per se* do not lead to democracy and human dignity and peace. There must be a fundamental willingness to make it work and then to seek such aids as freedom of the press, an independent judiciary, police that are for the nation and not the government, and a Ministry of Justice that does not protect corrupt government officials.

For our purposes, two things in particular are important for understanding religious human rights in Nigeria: corruption and religious pluralism. It is no secret that corruption has permeated the fabric of the Nigerian national polity, and corruption has been institutionalized and systematized. History teaches that saints are not made by acts of parliament; religious institutions are meant to be the moral conscience of society. They are key players in the fight against corruption, which necessarily denies some people their dignity. It follows that the right and freedom to live one's religion is an important aspect of national life.

Nigeria has for long been religiously pluralistic. In 1921, tribal religions comprised 56.8% of the population, Islam 39%, and Christianity 4.3%. These ratios have changed dramatically over time. In 1931, tribal religions comprised 50% of the population, Islam 43.6%, Christianity 6.3%. In 1953, the ratios were 32.8% tribal, 45.3% Islam, and 21.9% Christian; in 1963, 18.7% tribal, 43.4% Islam, 37.9% Christian; in 1975, 8.0% tribal, 44.5% Islam, 47.2% Christian; and in 1980 5.6% tribal, 45% Islam, 49% Christian. So Islam and Christianity are key players in national life. And indeed, in all the upheavals that the nation has been through, it has been made out that it is in part a struggle between the Islamic North and Christian South.

The administration of General Babaginda quietly and without public debate joined Nigeria to the Organisation of Islamic States. That rankled Christians. There were riots in the North in which many Christians and some Muslims died. Against that background came the famous clause 6 of the 1989 draft constitution in which it was proposed to introduce Shari'a law into the Constitution.[20] The Shari'a law has been in this century a politically inspired imposition which has been as damaging to Muslim-Christian relations as have been the imperialization of Christianity and Islam and the crusades. In the ensuing debate it was decided that the state was not to adopt any religion as the religion of the state. Further, every Nigerian was to be free to practice his or her own religion undisturbed.

Every time the issue of incorporation of the Shari'a is raised, a lot of heat, often irrational, is generated. But that issue has to be faced in pluralistic Nigeria as elsewhere. Let Dr. Abdul Lateef Adegbite, the Secretary General of the Nigerian Supreme Council of Islamic Affairs, speak the plea of the Muslims in Nigeria. He says that the 1989 proposal for the inclusion of the Shari'a "provides that those states (in Nigeria) that operate Shari'a courts are free to retain them if they so wished, just as those states which do not have the courts may establish theirs, if their respective state assemblies so resolve, and the state governors concerned give their consent."[21] The magazine *West Africa* goes on: "He explained that Shari'a courts could only exercise jurisdiction over Moslems. According to him, non-Moslems 'have nothing to fear from this enlightened arrangement for it would not prejudice them in any way.' Dr. Adegbite then called on Moslem organizations to work for the unity of the *Ummah*

[20] Antony N. Aniagolu, *The Making of the 1989 Constitution in Nigeria* (Ibadan, 1993).

[21] Cited in *West Africa* No. 3985 (1994).

[Moslem community] but 'at the same time support the unity of the nation so that neither religion or ethnic differences would be allowed to divide the country.'"[22]

Thus far I have no quarrel. But what is the real value of those provisions? For one thing, the laws of the nation inherited from the British colonial administration have a heavy dose of Christianity. So whatever else may be said, Christianity has a head-start on other religions in Nigeria, and Christian ideas have become part of the consciousness of the nation. Against that background, what does it mean to talk of freedom to practise one's religion? There is a real problem of the legacy of history.

I have no blueprint to offer, but will underline the following guideposts. First, freedom of conscience must be respected, fostered, and secured. Second, freedom of conscience must be consistent with the dignity for all the people in the society and nation. Third, we must be bold to dare to do the right things that foster human dignity.

Sudan. Jumhuriyat as-Sudan ad-Dimuqratiyah, the Democratic Republic of the Sudan, an area of 967,500 square miles, has been in a persistent civil war for about twenty years. It is a war between the Arabic North and the Nilotic South, which is co-extensive with Muslims, on the one hand, and Christians and Animists, on the other. Obviously here race, ethnicity, and religion have been thoroughly interwoven.

The political history of the Sudan is worth recalling. In 1820, it was under Ottoman rule. In 1885, it became an independent Mahdist state. In 1899, it became an Anglo-Egyptian condominium. In 1956, it became a republic. From being under a military junta in 1958, it came to civilian rule in 1964 and back to military rule in 1969. Since 1971, it has become a one-party state.

Alongside this political history, we must put the religious demography of the Sudan. In 1900, tribal religions occupied 38% of the population, Islam 62%, Christianity none at all. In 1970, tribal religion comprised 20.8%, Islam 71%, and Christianity 7.4% of the population. In 1980, the ratios stood at 16.7% for tribal religions, 73% for Islam, 8.3% for Christianity. Obviously, Islam is the dominant religion in the Sudan. Most of the Muslims are Sunnis, mostly of the Malikite rite. But there are some Shafiites. In 1971 the intelligentsia who professed to be atheist and communist were suppressed.

The Self-Government Statute of 1953 (section 5.2) stated: "All persons shall enjoy freedom of conscience and the right freely to profess their religion, subject only to such conditions relating to morality, public order or health as may be imposed by law." The Republican Order No. 1, is-

---

[22] Ibid.

sued after the May 1969 *coup d'etat*, however, suspended the constitution and also made no reference to religious freedom. The Constitution of April, 1973 refers to God as "the creator and guarantor of freedom." Article 9 of Part I also states: "The Islamic law and custom shall be the main sources of legislation. Personal matters of non-Muslims shall be governed by their personal laws." Article 16 further states: "In the Democratic Republic of the Sudan, Islam is the religion, and the society shall be guided by Islam being the religion of the majority of its people, and the state shall endeavor to express its values." Thus the nation adopted the Islamic penal code, and General Numeiry imposed his own interpretation of Shari'a law on the nation. The same Article 16, however, recognized the religious pluralism of the nation and religious freedom:

> Islam is the religion in the Democratic Republic of the Sudan, being professed by a large number of its citizens who are guided by Islam and the state shall endeavor to express its values. (c) Heavenly religions and the noble aspects of spiritual beliefs shall not be insulted or held in contempt. (d) The state shall treat followers of religions and noble spiritual beliefs without discrimination as the rights and freedoms guaranteed to them as citizens by this Constitutions. . . . (e) The abuse of religions and noble spiritual beliefs for political exploitation is forbidden. . . .

The Constitution, in spite of the adoption of Shari'a as the law of the land, provides religious tolerance, at least on paper. But the point is the gap between theory and reality. In reality, there has been social discrimination against ethnic and religious minorities. There has been institutional injustice both private and communal, inequalities in which religion and ethnic groups are disadvantaged. Some Muslims have blamed these on the peculiar interpretation of Shari'a by General Numeiry and disowned that particular interpretation and have even died for their concerns. Numeiry's policy was the expression of a vision of unification of the Sudan. That was rejected by the Christian South which saw itself as different and sought to reserve the right to be different. Nevertheless, the war has continued till now, and there are signs of anti-Christian acts.

The state of Sudan has been torn apart by civil war. In 1972, the All Africa Conference of Churches brokered a peace settlement and reconciliation. Unfortunately, it did not last. Originally it was not a religious war. But the leadership of the South was Christian and that of the north was Muslim. "President Omar Hassan al-Bashir, who heads the National Islamic Front government and came to power in 1989 with the help of [a] Fundamentalist-backed coup d'etat, staked his future on defeating the rebels. . . . His survival depends on it. He is fairly desperate."[23] He seeks a decisive victory in what he calls a jihad or holy war in a situation where there are profound divisions between north and south which are respectively Arab and African, Muslim and Christian.

What is the way forward in the Sudan? The first step is to identify the harms done to the smaller parties in the struggle and to correct them, as a basis for peace. In other words, what are the legitimate grievances of the peoples—Christians and Animists of the South which have issued in the war with the consequences of massive destruction, death, population displacements? The second step is to help the Shari'a law to acquire a human face. In other words, how do we help to update it into the twentieth century? Can we continue to do amputations of hands as punishment for stealing? In 1993, an Anglican bishop was flogged in public for alleged adultery. Can this be justified in any way, not to mention the truth or otherwise of the allegation? The third step is to develop a national ethic in this particular context of Islamic predominance in a pluralistic state that will weld the various groups into a coherent nation in this twentieth century.

Namibia. In 1884, South West Africa (named Namibia in 1966 by the United Nations) became a German colony. In 1920, it became a South African mandated territory, and in 1949 it was annexed by South Africa and was, until independence, a self-governing dependency of the Republic of South Africa.

The religious demography of Namibia is as follows. In 1900, 91.3% of the population belonged to traditional religions, 8.7.% to Christianity. In 1970, only 5.2% of the population was still traditional, 94.6% Christian. In 1980, the ratio stood at 3.5% and 96.3%. Namibia is now a predominantly Christian country. Of the Christian population, more than half are Lutherans, which gave their leadership special authority, especially as they took the side of the oppressed in the struggle for political freedom from apartheid South Africa. Far below them are the Anglicans who nevertheless were very active in the liberation struggle on the side of the oppressed. Roman Catholics are few.

With this religious composition of the nation, tribal religions, Jews and Baha'is were too few to be in the picture. So religious freedom has been focused on relations among Christians. In the struggle, however, the majority of Christians retained their capacity to provide a point of view other than that of the racist party in power. It is this that gave the Lutherans in particular, but also Anglicans and the Christian Council of Na-

---

[23] Andrew Purvis "Sudan To Kill a People" *Time*, no. 8 (February 21, 1994): 311

mibia, the great visibility and influence they had in the struggle against apartheid.

There is one consequence that needs watching. Because the major churches took up the cause of the oppressed masses, they became bedfellows with the liberation movement called SWAPO. It is often said that the staff of the Council of Churches is SWAPO, and that sometimes raises questions about the independence and objectivity of such bodies. So a major concern is how churches retain their independence from the party in power, so they can be seen to be an independent, honest broker in the cause of peace with justice. This is a problem of success.

Articles 10, 19, and 21 of the Constitution guarantee the fundamental freedoms—speech, expression, thought, conscience, and belief—including freedom "to practise any religion and to manifest such practice," and freedom of association. Namibia represents another version of the task of achieving religious human rights in Africa. Here the question is how religious human rights may be generated and secured in a case where one Christian denomination is predominant and, indeed, the Deputy Speaker of the House of Assembly comes from the majority church. In addition, there is a question of the rights of the Animists.

Because religion is ultimately about what it is to be human, it is vital that the church should stand guard over humanity, especially after the horrendous age of apartheid. That human dignity should cover freedom from fear of or reality of retaliation and freedom to join any political party, however unrevolutionary. At the moment, political parties include SWAPO, the majority party, DTA, United Democratic Front, Aksie Christerlik Nasionaal, National Patriotic Front of Namibia, Federal Convention of Namibia, and Namibian National Front. It will be a matter of human rights, and therefore a religious and moral matter, whether these others are bludgeoned into submission to SWAPO or driven underground, as long as they keep within the legitimate laws of the land.

Ghana. I now come home to Ghana. I choose Ghana not only because it is my home but also because it is the first black African country in this century to gain political independence from colonial rule—from the British in 1957. At its independence, Ghana was called the "Star of Freedom" and because of the dynamism and vision of Dr. Kwame Nkrumah, the prince of African nationalism, Ghana's influence on the African continent reached far and wide.

The religious composition is as follows. In 1900, traditional African religion comprised 90.3% of the population, Christianity 4.7%, Islam 5%. In 1949, the ratios stood at 66% traditional, 30% Christian, 4% Islamic. In 1960, they stood at 38.2% traditional, 42.8% Christian, 12% Islamic; in

1970, 33.2% traditional, 52.7% Christian, 13.9% Islamic. In 1980, the ratio stood at 21.4% traditional, 62.6% Christian, and 15.7% Islamic.

Let me interpret these data. First, religion is a notable feature of African social life in Ghana, which means discussions of human rights cannot ignore religion. Second, Christianity is the largest single religious institution. Besides, its growth rate evidences a significant vitality of this institution. It is also true that because of the churches' involvement in social services, its influence goes beyond the numbers of the avowed adherents to a sizeable population of the population who represent diffused Christianity. Third, Ghana is religiously pluralistic. Fourth, there has been an increase in the numbers of African Instituted Churches.

These religions operated in a context of highly charged political activity. There are three things I wish to stress for our purposes. First, if the church was a critical actor in society, so too was the Convention People's Party of Kwame Nkrumah, which claimed to hold Leninist-Marxist ideology called Consciencism. That rhetoric made relationships between church and state anything but easy, especially as the government became more and more dictatorial.[24] Second, Nkrumah's government turned dictatorial for a number of reasons. But one important reason is that "it was concerned with national rather individual rights, and its primary concern is still with safeguarding the independence of the state rather than with the liberation of individuals."[25] Clearly the Church's task of human rights was cut out for it.

Third, is the constitutional situation. Since independence in 1957 Ghana has made the following political journey: 1st Republic: March 6, 1957 to February 24, 1966; 1st Military Government: February 24 to September 1969; 2nd Republic (Busia Government): September 1969 to January 13, 1972; 2nd Military Government: General I.K. Acheampong and Akuffo and 1st Rawlings administration January 1972-1979; 3rd Republic (Hilla Limann) September 1979 to 1981; 3rd Military Government: 2nd J.J. Rawlings administration 1981-January 1993; 4th Republic: President J.J. Rawlings January 1993 to date. Throughout this period, and in spite of the assortment of civilian and military governments, freedom of conscience and of religion have been part of the fabric of Ghanian governance. The 1992 constitution states: "Every person in Ghana, whatever his race, place of origin, political opinion, colour, religion, creed or gender shall be entitled to the fundamental human rights and freedoms of the individual . . . but subject to respect for the rights and freedoms of others and for the public interest" (Articles 12:2, 21). Article 17 also mandates

[24] Pobee, *Kwame Nkrumah and the Church in Ghana*.

[25] D. Austin, "Strong Rule in Ghana," *The Listener* LXVII (173) (January 25, 1962): 152.

equality and freedom from discrimination. In other words, on paper at any rate, religious pluralism is recognized and respected in Ghana.

However, there have been occasions for friction between church and state. I will take three examples. The first is the controversy about whether the traditional rite of libation could be poured at the celebrations marking the independence of Ghana. The churches protested to the proposal to pour libation and stayed away from that particular function. In my view, the historic churches' protest reflected a lack of sensitivity to the pluralism of the nation, in which even traditional religionists are entitled to their space. Further, the clash was also over cultural self-consciousness of the nationalist government in contrast to the seeming lack of it in the historic churches. The basic issue is whether theological disagreement justifies the church to deny others their religious commitment.[26]

The issue is when religious freedom becomes religious subversion. This issue was crystallized in a controversy involving the Roman Catholic Bishop of Kumasi, Bishop Bronk. The *Ghanaian Times* of 20 December 1961 carried an attack on him as follows: "He [de Bronk] has turned the altar into a political platform where decisions and actions of government of the people are condemned with the cheeky indiscretion of an imperialist spy paid to subvert our people's mind. . . . Religious freedom is one thing. Religious subversion or the freedom to use religious freedom for subversive activities, is another and an entirely difficult thing. . . ." The bishop's alleged crime was to have criticized the C.P.P. government for sending Ghana's youth to Eastern and Central Europe for education and expressed fears of communist indoctrination. This is not the place to apportion blame. But for now, I wish to highlight the issue at stake: when may the legitimate right to propagate one's beliefs become subversion that must be disallowed, if not punished? When does the missionary vocation of the church begin to violate the rights of others in the state? I would, however, warn against a wholesale condemnation of subversion, for there is a sense in which good education is subversion.

A perennial issue has been the right of the churches to run schools and hospitals in Ghana. Nkrumah had taken the position that education of the people may not be divorced from the struggle of the people. For the churches this was identified as a cornerstone of Leninist socialist ideology and therefore, suspected Nkrumah's bid for the government to take over church schools and hospitals as a ploy to indoctrinate the people. I have elsewhere discussed the merits and demerits of this issue.[27]

---

[26] Pobee, *Kwame Nkrumah and the Church in Ghana*, 55ff.

[27] Ibid., 86-96.

For now, the issue I wish to raise is this: in a pluralistic context, what are the rights of the government vis-à-vis the rights of religious institutions in respect of the social services? This is an issue recurring in Africa.

The Way Forward

Several factors are critical to charting the way forward toward a fuller recognition of religious human rights in Africa and elsewhere.

Renewed Spirituality. We have assumed that religion is a living stream that can nurture human dignity and human rights. However, as one watches the world, we can identify a threefold crisis: crisis of church, crisis of faith, and crisis of culture.

With respect to the *crisis of church,* the indications include the loss of membership and general sense of the irrelevance of the church. If religion is to be taken seriously as an important institution which can nurture human dignity, then it must get its act together. The church needs to face the question: does the church make a difference whether it is there or not? The church does make a difference when the church is the "voice of the voiceless"—as in El Salvador through the witness of Archbishop Romero, or in the Republic of South Africa through the witness of Beyers Naudé and Desmond Tutu—because the church has heard, understood, embraced, and lived the insight of "God's preferential option for the poor." This is the testimony of Beyers Naudé: "What really annoyed the leaders of Afrikaner nationalism when I broke ranks was that I was every bit as much a white Afrikaner as they were. I think I reminded them of that side of Afrikanerdom which they have never been able to tame. It is an Afrikaner willingness to cross frontiers—relating the Afrikaner experience of exploitation, poverty and struggle to others who face similar experiences."[28] We can also cite persons of other faiths or of no faith who have travelled that route—people like Fatima Meer, a South Africa Muslim, Ela Gandhi, a Hindu Socialist also from South Africa.[29]

The *crisis of faith* is evident in the great confusion surrounding several faith traditions. The rise of so-called religious fundamentalism is an attempt to recover from that— though in the process it has gone overboard into inhumane acts. As Frances Brienen puts it: "[T]he crisis of faith can be described by having lost sight of God. Or may be we should ask the question: Has God hidden his/her face from us?"[30]

---

[28] Cited in Villa-Vicencio, *The Spirit of Hope*, 220.

[29] Ibid.

[30] Frances Brienen, "In the Matter of Resources We in the North Live in a Desert," in John S. Pobee, ed., *Ministerial Formation for Missions Today* (Asempa, 1993), 66.

The *crisis of culture* has come largely from the heavy impact of technocracy and economics on our age and world, leading to a certain dehumanization and depersonalization. Religion and culture are very much interrelated and belong to the living wells of a society. Therefore, the crisis of cultures experienced in varying degrees in various contexts of the world must be faced and rehabilitated if the living wells of tradition can be efficacious in being the underpinning of human dignity and human rights.

Inside this threefold crisis stands an issue: There is a need for religious people to recover the sense that it is a religious and spiritual matter whether people have dignity or not. As Desmond Tutu puts it:

> Obedience to God is very important to me. Perhaps it is my attempt to respond to the living, dynamic God that makes me appear unpredictable. Maybe this makes me ungovernable. What I am suggesting is that the Church must sit a little loose to political ideology and never be too concerned about being politically correct. Our task is to be agents of the Kingdom of God, and this sometimes requires us to say unpopular things.[31]

Tutu adds:

> [I]t is extremely difficult to know and discern the will of God. It involves thoughtfulness, a willingness to search the scriptures, an ability to plumb the depths of the Christian tradition, and consultation. God's will has to do with what is healing of the wounds of society—right, just and decent. To know what this means, we need to cleanse ourselves of our ourselves—of our fears, greed, ambitions and personal desires. This is where prayer, fasting, meditation and the sacraments come into the picture. Honest prayer and disciplined living are incredibly illuminating and revealing.[32]

Metanoia. Forgive my use of a Greek word, but the normal English word "repentance" has been so trivialized, that I wish to avoid it here. One of the penetrating analyses of the human condition is the assertion of the human capacity and proclivity for sin—sins of commission and sins of omission, the acts that deny love of God as of neighbor. It is against that background that there is a call for *metanoia*. The basic meaning of the word is change of mind. But in its biblical usage it has religious and ethical significance, a complex of feeling sorry, changing one's mind, and doing acts of expiation for wrongs committed—in short, a quest after

[31] Villa-Vicencio, *The Spirit of Hope*, 276.

[32] Ibid., 281-282.

radical change in relation to God and humanity.[33] A serious discussion of human rights must include creating awareness of past errors, without necessarily making people feel embattled; confession of guilt, forgiveness, and penance.

In the matter of human dignity and rights almost every person and religious institution needs *metanoia* in its different elements. There are two particular areas that I wish to single out. The first is the violence with which Christians met so-called heretics, schismatics, and unbelievers. Suffice it here only to quote Thomas Aquinas (1225-1274), *doctor communis* and *doctor angelicus*: "[F]rom the point of view of heretics there is their sin by which they have desired not only to be separated from the Church, but to be eliminated from the world by death. For it is a far graver matter to corrupt the faith which is the life of the soul than to falsify money which sustains temporal life. So if it be just that forgers and other malefactors are put to death without mercy by the secular authority, with how much greater reason may heretics be not only excommunicated but also put to death, when once they are convicted of heresy."[34] If freedom of conscience, thought and expression are part of human identity and dignity, then the position of the revered Saint Thomas must be abandoned. Ideas of Christendom and the theology of the absoluteness of Christ often issued in intolerance and persecution of dissenters, people of other faith traditions or no faith at all. But that development is an aberration of the true vocation of the people of God. *There is a prerequisite of repentance, confession of guilt and forgiveness as well as a resolution not to repeat these errors.* Since all religionists at one point or other have been cruel to others, there should be *mutual* confession of guilt and *mutual* forgiveness. These are a precondition for peace in which human dignity and human rights can be nurtured.

The second area I wish to highlight is the rampant tendency to creating enemy images. We seem to be unable to live without enemy images and demonizing those who differ from us or disagree with us.[35] Such enemy images lead to violence and massive suffering. *There is need for a theology of religious pluralism as the underpinning of a culture of religious pluralism.* For religious bigotry and intolerance are rooted in narrow notions of God. This task is at once a theological and pastoral and deeply spiritual quest. One aspect of this is the need for the churches to move from a missiological understanding of people of other faiths to a theo-

---

[33] J. Behm, "Metanoia," in G. Kittel, ed., *Theological Dictionary of the New Testament* F.W. Bromiley, trans. (Grand Rapids, 1967), 4:999-1022.

[34] Summa Theologica, II-II, 14, q. 2. art. 3.

[35] John S. Pobee, "Images of the Enemy," *One World* 178 (August/September, 1992): 15-17

logical understanding of people of other faiths and that includes a review of the traditional interpretation and understanding of scripture.

Such a culture of religious pluralism demands the development of the capacity for dialogue in all peoples and helping people to be convinced that such flexibility is not *ipso facto* negotiating away truth. That culture demands commitment to partnership and advocacy. Religious institutions must take the role of advocates of human rights in the light of the "gospel" and in so doing, they will be travelling in one boat with political parties on what they should be doing. All told, the vocation is to build a common framework with justice as the basis for interaction in society. Religious people and institutions should serve disinterestedly on behalf of people and their dignity, irrespective of their religion.

Education and Formation. It is a tall order of things to be worked at, but it will not happen by itself. There is need for peoples to be formed into that culture of religious plurality and that anthropological question. In this quest education, religious and theological, is key. Religious education must include mission education which focuses on a culture of pluralism, in which the plurality of humanity in God's creation and image is fostered and refurbished. In that plurality of humanity we should be concerned not only with religious and racial identities but also with gender identity. I also would underscore the importance of the education of the young; for they are not only the church or leaders of the future—they are the energy and enthusiasm of today.

This is not the time to wax eloquent on education and formation. Forgive me for reverting to a statement of 1955, but it is most apposite still for today. Niblett writes: "the process of education . . . includes all the influences brought by a community to bear upon the human beings growing within it. Every developing human being must be deeply affected by his environment. This is true of outward environment—climate, physical surroundings, the material gadgets and inventions available; but it is far more true of inward environments—the climates of affection, enterprise, loyalty, or on the other hand, of shallowness, lack of purpose, lack of zeal, in which he is reared . . . a change of physical surrounding will have its effects, but a change of mental and spiritual climate will have many more."[36] Religious education must be contextual in the sense that it addresses the "external environment," such as the structures of injustices and inhumanity, as well as the "internal environment," which includes as well the layers of customs and prejudices that can obscure reality. On the positive side of the internal environment is the human need to be loved and to belong, which includes the symbols,

[36] W.R. Niblett, "Neutrality or Profession of Faith," in *Science and Freedom. The Proceedings of a Conference Convened by the Congress of Cultural Freedom* (London, 1955), 234.

stories, memories, and practices which weld the community together. But it should be an inclusive community. It includes the human yearning for what is just and honorable. *Religious and theological education at all levels is a key instrument for fostering human rights, religious or otherwise.* But that education should be contextually relevant, participatory and dialogical not only in the sense of promoting dialogue between persons of different faith traditions but also of holding dialogue with sociology.

The Place of Law. The word "right" is normally laid out in terms of law. But I submit that law should undergird an ethos created by education and formation. Law is an instrument for refurbishing an ethos that the people, by and large, accept as something for the good, for the peace and coherence of the community. But even here we need to be sensitive to the cultural elements in the attitudes to law. The British, for example, tend to shy away from statutes and to stick to common law. The Italians and Germans have different attitudes to law. So too the Africans. So it is not enough to rush to formulate laws. It is important for the law to be taken with the education of society. *There is need to negotiate ecumenically for laws that have the capacity to win the commitment of peoples in their plurality.*

Conclusion

In conclusion, let me reiterate several themes which I have highlighted in the course of my search for religious human rights, particularly in Africa: *First,* religion of one type or other is a living spring of life, especially of *homo africanus* and therefore has a special place in the nurture and fostering of human rights, religious or otherwise. *Second,* there is a need to revisit the contours of the origins of the concept of human rights, given the new sense of a wider *oikoumene* than when they were first articulated. *Third,* critical to the pursuit of religious human rights is the ecumenical broaching of what it is to be human today. *Fourth,* the credibility of the quest rests, to some extent, on a perceived congruence and consistency between the rhetoric and practice of human rights. *Fifth,* a tested and renewed tradition, often undergirded by religion, is the living well from which the stream of human rights will rise and flow. *Sixth,* religious human rights includes the freedom not to be religious or not to believe, without suspicion, prejudice, or fear of retribution. *Seventh,* freedom of conscience and self-expression is essential to human and religious rights. *Eighth,* a responsible quest after religious human rights must include addressing the issues that turned some religious groups to violent activities in the name of a return to the fundamentals of the faith. *Ninth,* since the two most populous religions of Africa, namely Christianity and

Islam, are missionary religions, the quest for religious human rights must search for models of mission which from start to finish, respect and foster human dignity. I opt for a model of mission that builds communities that are guided by the values of God's rule, namely sacrificial love, truth, righteousness and justice, freedom, reconciliation, and peace. Religious human rights can be fostered when the unique claims of each and every religion are taken seriously and engaged. This means a rejection of the temptation to define the other only on one's own terms. *Tenth*, given the fact that all religious institutions have erred at one time or another and in the process have denied their membership or the other their human dignity, there is need for *metanoia* which is repentance, mutual confession of guilt and mutual forgiveness as well as a resolve not to repeat the error. *Eleventh*, religious human rights will flourish only in a culture of religious pluralism which can be fostered by a theology of religious pluralism. *Twelfth*, religious and theological education and formation should be key instruments for fostering human rights, religious or otherwise. Such education must not be proselytizing; it should be contextually relevant, participatory, and dialogical. *Finally*, religious human rights should be refurbished by laws that would have been negotiated ecumenically.

Limitations on Religious Rights: Problematizing Religious Freedom in the African Context

MAKAU WA MUTUA[1]
Harvard University

It is not my intention in this chapter to discuss what limitations, if any, should or could be placed on religious rights per se. Rather, I propose to explore the historical experience of religious penetration and advocacy in a very specific context and demonstrate the possibilities of conflict between certain forms of evangelistic advocacy and some human rights norms. With the African theater as the basic laboratory, I intend to unpack the meaning of religious freedom at the point of contact between the messianic faiths and African religions and illustrate how that meeting resulted in a phenomenon akin to cultural genocide. The main purpose here is not merely to defend forms of religion or belief but rather to problematize the concept of the right to the free exercise of messianic faiths, which includes the right to proselytize in the marketplace of religions. In societies, such as the African ones where religion is woven into virtually every aspect of life, its delegitimization can easily lead to the collapse of social norms and cultural identities. The result, as has been

[1] I am grateful to Professor John Witte, Jr. for his unwavering support of my scholarly and professional endeavors. I express my sincere thanks to him for involving me in the processes that led to the religious human rights conference and for giving me an opportunity to provide a point of view not commonly heard. His comments on an earlier draft of this paper and his continuing interest in my research helped me sharpen my focus and further contextualize my critique. I am also grateful to Professor Henry Steiner, my colleague and friend at Harvard, who kindly read an initial draft of this article and as always helped me think through some of the complex issues raised by this contentious subject. My thanks also go to Professor Harriet King and Professor Michael Broyde, both of Emory University, for their insightful comments. Finally, I am deeply indebted to Athena, my wife, for her critical but compassionate views on several drafts of the article. I am, however, responsible for all the views expressed in this chapter.

J.D. van der Vyver and J. Witte, Jr. (eds.), Religious Human Rights in Global Perspective, 417-440.

the case in most of Black Africa, is a culturally disconnected people, neither African nor European nor Arab. In other words, I shall argue that imperial religions have necessarily violated the individual conscience and the communal expressions of Africans and their communities by subverting African religions. In so doing, they have robbed Africans of essential elements of their humanity. In as much as this chapter is a protest, it is also a plea for the better understanding of African religions, their freedom from imperial faiths, and the necessity for the rights regime to devise norms and mechanisms for protecting them. I base this argument on several premises.

Since the right to religious freedom includes the right to be left alone—to choose freely whether and what to believe—the rights regime by requiring that African religions compete in the marketplace of ideas incorrectly assumes a level playing field. The rights corpus not only forcibly imposes on African religions the obligation to compete—a task for which as non-proselytizing, non-competitive, creeds they are not historically fashioned—but also protects evangelizing religions in their march towards universalization. In the context of religious freedom, the privileging by the rights regime of the competition of ideas over the right against cultural invasion, in a skewed contest, amounts to condoning the dismantling of African religions. I also argue that the playing field, the one crucial and necessary ingredient in a fair fight, is heavily weighted against Africans. Messianic religions have either been forcibly imposed or their introduction was accomplished as part of the cultural package borne by colonialism. Missionaries did not simply offer Jesus Christ as the savior of benighted souls; his salvation was frequently a precondition for services in education and health, which were quite often the exclusive domain of the church and the colonial state.[2] It makes little sense to argue that Africans could avoid acculturation by opting out of the colonial order; in most cases the embrace of indigenous societies by the European imperial powers was so violent and total that conformity was the only immediate option. In making this argument I shall also rely on notions of human rights law which, as I shall seek to show, suggest that indigenous

---

[2] The case of the Akamba, a Kenyan community targeted by European missionaries for conversion and colonization, was typical. As told by a European writer, for "most Africans the turn to education [formal European education] brought a new involvement with the Christian religion. School and church were closely intertwined because almost everywhere missionary organizations had a monopoly on educational facilities and expertise. Problems of educational mobilization, therefore, could not be separated from the problem of adjustment to a new faith and values. School and church affairs were of vital concern to Africans seeking to come to terms with the colonial situation. . . ." See F. Munro, *Colonial Rule Among the Kamba: Social Change in the Kenya Highlands 1889-1939* (Oxford, 1975), 147-148.

beliefs have a right to be respected and left alone by more dominant external traditions.

This reasoning poses serious questions that go to the root of the rights regime. Some difficulties are obvious. A key ideal of the human rights movement, and indeed of liberalism, is the unwavering commitment to the open society in which the freedom to advance, receive, and disseminate ideas is assumed necessary for the greater social good. Though not absolute—permissible limitations can be placed on what ideas and under what circumstances advocacy is allowed by the law—this commitment creates a rights regime conundrum in conversations about the universality of human rights norms. Questions arise about the validity of the advocacy of certain norms beyond the borders of their origin. The right of advocacy itself and its centrality in the human rights corpus becomes an issue. Is it possible, for instance, to question advocacy in connection with other creeds, ideologies, and institutions? Should advocacy by the industrial West to spread free markets and democracy to non-democratic, non-Western cultures, complete with their power to transform and fundamentally change economic, social, and political systems, be protected under the human rights regime? Could theocratic states, for example, seek protection for their political orders and social systems under the rights corpus? Other examples come to mind: should human rights law invade cultures that subordinate women and seek to eradicate gender bias through advocacy? Are these acceptable forms of advocacy which the human rights movement should protect? Ultimately, one must ask, who decides what is good for the universe and what should be advocated transnationally?

I mention these problems only to indicate the scope of the dilemma posed by this chapter; it would require another exercise to address them. My particular concern here is with a certain historical experience and the results of that experience: specifically, I shall address the nature and forms of religious advocacy employed by the two major messianic religions—Christianity and Islam—in Africa and the tension between those forms of advocacy and certain norms and ideals of the human rights movement.

I have organized the paper into several parts. First, I briefly sketch the history of the human rights movement and outline those ideals within it that are relevant for my purposes. Secondly, I discuss the view of the messianic religions towards human rights and other religious traditions, particularly indigenous religions. My goal here is to indicate some of the bases for demonizing "the other" and draw attention to possible contradictions between the human rights corpus and some of the positions taken by messianic religions. Thirdly, I briefly review the human rights, constitutional, and other legal bases for religious freedom and the protection of indigenous religions in Africa. I then explore the forms of proselytization preferred by both Islam and Christianity in Africa and the use of coercion, both physical and cultural, as a tool in that process. The last segment addresses the tension inherent in the rights regime and the dilemmas posed to the human rights movement by the practical and historical experience of evangelization in Africa.

A discussion about limitations on religious rights at first blush appears to frustrate some of the major ideals of the human rights movement. It raises the question about the tension between the restriction of the right to evangelize or advocate a point of view and one of the central ideals of the human rights movement, the promotion of diversity and the right to advocate ideas or creeds.[3] An exploration of the manner in which the human rights corpus ought to view religious rights—whether further to limit or to expand the protections they currently enjoy—raises this fundamental tension: how does a body of principles that promotes diversity and difference protect the establishment and manifestation of religious ordering that seeks to destroy difference and forcibly impose an orthodoxy in Africa—as both Christianity and Islam, the two major proselytizing religions, attempted, and in many cases successfully did? Precisely because of the ethos of universalization common to both, the messianic faiths sought to eradicate, with the help of the state, all other forms of religious expression and belief and close off any avenues through which other competing faiths could be introduced or sustained. This coerced imposition of a religious orthodoxy implies a desire and a social philosophy to seek the forcible destruction of that which is different. Yet, it seems inconceivable that the human rights movement would have intended to protect the "right" of certain religions to "destroy" others. In this chapter, I shall attempt to explore this tension—between protecting the right to proselytize in Africa while limiting the circumstances

---

[3] The movement's emphasis on respect for diversity and tolerance of difference implies that societies remain permanently open to inquiry, change, and challenge; it could be argued that this philosophy betrays the bias of the human rights corpus for a liberal, democratic society, a favoritism that could diminish the movement's claim of universality. But scholars of the movement argue that with the possible exception of itself, "That movement institutionalizes no one ideal of social order. To the contrary, it explicitly allows for many faiths and ideologies while denying to any one among them the right or power to impose itself by force. It expresses a humanistic commitment to ongoing inquiry and diversity, as well as a deep skepticism about any final truth. It denies governments the right to close avenues of reflection, criticism, advocacy, and innovation in order to impose an orthodoxy. . . ." Henry Steiner, "Ideals and Counter-Ideals in the Struggle over Autonomy Regimes for Minorities," *Notre Dame Law Review* 66 (1991): 1552. Steiner's comment would seem to give credence to the view that the movement institutionalizes liberalism as a political order because the "openness" required by the movement appears to be one of the essential qualities of a liberal society.

in which that right can be exercised—within the confines of the human rights corpus.

It is my argument that the free exercise of religion and belief should find protection within the human rights universe in the context of respect for diversity without giving license to the destruction of other religions and cultures. While I attempt to explore the nature, context, and purposes of proselytization in Africa from a rights perspective, I also seek to see whether proselytization in that context constituted a human rights violation, and if so, what the response of the human rights regime should be.

I shall briefly sketch the history of the development of human rights movement to situate my discussion and provide a context for my views on religious rights in the African setting. The human rights movement—that collection of norms, processes, and institutions—is largely a product of the horrors of the devastating war of 1939-45. Its rise, development, and elaboration cannot be understood without resort to the abominations committed by European states and their agents during that war. Drawing on the Western liberal tradition, the movement arose primarily to control and contain state action against the individual. The two principal instruments on which it is based—the 1948 Universal Declaration of Human Rights (UDHR) and the 1966 International Covenant on Civil and Political Rights (ICCPR)—establish negative rights that either limit or prohibit altogether governmental reach into the private and individual realms. Primarily, the movement has been restrictive of state power. In the recent past, however, as the traditional human rights movement has grown in strength and effect, its language has been appropriated by other causes which recognize its legitimizing power. Women's groups, gay and lesbian organizations, environmentalists, and advocates of economic, social, and cultural rights, all seek recognition by the "official" human rights movement.

There is a growing realization internationally that the struggle for human rights is a quest for the reduction of conditions that engender weakness; in effect, it is a push against the denial of certain fundamental rights[4] by any individual or institution regardless of its relationship to

[4] What constitutes a fundamental human right is a subject of great tension and disagreement within and without the human rights movement. The more traditional activists in the movement only recognize as legitimate those rights that implicate raw state power, such as freedom from torture, extra-judicial executions, arbitrary arrest and detention, denials of procedural due process, and the suppression of free speech, and assembly and association. More recently, non-Western scholars and activists have insisted on the indivisibility of human rights and have emphasized the importance of economic, cultural, social, and group rights. Many in the West still refuse to recognize these as rights, referring to them instead as "equities." This dichotomization of rights is also a legacy of the logic and struggles of the Cold War.

the state. Certain institutions, such as the family which traditionally have been part of the private realm, are now coming under increasing scrutiny to comply with international human rights standards. The state—the political instrument that gives legal personality and protection to private institutions—is being pressed to intervene to secure basic rights for individuals under the control or influence of entities in the private realm. Advocates base their claims on the influence or control that the state ought to exercise over such entities. The challenge for the human rights movement is to move beyond the singular obsession with wrongs committed directly by the state—although it remains the most important obligee of the discourse—and invade non-state actors in order to contain and control human rights violations in the private sphere. To do so, the movement has to take on powerful private institutions in the private realm, including established religion. In this paper, I argue that although religious human rights must be defined, secured, and protected, there is a correlative duty on the part of religions to respect the human rights of non-believers and adherents of other religions or faiths and not to seek their coerced conversion either directly or through the manipulation and destruction of other cultures. Although Article 18 of the ICCPR guarantees the "right to freedom of thought, conscience and religion," and provides for certain limitations, it does not spell out the duties that must be borne by proselytizing religions. I attempt in this chapter to balance the interests of these religions with those of African societies, both individual and collective, and to explore ways, if possible, in which the respectful co-existence between these radically different spiritualities could be imagined and worked out.

Demonization: The Unholy View of "the Other"

The two most geographically diverse religions—Christianity and Islam—are also the most imperial: they are proselytizing and universalist, that is, they seek to convert into their faith the entire human race.[5] Although these religions are not spread through physical violence today, they have historically been forcibly introduced. They have also been negatively competitive against each other as well as other creeds as they

[5] The designation of non-believers—individuals who do not profess the trinity of Judaism, Islam, or Christianity—by both Muslims and Christians as either pagans or infidels is one manifestation of belief in their own superiority over other religions. Christian missionaries and Islamists evidence this zeal and drive to universalize through the conversion or salvation of unbelievers from what they regard as eternal damnation. For a more detailed analysis of the attitude of Shari'a, or Islamic jurisprudence, towards non-believers see generally Abdullahi Ahmed An-Na'im, "Human Rights in the Muslim World: Socio-Political Conditions and Scriptural Imperatives," *Harvard Human Rights Journal* 3 (1990): 13.

have fought over the souls of third groups and individuals.[6] But central to them is the belief in the racial superiority of the proselytizers; the other is quite often depicted as inferior. Arab Muslims, for example, have historically viewed Black Africans as racially inferior; Islamized Africans are regarded as having taken an important step towards overcoming that inferiority. The capture and enslavement of millions of Africans by Arab Muslims over the centuries bore the trademarks of this theological and racial justification. It does not require a profound knowledge of history to prove that both Arab and European perceptions of Africa have been decidedly racist over the centuries. Asserting that the "Bantu mind" was inferior to that of the "civilized man," a leading European missionary described Africans thus:

> It is suggested that the mere possession on the part of the Bantu of nothing but an oral tradition and culture creates a chasm of difference between the Native "mind" and that of civilized man, and of itself would account for a lack of balance and proportion in the triple psychological function of feeling, thinking and acting, implying that thinking is the weakest of the three and that feeling is the most dominant. The Native seeks not truth nor works, but power —the dynamical tool.[7]

Writing about the importance of evangelization in Africa, another European missionary asserted that the "Mission to Africa was the least that we [Europeans] can do to strive to raise him [the African] in the scale of mankind."[8] The catalog of writing by pioneer missionaries in Africa is inexhaustible and uniquely similar. Paternalistic at best, African mission-

---

[6] The wars between the Christian Portuguese and Moslem North Africans are well documented. In the fifteenth century, the Portuguese under the command of Prince Henry carried the crusades to Africa as part of the campaign to win back the continent from Muslims. An admiring portrait of Prince Henry said that the "flame that lit the Soldier of the Cross was kindled in his heart in early youth, and to win back Morocco from the Moors was the ambition of his life. He never drew his sword in any other cause. . . ." See H. Debrunner, *A History of Christianity in Ghana* (Accra, 1967), 15. Elsewhere, he is called the "commander of the Portuguese Crusaders' Order of the Knight of Christ." Ibid. Even among different Christian denominations, competition for souls often turned violent as evidenced by the conflict in 1637 between the Dutch and the Catholic Portuguese at historic Elmina, part of what is today Ghana. A Catholic account of the conflict said that the "new conquerors, the Dutch, were then bitter enemies of Catholicism. Wherever they came, they burnt and destroyed the churches and would not allow a Catholic priest to preach to the people." See H. Pfann, *A Short History of the Catholic Church in Ghana* (Cape Coast, 1965), 8 .

[7] D. Shropshire, *The Church and the Primitive Peoples* (London, 1938), xix. The author goes on to write that: "Though he [the Native] relies a good deal on what he has observed, he will always seek the true cause in the world of unseen powers above and beyond what we call 'Nature'—in the metaphysical realm in the literal sense, and his peculiar mental activity is largely due to his lack of distinction between what is actually present to sense and what is beyond." Ibid.

[8] A.H. Barrow, *Fifty Years in West Africa* (London, 1900), 29.

aries left no doubt of their belief in the superiority of their race, religion, and culture, and the necessity of "freeing" the African from his heathen and sub-human belief and status.

Such attempts, often quite successful, at the universalization of the messianic faiths have resulted in untold suffering throughout history. The religious crusades and jihads waged by both Muslims and Christians, in which millions were killed and enslaved, are just one example of the destruction that accompanied or was the excuse for proselytization. In strange symbolism, the cross, with its linear structure, becomes a sword once turned on its side.[9] The causal link, historically, between evangelization and war appears to be indisputable.[10] The philosophy and practice of re-making "the other" appears therefore to be based on the contempt for that which is different and belief in the superiority of the aggressive creed. Major bodies of both Christian and Islamic jurisprudence directly assert the inferiority of and disrespect for non-believers. Although some scholars argue that Shari'a, for example, is just one particular interpretation of the Qur'an, the definitive word of God and Muhammad, his Prophet, it is the only coherent, unified body of law for the world's Muslims.[11] Other, more liberal interpretations of Islam have been of little consequence to the lives of Muslims. Yet Shari'a itself contradicts basic human rights standards by discriminating against non-Muslims. Abdullahi An-Na'im, a leading advocate for reform of Islamic jurisprudence to bring it into conformity with international human rights standards, has written:

> The claim that Shari'a is fully consistent with and has always protected human rights is problematic both as a theoretical and a practical matter. As a theoretical matter, the concept of human rights as rights to which every human being is entitled by virtue of being human was unknown to Islamic jurisprudence or social philosophy until the last few decades and does not

---

[9] M. Fox, *A Spirituality Named Compassion* (San Francisco, 1990), 112: "Crusades, inquisitions, witch burnings—which invariably meant the burnings of heretics and gay people, of fellow Christians and of infidels—all in the name of the cross. It is almost as if Constantine, and his empire's conversion to Christianity in the fourth century, uttered a well-fulfilled prophecy when he declared: 'in the name of this cross we shall conquer'. The cross has played the role of weapon time and time again in Christian history and empire building." Ibid.

[10] Christian armies, much in the same way that Muslim crusaders saw themselves, considered it an honor to die for Christianity. According to many, "the supreme sacrifice was to die fighting under the Christian emperor. The supreme self-immolation was to fall in battle under the standard of the cross. . . . But by the time Christianity was ready to meet Asia and the New World, the Cross and the sword were so identified with one another that the sword itself was a cross. It was the only kind of cross some conquistadors understood." Ibid.

[11] Shari'a, the legal and ethical regime of Islam, is derived from both the Qur'an and the Sunna, the Prophet's elaboration of the Qur'an through his statements and actions.

> exist in Shari'a. *Many rights are given under Shari'a in accordance with a strict classification based on faith and gender and are not given to human beings as such.* As a practical matter, fundamental inconsistencies exist between Shari'a as practiced in Muslim countries and current standards of human rights.[12]

A number of theoretical and scriptural examples illustrate this point. Unbelievers, defined by Shari'a as non-Muslims except Jews and Christians or those who do not believe in the "revealed heavenly" scriptures,[13] are not regarded as fully human and could be legally enslaved. Shari'a only discusses the manner in which slaves ought to be treated; it does not prohibit the enslavement of non-believers.[14] In addition, according to Shari'a, only Muslims can fully enjoy the benefits of citizenship in an Islamic state. Even members of other revealed faiths such as Jews or Christians are only entitled to the lesser status of *dhimma* under which their security of person and property is guaranteed with some freedom to practice their own religion. In return, they have to pay taxes and submit to Islamic rules in all public matters.[15] Shari'a also punishes by execution Muslims who repudiate their faith.[16] The assumption of the "right" to Islamize and then prevent others from converting—or counterpenetrating—is at the very least a manifestation of intolerance for difference and diversity.

Bigoted clergymen and their followers, from South Africa to the United States, have continuously searched the scriptures for references to the sub-humanity of Africans to justify apartheid, slavery, and other violations of basic freedoms based solely on race and skin color. In the United States and the European colonies and possessions in Africa, law and religion were often synthesized to create an oppressive social philosophy in order to justify the institutionalization of slavery, colonialism, and the ubiquity of white or European power over blacks. Many settled on the story of the curse of Noah's son, Ham, in Genesis 9 as the divine curse on all people of African descent. Religion and pseudo-science were

---

12 See An-Nai'm, "Human Rights in the Muslim World," 22 (emphasis added).

13 Not surprisingly, the revealed scriptures are only the Bible, the Qu'ran, and Torah or the Old Testament, the holy books of Christianity, Islam, and Judaism, respectively. It is inexplicable that Shari'a would disregard all other religious persuasions such as Hinduism and indigenous African or native American religions, among others, as illegitimate.

14 An-Nai'm, "Human Rights in the Muslim World," 22-23.

15 Ibid., 24. An-Nai'm adds that, "non-Muslim subjects of an Islamic state can aspire only to the status of *dhimma* under which they would suffer serious violations of their human rights. *Dhimmis* are not entitled to equality with Muslims. Their lives are evaluated as inferior in monetary terms as well: they are not entitled to the same amount of diya or financial compensation for homicide or bodily harm as Muslims." Ibid.

16 The crime of apostasy, which disallows individuals from freely changing their faith, violates human rights standards by preventing the freedom of choice.

often hand-woven to "prove" the bestial, sub-human characteristics of Africans. These philosophies and practices allowed "good" Christians brutally to subjugate or to acquiesce with a clear conscience in the subjugation of African cultures and religious traditions.

The Processes and Effects of Proselytization in Africa

In this segment, I explore the views of the evangelizer and the processes of evangelization in Black Africa and raise some of the human rights issues implied by their penetration of the continent. I attempt to highlight the tension between proselytization, coupled with force and power, and respect for difference and cultural identity. Islam was introduced to Africa through military conquest by the Arabs. Thereafter, the processes of Arabization (in North Africa and the Nile Delta) and Islamization (in East and West Africa) proceeded simultaneously through force, the slave trade, and general commerce. The entry of Christianity into the continent was no less violent, coming as it did in partnership with the colonial imperial powers.[17] Most European missionaries saw their duty in the image painted by Rudyard Kipling in 1899: "Take up the White Man's burden, send forth the beast ye breed. Go bind your sons to exile to serve your captives' need. To wait in heavy harness on fluttered folk and wild your new-caught, sullen peoples, half-devil, half-child."[18] A missionary who worked among Zimbabweans early in the twentieth century exemplified these beliefs; to him, "unlettered" Natives were in "the technically barbaric and pre-literacy stage of cultural and social development."[19] In a book written for those "responsible for the development of a primitive people or are concerned for their progress—missionary and administrator, government official and teacher, employer and civilian,"[20] the missionary stated starkly:

---

[17] Many African communities did not see any functional distinctions between the colonial administrators and the missionaries. "The political factor [colonialism] worked to the disadvantage of the missionaries in that the Kamba [an ethnic community in Kenya] like all other Africans, viewed the newcomers in terms of their local political situation. They identified the missionaries, arriving with the colonial power which gave them its support and approval, as part of the colonial authority system, barely distinguishable from administrative officers. In 1913, for example, elders in Mwala [area of Kenya inhabited by the Akamba] went to the mission at Kabaa to obtain licenses for sugar-mills." Munro, *Colonial Rule Among the Kamba*, 104.

[18] Quoted in K. Kiteme, *We, The Pan-Africans: Essays on the Global Black Experience* (New York, 1992), 94.

[19] Shropshire, *The Church and the Primitive Peoples*, xiii.

[20] Ibid. The author develops a methodology for evangelization in "primitive" cultures and pleads for the "careful discrimination, preservation, transmutation and transformation of the religious and cultural institutions and beliefs of the Southern Bantu [the African peoples

> Indeed, primitive people all over the world who have not yet acknowledged a sovereignty of reason arm themselves with similar weapons against their physical and spiritual foes and have the same elemental passions, emotions and instincts. Institutions and beliefs such as initiation ceremonies, the medicine-man, witchcraft, and all the magico-religious assumptions are part and parcel of the lives of such peoples.[21]

In contrast, Christianity which has undergone "centuries of theological learning," "labour of intellect, and subtlety of reasoning throughout its whole history, stands for a literary type of religion giving prominence to beliefs that can be put into ideas as dogma and doctrine."[22] That is why, according to the missionary, he was "amazed at my own impertinence in desiring to impose a new and strange religion and culture upon a primitive people with whose cultural inheritance I was quite unacquainted."[23] Hence he advises, "Before sowing, know your ground."[24] He emphasizes that the purpose of the evangelist is not "merely to civilize but to Christianize, not merely to convey the Gifts of Civilization."[25]

European missionaries, sociologists, and anthropologists have historically treated African religions as bizarre and primitive phenomena completely different from and inferior to the messianic faiths. Part of this process of demonization betrays the prejudice, ignorance, and the cultural vantage point of the outsider. Hence the description of Africans as heathens and pagans. Many of the writers and missionaries describe African religions as superstitious, unscientific, and without reason.[26] Missionaries therefore sought to discredit and dismantle those African religions and cultural expressions that they deemed un-Christian or resistant to Christianization and Westernization. Some missionaries, however, did not advocate the full destruction of "false religions" but rather a process of "assimilation":

---

of southern Africa], by and within a full-orbed presentation of the Christian religion." Ibid., xix.

21 Ibid., xiii-xiv.

22 Ibid., xxiv.

23 Ibid., xiii.

24 Ibid.

25 Ibid., 425.

26 Ibid. See E. Ayisi, *An Introduction to the Study of African Culture* (London, 1972), 57: "It has been said that they [African religions] lack any theological ideas and all the elements which make Judaism, Islam or Christianity sublime are lacking in African religion. People who should have known better, especially missionaries, were completely misguided about African religion, and by their muddled thinking propagated erroneous ideas about African religious beliefs."

> It is becoming increasingly clear, and governors and missionaries alike are coming to realize, that the method of the destruction of religion and culture of primitive races, as happened in the cases of the Tasmanians, Australians, . . . and American Indians is both scandalous and futile. For such a method destroys all the values that give meaning and zest to their lives, rendering them impotent and ill-equipped to face the future, cutting them loose from all their moorings on a vast and uncharted sea where they drift to despair and finally destruction.[27]

This paternalistic approach, which sought to "secure, at whatever cost, the fullness of the development of the personality of the African," would not simply target African religions but would be a "concerted attempt" in the "spheres of religion, law, medicine, politics and economics for the simple reason that the life of those we are seeking to transform is all of a piece."[28] In this process of re-education, missionaries ended up denouncing as satanic African ceremonies and actions of worship for the spirit world. African dances, marriage ceremonies, female circumcision, and polygamy were deemed pagan or heathen practices incompatible with Christianity. Among the Kikuyu and Akamba of Kenya, for example, parents who permitted female circumcision were not allowed access to churches and schools, although the practice was deeply bound up with other cultural norms.[29] As one writer has mildly put it:

> The missionaries, as even devout Christians will admit, were extremely narrow in outlook. They taught that Christianity was the only right religion and that all other religions and practices must stop. Such teaching confused the Africans, who believed that all religions were good.[30]

---

[27] Shropshire, *The Church and the Primitive Peoples*, 425.

[28] Ibid. A more forceful method was favored by others as this description of Henry the Navigator reveals: "The heathen lands were kingdoms to be won for Christ, and the guidance of their backward races was a duty that must not be shirked. Henry shouldered this responsibility. If he had the spirit of a crusader, he had that of a missionary as well. Wherever he explored, his aim was to evangelise, to civilise, and to educate the simple natives. . . . He sent out teachers and preachers to the black men on the Senegal [river]." Debrunner, *A History of Christianity in Ghana*, 15.

[29] In most African cultures, the private/public distinction appears to have been absent or insignificant in the construction of social and political reality. Earthly existence constituted one whole: life was at once social, political, religious, cultural, and economic. The state (or the socio-political organism for the orderly running of the community, such as the council of elders) among many of the Bantu peoples of East Africa, was not apart from the community or contradictory to it. Life was one continuum, neither wholly private nor completely public. Religion was permeated every aspect of life.

[30] L. Clark, ed., *Through African Eyes: The Colonial Experience* (New York, 1970), 81. See also A. Mazrui, "Africa and Other Civilizations: Conquest and Counterconquest," in J. Harbeson, ed., *Africa in World Politics* (Boulder/San Francisco, 1991), 77-78: "Indigenous African religions, on the other hand, are basically communal rather than universalist. As with Hin-

The deliberate destruction of African values was epitomized by the introduction of a "white" god and Jesus Christ and a "black" devil or satan. The visual images displayed and popularized by missionaries to date—drawings and other impressions of Jesus Christ, the Virgin Mary, and God—are those of whites with blue eyes and long, usually blond, hair. Verbal and written descriptions of these figures also gave the impression that they were European. Growing up in Africa as a young boy—and my experience was typical—I thought that God was a silver-haired white sage resident somewhere in the deep blue sky. The system of formal education introduced by the missionaries and the colonial authorities emphasized the superiority of Europe over the rest of the world. This educational and religious orientation was meant to disembowel, and did so, African traditional outlooks and replace them with Western, Judeo-Christian conceptions of life.

The alliance between, and in many cases the practical fusion of the Church and the colonial flag, even where naked force was not applied, served to quash African values. As a reaction to the Eurocentric and racist curricula of the mission schools, together with their opposition to African cultural and religious practices such as female circumcision, Africans in Kenya started in the late 1920s to establish independent schools under the leadership of Jomo Kenyatta, later the first president of Kenya. This frontal attack on religious values and practices and ethnic and racial identities developed over hundreds of years was particularly damaging because religion was an integral part of being African.[31] African religious beliefs centered individual and group existence; their subversion overthrew ethnic identities. The devaluation of their culture dehumanized Africans and created a self-hatred that continues to devour the continent today.

Predictably, different denominations of Christianity, primarily the Protestant and Roman Catholic, introduced bitter rivalries between African communities. The rivalry engendered by the competition for converts

duism and modern Judaism—and unlike Christianity and Islam —indigenous African traditions have not sought to convert all of mankind. The Yoruba do not seek to convert the Ibo to the Yoruba religion, or vice-versa. Nor do the Yoruba or the Ibo compete with each other for the souls of a third group. By not being proselytizing religions, indigenous African creeds have not fought with each other." Mazrui thinks that Africa probably did not experience religious wars before the arrival of Christianity and Islam. He attributes the lack of religious wars in pre-Islamic, pre-Christian Africa to the non-proselytizing nature of indigenous religions and traditions.

[31] According to a leading African scholar, religion is an essential element of African culture. "Africans are notoriously religious, and each people has its own religious system with a set of beliefs and practices. Religion permeates into all the departments of life so fully that it is not easy to isolate it." J. Mbiti, *African Religions and Philosophy* (Garden City, NY, 1970), 1.

created deep political antagonisms between ethnic groups and introduced one more cleavage in societies already destabilized by colonization. In countries like Uganda, these sectarian rivalries have periodically erupted into ethno-political violence. In countries such as Sudan or Nigeria, the primary source of violence has been inter-religious: between Muslims and Christians.[32]

It was not the purpose of this segment to document the destruction of African religions and cultural values through the agencies of the messianic religions and colonialism. My purpose was to explore the views of the missionaries and the methods employed in their work. There is little doubt that the coupling of Islam with force and Christianity with the colonial state—with a technologically superior base—virtually assured the decimation of indigenous religions or, at the very least, the imposition of alien religions. The material and military resources available to the colonial administrators enabled them to crush resistance and establish political hegemony. From their privileged vantage points, the missionaries—utilizing equally sophisticated means of pacification and communication—were able to force and pressure whole communities to abandon their indigenous faiths if they hoped to benefit from the new order. In all probability, the dismantling of African religions and cultures—even under colonialism—would have been much more difficult without the combination of proselytization with racism. According to Basil Davidson, the Africanist, none of this was an accident or a mistake:

> By racism I mean the conscious and systematic weapon of domination, of exploitation, which first saw its demonic rise with the onset of the trans-Atlantic trade in African captives sold into slavery, and which, later, led on to the imperialist colonialism of our yesterdays.
>
> This racism was not a "mistake," a "misunderstanding" or a "grievous deviation from the proper norms of behavior." It was not an accident of human error. It was not an unthinking reversion to barbarism. On the contrary, this racism was conceived as the moral justification—the necessary justification, as it was seen by those in the white man's world who were neither thieves or moral monsters—*for doing to black people what church and state no longer*

[32] Since independence, successive Sudanese governments—which have been dominated exclusively by Sudanese Arabs—have sought to force Islam on Black Africans who are adherents of African traditional religions and Christianity in the south. In Nigeria, political instability—and the resultant inability to create a viable, economically prosperous society in spite of enormous material and human resources—must be attributed, at least partially, to the religious animosities between Muslims in the north and Christians in the south, a cleavage that also corresponds with ethnicity.

thought it permissible to do to white people: the justification for enslaving black people. . . .[33]

Indigenous Religions and the Law: A Lacuna

The subject of indigenous religions is one of the most underdeveloped areas of inquiry in human rights. Indeed, it remains a question whether the view adopted by the human rights corpus on the freedom of religion, belief, and conscience—in Article 18 of both the UDHR and ICCPR—took into account indigenous religions and their historical relationship with messianic faiths. In this segment, I shall briefly examine what protections, if any, are afforded indigenous religions in the human rights regime and in several African countries. For the purposes of my argument, I shall not attempt to define the complex and contentious term "indigenous peoples." Instead, I shall focus my attention on "indigenous religions" which I define as non-messianic faiths but excluding dominant and politically established religions such as Judaism, Buddhism, and Hinduism. The key to the inclusion of a religion as indigenous is its history of attack and domination by the imperial faiths and colonialism and its status as the cultural inheritance and spiritual expression of the original, non-white, non-Arabic peoples of Africa.[34] But I also examine United Nations documents regarding the cultural rights of indigenous peoples to indicate how the human rights regime might consider thinking about the protection of indigenous religions.

The UDHR and the ICCPR do not specially recognize indigenous religions in relation to dominant faiths or cultures; they do not even refer to them. Article 18 simply provides the right of everyone "to freedom of thought, conscience and religion" and prohibits the use of coercion to "impair" the freedom of others to have or to adopt a religion or a belief of their choice. The freedom to "manifest one's religion or beliefs may be subject to such limitations as are prescribed by law" or limited to protect public "morals or the fundamental rights and freedoms of others."[35] This provision prohibits the use of force to make converts as was the case in early European crusades in Africa and the conquest of parts of the continent by Arab Muslims. It would also appear to disallow using state resources—such as educational, health, and other services—to

---

[33] B. Davidson, *African Civilization Revisited* (Trenton, NJ, 1991), 3-4 (emphasis added).

[34] Simply put, I define as indigenous all African traditional religions which predated Islamization and Christianization. Similarly, the term could also be used to denote the religious beliefs of native, non-settler peoples in the Americas and parts of Asia.

[35] ICCPR, Article 18.

disadvantage particular faiths. Missionaries who worked against other religions with the help of colonial regimes would seem to be in violation of this provision.

While no authoritative human rights body has issued a definitive interpretation of such construction, the Human Rights Committee[36] recently adopted a General Comment[37] on Article 27 of the ICCPR,[38] providing that states are under an obligation to protect the cultural, linguistic, and religious rights of minorities. It said, in part:

> Although the rights protected under Article 27 are individual rights, they depend in turn on the ability of the minority group to maintain its culture, language or religion. Accordingly positive measures by States may also be necessary to protect the identity of a minority and the rights of its members to enjoy and develop their culture and language and to practice their religion, in community with other members of the group.[39]

In its 1981 Declaration on the Elimination of all Forms of Intolerance and of Discrimination Based on Religion and Belief,[40] the United Nations did not address the subject of indigenous religions. The Declaration was little more than an elaboration of article 18 of the ICCPR.

Some more recent developments, however, indicate a willingness to recognize indigenous religions within the ambit of the United Nations. Through the relentless and focussed advocacy of indigenous peoples and their supporters, the General Assembly in 1992 instructed the Working Group on Indigenous Populations to draft a Declaration on the Rights of Indigenous Peoples for consideration by the Commission on Human Rights.[41] The Draft Declaration, which now awaits action by the Commis-

---

[36] The ICCPR, the principal civil and political rights human rights treaty, establishes the Human Rights Committee, the body responsible for the elaboration, interpretation, and the encouragement of the implementation of the treaty. See ICCPR, Article 28.

[37] Article 40(4) of the ICCPR directs the Human Rights Committee to "study" state reports and to "transmit its reports, and such general comments as it may consider appropriate." The general comments are meant to be authoritative interpretations of the ICCPR's provisions.

[38] Article 27 of the ICCPR provides that "In those States in which ethnic, religious or linguistic minorities exist, persons belonging to such minorities shall not be denied the right, in community with others members of the group, to enjoy their own culture, to profess and practice their own religion, or to use their language."

[39] General Comment No. 23, para 6.2, U.N. Doc. CCPR/C/21/Rev.1/Add.5, 1994.

[40] Proclaimed by the General Assembly Resolution 36/55 of November 25, 1981. United Nations, *Human Rights: A Compilation of International Instruments* (New York, 1993), 122-125 .

[41] The Working Group on Indigenous Populations was established in 1982 by the United Nations as a subsidiary body of the UN Sub-Commission on Prevention of Discrimination and Protection of Minorities, itself an expert body of the UN Commission on Human Rights.

sion on Human Rights, explicitly recognizes indigenous religions and goes further than any other United Nations document in recognizing the rights of indigenous peoples and protecting their indigenous religions.

The Draft Declaration, in dramatic and definitive language, affirms in the preamble that: "all doctrines, policies and practices based on or advocating superiority of peoples or individuals on the basis of national origin, racial, religious, ethnic or cultural differences are racist, scientifically false, legally invalid, morally condemnable and socially unjust. . . ."[42]

The Draft Declaration would find unacceptable the philosophical and theological assumptions propagated by missionaries in Africa; the demonization of African religions as backward and inferior would violate the letter and spirit of the document. Elsewhere, the Draft Declaration protects indigenous peoples from any "adverse discrimination, in particular based on their indigenous origin and identity."[43] More importantly, the Draft Declaration prohibits "cultural genocide" and disallows "any form of assimilation or integration by other cultures or ways of life imposed on them . . . ."[44] In a sweeping assertion of sovereignty, the Draft Declaration appears to prohibit all forms of advocacy or proselytization by agents external to the indigenous culture when it calls for the "prevention of and redress for," among other things, "any form of propaganda directed at them [that is, indigenous peoples]."[45] The objective of this reasoning is to create space in which indigenous peoples and their cultures are left alone by external agents including imperial religions. If adopted, the Draft Declaration would provide guidance for the human rights movement in understanding indigenous religions and creating processes to protect them.

While the protection of indigenous cultures appears to be gaining international currency, African states remain uninterested in reclaiming the pre-colonial past and restoring those aspects of traditional norms and values, including elements of spirituality, which were discredited during the colonial era. The lack of interest in the past is partially due to its thorough demonization and the shame and backwardness with which the Westernized and Christianized or Islamized ruling African elites associate it. Good culture in Africa today is defined by its distance from traditional cultures and proximity to Western values. In many instances,

---

[42] See Draft Declaration on the Rights of Indigenous Peoples, U.N. ESCOR, Commission on Human Rights, Sub-Commission on Prevention of Discrimination and Protection of Minorities, 46th Session, Agenda Item 15, U.N. Doc. E/CN.4/Sub.2/1994/Add.1 (1994). [hereinafter Draft Declaration].

[43] Draft Declaration, Article 2.

[44] Ibid., Article 7(d).

[45] Ibid., Article 7(e).

African states continue to carry out "modernization" campaigns against "backward peoples" such as the Masai of Kenya and Tanzania. So-called African customary laws, for example, are ordinarily overridden by received colonial laws in most legal systems and jurisdictions in Africa. In many African countries, there have been no national debates to evaluate and contextualize African customs and laws within the modern state. Many traditional practices, from polygamy to traditional healing and worship, which were discredited by the colonial state, are actively prohibited and punished by the new African-led governments. In this process of continued acculturation, African religions have been one of the major casualties of the culture of imitation.

The exception to the general disregard of the African past is the African Charter on Human and Peoples' Rights, the continental human rights instrument adopted by the Organization of African Unity in 1981.[46] In its preamble, the African Charter recognizes the "virtues" of Africa's traditions and its civilization. Elsewhere, it imposes upon individual Africans the "duty to preserve and strengthen positive African values" although it neither spells out those values or mentions African religions.[47] But its use of the word "positive" betrays a Eurocentric bias and implies that there is much that is negative in African culture. The only reference to religion is a boiler plate provision, taken mainly from the ICCPR, that protects religious freedom.[48]

Predictably, African constitutions and laws have since independence from colonial rule been of little help in addressing the problem. A survey of the constitutions of several African states make no mention of indigenous religions choosing instead to provide the generic protection of religious freedom contained in international human rights instruments.[49] The wording of several other constitutions suggests that some forms of evangelization may be restricted.[50] The constitution of Zambia, for example, guarantees the freedom of religion except that limitations could be placed to "ensure that the enjoyment of the said rights and freedoms of any one individual does not prejudice the rights and freedoms of oth-

[46] The African Charter on Human and Peoples' Rights [hereinafter the African Charter] came into force in 1986. It establishes a continental human rights system by creating the African Commission on Human and Peoples' Rights, its implementing body. Although widely criticized as lacking in effectiveness, the Commission remains the only continent-wide human rights body.

[47] Ibid., Article 29(7).

[48] Ibid., Article 8.

[49] See, e.g., The Constitution of the Republic of Ghana, 1979, Section 27(1); The Constitution of Mozambique, 1975, Article 33; The Constitution of Mali, 1977, Section 11.

[50] See The Constitution of Mauritius, 1971, Section 11 5(b); The Constitution of Zimbabwe, 1980, Section 19 5(b).

ers."[51] The constitution of Mauritius seems to limit attempts at proselytization by protecting "the right to observe and practice any religion or belief without the unsolicited intervention of persons professing any other religion or belief."[52] Although the laws respecting indigenous religions is quite thin if not lacking, the general orientation of the policies of most African states has been hostile to pre-colonial, pre-Islamic, or pre-Christian values but very protective of one or both of the messianic faiths. In many cases, states continue to actively prosecute campaigns to root out "unenlightened" customs and traditions.

Ideals Versus Realities: The Dilemma

The two basic human rights documents—the Universal Declaration of Human Rights and the International Covenant on Civil and Political Rights—seek to entrench and encourage the free exchange of ideas[53] and the respect for difference and diversity. The emphasis placed on the importance of creating and maintaining a diverse society is one of the most striking characteristics of human rights law. Diversity is encouraged, though not required, by the rights corpus in cultural, religious, political, and other endeavors and pursuits. Through this emphasis, human rights law "evidences throughout its hostility to imposed uniformity."[54] According to Henry Steiner:

> The ideal of encouraging and protecting diversity informs many human rights provisions. No other norm in the human rights corpus plays as vital a role in the struggle to realize that ideal as the principle of equal protection, perhaps the preeminent human rights norm. *Its premise of the equal worth of individuals and their right to equal respect necessarily applies to the ethnic groups with which individuals are associated, for discrimination has the same systemic character whether it is directed against a group or selectively against a member.*[55]

---

[51] The Constitution of Zambia, 1974, Section 13.

[52] The Constitution of Mauritius, 1971, Section 11 5(b). The Constitution of Zimbabwe, 1980, Section 19 5(b), repeats almost verbatim the corresponding section of the constitution of Mauritius.

[53] Article 19 of the UDHR provides: "Everyone has the right to freedom of opinion and expression; this right includes the freedom to hold opinions without interference and to seek, receive and impart information and ideas through any media and regardless of frontiers." Article 19 of the ICCPR is the equivalent provision although it warns that these rights carry "special duties and responsibilities" and are therefore subject to "certain restrictions" for the "respect of the rights . . . of others" and for the protection of "national security or of public order (*ordre public*), or public health and morals."

[54] Steiner, "Ideals and Counter-Ideals," 1548.

[55] Ibid. (emphasis added).

Indeed, Article 26 of the ICCPR prohibits discrimination on the basis of race, color, sex, language, religion, political or other opinion, national or social origin, property, birth, or other status. Article 27 affirms the same philosophy by requiring states to make sure that minorities shall not be denied the right to enjoy their own culture and to profess and practice their own religion.[56] Elsewhere, the ICCPR repeatedly confirms its adherence to difference by protecting the rights of persons to assemble peacefully[57] and to associate freely with others.[58] Lawful restrictions, however, could be imposed on the basis of national security, the protection of public health or morals, or the protection of the rights and freedoms of others.[59] Although it is clear that human rights law is obsessed with the creation, protection, and preservation of diversity, it is also clear that rights advancing this ideal—which is central to the movement—could also be curtailed to protect the rights of others.

This propagation of diversity through the freedom to exchange ideas and to associate across divides and traditional cleavages such as race, religion, culture, national origin, and gender by human rights law assumes—an assumption that is still being tested—that there is inherent benefit in cross-fertilization or contact with "otherness." When the ICCPR declares, for example, the "freedom to seek, receive, and impart information and ideas of all kinds, regardless of frontiers,"[60] it presupposes, without final proof, an ultimate good in the exercise of that right. There are presumed "goods"—growth, vitality, search for truth, and new challenges—that would benefit humanity from interaction, difference, and diversity. Ethnic separation—whether voluntary or enforced—is not preferred; instead, openness and transparency towards "the other" might nurture respect for difference and reduce bigotry and demonization. These assumptions raise certain difficulties that I will return to later.

With regard to the right to religious belief, the ICCPR grants a wide latitude:

> Everyone shall have the right to freedom of thought, conscience and religion. This right shall include freedom to have or to adopt a religion or belief of his choice, and freedom, either individually or in community with others and in public or private, to manifest his religion or belief in worship, observance, practice and teaching.[61]

---

[56] ICCPR, Article 27.
[57] Ibid., Article 21.
[58] Ibid., Article 22.
[59] Ibid., Article 22(2).
[60] Ibid., Article 19(2).
[61] Ibid., Article 18(1).

Significantly, the covenant also provides that no one shall "be subject to coercion which would impair his freedom to have or to adopt a religion or belief of his choice."[62] Additionally, the freedom to "manifest one's religion or beliefs," could be lawfully limited on the grounds of public safety, order, health, or morals or "the fundamental rights and freedoms of others."[63] Article 18 of the UDHR also provides for the "right to freedom of thought, conscience and religion."

Taken together, the provisions advocating difference and diversity and those providing explicitly for religious rights, would seem to allow proselytization by the messianic religions, although they also provide for certain limitations which might be read as possibly excluding certain modes of evangelization. For example, proselytization through force, coercion, or in the context of colonization would appear to be excluded.

Although human rights law amply protects the right to proselytize through the principles of free speech, assembly, and association, the "pecking" order of rights problematizes the right to evangelize where the result is the destruction of other cultures or the closure of avenues for other religions. It is my argument that the most fundamental of all human rights is that of self-determination[64] and that no other right overrides it. Without this fundamental group or individual right, no other human right could be secured, since the group would be unable to determine for its individual members under what political, social, cultural, economic, and legal order they would live. Any right which directly conflicts with this right ought to be void to the extent of that conflict. Traditionally, the self-determination principle has been employed to advance the cause of decolonization or to overcome other forms of external occupation. The principle was indispensable to the decolonization process. This usage of the principle—as a tool for advancing demands for external self-determination—could be expanded to disallow cultural and religious imperialism or imposition by external agencies through acculturation, especially where the express intent of the "invading" culture or religion, as was the case in Africa, is to destroy its indigenous counterparts and seal off the entry or growth of other traditions. Furthermore, the principle could also be read to empower internal self-determination, that is, the right of a people to "cultural survival."[65] This usage of self-determination

---

62 Ibid., Article 18(2).

63 Ibid., Article 18(3).

64 ICCPR, Article 1: "All peoples have the right of self-determination. By virtue of that right they freely determine their political status and freely pursue their economic, social and cultural development." Article One of the International Covenant on Economic, Social and Cultural Rights, the other treaty which together with the ICCPR and the UDHR makes the so-called International Bill of Human Rights, is identically worded.

65 See Steiner, "Ideals and Counter-Ideals," 1545-1547.

is advanced by the Draft Declaration on the Rights of Indigenous Peoples. It is also an argument against cultural genocide. It is one of the ideas advanced by advocates of autonomy regimes for minorities: unless groups are given protection against invasion and control by others, their cultural and ethnic identities could be quashed by more powerful cultures and political systems. The violent advocacy of the messianic religions in Africa could be seen as a negation of this right particularly because religion is often the first point of attack in the process of acculturation.

Christianity and Islam forcibly entered Africa not as guests but as masters.[66] The two traditions came either as conquerors or on the backs of conquerors. As they had done elsewhere, they were driven by the belief and conviction of their own innate superiority—and conversely what they saw as barbaric African religions and cultures. This belief was not a function of an objective assessment and reflection about African religions and cultures. It was born of the contempt and ignorance of that which was different and the exaggerated importance of the messianic faiths. The messianic religions—Christianity to be precise—came to Africa at a time of great technological and scientific imbalance between the West and the continent. Already the beneficiaries of the industrial revolution, the colonial church and state commanded superior resources in the areas of the military, economic organization and finance, the media, and other social and political spheres. Africa was no match, and the successful imposition of colonialism is proof of that fact. The West was able through coercion, intimidation, trickery, and force to impose a new political, social, cultural, and thanks to the missionaries, religious order in Africa. African political, social, and religious traditions were delegitimized virtually overnight.

Thus begun the process of de-Africanization through large-scale cash-crop farming for European industries, industrialization, urbanization, and the wholesale subversion of traditional values and structures. Africa—from top to bottom—was re-made in the image of Europe complete with Eurocentric modern states. Christianity played a crucial role in this process: weaning Africans from their roots and pacifying them for the new order. Utilizing superior resources, it occupied most political space and practically killed local religious traditions and then closed off society from other persuasions. It is in this sense that the practice of colonial Christian advocacy constituted a violation of the fundamental freedoms of Africans. Islam, which had invaded Africa at an earlier date, was

[66] Christians and Muslims came to Africa to holy wage war, as it were, and to subjugate and eradicate indigenous religions and cultures. They did not come to persuade; they came to conquer and did indeed conquer. This is a contradiction of the right to self-determination.

equally insidious and destructive of local religions. Its forceful conversions and wars of conquest together with its prohibition of its repudiation, were violative of the rights of Africans as well.

Conclusions

Individuals do not exist in the atomized language prevalent in the human rights movement. Usually, individuals, even in the industrial democracies of the West, are members of an ethnic, social, religious, or political group. Quite often, a single individual will fall under several classifications. Although many of the rights enumerated in human rights law attach to individuals, they only make sense in a collective, social perspective. This is the case because the creation or development of a culture or a religion are societal, not individual, endeavors. I make this point to underline the importance of culture or religion to individuals and groups. An individual's morals, attitudes towards life and death, and identity come from this collective construction of reality through history.

No one culture or religion is sovereign in relationship to any other culture or religion. From the perspective of the human rights movement, all cultures are equal. This view rejects the notion that there is a hierarchy of cultures or religions; that some cultures are superior to others even though technologically they may be more advanced. Belief in the contrary has led to military invasions to "civilize," colonize, and enslave, as was the case with Christianity in Africa. Cultures, however, have always interacted throughout history; there are no pure cultures, as such, although many traditions retain their distinctive personality. In many cases, the voluntary, unforced commingling of cultures has led to a more vital and creative existence. Several lessons can be drawn from this premise. The human rights movement should encourage the cross-breeding of cultures and tolerance for diversity. It should also frown upon homogenization and the imposition of uniformity.

As I mentioned at the beginning, the human rights movement is premised on societies being open to new ideas and challenges; even when a creed seeks homogenization, it must be open to persuasion from other traditions. Although I agree with and share this basic ideal of the human rights corpus, I am deeply concerned that the movement's central tenets may support forms of advocacy that negate certain rights and give legitimacy to abusive conduct. In the case of Africa, the arrival of Christianity, for example, was so violent towards indigenous traditions that the possibility of the free exchange of values and a voluntary commingling was non-existent. The missionaries and the colonial authorities defined local cultures as demonic; one had to choose between the old and the new. The new ways were promoted as the salvation from a satanic past. Progress, culture, and humanity were identified entirely in Islamic or Christian terms, never with reference to indigenous traditions. But the new converts could not become fully "Christian" or "European"; many, to this day, remain suspended between a dim African past and a distorted, Westernized existence. Many have been robbed of their humanity.

It was not the intention of this chapter to circumscribe religious human rights. I share with other scholars and activists in the human rights movement the importance of protecting religious human rights and enjoining governments from unduly burdening or prohibiting the free exercise of religion. But I am concerned by those dimensions of messianic religions that claim a right not merely to persuade individuals or groups of peoples of the "truth" as they see it but rather actively demonize, systematically discredit, and forcibly destroy and eventually replace non-universalist, non-competitive, indigenous religions. Quite often, indigenous religions anchor a total worldview and their destruction usually entails a fundamental distortion of ethnic identities and history.

Perhaps there is nothing that can be done today to reverse the negative effects of forced or coerced religious proselytization during the era of colonialism in Africa. Nor is it possible to reclaim wholly the African past as though history has stood still. This does not mean, however, that we should simply forget the past and go on as if nothing happened. The anguish and deprivation caused by that historical experience is with me—and millions of other Africans—today. We bear the marks of that terrible period. For those Africans who choose not to be Christians or Muslims, the past is not really an option: it was so effectively destroyed and delegitimized that it is practically impossible to retrieve. It is this loss that I mourn and for which I blame Christianity and Islam. The human rights corpus should outlaw those forms of proselytization used in Africa, because their purpose and effect have been the dehumanization of an entire race of people. It could do so by elaborating a treaty that addresses religious human rights but provides for the protection and mechanisms of redress for forms of proselytization that seek to unfairly assimilate or impose dominant cultures on indigenous religion.

Religious Human Rights in South Africa

LOURENS M. DU PLESSIS
University of Stellenbosch

The signs of the times in the new South Africa have determined the spirit and purport of this chapter. The apartheid past is not forgotten, but most South Africans are no longer in sackcloth and ashes about it. They are looking forward to a better future with enthusiasm, but the euphoria reigning the election and its aftermath has begun to make way for level-headed realism. Hard work and profound thinking will be needed to optimize the effectiveness of the negotiated structures and institutions which came into place with the commencement of a transitional Constitution on April 27, 1994.[1] Some of these novelties, and particularly those discussed in this chapter, are temporary and transitional. The trial run will nevertheless be crucial. It will determine the success or failure of a "final" dispensation which will not differ substantially from the transitional phase. This is due to the entrenchment, in the transitional Constitution itself, of 33 constitutional principles on which the final constitution will have to be based.

In this chapter, I shall focus on the future implementation of provisions in the Constitution which could have a direct or indirect impact on the protection of religious rights without, however, ignoring the past. The process through which the Constitution came into existence will also be reviewed and a possible approach to the interpretation of the Constitution considered. Such a contextualization of the constitutional text is necessary to facilitate the fullest possible understanding of those provisions that will be looked at in particular.

[1] The Constitution of the Republic of South Africa 200 of 1993.

J.D. van der Vyver and J. Witte, Jr. (eds.), Religious Human Rights in Global Perspective, 441-465.

The Religious Demography of South Africa

The 1991 population census, adjusted for undercount, provides a good summary of the religious demography of South Africa.[2] A clear majority of the population profess to have religious affiliations. Of the 21,778,868 people (comprising almost 70% of the population) stating such affiliations, 94.5% are Christian. 29.7% of the total population, however, failed to mention their religious affiliation or objected to doing so. Should nobody in this group be Christian (which is probably not a realistic assumption) the percentage of Christians in relation to the total population could be as low as 66.4%.

The second largest religious group in South Africa is African traditionalists. They constitute the majority of the 6,000,000 South Africans, or more than 15% of the total population, who claim no affiliation to any formal religious organization. Many black South Africans find themselves in transition somewhere between traditional African religion and Christianity.[3]

The almost 7,000,000 members of the more than 4,000 African Indigenous Churches constitute the majority of Christians in South Africa, namely 22.2% of the total population. The second largest group is the Dutch Reformed Church "family" consisting of the white Dutch Reformed "mother church" and the colored, Indian, and Black "daughter churches." These "daughter churches" recently formed a single United Reformed Church. 10.4% of the total population (of which the majority are people other than whites) belongs to churches in the Dutch Reformed family, making it the second largest Christian denomination in South Africa. The other two Afrikaans churches which, together with the "white" Dutch Reformed Church, helped shape apartheid and justified it theologically, constitute decided minorities of the population.[4]

Further significant Christian denominations in South Africa are the Roman Catholic Church (7.6% of the total population, of which more than 80% is black), the Methodist Church (5.9% of the total population), and various Pentecostal churches (4.4%). Hinduism is the second largest non-Christian religious grouping, namely 1.3% of the total population, followed by Islam at 1.1%. Jews, of whom the majority are orthodox, constitute 0.2% of the total population.[5] Only 1.2% of the total population stated that they have no religion and belong to no church.

---

[2] Central Statistical Service, *South African Statistics 1993* (Pretoria, 1993), par. 1.18.

[3] Elise Keyter, ed., *Official Yearbook: South Africa 1993* (Pretoria, 1993), 263

[4] The all-white *Nederduitsch Hervormde Kerk* has but 0.9% of the total population as its members, and the *Gereformeerde Kerk* only 0.5% (including a minority of blacks and coloreds).

[5] Keyter, ed., *Official Yearbook*, 263-264.

Christianity thus has a majoritarian position in South Africa, but with great denominational diversity spread over more than 34 religious groupings and several thousand denominations. This clearly indicates religious pluralism.[6]

Religion and the Law Until April 27, 1994

Until April 27, 1994, when the transitional Constitution entered into force, South Africa had no legislative instrument remotely resembling a supreme constitution with a bill of rights. Constitutional law was premised on the British concept of parliamentary sovereignty. Section 34(3)—read with section 34(2)—of the previous Republic of South Africa Constitution Act,[7] like its predecessors,[8] restricted the Supreme Court's competence to pronounce on the validity of Acts of Parliament to "manner and form" issues. The question whether procedural requirements stipulated by, *inter alia*, the Constitution[9] had been satisfied in passing an act was, in other words, the only issue which a court could review.[10]

Matters relating to religion were regulated either by enactments of the (supreme) legislature or by the common law. South Africa's common law originated from Roman-Dutch law but has to a large extent been amplified—and in some areas transformed—by English law.[11] The common law has been developed mainly through case law.

There is also provision in South Africa for the recognition of customary law. A custom fulfilling certain requirements can after some time acquire the force of law.[12] The law observed by indigenous South African blacks conserving their "traditional lifestyle" is recognized as customary law—presently in terms of the Law of Evidence Amendment Act,[13] section 2 of which stipulates that judicial notice can be taken of customary law (just as in the case of the law of a foreign country) provided that it is not in conflict with "the principles of public policy or natural justice."

Christian Bias in South African Law. Both South African statute and common law have shown (and still show) a Christian bias. The South Af-

---

6 See also ibid., 261.

7 Section 110 of 1983.

8 Section 2 of the South Africa Act Amendment Act 9 of 1956 (introduced after a constitutional debacle in the early fifties) and sec. 59(2) of the Republic of South Africa Constitution Act 32 of 1961.

9 Mostly in sec. 99(2).

10 Lourens M. du Plessis, *The Interpretation of Statutes* (Durban, 1986), 6-7.

11 Lourens M. du Plessis and A.G. du Plessis, *An Introduction to Law* (Cape Town, 1992), 16-18.

12 Ibid., 183-184.

13 Section 45 of 1988.

rican common law, during its earliest formative period, was exposed to the same Christian influences which helped shape Roman law in Western Europe since the time of the emperor Constantine (306-337). After the Dutch colonization of the Cape in 1652, these influences were enhanced by legislation.

A few examples of this Christian bias will suffice. A series of Sunday observance laws, of which some are still in force, was passed mostly by legislatures at a provincial level.[14] While the main body of censorship legislation in the Publications Act[15] purports to afford protection to the religious convictions or feelings of all religious groups,[16] it also introduces blasphemy as a criterion for censorship, and blasphemy has been understood with a definite Christian bias.[17] Section 1 of the Publications Act furthermore states that "[i]n the application of this Act the constant endeavor of the population of the Republic of South Africa to uphold a Christian view of life shall be recognised." Two statutes dealing with education policy, namely the National Education Policy Act[18] for whites and the Education and Training Act[19] for blacks, prescribe a Christian orientation in education. The first act requires education to be Christian national and the second act requires it to be Christian in character. Limited concessions are made to non-Christian religions in the sense that respect for the religious convictions of parents and pupils in regard to religious instruction and religious ceremonies is required.[20] These two Acts are apparently contradicted by the National Policy for General Education Affairs Act,[21] which seems to favor religious neutrality and impartiality in the formulation of education policy. Until 1977, witnesses in both criminal and civil proceedings were allowed to take an oath in the form which they considered binding upon their conscience. Section 162(1) of the Criminal Procedure Act,[22] however, makes allowance for the Christian form of the oath only. Witnesses objecting to this are allowed to make an affirmation in lieu of the oath.

This Christian bias was also reflected in constitutional law. Section 2 of South Africa's 1983 Constitution includes a constitutional confession of

---

14 Johan D. van der Vyver, "Religion," in W.A. Joubert and T.J. Scott, eds., *The Law of South Africa* (Durban/Pretoria, 1986), 23:175-202, esp. 198-199.

15 Section 42 of 1974.

16 Section 47(2)(b).

17 Blasphemy as a common law offence, for instance, consists of the desecration of *the God confessed by Christianity*. See van der Vyver, "Religion," 199-200.

18 Section 9 of 1967.

19 Section 90 of 1979.

20 van der Vyver, "Religion," 197-198.

21 Section 76 of 1984.

22 Section 51 of 1977.

faith: "The people of the Republic of South Africa acknowledge the sovereignty and guidance of Almighty God." It has been argued quite convincingly that such a confession of faith does not constitute a binding and enforceable rule of law.[23] The preamble to the 1983 Constitution also contained a number of statements of a religious nature not only showing a Christian bias but arguably also a bias for Christianity as understood by South African whites and Afrikaners in particular. However, according to the law as it then stood the preamble to the constitution was not an authoritative legal statement. It is interesting that in the opening sentence of the (legally more authoritative) preamble to the 1994 (transitional) Constitution the phrase "In humble submission to Almighty God" has remained. No further references of a religious nature, however, follow and the opening statement is at any rate phrased in a broad, denominationally neutral way.

Church and State. Since 1902 there has been no established church in South Africa enjoying preferential treatment. Statutory provisions relating to different church denominations and enacted since the unification of the four colonies in 1910 made no attempt to favor any denomination, nor did they detract from the internal sovereignty or autonomy of the churches.[24]

Under South African law, a church is a juristic person. This means that it has rights and obligations of its own, distinct from those of its members. It can own property, it has the capacity to enter into legal transactions and it can sue (and be sued) in its own name. Depending on the internal organization of a church, legal personality could be conferred on either the church as denomination, a particular congregation of the church, or both. Apart from external legal recognition as reflected in, among others, its legal personality, a church also has its own internal legal structure and can make its own rules and regulations. These rules and regulations have legal force by virtue of the fact that from a legal point of view churches are regarded as voluntary associations. This means that the domestic tribunals of churches must comply with the precepts of natural justice should they "hear cases" and make decisions which affect the rights and legitimate expectations of their members.[25]

Section 10(1)(d) of the Income Tax Act[26] exempts from income tax the receipts and accruals of all religious, charitable, and educational institutions of a public character, whether or not supported by grants from the public revenue. The same applies to the income received by a trust for

---

[23] See, inter alia, van der Vyver, "Religion," 193, n.5.

[24] Ibid., 179-180.

[25] Ibid., 182.

[26] Section 58 of 1962.

the purpose of distributing it among such institutions[27] or the income of a fund doing the same. Such a fund must, however, have a written constitution, must have been approved by the Commissioner of Inland Revenue, and must comply with a number of formal requirements.[28] The exemption is not limited to institutions in South Africa and includes income derived by an institution from carrying on a business.[29] Donations or contributions made by individuals and organizations to religious organizations are, however, not deductible for the purpose of determining taxable income. Finally, local governments mostly exempt religious organizations from property tax.

Patterns of Religious Tolerance in South Africa

Religion Under Apartheid. Religious intolerance in South Africa has not really been manifested in confrontations between different religions or denominations—although there has been the occasional rubbing of shoulders which is normal in a religiously pluralistic society. However, it can hardly be said that religious freedom has prevailed in a society where the teargassing and arrest of worshippers, the banning and breaking up of religious services, and the dousing of church leaders by water cannons have occurred from time to time.[30] These manifestations of religious intolerance stemmed from socio-political conflict and from the claim of "both sides" to religious justification for their cause.[31]

Afrikaner civil religion, which was tolerated and through acquiescence (and complicity) promoted in particular the three Afrikaans churches, offered religious justification for whites' and Afrikaners' self-assumed position of superiority in relation to the "non-white" population and thus also for the policy and ideology of apartheid.[32] This sense of superiority was expressed in racially discriminatory statutes, mostly condoned by white Christians and their churches and in some instances even adopted at their behest. The notorious "church clause," for instance, which was section 9(7) of the Blacks (Urban Areas) Consolidation Act,[33] authorized the prohibition of blacks from, attending church services and functions in urban areas occupied by "non-blacks." Religious organiza-

[27] A.P. de Koker and G.A. Urquhart, *Income Tax in South Africa* (Durban, 1989), 9-8(6).

[28] Section 10(1)(fA).

[29] de Koker and Urquhart, *Income Tax in South Africa*, 9-8(5).

[30] Mike Robertson, ed., *Human Rights for South Africans* (Cape Town, 1991), 127.

[31] G.C. Oosthuizen et al., *Religion, Intergroup Relations and Social Change in South Africa. Work Committee: Religion, Human Sciences Research Council (HSRC) Investigation into Intergroup Relations* (Pretoria, 1985), 37-38.

[32] Ibid., 38-40.

[33] Section 25 of 1945.

tions were also not immune from being declared unlawful (and banned) or "affected" (and thus cut off from external funding) in terms of "security" legislation.[34] Legislation of a not so overtly religious nature, such as the infamous Prohibition of Mixed Marriages Act[35] and the controversial section 16 of the Immorality Act,[36] were enacted at the behest of, amongst others, the Afrikaans churches in an attempt to prevent "miscegenation."

The apartheid authorities did not, however, resort to "legal means" only in order to suppress churches and religious organizations opposing their policies. In the early hours of August 31, 1988, one of the worst bomb blasts in the history of South Africa damaged beyond repair Khotso House, headquarters of the South African Council of Churches (S.A.C.C.). The S.A.C.C., an ecumenical organization affiliated with the World Council of Churches, was actively involved in the struggle against apartheid. The "mystery" of the bomb has never been solved, but there is strong evidence that the event was orchestrated by factions in the "security" community.[37]

There were also religious responses, from the victims of apartheid, to theological justifications for a system of white superiority. These responses came in a variety of forms. At various ecclesiastical meetings and church synods, resolutions were adopted condemning apartheid in the strongest possible theological terms.[38] At its 1982 synod the Dutch Reformed Mission Church, one of the "daughter" churches within the Dutch Reformed "family," for instance, resolved to declare a *status confessionis* and condemned the theological justification of apartheid as a heresy. This unequivocal denunciation came from a theologically conservative reformed church. Almost twelve years later, the majority of the members of this church voted for the National Party in South Africa's first democratic election!

One of the most scathing theological attacks on apartheid and churches' acquiescence in it is *The Kairos Document*, dated September 25, 1985. Not only does it condemn what it calls "state theology" and its God who is described as an "idol," but it also rejects the "false peace" and "counterfeit reconciliation" of the "church theology" preached in the so-

---

[34] van der Vyver, "Religion," 191-192.

[35] 55 of 1949.

[36] 23 of 1957.

[37] See e.g. *The Sowetan* (September 1, 1988): 1; *The Star* (September 1, 1988): 3; *South African Outlook* (October, 1988): 146.

[38] Oosthuizen et al., *Religion, Intergroup Relations and Social Change in South Africa*, 143-146.

called "English-speaking churches." The document offers a liberationist "prophetic theology" as an alternative.

I have thus far highlighted some of the intra-religious and intra-denominational conflicts caused by apartheid. For sake of completeness, it should, however, also be pointed out that some religious opponents of apartheid sought within their religious traditions ways and means of reconciling the opposing factions in South Africa. This trend manifested itself in, for instance, the *Koinonia Declaration* issued on November 16, 1977, two weeks before an all-white "general" election, by a group of Christians from the conservative Potchefstroom University for Christian Higher Education and members of The Loft, a Germiston-based Christian organization. This document condemned various aspects of the apartheid policy, the murder of Steve Biko by the Security Police, and the banning of several organizations, among which was the Christian Institute of Beyers Naudé, in October of that year. In spite of this critical tone, the declaration had as its first objective the reconciliation of political adversaries in South Africa on the basis of their common Christian faith. However, once political negotiations got underway in the early 1990s, religious groups and, indeed, religion as such has played a less visible reconciliatory role in politics.

The W.C.R.P.-S.A. Conferences and Declaration. An acid test for inter-religious tolerance is the extent to which various religions and religious groupings can agree on the conditions for the exercise of religious freedom. With the apartheid system crumbling and a new dispensation in sight, the representatives of a diversity of organized religious communities in South Africa held a National Inter-Faith Conference in Pretoria (November 22-24, 1992) under the auspices of the South African Chapter of the World Conference on Religion and Peace (W.C.R.P.-S.A.). At a similar conference in 1990, the idea of a charter on religious freedom in a "new" South Africa was mooted, and the W.C.R.P.-S.A. was mandated to set in motion a representative process for its drafting.[39] This process resulted in the adoption of a Declaration on Religious Rights and Responsibilities at the 1992 conference. A freedom of religion clause for a bill of rights (hereinafter referred to as "the W.C.R.P.-S.A. proposed clause") was included as an addendum to the Declaration. Both the Declaration and the proposed clause were of great assistance in drafting the provisions on religious rights in South Africa's transitional constitution.

The W.C.R.P.-S.A. proposed clause reads as follows: "1. All persons are entitled: 1.1 to freedom of conscience, 1.2 to profess, practise, and

[39] World Conference on Religion and Peace—South African Chapter, *Believers in the Future. Proceedings of the National Inter-Faith Conference on Religion-State Relations, December 2-4 1990, Johannesburg* (Johannesburg, 1991), viii.

propagate any religion or no religion, 1.3 to change their religious allegiance. 2. Every religious community and/or member thereof shall enjoy the right: 2.1 to establish, maintain and manage religious institutions; 2.2 to have their particular system of family law recognized by the state; 2.3 to criticize and challenge all social and political structures and policies in terms of the teachings of their religion." This clause and, to a lesser extent, some of the articles of the Declaration will be taken into account when, in the course of this chapter, the freedom of religion provisions in South Africa's transitional Bill of Rights are assessed.

Note, however, that the Declaration and the proposed clause do not necessarily reflect the unanimous viewpoint of all religious communities in South Africa. Some more fundamentalist and/or politically conservative Christian groups, such as the Kwasizabantu Ministers' Conference of September 1992, the Dutch Reformed Church, and the Gospel Defence League, reacted to the outcome of the 1992 National Inter-Faith Conference with varying degrees of apprehension. It is a pity that these reactions do not always focus on the preconditions for the exercise of religious freedom *by all religious communities* in a religiously pluralistic society but prefer to concentrate on the theology informing the notion of *inter-faith* deliberations. By thus emphasizing the differences between religions, instead of identifying the common everyday needs of diverse religious communities in exercising their religious freedom, the development of meaningful ideas on how religious rights are to be protected under a supreme constitution is inhibited.

The Protection of Religion and Religious Rights Under South Africa's Transitional Constitution

Background to Chapter on Fundamental Rights. The Multi-Party Negotiating Process (M.P.N.P) at the World Trade Centre in Kempton Park got underway early in March, 1993 as the successor to CODESA II,[40] which miscarried in May, 1992. The negotiators agreed on a supreme, transitional Constitution which includes a justiciable Chapter on Fundamental Rights (Chapter 3). South Africa's final constitution, which will be negotiated during the next two years, will include a similar chapter.[41] The introduction of a supreme constitution heralded a Copernican revolution in South African public law.

Negotiations on the Chapter on Fundamental Rights were conducted mainly in a Negotiating Council where each party was represented by

---

[40] "CODESA" stands for a "Conference for a Democratic South Africa."

[41] Constitutional Principle II in sch. 4 to the transitional Constitution.

two delegates (one of whom had to be a woman) and two advisers. The Negotiating Council, in turn, appointed a twelve person Planning Committee which was responsible for the smooth running of the process and which appointed its own "executive," namely a three person Sub-Committee.

Seven technical committees assisted and advised the Council. A nine person Technical Committee on Constitutional Issues was responsible for the drafting of the transitional Constitution, but the Chapter on Fundamental Rights was the responsibility of a five person Technical Committee on Fundamental Rights during the Transition. When critical differences among the parties on the contents of the Chapter on Fundamental Rights started to impede progress, the Planning Committee set up a six person Ad Hoc Committee representative mainly of those parties in the Negotiating Council who had expressed strong views on contentious matters, in order to try and facilitate agreement. The Technical Committee aided the Ad Hoc Committee with expert advice, couched agreements reached by the latter in technical language, and channeled them to the Planning Committee for submission to the Negotiating Council. Many contentious issues were resolved in bilateral discussions mostly between powerful role players such as the South African Government/National Party and the African National Congress alliance. The process of drafting Chapter 3 took more than six months.

Three ideological tensions had an impact on negotiating Chapter 3—tensions between *libertarianism* and (*egalitarian*) *liberationism*, between *progressivism* and *traditionalism*, and between *feminism* and *patriarchy*. Only the first tension, however, remained visible in the end-product and will now be considered more closely. Libertarians favor a bill of rights centered on individual liberty rather than on equality. In respect of state authority vis-à-vis individual autonomy, they assume an abstentionist (or "hands-off") attitude. Egalitarians, on the other hand, prefer equality as a core value in a bill of rights without, however, dispensing with tried "liberal values." It tolerates an interventionist state to the extent that it is necessary to help ensure even-handedness in the distribution of material means among the population as well as equal opportunity for all.

Mainstream egalitarianism in South Africa nurtures a spirit of "freedom fighting" which requires the struggle against oppression, prejudice, and discrimination to grow to fruition through the acquisition and exercise of political power. This form of egalitarianism is therefore better described as, for want of a better word, *liberationism*. Egalitarians normally contend for a "fuller" bill of rights than libertarians because, in their view, a bill of rights must, in seeking the achievement of socio-economic equilibrium, provide mechanisms which give effect to the claims on which second and third generation human rights are premised. Liberationism and libertarianism in South Africa, however, share an ingrained commitment to a quintessence of time-honored, liberal-democratic values, including freedom of conscience, religion, and belief. This commitment is reflected in South Africa's first Bill of Rights too.

The tension between libertarianism and liberationism shows in, amongst others, the interpretation and limitation formulas in Chapter 3. Section 35(1) enjoins a court of law interpreting Chapter 3 to promote the values which underlie an open and democratic society based on *freedom and equality*. The same value statement is applied as a "test" for determining the justifiability of the limitation of any right "by law of general application."[42] The tension between liberty and equality[43]—or freedom and social justice[44]—has thus been written into Chapter 3. As a result, constitutional hermeneutics in South Africa will require an alertness to the tension between libertarianism and liberationism in Chapter 3. Neither an invariably libertarian ("freedom-centered") nor an invariably liberationist ("equality-centered") understanding of Chapter 3 is warranted.

In some instances, a "freedom-centered" approach will be justified, for instance when provisions entrenching traditional freedoms such as the freedom and security of the person,[45] freedom of religion, belief, and opinion,[46] and freedom of expression[47] are interpreted. In other instances, an "equality-centered" approach will be more appropriate, for instance when provisions entrenching the right to equality and providing for affirmative action,[48] children's rights[49] and educational rights[50] are interpreted.

The real difficulty, however, will be to achieve a hermeneutical equilibrium when "affected" provisions, which evidently harbor the tension between liberty and equality, are interpreted. Examples of such provisions are section 26 (the right to free economic activity) and section 28 (property rights). In these instances in particular it would be unwarranted to lend precedence to either libertarian or egalitarian sentiments.

---

42 Section 33(1).

43 Liezl L. van Zyl, *Gesondheidsorg en Geregtigheid: 'n Filosofies-etiese Ondersoek* (Stellenbosch, 1993), 51-113.

44 Max Horkheimer, *Die Sehnsucht nach dem ganz Anderen; ein Interview mit Kommentar von Helmut Gumnior* (Hamburg, 1970), 86 and *Verwaltete Welt? Ein Gespräch* (Zürich 1970), 22 and 30.

45 Section 11.

46 Section 14.

47 Section 15.

48 Section 8.

49 Section 30.

50 Section 32.

The same difficulty will arise when "freedom rights" will have to be weighed against "equality" rights. In these instances a general assumption in favour of either liberty or equality will not be warranted.

There was a tug of war between *minimalists* and *optimalists* in deciding which fundamental rights to entrench during the transition. The minimalists argued that only rights indispensable to the political process of transition should be included in Chapter 3 while the optimalists contended for the fullest possible catalogue of rights. The *minimalist* position was adopted by parties, such as the A.N.C., enjoying majority support among the population. This position coincided with the view that the insufficiently representative Multi-Party Negotiating Process could at most produce a *transitional* constitution. An elected constitutional assembly then had to decide on a final constitution. The *optimalist* position was based on the view that a constitution guaranteeing as much as possible should result from the Multi-Party Negotiating Process. This view was held by parties with vested political interests but limited popular support, who feared marginalization in a proportionally representative constitution-making process. They included the Inkatha Freedom Party (I.F.P.) and the governments of some independent homelands, such as Ciskei and Bophuthatswana.[51] Given the ideological underpinnings of the various negotiating parties' conceptions of human rights, the minimalist stance assumed by the liberationists and the optimalist stance assumed by the libertarians were both *atypical* positions: liberationists as egalitarians would "normally" contend for a "fuller" bill of rights than libertarians.

The S.A. Government/NP signalled its preference for the optimalist position but not at all costs. This somewhat ambivalent attitude of a major role player in the process ultimately helped facilitate agreement on a final list of rights which, from a jurisprudential point of view, is neither fatally anorexic nor satisfactorily comprehensive. Chapter 3 can, however, not be described as a full Bill of Rights. It is important to note that the inclusion of religious rights in Chapter 3 was not controversial.

On Reading and Understanding Chapter 3. The interpretation of Chapter 3 calls for an approach which coincides with recognized procedures of constitutional interpretation and yet honors the peculiarity of the Chapter. This will facilitate a comprehension of the full breadth of religious rights as dealt with in the Chapter. Chapter 3 is supreme law[52] which trumps "all law in force" and to which all administrative action is ultimately subordinate.[53]

---

[51] But not Transkei and Venda who sided with the ANC.

[52] See sec. 4 of the transitional Constitution.

[53] Section 7(2).

Its interpretation thus involves: (1) defining rights or entitlements and determining their scope; (2) understanding the law in force or the administrative action subordinate to Chapter 3 by: (a) construing "ordinary" legislation and interpreting applicable common and customary law so as to determine their scope and effect, and/or (b) comprehending the effects of administrative action; (3) determining whether, on the face of it, law in force or administrative action limits rights; and (4) adjudicating the constitutionality of limitations in (3).

These four elements of interpretation are realized through five methods (or techniques) of constitutional interpretation.[54] First, *grammatical interpretation* is required, which is a philological or linguistic exposition of the text. Words, phrases, sentences, and paragraphs are analyzed in terms of linguistic "rules of meaning." This could include reference to dictionaries to determine the meaning of words and phrases but should also proceed beyond the verbal aspect of the text to the acknowledgement of the structural dimensions of the language as well. Syntax is therefore as important. Second, *systematic interpretation* is required, which seeks to determine the meaning of a particular provision in relation to the constitution as a whole and the context or environment within which it functions. Third, *teleological interpretation* is required, through which the *ratio legis* or "the intention of a hypothetically permanent constitution-maker" is determined. The direct influence of "present circumstances" is thus recognized. Fourth, *historical interpretation* is required, which accounts for the historical context in which the constitution took shape. In so far as this method involves the essentially *subjective* exercise of consulting *travaux préparatoires* in order to determine what the original drafters of the constitution had in mind, it is invoked only as a secondary interpretive aid to confirm results arrived at via more objective methods. Fifth, *comparative interpretation* is required, which takes into account international human rights jurisprudence and the constitutional jurisprudence of other jurisdictions. Section 35(1) of South Africa's transitional Constitution *enjoins* a court of law interpreting Chapter 3 to "have regard to international law" and *allows* it to be convinced by the persuasive force of "comparable foreign case law."

---

[54] See e.g. BVerfGE 35, 263 279; Donald P. Kommers, *The Constitutional Jurisprudence of the Federal Republic of Germany* (Durham/London, 1989), 48-49; Lourens M. du Plessis and J.R. de Ville, "Bill of Rights Interpretation in the South African Context (2): Prognostic Observations," *Stellenbosch Law Review*, 4(2) (1993): 199-218, 211-217; Lourens M. du Plessis and J.R. de Ville, "Bill of Rights Interpretation in the South African Context (3): Comparative Perspectives and Future Prospects," *Stellenbosch Law Review* 4(3) (1993): 356-393, 357; J.R. de Ville, *Moontlike Veranderinge in die Suid-Afrikaanse Administratiefreg na aanleiding van 'n Menseregteakte* (Stellenbosch, 1992), 102-104 and 121-127.

Defining Rights and Other Entitlements. Grammatical interpretation initiates the definition of rights but cannot fully satisfy its demands, since Chapter 3 is couched in broad and inclusive terms which makes a purely grammatical reading of the text impossible. Entitlements in Chapter 3 were deliberately expressed as general norms, as broadly as possible, and reliance on lists of specific and detailed guarantees and conditions was avoided as far as possible.[55] Provisions not couched in a broad and inclusive style reflect areas of contention and compromise among the negotiating parties. The definitional function of systematic interpretation is to reveal distinctions between but also the interconnectedness of rights. Teleological interpretation builds on systematic interpretation in fostering an understanding of particular provisions in the light of the aims and objects of the Bill of Rights and the Constitution as a whole. Historical interpretation could affirm the definitional outcome of systematic and teleological interpretation. Comparative interpretation, on the other hand, could contribute substantially to determining the definitional content and scope of a right.

Understanding Law in Force or Administrative Action. The meaning of legislation subject to Chapter 3 has to be determined through techniques of statutory interpretation. The traditional South African view is that statutory interpretation is an exercise in ascertaining the intention of a legislature. The days of this belief are numbered. Since April 27, 1994 the supreme Constitution trumps the will or intention of the legislature. Statutory interpretation can thus not be guided by what the legislature wanted or meant but rather by what the Constitution allows. This conclusion is borne out by section 35(2), which requires a law capable of being construed in such a way that it is in conformity with Chapter 3 and thus valid, to be so construed. A court is, in other words, enjoined to construe any enactment in such a way that both constitutionality and legal certainty are enhanced no matter what the legislature intended.

Constitutional jurisprudence and constitutional interpretation will hopefully also have a positive effect on a hitherto deficient literalist and technical approach to statutory interpretation in South Africa.

Section 7(1) of the Constitution makes Chapter 3 directly binding on all legislative and executive organs of state at all levels of government. This means that legislation as "state action" is always directly subject to Chapter 3. Common and customary law, on the other hand, could either be directly or indirectly subject to Chapter 3. Section 7(2) makes Chapter 3 applicable to "all law in force." This includes both common and cus-

---

[55] Hugh Corder et al., *A Charter for Social Justice: A Contribution to the South African Bill of Rights Debate* (Cape Town, 1992), 17-18; South African Law Commission, *Working Paper on Group and Human Rights* (Pretoria, 1989), pars 14.2-14.5.

tomary law. However, if section 7(2) is understood in the light of section 7(1), it follows that only common and customary law applicable in the context of the "vertical" relationships envisaged in section 7(1) is directly subject to Chapter 3.

The indirect application of Chapter 3 to common law and customary law in the context of "horizontal" relationships is achieved through section 35(3). According to this provision a court which interprets, applies, and develops the common law and customary law "shall have due regard to the spirit, purport and objects" of the Chapter.

The preponderantly vertical operation of Chapter 3 has important consequences for the protection of religious rights. Constitutional provisions entrenching religious rights are directly enforceable against legislative or executive organs of state only. The application of these provisions to horizontal relationships, for instance the relationship between a church and its members, is mediated through section 35(3) and is thus indirect.

The transitional Constitution will predictably also have an effect on how the courts will comprehend administrative action and what they will allow under it. The principle of legality or conformity to the norms of the supreme Constitution will henceforth guide the judiciary's understanding of administrative action. Legality will also be promoted as a result of the requirement in section 33(1) that only non-constitutional "*law* of general application" can limit rights in Chapter 3. This means that non-legislative administrative action cannot limit rights unless clearly authorized by law (of general application).

Determining Whether There is a Limitation. Here the question is whether, on the face of it, law in force or administrative action as understood in the foregoing terms is inconsistent with a right or rights as defined using the interpretative methods just set forth. A qualitative assessment of the constitutionality of the limitation is not made at this stage.

Adjudicating the constitutionality of limitations. Constitutionally tenable or justifiable limitations of rights can be effected (1) by a provision or provisions of the supreme Constitution itself (*intra-constitutional limitation*); or (2) by "non-supreme, non-constitutional" law "of general application" in accordance with the general limitation clause, section 33(1)) (*extra-constitutional limitation*).

As to the first, intraconstitutional limitation, all five methods of interpretation can help determine whether the Constitution itself limits rights. First, an inherent limitation of a right is normally effected through restrictive formulation and appears quite readily through grammatical interpretation. Second, systematic interpretation helps determine whether a right entrenched in one provision is limited by another provision or whether rights have a reciprocally limiting effect. Third, the teleological method draws attention to limitations necessitated by the aims and objects of the Constitution and the Bill of Rights as a whole. Fourth, historical interpretation could affirm limitations exposed by the previous three methods. Fifth, comparative interpretation can indicate how intra-constitutional limitations are dealt with both internationally and in other jurisdictions.

As to the second form limitation, it must be said that limitations under section 33(1) are not wholly *extra*-constitutional because the Constitution still prescribes *how* they are to be achieved. The section is a general circumscription clause providing for the limitation of *all the rights* entrenched in Chapter 3 and therefore also the religious rights entrenched in section 14. The limitation of any right can be achieved through "laws of general application" (in other words, legal rules which apply generally and not solely to an individual case) provided that: (1) the right in question is limited only to the extent that it is reasonable *and* "justifiable in an open and democratic society based on freedom and equality" (section 33(1)(a)); and (2) its essential content is not negated (section 33(1)(b)).

A list of illimitable rights is included in some bills of rights. Illimitability in this sense, however, only means that an *extra-constitutional* limitation of a right (by law of general application other than the supreme constitution) is not possible. Illimitable rights can still be limited intra-constitutionally.[56] Since Chapter 3 of the transitional constitution is not a full bill of rights, it was deemed inadvisable to include a list of illimitable rights in the limitation clause. The limitation of such rights in terms of the incomplete list of rights included in Chapter 3 would have been ineffectual. Instead a stricter limitation test was introduced for some rights. The limitation of these rights must, in addition to being reasonable, also be *necessary*. The rights to freedom of religion, belief and opinion entrenched in section 14(1) are among the rights enjoying this enhanced protection (see section 33(1)(aa)(bb)).

Section 33(1) must be construed *in relation* to the limitation sought to be achieved in order to determine the constitutionality of the latter. For this purpose all five methods of constitutional interpretation can once again be relied on. First, grammatical interpretation is the point of entry to the meaning of section 33(1) but can by no means be conclusive. This section clearly invites an application of the other methods as well. Second, Section 33(1) should be understood systematically in the light of, for instance, (other) statements of value in the Constitution. It should also be seen in comparison with section 34 in order to understand why the limi-

---

[56] du Plessis and de Ville, "Bill of Rights Interpretation in the South African Context (3)," 385.

tation of a right is different to its suspension. Third, the section must be understood teleologically, in view of the aims and objects of the Constitution and the Bill of Rights, in order to prevent an "over-active" limitation of rights. A value-statement has therefore been introduced to "limit the limitation" of rights: a limitation is permissible *only to the extent that* it is reasonable and justifiable in an open and democratic society based on freedom and equality. Fourth, a historical perspective of section 33 is necessary in order to understand the reasons for its very existence but, in particular, also why a stricter limitation test in respect of certain rights was introduced. Finally, there is a vast body of jurisprudence and literature, both internationally and in other jurisdictions, on the extra-constitutional limitation of rights. It is therefore predictable that comparative interpretation will play a very important role in the construction of section 33.

Provisions in Chapter 3 Protecting Religious Rights. Section 14(1) of South Africa's transitional Constitution refers explicitly to religious freedom in the following terms:

> Every person shall have the right to freedom of conscience, religion, thought, belief and opinion, which shall include academic freedom in institutions of higher learning.

On a mere grammatical reading of the section, it is clear that it entrenches more than religious rights. It also guarantees freedom of *conscience* and *thought* and *belief* and *opinion* and most probably includes the right not to observe any religion and not to believe. The epicenter of the debate on the cluster of rights entrenched in section 14(1) has, however, been religious rights. It was clear that the multi-party negotiators had no intention whatsoever of using the Constitution or the Bill of Rights to erect a wall of separation between church and state.

The economy of language characterizing Chapter 3 invites a systematic, teleological, historical, and comparative interpretation of section 14(1) which itself makes no elaborate and detailed reference to religious rights and freedoms. In order to understand the section systematically and teleologically, other provisions in Chapter 3 which could amplify and enhance it must therefore first be identified. Reference will be made to standards laid down in the W.C.R.P.-S.A. Declaration on Religious Rights and Responsibilities. Sections 14(2) (religious observances in state or state-aided institutions) and 32(c) (religiously based educational institutions) will be discussed later.

Article 2 of the Declaration on Religious Rights and Responsibilities is adamant in proclaiming the *equality* before the law of religious communities. Section 8 of the transitional Constitution is equally adamant in proclaiming every person's "equality before the law and . . . equal protection of the law"[57] in pursuance of which discrimination on the grounds of (amongst others) religion, conscience, or belief are precluded.[58] However, the vast majority of the submissions on the equality clause made on behalf of religious communities during the negotiating process did not address the issue of religious equality but rather the stipulation (in section 8(2)) that "no person shall be unfairly discriminated against" on the ground of "sexual orientation."

The freedom of expression provision[59] also caters to the need of religious communities to "criticize and challenge all social and political structures and policies in terms of the teachings of their religion" (see 2.3 of the W.C.R.P.-S.A. proposed clause). The right to "assemble and demonstrate with others . . . and to present petitions" entrenched in section 16 also includes forms of "expression" which religious groups can use in order to convey their message.

Section 15(2) furthermore provides that "media financed by or under the control of the state shall be regulated in a manner which ensures impartiality and the expression of a diversity of opinion." This goes a long way in addressing religious communities' concern about having "reasonable access to . . . publicly-owned communications media" (see article 7 of the Declaration on Religious Rights and Responsibilities).

As will be argued in due course, the entrenchment of freedom of association enhances the *institutionalized* exercise of religious freedom—as does section 31 (on language and cultural rights) for religious communities to whom the exercise of their religious freedom is closely related to or dependent on language and culture.

Members of religious communities, like all other bodies and persons, "shall have the right to have justiciable disputes settled by a court of law or, where appropriate, another independent and impartial forum."[60] This means that members of a religious community can (as of right) have recourse to either a court of law or "an outside referee" should they not be able to resolve their disputes among themselves. Strictly speaking, the section in the transitional constitution on administrative justice[61] does not bind religious communities, since the Chapter on Fundamental Rights operates predominantly vertically. However, the requirement that religious communities should comply with the precepts of natural justice in instances where the rights of any of their members stand to be affected by

[57] Section 8(1).

[58] Section 8(2).

[59] Section 15(1).

[60] Section 22.

[61] Section 24.

decisions, forms part of the law as it stands. The provision in the transitional constitution allowing for a seepage of the provisions of Chapter 3 to horizontal relationships[62] could therefore well be taken as reinforcing the right of any member of a religious community to the application of the rules of natural justice in instances where intra-institutional disputes are to be resolved.[63]

Section 14(1) is libertarian in its purport and thus provides, in a highly individualized way, for freedom of conscience, the right to profess, practice, and propagate any religion and the right to change one's religious allegiance. To this extent it is in conformity with the first subclause of the W.C.R.P.-S.A. proposed clause.

Teleologically understood, section 14(1) also guarantees the rights not to believe and not to observe any religion. This follows from the statement of purpose in the interpretation section.[64] The values underlying an open and democratic society based on *freedom* and *equality* require section 14(1) to be read, first, as promoting optimal freedom. This is best achieved if the section is given a wide berth. Secondly, equality is promoted if the section is understood inclusively rather than exclusively: both "non-believers" and "believers" enjoy the protection it offers and one category of persons is thus not discriminated against.

The combination of religious and academic freedom in section 14(1) is unusual. The example (and, indeed, the wording) of article 21(b) of the Constitution of the Republic of Namibia was followed. In the Namibian article, academic freedom and the freedom to practice religion are, however, entrenched in two different sub-articles, namely articles 19(b) and (c) respectively. Because of the tug of war between minimalists and the optimalists at the negotiations, the Technical Committee refrained from explicitly referring to academic freedom in the initial drafts of Chapter 3. It was of the opinion that "freedom of . . . thought, belief and opinion" at any rate includes academic freedom. A number of submissions were then made in which the explicit constitutionalization of academic freedom and of the freedom of artistic creativity and scientific research were advocated. The Technical Committee recommended to the Negotiating Council that explicit reference be made to academic freedom in section 14(1) and to freedom of artistic creativity and scientific research in the freedom of expression clause, section 15(1). This the Council accepted. Note, however, that in both instances the wording (introduced by the phrase

62 Section 35(3).

63 Adjudication in the context of religious communities is at any rate fraught with problems, as van der Vyver, "Religion," 183-187 clearly shows. Only time will tell whether the introduction of Chapter 3 will add to or help solve these problems.

64 Section 35(1).

"which shall include") suggests that the particular freedoms explicitly mentioned are at any rate included in the entitlements initially entrenched in broad and non-specific terms.

Religion has, in addition to its *personal* or *individual* dimension, an *institutional* or *associative* dimension. Section 2.1 of the W.C.R.P.-S.A. proposed clause explicitly refers to the right "to establish, maintain and manage religious institutions." Does the absence of such an explicit reference in section 14(1) of the Constitution exclude the institutional dimension of religion from the ambit of the section? I think not.

The protection of the institutional dimension of religion is inherently part of section 14(1) for three reasons. *First*, religious freedom, by its very nature, includes what is necessary for a person to be involved in a religious community of her or his choice. The right to religious freedom will thus include a right to its associative or institutional element. Churches in South Africa are juristic persons, and section 7(3) entitles juristic persons to the rights entrenched in Chapter 3 "where, and to the extent that, the nature of the rights permits." A cogent argument can be made that the very nature of the rights in section 14(1) "permits" a church to have them, albeit in a capacity different to that of an individual. The opposite can hardly be argued, namely that a church has no religion or no beliefs and opinions of its own. Should churches enjoy a weaker form of religious freedom than individuals, or should it be easier for the State to control their beliefs and opinions? To answer this question in the affirmative would be to deny the essential nature of at least three of the five rights mentioned in section 14(1). *Second*, a systematic reading of section 14(1) is not optional. *It has to be* understood in conjunction with the right to freedom of association in section 17. The right "to establish, maintain and manage religious institutions" is thus inherent in section 14(1) by virtue of its essential interconnectedness with section 17. *Third*, Section 14(1) mentions academic freedom with reference to its concretization in *institutions* of higher learning. Since academic freedom is a section 14(1) freedom and its personal and institutional dimensions have both been made explicit, an analogous dual understanding of religious freedom is warranted.

The three examples next discussed pertain to the institutional dimension of religious freedom in institutions other than religious communities. The *first example* concerns religious observances in state or state-aided institutions. Article 5 of the W.C.R.P.-S.A. Declaration on Religious Rights and Responsibilities is concerned with people's enjoyment of religious rights in state institutions. Section 14(2) constitutionalizes this right as follows: "(2) Without derogating from the generality of subsection (1), religious observances may be conducted at state or state-aided institutions under rules established by an appropriate authority for that purpose, provided that such religious observances are conducted on an equitable basis and attendance at them is free and voluntary."

Section 14(2) attests to the negotiators' *unwillingness* to erect a wall of separation between church and state. It allows for the conduct of religious observances at *all state or state-aided institutions*, for example, educational institutions, prisons, and state hospitals. Some libertarian negotiators voiced their concern at the inclusion of such a provision and not even the requirements that the observances must be conducted on an *equitable basis* and that *attendance must be free and voluntary* could set their minds at ease. They argued that in practice actual equity and voluntariness have proved to be difficult if not impossible to achieve. These concerns certainly emphasize the need to apply section 14(2) with circumspection.

A *second example* concerns educational institutions that are organized on a religious basis. Section 32 guarantees individuals' rights to a basic education, to equal access to education,[65] and to instruction in a language of choice where reasonably practicable.[66] Section 32(c) then proceeds to give "every person" the right "to establish, where practicable, educational institutions based on a common culture, language *or religion*, provided that there shall be no discrimination on the ground of race" (emphasis added).

Section 32(c) adequately addresses the sentiments of religious groups articulated in articles 4.5 and 4.6 of the Declaration on Religious Rights and Responsibilities, because it enables religious communities to establish and maintain their own educational institutions at pre-school, primary, secondary, and tertiary levels. The nature of this right also makes it possible for churches as juristic persons to be entitled to exercise it.[67] The inclusion of section 32(c) was more controversial than the inclusion of the first two subsections. Some evidence does suggest that section 32(c) was used a "bargaining chip" in bilateral negotiations between the N.P./S.A. Government and the A.N.C.

The provision has both a linguistic/cultural dimension as well as a religious dimension (even though all three are mentioned in the alternative). Of these two, the latter is the least controversial, and it ties in with the sentiments of religious groups articulated in, for instance, articles 4.5 and 4.6 of the W.C.R.P.-S.A. Declaration on Religious Rights and Responsibilities which was previously referred to. The provision makes it possible for religious communities to establish and maintain their own

---

[65] Section 32(a).

[66] Section 32(b).

[67] Section 7(3).

educational institutions at pre-school, primary, secondary and tertiary levels. That these institutions will have *a right* to financial support by the state (subject to compliance with minimum academic norms laid down by educational authorities) is, however, not a foregone conclusion. Language and cultural communities have a similar right, but the section expressly excludes recourse to religious freedom or to language and cultural rights as a pretext for "privatized" racial (but not gender) discrimination. No reference was made to gender discrimination in order not to preclude the possibility of having single-sex schools within the framework of the differentiations catered to by section 32(c).

Article 13(3) of the International Covenant on Economic, Social and Cultural Rights guarantees the right of parents to "ensure the religious and moral education of their children in conformity with their own convictions" and provides, at the same time, that this right can be exercised by parents choosing "schools . . . other than those established by the public authorities." From this it follows that "[t]he state is not obliged to finance such education but only to tolerate it if the parents wish to provide for it or pay for it."[68] South Africa will thus not be out of step with international human rights standards should the government withhold financial support from religiously oriented educational institutions. On the other hand, the fact that section 32(c) rights were regarded as of sufficient significance to constitutionalize them explicitly, may be understood as an indication that the State thereby assumed the obligation to help provide financially for such institutions.

A *third example* concerns religious personal and family law. Section 14(3) of the transitional Constitution reads as follows: "(3) Nothing in this Chapter shall preclude legislation recognising— (a) a system of personal and family law adhered to by persons professing a particular religion; and (b) the validity of marriages concluded under a system of religious law subject to specified procedures."

This section caters to the concern about systems of family law reflected in 2.2 of the W.C.R.P.-S.A. proposed clause. A person's *right* to have her or his system of family law recognized by the state is, however, not constitutionalized. Instead the legislature is authorized to pass legislation recognising this right. The provisional nature of section 14(3) is due to the fact that the issues for which it caters were raised during the very last phases of the negotiating process.

Traditional African leaders participating in the negotiating process attempted to have African customary law exempted from the effects of

[68] Karl Josef Partsch, "Freedom of Conscience and Expression, and Political Freedom," in Louis Henkin, ed., *The International Bill of Rights: The Covenant on Civil and Political Rights* (New York, 1981), 207-245, at 213.

Chapter 3 and, in particular, section 8 (the equality clause). They feared that certain aspects of customary law would not survive constitutional review, because a "Western court" may regard them as discriminatory against women. This, they argued, could uproot traditional communities. The Traditional Leaders' attempts were vigorously resisted, especially by female negotiators. In the end, any suggestion intimating an insulation of customary law was excluded from Chapter 3.

The ease with which the negotiators accepted section 14(3) is therefore remarkable. They did it at the behest of the legal representative of a fundamentalist Islamic faction who lobbied them during the very final stages of the negotiating process. Muslim personal and family law, like African customary law, can be seen to be discriminatory against women. The negotiators (including the women) were nevertheless amenable to its recognition in some form but proceeded with circumspection. Religious groups now still have to lobby the legislature to pass the constitutionally-authorized legislation which recognizes their personal and family law.

Religious freedom is no doubt high on the priority list of basic freedoms singled out for protection in national as well as international human rights instruments. Some regard it as "the most sacred of all freedoms,"[69] and it "appeared as the first fundamental human right in political instruments of both national and international character long before the idea of systematic protection of civil and political rights was developed."[70] Rights which are so eminently fundamental are, in terms of international human rights standards, usually regarded as non-derogable,[71] which means that they cannot be suspended even in time of a publicly proclaimed emergency when the life of the nation is threatened.[72] Accordingly, article 4(2) of the International Covenant on Civil and Political Rights explicitly provides for the non-derogatibility of the religious rights and freedoms enshrined in article 18. The rule of non-

[69] Robertson, ed., *Human Rights for South Africans*, 124.

[70] Partsch, "Freedom of Conscience and Expression, and Political Freedom," 209; see also Robertson, ed., *Human Rights for South Africans*, 124. See also e.g. the first paragraph of the Agreement of the People (of England) of 28 October 1647. The First Amendment to the U.S. Constitution, which deals with religious freedom at a federal level, was proposed in 1789 (the same year in which the constitution itself came into operation) and was ratified shortly after the commencement of the constitution. See Johan D. van der Vyver, *Die Juridiese Funksie van Staat en Kerk* (Durban 1972), 104.

[71] With reference to sec. 34 of South Africa's transitional constitution "non-derogatable" must be read as "non-suspendable."

[72] See also B.G. Ramcharan, "The Concept and Dimensions of the Right to Life" in B.G. Ramcharan, ed., *The Right to Life in International Law* (Dordrecht/Boston/Lancaster, 1985), 1-32, at 14-17 and W.P. Gormley, "The Right to Life and the Rule of Non-gerogatability: Peremptory Norms of *Jus Cogens*," in ibid., 120-159 with regard to the non-derogatability of the right to life.

derogatibility has probably also become part of customary international law binding on every state irrespective of whether it is a party to any international convention or covenant.[73]

Section 34 of South Africa's transitional Constitution provides for decidedly strict conditions on which rights can be suspended during a state of emergency. Some rights are, however, non-suspendable or non-derogable.[74] *All section 14 rights* have been included in this category. Chapter 3 thus conforms to internationally recognized standards. Permissible limitations or circumscriptions of religious rights mostly seem to apply exclusively to the freedom to *manifest* religious beliefs and not to the freedom to *hold* them.[75] In the same vein, freedom of conscience, thought and opinion, in so far as it has not been concretely manifested, is probably also illimitable.

The limitation of religious rights could prove to be more problematic than may appear at first sight. No state could possibly permit, for example, enforced polygamy, ritual murders, or public disturbance in the name of exercising religious freedom: such religious practices that endanger life or health or contravene public morals should somehow be subject to state limitations.[76]

On the other hand, oppressive regimes often profess to guarantee the free exercise of religion while, at the same time, they suppress full expression of the political and social manifestations of religion, and do so in the name of justifiably circumscribing concrete manifestations of religious freedom.[77] This happened, to a large extent, in South Africa under the apartheid regime.[78] The subjection of religious rights to a stricter limitation test, as is done in South Africa's transitional Constitution, is one way of averting the abuse of political power to suppress full expression of the political and social consequences of religion. At the same time it still leaves the door open for a court to conclude that the freedom to *manifest* religion or beliefs is limitable but that the freedom to *hold* them is not.

---

[73] Louis Henkin, "Human Rights," in *Encyclopedia of Public International Law* (Amsterdam/New York/Oxford, 1985), 8:268-274, at 271.

[74] Section 34(5)(c).

[75] Partsch, "Freedom of Conscience and Expression, and Political Freedom," 207, 210.

[76] Ibid., 212 n. 11 at 447. Partsch, in his discussion of the protection of religious freedom under the International Covenant on Civil and Political Rights, observes that astonishingly ample and broad limitations of the right to manifest one's religion have been admitted. He does not, however, spell out exactly why he thinks so.

[77] Robertson, ed., *Human Rights for South Africans*, 124. For a deserving exposition of the interaction between (and, indeed, interdependence of) law/politics and religion, see John Witte, Jr., *Towards an Integration of Law and Religion* (Pretoria, 1993).

[78] Robertson, ed., *Human Rights for South Africans*, 126-127.

Conclusions

Chapter 3 of South Africa's transitional Constitution entrenches religious rights and freedoms (and rights relating to them) within a broad framework. It is now up to religious communities themselves to work out in practical terms exactly what these rights and freedoms mean. The W.C.R.P.-S.A. Declaration on Religious Rights and Responsibilities is a good starting point. The courts (and the Constitutional Court in particular) could well consult declarations or charters of this nature in order to give content to the religious (and related) rights and freedoms entrenched in broad terms in the transitional Bill of Rights.

Religious communities, furthermore, should make their members aware of their rights and of the implications of the entrenchment of those rights in Chapter 3. Rights are worth nothing if they remain only lofty statements. They are there to be used in order to help optimize the exercise of the freedoms they embody.

Resort to constitutional rights will probably result in challenges to the constitutionality of many common law and statutory provisions in South Africa, particularly those showing a Christian bias. A number of these provisions will not likely survive constitutional review. I am convinced, however, that a visible trend towards greater inter-religious and inter-denominational equality will serve the cause of all religions in a religiously pluralistic society. This, I believe, is the most sensible way of promoting religious tolerance. I trust that, in time to come, this will also be true of South Africa.

Religious Human Rights in Latin America

PAUL E. SIGMUND
Princeton University

The basic thesis of this chapter is that religious human rights, in the sense of freedom to exercise and practice one's religion, are almost universally guaranteed in the laws and constitutions of Latin America today, although they are not universally observed in practice. However, it has taken Latin America much longer than other parts of the West—and I count Latin America as part of the West—to accept religious rights in theory and in practice, and the habit of respect for those rights, along with other human rights, is only gradually being developed. For most of the history of Latin America, religious rights were regularly violated, and while the prospects for religious freedom are better now than they have ever been, tensions and conflict in the area of religion remain.

Historical Background

The late arrival of religious freedom in Latin America is related to its colonial heritage and to its post-colonial history. Before analyzing and evaluating the present state of religious rights, I would like to review that history, since it continues to influence the contemporary situation. I shall divide my discussion into five periods: (1) Iberian colonization; (2) the post-Independence liberal-conservative conflict; (3) the rise of democracy and populism between the 1930s and the 1960s; (4) the cold-war period of military intervention and rule between 1960 and 1990; and (5) the triumph of liberal democracy.

Iberian Colonization. Even before the arrival of the Spaniards, the great pre-Columbian empires, centered in Peru and Mexico, used religion to support their authority and power. It was relatively easy, therefore, for the European conquerors to replace native religious structures with those

J.D. van der Vyver and J. Witte, Jr. (eds.), Religious Human Rights in Global Perspective, 467-481.

of a Catholicism that was closely linked to the Spanish throne. Religious uniformity was central to the post-*Reconquista* Spanish monarchy, and the papacy, threatened by the spread of Protestantism, was willing to cede vast authority to the Spanish rulers in their colonies. The missionaries accompanied the *conquistadores* who saw their role as converting the heathen, by force if necessary. "The cross and the sword" were thus closely linked in the Spanish empire. The monarch had extracted from the papacy the right of patronage, *jus patronatus* or *patronato*, that is, control over the appointment of bishops—elements of which have survived in some of the legal systems of Latin America until the last part of the twentieth century. In turn, the church received a religious and educational monopoly, control over its own courts, and vast landholdings. The Inquisition was active, and religious dissidence was repressed. Neither in theory nor in practice was there recognition of religious human rights.

Liberal-Conservative Conflict. After independence was achieved in the period between 1810 and 1830, most of the newly independent Latin American states concluded concordats or treaties with the Vatican, often claiming succession to the right of patronage. The Vatican was initially resistant even to recognition of Latin American independence because of the opposition of Spain, but formal relations were established in the 1830s, although the issue of the *patronato* remained to be settled on a case-by-case basis. The problem was complicated by the emergence of a liberal-conservative split in many Latin American republics with the liberals sharing to a greater or lesser degree the anti-clericalism of the French Revolution which had inspired them, and the conservatives generally supporting the establishment of Catholicism as the state religion. Issues of control over marriage, education, and cemeteries, plus the large landholdings of the church complicated the relationship. Although most constitutions of the nineteenth century recognized Catholicism, the specifics of the relations in each country were fought over throughout the century with the liberals taking the lead when they were in power in reducing church power and financial support. The formal separation of church and state would only take place in the twentieth century, and legislation regarding the *patronato* was only repealed in Bolivia and Argentina in the 1960s. The provision of the Argentine constitution that the president must be a Catholic and obsolete references to the conversion of the Indians and to presidential control over the appointment of bishops and the promulgation of papal legislation were only removed in 1994.[1]

---

[1] For the situation in the 1960s, see J. Lloyd Mecham, *Church and State in Latin America*, rev. ed. (Chapel Hill, 1966). For the contemporary scene, see Edward L. Cleary and Hannah Steward-Gambino, *Conflict and Competition: The Latin American Church in a Changing Environ-*

Two examples might illustrate the extremes to which the liberal-conservative split on the role of the church could go. In Mexico, the 1857 *Reforma* of liberal President Benito Juarez confiscated all church lands except those used directly for worship, removed clerical judicial privileges, and asserted a general right of the Mexican state to control religious activities. Later legislation suppressed religious orders, broke relations with Rome, secularized cemeteries, and required civil marriage. At the other extreme, Ecuador under Gabriel Garcia Moreno, president between 1859 and 1874, signed a concordat with Rome that gave the Church complete control of education and made Catholicism a requirement for citizenship. Indeed in 1873, two years before he was assassinated, Garcia Moreno dedicated Ecuador to the Sacred Heart of Jesus.[2]

The Rise of Democracy and Populism. In the first part of the twentieth century, the general pattern is one of partial separation of church and state, although constitutional provisions recognizing Catholicism often remained. In Mexico, the old split between clericals and anti-clericals was intensified by the Constitution of 1917 that in effect nationalized *all* church property, laicized education and marriage, took the vote from the clergy and strictly controlled religious publications, forbidding all political activity by churchmen, provisions that remained in the Constitution until 1992. Anti-clerical legislation was also adopted in Guatemala and Uruguay, but the more common pattern was the adoption of constitutional provisions that guaranteed the free practice of religion to all citizens. In this period, Protestant missionary activity was intensified in Central America, especially in Guatemala. As late as the 1950s, Protestant missionaries in Colombia, one of the most Catholic countries in America, were opposed by fanatical Catholics who burned churches, closed schools, and in 1959 killed over 100 Protestants.[3] Also in Colombia, down to the 1950s the Liberal and Conservative Parties divided along religious lines, but the 1958 agreement between the two parties to share power and the advance of ecumenical cooperation in Catholicism have meant that since the 1960s religion is no longer a source of conflict, except for isolated instances.

The period from the 1930s to the 1960s saw the rise of democratic populist parties all over Latin America. Some were secular social democratic groups like the *Apristas* in Peru and *Acción Democratica* in Venezuela that initially were influenced by Marxism and opposed to any official recognition of Catholicism, but they did not share the intense

---

ment (Boulder, CO, 1993). The requirement of the 1853 Argentine constitution that the president be Catholic was linked to his role in naming bishops, which was formally ended in 1966.

[2] For details see Mecham, *Church and State*, chaps. 6 and 15.

[3] Ibid., 135.

anti-clericalism of earlier laicist groups. On the other side, beginning in the 1930s and intensifying in the 1950s, Christian Democratic parties were founded in many Latin America countries, which broke with the clericalism of the conservatives and specifically endorsed religious freedom, human rights, and democracy. With the *Declaration on Religious Freedom*, adopted by the Second Vatican Council in 1965, there were no longer obstacles on the Catholic side to cooperation with their former liberal and social democratic opponents, although there remained issues of government support for religious schools, and of divorce, as areas of disagreement. In the mid-1950s there was a brief flareup of anti-clericalism, organized by the Argentine strongman, Juan Peron, but his attack on the church was one of the factors that contributed to his overthrow in 1955.

The Cold War Period. With the spread of democracy in Latin America after World War II, and the changes on the part of liberals, social democrats, and Catholics, one might have expected that religious liberty would become the rule in Latin America. Probably this would have been the case, had it not been for the Cuban Revolution and the polarization associated with the extension of the Cold War to Latin America. In Cuba itself, the Catholic church, never very strong in that country, took a position opposed to Castro after he moved toward Marxism in 1960, and active Catholics, Protestants, and Jehovah's Witnesses were persecuted as enemies of the state. Church schools were closed, and religion became one of the reasons for the successive waves of Cuban emigration. Elsewhere in Latin America some Catholic intellectuals, clergy, and students were attracted to liberation theology, and its support for cooperation with Marxists in the establishment of socialism. On the other side, the military governments that had taken over in many countries in response to the perceived threat of Communism attempted, usually unsuccessfully, to enlist the support of the Catholic Church for their crusade against Marxism in the interests of national security. Christians who were politically active on the left or defended human rights were tortured or "disappeared." Conservative Catholics and many Evangelicals either supported the military because of their opposition to Marxism or became politically apathetic. In Central America, Christian-Marxist alliances were established in Nicaragua and El Salvador, and gained power in Nicaragua in 1979. After the Sandinistas came to power in Nicaragua, a process of polarization took place among Christians, with the government giving support to left Christian groups, but limiting the official Catholic church hierarchy and opposition Protestant groups, especially on the Atlantic coast. Military regimes elsewhere often encouraged the spread of more conservative versions of Protestantism, and allowed the establishment of private schools and universities by church and business groups to compete with the public institutions that had been influenced by the left. The churches, like the societies in which they were working, were deeply divided along ideological lines.[4]

The Triumph of Liberal Democracy. In the late 1970s, the military began to surrender power. By the 1990s every country in Latin America except for Cuba had a civilian constitutional government based on competitive elections governed by constitutions that guaranteed political and civil rights, including the right of freedom of religion. During the military period, the Organization of American States Human Rights Commission had become active, and non-governmental human rights organizations emerged in many countries, in response to the military repression. New constitutions were adopted in Brazil (1988), Ecuador (1989), Colombia (1991), Paraguay (1992) and Argentina (1994) guaranteeing religious freedom. Mexico amended its constitution in 1992 to remove the anti-clerical clauses, and there was discussion in Bolivia of amending Article 3 of the 1967 constitution that, although it guarantees the public exercise of all religions, gives official recognition to the "Roman Catholic, Apostolic religion." In the cases of Paraguay and Colombia, the new constitutions omitted the provisions of earlier constitutions that gave special recognition to Catholicism.[5]

During the period of military rule, Protestantism, especially of the evangelical, pentecostal, or fundamentalist kind (the word used for Protestant in Latin America is *evangelico*), began to make spectacular advances in many parts of Latin America. These advances were often related to the shift in the 1960-1990 period in Latin America from a largely rural to a predominantly urban population. The migration to the cities made many Latin Americans available for conversion to evangelical religion, which offered spiritual direction, support of small communities, strong moral teachings and practice that emphasized hard work, abstention from alcohol, and family responsibility. In addition, in Central America, and Colombia, there was U.S. financial support and proselytism through American television evangelists, but it should be emphasized that contrary to some critics both on the left and in the Catholic hierarchy, the bulk of the expansion and organization of the evangelicals has been carried on by Latin Americans, and evangelical Protestantism now has strong indigenous roots.

---

[4] On this period, see my book, *Liberation Theology at the Crossroads: Democracy or Revolution?* (New York, 1990; paperback, 1992).

[5] See Pedro C. Moreno "Constitutional Reforms in Latin America Promoting Religious Association," Interamerican Bar Association, Santiago, Chile, April 18-23, 1993 (unpublished manuscript), and the Appendix to this article.

Evangelical Protestantism has already made a political impact in Latin America, despite the widespread belief that evangelicals tend to be apolitical. The vice-president of Peru is Protestant, and Alberto Fujimori, the president, was elected with public support from evangelical pastors. José Serrano, the president of Guatemala, until his removal after an unsuccessful "self-coup" in June, 1993, was an evangelical Protestant. General Efrain Rios Montt, president of Guatemala in 1982-1983, before the transition to democracy, was a member of a California-based sect, the Church of the Word, and was so active in promoting its members and doctrines in his administration that he was removed by the other military after seventeen months in power—during which he regularly gave a Sunday night quasi-sermon promoting "the three fingers"—"I will not rob, I will not lie, and I will not abuse authority." His party won the most seats in the August 1994 congressional elections in Guatemala. In the Salvadoran elections in March 1994, there were two evangelical parties, and one of them won a congressional seat.

There is considerable debate about the actual number of Protestants in Latin America. Everyone agrees that percentage-wise, Guatemala has the largest Protestant community with estimates of up to 38% and projections of a majority by the year 2000. El Salvador and Chile are estimated to be about 20% Protestant, and Brazil, Costa Rica, and Mexico over 15%, but some critics argue that the figures are inflated since they are based on conversions and do not track the numbers who actually continue to attend services. The most common estimate for Latin America as a whole is that it is 10% Protestant.[6]

While the conspiracy theories of the left about the evangelicals as agents of American imperialism are less frequently heard today, the Catholic church continues to be concerned about the advances of what the Catholic bishops at their 1992 Conference in Santo Domingo called "the sects." Referring to the challenge posed by "proselytizing fundamentalism by sectarian, Christian groups who hinder the sound ecumenical path," they accused them of hostility to Catholicism and of resorting "to defamation and to material inducements," adding that, "although they are only weakly committed to the temporal realm, they tend to become involved in politics with a view to taking power."[7]

---

[6] See "Forty Million and Counting," *The Christian Century* 36 (4) (April 6, 1992): 32 and "The Pastor is Faster," *The Economist* (April 17, 1993): 42. For analyses of the recent expansion of Protestantism in Latin America see David Martin, *Tongues of Fire: The Explosion of Protestantism in Latin America* (Oxford, 1990); David Stoll, *Is Latin America Turning Protestant?* (Berkeley, CA, 1990); Virginia Garrard-Burnett and David Stoll, eds., *Rethinking Protestantism in Latin America* (Philadelphia, 1993).

[7] Secretariat, Bishops' Committee for the Church in Latin America, National Conference of Catholic Bishops, *New Evangelization, Human Development, Christian Culture [English Trans-*

The State of Religious Human Rights

The spread of Protestantism has created problems for religious rights in Latin America. In some rural areas, there are deep divisions between Catholics and evangelicals. Issues such as participation in traditional folk festivals with a heavily Catholic flavor, for example, processions and fiestas in honor of the town's patron saint, have caused problems. Mormon missionaries are harassed; in one case a Mormon missionary in Bolivia was murdered, and Mormon temples have frequently been bombed by leftist revolutionaries in Chile. Despite constitutional guarantees, Protestant groups do not receive the same legal recognition in public law as do Catholics. While David Martin[8] overstates the situation in predicting the kind of conflicts associated with the Reformation in Europe, there is no question that there are problems in the shift from a heavily Catholic culture (Catholic practice is much lower, estimated at between 5% and 20% depending on the country) to one that is more religiously pluralistic—and secular.[9]

In the early 1990s, the two exceptions to the general advance of religious rights in Latin America, Mexico and Cuba, took steps to bring their legal systems in line with the rest of the continent. As noted earlier, the 1917 constitution of Mexico nationalized church property, abolished religious orders and forbad church garb, and excluded the church from education. These provisions were circumvented through a variety of devices, but only in 1992 did the government of Carlos Salinas amend the anti-clerical, and indeed anti-religious, constitutional provisions. Now the churches, if they are officially registered as "religious associations"—and by April 1994, 2000 such associations had applied for recognition — can own property and operate educational institutions, although the property must be used for "religious" purposes. Members of the clergy can now vote, but they may not run for, or hold, public office unless they have given up their church positions for a period of five years. The churches may not own or operate radio or television stations, or carry out

---

lation of Conclusions of Fourth General Conference of Latin American Bishops, Santo Domingo] (Washington, 1993), 95-97.

8 Martin, *Tongues of Fire*.

9 See, e.g., David Clark Schott, "Christian Sects Clash in Latin America," *The Christian Science Monitor* (April 1, 1992): 14, and the publications of the Rutherford Institute, based in Charlottesville, Va. (P.O. Box 17482) that publicizes violations of religious rights. For an account of atrocities in El Salvador involving evangelicals, see Mark Danner "The Truth of El Mazote," *The New Yorker* (December 6, 1993) and id., *The Massacre of El Mazote* (New York, 1994).

political activities. To be registered they must have been active in Mexico for at least five years.[10]

In the case of Cuba, while the Catholic church has been tolerated, its schools have been closed (although there is still a Catholic seminary in Havana), and government and party youth programs are regularly scheduled on Sunday mornings at the time of religious services. The Castro government has persecuted and imprisoned Jehovah's Witnesses who along with homosexuals have been singled out for repression. Moreover, it has been announced public policy that religious believers were excluded from government, education, and professions like psychology. In 1992, however, the rubber stamp Cuban People's National Assembly amended the constitution to guarantee religious freedom and to prohibit any form of religious discrimination, although it did not change the constitutional article that states that no constitutional liberty may be exercised "contrary to the Cuban people's decision to build socialism and communism."

In Haiti, before the U.S. intervention in October 1994, there was also a problem of religious human rights that was part of a broader pattern of repression. Religious leaders, identified with President Aristide after his overthrow in 1992, were persecuted and even killed. With the return to constitutional democracy in that country, religious as well as other human rights should now be respected.

There also continue to be debates over public policies that are seen as violative of religious doctrines. This is particularly true in the area of sex and marriage. Catholic opposition to divorce meant that laws allowing the dissolution of marriage were adopted later in Latin America than elsewhere and as late as the 1960s, five countries still prohibited divorce. Today, only Chile does so, and there is active discussion of a divorce law in that country—although many Chileans prefer the present widespread mechanism of fraudulent annulment as easier than a presumably more restrictive law on divorce. Government-supported contraception programs in Latin America were also opposed by the Catholic church in the 1960s, but it now tolerates them as preferable to the alternative of wholesale abortion. Abortion itself has not become the object of public controversy as yet, and both Catholics and evangelicals are strongly opposed to its legalization.

---

[10] For background, see Allan Metz, "Mexican Church-State Relations under President Carlos Salinas de Gortari," *Journal of Church and State* 34 (1992): 111-130. The 1992 Law on Religious Associations and the relevant constitutional amendments, as well as a list of churches that have applied for registration, are published in Instituto de Investigaciones Juridicas, *Estudios Juridicos en Torno a la Ley de Asociaciones Religiosas y Culto Publico* (Mexico City, 1992), 175-265. See also Armando Méndez Gutiérrez, ed., *Una Ley para la Libertad Religiosa* (Mexico City, 1992).

There is also the question of the financial relationship of the government to the churches. Three constitutions, those of Argentina, Bolivia, and Costa Rica, refer to state support (*sustentar*) for Catholicism. In the 1960s Bolivia and Costa Rica allocated small amounts to that church from their national budget.[11] In the 1994 budget of Argentina, $11,000,000 was assigned to Catholic bishops and seminarians. In addition, since 1979 bishops have received a state salary equivalent to 80% of the salary of a federal judge. Elsewhere in Latin America, non-discriminatory aid is given to church-owned schools, hospitals, and charitable institutions, and church property used for religious purposes is exempt from taxation.

This chapter has not discussed the Jewish minority in Latin America. Since the Jewish community is not large in most Latin American countries, the problems of anti-semitism and violent acts against Judaism are not as salient. The one exception would be Argentina, which has the largest Jewish community in Latin America, where part of the ideology of the military government which carried out the "dirty war" was directed at a mythical international Jewish conspiracy, and anti-semitism has characterized the far right for many years.[12] There was also a significant Jewish community in pre-Castro Cuba, but all but a few Jews have emigrated.

In summary, religious human rights today are better guaranteed from a legal and constitutional point of view than they have ever been in Latin America. We have not arrived at the end of history, but, at least formally, the ideals of liberal constitutional democracy and religious freedom are accepted throughout Latin America, even by Cuba. Religious minorities, especially evangelicals and pentecostals, are more active and self-confident than in the past, and discrimination against Protestants and Jews is rare. There are still hurdles to be overcome, including, for example, the excessively complex process of registration of new religious groups in some countries, minimal state financial support to Catholicism in a few countries, and controversies over proselytization, but the principal battles for religious liberty have been won, although only in recent times. The outlook for religious human rights in Latin America is the one of guarded optimism.

[11] Mecham, *Church and State*, 184 and 334.

[12] See Jacobo Timerman, *Prisoner Without a Name, Cell Without a Number* (New York, 1981) and Sandra McGee Deutsch and Ronald H. Dolkart, eds., *The Argentine Right* (Wilmington, DE, 1993), 9-12, 79-81, 126-128, 131-140.

APPENDIX

Constitutional Provisions on Church and State in Latin America[13]

ARGENTINA.
POLITICAL CONSTITUTION OF THE ARGENTINEAN NATION (1853, as amended 1994)

Article 2. The federal government supports the Roman Catholic Apostolic, Religion.

Article 14. All the inhabitants of the Nation enjoy the following rights in conformity with the laws that govern their exercise; to work and exercise every legal industry; to sail and trade; to petition the authorities; to enter, stay, and leave the Argentinean territory; to publish their ideas through the press without previous censorship; to use and dispose of their property; to associate for useful purposes; to profess their religion freely; to teach and learn.

Article 73. The regular clergy cannot be members of the Congress, nor can provincial governors while in office.

BOLIVIA.
POLITICAL CONSTITUTION OF THE STATE (1967)

Article 3. The State recognizes and supports the Roman Catholic, Apostolic, religion. It guarantees the public exercise of all other religions. The relationship with the Catholic Church will be governed by concordats between the Bolivian State and the Holy See.

---

[13] For sources, see Pedro C. Moreno, "Constitutional Reforms in Latin America," 14-18 (with minor linguistic changes) and apppendix hereto with translations by the author of published texts of amended constitutions of Argentina (1994) and Mexico (1992). The 1992 amended Cuban constitution is translated in Foreign Broadcast Information Service (LAT-92-2265), 23 November, 1992.

BRAZIL.
FEDERAL REPUBLIC OF BRAZIL, CONSTITUTION (1988)

Article 5. VI. Freedom of conscience and belief is inviolable, assuring the free exercise of religious groups and guaranteeing, by law, the protection of places of worship and liturgy.

VII. The provision of chaplains in civil and military prisons is assured by law.

VIII. No one will be deprived of rights due to religious belief or philosophical or political convictions, unless he claims them in order to exempt himself from legal obligations enforced on all and refuses to fulfill the alternative duty, established by law.

Article 210. I. Optional religious education shall be available during normal school hours in public elementary schools.

Article 213. Public funds shall be provided for public schools, but they may be allocated to community, religious, or charitable schools, provided that they (1) attest to non-profit status and invest their financial surpluses in education.

CHILE.
POLITICAL CONSTITUTION OF THE REPUBLIC OF CHILE (1980)

Article 19. The Constitution guarantees for every person:

6th. Freedom of conscience, the manifestation of all beliefs, and the free exercise of all religions that do not oppose morality, good customs, or public order. Religious communities can build and maintain churches and their facilities in accordance with the safety and hygiene conditions established by the laws and regulations. The churches, religious communities, and institutions of any denomination will have the rights regarding their property that are granted by the laws currently into effect. Church buildings and their facilities exclusively devoted to worship will be exempt from any kind of taxes.

COLOMBIA.
POLITICAL CONSTITUTION OF COLOMBIA (1991)

Article 18. Freedom of conscience is guaranteed. No one will be adversely affected because of his convictions or beliefs or forced to reveal them or forced to act against his conscience.

Article 19. Freedom of worship is guaranteed. Every person has the right to profess his religion freely and to spread it in individual or collective form. All religious confessions and churches are equally free before the law.

COSTA RICA.
POLITICAL CONSTITUTION OF THE REPUBLIC OF COSTA RICA (1949)

Article 75. The Roman Catholic, Apostolic religion is that of the state, which contributes to its support, without preventing the free exercise in the Republic of other religions that are not opposed to universal morals or good customs.

CUBA.
CONSTITUTION OF THE REPUBLIC OF CUBA (1976, as amended 1992)

Article 8. The State recognizes, respects, and guarantees religious freedom. In the Republic of Cuba, religious institutions are separate from the State. The different creeds and religions enjoy equal consideration.

Article 42. Discrimination based on race, skin color, sex, national origin, religious belief, or of any other kind offending human dignity, is prohibited, and punishable by law.

Article 55. The State, which recognizes, respects, and guarantees freedom of conscience and religion, simultaneously recognizes, respects, and guarantees the freedom of all citizens to change religious creeds, or to have no religion, and to profess the religion of their choice, based on respect for the law. The law regulates the State's relations with religious institutions.

Article 62. None of the freedoms recognized for citizens may be exercised contrary to the stipulations of the Constitution and the laws, or contrary to the existence and goals of the socialist State, or contrary to the Cuban people's decision to construct socialism and communism. The infraction of this principle is punishable.

ECUADOR.
CONSTITUTION OF THE REPUBLIC (1989)

Article 19. Without affecting other rights needed for the clear moral and material development that derives from the nature of the person, the State guarantees:

6) Liberty of conscience and of religion, in individual or collective form, in public or private. Persons will practice the religion they profess freely with only the limitations that the law prescribes to protect security, public morality, or the fundamental rights of the rest of the people.

MEXICO.
POLITICAL CONSTITUTION OF THE UNITED STATES OF MEXICO
(1917, as amended 1992)

Article 3 I. As guaranteed by article 24 on religious freedom, (public) education will be secular, and therefore will remain free of any religious doctrine.

Article 24. Every man is free to profess the religious belief that he prefers and to practice its ceremonies, devotions, and acts of worship, provided that they do not constitute a crime or offense punishable by law. The Congress can not adopt laws that establish or prohibit any religion. Religious acts of public worship will ordinarily be celebrated in churches. Those that on special occasions are carried out outside of churches will be subject to legal regulation.

Article 27 II. Religious associations which are constituted in accordance with article 130 and its implementing law will be able to acquire, possess, or administer in exclusivity the property that is indispensable for their purposes, subject to the requirements and limitations that the law establishes.

Article 130. The historical principle of the separation of church and state provides the orienting principle of the provisions of this article. Churches and other religious groups are subject to the law. It is the exclusive right of the federal Congress to legislate on public worship, churches, and religious groups. The implementing legislation regarding public order will carry out and apply the following provisions:

a) Churches and religious groups will receive legal recognition as religious associations as soon as they have been registered. The law will regulate these associations and establish the conditions and requirements for their registration.

b) The authorities will not intervene in the internal life of religious associations.

c) Mexican citizens can exercise the ministry of any religion. Both Mexicans and foreigners must satisfy the requirements of the law in order to do so.

d) The regulations will provide that religious ministers may not hold public office. As citizens they have the right to vote but they may not be candidates. Those who have ceased to be ministers of religion for the period and in the manner provided by law may run for office.

e) Ministers may not organize for political purposes or campaign for or against any candidate, party, or political organization. Nor may they, in public meetings, acts of worship, or religious preaching, oppose the laws or institutions of the country, or attack in any way its patriotic symbols. The establishment of any kind of political group whose title contains any word or indication relating to any religious creed is strictly prohibited. Meetings of a political nature may not be held in a church.

PANAMA.

POLITICAL CONSTITUTION OF THE REPUBLIC OF PANAMA (1972)

Article 35. The profession of all religions is free as is the exercise of all other worship groups, without any limitation other than respect for Christian morals and for public order. It is recognized that the Catholic religion is that of the majority of Panamanians.

Article 36. Religious associations have legal capacity and order, and administer their properties within the limits established by the law in the same way as other juridical persons.

PARAGUAY.

CONSTITUTION OF THE REPUBLIC OF PARAGUAY (1992)

Article 24. Religious liberty, freedom of worship, and ideological liberty are recognized without more limits than those established in this Constitution and the law. No confession shall have official status.

The relationship of the State with the Catholic church is based on independence, cooperation, and autonomy.

The independence and autonomy of the churches and religious confessions are recognized without any limitations other than those imposed in this Constitution and the laws.

No one can be harassed, investigated, or forced to testify concerning his beliefs or his ideology.

PERU.

POLITICAL CONSTITUTION OF PERU (1993)

Article 2. Every person has the right:

3) To freedom of conscience and of religion, in individual or associated form. There is no persecution due to ideas or beliefs . . . . The public exercise of all creeds is free, whenever it does not offend morality or threaten public order.

18) To the privacy of political, philosophical, religious, or any other beliefs, as well as to the maintenance of professional secrecy.

VENEZUELA.

CONSTITUTION OF THE REPUBLIC OF VENEZUELA (1961)

Article 65. Every person has the right to profess his religious faith and to worship, privately or publicly, whenever it is not contrary to public order or good morals. Religion will be subject to the supreme inspection of the National Executive, according to law. No one can claim beliefs or religious teachings to avoid obeying the law or to prevent others from the exercise of their rights.

Religious Human Rights in Central America

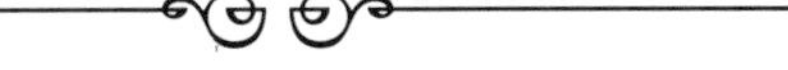

STANLEY MUSCHETT IBARRA
Universidad Santa María La Antigua, Panama

To address the topic of religious human rights in Central America requires some preliminary understanding of the region. First, we must recognize the predominant Catholic legacy and identity, if one may say so, of the region, which began already with the Hispanic Catholic project of the fifteenth century. Only starting in the nineteenth century did the presence and proselytizing of non-Catholic groups present the first sustained challenge for religious tolerance, and this has been solved fairly in legal and functional terms.[1] The recent arrival of what have been called the "fundamentalist sects,"[2] some of whom are apparently both politically motivated and anti-Catholic in character, are clear signs that there are new challenges for the evaluation and reformulation of the law of religious freedom. The cases of Guatemala and Panama are good examples of not so much a new process of "conversion" to fundamentalism as a new reality marked by a process of cultural, political, and religious transformation. The new sects sooner or later will demand a new restatement from civil and political society of religious freedom and tolerance which is a challenge we must all face together.

Second, although we speak of Central America as part of the Latin American subcontinent, we must also be aware of the historical condi-

[1] This assertion is not to overlook the treatment of native religions after the arrival of the Spaniards, a theme which cannot be taken up here.

[2] It is very important, at the outset, to stress the differences that North Americans and Latin Americans attach to the term "sect." North Americans tend to distinguish "sects" from "cults," while Latin Americans use the term "sect" in a wide generic sense, which is how I use the term herein. This semantic difference might be explained, in part, by the Catholic hegemony in the region, which treated all non-Catholics alike as "sects," even though there are clear functional distinctions between the Historical Protestant Churches and the new fundamentalist sects in the region.

J.D. van der Vyver and J. Witte, Jr. (eds.), Religious Human Rights in Global Perspective, 483-495.

tions under which the different nations of the region came to their current religious identities. Each nation has had its own particular religious tradition in the years since the experiment with the Central American Federation, attempted after the region gained independence from Spain. Each nation has had to develop its own distinctive constitutional and legal provisions on religious freedom. We need to understand the particularities that have shaped their religious and constitutional identities in order to draw a picture as close as possible to reality. The purpose of this chapter is to offer, from a comparative perspective, criteria and elements to enhance the reading and understanding of religious human rights in Central America.

The Advent of a Religious Identity

What is known today as Central America was "incorporated" into the history of the modern West in 1502 by Columbus on his fourth trip. History written by natives and general data clearly state that the "native Central American population had a well defined historical conscience"[3] as well as resources and means to express it. By the time the Spanish arrived, their tales and traditions were no longer written only in stone; hieroglyphic texts were also engraved in ceramic and wood.[4] The Mayan influence over the culture and identity of the social realm of Central America, from the Yucatan peninsula to the Isthmus of Panama, was accepted without reservation. The Mayans brought a high level of cultural sophistication and development, even though it was a tropical community of the low lands.

It must be stressed, however, that by the time of the arrival of the Spaniards there was no such thing as a unified Central American world. This fact is an important clue to understand the ensuing behavior and performance of the region in later years. The strength and dominion of the pre-Hispanic Central American people continued very much into colonial times and into the republican era, even when countries such as Costa Rica and Panama developed rather isolationist behavior, illustrated by Panama's exclusion from the Audiencia of Guatemala. In general terms, natives reacted to foreigners by becoming a "closed corporation." This was a means of protection, enabling them also to react through and

---

[3] Robert Carmack, ed., *Historia General de Centroamérica. Historia Antigua* (Proyecto elaborado por FLACSO, La Sociedad Estatal V Centenario y la Comisión de las Communidades Europeas, 1993), 1:32.

[4] Of the thousands of such manuscripts that were written, only four have been preserved.

with actions of force and also to influence the formation of new social relations through the preservation of much of their cultural inheritance.

This diversity and localism of Central America persisted during the *"Conquista,"* a period that featured what some have called the process of "homogenization." In its religious dimension, this process drew little distinction between the preaching of the missionaries and the imposition of an ethical-religious system as part of a major scheme of social organization. But in Central America, this process did not have a central and homogeneous character. Not only did the *Conquista* lack a dominant military and personal figure, as in the cases of Cortés in Mexico or Pizarro in Perú. There was also no major commercial activity that could bring and bind people together, and no civil and political unity through a permanent city or administrative unit. The end result was almost a state of administrative chaos and the growing might of local and private interests, sometimes native, sometimes not. In Costa Rica, for example, whose *Conquista* did not begin until the second part of the sixteenth century, an almost total absence of native presence made possible a predominance and a type of colonization driven by whites and mestizos. This helps to explain why, from the beginning, Costa Rica has in many respects been different from other countries in the region.

Any account of the state of religious human rights in the region must consider the process of "evangelization"[5] that accompanied the installation of a new political system and that until the nineteenth century imposed an almost monolithic Catholicism. This process of evangelization found in the *"encomiendas"* an efficient means to promote the new religion, even though in its essence the *encomiendas* were nothing more than allocations of "Indians" to someone by the authorities as either a reward or an incentive. In return for the services and attention received from the Indians entrusted to him, "the *encomendero* had to protect them and to allow for their instruction in Catholicism. . . . The *'encomienda'* was an attempt to reconcile the wish of the Crown to 'christianize' the Indians with the demands of the *'conquistadores'* for a labor force."[6] There were, of course, ample abuses in this system, which cannot be considered here. It must be said, however, that the evolution of the juridical order allowed for a progressive humanization in the treatment of Indians. For example, the Indians in towns were also subject to the *"reducciones"*—forms of con-

---

[5] This was the term used by the Catholic Church, at the 500th anniversary, to describe the arrival of Columbus in America. It aimed to convey the Church's commitment to the preaching of a new faith and the promotion of human dignity, acknowledging the "light and shadows" that occured in the process.

[6] Julio César Pinto Soriá, ed., *Historia General de Centroamérica. El Regimen Colonial* (Proyecto elaborado por FLACSO, La Sociedad Estatal V Centenario y la Comisión de las Communidades Europeas, 1993), 2:40.

centrating Indians, in which event members of religious orders were able to do a better job than civil servants in caring for the Indians. There were also the *"cofradías"* where the natives found an opportunity to incorporate and preserve elements of their own religiosity: after advancing the cause of a given saint or *"patrón"* all year long, the *cofradías* fostered celebrations, supported by the work of the natives, who were allowed to add expressions of their religious traditions in a clear exercise of religious syncretism.

A retrospective look at the presence of the Catholic Church and of Catholicism in the region since the *Conquista*, shows that in their missionary work the clergy had to cope with many difficulties. They used a variety of means, not always in accordance with their core values of faith and missiology. On many occasions, the Church "played the role of the arm of the State, participating in the process of also ruling the colonies. In the Hispanic world, church and state helped and reinforced each other. The state defended the Church's authority whereas the former submitted to the divine right of the king."[7] Given this relationship it will not be difficult to understand how Catholicism became the official religion, the State religion, from then on. This relationship did not render the Church entirely passive and corrupt. Many times, Church leaders criticized and denounced state policies that violated the religious human rights not only of Catholics but of the native population as well. Moreover, the Church even incorporated and accepted native religious expressions in liturgical celebrations, in an attempt to attend to the claims of the native populations. Nevertheless, Indians still resisted the process of faith inculturation in the *Conquista* period. "Spaces of evangelization" remained, particularly in the Caribbean regions of Costa Rica, Nicaragua, and Guatemala, where, together with the presence of English pirates and contraband commercial activities, native resistance was particularly strong, despite repeated missionary campaigns.

The one hundred year period between 1750 and 1850 signaled the end of Spanish dominion in the region, fostered in part by reforms of the Borbonic House in Spain. It also signalled the beginning of a process of independence in which foreign influences, political and religious, were very important. Particularly influential were the new liberal and secular ideas of the Enlightenment, not least its strong anti-clericalism and anti-Catholicism. Catholic influence and predominance weakened in the entire region, not only religiously but also socially. The early years of the nineteenth century brought new practices tolerating "civil marriage and divorce, the right of 'illegitimate' children to inherit, lay education, and

[7] Ibid., 2:170.

support for European Protestant immigration as an avenue for economic development of the region."[8]

Protestants came to the region not only for ideological and religious reasons, but also with an interest in "developing the economy of the region, particularly with regard to the desolated lower lands of the Atlantic."[9] The progressive diversification of the agricultural activity, whereby coffee had to share with, and in some cases lose its predominance to, the banana industry by the end of the nineteenth century, offered an avenue for new religious actors to come to the isthmus. Protestantism came hand in hand with North Americans who came as directors and managers of the banana plantations, bringing along their way of life and their religious practices. Protestantism also came with the introduction of a new kind of labor force, mostly from Jamaica, whose workers introduced their Protestant identity and their varied religiosity into the region.

By the end of the nineteenth century the political organization of Central American States was transformed, and church-state relations were constitutionally redefined along the lines of liberalism. The Federal Constitution of 1824—which had declared the official religion of the region to be "the Roman, Apostolic, Catholic religion with the exclusion of any public expression of any other"—was radically changed. For example, the El Salvador Constitution, proclaimed by General Santiago González (1872-1876), "resolved the secularization of cemeteries and of education, as well as the tolerance of religious cults [even though the] Catholic religion continued as the official one."[10] González's successor, Rafael Zaldívar completed the secularization of the state. The Honduran Constitution of 1880 underscored the doctrine of the separation of church and state, fostering laws "that suspended the tithe . . . of the '*cofradías*' and ecclesiastical privileges, the creation of the civil registering office and the secularization of the cemetery, marriage and education"[11] and allowing for religious tolerance. Starting with the Constitution of 1858, Nicaragua passed a series of legal instruments whereby under Adán Cardenas (1883-1887) the civil registration office was created, and the Church was forced to sell its non-cultivated lands. "Nevertheless, privileges were maintained . . . with an official recognition of the Catholic Church, even when the tithe was banned, and the Jesuits were consid-

---

[8] Hector Pérez Brignoli, ed., *Historia General de Centroamérica. De la Ilustració al Liberalismo* (Proyecto elaborado por FLACSO, La Sociedad Estatal V Centenario y la Comisión de las Communidades Europeas, 1993), 3:230.

[9] Ibid., 3:233.

[10] Victor Hugo Acuna Ortega, ed., *Historia General de Centroamérica. Las Repúblicas Agroexportadoras* (Proyecto elaborado por FLACSO, La Sociedad Estatal V Centenario y la Comisión de las Communidades Europeas, 1993), 4:185.

[11] Ibid., 4:192.

ered to be instigators of native revolts."[12] The new 1871 Constitution of Costa Rica laicized high school and college education. In 1884, a reform brought further secularization to Costa Rica by prohibiting the Church from receiving inheritances, "banning monastic and religious orders, secularizing cemeteries, laicizing education more clearly, prohibiting public religious expressions outside the temples [and] suppressing the Concordat with the Holy See."[13] In 1894, as a result of the activity of a political party named the "Union Catholic Party," a constitutional reform prohibited political propaganda in the name of religion or conducted by the clergy. Panama, which gained independence from Spain in 1821 but remained united to Colombia until 1903, included religious freedom provisions in the Constitution of 1863, which was changed in 1886. The latter, however, allowed the Catholic Church to organize and cooperate with public education, to have the right to organize civil and public acts, and to be exempt from taxes on churches, seminaries, and the homes of episcopals and priests.

Liberalism thus did not signal a rejection of Catholicism as a religion but rather a restatement of clerical rights and performance as well as a redefinition of the Church's role as a civil actor in society and Catholicism's role as an official religion of the State.

The "Sects"

In his final remarks at the 1991 "Christianity and Democracy" conference at Emory University in Atlanta, the Most Reverend Archbishop Marcos McGrath said: "[V]arious religious fundamentalist groups, some Christian, others not, mostly originating in the United States, present three problems for ecumenical and therefore democratic understanding: (1) lack of a clearly defined doctrine of Church and apostolic continuity; (2) sometimes an aggressive proselytizing vis-à-vis other (including Christian) religious groups; and (3) a marked disinterest in the social and economic problems of our people."[14]

The new sects are, indeed, new political and religious actors in Central America, alongside the Catholic and the "historical" Christian churches—Lutheran, Calvinist, Anglican, Episcopal, Presbyterian, Methodist, Baptist, and Congregationalist—as well as Jews, Muslims, and native religions. The behavior of these sects, though religious in principle,

---

[12] Ibid., 4:196.

[13] Ibid., 4:198.

[14] Marcos McGrath, c.s.c., "Democracy and Christianity in Latin America," in John Witte, Jr., ed., *Christianity and Democracy in Global Context* (Boulder, CO/San Francisco, 1993), 173, 185.

has clearly transcended the realm of religion alone. Many of them are separatist movements, originating mostly in the United States. Many have a deep attachment to a literal and narrow interpretation of the Bible, often promoting in their members a feeling of fatalism, without any real social commitment. Liturgical celebration and religious participation are emotionally oriented in search of psychic satisfaction.

Traditionally, the Catholic and historical Protestant churches accommodated new religions, even the free-thinking anti-clericals and Masonic lodges, both associated with liberal ideas of the nineteenth century. The legacy of the Catholic religion was shared with the new actors from the nineteenth century onward. Central America has not known real episodes of religious persecution and its ensuing consequences of war and discrimination. To be sure, there was some hierarchical recrimination, and social stigmatization, of the new religions. But there has been a longstanding practice of religious toleration, both in legal and functional terms, with no real evidence of major religious intolerance in the region.

In the past 25 or 30 years, however, the religious demography of Central America has changed dramatically. A study of the sects prepared by the Central American Bishops Secretariat (SEDAC) identifies among the prominent new groups Evangelicals, Pentecostals, Nazarenes, Jehovah's Witnesses, Christian Scientists, and Mormons, among others. Evangelicals and Pentecostals are now the largest and strongest presence in Guatemala, Costa Rica, Panama, and El Salvador. In general, the sects have a stronger presence among the rural poor, some 56% of whom have embraced the new sects. Their conversion has been self-conscious. Even in the predominantly Catholic regions of Central America, some 85% of both lay members and clergy are able to distinguish the presence and proselytizing of these new sects from that of the Historical Protestant Churches.

The SEDAC study attributes this new flourishing of the sects in Central America to two main factors. First, from an internal Catholic perspective, the sects seem to have provided greater opportunities for participation in the liturgy and leadership of the church. Moreover, in Nicauragua, El Salvador, and Guatemala, the sects have addressed more effectively religion's social needs—particularly alcohol and drug abuse and issues of war and peace—in an open and spontaneous environment free of demands for social commitments and reprimands for their breach. Second, from an external perspective, the sects have imported to the region new cultural values, which are attractive in part because of their novelty. Some view this cultural importation as a process of cultural alienation from the traditional Catholic and other religious values that shaped the identity of the nations and peoples of the region.

The flourishing of the new sects in Central America also has a political dimension. It was part of the attempt to weaken the influence of the Catholic Church and some Protestant churches[15] in the region because of their social agenda and commitment, expressed particularly through the Theology of Liberation that emerged out of the Second Vatican Council and the Medellín Conference. The notorious Rockefeller Report, submitted to President Nixon after Rockefeller's Latin American tour in the 1960s and used as the basis for U.S. policy in the region, already identified the Catholic Church with the radical university students of the region and as a threat to U.S. national interests. Similarly, the Santa Fe Pact I and II, developed under President Reagan, criticized the "use of media information by Church-affiliated human rights groups" and called for U.S. foreign policy to counter liberation theology and to "view the church as being used as a political weapon by the communists." There is a widespread consensus within Central American nations that U.S. strategy promoted and supported the actions of military regimes through the advancement of those fundamentalist sects which eschewed such involvement in politics. According to the SEDAC study, 93.9% of those asked in Costa Rica felt this way, along with 52.7% in El Salvador, 82.7% in Guatemala, 87.7% in Honduras, and 87.6% in Panama. Even when this is no longer the case, this speaks at least to the extent to which it could explain the initial presence of the sects.

Legal Aspects

Even though the current population of Central America still declares itself in general terms to be Catholic, the constitutional and legal provisions of the region follow the general patterns set out in the later nineteenth century. After invoking the name and protection of God, most constitutions of the region are generally framed in a commercial and open fashion, acknowledging freedom of religious worship and respect for religious creeds.

Both Costa Rica and Panama have similar constitutional patterns. Costa Rica still recognizes Catholicism as the official religion to be maintained by the State, though all other religious groups are accepted. As part of the Concordat with the Vatican, the Catholic religion is taught in public schools, and the state pays for these teachers. Non-Catholic students are free to request, through their parents, to be released from these religion courses. Article 28 maintains an earlier drafted provision underscoring that "no political propaganda may be carried on in any way by

[15] The contribution of Protestant theologians, such as Rubem Alves and José Miguez Bonino, to the Liberation theology are often forgotten, by scholars and politicians alike.

clerical or secular persons invoking religious motives or making use of religious beliefs." Panama's Constitution similarly prescribes freedom of all religions, but acknowledges Catholicism as the religion of most of the Panamanians. This provision was a compromise formula adopted in 1972 to replace the previous provision that recognized Catholicism as the official religion of the nation. Throughout the Constitution, one finds reference to the Catholic Church and the other churches. The Catholic religion is to be taught in public schools following the model of Costa Rica. All churches are subject to a special tax regime for income from their religious activities, though this provision does not cover the teaching-related activity of religious orders.

The constitutional provisions of religious human rights in Costa Rica and Panama differ from those of the rest of the region. The Constitution of El Salvador acknowledges that all men are created equal before the law, outlaws restrictions based on differences of nationality, sex, race, or religion, grants the free exercise of all religions, and rejects the use of religion to define the civil status of persons. Religion is not to be taught in public schools. The constitution clearly states that the capacity to hold and administer real property is not intended to benefit civil or ecclesiastical corporations or foundations, regardless of their denomination, with the exception of property used immediately and directly for the service or purposes of the institution. The only preferential treatment given to any religion has to do with the *de facto* acceptance and recognition of the juridical personality of the Catholic church, whereas other churches have to file for it.

Keeping in mind that Nicaragua's constitution is that of the Sandinistas, many of the provisions on religious matters are not surprising. While the preamble makes special reference to "those Christians who because of their faith in God have committed themselves and have participated in the fight for liberating the oppressed," Article 14 flatly states that the state has no official religion. Religiously-based discrimination is outlawed. Freedom of religious worship is protected. Public education is lay. In order to overcome what it considers to be a decade of negative Sandinista rulership, and particularly the lack of moral values in society, the current Minister of Education is considering the introduction of religious teaching in the public schools, though with no intention of imposing any given religion. The intention is to reach an agreement with the parents and to teach whatever religious values can be agreed upon in the dialogue.

Honduras has a long tradition of not acknowledging any official religion. Its constitution grants freedom of worship for all religions, subject only to the limits of public morality and public order. No one may be discriminated against because of his or her religious conviction. No kind of official association or relationship can be devised in favor of any given religion. Religion may not be taught in public schools.

Though the preamble to the Constitution of Guatemala starts by invoking God's name and identifying the nation as Catholic, the Constitution provides for freedom of religious worship and demands respect for all religions. As in the case of El Salvador, the Catholic Church is granted juridical personality whereas other churches have to file for it. The Catholic Church is also singled out for special property rights, including a State entitlement to receive certification of ownership, free of charge, "as long as they were owned in the past." Church property devoted to worship, education, and social relief programs is exempted from taxation. Religion may be taught in public schools without any discrimination. The State is committed to support religion, but without discrimination or favoritism.

Interpretation

It should be evident from the foregoing that religious human rights in Central America are still today colored by the Catholic evangelization of the fifteenth century. Many people in the region still proudly declare themselves to be Catholics. Non-Catholics, however, do not suffer because of this. A climate of coexistence and of religious toleration has generally been the norm in Central America—though, on occasion, earlier Catholic authorities felt their hegemony threatened and issued Bishops' Pastoral Letters to the faithful condemning certain aspects of the growing religious diversity. Especially since the Second Vatican Council, however, the spirit of ecumenism has grown. Those nations that had to endure the abuses of military rulership have witnessed, many times, that Catholics and Protestants have joined together in the common cause of defending freedom and the dignity of human beings.

A fundamental paradox, however, still persists in the religious human rights regime of Central America. On the one hand, there is neither legal nor empirical evidence of abuses of religious freedom, or to show that religious identity is being used to discriminate or to persecute anyone. Furthermore, as we already underscored, most Central American nations, except Costa Rica and Panama, have adopted a secular constitution, founded on the doctrine of separation of church and state. On the other hand, and here lies the paradox, all public performances by civil servants and authorities reveal what could be called the "Catholicization" of public life in Central America. This is very well expressed in the celebration of traditional public festivities (where Catholics either preside or attend as authorities) and in the public celebration of liturgical acts such as the *Te Deum* and thanksgiving masses during national holidays. Some have argued that this Catholicization is itself a form of religious discrimination, a preference for the rights and rites of one religion, and against all others. To me, this situation is more of a simple acknowledgement and accommodation of the people's Catholic cultural and national identity.

A related paradox of religious rights in the region is that, while Catholicism is culturally prominent, its members have been confronted with increasing animosity—indeed, in the view of some Catholics, subject to outright religious persecution. In some countries such as El Salvador and to a lesser degree Guatemala, this animosity has escalated to expressions of harassment, conflict, and murder of lay and religious members of the Catholic Church. How can this be approached and explained? Is this really religious persecution? Despite my personal sympathy with the issue and the commitment with which we have advanced the cause of justice and reconciliation as a member of the Commission on Justice and Peace in my country of Panama, I must say that this is no black and white situation. There is no doubt that sectors within the Catholic Church, including some members of the hierarchy, have clearly sided with the oppressed in several countries in the region. Through criticism, vigorous public statements, rallies, and other legal means they have presented their cause. Other sectors—groups of priests, laymen, and nuns that do not represent the official behavior of the Catholic Church—have also participated in armed struggle and violent means, thus alienating the authorities. There is at least room to argue that the hostile reaction against these sectors is something which they have invited by "intervening in politics." The response from the authorities has been not against the religious dimension or identity of the whole body, the argument goes, but against the political intervention that "threatens" the system.

Do not misunderstand me. This argument respecting the ill plight of these people has been presented by people interviewed in this respect and who have expressed their support of it, saying at the time that they too are Catholics. To say the least, it is difficult to deal with the assassinations of Archbishop Romero and of the Jesuits of the Simeon Canas University in El Salvador with this approach and explanation. However, to many, this is good enough. They underscore that some other sector of the Catholic Church not only did not support this attitude but sided with the opposite group, the government authorities and the powerful.

We must say a word about the political projection of not only Catholics but also some of the sect leaders in countries such as Guatemala and

Panama. The case of General Efrain Rios Montt, a leader and chairperson of the "Church of the Word" who ran for president, is well known. The question is whether he was running as a member of this religious group or just taking political advantage of his religious situation? Can a separation be drawn between the civil and the religious leader? Should separate religious rights protection be afforded to the political activities of a religious group? Rios Montt's discourse makes no explicit reference to religious elements or symbols, makes no effort at proselytizing, and makes no reference to the plight of the poor or to social sin, which is so characteristic of Catholic teaching today. On the contrary, his was a message addressed to common people and issues. It presented the material needs of security, health, education, and job opportunities, through the constant reference to discipline, a lost value in need of recuperation. It remains to be seen whether his access to Congress in the recent elections in the powerful position of leader of the most popular coalition will bring any change to the way he deals with these civil and religious dimensions.

While Rios Montt's religious sentiments have so far not marked his politics, this was not the case with a political party identified, both from inside and outside, as a religiously-oriented group, associated with a fundamentalist sect, the Assembly of God. To the surprise of many in Panama, this party participated in the last political campaign. Its leadership was drawn from the Assembly of God sect. A great majority of the party members also came from this sect, but a large number of members were also disenchanted Catholics, disenchanted not only with the traditional political offerings but also with the Catholic Church's participation in politics in confronting Noriega. The new religiously-based party thus gained quick and massive support in the campaign, and all kinds of predictions were made about their political success. From the beginning, however, there was some uneasiness with the party's logo, which bore close resemblance to a Catholic symbol. A legal complaint charged that this logo might be used to attract and deceive new members, and the party was ordered to change its logo. Even though the party denied any subtle religious orientation or manipulation, this fact haunted them. They did not do well in the elections, and the party was officially declared non-existing according to voting laws. It remains to be seen if the controversy over the party logo had more to do with appropriation of the Catholic Church's copyright in a religious symbol, or if some sort of Catholic spite was at the root of the action. No one ever thought that a religious group would participate so overtly in politics and political strategm.[16]

---

[16] As President of the Commission on Justice and Peace of the Catholic Church and in the context of an ethical agreement promoted among political parties for the presidential

I draw attention to these cases to illustrate the new religious scene of Central America, in which new religious sects have emerged, making strong political claims and prompting various questions and reactions. Unlike the Historical Protestant Churches, fundamentalist sects have strong political linkages and aspirations, and this has become a clear mark against these groups—subtly in the social and religious realms, though not officially in the constitutional and legal realms. The question is whether in the near future this stigma will be overcome, whether the threat these groups seem to pose in Central America will disappear, and whether persistence of the stigma will be seen as a violation of their religious human rights?

The assessment of religious human rights in Central America, however, cannot be reduced, as it so often is, to the question of how these fundamentalist sects are being treated. Their treatment is not so important an issue on the agenda of the countries and people of the region, and their presence has not altered the general climate of religious tolerance and mutual respect that has been observed throughout most of the history of the region. Nothing suggests an imminent change either in the legal provisions, nor in the hearts of the people, toward religious human rights. For the present at least, Central America continues to know little of, what Pope John Paul II called, "the plight that rises continually to God from the sanctuary of their conscience" because of the denial "of the right to worship and educate the children according to the faith of their parents."

campaign, I was witness to a discussion in which demands by representatives of this group were countered with the argument that this was not possible because of the Catholic tradition of Panamanians.

The American Constitutional Experiment in Religious Human Rights: The Perennial Search for Principles

JOHN WITTE JR.
Emory University
and
M. CHRISTIAN GREEN
University of Chicago

President Thomas Jefferson once described the religion clauses of the First Amendment to the United States Constitution as a "fair" and "novel experiment" in religious rights and liberties.[1] The religion clauses, declared Jefferson, defied the millennium-old assumptions inherited from Western Europe—that one form of Christianity must be established in a community, and that the state must protect and support it against other religions. The religion clauses, Jefferson argued, suffer neither prescriptions nor proscriptions of religion. All forms of Christianity must stand on their own feet and on an equal footing with all other religions. Their survival and growth must turn on the cogency of their word, not the coercion of the sword, on the faith of their members, not the force of the law.

This bold constitutional experiment in religious liberty, though neither as fair nor as novel as Jefferson believed,[2] remains intact and in pro-

---

[1] Thomas Jefferson, "Letter of November 21, 1808," in Thomas Jefferson, *The Complete Jefferson, Containing His Major Writings*, Saul K. Padover, ed. (New York, 1943), 538. See discussion in Sidney E. Mead, *The Lively Experiment: The Shaping of Christianity in America* (New York, 1963).

[2] For prototypes, see, e.g., the religious liberty clauses cast in the aftermath of the Dutch Reformation in the 1570s and 1580s, collected in E.H. Kossmann and A.F. Mellink, *Texts Concerning the Revolt of the Netherlands* (New York/London, 1974) with discussion in O.J. DeJong, "Union and Religion," *The Low Countries History Yearbook* (1981): 29 and Gerhard Güldner, *Das Toleranz-Problem in den Niederlanden im Ausgang des 16. Jahrhunderts* (Lübeck/Hamburg, 1968). For other European prototypes, see K. Schwarz "Der Begriff Exercitium Religionis

J.D. van der Vyver and J. Witte, Jr. (eds.), Religious Human Rights in Global Perspective, 497-557.

gress in the United States. The First Amendment religion clauses, drafted in 1789 and ratified in 1791, remain the predominant federal constitutional text to govern religious rights and liberties in America.[3] Principal governance of this experiment—initially left to state legislatures and state courts—has since the 1940s fallen largely to the United States Supreme Court and lower federal courts, which have interpreted and applied these religion clauses in hundreds of cases.[4]

The American experiment in religious liberty initially inspired exuberant rhetoric throughout the young republic and beyond. Elhanan Winchester, a Baptist preacher turned Universalist, declared proudly to a London audience in 1789:

> There is but one country in the world where liberty, and especially religious liberty, is so much enjoyed as in these kingdoms, and that is the United States of America: there religious liberty is in the highest perfection. All stand there on equal ground. There are no religious establishments, no preference of one denomination of Christians above another. The constitution knows no difference between one good man, and another. A man may be chosen there to the highest civil offices, without being obliged to

---

Privatum," *Zeitschrift der Savigny-Stiftung (Kan. Ab.)* 105 (1988): 495. James Madison, an equally important architect of the American experiment alongside Jefferson, was aware of these Dutch prototypes. See, e.g., Letter to Rev. Adams (1832), in James Madison, *The Writings of James Madison*, G. Hunt ed. (Washington, 1910), 9:484-487 (referring to Holland's "experiment . . . of liberal toleration").

[3] U.S. Const. amend. I. The only other explicit constitutional provision, the prohibition against religious test oaths, U.S. Const. art. VI, S. 3, cl. 2 has been subject to only modest judicial interpretation. See Gerald V. Bradley, "The No Religious Test Clause and the Constitution of Religious Liberty: A Machine That Has Gone of Itself," *Case Western Law Review* 37 (1987): 674; Michael E. Smith, "The Special Place of Religion in the Constitution," *Supreme Court Review* (1983): 83.

[4] See Carl H. Esbeck, "Table of United States Supreme Court Decision Relating to Religious Liberty 1789-1994," *Journal of Law and Religion* 10 (1993-1994): 573 (listing 142 Supreme Court cases); three more have been decided since Esbeck's article was published: *Board of Education of Kiryas Joel Village School District v. Grumet*, 114 S.Ct. 2481 (1994); *Rosenberger v. Rector and Visitors of the University of Virginia*, 1995 LW 382046 (West Law); *Capitol Square Review and Advisory Board v. Pinette*, 1995 LW 382063. See also *E.E.O.C. v. Townley Eng'g & Mfg. Co.*, 859 F.2d 610, 625-629 (9th Cir. 1988), cert. denied 489 U.S. 1077 (1989) (Noonan, J. dissenting, providing a detailed table of federal free exercise cases); James E. Ryan, "*Smith* and the Religious Freedom Restoration Act," *Virginia Law Review* 78 (1992): 1407, 1458 (summarizing free exercise cases in federal courts from 1963-1990), with corrections in Thomas C. Berg, ""What Hath Congress Wrought? An Interpretive Guide to the Religious Freedom Restoration Act," *Villanova Law Review* 39 (1994): 1, 11-12.

> give any account of his faith, subscribe [to] any religious test, or go to the communion table of any church.[5]

Yale President Ezra Stiles predicted robustly in 1793:

> The United States will embosom all the religious sects or denominations in christendom. Here they may all enjoy their whole respective systems of worship and church government, complete. . . . All religious denominations will be independent of one another . . . and having, on account of religion, no superiority as to secular powers and civil immunities, they will cohabit together in harmony, and I hope, with a most generous catholicism and benevolence.[6]

Dozens of such confident panegyrics can be found in the sermons, pamphlets, and monographs of the young American republic.

Today, the American experiment in religious liberty inspires far more criticism than praise. The United States does "embosom" all religious sects and denominations, as President Stiles predicted, not only from Christendom, but from around the world. American citizens do enjoy remarkable freedom of thought, conscience, and belief—too much freedom, according to some commentators.[7] But the laboratory of the United States Supreme Court, which has directed the American experiment for the past fifty years, no longer inspires confidence. Not only have the Court's recent decisions on the religious rights of Jews, native American Indians, Muslims, and school children evoked withering attacks in the popular and professional media. The Court's entire record on religious liberty has become vilified for its lack of consistent and coherent principles and its uncritical use of mechanical tests and empty metaphors.[8] "Religion Clause jurisprudence," writes one leading commentator "has been described on all sides, and even by Justices themselves, as unprincipled, incoherent, and unworkable. . . . [T]he Court must now grapple se-

---

[5] Elhanan Winchester, *A Century Sermon on the Glorious Revolution* (London, 1789), reprinted in Ellis Sandoz, ed., *Political Sermons of the American Founding Era, 1730-1805* (Indianapolis, 1991), 969, 988-989.

[6] Ezra Stiles, *The United States Elevated to Glory and Honor* (New Haven, 1793), 55 (with modernized spelling and italics in original removed).

[7] See, e.g., Leonard W. Levy, *Blasphemy: Verbal Offenses Against the Sacred From Moses to Salman Rushdie* (New York, 1993), 568ff. ("We have become not only a free society, but also a numb society. We are beyond outrage."); Harold J. Berman, "Some Reflections on the Differences Between Church and State," *Christian Legal Society Quarterly* 5(2) (1984): 12 ("Today it is by no means clear that the experiment [proposed by Jefferson] has succeeded.").

[8] See discussion and sources in Michael W. McConnell, "Religious Freedom at a Crossroads," *University of Chicago Law Review* 59 (1992): 115; John Witte, Jr., "Toward an Integration of Religious Liberty," *Michigan Law Review* 91 (1992): 1363.

riously with the formidable interpretive problems that were overlooked or given short shrift in the past. The task is an urgent one, for it concerns nothing less than the cultural foundations of our experiment in ordered liberty."[9]

The United States Supreme Court is not the only body that is now "grappling" with the experiment. In the past few years, the "laboratory" seems to be shifting away from the courts to the legislatures, and away from the federal government to the states—a trend encouraged by the dicta of several recent Supreme Court opinions.[10] Congress has issued a number of acts to define the free exercise rights of various religious individuals and groups, and even to determine the appropriate free exercise test to be used in future constitutional cases.[11] At the same time, state legislatures have become bolder in conducting their own experiments in religious liberty that seem calculated to revisit, if not rechallenge, prevailing Supreme Court interpretations of the establishment clause. State courts have begun to develop their own independent laws on religious liberty that sometimes depart dramatically from prevailing Supreme Court opinions.[12] These trends have only served to exacerbate the incoherence and indeterminacy of the American experiment in religious rights and liberties.

When an experiment becomes a "kind of wandering inquiry, without any regular system of operations," wrote Francis Bacon, the so-called father of the experimental method, "prudence commends three correctives."[13] First, said Bacon, we must "return to first principles and axioms," reassess them in light of our experience, and "if necessary refine them." Second, we must assess "our experience with the experiment" in light of these first principles, to determine where "the experiment should be adjusted." Third, we must "compare our experiments" and experi-

---

9 Mary Ann Glendon & Raul F. Yanes, "Structural Free Exercise," *Michigan Law Review* 90 (1991): 477, 478; see also Mary Ann Glendon, "Law, Communities, and the Religious Freedom Language of the Constitution," *George Washington Law Review* 60 (1992): 672.

10 See the cases and discussion in Stuart D. Poppel, "Fundamentalism, Fairness, and the Religion Clauses," *Cumberland Law Review* 25 (1994-1995): 247.

11 See, e.g., American Indian Religious Freedom Act (1978), 42 U.S.C. 1996 (amended 1994, H.R. Rep. 103-675); Religious Freedom Restoration Act (1993), 42 U.S.C. 2000bb; Military Apparel Act, 10 U.S.C. 774; Equal Access Act (1984), 20 U.S.C. S. 4071-4074. There is, at the time of this writing, a movement in Congress to prepare a constitutional amendment to reintroduce prayer into public schools, as well as an amendment, or statute, to guarantee equality of treatment for all religious organizations. See briefly Gregory S. Baylor, "The Religious Equality Amendment," *Christian Legal Society Quarterly* 16(3) (1995): 4.

12 See sources and discussion in Angela C. Carmella, "State Constitutional Protection of Religious Exercise: An Emerging Post-Smith Jurisprudence," *Brigham Young University Law Review* (1993): 275.

13 Francis Bacon, *The Great Instauration* (1620), preface, reprinted in id., *The New Organon and Related Writings*, Fulton H. Anderson, ed.(Indianapolis, 1960), 3, 11.

ences with those of fellow scientists, and where we see in that comparison "superior techniques," we must "amend our experiments," and even our first principles, accordingly.[14] Though Bacon offered these prudential instructions principally to correct scientific experiments that had gone awry, his instructions commend themselves to legal and political experiments as well—as he himself sought to demonstrate in seventeenth century England.[15]

This chapter applies Bacon's prudential instructions to the American constitutional experiment in religious rights and liberties—an experiment that today is, indeed, "wandering, without any regular system of operations." Applying Bacon's first instruction, Part I distills from the diverse theological and political traditions and experiences of the eighteenth century the most widely embraced "first principles" of the American constitutional experiment—liberty of conscience, free exercise of religion, confessional and structural pluralism, equality of religions before the law, separation of the institutions of church and state, and disestablishment of religion. Applying Bacon's second instruction, Part II analyzes the American constitutional experience in light of these first principles, lifting these principles out of the familiar free exercise and establishment clause cases of the past half century. Applying Bacon's third instruction, the Conclusion considers the principles and practice of the American experiment against prevailing international norms of religious rights and liberties.

The Genesis of the American Constitutional Experiment

The religion clauses of the state constitutions and of the First Amendment, forged between 1776 and 1791, express both theological and political sentiments. They reflect both the convictions of the religious believers of the young American republic and the calculations of their political leaders. They manifest both the certitude of theologians such as Isaac Backus and John Witherspoon, and the skepticism of philosophers such as Thomas Jefferson and Thomas Paine. A plurality of theological and political views helped to inform the early American constitutional experiment in religious rights and liberties, and to form the so-called original intent of the constitutional framers.

The American experiment in religious rights and liberties cannot, in our view, be reduced to the First Amendment religion clauses alone, nor

---

[14] Francis Bacon, *The New Organon* (1620), Aphorisms Book One, 70, 82, 103, 104, in ibid., at 31, 67-69, 78-80, 97-98.

[15] See generally Barbara Shapiro, "Sir Francis Bacon and the Mid-Seventeenth Century Movement for Law Reform," *American Journal of Legal History* 24 (1980): 331-362.

can the intent of the framers be determined simply by studying the cryptic record of the debates on these clauses in the First Session of Congress—however valuable that source is still today.[16] Not only are these Congressional records woefully incomplete, but the First Amendment religion clauses, by design, reflect only a small part of the early constitutional experiment and experience. The religion clauses, on their face, define only the outer boundaries of appropriate government action respecting religion—government may not prescribe ("establish") religion nor proscribe ("prohibit") its exercise. This leaves wide open for debate and development precisely what governmental conduct short of outright prescription or proscription of religion is constitutionally permissible. Moreover, the religion clauses on their face bind only the federal government ("Congress"), rendering prevailing state constitutional provisions, and the sentiments of their drafters, equally vital sources of original intent. Finally, the drafters of the religion clauses urged interpreters to look not to the drafters' intentions, but, in James Madison's words, "to the text itself [and] the sense attached to it by the people in their respective State Conventions, where it received all the authority which it possesses."[17] The understanding of the state conventional delegates was derived from their own state constitutional experiments and experiences, which are reflected in contemporaneous pamphlets, sermons, letters, and speeches. A wide range of eighteenth century materials must be consulted to come to terms with the prevailing sentiments on religious rights and liberties in the young American republic.

Theological and Political Perspectives. Within the eighteenth century sources at hand, two pairs of theological perspectives on religious liberties and rights were critical to constitutional formation: those of congregational *Puritans* and of free church *evangelicals*. Two pairs of contem-

[16] For a range of interpretations of these debates, see, e.g., Michael Malbin, *Religion and Politics: The Intentions of the Authors of the First Amendment* (Washington, 1978); Michael W. McConnell, "The Origins and History of Free Exercise of Religion," *Harvard Law Review* 103 (1990): 1473; Douglas N. Laycock, "Non-Preferential Aid to Religion: A False Claim About Original Intent," *William and Mary Law Review* 27 (1986): 875; Rodney K. Smith, "Getting Off on the Wrong Foot and Back on Again: A Reexamination of the History of the Framing of the First Amendment and a Critique of the *Reynolds* and *Everson* Decisions," *Wake Forest Law Review* 20 (1984): 569; Walter Berns, "Religion and the Founding Principle," in Robert H. Horwitz, ed., *The Moral Foundations of the American Republic,* 3d ed. (Charlottesville, 1986), 204.

[17] James Madison, "Letter from James Madison to Thomas Richie (September 15, 1821)," in id., *Letters and Other Writings of James Madison* (Philadelphia, 1821), 3:228 . See similar sentiments in James Madison, "Letter from James Madison to Major Henry Lee (June 25, 1824)," in ibid., 442; J. Gales, ed., *Annals of Congress* (Washington, 1796), 5:776 (where Madison writes: "As the instrument came from [the drafter] it was nothing more than the draft of a plan, nothing but a dead letter, until life and validity were breathed into it by the voice of the people, speaking through their several State conventions."). See discussion in B.N. Ong, "James Madison on Constitutional Interpretation," *Benchmark* 3 (1987): 18-20.

poraneous political perspectives were equally influential: those of *enlightenment* thinkers and civic *republicans*.[18] Exponents of these four perspectives often found common cause and used common language, particularly during the constitutional convention and ratification debates. Yet each group cast its views in a distinctive ensemble, with its own emphases and its own applications.

It must be emphasized that this is a heuristic classification, not a wooden taxonomy, of the multiple opinions on religious rights and liberties in the early republic. Other views besides these circulated, and other labels besides these were sometimes used to describe these four views. Moreover, individual writers of the eighteenth century often straddled two or more perspectives, shifted their allegiances or alliances over time, or changed their tones as they moved from formal writing to the pulpit or to the political platform. John Adams, for example, expounded both Puritan and civic republican views. John Witherspoon moved freely between evangelical and civic republican camps. Jonathan Edwards, at least in his political and ethical writings, toed the line between old light Puritan and new light evangelical perspectives. James Madison's early writings on religious liberty had a strong evangelical flavor; his political speeches in the early sessions of Congress often pulse with civic republican sentiments; his later writings, particularly after his Presidency, were of firm Enlightenment stock.

Nonetheless, there four perspectives had distinctive and distinguishable teachings on religious rights and liberties. The so-called original intent of the American constitutional framers respecting government and religion cannot be reduced to any one of these views. It must be sought in the tensions among them and in the general principles that emerge from their interaction.[19] What follows is (1) a summary of each of these four views; and (2) a distillation of the general principles of religious rights and liberties that these four groups and others propagated.

Puritan Views. "At the time of the [American] Revolution, at least 75 percent of American citizens had grown up in families espousing some form of Puritanism."[20] The Puritans were direct heirs to the theology and

---

[18] For other classifications of the framers' perspectives, see, e.g., Arlin M. Adams and Charles J. Emmerich, *A Nation Dedicated to Religious Liberty* (Philadelphia, 1990), 21-31 (distinguishing enlightenment separationists, political centrists, and pietistic separationists); McConnell, "Free Exercise," 1430-1455 (contrasting Lockeian-Jeffersonian, various evangelical, and Madisonian views).

[19] See a comparable caveat in Adams and Emmerich, *A Nation Dedicated to Religious Liberty*, 21-22, 31.

[20] A.J. Reichley, *Religion in American Public Life* (Washington, 1985), 53; Sidney Ahlstrom, *A Religious History of the American People* (New York, 1975), 1:169. This percentage is overstated, but the quote signals the importance of Puritanism in eighteenth century America. For a more nuanced religious demography, see Edward S. Gaustad, "Colonial Religion

ethics of European Calvinism. They had revised and refined this European legacy through the efforts of John Winthrop, John Cotton, Cotton Mather, Jonathan Edwards, Charles Chauncy, Jonathan Mayhew, and a host of other eminent writers. Since the 1630s, the Puritans had dominated the New England colonies and thus had ample occasion to cast their theological and political principles into constitutional practice.[21]

The Puritans who wrote on religious liberties and rights were concerned principally with the nature of the church, of the state, and of the relationship between them.[22] They conceived of the church and the state as two separate covenantal associations, two seats of Godly authority in the community. Each institution, they believed, has a distinctive polity and calling. The church was to be governed by pastoral, pedagogical, and diaconal authorities who were called to preach the word, administer the sacraments, teach the young, care for the poor and the needy. The state was to be governed by executive, legislative, and judicial authorities who were called to enforce law, punish crime, cultivate virtue, and protect peace and order.

In the New England communities where their views prevailed, the Puritans adopted a variety of safeguards to ensure the basic separation of the institutions of church and state. Church officials were prohibited from holding political office, from serving on juries, from interfering in governmental affairs, from endorsing political candidates, from censuring the official conduct of a statesman. Political officials, in turn, were prohibited from holding ministerial office, from interfering in internal ecclesiastical government, from performing sacerdotal functions of clergy,

---

and Liberty of Conscience," in Merrill D. Peterson & Robert C. Vaughn, eds., *The Virginia Statute for Religious Freedom: Its Evolution and Consequences in American History* (Cambridge, 1988), 23ff.; Thomas J. Curry, *The First Freedom: Church and State in America to the Passage of the First Amendment* (Oxford, 1986).

[21] Portions of the following section are drawn from John Witte, Jr., "Blest Be the Ties that Bind: Covenant and Community in Puritan Thought," *Emory Law Journal* 36 (1987): 579-601; id., "How to Govern a City on a Hill: The Early Puritan Contribution to American Constitutionalism," *Emory Law Journal* 39 (1990): 41-64. For samples of Puritan writings, see P. Miller and T. Johnson, *The Puritans* (New York, 1938) and Edmund S. Morgan, *Puritan Political Ideas, 1558-1794* (Indianapolis, 1965).

[22] The Puritan contribution to the American tradition of religious liberty, though generally ignored by current commentators, was well understood in the eighteenth century. See, e.g., John Adams, *Dissertation on the Canon and the Feudal Law* (1765), reprinted in John Adams, *Papers of John Adams*, R. Taylor, M. Kline, and G. Lint, eds. (Cambridge, 1977), 1:115-116 (describing the Puritans as "apostles of religious liberty" who were the first in America "to establish a government of the church more consistent with the scriptures, and a government of the state more agreable to the dignity of humane nature); Joseph Priestly, *An Address to Protestant Dissenters of all Denominations* (Boston, 1774), 5-6 (arguing that "Religious liberty . . . cannot be maintained except on the basis of civil liberty" and that "the Puritans and Nonconformists were equally distinguished for their noble and strenuous exertions in favour of them both").

from censuring the official conduct of a cleric.[23] To permit any such officiousness on the part of church or state officials, Governor John Winthrop averred, "would confounded those Jurisdictions, which Christ hath made distinct."[24]

Although church and state were not to be confounded, however, they were still to be "close and compact."[25] For, to the Puritans, these two institutions were inextricably linked in nature and in function. Each was an instrument of Godly authority. Each did its part to establish and maintain the community. As one mid-eighteenth century writer put it, "I look upon this as a little model of the Gloriou[s] Kingdome of Christ on earth. Christ Reigns among us in the Common wealth as well as in the Church, and hath his glorious Interest involved and wrapt up in the good of both Societies respectively."[26] The Puritans, therefore, readily countenanced the coordination and cooperation of church and state.

State officials provided various forms of material aid to churches and their officials. Public properties were donated to church groups for meeting houses, parsonages, day schools, and orphanages. Tax collectors collected tithes and special assessments to support the ministers and ministry of the congregational church. Tax exemptions and immunities were accorded to some of the religious, educational, and charitable organizations that they operated. Special subsidies and military protections were provided for missionaries and religious outposts. Special criminal laws prohibited interference with religious properties and services. State officials also provided various forms of moral support to the church. Sabbath day laws prohibited all forms of unnecessary labor and uncouth leisure on Sundays and holy days, and required faithful attendance at worship services.

Church officials, in turn, provided various forms of material aid and accommodation to the state. Church meetinghouses and chapels were used not only to conduct religious services, but also to host town assemblies, political rallies, and public auctions, to hold educational and vocational classes, to house the community library, to maintain census rolls and birth, marriage, and death certificates. Parsonages were used not

---

23 See, e.g., *The Book of the General Laws and Liberties of Concerning the Inhabitants of Massachusetts (1648)*, Max Farrand, ed. (Cambridge, 1929), 18-20; "The Cambridge Synod and Platform (1648)," in Williston Walker, ed., *The Creeds and Platforms of Congregationalism* (New York, 1960), 234-237.

24 Quoted by Timothy Breen, *The Character of the Good Ruler, 1630-1730* (New Haven, 1970), 42.

25 John Cotton, "Letter from The Rev. John Cotton to Lord (1636)," in Miller and Johnson, *The Puritans*, 209.

26 Uriah Oakes, *New England Pleaded with, and Pressed to Consider the Things Which Concern Her* (Boston, 1673), 49.

only to house the minister and his family, but also to harbor orphans and widows, the sick and the aged, victims of abuse and disaster. Church officials also afforded various forms of moral support to the state. They preached obedience to the authorities and imposed spiritual discipline on parishioners found guilty of crime.[27] They encouraged their parishioners to be active in political affairs and each year offered "election day sermons" on Christian political principles. They offered learned advice on the requirements of Godly law, and occasionally offered advice to legislatures and courts.

Puritan leaders of colonial New England left little room for individual religious experimentation. Despite their adherence to a basic institutional separation of church and state, the New England authorities established a form of Calvinist congregationalism. Already in the 1630s, dissidents from this faith, such as Anne Hutchinson and Roger Williams, were summarily dismissed from the colony. Immigration restrictions in Massachusetts Bay throughout the seventeenth century left little room to Quakers, Catholics, Jews, "Familists, Antinomians, and other Enthusiasts."[28] Although in the eighteenth century, religious dissidents of all kinds came to be tolerated in the New England colonies, they enjoyed only limited political rights and social opportunities and were subject to a variety of special governmental restrictions, taxes, and other encumbrances.[29]

Evangelical Views. Though the evangelical tradition claimed early exponents like Roger Williams and John Clarke, it did not emerge as a strong political force until after the Great Awakening of circa 1720-1780.[30] Numerous spokesmen for the evangelical cause rose up in the course of the later eighteenth century all along the Atlantic seaboard—Isaac Backus, John Leland, John Wesley, and a host of other pastors and pam-

---

[27] See generally Emil Oberholzer, *Delinquent Saints: Disciplinary Actions in the Early Congregational Churches of Massachusetts* (New York, 1956); Ronald A. Bosco, "Lectures at the Pillory: The Early American Execution Sermon," *American Quarterly* 30 (1978): 156 (describing the practice of New England preachers of offering lectures on the importance of moral and legal principles on the occasion of public executions).

[28] Nathaniel Ward, *The Simple Cobler of Aggawam in America*, 5th ed. (Boston, 1713), 43.

[29] See William C. McLoughlin, *New England Dissent 1630-1833* (Cambridge, MA, 1967), 2 vols.

[30] On evangelical views, see, generally, Curry, *The First Freedom*, 134-222; J. William Frost, *A Perfect Freedom: Religious Liberty in Pennsylvania* (Cambridge, 1990); E.S. Gaustad, *Liberty of Conscience: Roger Williams in America* (Grand Rapids, 1991); William Lee Miller, *The First Liberty: Religion and the American Republic* (New York, 1986); Perry Miller, "The Contributions of the Protestant Churches to Religious Liberty in Colonial America," *Church History* 4 (1935): 65-88. For representative evangelical writings, see Isaac Backus, *Isaac Backus on Church, State, and Calvinism: Pamphlets, 1754-1789*, W. McLoughlin, ed. (Cambridge, MA, 1968); John Leland, *The Writings of the Late Elder John Leland* (Privately Published, 1845); Roger Williams, *The Complete Writings of Roger Williams* (New York, 1963), 7 vols.

phleteers. Though the evangelicals had enjoyed fewer opportunities than the Puritans to institutionalize their views, they nonetheless had a formidable influence on the early American constitutional experiment.

Like the Puritans, the evangelicals advanced a theological theory of religious rights and liberties. They likewise advocated the institutional separation of church and state—the construction of "a wall of separation between the garden of the Church and the wilderness of the world," to quote their early leader, Roger Williams.[31] The evangelicals went beyond the Puritans, however, both in their definition of individual and institutional religious rights and in their agitation for a fuller separation of the institutions of church and state. The evangelicals sought to protect the liberty of conscience of every individual and the freedom of association of every religious group. Their solution was thus to prohibit all legal establishments of religion, and, indeed, all admixtures of religion and politics. As John Leland, the fiery Baptist preacher, put it in a proposed amendment to the Massachusetts Constitution:

> To prevent the evils that have heretofore been occasioned in the world by religious establishments, and to keep up the proper distinction between religion and politics, no religious test shall every be requested as a qualification of any officer, in any department of this government; neither shall the legislature, under this constitution, ever establish any religion by law, give any one sect a preference to another, or force any man in the commonwealth to part with his property for the support of religious worship, or the maintenance of ministers of the gospel.[32]

Later, Leland put the matter even more bluntly: "The notion of a Christian commonwealth should be exploded forever."[33]

Religious voluntarism lay at the heart of the evangelical view. Every individual, they argued, must be given the liberty of conscience to choose or to change his or her faith. "[N]othing can be true religion but a voluntary obedience unto [God's] revealed will," declared the Baptist Isaac

---

[31] Roger Williams, "Letter from Roger Williams to John Cotton (1643)," in ibid., 1:392. For discussion of the use of the metaphor of a wall of separation among evangelicals, and its transmutation by Thomas Jefferson and the United States Supreme Court, see Mark D. Howe, *The Garden and the Wilderness: Religion and Government in American Constitutional History* (Chicago, 1965).

[32] Jack Nips [John Leland], *The Yankee Spy* (Boston, 1794), reprinted in Charles Hyneman and Donald S. Lutz, eds., *American Political Writing During the Founding Era 1760-1805* (Indianapolis, 1983), 2:971, 989.

[33] Leland, *The Writings*, 118. See further discussion in McConnell, "Free Exercise," 1437-1443.

Backus.[34] State coercion or control of this choice—either directly through persecution and forced collection of tithes and services, or indirectly through withholding civil rights and benefits from religious minorities—was an offense both to the individual and to God. A plurality of religions should coexist in the community, and it was for God, not the state, to decide which of these religions should flourish and which should fade. "Religious liberty is a divine right," wrote the evangelical preacher Israel Evans, "immediately derived from the Supreme Being, without the intervention of any created authority. . . . the all-wise Creator invested [no] order of men with the right of judging for their fellow-creatures in the great concerns of religion."[35]

Every religious body was likewise to be free from state control of their assembly and worship, state regulations of their property and polity, state incorporation of their society and clergy, state interference in their discipline and government. Every religious body was also to be free from state emoluments like tax exemptions, civil immunities, property donations, and other traditional forms of state support for the church, countenanced by Puritan and other leaders. The evangelicals feared state benevolence towards religion and religious bodies almost as much as state repression. For those religious bodies that received state benefits would invariably become beholden to the state. "[I]f civil Rulers go so far out of their Sphere as to take the care and Management of religious affairs upon them," reads a 1776 Baptist Declaration, "Yea . . . Farwel to 'the free Exercise of Religion'."[36]

The chief concern of the evangelicals was theological, not political. Having suffered for more than a century as a religious minority in colonial America, and even longer in Europe, they sought a constitutional means to free all religion from the fetters of the law, to relieve the church from the restrictions of the state. In so doing, they developed only the rudiments of a political theory. They were content with a state that created a climate conducive to the cultivation of a plurality of religions and accommodated all religious believers and religious bodies without conditions or controls.

Enlightenment Views. Exponents of the enlightenment tradition in America provided a political theory that complemented the religious rights theology of the evangelicals. Though American exponents of the

---

[34] Isaac Backus, *A Declaration of the Rights, of the Inhabitants of the State of Massachusetts-Bay in New England* (1779), in Backus, *Church, State, and Calvinism*, 487.

[35] Israel Evans, *A Sermon Delivered at Concord, Before the Hon. General Court of the State of New Hampshire at the Annual Election* (Concord, 1791), reprinted in Sandoz, ed., *Political Sermons*, 1062-1063.

[36] "Declaration of the Virginia Association of Baptists (December 25, 1776)," in Thomas Jefferson, *The Papers of Thomas Jefferson*, Julian Boyd, ed. (Princeton, 1950), 1:660-661.

enlightenment claimed early European visionaries such as John Locke and David Hume, they did not emerge as a significant political voice until the mid-eighteenth century. Particularly the American Revolution served to transform the American enlightenment tradition from scattered groups of elite philosophers into a sizeable company of intellectual and political lights. Members of this company, though widely divergent in theological perspective and social position, were united in their efforts to convert enlightenment ideals into constitutional imperatives and in their adherence to the political views of Thomas Jefferson, Thomas Paine, and others.[37]

The primary purpose of enlightenment writers was political, not theological. They sought not only to free religion and the church from the influence of politics and the state, as did the evangelicals, but, more importantly, to free politics and the state from the influence of religion and the church. Exponents of the enlightenment taught that the state should give no special aid, support, privilege, or protection to organized religion, in the forms of tax exemptions, special criminal protections, administrative subsidies, or the incorporation of religious bodies. Nor should the state predicate its laws or policies on explicitly religious grounds or religious arguments, or draw on the services of religious officials or bodies to discharge state functions. As Madison put it in 1822: "[A] perfect separation between ecclesiastical and civil matters" is the best course, for "religion and Government will both exist in greater purity, the less they are mixed together."[38]

Such views were based on a profound skepticism about organized religion and a profound fear of an autocratic state. To allow church and state to be unrestricted, it was thought, would be to invite arbitrariness and abuse. To allow them to combine would be to their mutual disadvantage—to produce, in Thomas Paine's words, "a sort of mule-animal, capable only of destroying and not of breeding up."[39] Such enlightenment views were also based on the belief that a person is fundamentally an individual being and that religion is primarily a matter of private reason and conscience and only secondarily a matter of communal association and corporate confession. Every person, James Madison wrote, has

[37] On Enlightenment views, see generally Henry May, *The Enlightenment in America* (New York, 1976); A. Koch, ed., *The American Enlightenment: The Shaping of the American Experiment in a Free Society* (New York, 1965); R. Sher, *Scotland and America in the Age of the Enlightenment* (Princeton, 1990); P. Spurlin, *The French Enlightenment in America: Essays on the Times of the Founding Fathers* (Athens, GA, 1984). For samples of their writings, see P. Kurland and R. Lerner, eds., *The Founders' Constitution* (Chicago, 1987), 5:43-111.

[38] Letter to Edward Livingston (July 10, 1822), in Madison, *Writings*, 9:103.

[39] Thomas Paine, *The Complete Writings of Thomas Paine*, Philip Sheldon Foner, ed. (New York, 1945), 1:292.

the right to form "a rational opinion" about the duty he owes the Creator and the manner in which that duty is to be discharged.[40] Whether that religious duty is to be discharged individually or corporately is of secondary importance.[41]

Post-revolutionary Virginia proved to be fertile ground for political exponents of the enlightenment tradition to cultivate these views. Article 16 of the 1776 Virginia Bill of Rights, influenced in part by James Madison, provided: "That religion, or the duty which we owe to our Creator, and the manner of discharging it, can be directed only by reason and conviction, not by force or violence; and therefore, all men are equally entitled to the free exercise of religion, according to the dictates of conscience; and that it is the mutual duty of all to practise Christian forbearance, love, and charity, towards each other."[42] The famous Virginia Statute on Religious Freedom, drafted by Thomas Jefferson in 1777 and ultimately passed in 1786, provided even stronger Enlightenment language. The statute begins by celebrating that "almighty God hath created the mind free; that all attempts to influence it by temporal punishments or burthens, or by civil incapacitations, tend only to beget habits of hypocrisy and meanness, and are a departure from the plan of the Holy author of our religion." The statute recounts the ravages of religious establishment and repression, and their resulting injuries to God, religion, churches, states, and individuals. It then guarantees: "That no man shall be compelled to frequent or support any religious worship, place, or ministry whatsoever, nor shall be enforced, restrained, molested, or burthened in his body or goods, nor shall otherwise suffer on account of his religious opinions or belief; but that all men shall be free to profess, and by argument to maintain, their opinion in matters of religion, and that the same shall in no wise diminish, enlarge, or affect their civil capacities."[43]

These lofty protections of individual religious rights and liberties went hand-in-hand with the close restrictions on the rights of religious groups that were also advocated by Enlightenment exponents. Before the

---

[40] James Madison, *Memorial and Remonstrance Against Religious Assessments* (1785), sec. 1, in id., *The Papers of James Madison*, Robert A. Rutland and William M.E. Rachal, eds., Chicago, 1973), 8:298.

[41] In his *Detached Memoranda* of circa 1817, Madison highlighted his distaste for corporate organized religions by criticizing laws that allowed ecclesiastical bodies to incorporate, to be exempt from taxation, to accumulate property, and to gain political access through chaplains and other means. See Elizabeth Fleet, "Madison's, 'Detached Memoranda'," *William and Mary Quarterly* 3, 3d ser. (1946): 554.

[42] Reprinted in *The Papers of James Madison*, 1:175.

[43] W.W. Hening, ed., *The Statutes at Large . . . of Virginia* (1823), 12:84-86 [hereafter *Virginia Statutes*].

turn of the nineteenth century, the Virginia legislature outlawed religious corporations (a feature still in place in Virginia and West Virginia).[44] It also confiscated substantial tracts of vacant glebe lands held by the Anglican church, and restricted severely the tax exemptions and immunities accorded to the remaining religious properties.[45] The law of Virginia did not live entirely by the gospel of the enlightenment, however. Even Jefferson supported the revision of Virginia's post-revolutionary laws, which included A Bill for Punishing Disturbers of Religious Worship and Sabbath Breakers; A Bill for Appointing Days of Public Fasting and Thanksgiving; and a Bill Annulling Marriages Prohibited by the Levitical Law, and Appointing the Mode of Solemnizing Lawful Marriage [in Church].[46]

Civic Republican Views. The so-called "civic republicans" were an eclectic group of politicians, preachers, and pamphleteers who strove to cultivate a set of common values and beliefs for the new nation. Their principal spokesmen were John Adams, Samuel Adams, Oliver Ellsworth, George Washington, James Wilson, and other leaders, though the movement attracted considerable support among the spiritual and intellectual laity of the young republic as well. Just as the Enlightenment leaders found their theological analogues among the evangelicals, so the republican leaders found their theological analogues among the Puritans.[47]

To be sure, civic republicans, like evangelical and enlightenment exponents, advocated liberty of conscience for all and state support for a plurality of religions in the community. They, too, opposed religious intrusions on politics that rose to the level of political theocracy and political intrusions on religion that rose to the level of religious establishment. But, like the Puritans, the civic republicans sought to imbue the public square with a common religious ethic and ethos—albeit less denominationally rigorous than that allowed by their Puritan brethren.

---

44 See discussion in Paul B. Kauper and Stephen B. Ellis, "Religious Corporations and the Law," *Michigan Law Review* 71 (1973): 1499, 1529ff.

45 See H.J. Eckenrode, *Separation of Church and State in Virginia: A Study in the Development of the Revolution* (Richmond, 1910), 116ff.

46 *Papers of Thomas Jefferson*, 2:555-558, with discussion in Adams and Emmerich, *A Nation Dedicated to Religious Liberty*, 23-24.

47 On civic republican views, see, generally, Nathan O. Hatch, *The Sacred Cause of Liberty* (New Haven, 1977); Gordon S. Wood, *The Creation of the American Republic, 1776-1787* (New York, 1969), and the critical summary of more recent literature in Richard H. Fallon, Jr., "What is Republicanism, and is it Worth Reviving?" *Harvard Law Review* 102 (1989): 1695.

"Religion and Morality are the central pillars of Civil society," George Washington declared.[48] "[W]e have no government," John Adams echoed, "armed with power capable of contending with human passions unbridled by morality and religion."[49] "Religion and liberty are the meat and drink of the body politic," wrote Yale President Timothy Dwight.[50] According to the civic republicans, society needs a fund of religious values and beliefs, a body of civic ideas and ideals that are enforceable both through the common law and through communal suasion. This was what Benjamin Franklin had called the "Publick Religion"[51] (and what is now called the "civil religion") of America, which undergirded the plurality of sectarian religions.[52] This civil religion taught a creed of honesty, diligence, devotion, public spiritedness, patriotism, obedience, love of God, neighbor, and self, and other ethical commonplaces taught by various religious traditions at the time of the founding. Its icons were the Bible, the Declaration of Independence, the bells of liberty, the Constitution. Its clergy were public-spirited Christian ministers and religiously-devout politicians. Its liturgy was the proclamations of prayers, songs, sermons, and Thanksgiving Day offerings by statesmen and churchmen. Its policy was government appointment of legislative and military chaplains, government sponsorship of general religious education and organization, and government enforcement of a religiously-based morality through positive law.

This civic republican policy perforce produced some level of state support and accommodation for clerics and churches. "[R]eligion and its institutions are the best aid of government," declared Nathan Strong, "by strengthening the ruler's hand, and making the subject faithful in his place, and obedient to the general laws."[53] Similarly, the Connecticut

---

[48] George Washington, "Letter of George Washington to the Clergy of Philadelphia (March 3, 1797)," in id., *The Writings of George Washington From the Original Manuscript Sources, 1745-1799*, J.C. Fitzpatrick, ed. (Washington, DC, 1931), 30:416.

[49] John Adams, "Letter of John Adams to a Unit of the Massachusetts Militia (1798)," in *The Works of John Adams*, 9:229.

[50] Timothy Dwight, *The Duty of Americans at the Present Crisis, Illustrated in a Discourse Preached on the Fourth of July, 1798* (New Haven, 1798), reprinted in Sandoz, ed., *Political Sermons*, 1365, 1380.

[51] See Benjamin Franklin, *Benjamin Franklin: Representative Selections*, C. Jorgenson and F. Motts, eds. (New York, 1962), 203, quoted and discussed in Martin E. Marty, "On a Medial Moraine: Religious Dimensions of American Constitutionalism," *Emory Law Journal* 39 (1990): 9, 16-17. On the later influence of these sentiments in America, see generally Martin E. Marty, *Pilgrims in Their Own Land: 500 Years of Religion in American* (Harmondsworth, 1984).

[52] See Robert N. Bellah, *The Broken Covenant: American Civil Religion in Time of Trial* (New York, 1975); Sidney E. Mead, *The Old Religion in the Brave New World: Reflections on the Relation Between Christendom and the Republic* (Berkeley, 1977); Ellis Sandoz, *A Government of Laws: Political Theory, Religion, and the American Founding* (Baton Rouge, LA, 1990).

[53] Nathan Strong, *Election Sermon* (Hartford, 1790), 15.

Senator Oliver Ellsworth declared: "Institutions for the promotion of good morals, are objects of legislative provision and support: and among these . . . religious institutions are eminently useful and important."[54] Civic republicans, therefore, endorsed various forms of general support for religious institutions, particularly tax exemptions for church properties and tax support for religious schools, charities, and missionaries, donations of public lands to religious organizations, and criminal protections against blasphemy, sacrilege, and interruption of religious services.[55] In theory, such state emoluments were to be given non-preferentially to all religious groups; in practice, certain Protestant groups received the preponderance of such support, while Quakers, Catholics, and the few Jewish groups about were routinely excluded.

Post-revolutionary Massachusetts proved to be fertile ground for the cultivation of these civic republican views. The 1780 Constitution of Massachusetts, for example, proclaimed that "[i]t is the *right* as well as the *duty* of all men in society, publicly and at stated seasons, to worship the SUPREME BEING, the great Creator and preserver of the universe."[56] For "the public worship of God and instructions in piety, religion, and morality, promote the happiness and prosperity of a people, and the security of a republican government."[57] The same constitution also insisted that all persons, particularly political leaders, maintain rigorous moral and religious standards: "A frequent recurrence to the fundamental principles of the constitution, and a constant adherence to those of piety, justice, moderation, temperance, industry, and frugality, are absolutely necessary to preserve the advantages of liberty, and to maintain a free government."[58]

These civic republican views also found favor in the Continental Congress, which authorized the appointment of tax-supported chaplains to the military, tax appropriations for religious schools and missionaries, diplomatic ties to the Vatican, and recitations of prayer at its opening ses-

---

[54] Oliver Ellsworth, "Report of the Committee to whom was referred the Petition of Simeon Brown and others. . . ." (1802), in *The Public Records of the State of Connecticut*, Christopher Collier, ed. (Hartford, 1967), 11:371, 373. See discussion in William Casto, "Oliver Ellsworth's Calvinism: A Biographical Essay on Religion and Political Psychology in the Early Republic," *Journal of Church and State* 36 (1994): 506, 525.

[55] See Chester J. Antieau, Arthur T. Downey and Edward C. Roberts, *Freedom from Federal Establishment: Formation and Early History of the First Amendment Religion Clauses* (Milwaukee, 1964), 62-91; John Witte, Jr., "Tax Exemption of Church Property: Historical Anomaly or Valid Constitutional Practice," *Southern California Law Review* 64 (1991): 363, 368-395.

[56] Constitution or Form of Government for the Commonwealth of Massachusetts (1780), Part I, art. 2. (emphasis added).

[57] Ibid., Amendment, art. 11, which replaced Part I, art. 3 in the 1780 Constitution.

[58] Ibid., Part I, art. 18.

sions and during the day of Thanksgiving.[59] The Continental Congress also passed the Northwest Ordinance in 1787, which provided, in part, "Religion, morality, and knowledge, being necessary to good government and the happiness of mankind, schools and the means of education shall forever be encouraged."[60]

These four views—Puritan, evangelical, enlightenment, and republican—helped to inform the early American experiment in religious rights and liberties. Each view was liberally espoused by federal and state leaders in the early American republic, informally in their letters and pamphlets, and formally in the constitutional convention and ratification debates.

The Essential Rights and Liberties of Religion. Despite the tensions among them, exponents of these four groups could generally agreed upon, what the New England Puritan jurist and theologian Elisha Williams called, "the essential rights and liberties of [religion]."[61] To be sure, these "essential rights and liberties" never won uniform articulation or universal assent in the young republic. But a number of enduring and interlocking principles found widespread support, many of which were included in state and federal constitutional discussions—liberty of conscience, free exercise of religion, pluralism, equality, separationism, and disestablishment of religion. Such principles remain at the heart of the American experiment today.

The common goal of these principles was to replace the inherited tradition of repressive religious establishments with a new experiment in granting religious rights and liberties for all. To be sure, a number of writers were reluctant to extend religious liberty to Catholics and Jews, let alone to Muslims and Indians—and these prejudices are sometimes betrayed in the earliest drafts of the state constitutions. For many eighteenth century writers, the term "religion" was synonymous with Christianity (or even Protestantism), and the discussion of "religious liberty" was often in terms of the "liberty or rights of Christians."[62] And to be sure, some Puritans and civic republicans continued to support what

---

59 See generally Isaac A. Cornelison, *The Relation of Religion to Civil Government in the United States of America: A State Without a Church, But Not Without a Religion* (New York, 1895).

60 Article III, 1 Stat. 50, 51-53, ch. 8.

61 Elisha Williams, *The Essential Rights and Liberties of Protestants: A Seasonable Plea for The Liberty of Conscience, and the Right of Private Judgment in Matters of Religion, Without any Controul from Human Authority* (Boston, 1744), reprinted in Sandoz, ed., *Political Sermons*, 51. Madison also used the phrase "essential rights and liberties" of religion in the Congressional debates about the First Amendment. See, e.g., Gales, *Annals of Congress*, 1:784.

62 Robert T. Handy, "Why it Took 150 Years for Supreme Court Church-State Cases to Escalate," in R. White and A. Zimmermann, eds., *An Unsettled Arena: Religion and the Bill of Rights* (Grand Rapids, 1990), 54.

John Adams called a "slender" form of congregationalist establishment in some of the New England states—consisting principally of tax preferences for the congregational churches and schools.[63] But such "compromises" do not deprive the early American experiment, and the sentiments that inspired it, of their ongoing validity or utility. By eighteenth century standards, this experiment was remarkably advanced, and calculated to benefit the vast majority of the population. Many provisions on religious rights and liberties were cast in broad terms, and those that were more denominationally specific could easily be extended to other religious groups, as later state courts repeatedly demonstrated. The "slender" New England establishments, which ended in 1833, were a far cry from the repressive, bloody regimes of the American colonies and of post-Reformation Europe, and the maintenance of such soft establishments was not seen as inconsistent with guarantees of essential rights and liberties of all citizens within the state.[64]

Virtually all writers embraced religious liberty as the "first liberty" and the "first freedom."[65] It is "the most inalienable and sacred of all human rights," wrote Thomas Jefferson.[66] "Religious liberty, both civil and ecclesiastical, is the greatest blessing of the kind, that we can enjoy," wrote the congregationalist preacher Jonathan Parsons, "and thereby to be deprived of either, is the greatest injury that we can suffer."[67] At the same time, virtually all writers also denounced the bloody religious establishments of previous eras. James Madison reflected commonplaces of the day when he wrote: "[E]xperience witnesseth that ecclesiastical establishments, instead of maintaining the purity and efficacy of Religion, have had a contrary operation. During almost fifteen centuries has the legal establishment of Christianity been on trial. What have been its fruits? More or less in all places, pride and indolence in the Clergy, igno-

---

[63] Quoted by Gaustad, "Colonial Religion and Liberty of Conscience," 39.

[64] The 1780 Massachusetts Constitution, Part I, art. 2, for example, guaranteed that "no subject shall be hurt, molested, restrained, in his person, liberty, or estate, for worshipping God in the manner and season most agreeable to the dictates of his own conscience." See similar provisions in the Constitution of Vermont (1793), chap. 1, art. 3; Constitution of New Hampshire (1784), Part I, arts. 4-5. When it finally adopted a constitution in 1818, Connecticut provided expansively: "Sec. 3. Religious Liberty. The exercise and enjoyment of religious profession and worship, without discrimination, shall forever be free to all persons in this state. . . . Sec. 4. No preferences in Christian sects or modes of worship. No preference shall be given by law to any Christian sect or mode of worship."

[65] See Miller, *The First Liberty;* James E. Wood, Jr., *The First Freedom: Religion and the Bill of Rights* (Waco, TX, 1990).

[66] Thomas Jefferson, "Freedom of Religion at the University of Virginia (Oct. 7, 1822)," in *The Complete Jefferson*, 958.

[67] Jonathan Parsons, *Freedom from Civil and Ecclesiastical Slavery* (Newbury-Port, 1774), 10.

rance and servility in the laity, in both, superstition, bigotry, and persecution. . . . Torrents of blood have been spilt in the old world, by vain attempts of the secular arm, to extinguish Religious discord, by proscribing all differences in Religious opinion."[68]

Liberty of Conscience. Liberty of conscience was the general solvent used in the early American experiment in religious liberty. It was almost universally embraced in the young republic—even by the most churlish of Erastians and establishmentarians.[69] The term "liberty of conscience" was often conflated with the terms "free exercise of religion," "religious freedom," "religious liberty," "religious privileges," and "religious rights." James Madison, for example, simply rolled into one linguistic heap "religious freedom" or "the free exercise of religion according to the dictates of conscience."[70] Later he spoke of "religious liberty" as the "religious rights . . . of a multiplicity of sects."[71] Such patterns of interwoven language appear regularly in later eighteenth century writings: one term often implicated and connoted many others.[72] Liberty of conscience, however, also had distinctive content.

First, liberty of conscience served to protect *voluntarism*—"the unalienable [and divine] right of private judgment in matters of religion," the unencumbered ability to choose and to change one's religious beliefs and adherences.[73] Already Elisha Williams put this matter very strongly for Christians in 1744: "Every man has an equal right to follow the dictates of his own conscience in the affairs of religion. Every one is under an indispensable obligation to search the Scriptures for himself . . . and to make the best use of it he can for his own information in the will of God, the nature and duties of Christianity. As every Christian is so bound; so he has the inalienable right to judge of the sense and meaning of it, and to follow his judgment wherever it leads him; even an equal right with any

---

68 Madison, *Memorial and Remonstrance*, secs. 7, 11.

69 For a good collection of prevailing sentiments, see *The Palladium of Conscience, or, The Foundation of Religious Liberty Displayed, Asserted and Established, Agreeable to its True and Genuine Principles* (Philadelphia, 1773) (frequently reprinted).

70 Virginia Bill of Rights, Art. 16.

71 Quoted by Anson P. Stokes and Leo Pfeffer, *Church and State in the United States*, rev. ed. (Boston, 1967), 61.

72 See examples in McConnell, "Free Exercise," 1455ff. 1480ff. For a catalogue of such terms, see, e.g., John Mellen, *The Great and Happy Doctrine of Liberty* (Boston, 1795), 17-18; Amos Adams, *Religious Liberty an Invaluable Blessing* (Boston, 1768), 39-40, 45-46; *A Manual of Religious Liberty*, 3d ed. (London/New York, 1767).

73 Williams, *Essential Rights and Liberties*, 94-95. See also John Lathorp, *A Discourse on the Peace* (Boston, 1784), 29. The phrase "divine right of private judgment" in matters of religion was commonplace in the eighteenth century. See, e.g., Hugh Fisher, *The Divine Right of Private Judgment, Set in a True Light* (Boston, 1731; repr. ed., Boston/Philadelphia, 1790).

rulers be they civil or ecclesiastical."[74] James Madison wrote more generically in 1785: "The Religion then of every man must be left to the conviction and conscience of every man; and it is the right of every man to exercise it as these may dictate." "Every man must give an account of himself to God," echoed the evangelical leader John Leland in 1791, "and therefore every man ought to be at liberty to serve God in that way that he can be reconcile it to his conscience. . . . It would be sinful for a man to surrender to man which is to be kept sacred for God. A man's mind should be always open to conviction, and an honest man will receive that doctrine which appears the best demonstrated; and what is more common for the best of men to change their minds?"[75] Puritan, *philosophe,* and evangelical alike could agree on this core meaning of liberty of conscience.

Second, and closely related, liberty of conscience *prohibited* religiously-based *discrimination* against individuals. Persons could not be penalized for the religious choices they made, nor swayed to make certain choices because of the civil advantages attached to them. Liberty of conscience, Ezra Stiles opined, permits "no bloody tribunals, no cardinal inquisitors-general, to bend the human mind, forcibly to control the understanding, and put out the light of reason, the candle of the Lord in man."[76] Liberty of conscience also prohibits more subtle forms of discrimination, prejudice, and cajolery by state, church, or even other citizens. "[N]o part of the community shall be permitted to perplex or harass the other for any supposed heresy," wrote a Massachusetts pamphleteer, ". . . each individual shall be allowed to have and enjoy, profess and maintain his own system of religion."[77]

Third, in the view of some eighteenth century writers, liberty of conscience guaranteed "a freedom and exemption from human impositions, and legal restraints, in matters of religion and conscience."[78] Persons of faith were to be "exempt from all those penal, sanguinary laws, that generate vice instead of virtue."[79] Such laws not only included the onerous criminal rules that traditionally encumbered and discriminated against

---

74 Williams, *Essential Rights and Liberties*, 61.

75 See esp. John Leland, *The Rights of Conscience Inalienable* (New London, 1791), reprinted in Sandoz, ed., *Political Sermons*, 1079. See similar themes in Issac Backus, *An Appeal to the Public for Religious Liberty* (Boston, 1773), in ibid., 327; Evans, *A Sermon Delivered at Concord*, 1063ff.

76 Stiles, *The United States Elevated to Glory*, 55.

77 *Worcestriensis, Number IV* (1776), in Hyneman and Lutz, *American Political Writing*, 1:449. The typical caveat follows: "provided it does not issue in overt acts of treason against the state undermining the peace and good order of society." Ibid.

78 John Mellen, *The Great and Happy Doctrine of Liberty* (Boston, 1795), 17.

79 Ibid., 20.

religious non-conformists, and led to fines, whippings, banishments, and occasional executions of dissenting colonists. They also included more facially benign laws that worked injustice to certain religious believers—conscription laws that required religious pacificists to participate in the military, oath-swearing laws that ran afoul of the religious scruples of certain believers, tithing and taxing laws that forced believers to support churches, schools, and other causes that they found religiously odious.[80] Liberty of conscience required that persons be exempt or immune from civil duties and restrictions that they could not, in good conscience, accept or obey.[81] As Henry Cumings put it: "Liberty of conscience requires not [only] that persons are . . . exempt from hierarchical tyranny and domination, from the usurped authority of pope and prelates, and from every species of persecution on account of religion." It requires also that they "stand on equal ground, and behaving as good members of society, may equally enjoy their religious opinions, and without molestation, or being exposed to fines or forfeitures, or any other temporal disadvantages."[82] It was commonly assumed that the laws of conscientious Christian magistrates would not tread on the religious scruples of their predominantly Christian subjects.[83] As George Washington put it in a letter to Quakers: "[I]n my opinion the conscientious scruples of all men should be treated with great delicacy and tenderness: and it is my wish and desire, that the laws may always be as extensively accommodated to them, as a due regard for the protection and essential interests of the nation may justify and permit."[84] Where general laws and policies did intrude on the religious scruples of an individual or group, liberty of conscience demanded protection of religious minorities and exemption.[85]

---

[80] See, e.g., Jonathan Parsons, *Freedom from Civil and Ecclesiastical Slavery* (Newbury-Port, 1772); Backus, *Appeal to the Public for Religious Liberty*. See McConnell, "Free Exercise," 1466-1473.

[81] Henry Cumings, *A Sermon Preached at Billerica* (Boston, 1797), 12-13. These arguments for exemptions from civil impositions were sometimes extended to claiming "exemptions" and "immunities" from the jurisdiction, discipline, and confessional statements of a local church. See, e.g., Isaac Foster, *A Defense of Religious Liberty* (Worcester, MA, 1780) (a 192 page tract arguing for an exemption from the new imposition of a new confession, the Saybrook Platform, in a local church).

[82] Ibid.

[83] See Carol Weisbrod, "Commentary on Curry and Firmage Articles," *Journal of Law and Religion* 7 (1989): 315, 320-321 (arguing for such presumptive accommodation of religious scruples, without express mention in legislation and without necessity for judicial intervention).

[84] *The Writings of George Washington*, 30:416.

[85] For contrary sentiments, see, e.g., Madison, *Memorial and Remonstrance*, sec. 4 (arguing that equality was compromised by granting certain religious groups "peculiar exemptions"). Even early writers who thought exemptions were necessary to protect religious liberty were fully aware that such guarantees could be abused. Thus, on the one hand, they

Whether such exemptions should be accorded by the legislature or the judiciary, and whether they were per se a constitutional right or simply a rule of equity—the principal bones of contention among recent commentators[86]—the eighteenth century sources simply do not clearly say.

All the early state constitutions include a guarantee of liberty of conscience for all.[87] The Delaware Constitution provides typical language: "That all men have a natural and inalienable right to worship Almighty God according to the dictates of their own consciences and understandings; and that no man ought or of right can be compelled to attend any religious worship or maintain any religious ministry contrary to or against his own free will and consent, and that no authority can or ought to be vested in, or assumed by any power whatever that shall in any case interfere with, or in any manner controul [sic] the right of conscience and free exercise of religious worship."[88] The Pennsylvania Constitution adds a protection against religious discrimination: "Nor can any man, who acknowledges the being of a God, be justly deprived or abridged of any civil right as a citizen, on account of his religious sentiments or peculiar mode of worship." It also provides an exemption for conscientious objectors: "Nor can any man who is conscientiously scrupulous of bearing arms, be justly compelled thereto, if he will pay such equivalent."[89] The Constitution of New York was concerned to guard against both state and

---

insisted that liberty of conscience could not be used to excuse breaches of the peace or of the public order—a caveat that found its way into almost all state constitutions. On the other hand, they insisted that liberty of conscience not be used as a sham to shirk one's civil duties. In the same passage where he defends the importance of religious exemption, Henry Cumings writes: "[T]o admit the plea of conscience, when urged, in order to excuse persons from contributing, in any way to the necessary defence, support, and well-being of the community to which they belong would evidently be inconsistent with civil union and terminate in the abolition of society: and it would encourage people to sanctify their sordid selfishness and avarice by the sacred name, conscience, in order to free themselves from public expences [sic]." Cumings, *A Sermon Preached at Billerica*, 13-14. It was thus assumed that the conscientious objector would pay for his replacement and the oath-forsaker would provide other guarantees of veracity.

[86] See Philip A. Hamburger, "A Constitutional Right of Religious Exemption: An Historical Perspective," *George Washington Law Review* 60 (1992): 915; Ellis West, "The Right to Religion-Based Exemptions in Early America: The Case of Conscientious Objectors to Conscription," *Journal of Law and Religion* 10 (1994): 367; William P. Marshall, "The Case Against the Constitutionally Compelled Free Exercise Exemption," *Case Western Reserve University Law Review* 40 (1990): 357; Kurt T. Lash, "The Second Adoption of the Free Exercise Clause: Religious Exemptions Under the Fourteenth Amendment," *Northwestern University Law Review* 88 (1994): 1106; Michael W. McConnell, "Accommodation of Religion: An Update and a Response to the Critics," *George Washington Law Review* 60 (1992): 685.

[87] For good summaries of these state developments, see Antieau et al., *Religion Under the State Constitutions*; John K. Wilson, "Religion Under the State Constitutions, 1776-1800," *Journal of Church and State* 32 (1990): 753.

[88] Delaware Declaration of Rights (1776), sec. 2.

[89] Constitution of Pennsylvania (1776), II.

church intrusions on conscience, and endeavored "not only to expel civil tyranny, but also to guard against that spiritual oppression and intolerance wherewith the bigotry and ambition of weak and wicked priests have scourged mankind [and thus] declare, that the free exercise and enjoyment of religious profession and worship, without discrimination or preference, shall forever be allowed, within this state, to all mankind."[90] The Constitution of New Jersey provided exemptions from religious taxes, using typical language: "nor shall any person . . . ever be obliged to pay tithes, taxes, or any other rates, for the purpose of building or repairing any other church, . . . or ministry, contrary to what he believes to be right."[91]

The principle of liberty of conscience also informed some of the federal constitutional debates on religion. Article VI of the Constitution explicitly provides: "[N]o religious Test [oath] shall ever be required as a qualification" for public office, thereby, *inter alia*, protecting the religiously scrupulous against oath-swearing.[92] Early versions of the First Amendment religion clauses included such phrases as: "That any person religiously scrupulous of bearing arms ought to be exempted, upon payment of an equivalent to employ another to bear arms in his stead";[93] "The Civil Rights of none shall be abridged on account of religious belief or worship . . . nor shall the full and equal rights of conscience be in any manner, nor on any pretext, infringed";[94] "Congress shall make no law . . . to infringe the rights of conscience."[95] Such phrases were ultimately abandoned (though not argued against in the extant records[96]) for the more pregnant language: "Congress shall make no law . . . prohibiting the free exercise [of religion]." This language does not leave conscience unprotected, but more protected. Since Congress cannot "prohibit" the free exercise, the public manifestation, of religion, a fortiori

[90] Constitution of New York (1777), art. xxxviii.

[91] Constitution of New Jersey, (1776), art. xviii.

[92] See Joseph Story, *Commentaries on the Constitution* (Boston, 1833), 3:703, and discussion in Adams & Emmerich, *A Nation Dedicated to Religious Liberty*, 61-62.

[93] Virginia Version (June 27, 1788), *Documentary History of the United States of America* (Washington, 1894), 2:380.

[94] James Madison's First Proposal, introduced in the House on June 7, 1789, in Gales, *Annals of Congress* (1834), 1:434.

[95] Draft proposed by Fisher Ames of Massachusetts on August 20, 1789 for debate in the House. Ibid., 1:766.

[96] Indeed the prevailing assumption in the House Debates of August 15, 1789 about the religion clauses was, in Representative Carroll's words, that "the rights of conscience are, in their nature, of peculiar delicacy and will little bear the gentlest touch of governmental hand" and that "many sects have concurred in [the] opinion that they are not well secured in the present constitution," lacking a bill of rights. Ibid., 1:783.

Congress cannot "prohibit" a person's private liberty of conscience, and the precepts embraced therein.

Liberty of conscience was the cardinal principle for the new experiment in religious liberty. Several other "essential rights and liberties of religion" built directly on this core principle.

Free Exercise of Religion. Liberty of conscience was inextricably linked to free exercise of religion. Liberty of conscience was a guarantee to be left alone to choose, to entertain, and to change one's religious beliefs. Free exercise of religion was the right to act publicly on the choices of conscience once made, without intruding on or obstructing the rights of others or the general peace of the community. Already in 1670, the Quaker leader William Penn had linked these two guarantees, insisting that religious liberty entails "not only a mere liberty of the mind, in believing or disbelieving . . . but [also] the exercise of ourselves in a visible way of worship."[97] By the next century, this organic linkage was commonly accepted. Religion, Madison wrote, "must be left to the convictions and conscience of every man; and it is the right of man to exercise it as these may dictate."[98] For most eighteenth century writers, religious belief and religious action went hand-in-hand.

Though eighteenth century writers, or dictionaries, offered no clear definition of "free exercise," the phrase generally connoted various forms of free public religious action—religious speech, religious worship, religious assembly, religious publication, religious education, among others. Free exercise of religion also embraced the right of the individual to join with like-minded believers in religious societies, which religious societies were free to devise their own modes of worship, articles of faith, standards of discipline, and patterns of ritual.[99] Eighteenth century writers did not speak unequivocally of what we now call group rights, or corporate free exercise rights, but they did regularly call for "ecclesiastical liberty," "the equal liberty of one sect . . . with another," and the right "to have the full enjoyment and free exercise of those spiritual powers . . . which, being derived only from CHRIST and His

---

97 William Penn, "The Great Case of Liberty of Conscience (1670)," reprinted in William Penn, *A Collection of the Works of William Penn* (London, 1726), 1:443, 447.

98 Madison, *Memorial and Remonstrance*, sec. 1. See also Levi Hart, *Liberty Described and Recommended* (Hartford, 1775), 14-15 (distinguishing religious liberty, ecclesiastical liberty, and spiritual liberty).

99 See, e.g., Williams, *Essential Rights and Liberties*, 99ff.; Backus, *Church, State, and Calvinism*, 348ff.; Parsons, *Freedom from Civil and Ecclesiastical Slavery*, 14-15; Stiles, *The United States Elevated to Glory*, 55ff.; Adams, *Religious Liberty an Invaluable Blessing*, 38-46.

Apostles, are to be maintained, independent of every foreign, or other, jurisdiction, so far as may be consistent with the civil rights of society."[100]

Virtually all of the early state constitutions guaranteed "free exercise" rights, with the familiar caveat that such exercise not violate the public peace or the private rights of others. Most states limited their guarantee to "the free exercise of religious worship" or the "free exercise of religious profession," presumably thereby leaving the protection of other forms of religious expression and action to other constitutional guarantees. A few states provided more generic free exercise guarantees. Virginia, for example, guaranteed flatly "the free exercise of religion, according to the dictates of conscience."[101] The Georgia constitution provided: "All persons whatever shall have the free exercise of their religion; provided it be no repugnant to the peace and safety of the State."[102] The First Amendment drafters chose equally embracive language of "the free exercise" of religion. Rather than using the categorical language preferred by state drafters, however, the First Amendment drafters guaranteed protection only against Congressional laws "prohibiting" the free exercise of religion. Whether Congress could make laws "infringing" or "abridging" the free exercise of religion—as earlier drafts sought to outlaw—was left open.

Pluralism. Eighteenth century writers regarded "multiplicity," "diversity," or "plurality," as an equally essential principle of religious rights and liberties. Pluralism was not just a sociological fact for them; it was a constitutional condition for the guarantee of true religious rights and liberties.

Two kinds of pluralism were distinguished. Evangelical and Enlightenment writers urged the protection of *confessional pluralism*—the maintenance and accommodation of a plurality of forms of religious expression and organization in the community. Evangelical writers advanced a theological argument for this principle, emphasizing that it was for God, not the state, to decide which forms of religion should flourish and which should fade. "God always claimed it as his sole prerogative to determine by his own laws what his worship shall be, who shall minister in it, and how they shall be supported," Isaac Backus wrote.[103] "God's

---

[100] See respectively, Hart, *Liberty*, 14; Backus, *Church, State, and Calvinism*, 348-349; *A Declaration of Certain Fundamental Rights and Liberties of the Protestant Episcopal Church in Maryland*, quoted in Anson P. Stokes, *Church and States in the United States* (New York, 1950), 1:741.

[101] Virginia Declaration of Rights, Art. 16.

[102] Constitution of Georgia (1777), art. lvi.

[103] Backus, *Church, State, and* Calvinism, 317. See also, e.g., *The Freeman's Remonstrance Against an Ecclesiastical Establishment* (Williamsburg, 1777), 13.

truth is great, and in the end He will allow it to prevail."[104] Confessional pluralism served to respect and reflect this divine prerogative. Enlightenment writers advanced a rational argument. "Difference of opinion is advantageous in religion," Thomas Jefferson wrote. "The several sects perform the office of a *Censor morum* over each other. Is uniformity attainable? Millions of innocent men, women, and children, since the introduction of Christianity, have been burnt, tortured, fined, imprisoned; yet we have not advanced one inch towards uniformity. . . . Reason and persuasion are the only practicable instruments."[105] Madison wrote similarly that "the utmost freedom . . . arises from that multiplicity of sects which pervades America, . . . for where there is such a variety of sects, there cannot be a majority of any one sect to oppress and persecute the rest."[106] Other writers added that the maintenance of multiple faiths is the best protection of the core guarantee of liberty of conscience.[107]

Puritan and civic republican writers insisted on *social pluralism*—the maintenance and accommodation of a plurality of associations to foster religion. Churches and synagogues were not the only "religious societies" that deserved protection. Families, schools, and charities were equally vital bastions of religion and equally deserving of the special protections of religious rights and liberties. These diverse social institutions had several redeeming qualities. They provided multiple forums for religious expressions and actions, important bulwarks against state encroachment on natural liberties, particularly religious liberties, and vital sources of theology, morality, charity, and discipline in the state and broader community.[108] As John Adams put it: "My Opinion of the Duties

---

104 Isaac Backus, *Truth is Great and Will Prevail* (Boston, 1781). See also John R. Bolles, *A Brief Account of Persecutions, in Boston and Connecticut Governments* (New London, 1758), 47, 59.

105 Jefferson, *Notes on the State of Virginia* (1784), query 17. See also Stiles, *The United States Elevated to Glory*, 55-56; Thomas Paine, *Common Sense* (1776), in id., *Common Sense and the Crisis* (New York, 1960), 50.

106 See Debates of June 12, 1788, in J. Elliot, ed., *The Debates in the Several State Conventions on the Adoption of the Federal Constitution*, 2d ed. (Washington, 1836), 3:330. See discussion in Smith, "Getting off on the Wrong Foot and Back on Again," 576ff.; Christopher L. Eisgruber, "Madison's Wager: Religious Liberty in the Constitutional Order," *Northwestern University Law Review* 89 (1995): 347, 373ff.

107 See Williams, *Essential Rights and Liberties*, 92-93; Stiles, *The United States Elevated to Glory*, 55ff.

108 See, e.g., James Wilson, *The Works of James Wilson*, R.G. McCloskey, ed. (Cambridge, 1967), 197 and general discussion in W.C. McWilliams, *The Idea of Fraternity in America* (Berkeley, 1973), 112-123; Clinton Rossiter, *The Political Thought of the American Revolution* (New York, 1963), 204. For earlier pluralist theories rooted in the work of the sixteenth-century Dutch political theorist Johannes Althusius and in Puritan covenant theology, see respectively C.J. Friedrich, *Trends of Federalism in Theory and Practice* (Cambridge, 1958), 11-25 Witte, "Blest be the Ties That Bind." For later formulations, see Johan van der Vyver, "Sphere Sovereignty and the American Concept of Religious Freedom," in id., *Reformed Chris-*

of Religion and Morality comprehends a very extensive connection with society at large. . . . The Benevolence, Charity, Capacity and Industry which exerted in private Life, would make a family, a Parish or a Town happy, employed upon a larger Scale, in Support of the great Principles of Virtue and Freedom of political Regulations might secure whole Nations and Generations from Misery, Want and Contempt."[109]

Equality of Religion. Liberty of conscience, free exercise of religion, and confessional pluralism depended for their efficacy on a guarantee of equality of all peaceable religions before the law. For the state to single out one pious person or one form of faith for either preferential benefits or discriminatory burdens would skew the choice of conscience, encumber the exercise of religion, and upset the natural plurality of faiths. Many of the framers therefore inveighed against the state's unequal treatment of religion. Madison captured the prevailing sentiment: "A just Government . . . will be best supported by protecting every Citizen in the enjoyment of his Religion with the same equal hand which protects his person and property; by neither invading the equal rights of any Sect, nor suffering any Sect to invade those of another."[110]

This principle of equality found its way into a number of early state constitutions. The Constitution of New Jersey insisted that "there shall be no establishment of any one religious sect in . . . preference to another."[111] Delaware guaranteed Christians "equal rights and privileges."[112] Maryland insisted that Christians "are equally entitled to protection in their religious liberty."[113] Virginia guaranteed that "all men have an equal . . . right to the free exercise of religion."[114] New York guaranteed all persons "free exercise and enjoyment of religious profession and worship, without discrimination or preference."[115] Even Massachusetts, which main-

---

tians and Social Justice (Sioux Center, IA, 1988), 1; W. Cole Durham, Jr. and Alexander Dushku, "Traditionalism, Secularism, and the Transformative Dimensions of Religious Institutions," *Brigham Young University Law Review* (1993): 421

[109] Letter from John Adams to Abigail Adams (October 29, 1775), quoted in John R. Howe, *The Changing Political Thought of John Adams* (Princeton, 1966), 156-157.

[110] Madison, *Memorial and Remonstrance*, sec. 8; see also ibid., sec. 4 (arguing that the general assessment bill in Virginia "violates equality by subjecting some to peculiar burdens [and] by granting others peculiar exemptions"). See discussion in Paul J. Weber, "James Madison and Religious Equality," *Review of Politics* 44 (1982): 163. For comparable sentiments, see, e.g., *The Freeman's Remonstrance*, 5, 10-13 (arguing that "every society of Christians [should be] allowed full, equal, and impartial liberty," and that it "contrary to scripture, reason, and experience . . . that one society of Christians should be raised to domination over all the rest").

[111] Art. XIX.

[112] Declaration of Rights, Sect. 3.

[113] Declaration of Rights, Sec. XXXIII.

[114] Declaration of Rights, Art. 16.

[115] Constitution, Art. XXXVIII.

tained a "slender" establishment, nonetheless guaranteed that "all religious sects and denominations, demeaning themselves peaceably, and as good citizens of the commonwealth, shall be equally under the protection of the law; and no subordination of one sect or denomination to another shall ever be established by law."[116]

The principle of equality also found its place in early drafts of the First Amendment religion clauses, yielding such phrases as: "nor shall the full and equal rights of conscience be in any manner, nor on any pretext, infringed";[117] "Congress shall make no law establishing one religious sect or society in preference to others. . . .";[118] and "Congress shall make no law establishing any particular denomination of religion in preference to another. . . ."[119] These provisions were abandoned (again without explicit criticism in the extant records), for the more generic guarantees of disestablishment and free exercise, which presumably apply equally to all religions. Of course, these constitutional principles of equality were not fully realized in practice. Majoritarian Protestantism overshadowed Catholicism, Judaism, and indigenous faiths, and discrimination on grounds of gender, race, culture, nationality, and economics persisted, despite the guarantees of equality.[120]

Separationism. The principle of separationism was designed to protect religious bodies and religious believers. On the one hand, separationism guaranteed the independence and integrity of the internal processes of religious bodies. Elisha Williams spoke for many churchmen when he wrote: "[E]very church has [the] right to judge in what manner God is to be worshipped by them, and what form of discipline ought to be observed by them, and the right also of electing their own officers."[121] In the mind of most framers, the principle of separation of church and state mandated neither the separation of religion and politics nor the secularization of civil society. None of the framers—save the most radical enlightenment and evangelical separationists[122]—intended to preclude

---

[116] Constitution or Form of Government for the Commonwealth of Massachusetts (1780), Part I, Art. 3, as amended by Art. 12. Originally, Art. 3 applied this guarantee only to "every denomination of Christians."

[117] James Madison's First Proposal, introduced in the House on June 7, 1789. Gales, *Annals*, 1:434..

[118] Version first rejected by the Senate, then reconsidered and passed by the Senate, on September 3, 1789. *Journal of the First Session of the Senate* (Washington, 1802), 1:70.

[119] Version rejected by the Senate on September 3, 1789. Ibid.

[120] See generally Morton Borden, *Jews, Turks, and Infidels* (Chapel Hill, 1984); Timothy Hall, "Religion, Equality, and Difference," *Temple Law Review* 65 (1992): 1.

[121] Williams, *Essential Rights and Liberties*, 99, 101.

[122] See, e.g., Madison, *Detached Memoranda* (urging the separation of religion and government, and urging the abolition of religious corporations, tax protections, appointments of chaplains, and other governmental support for religion).

religion altogether from the public square or the political process. The principle of separationism was directed to the institutions of church and state, not religion and culture.

The principle of separationism was also designed to protect the liberty of conscience of the individual. President Thomas Jefferson, for example, in his famous 1802 Letter to the Danbury Baptist Association, tied the principle of separationism directly to the principle of liberty of conscience:

> Believing with you that *religion is a matter which lies solely between a man and his God,* that he owes account to none other for his faith or his worship, that the legislative powers of government reach actions only, and not opinions, I contemplate with sovereign reverence that the act of the whole American people which declared that their legislature should "make no law respecting an establishment of religion, or prohibiting the free exercise thereof," *thus building a wall of separation between church and State.* Adhering to this expression of the supreme will of the nation *in behalf of the rights of conscience,* I shall see with sincere satisfaction the progress of those sentiments which tend *to restore to man all his natural rights,* convinced he has no natural right in opposition to his social duties.[123]

Separatism thus assured individuals of their natural, inalienable right of conscience, which could be exercised freely and fully to the point of breaching the peace or shirking social duties. Jefferson is not talking here of separating politics and religion. Indeed, in the very next paragraph of his letter, President Jefferson performed an avowedly religious act of offering prayers on behalf of his Baptist correspondents: "I reciprocate your kind prayers for the protection and blessing of the common Father and Creator of man. . . ."[124]

The principles of pluralism, equality, and separationism —separately and together—served to protect religious bodies, both from each other and from the state. It was an open question, however, whether such principles precluded state support of religion altogether. Evangelical and enlightenment writers sometimes viewed such principles as an absolute bar on state support of religious beliefs, believers, and bodies.[125] James Madison, for example, wrote late in his life: "Every new & successful ex-

---

[123] *The Writings of Thomas Jefferson*, H. Washington, ed. (Washington, 1853-1854), 8:113-114 (emphasis added).

[124] Ibid., 114.

[125] See, e.g., Laycock, "Non-Preferential Aid"; Leo Pfeffer, *Church, State and Freedom*, rev. ed. (Boston, 1967).

ample . . . of a perfect separation between ecclesiastical and civil matters, is of importance. And I have no doubt that every new example, will succeed, as every past one has done, in shewing that religion & Govt. will both exist in greater purity, the less they are mixed together."[126] Similar sentiments can be found in contemporaneous Baptist tracts,[127] particularly those of Isaac Backus and John Leland.

Puritan and republican writers often viewed such principles only as a prohibition against *preferential* state support of religion; general support for religion was licit, and indeed necessary for good governance.[128] As Joseph McKeen put it in 1793:

> Though some modern politicians may think religion of no importance to the state, it is clear that the experience of all ages and nations is against them. . . . The more, therefore, that the principles of piety, benevolence, and virtue are diffused among a people, the milder may their government and laws be, and the more liberty are they capable of enjoying because they govern themselves. But if there be little or no regard to religion or virtue among a people, they will not govern themselves, nor willingly submit to any laws, which lay restraint upon their passions; and consequently they must be wretched or be governed by force: they cannot bear freedom, they must be slaves."[129]

There are ample eighteenth century voices on hand to support either a "non-preferentialist" and a "strict separationist" account of religion and government in America. The persistent practice of every state, and of Congress, however, fell short of the absolutist claims of either party. In the early republic, state and federal officials both furnished at least minimal material and moral support for religion.

Disestablishment of Religion. For some eighteenth century writers, particularly the New England Puritans who defended their "slender establishments," the roll of "essential rights and liberties" ended here. For other writers, however, the best protection of all these principles was through the explicit disestablishment of religion. The term

---

126 James Madison, Letter to Edward Livingston (1822), quoted by Kurland and Lerner, *The Founders' Constitution*, 5:105-106.

127 See, e.g., *The Freeman's Remonstrance*, 5-11; Isaac Backus, *The Infinite Importance of the Obedience of Faith, and of a Separation from the World, Opened and Demonstrated* (Boston, 1791), 15-31; id., *Policy as well as Honesty Forbids the Use of Secular Force in Religious Affairs* (Boston, 1779).

128 See Antieau, et al., *Freedom From Federal Establishment*; Robert L. Cord, *Separation of Church & State: Historic Fact and Current Fiction*, rev. ed. (Grand Rapids, 1988).

129 Joseph McKeen, *Sermon Preached on the Public Fast in the Commonwealth of Massachusetts* (Salem, 1793). See also Adams, *Religious Liberty an Invaluable Blessing*, 52.

"establishment of religion" was a decidedly ambiguous phrase—in the eighteenth century, as much as today. The phrase was variously used to describe compromises of the principles of separationism, pluralism, equality, free exercise, and/or liberty of conscience. The guarantee of "disestablishment of religion" could signify protection against any such compromise.

According to some eighteenth century writers, disestablishment of religion meant foreclosing government from compromising the principles of separationism. In Jefferson's words, it prohibited government "from intermeddling in religious doctrine, with religious institutions, their doctrines, discipline, or exercises. . . and from the power of effecting any uniformity of time or matter among them. Fasting & prayer are religious exercises. The enjoining of them is an act of discipline. Every religious society has a right to determine for itself the times for these exercises, & the objects proper for them, according to their own peculiar tenets. . . ."[130] This view of disestablishment of religion was posed in the penultimate draft of the establishment clause: "Congress shall make no law establishing articles of faith or a mode of worship. . . ."[131] It was ultimately supplanted with vaguer language prohibiting Congress from making law "respecting an establishment of religion."

For other eighteenth century writers, disestablishment of religion meant foreclosing government from singling out certain religious bodies for preferential treatment in defiance of the principles both of equality and pluralism. This concept of disestablishment came through repeatedly in both federal and state constitutional debates. Three drafts of the religion clauses repeated this formulation: "Congress shall make no law establishing one religious sect or society in preference to others";[132] "Congress shall not make any law . . . establishing any religious sect or society";[133] "Congress shall make no law establishing any particular denomination of religion in preference to another."[134] A similar provision appears in the New Jersey Constitution: "[T]here shall be no establishment of any one religious sect . . . in preference to another."[135] This view of disestablishment confirmed the principles of pluralism and equality of religions before the law.[136]

---

130 Thomas Jefferson, Letter to Rev. Samuel Miller (1808), in Jefferson, *Works*, 11:7-9.

131 Version sent from Senate to House on September 9, 1789. *Journal*, 1:77.

132 Version first rejected by the Senate, then reconsidered and passed by the Senate, on September 3, 1789. Ibid., 1:70.

133 Version defeated by the Senate on September 3, 1789. Ibid.

134 Version rejected by the Senate on September 3, 1789. Ibid.

135 Art. XIX.

136 For other examples, see Antieau, et al., *Freedom From Federal Establishment*, 111-142.

For still others, disestablishment of religion meant foreclosing government from prescribing mandatory forms of religious belief, doctrine, and practice. Such coercion of religion inflates the competence of government. As Madison wrote, it "implies either that the Civil Magistrate is a competent Judge of Religious Truth; or that he may employ Religion as an Engine of Civil policy. The first is an arrogant pretension falsified by the contradictory opinions of rulers in all ages, and throughout the world: the second an unhallowed perversion of the means of salvation."[137] Such coercion of religion also compromises the pacific ideals of most religions. Thomas Paine, who is usually branded as a religious skeptic, put this well:

> All religions are in their nature mild and benign, and united with principles of morality. They could not have made proselytes at first, by professing anything that was vicious, cruel, persecuting, or immoral. . . . Persecution is not an original feature in *any* religion; but it is always the strongly marked feature of all law-religions, or religions established by law. Take away the law-establishment, and every religion reassumes its original benignity.[138]

Such coercion of religion also compromises the individual's liberty of conscience. As the Pennsylvania Constitution put it: "[N]o authority can or ought to be vested in, or assumed by any power whatever, that shall in any case interfere with, or in any manner controul [sic], the right of conscience in the free exercise of religious worship."[139]

Interdependence of Principles. For all the diversity of opinion one finds in the constitutional convention debates, pamphlets, sermons, editorials, and broadsides of the eighteenth century, most writers embraced this roll of "essential rights and liberties of religion"—liberty of conscience, free exercise of religion, pluralism, equality, separationism, and disestablishment of religion. To be sure, many of these terms carried multiple meanings by the later eighteenth century. And to be sure, numerous other principles of religious rights and liberties were under discussion in the early republic. But in the range of official and unofficial sources at our disposal, these principles were the most commonly discussed and embraced.

On the one hand, eighteenth century writers designed these principles to provide an interwoven shield against repressive religious estab-

---

[137] Madison, *Memorial and Remonstrance*, sec. 5.

[138] Thomas Paine, *Rights of Man* (1791), pt. 1, quoted in Kurland and Lerner, *The Founders' Constitution*, 5:95-96.

[139] Declaration of Rights, II.

lishments. Liberty of conscience protected the individual from coercion and discriminatory treatment by church or state officials and guaranteed unencumbered, voluntary choices of faith. Free exercise of religion protected the individual's ability to discharge the duties of conscience through religious worship, speech, publication, assembly, and other actions, without necessary reference to a prescribed creed, cult, or code of conduct. Pluralism protected multiple forms and forums of religious belief and action, in place of a uniform mandated religious doctrine, liturgy, and polity. Equality protected religious individuals and bodies from special benefits and from special burdens administered by the state, or by other religious bodies. Separationism protected individual believers, as well as religious and political officials, from undue interference or intrusion on each other's processes and practices. Disestablishment precluded governmental prescriptions of the doctrine, liturgy, or morality of one faith, or compromises of the principles of liberty of conscience, free exercise, equality, pluralism, or separationism.

On the other hand, the framers designed these principles to be mutually supportive and mutually subservient to the highest goal of guaranteeing "the essential rights and liberties of religion." No single principle could by itself guarantee such religious liberty. Simple protection of liberty of conscience provided no protection of religious actions or organizations. Pure pluralism could decay into religious relativism and render the government blind to the special place of religion in the community and in the Constitution. Simple guarantees of the equality of religion could render the state indifferent to the widely divergent needs of different forms of religion. Pure separationism could deprive the church of all meaningful forms and functions, and deprive the state of an essential ally in government and social service. Pure non-establishment could readily rob society of all common values and beliefs and the state of any effective religious role. Eighteenth century writers, therefore, arranged these multiple principles into an interlocking and interdependent shield of religious liberties and rights for all. Religion was simply too vital and too valuable a source of individual flourishing and social cohesion to be left unguarded on any side.

It is in the context of this plurality of opinions and panoply of principles that the First Amendment religion clauses must be understood. The religion clauses were a vital, but only a small, part of this panoply of defense of essential rights and liberties of religion. They bound only the national government, and set only the outer boundaries to its conduct vis-à-vis religion—forbidding either prescriptions or proscriptions of religion. The religion clauses, together, were designed to legitimate, and to live off, the state constitutional guarantees of religious rights and liberties, and the principles which imbued them. The guarantees of disestablishment and free exercise depended for their efficacy, both on each other and on other "essential rights and liberties of religion." Such guarantees standing alone—as they came to be after the special incorporation doctrine of the 1940s—could legitimately be read to have multiple principles incorporated within them.

The Exodus of the American Constitutional Experiment

From Multiplicity to Uniformity. These cardinal principles of religious human rights came to ready application in the unfolding of the American experiment in the nineteenth and early twentieth centuries. Consistent with the federalist doctrine that informed the Constitution in general and the First Amendment religion clauses in particular, primary political responsibility for religion and the church was left to the states. By 1833, the constitution of every state guaranteed liberty of conscience and free exercise of religion for all, and many included further guarantees of pluralism, equality, separationism, and disestablishment. The most intrusive and overt forms of religious establishment and state control of religion fell away. A plurality of religious sects came to flourish in the states, many supporting their own religious schools, charities, clubs, and other voluntary associations.

To be sure, glaring vestiges of religious establishment and inequality of religion remained, despite these gilded constitutional guarantees. Virginia, for example, revoked the corporate charters of the Episcopal churches in the 1790s and 1800s and thereafter sought to confiscate or taxed large portions of their properties not devoted to religious uses.[140] Massachusetts and New Hampshire dealt similarly with the properties of Quakers, Baptists, and Episcopalians.[141] Massachusetts, New York and New Jersey dealt churlishly with Unitarians and Catholics throughout the nineteenth century. Both federal and state legislatures and courts showed little respect for the religious rights of Jews and Mormons, let alone those of native American Indians and African-American slaves.[142]

---

140 See Eckenrode, *Separation of Church and State in Virginia*, 116-155; Kauper and Ellis, "Religion Corporations and the Law," 1529-1533. In *Terrett v. Taylor*, 9 U.S. (Cranch) 249 (1815), the United States Supreme Court declared invalid the confiscation of property in Alexandria authorized by Virginia statutes of 1798 and 1801.

141 See, e.g., James Ellis, *A Narrative of the Rise, Progress, and Issue of the Late Law-Suits Relative to Property Held and Devoted to Pious Uses* (Warren, RI, 1795); [John Cosens Ogden], *A Short History of Ecclesiastical Oppressions in New-England and Vermont* (Richmond, 1799).

142 See generally Borden, *Jews, Turks, and Infidels*; Lawrence M. Fuchs, *The American Kaleidoscope: Race, Ethnicity, and the Civic Culture* (Middletown, CT, 1990); John Higham, *Strangers in the Land: Patterns of American Nativism, 1860-1925* (New Brunswick, NJ, 1988).

Such abridgements of religious rights and liberties are an ineradicable part of the American constitutional tradition.

The general guarantees of disestablishment and free exercise of religion in the federal and state constitutions did not foreclose officials from supporting religious believers and religious bodies, particularly those that were Christian. "A mass of organic utterances,"[143] as the Supreme Court later put it, testify to the presence of a vibrant civil religion, a *de facto* Christian establishment, in the America of the nineteenth and early twentieth centuries—a civil religion, rooted principally in Puritan and civic republican rationales.

Government officials, for example, regularly acknowledged and endorsed religious beliefs and practices. "In God We Trust" and similar confessions appeared on currency and stamps. Various homages to God and religion appeared on state seals and state documents. The Ten Commandments and favorite biblical verses were inscribed on the walls of court houses, schools, and other public buildings. Crucifixes and other Christian symbols were erected in state parks and on state house grounds. Flags flew at half mast on Good Friday and other high holy days. Christmas, Easter, and other holy days were official holidays. Sundays remained official days of rest. Government-sponsored chaplains were appointed to Congress, the military, and various governmental asylums, prisons, and hospitals. Prayers were offered at the commencement of each session of Congress and of many state legislatures. Thanksgiving Day prayers were offered by presidents, governors, and other state officials. These and numerous other instances of official endorsement of a civil religion were commonplace in the early unfolding of the American experiment.[144]

Government officials afforded various forms of aid to religious groups. Congress commissioned and subsidized the preparation of an official American edition of the Bible. States underwrote the costs of Bibles and liturgical books for rural churches and occasionally donated land and services to them. Federal and state subsidies were given to Christian missionaries who proselytized among the native American Indians. Property grants and tax subsidies were furnished to Christian schools and charities. Special criminal laws protected the property and clergy of the churches. Tax exemptions were accorded to the real and personal

---

143 *Church of the Holy Trinity v. United States*, 143 U.S. 457, 473 (1892).

144 See discussion and sources in Harold J. Berman, "Religion and Law: The First Amendment in Historical Perspective," *Emory Law Journal* 35 (1986): 778-93 ; Antieau, et al., *Religion Under the State Constitutions*; Cornelison, *Relation of Religion to Civil Government in America*; Philip Schaff, *Church and State in the United States, or the American Idea of Religious Liberty and Its Practical Effects* (New York, 1888); Stokes and Pfeffer, *Church and State*; Carl Zollmann, *American Civil Church Law* (New York, 1914).

properties of many churches, clerics, and charities. Numerous other forms of direct and indirect aid to religion and the church were countenanced.

Government officials predicated some of their laws and policies directly on the moral and religious teachings of the Bible and the church. The first public schools and state universities had mandatory courses in religion and theology and compulsory attendance in daily chapel and Sunday worship services. Employees in state prisons, reformatories, orphanages, and asylums were required to know and to teach basic Christian beliefs and values. Polygamy, prostitution, pornography, and other sexual offenses against Christian morals and mores were prohibited. Blasphemy, sacrilege, and false swearing were still prosecuted. Gambling houses, lotteries, fortune-telling, and other activities that depended on fate or magic were forbidden. In many jurisdictions, these and other laws and policies were predicated on explicitly religious, and usually Christian, grounds. It was a commonplace of nineteenth century thought that "Christianity is a part of the common law."[145]

The promulgation of these laws and policies gave rise to some great debates in legislatures across the country. The enforcement of these laws in the courts occasioned some vitriolic dissenting opinions. The arguments for these laws and policies often sounded in classic terms of Puritanism and republicanism; those against sounded in classic terms of evangelical theology and enlightenment politics. Those inclined to Puritan and republican perspectives saw these laws and policies as appropriate forms of non-preferential state aid and accommodation to the civic and sectarian religions of the nation. Those inclined to enlightenment and evangelical perspectives saw these laws and policies as vestiges of religious establishment and compromises of the ideals of separationism and voluntarism.

For much of the nineteenth and early twentieth centuries, the United States Supreme Court had little occasion to interpret and apply the First Amendment religion clauses. It was widely understood that state constitutions, not the federal constitution, governed most religious and ecclesiastical affairs.[146] The few attempts to develop a general church-state law applicable to the states and enforceable in the federal courts, most

---

[145] See Wilson, *Works*, 2:671, citing William Blackstone, *Commentaries on the Laws of England* (London, 1765), bk. 4, 59 (where Blackstone writes "Christianity is part of the laws of England"). For examples of these nineteenth century sentiments in America, see Harold J. Berman, *Faith and Order: The Reconciliation of Law and Religion* (Atlanta, 1993), 209-219.

[146] See, e.g., Joseph Story, *Commentaries on the Constitution*, 2d ed. (Boston, 1851), 2:597.

notably the Blaine Amendment of 1875-1876, were defeated.[147] Few cases involving religious questions, therefore, came to the United States Supreme Court—only 23 between 1789 and 1940.

These early Supreme Court cases did little to advance the American experiment in religious rights and liberties. The Court offered only rudimentary analysis of the subject in a handful of cases concerning the maintenance and division of church properties.[148] It offered an extremely narrow reading of the free exercise clause to uphold various Congressional restrictions on Mormon polygamous teachings and practice, arguing simplistically that the free exercise clause protects beliefs of conscience respecting polygamy, not the practice and preaching of the same.[149]

In a few of these early cases, the Court was more forthcoming. Consistent with traditional principles of equality of treatment and general governmental support for a plurality of religions, the Court upheld the allocation of federal funds to help build a Catholic hospital[150] and to help operate a Catholic mission school among the native American Indians.[151] Consistent with the principles of separationism and structural pluralism, the Court insisted that religious bodies may resolve their property disputes among themselves without state interference,[152] may hold monastic properties in community despite countervailing private property rules,[153] may appoint their clergy from abroad without Congressional interference,[154] and may teach their children without undue state intrusion or deprivation.[155] In *Watson v. Jones* (1872), a church property dispute case, Justice Miller offered a crisp rendition of the basics of individual and corporate religious rights and liberties that generally supported these holdings:

---

[147] See Alfred W. Meyer, "The Blaine Amendment and the Bill of Rights," *Harvard Law Review* 64 (1951): 939; F. William O'Brien, "The Blaine Amendment, 1875-1876," *University of Detroit Law Journal* 41 (1963): 137.

[148] *Speidel v. Henrici*, 120 U.S. 377 (1887); *Smith v. Swormstedt*, 57 U.S. (16 How.) 288 (1853); *Permoli v. Municipality No. 1 of New Orleans*, 44 U.S. (3 How.) 589 (1845); *Vidal v. Mayor of Philadelphia*, 43 U.S. (2 How.) 127 (1844); *Terrett v. Taylor*, 13 U.S. (9 Cranch) 43 (1815).

[149] *Reynolds v. United States*, 98 U.S. 145 (1879); *Davis v. Beason*, 133 U.S. 333 (1890); *Church of Jesus Christ of Latter Day Saints v. United States*, 136 U.S. 1 (1890). See similar result in *Cleveland v. United States*, 329 U.S. 14 (1946).

[150] *Bradfield v. Roberts*, 175 U.S. 291 (1899).

[151] *Quick Bear v. Leupp*, 210 U.S. 50 (1908).

[152] *Watson v. Jones*, 80 U.S. (13 Wall.) 679 (1872); *Bouldin v. Alexander*, 82 U.S. (15 Wall.) 131 (1872); *Gonzalez v. Roman Catholic Archbishop*, 280 U.S. 1 (1929).

[153] *Order of St. Benedict v. Steinhauser*, 234 U.S. 640 (1914).

[154] *Rector of Holy Trinity Church v. United States*, 143 U.S. 457 (1892).

[155] *Meyer v. Nebraska*, 262 U.S. 390 (1923); *Pierce v. Society of Sisters*, 268 U.S. 510 (1925); *Farrington v. Tokushige*, 273 U.S. 284 (1927); *Cochran v. Louisiana*, 281 U.S. 370 (1930).

> In this country the full and free right to entertain any religious belief, to practice any religious principle, and teach any religious doctrine which does not violate the laws of morality and property, and which does not infringe personal rights, is conceded to all. The law knows no heresy, and is committed to the support of no dogma, the establishment of no sect. The right to organize voluntary religious associations to assist in the expression and dissemination of any religious doctrine, and to create tribunals for the decision of controverted questions of faith within the association . . . is unquestioned.[156]

Justice Strong amplified the principles of liberty of conscience and separation of church and state in *Bouldin v. Alexander* the same term, stating for the Court: "[W]e have no power to revise or question ordinary acts of church discipline, or of excision of church membership. . . . [W]e cannot decide who ought to be members of the church, nor whether the excommunicated have been regularly or irregularly cut off."[157] These cases, though important ingredients for later judicial solutions of religious rights disputes, were largely incidental to the early experiment.

This pattern changed abruptly and dramatically in the 1940s. Under growing pressure to remove the disparities in treatment of religion among the states and to protect religious minorities like Jews and Jehovah's Witnesses, the Supreme Court breathed new life into the religion clauses. In the landmark cases of *Cantwell v. Connecticut* (1940)[158] and *Everson v. Board of Education* (1947),[159] the Court incorporated the free exercise and establishment clauses of the First Amendment into the due process clause of the fourteenth amendment. With matter-of-fact simplicity, Justice Roberts declared for the Court in *Cantwell*: "The fundamental concept of liberty embodied in that [Fourteenth] Amendment embraces the liberties guaranteed by the First Amendment."[160] This so-called "selective incorporation doctrine"[161]—which was applied to several other provisions of the 1791 Bill of Rights as well—made the religion clauses binding on both the federal and state governments. The doctrine allowed the Court for the first time to review state and local policies on religion and the church. Ignoring the federalist premises that supported

---

156 *Watson*, 80 U.S. at 728-729.

157 *Bouldin*, 82 U.S. at 139-140. Justice Strong elaborates these sentiments in his *Two Lectures Upon the Relations of Civil Law to Church Polity, Discipline, and Property* (New York, 1875).

158 310 U.S. 296 (1940).

159 330 U.S. 1 (1947).

160 *Cantwell*, 310 U.S. at 303.

161 See generally sources and discussion in Poppel, "Federalism, Fundamental Fairness, and the Religion Clauses."

and initially governed application of the religion clauses, the Supreme Court set out to create a uniform constitutional law of religious rights and liberties that would be enforceable throughout the nation. In more than 100 cases decided after 1940, the Supreme Court took firm control of the American experiment in religious rights and liberties. For the next several decades, the Court's directives in these cases bound not only the lower federal courts, but also many of the state courts.

Modern Free Exercise Law. In *Cantwell*, the Court incorporated the free exercise clause into the Fourteenth Amendment due process clause. Thereafter, the Court proceeded to incorporate into the free exercise clause (and sometimes also the free speech clause) a number of the "essential rights and liberties of religion" forged in the early republic. In *Cantwell* itself, the Court read the free exercise clause in capacious terms—as a protection for the beliefs of conscience and religious actions of all religious faiths, up to the familiar limits of public peace and order, and countervailing constitutional rights. As Justice Roberts put it in his majority opinion:

> The constitutional inhibition of legislation on the subject of religion has a double aspect. On the one hand, it forestalls compulsion by law of the acceptance of any creed or the practice of any form of worship. Freedom of conscience and freedom to adhere to such religious organization or form of worship as the individual may choose cannot be restricted by law. On the other hand, it safeguards the free exercise of the chosen form of religion. Thus the Amendment embraces two concepts—freedom to believe and freedom to act. The first is absolute, but, in the nature of things, the second cannot be. . . . [A] state may by general and nondiscriminatory legislation regulate the time, the places, and the manner of [religious exercise] . . . and may in other respects safeguard the peace, good order, and comfort of the community.[162]

"The essential characteristic of these liberties," Justice Roberts added, with a nod to the principle of confessional pluralism, "is, that under their shield many types of life, character, opinion and belief can develop unmolested and unobstructed. Nowhere is this shield more necessary than in our own country for a people composed of many races and many creeds."[163]

In more than a dozen subsequent cases over the next two decades, the Court expanded this multi-principled reading of the free exercise clause. "[N]o single principle can answer all of life's complexities," espe-

---

162 *Cantwell*, 310 U.S. at 303-304.

163 Ibid. at 310.

cially those surrounding the "right to freedom of religious belief," Justice Frankfurter wrote wisely (in an otherwise unwise opinion in 1940).[164] The Court took his maxim to heart. Consistent with the principle of liberty of conscience, the Court held that a public school could not require a student, who was conscientiously opposed, to salute the flag and recite the pledge,[165] but that a public school could allow religious children to be released from schools to attend religious services off school grounds.[166] It likewise held that a governmental official could not require a party, who was conscientiously opposed, to swear an oath before receiving citizenship status,[167] a property tax exemption,[168] or a state bureaucratic position.[169] "The struggle for religious liberty has through the centuries been an effort to accommodate the demands of the State to the conscience of the individual," Justice Douglas wrote for the Court in *Girouard v. United States* (1946). Accommodation of liberty of conscience sometimes requires exemption from generally applicable government prescriptions.

Consistent with the principle of equality of all peaceable religions before the law, the Court struck down several permit, licensing, and taxing ordinances that targeted, and burdened, the core proselytizing activities of Jehovah's Witnesses, who had emerged prominently in urban America in the early twentieth century.[170] The Court also struck down an ordinance that permitted church services, but prohibited other forms of religious speech in a public park.[171] Only indiscriminately applied permit requirements[172] or generally applicable criminal laws could be upheld

---

164 *Minersville School District v. Gobitis*, 310 U.S. 586, 594 (1940), rev'd by *West Virginia State Board v. Barnette*, 319 U.S. 624 (1943).

165 *West Virginia State Board v. Barnette*, 319 U.S. 624 (1943).

166 *Zorach v. Clauson*, 343 U.S. 306 (1952). Though this case is generally read as an establishment clause case, Justice Douglas viewed the practice under both religion clauses, finding no violation. With respect to the free exercise clause, he wrote: "It takes obtuse reasoning to inject any issue of the 'free exercise' of religion into the present case. No one is forced to go to the religious classroom and no religious exercise or instruction is brought to the classrooms of the public schools. He is left to his own desires as to the manner or time of his religious devotions if any." Ibid., 311.

167 *Girouard v. United States*, 328 U.S. 61 (1946). This case also turned on the test oath clause of Article VI.

168 *First Unitarian Church v. County of Los Angeles*, 357 U.S. 545 (1957).

169 *Torcaso v. Watkins*, 367 U.S. 488 (1961). But cf. *In re Summers*, 325 U.S. 561 (1945) (religiously scrupulous applicant received no free exercise right to exemption from a oath required to stand for the bar).

170 *Jamison v. Texas*, 318 U.S. 413 (1943); *Largent v. Texas*, 318 U.S. 418 (1943); *Jones v. Opelika (II)*, 319 U.S. 103 (1943); *Murdock v. Pennsylvania*, 319 U.S. 104 (1943); *Martin v. Struthers*, 319 U.S. 141 (1943); *Follett v. McCormick*, 321 U.S. 573 (1944); *Tucker v. Texas*, 326 U.S. 517 (1946).

171 *Fowler v. Rhode Island*, 345 U.S. 67 (1953).

172 *Cox v. New Hampshire*, 312 U.S. 569 (1941) (upholding general parade permit, offered on a sliding fee scale, for all processions).

against free exercise or (religious) free speech challenges.[173] Several times in its early opinions, the Court stressed the principle of equality and nondiscrimination towards religions. Even Justice Frankfurter and Justice Black, whose interpretations of the religion clauses were often criticized, defended this principle earnestly. "Propagation of belief—or even disbelief in the supernatural—is protected, whether in church or chapel, mosque or synagogue, tabernacle or meetinghouse," wrote Justice Frankfurter in the infamous *Gobitis* case. "Likewise the Constitution assures generous immunity to the individual from imposition of penalties for offending, in the course of his own religious activities, the religious views of others, be they a minority or those dominant in government."[174] The free exercise clause, Justice Black echoed in the controversial *Everson* case, mandates that government "cannot exclude individual Catholics, Lutherans, Mohammedans, Baptists, Jews, Methodists, Nonbelievers, Presbyterians, or the members of any faith, *because of their faith, or lack of it*, from receiving the benefits of public welfare legislation."[175]

Consistent with the principles of pluralism and separationism, the Court in the 1952 case of *Kedroff v. Saint Nicholas Cathedral* held that a religious organization has the free exercise right to resolve their own disputes over doctrine and liturgy, polity and property without interference by the state.[176] In striking down a New York religious corporation law, passed in the Cold War era, that rejected the authority of the Moscow Patriarch over the local Russian Orthodox Church, the Court declared: "Here there is a transfer by statute of control over churches. This violates our rule of separation of church and state."[177] It also violates "the spirit of freedom for religious organizations, an independence from secular control and manipulation, in short, power to decide for themselves, free from state interference, matters of church government as well as those of faith and doctrine. Freedom to select the clergy, where no improper methods of choice are proven, we think, must now be said have federal constitutional protection as a part of the free exercise of religion against state interference."[178]

In the landmark case of *Sherbert v. Verner* (1963), the Court cast these early multi-principled readings of the free exercise clause (and free

---

[173] See *Chaplinsky v. New Hampshire*, 315 U.S. 568 (1942) (breach of peace conviction for Jehovah's Witness using "fighting words" upheld against free speech and free exercise challenge); *Prince v. Massachusetts*, 321 U.S. 158 (1944) (child labor statute upheld against free exercise claims of both parent and minor arrested for religious soliciting).

[174] *Gobitis*, 310 U.S. at 593.

[175] *Everson*, 330 U.S. at 16 (emphasis in original).

[176] *Kedroff v. St. Nicholas Cathedral*, 344 U.S. 94 (1952).

[177] Ibid., 114.

[178] Ibid., 116.

speech clause) into a constitutional test.[179] The case raised a precise free exercise claim to receive a specific state benefit. A Seventh Day Adventist was discharged for employment, and foreclosed from reemployment, because of her conscientious refusal to work on Saturday, her Sabbath Day. She was denied unemployment compensation from the state, for she had been, according to the applicable statute, discharged "for cause" and was thus disqualified from the benefit. She appealed, arguing that the disqualifying provisions of the statute "abridged her right to the free exercise of her religion," and that the same statute, which explicitly exempted Sunday Sabbatarians from the same disqualification, was religiously discriminatory. The Supreme Court agreed, with Justice Brennan's majority opinion stating its principal rationale in terms of liberty of conscience: "To condition the availability of [state] benefits upon this appellant's willingness to violate a cardinal principle of her religious faith, effectively penalizes the free exercise of her constitutional liberties."[180] Moreover, to disqualify a Saturday Sabbatarian from such benefits but to grant them to Sunday Sabbatarians "compounds" the constitutional violation with "religious discrimination."[181]

The Court took this case as an occasion to craft a more nuanced free exercise test in lieu of the simple balancing tests that had prevailed in earlier cases. Henceforth, any governmental policy or law that was challenged under the free exercise clause had to meet four criteria to pass constitutional muster. The policy or law must: (1) serve a compelling state interest; (2) be narrowly tailored to achieve that interest with the least possible intrusion on free exercise rights; (3) be non-discriminatory against religion on its face; and (4) be non-discriminatory against religion in application. Governmental policies that met all four criteria could be enforced, even though they had an adverse impact on religion. Policies that did not meet such criteria were either to be struck down, or applied in a manner that minimized, or eliminated, their affront to religion.

This "compelling state interest test," as it was later called, served to draw together the classic principles of liberty of conscience, free exercise, equality, pluralism, and separationism, and to accord free exercise protection to both religious individuals and religious groups. It also served to mould the free exercise clause into a more delicate and flexible instrument that could counter both overt and covert forms of religious discrimination, and could accommodate both traditional and novel needs of the growing plurality of religious groups seeking First Amendment protection. Justice Douglas stated this purpose well in his concurring opin-

---

179 *Sherbert v. Verner*, 374 U.S. 398 (1963).

180 Ibid., 406.

181 Ibid.

ion in *Sherbert*: "Religious scruples of Moslems require them to attend a mosque on Friday and to pray five times daily. Religious scruples of a Sikh require him to carry a regular or a symbolic sword. Religious scruples of a Jehovah's Witness teach him to be a colporteur, going from door to door, from town to town, distributing his religious pamphlets. Religious scruples of a Quaker compel him to refrain from swearing [an oath] and to affirm instead. Religious scruples of a Buddhist may require him to refrain from partaking of any flesh. The examples could be multiplied . . . to show that many people hold beliefs alien to the majority of our society—beliefs that are protected by the First Amendment but which could easily be trod upon under the guise of 'police' or 'health' regulations reflecting the majority's views."[182] The American experiment in religious rights was being adjusted to accommodate the expanding religious scene.

As Justice Douglas predicted, the *Sherbert* compelling state interest test rendered the free exercise clause a formidable obstacle to both subtle and overt forms of religious prejudice and insensitivity against religious individuals. Consistent with the principle of liberty of conscience, the Court extended the technical *Sherbert* holding to instances where applicants who sought unemployment compensation had individual scruples, not shared by their co-religionists, against indirect production of military hardware,[183] were newly converted to their Sabbatarian beliefs,[184] or held highly individualized views of the Sabbath.[185] Neither the novelty nor the idiosyncrasy of a religious belief should deprive its adherent from free exercise protection and from receipt of unemployment compensation. In Chief Justice Burger's words: "Where the state conditions receipt of an important benefit upon conduct proscribed by a religious faith, or where it denies such a benefit because of conduct mandated by religious belief, thereby putting substantial pressure on an adherent to modify his behavior and to violate his beliefs, a burden upon religion exists" that violates the free exercise clause.[186] Similarly, the Court struck down state

---

[182] Ibid., 411 (Douglas, J. concurring).

[183] *Thomas v. Review Board of Indiana Employment Security Division*, 450 U.S. 707 (1981).

[184] *Hobbie v. Unemployment Appeals Commission of Florida*, 480 U.S. 136 (1987) (free exercise claimant who converted to Seventh Day Adventist Sabbatarian beliefs two years after employment).

[185] *Frazee v. Illinois Department of Employment Security*, 489 U.S. 829 (1989) (free exercise claimant who had a "personal professed religious belief" in Sabbath as a day of rest, though not a day of worship).

[186] *Thomas*, 450 U.S. at 717-718. This very same principle had, earlier, been denied to Jewish groups who sought free exercise exemptions from Sunday blue laws. Their argument was that state law prohibited Sunday work, religious law prohibited Saturday work. This put Jewish merchants and workers at a general commercial disadvantage, and required kosher establishments to be closed to Jewish communities for two days, instead of one. The Court

constitutional prohibitions against clerical participation in political office, arguing that: "The State is 'punishing a religious profession with the privation of a religious right'."[187]

Not only religious individuals, but also religious groups were able to claim the panoply of free exercise rights and liberties embraced in the "compelling state interest" test. In a series of cases over the past dozen years, the Court has held that voluntarily-organized groups of religious students must be given *equal access* to public university and high school facilities if such access is granted to non-religious student groups.[188] Voluntarily convened religious groups in the community must have equal access to public school facilities if they are made available to other non-religious groups.[189] Student-run religious publishing groups at a public university must have equal access to school subsidies made available to other religious and non-religious publishing groups.[190] In each of these cases, the principles of voluntarism, equality, non-discrimination, and religious pluralism, collectively, overrode the principle of separationism captured in the establishment clause.

The same free exercise principles have been extended to other religious groups. Thus religious schools are permitted to choose their teachers without general labor law controls,[191] and religious employers are permitted to engage in the religious discrimination that is mandated by their

---

was not convinced that such regulations burdened "Jewish religion" per se. See *Gallagher v. Crown Kosher Super Market of Massachusetts*, 355 U.S. 617 (1961); *McGowan v. Maryland*, 366 U.S. 420 (1961); *Braunfeld v. Brown*, 366 U.S. 599 (1961). See also *Two Guys from Harrison Allentown, Inc. v. McGinley*, 366 U.S. 582 (1961), holding that Sunday legislation did not violate the establishment clause. After these cases, most states revised their Sabbath day laws. See generally Barbara J. Redman, "Sabbatarian Accommodation in the Supreme Court," *Journal of Church and State* 33 (1991): 495; Jerome A. Barron, "Sunday in North America," *Harvard Law Review* 79 (1965): 42.

187 *McDaniel v. Paty*, 435 U.S. 618, 626 (1978).

188 *Widmar v. Vincent*, 454 U.S. 263 (1981). This "equal access" principle, which was based on both free exercise and free speech grounds, was later extended to public high schools. See Equal Access Act, 20 U.S.C. 4071-4071, which was upheld against establishment clause challenge in *Board of Education of the Westside Community Schools v. Mergens*, 496 U.S. 226 (1990).

189 *Lamb's Chapel v. Center Moriches Union Free School District*, 113 S. Ct. 2141 (1993). See also *Jews for Jesus v. Airport Commissioners of Los Angeles*, 482 U.S. 569 (1987) (holding that the free speech clause prohibits a ban on "First Amendment activities," including religious solicitation in an airport). But cf. *Lee v. ISKCON*, 112 S. Ct. 2701 (1992) (holding that regulations of religious solicitation in a limited forum like an airport need only satisfy "reasonableness" standards).

190 *Rosenberger v. Rector and Visitors of the University of Virginia*, 1995 WL 382046 (West Law). This case was decided on pure free speech grounds.

191 *National Labor Relations Board v. Catholic Bishop*, 440 U.S. 490 (1979). See also *St. Martin Lutheran Church v. South Dakota*, 451 U.S. 772 (1981) (applying the Federal Unemployment Tax Act to church schools).

faith—particularly in the employment of religious officials.[192] Similarly, religious organizations are permitted to resolve their own disputes over polity and property, without state intrusion.[193] In *Orthodox Diocese v. Milivojevich* (1976), which prohibited even "marginal review" by a civil court of an ecclesiastical decision, Justice Brennan speaking for the Court declared: "Indeed, it is the essence of religious faith that ecclesiastical decisions are reached and are to accepted as matters of faith whether or not rational or acceptable by objective criteria." The Constitution allows "religious organizations to establish their own rules and regulations for internal discipline and government, and to create tribunals for adjudicating disputes over these matters. When this choice is exercised and ecclesiastical tribunals are created to decide disputes . . . the Constitution requires that civil courts accept their decisions as binding."[194]

In its most far-reaching free exercise case, *Wisconsin v. Yoder* (1972), the Court required that Amish parents and communities be exempted from full compliance with compulsory school attendance laws for their children, in order to preserve their ascetic, agrarian communitarianism.[195] What seemed to impress the Court was that the Amish "lifestyle" was "not merely a matter of personal preference, but one of deep religious conviction, shared by an organized group, and intimately related to daily living," and that these "religious beliefs and attitudes towards life, family and home . . . have not altered in fundamentals for centuries." In the Court's view, compliance with the compulsory school attendance law "carries with it a very real threat of undermining the Amish community and religious practice as they exist today; they must either abandon belief and be assimilated into society at large, or be forced to migrate to some

---

[192] *Corporation of the Presiding Bishop v. Amos*, 483 U.S. 327 (1987) (upholding Civil Rights Act provision for religious discrimination by religious employers). The Civil Rights Act bans religious discrimination by private, non-religious employers, which the Court has held requires "reasonable accommodations" of employees' religious needs, at no more than "de minimis" cost. *Trans World Airlines, Inc. v. Hardison*, 432 U.S. 63 (1977); *Ansonio Board of Education v. Philbrook*, 479 U.S. 60 (1987). See David L. Gregory, "The Role of Religion in the Secular Workplace," *Notre Dame Journal of Law, Ethics Public Policy* 4 (1990): 749; Ira Lupu, "Free Exercise Exemption and Religious Institutions: The Case of Employment Discrimination," *Boston University Law Review* 67 (1987): 391.

[193] *Presbyterian Church v. Hull Memorial Presbyterian Church*, 393 U.S. 440 (1969); *Serbian East Orthodox Diocese v. Milivojevich*, 426 U.S. 696 (1976). But see *Maryland Churches of God v. Church of God as Sharpsburg, Inc.*, 396 U.S. 367 (1970) (allowing resolution of some property disputes not involving "doctrinal controversy"); *Jones v. Wolf*, 443 U.S. 595 (1979) (allowing secular disputes within the church to be resolved using "neutral principles of law").

[194] *Milivojevich*, 426 U.S. at 715, 724-725. See generally, Louis Sirico, "Church Property Disputes: Churches as Secular and Alien Institutions," *Fordham Law Review* 55 (1986): 335; Frederick M. Gedicks, "Toward A Constitutional Jurisprudence of Religious Group Rights," *Wisconsin Law Review* (1989): 99.

[195] *Wisconsin v. Yoder*, 406 U.S. 205 (1972).

other and more tolerant region."[196] Thus the free exercise clause compels an exemption from a law that clearly, and reasonably, fostered "a compelling state interest" to educate children.

The compelling state interest test—though it had been tailored, and sometimes stretched, in the foregoing cases—did not always yield judgments in favor of religious petitioners, even in what has been called the "golden age" of religious liberty from 1963 to 1986.[197] Where governmental policies met the criteria of the "compelling state interest" test, they were upheld despite their burden on free exercise interests. Thus a Jehovah's Witness child could receive a blood transfusion, despite the religious objection of conscientiously opposed parents.[198] Religious pacifists could not withhold their taxes just because a portion of them supported the military.[199] The Amish could not withhold social security taxes just because of their religious objections to social welfare.[200] Hare Krishnas and other proselytizers could not demand exemption from general restrictions on sale or distribution of religious goods or articles on state fair grounds.[201] An itinerant missionary could not claim free exercise exemptions from collecting state sale and use taxes on articles sold at crusades or through the mails.[202] A private religious university, which practiced racial discrimination on religious grounds, could not voice free exercise objections to the withdrawal of its federal tax exempt status as a penalty for violating national policy.[203] A religiously-affiliated charity could not claim free exercise exemptions from general labor standards.[204] A Scientologist could not take a tax deduction for "auditing or training" fees paid to the church,[205] nor could Mormon parents take a tax deduction for funds sent to support their sons' church-supervised mission work.[206]

The prevailing logic in these cases was that the free exercise clause is not a absolute license to freedom from all generally applicable governmental policies. It is a protection against repressive government policies, or those that strike at cardinal religious convictions and conduct. Where

---

[196] Ibid., 216-218.

[197] Ira G. Lupu, "The Lingering Death of Separationism," *George Washington Law Review* 62 (1994): 230. See also Lupu's critical review of these cases in "Where Rights Begin: The Problem of Burdens on the Free Exercise of Religion," *Harvard Law Review* 102 (1989): 933.

[198] *Jehovah's Witnesses v. King County Hospital*, 390 U.S. 598 (1968).

[199] *United States v. American Friends Service Committee*, 419 U.S. 7 (1974).

[200] *U.S. v. Lee*, 455 U.S. 252 (1982).

[201] *Heffron v. International Society for Krishna Consciousness, Inc.*, 452 U.S. 640 (1981).

[202] *Jimmy Swaggart Ministries v. Board of Equalization of California*, 493 U.S. 378 (1990).

[203] *Bob Jones University v. United States*, 461 U.S. 574 (1983).

[204] *Tony & Susan Alamo Foundation v. Secretary of Labor*, 471 U.S. 290 (1985).

[205] *Hernandez v. Commissioner of Internal Revenue*, 490 U.S. 6880 (1989).

[206] *Davis v. United States*, 495 U.S. 472 (1990).

one party's religious exercise violates the life, liberty and property of another, threatens public peace and order, or flouts pressing national policies respecting race, the military, or taxes—there state interests outweigh religious interests, constitutional power preeempts constitutional rights.

This logic does not explain—or excuse—the holdings of some of the Court's most recent free exercise cases. In *Goldman v. Weinberger* (1986),[207] the Court held that the First Amendment does not prohibit the air force from prohibiting a rabbi from wearing his yarmulke as part of his military uniform. The Court so held even though the petitioner served as a psychologist in the mental health clinic of a military base (not on the front lines), even though for three years earlier he was accorded this "privilege," and even though numerous other exemptions for religious garb were accorded by the military dress code. The requirements for military discipline and uniformity, in the Court's view, outweighed the countervailing religious interests. In *O'Lone v. Estate of Shabbaz* (1987),[208] the Court extended this logic from military officials to prison officials, holding that a change in prison policy that deprived Muslim inmates from attending Jumu'ah, the Friday collective worship service, did not violate their free exercise rights. Here the requirements for security, protection of other prisoners, and other "reasonable penological objectives," in the Court's view, outweighed the free exercise rights of the Muslim prisoners. In *Lyng v. Northwest Indian Cemetery Protective Association*,[209] the Court extend this logic to the U.S. Forest Service, holding that the free exercise clause does not prohibit the Forest Service's construction of a road through the middle of a sacred site used for centuries by Indians—notwithstanding the injunctions of the American Indian Religious Freedom Act,[210] and the Court's recognition that this action "will have severe adverse effects of the practice of their religion."[211] Justice O'Connor defended this holding with blunt and formalistic logic:

> The crucial word in the constitutional text is "prohibit": "For the Free Exercise Clause is written in terms of what the government

---

[207] 475 U.S. 503 (1986).

[208] 482 U.S. 342 (1987).

[209] 485 U.S. 439 (1988).

[210] 42 U.S.C. Sect. 1996 (1978). The Act provides, in pertinent part: "It shall be the policy of the United States to protect and preserve for American Indians their inherent right of freedom to believe, express, and exercise the traditional religions of the American Indians . . . including but not limited to access to sites, use, and possession of sacred objects, and the freedom to worship through ceremonials and traditional rites." See generally Christopher Vecsey, ed., *Handbook of American Indian Religious Freedom* (Washington, 1991); Ann E. Beeson, "Dances With Justice: Peyotism in the Courts," *Emory Law Journal* 41 (1992): 1121.

[211] Ibid., 447. See also ibid., 451 (recognizing "devastating effects on traditional Indian religious practices").

> cannot do to the individual." . . . However much we might wish that it were otherwise, government simply could not operate if it were required to satisfy every citizen's religious needs and desires. A broad range of government activities—from social welfare programs to foreign aid to conservation policies—will always be considered essential to the spiritual well-being of some citizens, often on the basis of sincerely-held religious beliefs. Others will find the very same activities deeply offensive, and perhaps incompatible with their own search for spiritual fulfillment and with the tenets of their religion. The First Amendment must apply to all citizens alike, and it can give to none of them a veto over public programs that do not prohibit the free exercise of religion. The Constitution does not, and courts cannot, offer to reconcile the various competing demands on government, many of them rooted in sincere religious belief, that inevitably arise in so diverse a society as ours.[212]

Within two years, the marginally tenable logic of *Goldman*—that the special needs of the military to protect discipline must outweigh individual rights claims—had been transmuted into the tenuous argument of *Lyng*—that busy governmental officials simply do not have time to accommodate the diverse religious interests of citizens, however sincere, long-standing, or widely prevalent those religious interests might be.

While these earlier cases may have been isolated to their facts, *Oregon Department of Human Resources v. Smith* (1990) wove their holdings into a new, and narrow, free exercise test.[213] Smith, a native American Indian, periodically ingested peyote as part of the sacramental rite of the native American church of which he was a bona fide member. Discharged from employment at a drug rehabilitation center because of this practice, he applied for unemployment compensation from the State of Oregon. Such compensation was denied, on grounds that peyote ingestion was disqualifying criminal misconduct. Smith appealed, ultimately to the Supreme Court. The Court denied his claim, even though it fell easily within the holdings of unemployment compensation cases inaugurated by *Sherbert v. Verner*. More importantly, the Court denied the validity of the *Sherbert* "compelling state interest" test altogether, and explained away its application in subsequent cases. Henceforth, Justice Scalia wrote for the majority, "the right of free exercise does not relieve an individual of the obligation to comply with a 'valid and neutral law of general applicability'. . . ."[214] Such laws, when promulgated under proper proce-

---

212 Ibid., 451-452 (citations omitted).

213 494 U.S. 872 (1990).

214 Ibid., 879 (quoting in part, *United States v. Lee*, 455 U.S. 252, Stevens, J. concurring).

dures, must prevail—regardless of the nature of the state's interest and regardless of any intrusion on the interest of a religious believer or body. Religious petitioners, whose beliefs or practices are burdened by such neutral, generally applicable laws, must seek redress in the legislatures, not the courts.[215]

Over the past five years, dozens of lower court cases, presenting local statutes and practices that are patently discriminatory against religion, have tested the logic of *Smith*.[216] The Supreme Court itself has only slightly blunted this logic in its most recent free exercise case, *Church of Lukumi Babalu Aye, Inc. v. City of Hialeah* (1993).[217] There the Court declared unconstitutional a city ordinance subjecting local followers of the Santerian faith to criminal punishment for engaging in the ritual slaughter of animals that is a central practice of their religion. Even applying the *Smith* test, the Court could strike down this law, for it was neither of general application, nor neutrally applied.

The effect of *Smith* has been further blunted by Congress's promulgation of the Religious Freedom Restoration Act (RFRA) in 1993.[218] The Act was specifically designed to repudiate the *Smith* approach to free exercise analysis, and to restore the "compelling state interest" test of *Sherbert v. Verner* and *Wisconsin v. Yoder*. It provides in pertinent part:

> (a) In General. Government shall not burden a person's exercise of religion, even if the burden results from a rule of general applicability, except as provided in subsection (b)
>
> (b) Exception. Government may burden a person's exercise of religion only if it demonstrates that application of the burden to the person:
>
> (1) is in furtherance of a compelling governmental interest; and

---

215 See critical commentary in Douglas Laycock, "Summary and Synthesis: The Crisis in Religious Liberty," *George Washington Law Review* 60 (1992): 841; Michael W. McConnell, "Free Exercise Revisionism and the *Smith* Decision," *University of Chicago Law Review* 57 (1990): 1109; Steven D. Smith, "The Rise and Fall of Religious Freedom in Constitutional Discourse," *University of Pennsylvania Law Review* 140 (1991): 149.

216 See sources and discussion in Douglas Laycock and Oliver S. Thomas, "Interpreting the Religious Freedom Restoration Act," *Texas Law Review* 73 (1994): 209; Berg, "What Hath Congress Wrought?"; W. Cole Durham, Jr., "Treatment of Religious Minorities in the United States," in European Consortium for Church-State Research, *The Legal Status of Religious Minorities in the Countries of the European Union* (Thessalanica/Milan, 1994), 323; and the collection of articles in "The James R. Browning Symposium for 1994: The Religious Freedom Restoration Act," *Montana Law Review* 56(1) (1995).

217 61 U.S.L.W. 4587 (1993).

218 Pub. L. No. 103-141 (Nov. 16, 1993), 107 Stat. 1488, codified at 42 U.S.C.A. 2000bb to 2000-4 (Supp. V 1993).

> (2) is the least restrictive means of furthering that compelled governmental interest.[219]

The statute has evoked strong commentary by scholars and judges alike. Some defend it as the only sensible constitutional remedy to end the contemporary "crisis of religious liberty,"[220] and have put its provisions to immediate use. Others denounce the statute as a violation of the principle of separation of powers, and have urged that the common law method of adjudication based on earlier free exercise cases be used to take the sting from *Smith*, and, if necessary, inter it.[221] So deep-seated and fundamental a constitutional issue will in due course have to come to the Supreme Court for resolution. Whether the Court, with two new judicial appointments, is ready to reconsider *Smith*, or to judge dispositively on the constitutionality of RFRA, is not at all clear at the time of this writing. Whatever the outcome, the controversies over free exercise law in the past decade have sparked renewed public debate over many of the traditional essential rights and liberties of religion.

Modern Disestablishment Law. While multiple principles informed much of the Court's interpretation of the free exercise clause, a single principle drove much of the Court's early analysis of the establishment clause—the principle of separationism. Justice Black announced this focus in the ringing dicta of *Everson*, the Court's first major establishment clause case:

> The "establishment of religion" clause of the First Amendment means at least this: Neither a state nor the Federal Government can set up a church. Neither can pass laws which aid one religion, aid all religions, or prefer one religion over another. Neither can force nor influence a person to go or to remain away from church against his will or force him to profess a belief or disbelief in any religion. No person can be punished for entertaining or professing religious beliefs or disbeliefs, for church attendance or non-attendance. No tax in any amount, large or small, can be levied to support any religious activities or institutions, whatever they may be called, or whatever form they may adopt to teach or

---

219 Ibid., sec. 3.

220 See especially the recent articles by the Act's principal draftsman, Douglas N. Laycock: "Summary and Synthesis: The Crisis in Religious Liberty"; id. "RFRA, Congress, and the Ratchet," *Montana Law Review* 56 (1995): 145; id. and Thomas, "Interpreting the Religious Freedom Restoration Act."

221 See sources and discussion in Marci A. Hamilton, "The Religious Freedom Restoration Act: Letting the Fox into the Henhouse under the Cover of Section 5 of the Fourteenth Amendment," *Cardozo Law Review* 16 (1994): 357. See also id., "The Belief/Conduct Paradigm in the Supreme Court's Free Exercise Jurisprudence: A Theological Account of the Failure to Protect Religious Conduct," *Ohio State Law Journal* 54 (1993): 713.

> practice religion. Neither a state nor the Federal Government can, openly or secretly, participate in the affairs of any religious organizations or groups, or *vice versa.* In the words of Jefferson, the clause against establishment of religion by law was intended to erect "a wall of separation between church and state."[222]

Justice Black, and Justice Rutledge in dissent in *Everson,* described these sentiments as the "original intent of the eighteenth century framers." The historiography of both Justices, however, was at best selective. For, in determining the intent of the framers of the establishment clause, they turned primarily to enlightenment writers—Jefferson, Madison, Paine, and others—and read primarily the constitutional history of Virginia, where these writers had their greatest influence. Henceforth, the Court declared, all government laws and policies would have to abide by the strict separationist principles advocated by this enlightenment tradition, or be struck down as unconstitutional.

Such dicta were an open invitation to litigation. All the state and local policies on religion and the church that were promulgated under a regime dominated by Puritan and republican sentiments and justified under the founders' sundry principles of religious human rights, besides separationism, were now open to challenge. Scores of establishment cases poured into the lower federal courts after the 1940s. The subject matter of these cases was predictable enough: challenges to traditional laws and policies involving government endorsements of religious symbols and services; challenges to traditional laws and policies that afforded governmental aid to religious missions, schools, charities, and others; challenges to traditional laws explicitly predicated on (Protestant) Christian morals and conventions. The new application of the First Amendment religion clauses to the states encouraged such extensive litigation. The Supreme Court's narrow enlightenment-based interpretation of the establishment clause in its earliest cases demanded it.

The Court chose to enforce this separationist principle primarily in cases involving public school education.[223] Privately-employed religious teachers could not hold classes in public schools.[224] Public schools programs could not maintain programs that required students to participate in daily prayer,[225] to receive daily instruction in the Bible,[226] or to hear

---

222 *Everson,* 330 U.S. at 15-16.

223 Indeed, nearly three-quarters of the 40 plus Supreme Court cases heard under the establishment clause since *Everson* have involved questions of education.

224 *Illinois ex rel. McCollum v. Board of Educucation,* 333 U.S. 203 (1948).

225 *Engel v. Vitale,* 370 U.S. 421 (1962).

226 *Abington Township School District v. Schempp,* 374 U.S. 203 (1963).

recitation of the Lord's prayer.[227] Traditional prohibitions against teaching an evolutionary theory, alongside a creation theory, of origins, could not be maintained.[228] The Court was not single-minded in its pursuit of separationism. Despite its strong separationist dicta, *Everson* itself upheld state policies of furnishing sectarian school children with public bus transportation. Later, the Court upheld policies that released religious students from public schools to participate in religious rituals,[229] and that furnished sectarian schools with textbooks on non-religious subjects.[230]

In the landmark case of *Lemon v. Kurtzman* (1971), the Court cast this tempered separationist impulse into a constitutional test for all cases arising under the establishment clause—not just education cases.[231] Building on the *Walz v. Tax Commission* case of the previous term, which had upheld tax exemptions of church property,[232] the Court declared that henceforth every government policy challenged under the establishment clause would meet constitutional muster only if it could satisfy three criteria. The policy must: (1) have a secular, non-religious purpose: (2) result in a predominantly secular, or non-religious effect; and (3) foster no excessive entanglement between church and state.[233] Incidental religious "effect" or modest "entanglement" of church and state was tolerable, but defiance of any one of these criteria was presumed constitutionally fatal.

This reification of the separationist principle rendered the establishment clause a formidable obstacle to many traditional forms and forums of collaboration between church and state in delivering education. Using this test, the Court disallowed state programs that provided salary and service supplements to religious schools.[234] The Court struck down state programs that reimbursed religious schools for most costs incurred to administer standardized tests and to prepare state records[235]—although the "actual costs" for certain tests could be recouped.[236] The Court disallowed, with one narrow exception,[237] various state tax schemes that would allow for deduction or reimbursement for payments of religious

---

227 *Chamberlin v. Dade County Board of Public Instruction*, 377 U.S. 402 (1964).

228 *Epperson v. Arkansas*, 393 U.S. 97 (1968).

229 *Zorach*, 343 U.S. at 306.

230 *Board of Education v. Allen*, 392 U.S. 236 (1968).

231 403 U.S. 602 (1971), reh'g denied, 404 U.S. 876 (1971).

232 397 U.S. 664 (1970).

233 *Lemon v. Kurtzman*, 403 U.S. 602 (1971), reh'g denied, 404 U.S. 876 (1971).

234 Ibid.

235 *Levitt v. Committee for Public Education*, 413 U.S. 472 (1973); *New York v. Cathedral Academy*, 434 U.S. 125 (1977).

236 *Committee for Public Education v. Regan*, 444 U.S. 646 (1980).

237 *Mueller v. Allen*, 463 U.S. 388 (1963).

school tuition.[238] The Court disallowed states from loaning or furnishing religious schools with textbooks, various supplies and films, and various counselling and other personnel, all of which were made mandatory by state policy.[239] The Court prohibited public schools to hold remedial educational programs to indigent children in classrooms leased from religious schools,[240] or to lease public personnel to teach remedial and enrichment courses in religious schools.[241] The Court prohibited public school policies of posting the Decalogue,[242] allowing student-led prayers,[243] or maintaining moments of silence for private prayer or meditation.[244] Very recently, the Court struck down a local school board practice of offering clergy-led prayers at a middle school graduation ceremony.[245] It also outlawed a state's creation of a single public school district within an exclusively Satmar Hasidic community.[246]

The results of these religion and education cases heard under the establishment clause were not simply autogenerated by wooden application of the *Lemon* test. Each case had its own distinctive facts, which affected the test's application. Moreover, from the collection of cases emerged a general rationale that was specific to establishment clause cases involving education. The public school is one of the most visible and well-known arms of the state in any community, the cases repeatedly argued. The principal purpose of the public school is to stand as a model of constitutional democracy, and to provide a vehicle for the communication of democratic values and abilities to its students. The state compels its students to be at schools; these students are perforce young and impressionable. The public schools must cling as jealously as possible to core constitutional and democratic values. One such value is the consistent separation of church and state taught by the establishment clause. Whereas some relaxation of constitutional values, even establishment clause values, might be possible in other public contexts—where mature adults can make informed assessments of the values being transmitted—public schools with its impressionable youths who are compelled to be

---

[238] *Committee for Public Education v. Nyquist*, 413 U.S. 756 (1973); *Sloan v. Lemon*, 413 U.S. 825 (1973).

[239] *Meek v. Pittinger*, 421 U.S. 349 (1975); for some exceptions, see *Wolman v. Walter*, 433 U.S. 229 (1977).

[240] *Aguilar v. Felton*, 473 U.S. 402 (1985).

[241] *Grand Rapids School District v. Ball*, 473 U.S. (1985).

[242] *Stone v. Graham*, 449 U.S. 39 (1980).

[243] *Treen v. Karen, B.*, 455 U.S. 913 (1982)

[244] *Wallace v. Jaffree*, 472 U.S. 38 (1985).

[245] *Lee v. Weisman*, 112 S. Ct. 2649 (1992).

[246] *Board of Education of Kiryas Joel Village School District v. Grumet*, 62 U.S.L.W. 4665 (1994).

there cannot afford such slippage. The constitutional values contained in sources like the establishment clause must be rigorously protected.[247]

This rationale did not prevent the Court, on occasion, from granting support for religious schools or students. The Court upheld state policies that provided educational subsidies,[248] construction grants,[249] or other benefits[250] generically to religious and non-religious institutions alike—so long as the benefits did not fall primarily to religious schools, or religious activities. Nor was *Lemon* violated when state-supported disability services and benefits were afforded to students who attended religious schools.[251] In some of these cases, the Court applied rather tortured and tenuous logic to the *Lemon* test, yielding results that did not readily square with precedent. This was not just the exercise of disingenuity that many commentators ascribed to the Court. What seemed to be at work was that the Court was incrementally importing other principles of religious rights, besides separationism, into its establishment clause jurisprudence. State subsidies to religious schools, alongside others, protected equality (neutrality) and structural pluralism. State disability services to the sectarian school student preserved the voluntarism and the free exercise right to associate with others of one's faith. The Court in the later 1970s and 1980s had imbued the *Sherbert* free exercise test with an array of increasingly discordant principles; the Court was applying the same method to its interpretation of the *Lemon* test.

This more multi-principled reading of the *Lemon* test became more noticeable in cases not involving education. The Court did use the *Lemon* test to strike down a state policy that effectively gave churches "veto" power over state decisions to grant liquor licenses to nearby establishments,[252] a state law guaranteeing a private sector employee the absolute right not to work on his Sabbath,[253] and a state law that granted sale and

---

[247] Within the vast literature, see, e.g., Paul Freund and Robert Ulich, *Religion and the Public Schools* (Cambridge, 1965); Edward M. Gaffney, *Private Schools and the Public Good: Policy Alternatives for the Eighties* (Notre Dame, 1981); Richard C. McMillan, *Religion in the Public Schools* (Macon, 1987); Lynn R. Buzzard, *Schools: They Haven't Got a Prayer* (Elgin, IL, 1982); Rockne M. McCarthy, James W. Skillen, and William A. Harper, *Disestablishment a Second Time: Genuine Pluralism for American Schools* (Grand Rapids, MI, 1982); Rodney K. Smith, *Prayer and the Constitution: A Case Study in Constitutional Interpretation* (Wilmington, 1987); "Symposium: How Much God in the Schools," *William and Mary Bill of Rights Journal* 4 (1995): 223.

[248] *Roemer v. Board of Public Works of Maryland*, 426 U.S. 736 (1976).

[249] *Tilton v. Richardson*, 403 U.S. 672 (1971).

[250] *Hunt v. McNair*, 413 U.S. 734 (1973).

[251] *Witters v. Washington*, 474 U.S. 481 (1976); *Zobrest v. Catalina Foothills School District*, 113 S.Ct. 2462 (1993).

[252] *Larkin v. Grendel's Den*, 459 U.S. 1156 (1982)

[253] *Estate of Thorton v. Caldor*, 472 U.S. 703 (1985).

use tax exemptions exclusively to religious publications.[254] But, in the past decade, the Court has held that the *Lemon* test was not violated when Congress afforded church-affiliated counselling centers, along with others, funding to participate in a federal family counseling program,[255] or when Congress exempted religious employers from full compliance with employment discrimination laws,[256] or when Congress granted public high school students equal access with other school to school facilities to perform their religious activities after school hours.[257] These cases not only reflected the Court's growing deference to Congress, and growing indifference to the rigors of the *Lemon* test.[258] They also reflected a growing appreciation for the principles of the voluntarism, pluralism, and equality of religions before the laws—the need for "neutrality among religions, and between religion and non-religion," as the Court put it.[259]

In recent cases involving governmental use of religious services and symbols, the Court invoked these principles without any pretense of using the *Lemon* test. In *Marsh v. Chambers* (1983), the Court upheld a state legislature's practice of sponsoring a chaplain and opening its sessions with prayer.[260] Writing for the Court, Chief Justice Burger invoked civic republican arguments about the utility and validity of supporting a civil religion: "In light of the unambiguous and unbroken history of more than 200 years, there can be no doubt that the practice of opening legislative sessions with prayer has become part of the fabric of our society. To invoke Divine guidance on a public body entrusted with making the laws is not, in these circumstances, an 'establishment' of religion [but] simply a tolerable acknowledgement of beliefs widely held among the people of this country. . . . '[W]e are a religious people whose institutions presuppose a Supreme Being'."[261] *Lynch v. Donnelly* (1984),[262] extended this logic to uphold a municipality's traditional practice of maintaining a creche on

254 *Texas Monthly, Inc. v. Bullock*, 489 U.S. 1 (1989).

255 *Bowen v. Kendrick*, 487 U.S. 589 (1988).

256 *Amos*, 483 U.S. at 327.

257 *Mergens*, 110 S. Ct. at 2356.

258 Today, in fact, the Lemon test is moribund, if not dead. See Michael Stokes Paulsen, "*Lemon* is Dead," *Case Western Reserve Law Review* 43 (1993): 795; David O. Conkle, "*Lemon* Lives," *Case Western Reserve Law Review* 43 (1993): 865; Carl H. Esbeck, "The *Lemon* Test: Should it be Retained, Reformulated, or Rejected?" *Notre Dame Journal of Law, Ethics & Public Policy* 4 (1990): 513.

259 *Kendrick*, 487 U.S. at 607, quoting *Grand Rapids School District*, 473 U.S. at 373. For the use of "neutrality" as an organizing First Amendment principle, see Douglas N. Laycock, "Formal, Substantive, and Disaggregated Neutrality Toward Religion," *DePaul Law Review* 39 (1990): 993.

260 *Marsh v. Chambers*, 463 U.S. 783 (1983).

261 Ibid., 792, quoting *Zorach*, 343 U.S. at 306.

262 *Lynch v. Donnelly*, 465 U.S. 668 (1984).

a public park as part of a holiday display in a downtown shopping area. "There is an unbroken history of official acknowledgment by all three branches of government of the role of religion in American life," Chief Justice Burger argued, giving an ample list of illustrations. Our "constitutional underpinnings rest on and encourage diversity and pluralism in all areas." Moreover, the creche, while of undoubted religious significance to Christians, is merely a "passive" part of "purely secular displays extant at Christmas" that "engender a friendly community spirit of good will," "brings people into the central city and serves commercial interests and benefits merchants."[263] Such benign governmental support for religion cannot be assessed by "mechanical logic" or "absolutist tests" of establishment. It is far too late in the day to impose a crabbed reading of the Clause on the country."[264]

Free exercise law imploded in the 1990s. The *Smith* Court reduced the discordant principles and precedents of the *Sherbert* test to a simple neutrality principle, which Congress is seeking to unmake. Establishment law, by contrast, has exploded. The Court has transmuted the *Lemon* test into at least four principles, which the Court is now seeking to integrate. Justice Souter has urged the principle of governmental neutrality toward religion.[265] Justice O'Connor would strike down policies that reflect governmental endorsement or condemnation of religion.[266] Justice Kennedy would strike only governmental action that coerces or compels an individual or a group to accept or adopt religion.[267] Justice Scalia and Thomas would accord great weight to historical practices and legislative preferences.[268] Though each of these new principles has captured a majority of the Court in an individual case, none of them has as yet come to dominate establishment clause jurisprudence. As a consequence, disestablishment law today, like free exercise law, is in a state of confusion, even crisis.

---

263 Ibid., 685.

264 Ibid., 678, 687. In *County of Allegheny v. ACLU*, 492 U.S. 573 (1989), the Court imposed limits on this sweeping rule, holding that a creche prominently displayed in a county court house, undiluted with other secular symbols, containing verbal religious messages, and with no obvious redeeming commercial value could not be countenanced. In the same case, however, it upheld display of a menorah that was located in a less public place of the county courthouse, was buffered by a Christmas tree, and had no verbal religious messages.

265 See especially *Kiryas Joel*, 62 U.S.L.W. 4667ff. (Souter, J.); *Lukumi Babalu*, 61 U.S.L.W. 4598 (Souter, J. concurring).

266 See especially *County of Allegheny v. ACLU*, 492 U.S. 573, 623 (O'Connor, J. concurring).

267 *Lee v. Weisman*, 112 S.Ct. 2549 (1992).

268 Ibid. (Scalia, J. dissenting); *Texas Monthly*, 489 U.S. at 29 (Scalia, J. dissenting).

Concluding Reflections

The vacillations in the Supreme Court's interpretations of the establishment and free exercise clauses can be explained, in part, on factual grounds. The Court's application of a cryptic constitutional clause to a diverse set of complex issues over the course of fifty years has inevitably led to different, and sometimes conflicting, lines of interpretation. "The life of the law has not been logic: it has been experience," Oliver Wendell Holmes reminds us.[269] The law of religious rights and liberties in America is no exception.

These vacillations, however, also betray the failure of the Court to develop a coherent and comprehensive framework for applying the principles and precepts of the religion clauses. The Court has tended to rely too heavily on its mechanical tests of free exercise and establishment, and to use these tests as a substitute, rather than as a guide, to legal analysis. The Court has tended to pit the establishment and free exercise clauses against each other, rather than treating them as twin guarantees of religious rights and liberties. The Court has been too eager to reduce the religion clauses to one or two principles, often thereby ignoring the range of interlocking principles that were originally incorporated into the religion clauses—liberty of conscience, free exercise, equality, pluralism, separationism, and disestablishment of religion, among them. Once proud masters of the American experiment in religious rights, the Court of late has left a legacy of discordant precedents and fractioned plurality opinions.

The Court needs to develop an integrated approach to First Amendment questions that incorporates the first principles of religious rights and liberties on which the American experiment was founded, and integrates them into the resolution of specific cases. Such a framework is easy enough to draw up in the sterility of the classroom, or on the pages of a law review article. In the context of the ongoing constitutional experiment in religious liberty—with its thorny tangle of federal and state courts and legislatures—deliberate and provisional steps are essential. It might well be necessary, as an interim step, that certain lines of cases simply continue. Individual subjects of religious rights law, such as income taxation, labor relations, intrachurch disputes, and others might need to be left for a time to develop their own integrated pockets of principles, precepts, and precedents. Religious incorporation, zoning, landmark preservation, property taxation, and other subjects that generally fall within state (not federal) jurisdiction might need to remain "selectively deincorporated" for a time and left to the experimentation of

[269] Oliver Wendell Holmes, Jr., *The Common Law* (Boston, 1881), 1.

state legislatures and courts. Recent imports into the Court's conceptual constellation, such as "equal access" and "substantive neutrality," should be permitted to leaven the jurisprudence a bit longer. Religion clause jurisprudence should build stronger bridges with other clauses of the First Amendment as well as with other amendments in the Bill of Rights.[270] There is great wisdom in Justice O'Connor's cautionary admonition in the *Kiryas Joel* case last term:

> It is always appealing to look for a single test, a Grand Unified Theory that would resolve all the cases that might arise under a particular [First Amendment] clause. . . . But the same constitutional principle may operate very differently in different contexts. . . . And setting forth a unitary test for a broad set of cases may do more harm than good. Any test that must deal with widely disparate situations risks being so vague as to be useless. . . . I think a less unitary approach provides a better structure for analysis. If each test covers a narrower and more homogeneous area, the tests may be more precise and therefore easier to apply. . . . Perhaps eventually under this structure we may indeed distill a unified, or at least a more unified [approach].[271]

Whatever interim steps are taken, the Court, with the help of the academy, must eventually strive toward the achievement of this "more unified approach." Such an approach must certainly embrace (as Justice Scalia urged in response to Justice O'Connor) "the longstanding traditions of our people"[272]—traditions that are best captured in the principles of liberty of conscience, free exercise, equality, pluralism, separationism, and disestablishment forged in the early republic. Such an integrated framework must also consider the traditions of *other* people—traditions that are captured in the human rights instruments of international and other constitutional laws. The way of integration is not only the way of the past, the original intent of the framers of the religion clauses. It is also the way of the future, the intent of the emerging international and world legal system, of which American constitutional law will eventually have to be a part.

To date, the budding international law of religious rights and liberties has had little currency in First Amendment jurisprudence. Not only

---

[270] See Glendon and Yanes, "Structural Free Exercise," 541-550; Akil Amar "The Bill of Rights as a Constitution," *Yale Law Journal* 100 (1991): 1131; Phillip E. Johnson, "Concepts and Compromise in First Amendment Religious Doctrine," *California Law Review* 72 (1984): 817.

[271] *Kiryas Joel*, 62 U.S.L.W. at 4673-4674 (O'Connor, J., concurring).

[272] Ibid., 4683 (Scalia, J., dissenting).

has the canon of international norms on religious rights and liberties developed slowly and sporadically since World War II.[273] Even as more fully developed in the 1980s and 1990s, this international law remains largely hortatory. The principal international provisions on religious rights do not formally bind the United States. Comparatively few cases have been adjudicated, and those that have been reported do not follow the conventional forms and format of American constitutional law. The international law of religious rights and liberties, together with the applicable constitutional law of other countries, has thus been largely ignored in First Amendment circles.

But to keep this parochial veil drawn shut is to deprive the American experiment with a rich new source of instruction and inspiration. Especially at this time of turmoil and transition in First Amendment law, comparative legal analysis might well be salutary. There are several distinctive principles of international law that confirm, refine, integrate, and elaborate prevailing First Amendment principles and cases. There is much to be learned from international and comparative constitutional practices that differ from our own. The refined hermeneutical principles of international and civil law systems might well be used to reform the somewhat chaotic common law case method.[274] The prioritizing of liberty of conscience, free exercise, non-discrimination, and equality principles at international law might well serve as a prototype for the integration of free exercise and establishment clause values.[275] The heavy emphasis on group religious rights in recent international instruments, might help provide greater protection to religious minorities in America.[276] The ready merger of public and private, constitutional and civil rights on religion in many legal systems today might prompt us to try to bridge the growing gaps between constitutional and statutory protections of religious rights. The international doctrine of "a margin of appreciation" for local religious practices could be put to good use in our federalist system with its local jury trials.[277] The eventual resolution of the international

---

273 See chapter by Natan Lerner herein.

274 See chapters by Natan Lerner, W. Cole Durham, Jr., Martin Heckel, and Lourens M. du Plessis herein. See also Steven D. Smith, "Idolatry in Constitutional Interpretation," *Virginia Law Review* 79 (1993): 583.

275 See the chapters by W. Cole Durham, Jr., David Little, and Dinah Shelton and Alexandre Kiss herein.

276 See chapters by Natan Lerner, W. Cole Durham, Jr., Makua wa Mutua, and Dinah Shelton and Alexandre Kiss herein.

277 See Johan van der Vyver's chapter herein.

debate between "universalism versus relativism" in human rights[278] has enormous implications for the distinctive American debate over federal and state jurisdiction over religious rights.

The great American experiment in religious rights and liberties has often been the envy of the world. Yet brief glimpses by foreigners into the Supreme Court laboratory, where much of the experiment has been conducted, have often produced both caricatures and characteristically optimistic assessments of this experiment. Not all is so simple, nor so well, as it might appear from afar. However bold in conception and execution, the experiment has occasionally sputtered in the past, and it is sputtering today. In the past, it was through landmark cases—*Cantwell, Everson, Sherbert,* and *Lemon*—that the Court could set the experiment right. Today, it might well be up to Congress or to individual states eventually to restore a coherent American rule of law on religion. Whatever branch of government assumes the responsibility for the experiment, it would do well to look out the windows of its laboratory on the rest of the world.

---

278 See sources and discussion in ibid. and the chapter by Abdullahi Ahmed An-Na'im in the companion volume hereto, John Witte, Jr. and Johan van der Vyver, eds., *Religious Human Rights in Global Perspective: Religious Perspectives* (Dordrecht/Boston/London, 1995).

A Draft Model Law on Freedom of Religion, With Commentary[1]

DINAH SHELTON
Santa Clara University
and
ALEXANDRE KISS
International Institute of Human Rights, Strasbourg

In the process of democratic transformation underway in many countries throughout the world, the issue of protecting religious liberty is a central concern due to extensively reported past denials of this basic freedom. The laudable efforts of new regimes to achieve democratic governance and respect for human rights require the development of laws and practices that conform to international standards. The situation in other countries is less positive, as widespread human rights abuses continue, including religious persecution and discrimination. The present text and commentary present an effort to meet the needs of newly democratic governments and those seeking to protect religious liberty. It provides model legislation on freedom of religion based on international

[1] The project to draft a model law dates to the Santa Clara conference on religious liberty, held with the generous support of the Rockefeller Foundation in 1979. The main focus of that conference was the proposal for a United Nations Declaration on Religious Liberty, subsequently adopted in 1981. Since that time, there has been considerable discussion of the need for an international treaty on freedom of religion. The model law is designed to by-pass the treaty-drafting process by directly incorporating existing international standards into domestic law. It is not intended to and does not preclude further work on an international agreement. The first draft of the model law was prepared, thanks to a Presidential grant from Santa Clara University, by Luis Jimenez, Office of the Legal Counsel, Organization of American States; Alexandre Kiss; Kalman Kulchar, Minister of Justice of Hungary; Dinah Shelton; and Richard Verches, United Nations Office of the High Commissioner of Refugees. Each of the drafters participated in an individual capacity; the affiliations are given only for the purpose of identification.

J.D. van der Vyver and J. Witte, Jr. (eds.), Religious Human Rights in Global Perspective, 559-592.

human rights standards and the findings of the United Nations Special Rapporteur on Religious Intolerance.[2]

Constitutional guarantees are essential, but broadly stated provisions may provide inadequate protection absent detailed implementing laws. Legislation may be particularly important in civil law countries where written law is the norm and the role of the judiciary in interpreting and implementing broad constitutional mandates is limited. Under international law, the obligation of states to protect religious liberty by law is clear. The United Nations Declaration on the Elimination of All Forms of Intolerance and of Discrimination Based on Religion or Belief[3] provides that the rights and freedoms set forth in the Declaration shall be accorded in national legislation in such a manner that everyone can avail themselves of such rights and freedoms in practice. Similarly, the Concluding Document of the Vienna follow-up meeting to the Helsinki Conference on Security and Cooperation in Europe obligates all states to "ensure in their laws and regulations and in their application the full and effective implementation of the freedom of thought, conscience, religion or belief."[4]

The Model Law is part of an effort to implement international guarantees of religious liberty currently denied in all parts of the world. In many cases the violations are based on existing legislation. The Special Rapporteur on Religious Intolerance noted in her 1987 report: "[T]here does seem to be an undeniable relationship between certain legislative provisions and the occurrence of incidents or measures that reveal intolerance in matters of religion or belief."[5] Many countries deny religious liberty by enacting and implementing measures clearly incompatible with the 1981 Declaration. Some states establish an official or state religion or ideology which results in discrimination towards members of non-established religions. In other states, legislation provides for recognition

---

2 In 1986, the United Nations Commission on Human Rights approved the appointment of a Special Rapporteur on implementation of the 1981 United Nations Declaration on the Elimination of All Forms of Intolerance and of Discrimination Based on Religion or Belief. There have been annual reports submitted to the Commission since 1987 under the title *Implementation of the Declaration on the Elimination of All Forms of Intolerance and of Discrimination based on Religion or Belief, Report submitted by Mr. Angelo Vidal d'Almeida Ribeiro, Special Rapporteur appointed in accordance with Commission on Human Rights Resolution 1986/20 of 10 March 1986* [hereinafter *Report on Religious Intolerance*].

3 United Nations Declaration on the Elimination of All Forms of Intolerance and of Discrimination Based on Religion or Belief, adopted November 25, 1981, G.A. Res. 36/55, 36 U.N. GAOR Supp. (No. 51) at 171, U.N. Doc. A/36/51 (1981) [hereafter Declaration on Religious Intolerance].

4 Bureau of Public Affairs, *U.S. Department of State: Selected Doc. No. 35, CSCE Vienna Follow-Up Meetings. A Framework for Europe's Future* (1989), 10-11.

5 UN Doc. E/CN.4/1987/35 of 24 December 1986 at 10.

of one or several dominant religions, to the detriment of minority religions or beliefs. Even those religions that are recognized may be hampered by being placed under state control. In contrast, some religions or denominations are declared unlawful *per se* and adherents are punished for belonging to or practicing them.

Where states lack specific legislation, governmental decrees or policy may implement religious discrimination or otherwise infringe upon religious liberty, banning certain religions or controlling all religious activities. Some countries have undertaken campaigns for the forced assimilation of religious minorities.[6] Others have instigated attacks on individuals belonging to unrecognized religions or sects and have restricted religious practices and attire associated with religious norms. Decrees may limit the periods during which religious activities and ceremonies may be performed.[7]

The Model Law is thus directed at states that are seeking to adopt legislation on religious liberty and at those whose laws and practices are incompatible with international human rights standards. The law does not attempt to protect all speech, political rights or the rights of ethnic, cultural, or racial minorities, although in general there seems to be a close relationship between enjoyment of religious liberty and the observance of other human rights. Additional legislation must address these broader human rights concerns. The proposals here stem from international recognition that views about the sacred play a special role in every society and should be protected by law.

MODEL LAW ON FREEDOM OF RELIGION AND BELIEF

PART I
GENERAL PROVISIONS

ARTICLE 1. Statement of legislative purpose

The purposes of this law are:

a. to guarantee freedom of religion and belief in conformity with international human rights standards contained in the Universal Declaration of Human Rights, the United Nations Covenant on Civil and Political Rights, other relevant international treaties, and customary international law;

---

[6] Ibid., 11.

[7] Ibid., 12.

b. to promote understanding, tolerance and respect in matters relating to freedom of religion or belief;

c. to establish offenses against freedom of religion or belief and to prohibit discrimination based on religion or belief;

d. to ensure the separation of the state and religion;

e. to define the status of religious organizations.

ARTICLE 2. Definitions

For purposes of this law

a. *"religion"* means the personal commitment to and serving of one or several beings or spiritual masters with worshipful devotion; a system or systems of belief, faith, creed or worship; the service of the divine; or to the sacred beliefs, observances and practices of traditional cultures.

b. *"discrimination on the basis of religion or belief"* means any distinction, exclusion, restriction, preference, omission or other difference of treatment based on religion or belief, which has the purpose or effect of nullifying or impairing, directly or indirectly, intentionally or unintentionally, the recognition, equal enjoyment or exercise of human rights and fundamental freedoms in civil, political, economic, social or cultural life.

PART II
FREEDOM OF RELIGION AND BELIEF

ARTICLE 3. Guarantee of freedom of religion and belief

Everyone has the right to freedom of religion and belief, including the freedom to have or not to have a religion and to change religions, and the freedom, either individually or in community with others in public or private, to manifest religion or belief through worship, observance, practice and teaching.

ARTICLE 4. Protection against compulsion

No one may be compelled to profess a religion or a belief or to participate in any way in the acts or ceremonies of any form of worship or other religious activity, nor to observe its days of rest.

No one may be compelled, directly or indirectly, to disclose his or her religious convictions or other beliefs.

No one may be compelled to take any oath which is contrary to his or her religion or belief.

No one may be compelled to perform armed military service contrary to his or her religion or belief. However, no one may refuse to perform public or unarmed military service for humanitarian purposes or in the interest of the general welfare.

No student may be compelled to participate in religious activities nor given religious instruction contrary to the student's religion or belief; however, no student is exempt from compulsory schooling or enrollment and participation in the normal academic program of a school.

ARTICLE 5. Manifestations of religion or belief

Freedom of religion and belief includes the right of all persons to manifest their religion or belief, either individually or with others, in public or in private, including, *inter alia*, the right

a. to carry out in daily life the tenets of their religion or belief;

b. to hold religious services, to acquire and maintain places for this purpose;

c. to establish, maintain and manage religious institutions, including institutions for charitable, educational and humanitarian purposes;

d. to make, acquire, import, export, and use the objects and materials related to the rites or customs of their religion or belief;

e. to write, issue and disseminate relevant publications;

f. to solicit and receive voluntary financial and other contributions from individuals and institutions;

g. to train, appoint, elect or designate appropriate leaders according to the requirements and standards of the religion or belief;

h. to propagate the religion or belief through teaching and observance;

i. to establish and maintain communication with other individuals and religious organizations in matters of religion or belief without regard to national boundaries;

j. to observe and practice their religion or belief without intervention or interference by members of another religion or adherents of another belief;

k. to have reasonable accommodation in employment, military or alternative service, schools and prisons, for manifestations of their religion or belief;

l. to discuss or criticize any religion or belief and its practices;

m. to determine the religious education of their children subject to international norms protecting the rights of the child.

n. to maintain the confidentiality of confessional or other communications between religious authorities and members of the religion;

o. to have free access to places of worship and places sacred to the religion or belief.

PART III
THE STATE AND RELIGION

ARTICLE 6. Relations between the state and religion

a. The state is secular and has no official or established religion.

b. Subject to (c), no religion or religious organization may receive any privileges from the state, nor exercise any political authority.

c. The state may financially support the medical activities and the educational, charitable, and social services of religious organizations provided this is done without any discrimination based on the religion or belief of the observing organizations and equality of treatment with non-religious organizations.

d. Public authorities are prohibited from involvement in the selection or role of religious officials, the structure of religious organizations, or the organization of worship or other rites.

e. Manifestations of religion or belief may be limited only based on law and when it is demonstrated by the appropriate authority to be necessary in the interest of public safety, public health, public morality, or for the purpose of protecting the rights and freedoms of other persons.

PART IV
EQUAL RIGHTS AND NON-DISCRIMINATION

ARTICLE 7. Equal rights

All persons, irrespective of their religion or belief, are equal before the law, and shall enjoy equal rights in all fields of civil, political, economic, social an cultural life. All legal and natural persons enjoy the full protection of the law.

ARTICLE 8. Non-discrimination

Discrimination on the basis of religion or belief is prohibited.

PART V
RELIGIOUS ORGANIZATIONS

ARTICLE 9. Legal status

Organizations formed on the basis of religion or belief may benefit from the status and privileges afforded other non-profit organizations and are subject to the provisions of this law and to the laws and regulations governing such entities.

ARTICLE 10. Activities of religious organizations

Religious organizations may

a. found enterprises, institutions, and associations, acquire and dispose of property, and undertake other activities as decided by their members;

b. produce, buy, import, export, and distribute religious literature, other printed or audio-visual materials and goods normally used in religious practice;

c. conduct cultural, educational, charitable, health, or other activities either directly or through the formation of affiliated or independent organizations and foundations;

d. establish and maintain international relations and contacts;

ARTICLE 11. Internal governance

Organizations formed on the basis of religion or belief may govern themselves according to their laws and doctrines, which shall have no civil law effect and shall not be enforced by the public authority or be applicable to non-members.

ARTICLE 12. Creation and administration of schools

The creation and administration of private schools shall not be denied or limited on the basis of religion or belief; all schools shall maintain the compulsory academic, health and safety standards set out in the education laws of the state.

In their admissions and their educational policies, schools maintained by religious organizations shall not discriminate on the basis of race, ethnic origin, language, disability, or gender.

ARTICLE 13. Taxation of religious organizations

Employees of religious organizations and their enterprises are subject to taxes on their income and to social security taxes according to the revenue laws of the state.

Donations to and income of religious organization are subject to the laws governing non-profit educational and charitable organizations.

PART VI
OFFENSES

ARTICLE 14. Discrimination on the basis of religion or belief

Any limitation of rights or benefits, direct or indirect, or establishing of privileges, direct or indirect, on the basis of religion or belief, is an offense subject to prosecution according to the law.

ARTICLE 15. Protection of religious sites

Willful actions aimed at destroying, damaging or profaning objects of religious worship and other religious symbols, objects, buildings and places, including those for the repose of human remains, are prohibited and subject to prosecution according to the law.

ARTICLE 16. Religious hatred

It is prohibited for any person or persons to give public expression to views intended to incite religious hatred or likely to disturb the peace.

ARTICLE 17. Civil actions

Any person subject to discrimination on the basis of religion or belief or to religious hatred may bring a civil action for damages and/or to enjoin such discrimination.

COMMENTARY ON THE MODEL LAW

Article 1. Statement of legislative purpose. Most texts on religious liberty were originally written to neutralize social conflict over doctrinal debates within the same religion. In the United States and in Western Europe, legal provisions protected minority Christian denominations from the dominant group. The practices of other religions were generally not included or even considered. Today, in spite of occasional government claims,[8] states are invariably heterogeneous, composed of different racial, ethnic, cultural, and religious groups. Such diversity throughout the world presents each country with far more complex and thorny issues of religious liberty. Instead of doctrinal disputes over transubstantiation and papal infallibility, current religious conflicts may involve

[8] In a strangely contradictory message to the Special Rapporteur on religious intolerance, the government of Saudi Arabia reported "The population of Saudi Arabia is 100 percent of the Islamic faith. Non-Muslims in Saudi Arabia are free to practice their own faith in their own homes." Report on Religious Intolerance, UN Doc. E/CN.4/1990/46 of 22 January 1990, at 25.

animal sacrifices, the status of women, religious objection to patriotic or civic duties, differences of dress, diet, days of rest and worship.

Facing such diversity, each state must decide how to maintain the social cohesiveness necessary to function. It could impose by law the views and beliefs of its dominant group or it could seek to reflect the pluralism of its society. It could also reject notions of group values and recognize only the claims and rights of individuals.[9] International protection of religious liberty expresses pluralistic values, protecting both the individual and the group. It calls for legal guarantees of individual religious belief, but also for free exercise of religion by the communities of believers. It embraces differences, calling for their conservation based on mutual respect and cooperation. Carrying out that approach, the Model Law aims to create norms by which diverse and often competitive groups can retain their distinct identities and coexist.

The Model Law is drafted to conform to international human rights standards on religious liberty. Protection of religious liberty is contained in all general human rights treaties: the International Covenant on Civil and Political Rights,[10] the American Convention on Human Rights,[11] the European Convention for the Protection of Human Rights and Fundamental Freedoms,[12] and the African Charter on Human and People's Rights.[13]

In addition to the provisions of international treaties, other texts contain guarantees of religious liberty. Some are general, including the Universal Declaration of Human Rights.[14] Others, most significantly the United Nations Declaration on the Elimination of Intolerance and Discrimination Based on Religion or Belief, detail specific aspects of religious liberty, while providing that nothing in the Declaration can be read to re-

---

[9] See V. Tumin & W. Plotch, eds., *Pluralism in a Democratic Society* (New York, 1977); R. Havignhurst, *Anthropology and Cultural Pluralism: Three Case Studies, Australia, New Zealand, and USA* (New York, 1974); R. Post, "Cultural Heterogeneity and Law: Pornography, Blasphemy, and the First Amendment," *California Law Review* 76 (1988): 297. There can be conflict not only between the dominant group and other groups, but between a group and individual members of it. For example, compulsory education laws may be a threat to the continued existence of a traditional group like the Amish, but Amish prohibition on schooling after age fourteen may raise conflicts with the rights of children. This issue is discussed infra.

[10] International Covenant on Civil and Political Rights, adopted December 19, 1966, entered into force March 23, 1976, G.A. Res. 2200(XXI), 21 U.N. GAOR, Supp. (No. 16) 52, U.N. Doc. A/6316 (1966).

[11] American Convention on Human Rights, O.A.S.T.S.No. 36, at 1, OEA/Ser.L/V/II 23, Doc. 21, rev. 6 (1979).

[12] European Convention for the Protection of Human Rights and Fundamental Freedoms, signed Nov. 4, 1950, entered into force Sept. 3, 1953, 213 U.N.T.S. 222.

[13] African Charter on Human and Peoples' Rights, adopted June 27, 1981, entered into force Oct. 21, 1986, O.A.U. Doc. CAB/LEG/67/3 Rev. 5 (1981).

[14] G.A. Res. 217A (III), U.N. Doc. A/810, at 71 (1948).

strict or derogate from rights defined in the Universal Declaration or the Covenants.[15] Most recently, the Vienna follow-up meeting to the Helsinki Conference on Security and Cooperation in Europe agreed to language on the protection of religious liberty. Principle 16 of the Concluding Document provides that in order to ensure the freedom of the individual to profess and practice religion or belief, states must eliminate discrimination against individuals or communities on the grounds of religion or belief in the exercise of all human rights and fundamental freedoms, and ensure the effective equality of believers and non-believers.[16]

The Vienna text also requires states to: (1) respect the right of religious communities to establish and maintain freely accessible places of worship or assembly, organize themselves according to their own hierarchical and institutional structure, select, appoint and replace their personnel in accordance with their respective requirements and standards as well as with any freely accepted arrangement between them and their state, solicit and receive voluntary financial and other contributions; (2) respect the right of everyone to give and receive religious education in the language of his or her choice, individually or in association with others; (3) respect the liberty of parents to ensure the religious and moral education of their children in conformity with their own convictions; (4) allow the training of religious personnel in appropriate institutions; (5) respect the right of individual believers and communities of believers to acquire, possess, and use sacred books, religious publications, and other articles and materials in the language of their choice related to the practice of religion or belief; (6) allow religious faiths, institutions, and organizations to produce, import, and disseminate religious publications and materials; and (7) favorably consider the interest of religious communities in participating in public dialogue through mass media.

In general the Model Law takes as a basis the most expansive international statements. It also is based upon the principle that religious liberty means that the government should avoid penalizing or unduly burdening conduct required by religious belief or coercing or unduly encouraging conduct forbidden by religious belief, as long as the rights and freedoms of others are not infringed.[17] Its aims also include promoting tolerance and mutual respect among the diverse members of society.

Article 2. Definitions. Whether a group, body, activity, or individual is "religious" may be decisive in granting or denying certain privileges extended to protect religious liberty, for example, tax exemptions, and

---

15 Declaration on Religious Intolerance, art. 8.

16 CSCE supra n. 4.

17 See Jesse Choper, "The Religion Clauses of the First Amendment: Reconciling the Conflict," *University of Pittsburg Law Review* 41 (1980): 673.

exemption from governmental regulation. Some international human rights instruments protect religious freedom even during times of national emergency, when other human rights, including political rights, may be suspended.[18] In order to define entitlement to religious rights and privileges, the scope of "religion" must be determined.

Defining *"religion"* is probably the most difficult exercise in drafting a law for religious liberty. One scholar has concluded that "no definition of religion for constitutional purposes exists, and no satisfactory definition is likely to be conceived."[19] No definition appears in the UN Declaration on religious intolerance. The *travaux préparatoires* of the Declaration indicate consensus that it embraces theistic, non-theistic, and atheistic beliefs, and, further, that some understanding that belief systems that are fundamentally political, philosophical, historical, scientific, or aesthetic should be excluded. The UN Special Rapporteur on religious liberty offered a working definition of religion as "an explanation of the meaning of life and how to live accordingly. Every religion has at least a creed, a code of action, and a cult."[20] Scholars have attempted other definitions. James Nafziger proposes "a practice of ultimate concern about our nature and obligations as human beings, inspired by experience and typically expressed by members of a group or community sharing myths and doctrines whose authority transcends both individual conscience and the state."[21]

Any definition adequately inclusive is likely to be so broad as to be nearly useless. However, the drafters of the Model Law decided to include a definition for several reasons. First, in every legal system that protects religious liberty in any manner, someone is deciding who is included and who is excluded in the guarantees and privileges afforded. The question is who should decide: the legislature, the judiciary or the executive? Many states, especially those with common law systems, leave it to the judiciary. However, in states that lack strong traditions of an independent and competent judiciary, it may be important to limit the discretion of judges to exclude religious groups from protection, by

[18] See, e.g., American Convention on Human Rights, Art. 27, which lists Article 12 on religious liberty as one of the articles that may not be suspended.

[19] Philip Johnson, "Concepts and Compromise in First Amendment Religious Doctrine," *California Law Review* 72 (1984): 817, 832.

[20] U.N. Doc. E/CN.4/Sub.2/1987/26, p. 4. Similarly, the United States Congress has adopted a definition of "religious training and belief" for the 1967 Military Service Act that excludes "essentially political, sociological, or philosophical views, or a merely personal moral code." 50 U.S.C. sec. 456 (1982).

[21] James A.R. Nafziger, "The Functions of Religion in the International Legal System," in Mark W. Janis, ed., *The Influence of Religion on the Development of International Law* (Dordrecht, 1991), 147, 150.

providing a broad legislative definition of religion. Even in the best of cases, judges frequently are members of the dominant culture or religion in a given society and have cultural if not legal biases.[22] Second, in states with strong statutory traditions limiting judges to applying the law as written, a definition, however defective, may be necessary. Third, in many countries, ministries or departments of religion and religious affairs are given discretion to register or approve religions. Only those approved by these executive departments benefit from religious liberty. Ideally, such authorities should be abolished as incompatible with religious liberty; at a minimum, their discretionary powers should be sharply reduced by including a broad legislative definition of religion and guarantees of judicial review of all decisions they make.

The concept of religious liberty points towards an expansive definition of "religion" in order not to omit groups that may not meet the majority (defining) group's expectations about religion. Any definitional constraint involves the danger of discrimination and bias against unknown or unpopular religions, precisely those in greatest need of legal protection. The state is obliged to protect the rights of individuals to have and propagate their religious beliefs and to put these beliefs into practice. The problem is to find a definition of religion that avoids the dangers of discriminatory bias and yet distinguishes meaningfully between religions and non-religious beliefs, conduct and bodies.

Courts in common law countries have struggled with articulating a definition and establishing appropriate criteria to determine religious beliefs. Most have rejected the idea of any inquiry into the "truth" or "falsity" of beliefs claimed to be religious, stating that there is no heresy in law.[23] Most have also affirmed that religion is broader than theistic beliefs.

The United States Supreme Court has adopted a test that looks to the sincerity of beliefs and the function they play in the adherent's life. In *United States v. Seeger*,[24] the court concluded that "[a] sincere and meaningful belief which occupies in the life of its possessor a place parallel to that filled by the God of those admittedly qualifying for the exemption [from military service] comes within the statutory definition."[25] There is an inevitable subjectivity built into the definition, when it inquires into

---

[22] See A. Bradney, *Religions, Rights, and Laws* (Leicester, 1993) for a discussion of bias in the application of laws relating to religion in England.

[23] "The courts are constrained to accord freedom to faith in the supernatural, for there are no means of finding upon evidence whether a postulated tenet of supernatural truth is erroneous. . . ." *Church of the New Faith v. Commissioner for Pay-roll Tax* (1983), 57 ALJR 785.

[24] 380 U.S. 163 (1965).

[25] Ibid., 176.

whether the beliefs are "in [the holder's] scheme of things, religious."[26] In *Welsh v. United States*,[27] a plurality of the court elaborated that "the central consideration in determining whether the registrant's beliefs are religious is whether these beliefs play the role of a religion and function as a religion in the registrant's life."[28] It is not clear how this avoids the problem of defining religion, because it would seem that to know whether beliefs "play the role of religion" it is necessary to know what religion is in the first place.

In Australia, the High Court has stated two criteria: (1) belief in a supernatural Being, Thing or Principle; and (2) the acceptance of canons of conduct in order to give effect to that belief."[29] The concept of "supernatural" seems key to the definition. According to one commentator, the court's definition encompasses a metaphysical concept of the transcendental order, beyond the bounds of individuals and of the physical world, and an epistemological concept of non-empirical cognition.[30] The court distinguishes between what might be called scientific knowledge and matters of faith, that is, supernatural. The use of this distinction to qualify religion has been criticized as being both under-inclusive and over-inclusive.[31]

The underlying purpose of legal protection must be kept in mind in any definition: it is to avoid governmentally-sanctioned orthodoxy, leaving the choice of belief systems to individuals without consequent penalties or privileges. In this regard, limiting definitions that are imposed from outside the believer may run afoul of the goal of protecting individual beliefs. Given this, the functional test of *Seeger* may be appropriate.

The definition in the Model Law is comprehensive and inclusive; some may find that it does not distinguish religious belief from non-religious belief. In this regard, it may be open to criticism. However, once again, the primary problem to be redressed by a definition is the exclusion of many religious groups from recognition around the world.[32]

---

26 Ibid., 185.

27 398 U.S. 333 (1970).

28 Ibid., 339.

29 *Church of the New Faith*, 57 ALJR 785, 789 (1983).

30 W. Sadurski, "On Legal Definitions of 'Religion'," 63 *Australian Law Journal* (1993): 834, 837.

31 Ibid., 838-839 notes that some Eastern religions and Protestant theologians postulate a non-supernatural notion of religion. In contrast, several philosophical and ideological belief systems general thought of as non-religious could meet the test.

32 Italy, among other countries, does not recognize the Church of Scientology and is prosecuting various members for ordinary criminal offenses. Spain has also brought charges against the group under its penal code and does not recognize it as a religion. Several Islamic

There is far less problem with over-inclusiveness. To the extent the proposed definition opens the way to bogus claims, objective tests of the sincerity of the beliefs may help limit abuse.

The definition of *"discrimination"* in the Model Law is based upon the definition of discrimination contained in international texts, in particular the 1981 UN Declaration on Religious Intolerance, the Convention on the Elimination of All Forms of Racial Discrimination,[33] and the Convention on the Elimination of All Forms of Discrimination against Women.[34]

The United Nations Charter speaks of human rights and fundamental freedoms "without distinction as to . . . religion." All human rights texts echo this norm. States are required to take effective measures to prevent and eliminate discrimination based on religion or belief, including adoption of legislation where necessary. Children, as well as adults, must be protected from discrimination based on religion or belief.

Complaints of religious discrimination increase with religious diversity, when "neutral" laws run afoul of at least one group's religious beliefs. They center on the degree of accommodation that should be made to exempt minority religions from "secular" laws reflect the values of the dominant culture/religion. This issue is discussed in regard to articles 4 and 5 below.

Article 3. Guarantee of freedom of religion and belief. The provisions of article 3 contain guarantees for both religious beliefs and practices. The Model Law follows the Universal Declaration of Human Rights and the Declaration on Religious Intolerance in stating that religious liberty includes the right to freely adopt, reject, or change a religion or belief.[35]

The freedom to have a religion means that the government does not prescribe orthodoxy or prohibit particular religions or beliefs. In practice, this is not always the case. Among the examples that may be cited, Indonesia bans the Jehovah's Witness religion because of "its aggressive manner in propagating its teachings, trying to convert other adherents to

---

countries do not recognize the Baha'is and states in several regions of the world exclude Jehovah's Witnesses.

[33] International Convention for the Elimination of All Forms of Racial Discrimination, opened for signature March 7, 1966, entered into force January 4, 1969, 660 U.N.T.S. 195.

[34] Convention on the Elimination of All Forms of Discrimination against Women, adopted Dec. 18, 1979, entered into force Sept. 3, 1981, G.A. Res. 34/180, 34 U.N. GAOR Supp. (No. 46) 193, U.N. Doc. A/RES/34/180 (1980).

[35] See, Declaration on Religious Intolerance, Art. 1 (everyone has the right to freedom of through, conscience and religion, including "freedom to have a religion or whatever belief of his choice"; "no one shall be subject to coercion which would impair" the freedom to choose a religion or belief).

this faith."[36] According to the government, "misleading cults" are banned in order to maintain peace and harmony between and among adherents of the various religions. "Without the Government's handling in the matter, the activities of 'cults' (including Jehovah's Witnesses and Baha'is) may create disturbances and disrupt the existing religious tolerance."[37] Similar justifications are put forward by other states that ban specific religions.[38] In some countries, coercion is employed to force renunciation of banned religions.[39]

Short of banning, laws may severely interfere with minority religions. In Pakistan, the Ahmadis are prevented by law from calling themselves Muslims and using Muslim practices in worship or in the public manifestations of their faith.[40]

Both bans and restrictions may be imposed when the state is viewed as the beneficiary or object of religious liberty. The Saudi Arabian government states "[o]ur view is that freedom of religion (which is a basic issue in the Universal Declaration of Human Rights) has double edges: (a) The freedom *of any country* to adhere to, protect and preserve its religion. (b) The respect and tolerance towards religious minorities of the country's citizens as long as they respect the constitutional tenets of their country."[41]

Among the protections afforded by the Model Law, the most controversial is likely to be the right to convert and the right of members of religious groups to attract new adherents through conversions. The Universal Declaration on Human Rights explicitly provides that freedom of religion "includes the freedom to change [one's] religion or convictions." In spite of this, some countries imprison or kill individuals for converting from one religion to another. For example, the Sudanese

---

36 *Report on Religious Intolerance,* 20. Indonesian law is based on the Constitution which stipulates that "the State shall be based upon belief in the One Supreme God," and which guarantees every resident the freedom to adhere to his respective religion and to perform his own religious duties in conformity with that faith. Ibid., 39. However, Article 1 of Law No. 1/PNPS/1965 on the Prevention of Abuse and/or the Defiling of Religions, prohibits anyone from deliberately making interpretations of any of the recognized religions in Indonesia or publicly engaging in activities which deviate from those religions; such interpretations and activities being contrary to, and deviating from the true teachings of those religions. Ibid., 40. Based on this, the Baha'i faith is banned in Indonesia "since its teaching and practices are contrary to, and deviating from the teachings of Islam." Ibid.

37 Ibid.

38 Cuba forbids the Jehovah's Witnesses as "an unlawful association, whose members are known for their anti-social behavior and who, in many cases, even engage in incitement to break the law and in the desecration of patriotic emblems...." *Report on Religious Intolerance,* E/CN.4/1993/62, at 25 [hereafter *1993 Report on Religious Intolerance*].

39 Ibid., 78.

40 Ibid., 81.

41 Ibid., 85 (emphasis added).

Criminal Act 1991 provides that every Muslim who propagates for the renunciation of the Creed of Islam or publicly declares his renunciation thereof commits apostasy and is punishable by death.[42] In Malaysia, where Islam is the religion of state, the Constitution provides that state law may control or restrict the propagation of non-Islamic religions among Muslims.[43]

The Model Law explicitly provides that every person has the right to adopt or renounce a religion and the right to change religions. It protects the beliefs of all individuals and manifestations of this belief. It does not support laws or practices that ban or declare illegal religious groups or organizations. Of course, individual conduct may be subject to properly enacted criminal or civil laws. In this regard, conflicts between individual beliefs or manifestations thereof and the dominant norms of society must be resolved by applying the limitations clause contained in Article 6 in light of Article 3.

Article 4. Protection against compulsion. The essential element of religious liberty is freedom from coercion in matters of religion or belief. This article thus begins with a general protection against being compelled to adhere to a religion or participate in religious activities. In addition, Article 4 protects individual privacy in matters of religion and belief in order to protect against forced declarations of religion or belief. Such compulsion not only violates religious liberty but also the right to privacy and has been basic to many cases of religious discrimination.

The remainder of the article provides for exemptions from particular laws that would otherwise compel behavior in violation of religion or belief. Laws often mandate specific behavior: payment of taxes, wearing of particular clothing (school uniforms, hard hats on construction sites, motorcycle helmets), military or civic service, attendance in school. Where such compelled conduct would violate religious beliefs, adherents may ask to be exempted as a matter of religious liberty. The problem is to reconcile religious dictates with the need for uniformity to fulfill the purposes of the law and with general requirements of equality of treatment.

---

42 Ibid., 89. In contrast to the law, many Muslim scholars state that freedom of religion implies that non-Muslims are free, not compelled, to convert to Islam and may not be hindered from practicing their own religious rites. Although the Shari'a does not distinguish between legal and religious norms, meaning religion, politics, law and economics are inseparable, all religionists are free to propagate their own religion and defend it against attack. See Mohammed Hashim Kamali, "Freedom of Religion in Islamic Law," *Capital University Law Review* 21 (1992): 63. Compulsion in religion is seen as prohibited by the Qur'an, thus, laws that prescribe penalties for apostasy are not dictated by religious doctrine. See Ibid., 65-67 for a general discussion of the conflict over the meaning of various Islamic legal sources touching on the subject of conversion from one religion to another.

43 *1993 Report on Religious Intolerance*, 25.

Various approaches can be taken to this very difficult subject. Religious objectors might be entitled to exemptions from generally applicable laws when there is a (substantial) burden on the observance of a central religious belief or practice without compelling governmental reasons. Alternatively, the range of exceptions may be narrower, permitted only where the government intends to coerce conformity to a dominant religious belief and enacts specifically religious laws. Third, there could be a very broad presumption of diversity and pluralism, with few laws generally applicable.

The present article does not contain a general exemption provision, although Article 5 calls for "reasonable" accommodation of religion in employment, school, the military, and prisons. The drafters' view is that neutral government regulations—ones that do not demand adherence to religion in general or a religion in particular—should generally apply to all persons in society. However, certain exemptions are recognized, where the governmental interest can be served by other means and where the demands of the law are particularly onerous on religious objectors. Thus, exemption is provided for those whose religious beliefs prohibit taking oaths. Oaths, including pledges of allegiance to secular political symbols, demand proclamations of belief that are akin to demanding profession of a religion. In the case of courtroom testimony, declarations of truth are adequate to serve the governmental interest without compelling individuals to violate their religious beliefs by swearing an oath.

A more controversial issue is the exemption from armed military service, provided in Article 4. Although many countries do not recognize the right of conscientious objection, both the special rapporteur on religious intolerance and a UN report prepared by two members of the Sub-Commission on Prevention of Discrimination and Protection of Minorities recommend that all states recognize conscientious objection to military service as a legitimate exercise of the right to freedom of thought, conscience and religion. Further, countries should consider introducing various forms of alternative service for conscientious objectors which are compatible with the reasons for their objection.[44]

Finally, special mention is made of the right of students not to be compelled to participate in religious activities or to receive religious instruction. Article 4 also provides, however, that no student is exempt

---

[44] See *Report on Implementation of the Declaration on the Elimination of All Forms of Intolerance and of Discrimination Based on Religion or Belief*, UN Doc E/CN.4/1989/44 of 30 December 1988, and *Conscientious Objection to Military Service: Report Prepared in Pursuance of Resolutions 14 (XXXIV) and 1982/30 of the Sub-Commission on Prevention of Discrimination and Protection of Minorities* (UN Pub E.85.XIV.1).

from the normal academic program of a school. In this regard, difficult issues arise where normal activities or requirements of the school, including dress codes, compel a student to act in contravention of religious beliefs. Clearly, the state has a legitimate interest in conducting a consistent and comprehensive educational program. If the religious beliefs result in seeking exemptions that would substantially disrupt the educational program or interfere with the rights of other students, the authorities may decide that exemption is not warranted, especially if alternative schooling is available that conforms to the religious dictates of the students. Rather than attempt to anticipate all the cases where exemptions may be claimed, the Model Law explicitly calls for only two in Article 4. Article 5, on manifestations of religion or belief, contains a more general provision that everyone has the right "to have reasonable accommodation in employment, in military or alternative service, schools and prisons, for manifestations of their religion or belief."[45]

Article 5. Manifestations of Religion or Belief. All the manifestations referred to in international documents are detailed here. In addition, measures are included to redress particular forms of abuse that have been encountered in various states. Until recently in many countries it was forbidden to pray in private or in public. Public worship was prevented by closing or converting to other uses places of worship and religious meetings. In one state, possession of photographs of a spiritual leader led to arrests; displaying articles of faith was held illegal. Limitations on religious publications exist in several countries. Teaching is often strictly controlled because of the impact it may have on young minds. Financial contributions have been seized and collections controlled. In a number of countries, state authorities designate religious officials and clergy. In one state, all clergymen must obtain a license issued by the state and all promotions must be approved by the authorities.

It may be difficult in some instances to separate the exercise of religion from the exercise of civil and political rights. States that restrict religious groups often suppress other significant social and economic organizations. Other states discriminate against ethnic minorities, whose differences include religions different from the majority faith. In both cases, religious organizations are likely to become focal points for both political and religious opposition to the state and thus be correctly perceived as a threat to the dominant power. Nonetheless, Article 5 guaran-

[45] For example, laws mandating motorcycle or bicycle helmets may exempt Sikhs from the requirement and school regulations may permit wearing of religious symbols or dress. In each case it must be determined whether the accommodation demanded is reasonable. It may be noted that in *Mandla (Sewa Singh) v. Dowell Lee, Weekly Law Reports* 3 (1982), 932, an English court held that to require a Sikh pupil to wear a cap as part of a school uniform would discriminate against him on the ground of race.

tees the right of individuals to carry out in daily life the tenets of their religion or belief. Independently, religious adherents have civil and political rights that are not waived or compromised because of their religious beliefs.

Several other provisions of Article 5 deserve mention. Paragraph (h) guarantees the right to propagate religion or belief through teaching and observance. Linked to this, paragraph (l) provides the right to discuss or criticize any religion or belief and its practices. Together, these provisions apply to religion the broad guarantees of freedom of speech. They open to public discourse and persuasion, without fear of government sanction, all matters of belief and opinion, subject to Article 16 on incitement to religious hatred.

The relationship of parents, state, and children in regard to religious education is contained in paragraph (m). The Declaration on Religious Intolerance, Article 5, and human rights treaties guarantee to parents the right to organize their family life in accordance with their religion or belief. This may be considered not only an aspect of religious liberty, but of the right to privacy and family life. Parents may dictate the religious education of their children and ensure that the children are not compelled to receive teaching that is contrary to the wishes of the parent or guardian.

The potential for conflict between religious beliefs and welfare of children is balanced in the Declaration by providing that "practices of a religion or beliefs in which a child is brought up must not be injurious to his physical or mental health or to his full development; limitations may be imposed in this regard, the best interests of the child being the guiding principle." The potential for abuse by a dominant religion and by parents whose adolescent or adult children may choose another belief system is obvious. Conflicts are inevitable between the state and parents, and between both and children, over issues of religion and belief. No provision has been included in this law that would allow parental "kidnapping" or other efforts to remove adult young people from new religious groups. The strong presumption is in favor of parental control of religion during minority; the state would need to demonstrate that any limitation on religious liberty is prescribed by law and necessary in a democratic society for the protection of the rights of the child.

It is worth noting that the Declaration on Religious Intolerance contains its own belief system. It requires that children be brought up "in a spirit of understanding, tolerance, friendship among peoples, peace and universal brotherhood, respect for freedom of religion or belief of others, and in full consciousness that his energy and talents should be devoted to the service of his fellow men" (Article 5(3)).

Article 6. Relations between the state and religion. There are almost unlimited varieties of religion-state relations. Paradigms include: (1) state control over religion, either allowing doctrinal dissent or determining the correctness of competing views; (2) state neutrality regarding religious affairs, where no privileged relationship exists between the state and any particular religion, although the religious in general may be allowed certain exemptions from law not afforded the non-religious; few countries actually have such a neutral system; (3) theocratic states where the dominant religion controls both the religious and secular sphere of society; (4) state hostility to all religion, which may result in expulsion of clergy and religious orders, seizure of property and prohibition of religious activities; and (5) state division of authority with religions, where religions are granted a range of control over activities—from determining personal status (marriage and divorce) to controlling the succession of the head of state—that others consider secular. Determining the boundaries of each realm is not easy.[46]

States may shift at different points from one to another form of relationship, and conflict between religion and state can be compounded by conflict among religions. It may even be that the latter is most often the origin of the former. Some churches have actively sought state protection for declining membership and resources. They may involve the state in collecting tithes or "contributions" and in maintaining membership. In most cases state involvement is limited to larger "recognized" religious groups. This allows existing churches to obtain a competitive advantage over newer or missionary religions that threaten membership bases and financial resources.

The constitutions of some states establish the primacy of a religion over the state, granting privileges that are incompatible with religious liberty and non-discrimination. Even in states with excellent human rights records, links between religion and state pose problems.[47] In Nor-

---

[46] It is rather like the problem in restrictive sovereign immunity in international law. To decide whether a state is amenable to suit, the appropriate nature and scope of "governmental" conduct must be determined.

[47] Italy and the Vatican approved a concordat in 1927, revised and reaffirmed in 1984, that recognized Catholicism as the religion of the Italian people. The state requires episcopal nominees to be Italian nationals. Religious education was required in Italian state schools with the possibility for opting out. Boundary changes in dioceses were subject to civil approval. Canon law was granted the force of civil law in some areas. Non-Catholic churches could operate in Italy with the approval of the state. The state supports the church through a system of voluntary taxation where citizens may opt to support the church with additional payment in their taxes. Under the revised concordat, Protestant children were required to take another class in school if they opted out of Catholic religion classes. The Italian Constitutional Court ruled this discriminatory and agreed with those contesting the requirement that the children should be released from school instead.

way,[48] the king and a majority of the cabinet are required to be members of the state church. Christianity is still a mandatory subject in the Norwegian public schools. Nonconformists have been permitted to teach it since 1969 as long as they do so in accordance with evangelical Lutheran doctrine.[49] Only in 1964 was the constitution amended to guarantee all inhabitants the free exercise of religion. A 1969 Law Concerning Religious Denominations extends the right to form denominations and stipulates that groups registered with the Department of Justice may receive financial aid from both the national and municipal governments on the same basis as parishes of the state church in proportion to their membership statistics. The majority remains opposed to disestablishment of the state church. It is seen as "a public institution in which membership does not require a commitment of faith and which presently has approximately equal numbers of atheists and 'personal Christians' on its rolls."[50]

In England, the Anglican Church remains at the center of public policy and has substantial support from the state. Prime ministers appoint bishops and the House of Lords contains 26 Anglican bishops who are the lords spiritual. The Parliament can rule on doctrinal and liturgical matters—most recently on the issue of ordination of women. Although there may be little real intervention in the internal affairs of the church, its strongly privileged position can be seen to discriminate against minority religions.

State budgets provide for some religious denominations in Spain, Italy, Greece, Belgium, and Luxembourg. Religious taxes exist in Austria, Switzerland, Denmark, Germany, Norway, and Finland. Indirect support is provided in France, Great Britain, the Netherlands, and Sweden.

Established religions exist in all parts of the world. In Africa, the constitutions of the Comores, Mauritania, Libya, and Somalia proclaim Islam as the religion of the state. Libya also declares that "the Holy Koran is the constitution of the Socialist People's Libyan Arab Jamahiriya."[51] In the Sudan, all legislation must conform to Islamic prescriptions.[52] The head of state must be a Muslim, and non-Muslims are incompetent to testify

---

[48] See Frederick Hale, "The Development of Religious Freedom in Norway" *Journal of Church and State* 23 (1981): 47, 56.

[49] Ibid., 64.

[50] Ibid., 66-67.

[51] Declaration of the Establishment of the People (1981), Article 2.

[52] Religiously-based punishments must still be tested by the international prohibition on torture and cruel, inhuman and degrading punishment. See Universal Declaration of Human Rights, Art. 5; International Covenant on Civil and Political Rights, Art. 7; African Charter on Human and Peoples Rights, Article 5.

against Muslims. Propagation of heretical beliefs is a crime.[53] In contrast, the constitution of Botswana specifically recognizes the individual's right to propagate his religion.[54] Proselytizing or converting others is permissible.[55]

Subordination of religion to the state can have pernicious effects on religious liberty equal to those in states where the government is subordinate to religion. Revolutionary governments sometimes repress religious activities, providing that no one may invoke religious liberty "to hinder the state in its work of establishing the socialist order."[56]

Some states limit the political activities of clergy or religious officials, on the pretext of maintaining the separation of religion and state.[57] Such exclusionary laws have sometimes placed legislatures or courts in the position of deciding who constitutes "clergy" or officials of religion.[58]

Mexico's constitution contains some of the more restrictive provisions. Its articles provide that no minister of any faith may be a candidate for elected office. Article 130 provides that ministers cannot form associations for political purposes or rally in favor of or against any candidate, political party or association. Neither can they oppose the laws of the country or its institutions, or attack in any way the patriotic symbols in their public meetings, religious ceremonies, religious propaganda or

---

[53] A leader of the Muslim Republican Brotherhood demanded repeal of the apostasy law as a distortion of Islam. He was publicly executed as a heretic in January 1985; his property was confiscated, and he was prohibited burial at a Muslim graveyard. See Moyiga Koroto Nduru, "Taha's Martyrdom," *New African* (March, 1985): 28.

[54] Constitution of Botswana, section 11(1).

[55] Among other provisions, section 11(2) permits a religious organization to establish and maintain educational institutions "at its own expense." The Education Act provides that religious instruction may be given at school but the parent of any student may request that the student be excused. Ministers of religion have the right of access, at such reasonable times as may be agreed on with the school administration, to any school for the purpose of providing religious instruction to students whose parents profess to be members of his religious group and who have not objected to this. If a parent desires the student to attend religious worship or receive religious instruction of a kind not provided at the school, the school administration must make arrangements as may be practicable to allow this at the parents' expense. Laws of Botswana, Chapter 58:01, section 23(1).

[56] Constitution of Madagascar, Art. 1. During one period in Equatorial Guinea, Francisco Macias Nguema required all religious services to begin "in the name of the president and his son." He ultimately banned the Roman Catholic Church to which 80 percent of the citizens belonged.

[57] The Liberian constitution disqualifies any person from holding any political office while he is serving as the leader of a religious denomination or faith. See Daniel Nsereko, "Religion, the State and the Law in Africa," *Journal of Church and State* 28 (1986): 269, 271.

[58] The exclusion was abolished in the state of Georgia in the United States after a Baptist minister who was delegate to a constitutional revision conference proposed amending the provision to disqualify lawyers from sitting in the legislature. Neither exclusion was included in the new constitution. See Reba C. Strickland, *Religion and the State in Georgia in the Eighteenth Century* (New York, 1939), 165.

publications. It is strictly forbidden to establish any kind of political associations. It is also forbidden to hold political meetings in the churches.[59] Implementing legislation approved in July 1992 subjects the churches to strong state intervention.[60]

Such laws may be seen as an improper burden on the exercise of religion. They deprive religious adherents of civil and political rights or make them choose between religious beliefs and political participation in the society in which they live. Rather than legislating such incompatibility, the issue is better left to the voters and religious institutions. They may decide whether holding secular office is a proper function of religious officials.

The Model Law proposes a system in which there is no official or established religion. Religious organizations and matters of religion are deregulated. Such a system promotes individual freedom of choice, basing religious affiliation on personal affinities rather than state-sanctioned inducements and coercion.[61] In many states, it would result in elimination of excessive costs imposed on those joining dissenting groups who now face the double financial burden of supporting the state religion plus paying for their religion of choice. Deregulation should also increase individual and local control over the religion, with more power to the laity. The result may be a reinforcement of democratic principles, as religious organizations are forced to be responsive to the needs of the community they serve if they wish to maintain their resources. Without state support, religious groups must actively seek recruits. Historically, this has actually resulted in an increase in numbers of members, rather than a decline.[62]

In theory it might be possible to have a non-coercive and non-discriminatory statement of religious affiliation by the majority in a state ("this is a Christian community"). However, in practice it does not ap-

---

[59] Ministry of the Interior, Diario Oficial, "Decreto por elque se reforman los art. 3, 5, 24, 130 y se adiciona el Art. 17 Transitorio de la Constitucion Poletica de los Estados Unidos Mexicanos," 28 January 1992. Constitutional amendments approved in 1991 do now allow religious teaching in private schools, the formation of religious orders, public worship, church ownership of property and the right to vote for priests. Government approval remains mandatory for all public worship outside churches and should involve "very special circumstances."

[60] Catholic bishops criticized it for attributing excessive and discretionary decision-making to the Interior Ministry. Among other things, the law requires registration of churches with the Ministry and prohibits ownership of mass media.

[61] Some argue that deregulation promotes religious individualism and strength of religious commitment, because for a religious organization to survive it must attract adherents in the open market, without the competitive advantage of state support. See Roger Finke, "Religious Deregulation: Origins and Consequences," *Journal of Church and State* 32 (1990): 609-26; John G. Francis, "The Evolving Regulatory Structure of European Church-State Relationships", *Journal of Church and State* 34 (1992): 775-804.

[62] Finke, "Religious Deregulation," 622-23.

pear that there is any state with an established or official religion that fails to award substantial legal benefits to the established religion. The inevitable result is coercive to dissidents and a violation of religious liberty.

According to paragraph (c), the government may aid religious organizations. However, aid should be given to programs. It should be neutral, not based on who the recipient is, but on what the money is to be used for. Similarly, religious beliefs should be accommodated when there is no meaningful threat to individual religious liberty. Thus, the government can erect a nativity scene during the Christmas season or a menorah during Hannukah. Coercion involves providing tax benefits to sustain a state-established faith, compelled observance, or governmental proselytizing in favor of religion. The law should be less concerned with reinforcing the views of the dominant religion and more protective of those without the numbers and influence to ensure significant and effective protection through the political process for their religious liberty.[63]

Paragraph (e) concerns limitations on the exercise of religious liberty. There can be no separation of freedom of religion from the protection afforded the exercise of other human rights. No right is absolute or unlimited. It is clear that some restrictions on human conduct, whether based on religious belief or not, are permissible in order to protect the rights and freedoms of others, including society at large.

Unfortunately, any law that provides an exception to the right it guarantees may be abused by those in power. To minimize this, the right should be detailed and broadly protected, as here, and exceptions should be narrowly drafted. Further, there must be the possibility of judicial review by an independent judiciary of any law or executive decision to apply the limitations clause against a particular religion or religious practice.

Regulation of religious activities, like other regulatory schemes, is a means to restrict abuses of power by the regulated institutions. Article 29 of the Universal Declaration of Human Rights provides the starting point for permissible limitations on religious liberty. Restrictions must be authorized by law and be required (necessary in a democratic society) (a) in the interests of defense, public safety, public order, public morality or public health; or (b) for the purpose of protecting the rights and freedoms of other persons.

Although an earlier draft of the Model Law contained a provision allowing organizations to be banned that promote, incite, or organize discrimination or hatred based on religion or belief, the present text omits

---

[63] See Jesse H. Choper, "Separation of Church and State: 'New' Directions by the 'New' Supreme Court," *Journal of Church and* State 34 (1992): 363, 366.

any provision that would target organizations as a whole rather than individual conduct. In general, such laws have been the source of considerable abuse of religious minorities. The Botswana Penal Code empowers the president to declare any society to be "a society dangerous to peace and order in Botswana."[64] It then becomes an offense to manage, assist in the management, or to be a member of such a society.[65] Under similar provisions, religious groups have been declared "dangerous" in Angola, Ethiopia, Ghana,[66] Malawi, Mozambique, Uganda, Tanzania, Zaire, and Zambia.[67] The Code similarly empowers the president to declare any publication prohibited which he considers "contrary to the public interest."[68] Similar provisions have led to seizures of religious materials, particularly those of Jehovah's Witnesses.[69]

Some states limit the religious activities of foreigners, although this should also be prohibited. In China, the constitution provides: "No one may make use of religion to engage in activities that disrupt public order, impair the health of citizens or interfere with the educational system of the State. Religious bodies or religious affairs are not subject to any foreign domination."[70] In addition: "No one may use religion to promote activities detrimental to the social order, injurious to citizens' health or liable to hamper the state educational system. Religious groups and activities may not be controlled by foreign powers."[71]

Provision of medical care is a case where religious liberty may be infringed for the protection of the rights of others. The UN Declaration on Religious Intolerance proclaims the child's welfare to be the paramount consideration in issues of religious liberty. It may be necessary to regu-

---

[64] Penal Code, Section 66(2)(b).

[65] Ibid. section 68.

[66] In Ghana, the military government passed a law in 1989, PNDC Law 221, the Religious Bodies Registration Law. Section 3 provided that "every religious body in Ghana shall be registered under this law and no religious body in existence in Ghana shall after three months from the commencement of the Law operate as such unless it is registered under this Law." Responsibility for the enforcement of the law was entrusted to the Religious Affairs Committee of the National Commission for Culture. The Committee's decisions are final and not appealable to any courts of law. The aim of the law was said to be to protect members of the public from "too many bogus churches" and to control corruption. "Ghana: Official Attacks on Religious Freedom," *News from Africa Watch* (18 May 1990).

[67] See Nsereko, "Religion, the State, and the Law in Africa," 269-87.

[68] Penal Code, section 47.

[69] See *Rex v. De Jeger*, [1931-37] Law Reports of Northern Rhodesia, 13 (prohibition of books containing "politico-religious propaganda").

[70] *Implementation of the Declaration on the Elimination or all Forms of Intolerance and of Discrimination Based on Religion or Belief*, Report submitted by Mr. Angel Vidal d'Almeida Ribeiro, Special Rapporteur appointed in accordance with Commission on Human Rights Resolution 1986/20 of 10 March 1986, E/CN.4/1993/62, at 10.

[71] Ibid., 11.

late charismatic leaders that proclaim the power of healing in order to prevent fraud and exploitation.

International texts that permit limitations on the exercise of rights indicate that the right is the rule, the limitation the exception. For this reason, the burden should be on the government to demonstrate with clear evidence the reasons for limiting religious liberty.

Article 12. Creation and administration of schools. The Model Law permits all religious groups to establish and maintain private schools, but requires that they maintain state standards in education, health, and safety. These laws serve to protect the rights of the children, as do the laws prohibiting discrimination in admissions and educational policy.

State practices are conflicting, although many states do freely permit schools to be founded by religious groups. In Botswana and several other states, the constitution provides that "every religious community shall be entitled, at its own expense, to establish and maintain places of education and to manage any place of education which it wholly maintains; and no such community shall be prevented from providing religious instruction for persons of that community in the course of any education provide at any place of education which it wholly maintains or in the course of any education which it otherwise provides."[72]

Article 13. Taxation of religious institutions. One of the key objections non-believers raise to government involvement with religion concerns use of taxation for sectarian purposes.[73] Does religious liberty require exemption from taxes or are such exemptions a breach of the neutrality required by the state in matters of religion and belief?

Tax exemptions for religions have long existed and are part of the legal traditions of many societies.[74] In others, ecclesiastical property, like all other property, was subject to taxation unless specifically exempted. In many cases, exemptions were given only to the property of state-established religions that was used for religious purposes. Minority religions were ineligible for tax exemption. Some laws exempt all charitable trusts and organizations, whether religiously based or not. These organizations perform activities deemed of benefit to society as a whole and provide substitute government services by maintenance of hospitals, educational institutions, museums, and other public services. Advancement of religion may itself be seen as a charitable, beneficial social pur-

---

72 Constitution of Botswana, Art. 11; see also Constitution of Kenya, Art. 78 .

73 Choper, "The Religion Clauses of the First Amendment," 677.

74 Recently, Hungary has agree to provide about 100 million dollars to 35 denominations over a three year period. According to a 1979 concordat between Spain and Vatican, and a 1984 concordat between Italy and the Vatican, citizens may donate a percentage of their income tax to the Catholic Church.

pose, providing moral cohesion and standards to the community and other similar benefits. Arguably the protections afforded religious liberty reflect the belief that religion is a social good; tax exemptions support this not because of individual liberty, but because "the religious and moral culture afforded by these societies is deemed to be beneficial to the public, necessary to the advancement of civilization and the promotion of the welfare of society."[75]

Exemptions for charitable, non-profit organizations are common and are generally drafted to include religious organizations within the broader term "charitable."[76] Where such statutes are non-discriminatory and do not single out any particular religious group or religion as a whole, there are few questions about state furtherance of religion or coercion of non-believers. Any state with a scheme of taxation, which is today universal, will face the question of taxing or exempting religious organizations and activities. In either event, there will be some degree of involvement with religion. Taxing religious property would require valuation of religious property, potential liens and foreclosures. It gives the state great power over religious activities and organizations. Exemptions require defining "religion" to determine entitlements to the exemptions;[77] there is also a risk that the state may decide to remove the exemptions if religious practices conflict with public policy.[78] Government evaluation of religious beliefs is generally to be avoided.

If exemptions are permitted, are they required? It appears they are not in the United States and in England, so long as the taxes are not exacted as a condition of exercising religious beliefs.[79] Commercial property and investments undertaken for profit may be taxed whatever use is

---

[75] Carl F.G. Zollmann, *American Civil Church Law* (New York, 1969), 647.

[76] See e.g. 26 U.S.C.A. 501(c)(3) (1989).

[77] Compare two cases in which persons claimed exemption from payment of social security taxes. The United States Internal Revenue Code, sec. 1402 (e), (h) (1988) permits ministers, members of religious orders and Christian Science practitioners to exempt themselves from payment of social security taxes on "self-employment income" and from and social security benefits if they are "conscientiously opposed to . . . the acceptance of" such benefits. Also laity and clergy may be exempt from such taxes if they are members of "a recognized religious sect" which rejects social insurance and looks after its own members' needs in old age and disability. Intended to cover monasteries and nunneries, the exemption was refused a petitioner who claimed to be a member of "the Body of Christ" and to preach the Gospel from his ice cream truck. The tax court rejected his claims because the statutory exemption was limited to recognized religious sects or divisions thereof. The holding places the government in the position of determining which religions or sects are "recognized."

[78] See *Bob Jones University v. United States*, 461 U.S. 574 (1983).

[79] See *Murdock v. Pennsylvania*, 319 U.S. 105 (1943), striking down a local ordinance that required a license tax prior to missionary activities. The Court found that "it is one thing to impose a tax on the income or property of a preacher. It is quite another thing to exact a tax from him for the privilege of delivering a sermon." Ibid., 113-14.

made of the income. Laying a tax directly on an essentially religious activity would burden the exercise of religion in an impermissible way. However, it has been argued that free exercise of religion requires such exemption because otherwise religious activities would be burdened. In addition, religious organizations would be forced to support activities that would violate their religious beliefs. Of course, the latter has not been held to permit individuals to withhold taxes.

Article 14-17. Offenses. There is enormous difficulty in identifying legitimate claims of harm caused by speech and conduct. Listeners may sometimes be protected from offensive speech, especially where they cannot avoid it. Lewd, obscene, profane, libelous, and insulting or "fighting" words have been seen as inflicting injury or tending to incite an immediate breach of the peace.[80] Moreover, it can be argued that they are not the exposition of ideas, that is, not properly a communication of information and opinion safeguarded by guarantees of freedom of expression.

Many countries go further and attempt to protect orthodoxy through laws against blasphemy.[81] In common law countries, blasphemy has been treated as a branch of criminal libel, akin to but different from obscenity, sedition, and defamation. Early blasphemy laws were most closely allied to sedition, because an attack on God and religion was viewed as equivalent to attacks on the social order which was based on an established religion.[82] In such systems, some of which remain today, it is not

---

[80] See e.g., the Botswana Penal Code which prohibits acts that constitute an insult to religion of any class of people. Laws of Botswana, Chapter 08:01, section 136. It prohibits disturbing of religious assemblies, trespassing on burial places, hindering the burial of dead bodies and "writing or uttering of any words with intent to wound religious feelings." Ibid., sections 137-140.

[81] In Pakistan, the constitution declares Islam the national religion. The Ahmadi sect denies one of the central tenets of Islam, the finality of the prophethood of Muhammad. The legislature added Article 260 to the Constitution which states that a person who does not believe in the absolute and unqualified finality of the prophethood of Muhammad or who claims to be a prophet, or who recognizes such a claimant is not a Muslim for purposes of the Constitution or law. Orthodoxy is thus prescribed by law. Acts offending the religious sentiments of any citizen are prohibited and are punishable under the Penal Code. For further discussion see the report of the UN Special Rapporteur on religious intolerance, E/CN.4/1985/45/Add.1, 25 February 1988.

[82] For example, it was earlier view that Christianity was parcel of the laws of England; therefore to reproach the Christian religion was to speak in subversion of the law. See *Taylor's Case*, 86 Eng. Rep. 189, 1 Vent. 293 (K.B. 1676). This approach was most clearly stated in Gathercole's Case, where the judge directed the jury that "A person may, without being liable to prosecution for it, attack Judaism, or Mahomedanism, or even any sect of the Christian Religion (save the established religion of the country); and the only reason why the latter is in a different situation from the others is, because it is the form established by law, and is therefore a part of the constitution of the country. In like manner, and for the same reason, any general attack on Christianity is the subject of criminal prosecution, because Christianity is the established religion of the country." *Gathercole's Case*, (1838) 2 Lewin 237, 254.

the manner of speech, but the content that is punished.[83] The law would offer no protection to minority religions; in fact, their teaching could be seen as in violation of the law.

By the nineteenth century, in most European countries it was no longer blasphemous to make a reasoned attack on the Christian religion; it had to be "a scurrilous vilification of that religion." If the tone and spirit is that of offense and insult and ridicule, which appeal to "the wild and improper feelings of the human mind, more particularly in the younger part of the community," then it is wrong: "This shift of policy seems to ignore the fact that reasoned and sober discussion is likely to have a greater effect in undermining religion than scurrilous insults which might be expected to be treated with the contempt they deserve."

Today's laws remain directed more at manner than substance. There is less question of heresy and more of respecting "the decencies of controversy" or of respect in general. This formulation tries to avoid the controversy that attends efforts to regulate the content of speech. However, it is often not possible to separate matter and manner. Moreover, it is the content that often offends. The style/content distinction is generally unworkable for these reasons and inequitable in punishing the inelegant or uneducated for views that others express without hindrance.[84]

Blasphemy laws are usually invoked where there is a state religion and attacks on it are deemed an attack on society; in this way it is similar to apostasy which is treated as a form of sedition.[85] In some states, genuine disputes over orthodoxy are permitted and the law represses only ridicule[86] or insult, akin to laws on breach of the peace and obscenity.

Many common law systems penalize blasphemy, although most do so by statute. Canada, New Zealand, and India have provisions in their Codes, although there are no reported recent cases. Canadian law provides that no one shall be convicted who in good faith and decent language attempts to establish by argument an opinion upon a religious

---

[83] In *Rex v. Woolston*, the Court of King's Bench stated: "the Christian religion is established in this kingdom; and therefore [it] would not allow any books to be writ, which should tend to alter that establishment." *Rex v. Woolston*, 94 Eng. Rep. at 113, 1 Barn. K.B. at 163.

[84] Attacks on Christianity by respected writers such as H.G. Wells and Bertrand Russell pass without prosecution, while similar content in cruder form risks violation of the law and punishment. See 234 Parl. Deb., H.C. (5th Ser.) 535 (1930) (remarks of Mr. Kingsley Griffith).

[85] See *The Law Commission Working Paper No. 79: Offenses Against Religion and Public* (1981), 5..

[86] In Scotland, blasphemy is a common law offense committed by the uttering of impious and profane things against God or the authority of the Holy Scriptures when it is done in a "scoffing or railing manner, out of a reproachful disposition in the speaker, and . . . with passion against the Almighty, rather than with any purpose of propagating the irreverent opinion." Ibid., 40.

subject.[87] Australian states retain the common law offence of blasphemous libel. The Indian Penal Code, section 298, provides that "[w]hoever, with the deliberate intention of wounding the religious feelings of any person, utters any word or makes any sound in the hearing of that person or makes any gesture in the sight of that person, or places any object in the sight of that person, shall be punished with imprisonment . . . for a term which may extend to one year, or with fine or with both."[88]

In civil law countries there is great variety. The German Penal Code, Article 196, penalizes anyone who, in public, or by publishing written, recorded, or pictorial material or representations insults in a manner likely to disturb the public peace either (a) religious or philosophical beliefs; or (b) any church in the country or other religious or philosophical society or their institutions or traditions. Neither the French nor Swedish penal codes contain provisions on this subject. The Norwegian code prohibits any word or deed that publicly insults or in an offensive or injurious way shows disdain for a religious creed permitted in Norway, or for the dogma or worship of any religious community lawfully existing there. The Greek code, Article 198-199, penalizes those who publicly and maliciously by any means blaspheme God and the Greek Orthodox Church or any other religion permitted in Greece. Article 173 of the Turkish code focuses on violation of religious services, but adds additional penalties on anyone who publishes material that humiliates or debases any religion or sect.

In *Gay News Ltd. & Lemon v. United Kingdom*[89] the European Commission of Human Rights found inadmissible a claim that the English common law offense of blasphemy violates the European Convention of Human Rights. The applicants had been convicted by a jury of the offense of common law libel for having "unlawfully and wickedly published or caused to be published a blasphemous libel concerning the Christian religion, namely an obscene poem and illustration vilifying Christ in His life and in His crucifixion."[90]

---

[87] Canadian Criminal Code, Section 260.

[88] Section 295A covers deliberate and malicious outrage on the religious feelings of any class of citizens of India by spoken or written words or by visible representations that insult or attempt to insult the religion or the religious beliefs of that class. Case law indicates that only clear and serious breaches of these provisions are prosecuted. See *Law Commission*, 49.

[89] Eur. Comm of H.R., *Gay News Ltd and Lemon v. United Kingdom,* (1983) 5 EHRR 123 (7 May 1982).

[90] The applicants were the publisher and editor of a magazine called "Gay News"; they had printed a poem and accompanying illustration ascribing promiscuous homosexual practices to Christ and describing in detail various sexual acts. Compare the 1991 Pakistani amendment to section 295C of the Penal Code which previously provided life imprisonment or the death penalty for the offence of defiling the name of the Prophet Mohammed. The amendment removed the option of life imprisonment, making the death penalty mandatory.

The applicants claimed, *inter alia*, that the conviction violated their freedom of expression guaranteed by Article 10 of the Convention, as well as their right to freedom of thought and religion contained in Article 9 of the Convention. In addition, they claimed that the interference with these freedoms was unjustified, not being necessary in a democratic society for any of the legitimate purposes enumerated in the Convention articles.[91]

The Commission agreed that the applicants' freedom of expression had been limited, but found the restriction justified, in the process accepting that the offense could be one of strict liability (that is, the prosecutors need only prove an intent to publish, not an intent to blaspheme). The grounds for the limitation invoked by the government were prevention of disorder, protection of morals, and protection of the rights of others. The first two were rejected by the Commission, because the authorities themselves did not institute the prosecution, finding no threat at the time. Instead, the case was initially brought by private prosecution and the justification had to be found in the protection of the complainant's rights. The Commission considered "that the offense of blasphemous libel as it is construed under the applicable common law in fact has the main purpose to protect the right of citizens not to be offended in their religious feelings by publications." There remained the question of necessity in a democratic society.

In this respect, the Commission first observed that the existence of an offense of blasphemy does not as such raise any doubts as to its necessity. If it is accepted that the religious feelings of the citizen may deserve protection against indecent attacks on the matters held sacred by him, then it can also be considered as necessary in a democratic society to stipulate that such attacks, if they attain a certain level of severity, shall constitute a criminal offense triable at the request of the offended person. It is in principle left to the legislation of the State concerned how it wishes to define the offense, provided that the principle of proportionality, which is inherent in the exception clause of Article 10(2) is being respected.

Here, there was no disproportionality; the fact of a specialized publication not directed at the private prosecutor was irrelevant. The Commission also gave short shrift to the claim of religious liberty, noting that "it

---

[91] Article 10 guarantees everyone the right to freedom of expression, but provides that "since it carries with it duties and responsibilities, may be subject to such formalities, conditions, restrictions or penalties as are prescribed by law and are necessary in a democratic society, in the interests of national security, territorial integrity or public safety, for the prevention of disorder or crime, for the protection of health or morals, for the protection of the reputation or rights of others, for preventing the disclosure of information received in confidence, or for maintaining the authority and impartiality of the judiciary." Article 9 contains similar language permitting limitations on the exercise of religious liberty.

has not been substantiated that the publication of the poem in question constituted the exercise of a religious or other belief protected by the above Convention Article." In any case, the Commission said the interference would have been justified on the same grounds as applied to the freedom of expression claim.

The problem of minority religions and blasphemy laws is reflected in the first English case of blasphemy concerning a religion other than Christianity. Brought in 1991, the private prosecutor invoked the common law of blasphemy to attack the publication of *The Satanic Verses*.[92] The magistrate refused to issue the summons on the grounds that the common law offense of blasphemy historically was restricted to the Christian religion. On judicial review, this decision was upheld, the Court noting that only Parliament could alter or extend the law, and this could not be done *ex post facto*. However, the Court described the controversy over the book and summarized the arguments for and against its blasphemous character. In this regard, the judge stated that "a statement will not necessarily be prevented from being a blasphemous libel simply because the statement is put into the mouth of a character, even a disreputable character, in a novel." Rushdie's lawyer argued that the passages complained of were not blasphemous because they did not amount to a scurrilous and insulting attack on the religion of Islam. Instead, the passages form part of a dream or nightmare sequence of a fictional character: "Nothing there is meant to be, and should not be taken to be, the views of the author."[93]

---

[92] *R. v. Chief Metropolitan Stipendiary Magistrate, ex parte Choudhury* [1991] 1 QB 429, [1991] 1 All ER 306, [1990] 3 WLR 986, 91 Cr App Rep 393. The Court notes that the book was banned in all Muslim countries, in South Africa, China and India.

[93] The problem was presented to the court as follows:

> 1. It is not blasphemous to describe God as the destroyer of men. While God is portrayed in scripture and the Koran as merciful and compassionate, he is also described, especially in the Old Testament and the book of Revelation, as an avenging and destructive God, particularly towards unbelievers and the enemies of the Jews.
>
> 2. The story of Abraham and Hagar is not one which reflects credit on Abraham, whether it is told in the Old Testament or the Koran. Abraham is not seen as without fault, either by the Judaic, Islamic, or Christian religion. The comment in words underlined in the information, though strong, is not unjustified. It cannot be blasphemous to say that pilgrims gather to worship and spend.
>
> 3. In relation to the complaint concerning Muhammad, the name Mahound is a name used by Christians for the prophet, though it appears to be used in a derogatory sense. Anyway, most of these matters complained of came from the mouth of a character in the book who is a drunken apostate. They cannot reasonably be taken to be the views of the author.

Traditionally, blasphemy law protected the dominant religion from affront and attack, irrespective of whether offense was caused to the feelings of believers. It is government enforcement of official beliefs. Pluralistic societies and neutral governments undermine the basis for traditional blasphemy laws. However, the unique position which religious beliefs hold among a very substantial number of persons in society may call for protection against disruption of the public order due to hostility and religious attacks. Taken beyond breaches of the peace, some argue that religion in itself is a good that the government should not allow to be disparaged. Thus, it is in the public interest to ensure that the feelings of people in relation to matters they hold sacred should not be outraged, because of the extreme distress such attacks may cause them.

The assumption of those favoring continued blasphemy laws seems to be that religious beliefs hold a preeminent position not held by political or social beliefs. The special reverence for the sacred makes people more susceptible to offence in relation to their religious beliefs. In this perspective, abusive attacks may be viewed as the verbal equivalents of acts of desecration. Moreover, in increasingly plural societies, it is argued it is necessary to respect different religious beliefs, feelings and practices and to protect them from vilification, ridicule and contempt. Perhaps in sharply divided societies, like India and Northern Ireland, such views are justified. However, in most societies such restrictions are not necessary and values of free speech should be given greater latitude. Freedom of speech should not be curtailed because of offense to the feelings of others. Certainly, protecting orthodoxy through blasphemy laws is neither appropriate nor necessary.

While infliction of gratuitous suffering on certain members of society may be thought sufficient to warrant imposition of criminal sanctions, there should be a demonstrated serious social need before such limita-

4. The passage in which the whores in the brothel assume the names of the prophet's wives cannot reasonably be taken to be derogatory or insulting of the wives, who were expressly said to be chaste. Rather it is a reflection on the perverted lusts of those in a decadent society such as Jahilia was portrayed to be before it submitted to the Islam faith.

5. As for the references to the companions of the prophet, these words came from the mouth of a decadent hack poet, who is hired by the ruler of Jahilia to denigrate Mahound and his companions. If a fictional work were written about the times of Christ, it could not...be blasphemous to put into the mouth of an opponent of Christ calumnies on the apostles; indeed it is clear that they were derided by such people as being simple ignorant fishermen.

6. It is not blasphemous to criticize the religion of Islam on the basis that there are too many rules sought to be laid down for the conduct of every day life. Although this passage complained of is in strong language, it does not amount to vilifying Islam.

tions on speech should be imposed. In this regard, production of material whose predominant purpose is to insult the feelings of religious believers does not appear common in most societies.

Finally, any offense that prohibits publicly insulting the feelings of religious believers would cast a net so wide as to cover everyone. It could prohibit any public discussion of artificial means of birth control, the use of blood transfusions to save life and the use of drugs for medical treatment, as well as restaurants serving pork or all meat. Any statement or behavior contradicting the doctrines of hundreds of sects might be capable of becoming a criminal offense.

In religion, as in politics, each person or group may claim to have truth and find the tenets of another to be false and dangerous. Persuasion and argument may lead to exaggerated claims or falsehoods, but the principle of freedom of expression assumes that in the long run a democratic society benefits from open exchange of views and information. Many opinions and beliefs can be expressed unhindered, even if others object to the views. One view focuses on the hearer, the other on the speaker. The latter view allows offense to be suffered so that new religious groups and views can be born. With the dynamic of individual choice new religions would continually evolve. The function of the law is to protect the capacity of individuals to form new and different groups.

The Model Law thus omits any reference to blasphemy or insults as an offense under the law.

As the examples given in the commentary indicate, religious liberty is far from being a reality in most parts of the world. Even in countries generally respectful of human rights, privileged positions are often reserved for established religions, resulting in discrimination against minority religious groups and their members. While legislation cannot solve problems of religious intolerance and disrespect, it is a necessary precondition to legal enforcement of religious rights. If the rights of all groups are respected, one hopes there will be fewer sources of conflict and, ultimately, greater respect for the diversity of beliefs created by the human mind.

The Tensions and the Ideals

JOHN T. NOONAN, JR.
United States Court of Appeals, Ninth Circuit

In the summer of 1789, as the Bill of Rights of the United States Constitution was being framed in Congress, a similar process was underway in France, where Lafayette, counselled by Jefferson, was active in preparing a declaration of rights to be considered by the National Assembly. The French acted first, adopting on August 23, 1789, Article 10 of the Declaration of the Rights of Man and of Citizen. It provided: "No one ought to be disturbed for his opinions, even religious ones, provided that their manifestation does not trouble the public order established by the law."[1] Article 10 was not so strong, not so unqualifiedly committed to free exercise as the First Amendment, but it was remarkable in a country that had never known such tolerance. It seemed sufficient to guarantee freedom of belief, set as it was in a document that began, "Men are born and remain free and equal in rights" and went on to say that these rights were "natural and imprescriptible."[2] The affirmation of such natural rights appeared to buttress and confirm the Declaration's promise of respect for variety in religion.

One year later the National Assembly adopted a plan for the selection and organization of the Catholic clergy of France. The National Assembly, just before it went out of existence, then adopted a Constitution which affirmed in so many words "the freedom of every man . . . to exercise the religion to which he is attached": the essence of the First Amendment put in positive terms.[3] Only months later, the newly-elected Legislative Assembly prescribed penalties for all clergy who did not

1 A. Debidiour, *Histoire des rapports de l'Église et l'etat en France de 1789-1870* (Paris, 1911), 38. For the text, incorporated in the constitution of 1791, see Léon Duguit, *Les constitutions et les principales lois politiques de la France depuis 1789*, 7th ed. (Paris, 1952), 2.

2 Article I, in ibid., 1.

3 The Civil Constitution of the Clergy, in Debidiour, *Histoire*, 653-663, enforced by the decree of November 29, 1790, in ibid., 101.

J.D. van der Vyver and J. Witte, Jr. (eds.), Religious Human Rights in Global Perspective, 593-605.

swear to abide by the Assembly's organization of the Church.[4] By the following year, 1792, religious war had broken out, and the national government was openly persecuting priests. Before it was over, more than 30,000 priests had been driven out of the country; some had been transported as felons to Guyanne; a substantial number had been shot, drowned, or guillotined; all monasteries and convents had been closed; a remarkable array of paintings, statutes, and altars had been defaced or demolished; and numerous churches and cathedrals had been employed for the celebration of the rites designed by the State. The Vendée, where the struggle raged most fiercely, was turned by the national army into a kind of Rwanda, devastated in its agriculture, its men, women and children killed by the tens of thousands.[5] The persecution went on without a word being changed in the Declaration of the Rights of Man and Citizen and in the Constitution of the country. When it was finally over, and Napoleon brought religious peace, persecution was succeeded by an administrative and financial union of Church and State that prevailed for over a century. A regime of regulation, not the free exercise of religion, was the rule in France.[6]

I recall these melancholy facts to make the points so palpable and yet so easily forgotten, that declarations are not deeds, that a form of words by itself secures nothing, and that the same words pregnant with meaning in one cultural context may be entirely barren in another. Against the backdrop of this reminder I propose to consider what seem to be the two inescapable elements in any protection of religious rights: their foundation and the tension of that foundation with the rights, duties, and nature of the State.

The foundation of religious rights is found in the human conscience, that capability of every human being to tell right from wrong. That this common capacity gives rise to a right, or rights, flows historically from conscience being conceived as having access to something beyond individual whim, inherited conventions, or community custom. Guide, witness, and judge in Stoic conceptions at least as old as Cicero, conscience is not only distinctively human; it is, as Cicero says to the senators judging Cluentius, received "from the immortal gods."[7] In the Christian rational-

[4] Title 1 of the Constitution of September 3, 1791, in Duguit, *Les constitutions*, 4.

[5] See Donald Greer, *The Incidence of the Terror During the French Revolution* (Cambridge, MA, 1937), 37 and 107 (on priests killed); Donald Greer, *The Incidence of the Emigration During the French Revolution* (Cambridge, MA, 1951), 83 (on priests forced to leave); Francois Souchal, *Le vandalisme de la Révolution* (Paris, 1993), 31-148 (on assault on religious art); Simon Schama, *Citizens* (New York, 1989), 791-792 (on destruction of the Vendée).

[6] Jean-Michel Leniaud, *L'Administration des cultes pendant la période concordataire* (Paris, 1988), 17.

[7] Cicero, *Pro Cluentio*, in Cicero, *Orationes*, Albert C. Clarke, ed. (New York, 1900).

ism of Thomas Aquinas, conscience is "in a certain way the dictate of reason, and what is proposed by reason is proposed as true" and therefore "as derived from God, from Whom is every truth."[8] "In this account, conscience can be mistaken; it is not an intuition of God or the voice of God speaking within. But conscience must be obeyed because what conscience proposes is what reason says is right, and "it is the same thing to flout the dictate of reason and the commandment of God."[9]

How do the special characteristics of conscience convert into moral rights? In two ways. To force anyone to act against conscience is to force that person to act against that person's reason and so against that person's nature. It is to compel an act in the strictest sense *contra naturam* if the nature of human beings is a rational nature. The second reason is, for any believer in God, stronger still. To command anyone to perform an action against conscience is to command that person to act against what is perceived as the command of God, to violate that person's duty of obedience to God. One has a moral right not to be forced to act against one's nature or against one's obligation to obey God.

Suppose, however, that conscience is mistaken, as the rationalist account concedes may happen. Objectively, what conscience now proposes is not rational and not in compliance with a commandment of God. Nonetheless, for the person whose conscience is at issue, there is no higher guide. To force that person to act against the mistaken conscience is to force an act *contra naturam*, to force a believer to sin against what the believer takes to be a commandment of God.

In a modern context where human rationality is doubted or seen as severely qualified and divine commandments are disbelieved, this foundational place of conscience will be challenged. But I know nothing to replace it. If conscience does not have a special role, if the duty to follow conscience does not trump all other considerations, including the laws of the State, I do not understand why religion—the duty to our Creator, as it used to be called—leads to moral rights that the State should recognize as legal rights. It is not necessary that the concept of God be exactly that of biblical Judaism or Christianity; but unless there is acknowledged a being or spirit distinct from, and superior to, any human being, it is difficult to see why a special sacredness should surround the human response of religion, and unless there is a spirit within human beings capable of some sort of grasp of this Other, there is not a firm basis for respecting the obligations that the insights of conscience impose. A Jew, a Christian, a Moslem would, of course, say a good deal more about the duties to God,

---

8 Thomas Aquinas, *Summa Theologiae*, I-II, q. 19, a. 5.

9 Id., ad 2.

and the role of conscience in fulfilling them, but, at a minimum, a zone within each person that is capable of transcending immediate material surroundings must be acknowledged if there is to be a foundation for the moral right to religious exercise that the State must respect.

In the sphere accorded conscience we find the State faced by what the Father of the First Amendment, James Madison, termed "a great Barrier," which the State cannot cross without making itself a tyrant and the citizen a slave.[10] That barrier is set at the edge of the sacred sphere of conscience because, as Madison phrased it, the duty to obey God is "precedent, both in order of time and in degree of obligation," to all the claims of the State and civil society.[11] As this architect of American religious freedom put it, a human being's relationship with God is "excepted from the grant on which all political authority is founded."[12] Excepted from the grant and therefore excepted from political authority that would leap the barrier and invade the sacred sphere, conscience is supreme. Moral rights, to be translated into legal rights, follow.

But will any State admit the existence of the "great Barrier?" In practice, can any State admit it? The answers to these questions appears to be No, and that for three reasons. First, the State must perform certain essential tasks if it is to be a State. It must collect taxes, and it must defend its people. These duties trump all others, are "precedent both in order of time and degree" to all claims of citizens and so, apparently, to all claims of conscience. Second, the State must operate by laws of a general character. Exceptions for religious rights endanger this generality. Taken to a logical conclusion, the right of each person to the free exercise of religion destroys the universal obligation of the laws. Madison's formula of exception from political authority is a prescription for anarchy. Third, to recognize religious duties and religious rights the State, through its organs such as the judiciary, must determine what is religion. The last word in theology must be the State's, for if the State does not see the right being exercised as religious, the State will not be bound by any barrier safeguarding religious observance.

Let me enlarge upon each of these reasons by example, the first a personal experience. In 1987, I sat as a judge in the case of a young man, an electrician with a wife and two children, who had read the United States Constitution in the Quincy, Massachusetts public library and had come to the conclusion that the prohibition of unreasonable searches in the

---

[10] James Madison, "To the Honorable the General Assembly of the Commonwealth of Virginia: A Memorial and Remonstrance," in William T. Hutchinson and William M. E. Rachal, eds., *Madison Papers* (Chicago, 1962), 8:298.

[11] Ibid.

[12] Ibid.

Fourth Amendment and the privilege against self-incrimination in the Fifth Amendment prevented the United States from requiring him to file an income tax return. He was perfectly willing to pay his taxes if he were sent a bill, and most of his income was subject to withholding anyway, but he refused to file. Encountering him was like encountering a figure from the seventeenth century who had received a special illumination as to God's will. With equal fervor and obstinacy this man asserted he had a constitutional right not to file a return.

A jury convicted him of the federal misdemeanor he had committed by not filing a return.[13] Following the advice of the probation officer, I sentenced him to probation doing community service as an electrician, adding only, as the educational part of the sentence, that he learn to understand American government by doing a book report on Tocqueville's *Democracy in America*. He performed the service and wrote an intelligent report. But a standard condition of every sentence of probation is that the probationer not violate another law during the period of probation. During this period the time arrived to file the income tax return for the past year. Reverting to his principles, he refused to file. A revocation-of-probation hearing became necessary.

At this hearing I gave the electrician the choice of filing or going to prison. I told him that he would not find prison a pleasant experience and that his wife and children would miss him greatly. I told him that millions of his fellow citizens, hundreds of thousands of lawyers, thousands of judges filed income tax returns and did not read the Constitution as he did. In short, I acted as an inquisitor might have acted in medieval Europe with one who clung to heresy—on the one hand pointing out the terrors of the penalties that could be imposed, on the other pointing out that all of Christendom, so to speak, was on my side. Who was he, lone heretic, to have a different position?

In the end, he capitulated. He filed the return. I was filled with relief. My federal role had dictated my conduct. I did not and do not regret what I did. I do ask, Would I have acted differently if, instead of claiming a personal insight into the Constitution, the electrician had claimed that a personal revelation from God had instructed him not to file, or if he had averred that his conscience told him that Sacred Scripture forbade such cooperation in the affairs of a heathen government? I doubt that I would have. "Taxes are the life-blood of government," as the Supreme Court has chosen to put it.[14] Without them the nation must die. The necessity for regularity without exception in their collection is absolutely paramount. Against this necessity the First Amendment is no shield.

---

13 *United States v. Campbell*, CR 88-00104-01 (D. Mass. 1988).

14 *Bull v. United States*, 295 U.S. 247, 259 (1935).

Military manpower occupies a similar position. It must be raised when the country needs it. Religion cannot stand in the way. On this subject, there is nothing more instructive than the famous letter of Roger Williams to the Town of Providence, written in 1660 when Baptists in his colony objected in the name of religious liberty to bearing arms to defend the colony against Indian attack. No one before Williams, and few after him, have been so sensitive to the claims of the religious conscience, so eloquent in the defense of religious liberty, of which he is justly acknowledged an Apostle. Yet Williams wrote:

> There goes many a ship to sea, with many hundred souls in one ship, whose weal and woe is common, and is a true picture of a commonwealth, or a human combination or society. It hath fallen out sometimes that both papists and protestants, Jews and Turks, may be embarked in one ship; upon which supposal I affirm, that all the liberty of conscience, that ever I pleaded for, turns upon these two hinges—that none of the papists, protestants, Jews, or Turks be forced to come to the ship's prayers or worship, nor compelled from their own particular prayers or worship, if they practice any. I further add, that I never denied that notwithstanding this liberty, the commander of this ship ought to command the ship's course, yea, and also command that justice, peace, and sobriety, be kept and practiced, both among the seamen and all the passengers. If any of the seamen refuse to perform their services, or passengers to pay their freight; if any refuse to help, in person or purse, towards the common charges or defence; if any refuse to obey the common laws and orders of the ship, concerning their common peace or preservation; if any shall mutiny and rise up against their common peace or preservation; if any shall mutiny and rise up against their commanders and officers; if any should preach or write that there ought to be no commanders or officers, because all are equal in Christ, therefore no masters nor officers, no laws nor orders, nor corrections nor punishments;—I say, I never denied, but in such cases, whatever is pretended, the commander or commanders may judge, resist, compel and punish such transgressors, according to their deserts and merits.[15]

Even for this great champion of religious freedom, this prophet a century ahead of his time, the common defense of the community prevailed over conscience. Functionally, the community was what was ultimately sacred.

The State, when it judges it prudent to do so, may graciously grant exceptions. It has done so in the United States, narrowly confining the exception to conscientious opponents of all war, carefully ensuring that

---

[15] "Roger Williams to the Town of Providence, January 1654-1655," in Perry Miller, ed., *The Complete Writings of Roger Williams* (New York, 1963), 6:278-279.

no large body of believers fit within the grace granted. The founding Fathers rejected a constitutional amendment safeguarding religious objection to bearing arms.[16] The First Amendment has never been found to protect the exercise of religion in this regard.[17] A sacred duty prescribed by many consciences not to kill has been securely subordinated to the secular interest of the State.

I omit enlarging on the obvious, that every exception as of right for conscience endangers the general application of the laws and, if taken far, leads to anarchy; and I turn to the third reason why the State is not bound in practice by the "great Barrier": the State determines when that barrier is present, the State says what is religious. Illustration is afforded by the theological commentary engaged in by the United States Supreme Court. The commentary began, harmlessly enough, with the observation that Sunday was a state holiday because a uniform day of rest was a secular desideratum; that Sunday coincided with a day special for Christians was irrelevant to the constitutional status of the day.[18] The commentary became more tendentious when the Supreme Court suggested that the civic celebration of Christmas (mysteriously called "the Holiday") had a secular purpose.[19] The commentary became dogmatic when Justice O'Connor made the remarkable statement that prayers solemnize public occasions, express confidence in the future, and encourage appreciation of the appreciable.[20] That was a recasting of the purposes of prayer, a theological recasting that appeared to take scant account of the purposes of those praying and to superimpose upon their prayers a meaning distinct from the declared intentions with which the prayers were said.

In the 1960s, the Court recognized a new religion for constitutional purposes. Hugo Black in a famous footnote setting out a list of nontheistic religions added to the list "Ethical Culture" and "Secular Humanism."[21] This identification was in the long-run to be an embarrassment both to the judiciary and to those who could be argued to fall within the category. If Secular Humanism was a religion, it was appropriate to search out where it might be established by the State and root it out. A religious non-religion was a problem.

More recently, in an easy step from the treatment of prayer as communal therapy, the Supreme Court invented a counterpart to Secular

16 Journal of the First Session of the Senate, September 4, 1789.

17 See, e.g., *Negre v. Larsen*, decided with *Gillette v. United States*, 401 U.S. 437 (1971).

18 *McGowan v. Maryland*, 366 U.S. 420 (1961).

19 *Lynch v. Donnelly*, 465 U.S. 668 (1984).

20 Ibid., at 693 (concurring opinion).

21 *Torcaso v. Watkins*, 367 U.S. 488, 495, n.11 (1961).

Humanism, a non-religious religion. The Court called it "ceremonial deism," uncapitalized. Ceremonial deism was the collective description of prayers by a legislature, prayer at the opening of a court, and of "In God We Trust" imprinted on the coinage.[22] Its contours could be expanded. Already it included prayers offered in the Nebraska Legislature to the Trinity in the name of Jesus—"deism" was stretched to include the Christian usage. The adjective "ceremonial" apparently was intended to draw the sting out of the practices described because they were governmental and a government should not be guilty of practicing religion; and the Court did not care to proscribe these practices. Just as Secular Humanism was nonreligious practice that was called a religion, ceremonial deism was religious practice that was not called a religion. The Court created a kind of American Shinto, a state religion that for establishment purposes was a non-religion because its purposes were secular. This kind of commentary, it may be concluded, is inescapable. If religious rights are to have a special place in the laws, then some legal agency of the State will have to determine what is religious.

If I were an Hegelian, I would be happy with the antimony: rights to religious freedom founded on a conscience beyond the authority of the State, set off against powers of the State that it cannot surrender without ceasing to exist. But I am more puzzled than pleased and have no neat synthesis to resolve the conflict. I even venture to think, on the basis of historical experience, that none exists. There is no single universal formula for reconciling religious rights and State authority. There are only ways of avoiding bloodshed, blunting the sharpness of the conflict, alleviating the tensions. Let me name seven such ways. They are not exclusive of each others, but complementary and converging.

First, the two fundamental positions should not be drawn out as logic might demand. To hold that religion is truly excepted from all political authority is more mad than Madisonian. James Madison, although he said it, did not act upon it. For all his strong views on the separation of the church from the State, we find him as a president issuing public prayers and authorizing federal gifts to support religious education.[23] Similarly, he abandoned his efforts to secure constitutional exemption from arms for Quaker and Mennonite objectors. Madison is as good an example as exists of the moderation with which religious rights must be vindicated.

---

[22] *Allegheny County v. American Civil Liberties Union*, 492 U.S. 573, 596, n.46.

[23] See, e.g., James Madison, "Proclamation, July 23, 1793," in *Annals of Congress* 27:2673-2674; see also 1 Stat. 50, 51-53 (1790) (on the gift for religious education in the Northwest Territory).

As for the State, it can exercise its powers with firm constitutional and cultural inhibitions restraining the plenitude of their reach. The State must tax and must use force and must have general laws. But almost all laws have exceptions, legislatively or judicially created. The Internal Revenue Code, our basic tax law, is honeycombed with provisions for special situations, most notably in this context with the proviso governing exemption for religious organizations.[24] The draft laws of this century have deferred ministers and theological students of all denominations and pacifists of the four historic Peace Churches and some others.[25] The State has not fallen apart because of such exceptions. The legislature could and should make more. The judiciary has expanded on the exceptions and could expand further. If the State is committed to the free exercise of religion, it can facilitate and empower that exercise so that it flourishes in countless varieties. Only a foolish uniformity, a bureaucratic insistence on regularity, a doctrinaire devotion to the logic of the State can choke off what conscientious response to the Spirit will bring.

The reason why logic—mere logic, one might say—is inappropriate here is that one is in the realm of values. Values can never be taken so far that Value A eats up Values B, C, and the rest. That is the way of tyranny. Values must always be held in balance, in an equilibrium that is analogous not to matching weights on a scale but to the harmony of a fit human person. "The over logical went mad alone," to paraphrase Auden, while "kisses brutalized the over-male."[26]

Values held in balance lead to the second point to be observed by both positions: a sense of proportion. Not every religious principle is worth dying for. No religion is so wedded to words as to take each of its truths with exact literalness. Although one cannot tell members of another religion what is essential to their belief, counsel can be conveyed that a sense of proportion (in my view the heart of the cardinal virtue of prudence) is necessary in the life of human beings. The State needs a sense of proportion, too. In the case where religious belief appears to threaten human life—the evangelicals who take literally the words of the Gospel of Mark that a believer can touch snakes without danger; the Jehovah's Witnesses who refuse blood transfusions, even in pregnancy; the

---

24 Internal Revenue Code, Sect. 503(c).

25 See, e.g., *Selective Draft Cases*, 245 U.S. 366, 376 and 389-390 (1918).

26 W.H. Auden, "The Quest," in *Collected Poems*, Edward Mendelson, ed. (New York, 1976), 228:

> The over-logical fell for the witch
> Whose argument converted him to stone,
> Thieves rapidly absorbed the over-rich,
> The over-popular went mad alone,
> And kisses brutalized the over-male.

Christian Scientists, who will not summon a medical doctor to treat a sick child—in all such cases, the State should respond as delicately as possible. What can guide the State here is not logic, but a sense of proportion. The State's duty to preserve human life does not have to be carried out by the criminal law. A proportionate response to a religious action will take into account the motivation, the good faith, the religious commitment of the actor and ordain no sanction that equates conscientious conduct with common criminality.

Proportionality is tied to analogy; the latter is not understood without the former; and the way of analogy is the third way of diminishing the tension. By analogy, one understands, one empathizes with, religions not one's own, and so acts to protect their rights. By analogy one understands what conscience demands in contexts not one's own. By analogy, religion, which varies from culture to culture, is grasped as a practice. As for the State, it can learn from all the State experiences of the past what is and is not invasive of religious rights. For example, the oath as a technique to control religious belief was as offensive to conscience in the seventeenth century when demanded as a test for public office in a country committed to the Church of England as it was in eighteenth century France when demanded by the Assembly from the Catholic clergy, as it was in nineteenth century America when required of jurymen or voters in federal territories bent on stamping out polygamy.[27] Or, to take a positive example, other countries have learned from us that the State will survive and prosper without stamping any religious body as heretical, without regulating its choice of its governing officers, and without forbidding it to engage in political activity. As every country has its own cultural components, these lessons on how usefully State power can be limited are learned by analogy.

Fourthly, in one's own culture one learns by experience. In America we have had over two hundred years of experience. Free exercise—let us as Americans assert it—was, in practice as distinguished from theory, an American invention. "Free exercise" was a phrase that as applied in 1791 to a federal government assumed to be without any power to interfere with religion was practically costless. Who gave up anything by adopting it? But for its principal author, Madison, it was not a cliché but a hope and even a program that would be worked out in time. For Madison, as he put it, it was "an experiment."[28]

The formula has been fruitful, functioning first as a national ideal even when it did not exist in every state, visible enough to catch the at-

---

[27] See sources in note 4 above on France and *Davis v. Beason*, 133 U.S. 333 (1890) on the enforcement of an anti-Mormon oath.

[28] James Madison to Frederick Adams, 1832, in *Madison Papers*, 9:485.

tention of that great foreign student of the subject, Alexis de Tocqueville. For a century and a half the development of the idea was the work of legislators and government officials, of schools and colleges, of churchmen and civic leaders, of treatise-writers and law professors. None of these has abandoned the field, but only in the last half century has development been accomplished by the activity of federal courts. In this era that began in 1940, particular judicial shapes have been given to free exercise. The results, inspected closely, appear chaotic. No mystery surrounds what is happening. By trial and error, by exaggeration and careful qualification, by broad declarations and hairsplitting distinctions, by retreats and reaffirmations, human beings in conflict are developing doctrine.

On the whole, the Supreme Court has moved in the direction of freedom. For that reason, especially for those acknowledging no other authority, the court is special; it seems even sacred. But no institutional guarantee has been given that the movement will continue or be uninterrupted. After all, until 1860 this court was the citadel of the Slave Power. As for religion, its early precedents declined to extend freedom to the Church of Jesus Christ of Latter-Day Saints and ratified the confiscation of that church's property.[29] Since 1940 the court has known three regressions: The first Flag Salute Case, the federal prosecution of Edna Ballard, the leader of the I Am movement, and the Sacramental Peyote Case.[30] The Ballard case has the peculiar interest of being an attack by the federal government on the core beliefs of a religion; it exhibits not only what could happen with the approval of the Supreme Court but what has happened.

Development is key to understanding the work of this court and other courts in relation to free exercise. The concept is borrowed from theology, specifically from John Henry Newman's *Essay on the Development of Doctrine*. In the course of time Christian doctrine has undergone many shifts and turns and is noticeably expanded from its evangelical form. How account for the changes? By supposing that the process has been one in which an idea or set of ideas have had their implications worked out, with the basic or dominant idea gradually driving out ideas incompatible with that dominant idea's mastery; or to put it in less Hegelian terms, human beings in conflict have come to see that commitment to certain basic principles excludes accommodations and deviations

[29] *The Late Corporation of the Church of Jesus Christ of Latter Day Saints v. United States*, 136 U.S. 1 (1890).

[30] *Minersville School District v. Gobitis*, 310 U.S. 586 (1940) (the first Flag Salute Case); *United States v. Ballard*, 322 U.S. 78 (1944) (prosecution of a religion as a fraud); *Employment Division v. Smith*, 494 U.S. 872 (1990) (the Sacramental Peyote Case).

once accepted as normal.[31] So, for example, Christianity has gone from endorsing slavery to abhorring it, all as a firmer grasp of the central commandment of charity has been had.[32] Something similar has happened, and is happening, in the realm of free exercise. The experiment is not over.

What is important now—and here is my fifth way—is self-consciousness. By that I mean self-consciousness on the part of religious men and women that they ask for very much when they ask any exemption from the requirements of the State. Modesty, a sense of proportion, charity are virtues that self-consciousness here might cultivate. Even Christ said, "Render unto Caesar what is Caesar's." Self-consciousness is equally desirable for the agents of the State when they enter into the area of others' consciences. It does not do, I suggest, for judges to pretend that they are neutrals somehow free from all prejudice when they decide intrachurch disputes, determine who has a religious claim, or balance the State's interest in relation to the First Amendment. Judges, to pursue this personal example, should be intensely conscious of the difficulty of reaching dispassionate decisions in such matters. It is my belief that here, as elsewhere, a mind conscious of the problem will work with greater success than a mind which denies that a problem exists or buries in conventions the new challenges that the conflicts of the State with the promptings of the Spirit are sure to engender.

Sixthly, a special kind of self-consciousness must be the memory of past atrocities committed in the name of religion at the urging of convinced believers. The State would often have taken little interest in points of doctrine or conduct if a body of believers had not induced the State to act. The blood of thousands is at the churches' doors. What an advance toward religious liberty that no major faith now prescribes acts of intolerance to be executed by the State! And on the State's side, it must be remembered not only how the State was manipulated by religions but how the State itself for its own ends has harried and hunted believers; the French Terror, the Russian Revolution, the Chinese Cultural Revolution are proof enough that the atheist State can be as cruel or crueller than the church-dominated one. Self-consciousness on each side must be

[31] See John Henry Newman, *An Essay on the Development of Doctrine*, Charles F. Harrold, ed. (New York, 1949), 1.1.6, p. 74.

[32] See John T. Noonan, Jr., "Development in Moral Doctrine," *Theological Studies* 44 (1993): 662, 673.

sin-consciousness, awareness of the evils that suppression of religious freedom has produced.

And I add, there is one more way: prayer. To quote Scripture once more: "Unless the Lord build the house, they labor in vain who build it. Unless the Lord guard the citadel the sentinel stands in vain."

Bibliography of Books and Articles Cited

Abu-Sahlieh, Albeeb, "Les droits de l'homme et l'Islam," *Revue Generale de Droit International Public* 89 (1985): 626

Adams, Amos, *Religious Liberty an Invaluable Blessing* (Boston, 1768)

Adams, Arlin M. and Charles J. Emmerich, *A Nation Dedicated to Religious Liberty: The Constitutional Heritage of the Religion Clauses* (Philadelphia, 1990)

——— and Sarah B. Gordon, "The Doctrine of Accommodation in the Jurisprudence of the Religion Clauses," *DePaul Law Review* 37 (1988): 317

Adams, John, *Papers of John Adams*, R. Taylor, M. Kline, and G. Lint, eds. (Cambridge, 1977)

———, *The Works of John Adams, Second President of the United States, with a Life of the Author, Notes, and Illustrations*, C. Adams ed. (Boston, 1850-1856)

Adler, Stephen J., "The Temple Mount in Court," *Biblical Archaeology Review* 5 (1991)

Advocates for Human Rights and the International Service for Human Rights, *The U.N. Commission on Human Rights, Its Sub-Commission, and Related Procedures: An Orientation Manual* (Minneapolis, 1993)

Afshari, Reza, "An Essay on Islamic Cultural Relativism in the Discourse of Human Rights," *Human Rights Quarterly* 16 (1994): 235

Ahlstrom, Sidney, *A Religious History of the American People* (Garden City, NY, 1975)

Akinpelu, J.A., *New Perspectives in Moral Education* (Lagos, 1983)

Albernathy, M. Glenn, *Civil Liberties under the Constitution*, 6th ed. (Columbia SC, 1993)

Alexander, Stella, *Church and State in Yugoslavia since 1945* (Cambridge, 1979)

Alley, Robert S., ed., *James Madison on Religious Liberty* (Richmond, 1985)

Alston, Philip, "The Commission of Human Rights", in Philip Alston, ed., *The United Nations and Human Rights* (Oxford/New York, 1992), 127

———, "The Committee on Economic, Social and Cultural Rights", in Philip Alston, ed., *The United Nations and Human Rights* (Oxford/New York, 1992), 473

———, ed., *The United Nations and Human Rights* (Oxford/New York, 1992)

Althusius, Johannes, *Politica Methodiae Digesta*, 3d ed. (1614)

Amanat, A., *Resurrection and Renewal. The Making of the Babi Movement in Iran, 1844-1850* (Ithaca/London, 1989)

A Manual of Religious Liberty, 3d ed. (London, 1767)

Amar, Akil, "The Bill of Rights as a Constitution," *Yale Law Journal* 100 (1991): 1131

Amnesty International, *Guatamala: The Human Rights Record* (New York, 1987)

———, "Saudi Arabia: Religious Intolerance, The Arrest, Detention and Torture of Christian Worshippers and Shi'a Muslims" (September 14, 1993)

An-Na'im, Abdullahi Ahmed, "Cross Cultural Support for Equitable Participation in Subsaharan Africa," in Kathleen E. Mahoney and Paul Mahoney, eds., *Human Rights in the Twenty-First Century: A Global Challenge* (Dordrecht/BostonLondon, 1993), 133

———, ed., *Human Rights in Cross-Cultural Perspectives: A Quest for Consensus* (Philadelphia, 1992)

———, "Human Rights in the Muslim World: Socio-Political Conditions and Scriptural Imperatives," *Harvard Human Rights Journal* 3 (1990): 13

———, "Religious Minorities Under Islamic Law and the Limits of Cultural Relativism," *Human Rights Quarterly* 9 (1987): 1

——— and Francis M. Deng, eds., *Human Rights in Africa* (Washington, 1990),

Anderson, Benedict, *Imagined Communities* (London, 1983)

Anderson, John, "Legislative and Administrative Control of Religious Bodies," in Eugene B. Shirley, Jr. and Michael Rowe, eds., *Candle in the Wind* (Washington, DC, 1989), 68

Anderson, Paul, *People, Church, and State in Modern Russia* (New York, 1944)

Aniagolu, Antony N., *The Making of the 1989 Constitution in Nigeria* (Ibadan, 1993)

Antieau, Chester J., Arthur T. Downey & Edward C. Roberts, *Freedom from Federal Establishment: Formation and Early History of the First Amendment Religion Clauses* (Milwaukee, WI, 1964)

Anwar, M. "Young Muslims in Britain: Their Educational Needs and Policy Implications", in M.W. Khan, ed., *Education and Society in the Muslim World* (London, 1981), 100

Arjomand, Said A., "Shi'ite Jurisprudence and Constitution-Making in the Islamic Republic of Iran," in Martin E. Marty and R. Scott Appleby, eds., *Fundamentalisms and the State: Remaking Polities, Economies, and Militance* (Chicago, 1993), 88-109

———, *The Political Dimensions of Religion* (Albany, NY, 1993)

———, "Unity and Diversity in Islamic Fundamentalism," in Martin E. Marty & Scott E. Appleby, eds., *Fundamentalisms Comprehended* (Chicago, 1995), 179-198

Armstrong, James, "A Conversation with Castro," *The Christian Century* (August 31, 1977): 743

Arzt, Donna, "The Application of International Human Rights Law in Islamic States," *Human Rights Quarterly* 12 (1990): 202

Ashburn, Daniel G., "The State of Religious Human Rights in the World: Preliminary Consultation," *Preliminary Documents of Religious Human Rights Project* 2 (1993)

Auden, W.H., *Collected Poems*, Edward Mendelson, ed. (New York, 1976)

Austin, Dennis, *Politics in Ghana 1946-1960* (London, 1964)

Ayisi, E., *An Introduction to the Study of African Culture* (London, 1972)

Backus, Isaac, *Isaac Backus on Church, State, and Calvinism: Pamphlets, 1754-1789*, William C. McLoughlin, ed. (Cambridge, Mass., 1968)

———, *Policy as well as Honesty Forbids the Use of Secular Force in Religious Affairs* (Boston, 1779)

———, *The Infinite Importance of the Obedience of Faith, and of a Separation from the World, Opened and Demonstrated* (Boston, 1791)

———, *Truth is Great and Will Prevail* (Boston, 1781)

Bacon, Francis, *The New Organon and Related Writings*, Fulton H. Anderson, ed. (Indianapolis, 1960)

Baha'i International Community, *The Baha'i Question. Iran's Secret Blueprint for the Destruction of a Religious Community* (1993)

Bailey, S.H., D.J. Harris, and B.L. Jones, *Civil Liberties: Cases and Materials*, 3d ed. (London, 1991)

Baka, András B., "The European Convention on Human Rights and the Protection of Minorities Under International Law," *Connecticut Journal of International Law* 8 (1993): 227

Barrell, G. R., *Teachers and the Law*, 5th ed. (London, 1975)

Barron, Jerome A., "Sunday in North America," *Harvard Law Review* 79 (1965): 42.

Barrow, A.H., *Fifty Years in West Africa* (London, 1900)

Baylor, Gregory S., "The Religious Equality Amendment," *Christian Legal Society Quarterly* 16(3) (1995): 4

Beck, Lewis White, *Early German Philosophy: Kant and His Predecessors* (Cambridge, MA 1969)

Beddard, Ralph, *Human Rights in Europe*, 3d ed. (Cambridge, 1993)

Beeson, Ann E., "Dances With Justice: Peyotism in the Courts," *Emory Law Journal* 41 (1992): 1121

Beeson, Trevor, *Discretion and Valour* (Glasgow, 1974)

Beetham, David, *Max Weber and the Theory of Modern Politics* (London, 1974)

Bellah, Robert N., *The Broken Covenant: American Civil Religion in Time of Trial* (Chicago, 1975)

Benito, Elizabeth Odio, *Study of the Current Dimensions of the Problems of Intolerance and Discrimination Based on Religion or Belief* (New York, United Nations, 1987)

Berg, Thomas C., "What Hath Congress Wrought? An Interpretive Guide to the Religious Freedom Restoration Act," *Villanova Law Review* 39 (1994): 1

Berger, Vincent, *Case Law of the European Court of Human Rights* (Sarasota, 1989)

———, *Jurisprudence de la cour européenne des droits de l'homme*, 3d ed. (Paris, 1991)

Berman, Harold J., "Christianity and Democracy in the Soviet Union," in John Witte, Jr., ed., *Christianity and Democracy in Global Context* (Boulder, CO/San Francisco, 1993), 287

———, *Faith and Order: The Reconciliation of Law and Religion* (Atlanta, 1993)

———, "Law and Logos," *DePaul Law Review* 44 (1994): 143

———, *Law and Revolution: The Formation of Western Legal Tradition* (Cambridge, MA, 1983)

———, "Religion and Law: The First Amendment in Historical Perspective," *Emory Law Journal* 35 (1986): 778

———, "Religious Foundations of Law in the West: An Historical Perspective," *Journal of Law and Religion* 1 (1983): 1

———, "Some Reflections on the Differences Between Church and State," *Christian Legal Society Quarterly* 5(2) (1984): 12

———, "The Interaction of Law and Religion," *Capital University Law Review* 8 (1979) 346

———, *The Interaction of Law and Religion* (Nashville, 1974)

———, "Toward an Integrative Jurisprudence: Politics, Morality, History," *California Law Review* 76 (1988): 779

———, Erwin N. Griswold & Frank C. Newman, "Draft USSR Law on Freedom of Conscience, with Commentary," *Harvard Human Rights Journal* 3 (1990): 137

Bernhardt, R., "Human Rights Aspects of Racial and Religious Hatred Under Regional Human Rights Conventions," *Israel Yearbook on Human Rights* 22 (1992): 17

Berns, Walter, "Religion and the Founding Principle," in Robert H. Horwitz, ed., *The Moral Foundations of the American Republic*, 3d ed. (Charlottesville, Va., 1986), 204

Bessmertnij-Anzimirov, A., "Freedom of Faith: Internal Norms and Stalinist Legislation," *Occasional Papers on Religion in Eastern Europe* (June, 1989)

Blackham, H. J., *Modern Humanism* (Neuchtael, 1964)

Bloed, Arie, ed., *The Conference on Security and Co-Operation in Europe: Analysis and Basic Documents* (Dordrecht, 1993)

Blum, N., *Die Gedanken Gewissens und Religionsfreiheit nach Artikel 9. der europäischen Menschen Rechts Konzepzion* (Berlin, 1990)

Bolles, John R., *A Brief Account of Persecutions, in Boston and Connecticut Governments* (Boston, 1758)

Borden, Morton, *Jews, Turks, and Infidels* (Chapel Hills, NC, 1984)

Bosco, Ronald A., "Lectures at the Pillory: The Early American Execution Sermon," *American Quarterly* 30 (1978): 156

Bossuyt, Marc, *L'interdiction de la discrimination dans le droit international des droits de l'homme* (Brussels, 1976)

Bourdeaux, Michael, *Gorbachev, Glasnost, and the Gospel* (London, 1990)

Boyle, Kevin, "Religious Intolerance and the Incitement of Hatred," in Sandra Coliver, ed., *Striking a Balance: Hate Speech, Freedom of Expression and Non-Discrimination* (London, 1992), 61

———, T. Hadden and P. Hillyard, *Law and State: The Case of Northern Ireland* (London, 1975)

Bradley, Gerald V., "The No Religious Test Clause and the Constitution of Religious Liberty: A Machine That Has Gone of Itself," *Case Western Law Review* 37 (1987): 674

Bradney, A., *Religions, Rights, and Laws* (Leicester, 1993)

———, "Taking Sides: Religion, Law and Politics," *New Law Journal* (March 26, 1993): 443

Brady, J.C., "Public Benefit and Religious Trusts: Fact or Fiction," *Northern Ireland Legal Quarterly* 25 (1974): 174

Breen, Timothy, *The Character of the Good Ruler, 1630-1730* (Cambridge, MA, 1970)

Brienen, Frances, "In the Matter of Resources We in the North Live in a Desert," in John S. Pobee, ed., *Ministerial Formation for Missions Today* (Asempa, 1993), 66

Brierley, Peter and David Longley, eds., *United Kingdom Christian Handbook* (London, 1992/1993)

Bright, S., "Charity and Trusts for the Public Benefit—Time for a Re-Think?" *Conveyancer and Property Lawyer* (January/February, 1989): 29

Brignolia, Hector Pérez, ed., *Historia General de Centroamérica. De la Ilustració al Liberalismo* (Proyecto elaborado por FLACSO, La Sociedad Estatal V Centenario y la Comisión de las Communidades Europeas, 1993)

Brolmann, Caherine, et al., eds., *Peoples and Minorities in International Law* (Dordrecht/Boston/London, 1993)

Broun, Janice, *Conscience and Captivity: Religion in Eastern Europe* (Washington, 1988)

———, "The Bulgarian Orthodox Church Schism," *Religion in Eastern Europe* 13(3) (June, 1993): 1

Browne, E.G., *Materials for the Study of the Babi Religion* (Cambridge, 1918)

Brownlie, Ian, ed., *Basic Documents in International Law*, 2d. ed. (Oxford, 1972)

Buergenthal, Thomas, *International Human Rights* (St. Paul, 1988)

———, "To Respect and to Ensure: State Obligations and Permissible Derogations," in Louis Henkin, ed., *The International Bill of Rights* (New York, 1981), 72

Buraku Liberation Research Institute, *Human Rights in Japan from the Perspective of the International Covenant on Civil and Political Rights: Counter-Report to the Third Japanese Government Report* (Osaka City, 1993)

Buzzard, Lynn R., *Schools: They Haven't Got a Prayer* (Elgin, IL, 1982);

Calebrese, Frank, "Equal Access Upheld as the *Lemon* Test Sours," *DePaul Law Review* 39 (1990): 1281

Calhoun, Craig, "Nationalism and Ethnicity," *Annual Sociological Review* 19 (1993): 229

Capotorti, Francesco, *Study on the Rights of Persons Belonging to Ethnic, Religious and Linguistic Minorities* (New York, 1991)

Carmack, Robert, ed., *Historia General de Centroamérica. Historia Antigua* (Proyecto elaborado por FLACSO, La Sociedad Estatal V Centenario y la Comisión de las Communidades Europeas, 1993)

Carmella, Angela C., "House of Worship and Religious Liberty: Constitutional Limits to Landmark Preservation and Architectural Review," *Villanova Law Review* 36 (1991): 401

———, "Landmark Preservation of Church Property," *Catholic Lawyer* 34 (1991): 41

———, "State Constitutional Protection of Religious Exercise: An Emerging Post-*Smith* Jurisprudence," *Brigham Young University Law Review* (1993): 275

Cassese, Antonio, "The General Assembly: Historical Perspective 1945-1989," in Philip Alston, ed., *The United Nations and Human Rights* (Oxford/New York, 1992), 37

Casto, William, "Oliver Ellsworth's Calvinism: A Biographical Essay on Religion and Political Psychology in the Early Republic," *Journal of Church and State* 35 (1994): 506

Central Statistical Service, *South African Statistics 1993* (Pretoria, 1993)

Choper, Jesse H., "Separation of Church and State: 'New' Directions by the 'New' Supreme Court," *Journal of Church and State* 34 (1992): 363

———, "The Religion Clauses of the First Amendment: Reconciling the Conflict," *University of Pittsburg Law Review* 41 (1980): 673

Cicero, *Pro Cluentio*, in Cicero, *Orationes*, Albert C. Clarke, ed. (New York, 1900)

Clark, L., ed., *Through African Eyes: The Colonial Experience* (New York, 1970)

Clark, Roger S., "The United Nations and Religious Freedom," *New York University Journal of International Law and Politics* 11 (1978): 197

Claude, Richard and Burns H. Weston, eds., *Human Rights in the World Community*, 2d ed. (Philadelphia, 1992)

Cleary, Edward L. and Hannah Steward-Gambino, *Conflict and Competition: The Latin American Church in a Changing Environment* (Boulder, CO, 1993)

Codevilla, Giovanni, "The Limits of Religious Freedom in the USSR," in Dennis J. Dunn, ed., *Religion and Communist Society* (Berkeley, CA, 1983), 67

Colbi, Saul A., *Christian Churches in Israel* (Jerusalem, 1969)

———, *Christianity in the Holy Land* (Tel Aviv, 1969)

Coliver, Sandra ed., *Striking a Balance: Hate Speech, Freedom of Expression and Non-Discrimination* (London, 1992)

Coll, A.R. and A.C. Arend, *The Falklands War* (London, 1985)

Conkle, David O., "*Lemon* Lives," *Case Western Reserve Law Review* 43 (1993): 865;

Connor, Walker, *Ethnonationalism: The Quest for Understanding* (Princeton, NJ, 1994)

Cord, Robert L., "Church-State Separation: Restoring the 'No Preference' Doctrine of the First Amendment," *Harvard Journal of Law and Public Policy* 9 (1986): 129

———, *Separation of Church & State: Historic Fact and Current Fiction*, rev. ed. (Grand Rapids, MI, 1988)

Corder, Hugh, et al., *A Charter for Social Justice: A Contribution to the South African Bill of Rights Debate* (Cape Town 1992)

Cormack, R.J. and R.D. Osborne, *Discrimination and Public Policy in Northern Ireland* (Oxford, 1991)

Cornelison, Isaac, *Relation of Religion to Civil Government in America: A State Without a Church, But not Without a Religion* (New York, 1895)

Cosic, Dorica, "Zbiva se civilizacijska revolucija," NIN 2045 (March 11, 1990): 60

Cotler, Irwin and F. Pearl Eliadis, eds., *International Human Rights Law* (Montreal, 1992)

Council of Europe, *Human Rights in International Law: Basic Texts* (Strasbourg, 1991)

Cox, Harvey and Arvind Sharma, "Positive Resources of Religion for Human Rights," in John Kelsay and Sumner B. Twiss, eds., *Religion and Human Rights* (New York, 1994), 61

"Cuba Courts the Black Churches," *Information Digest* (New York, August 3, 1984): 240

Cumings, Henry, *A Sermon Preached at Billerica* (Boston, 1797)

Curry, Thomas J., *The First Freedoms: Church and State in America to the Passage of the First Amendment* (Oxford, 1986)

Danner, Mark, "The Truth of El Mazote," *The New Yorker* (December 6, 1993)

———, *The Massacre of El Mazote* (New York, 1994)

Dart, John, and Jimmy Allen, *Bridging the Gap: Religion and the News Media* (Nashville, n.d.)

Davidson, B., *African Civilization Revisited* (Trenton, NJ, 1991)

Davidson, Scott, *Human Rights* (Buckingham, 1993)

de Silva, K.M., *Religion, Nationalism, and the State* (Tampa, FL, 1986)

de Ville, J.R., *Moontlike Veranderinge in die Suid-Afrikaanse Administratiefreg na aanleiding van 'n Menseregteakte* (Stellenbosch 1992)

de Koker, A.P. and G.A. Urquhart, *Income Tax in South Africa* (Durban 1989)

Debidour, A., *Histoire des rapports de l'Église et l'etat en France de 1789-1870* (Paris, 1911)

Debrunner, H., *A History of Christianity in Ghana* (Accra, 1967)

DeJong, O.J., "Union and Religion," *The Low Countries History Yearbook* (1981): 29

del Russo, Alessandra Luini, *International Protection of Human Rights* (Washington, 1971)

Deng, Francis, "The Tragedy in Sudan Must End: A Personal Appeal to Compatriots and to Humanity," *Mediterranean Quarterly* 5(1) (Winter, 1994): 47

Dengerink, Jan, *Critisch-Historisch Onderzoek naar de Sociologische Ontwikkeling der Beginsel der "Souvereiniteit in eigen Kring" in de 19e en 20e Eeuw* (Amsterdam, 1948)

Denning, A., *Freedom Under Law* (London, 1949)

Deutsch, Sandra McGee and Ronald H. Dolkart, eds., *The Argentine Right* (Wilmington, DE, 1993)

Dinstein, Yoram, "Freedom of Religion and the Protection of Religious Minorities," in Yoram Dinstein and Mala Tabory, eds., *The Protection of Minorities and Human Rights* (Dordrecht/Boston/London, 1992), 157

——— and Mala Tabory, eds., *The Protection of Minorities and Human Rights* (Dordrecht/Boston/London, 1992)

Dominguez, Jorge I., *Cuba: Order and Revolution* (Cambridge, MA, 1978)

Donnelly, Jack, "Cultural Relativism and Universal Human Rights," *Human Rights Quarterly* 6 (1984): 400

Dooyeweerd, Herman, *A New Critique of Theoretical Thought*, David H. Freeman and H. de Jongste, trans. (Toronto/St. Catharines, 1984), 4 vols.

———, *De Strijd om het Souvereiniteitsbegrip in de moderne Rechts- en Staatsleer* (Amsterdam, 1950)

———, *Verkenningen in de Wijsbegeerte, De Sociologie en de Rechtsgeschiedenis* (Amsterdam, 1962)

Drewry, G., "Select Committees and Back Bench Power", in G. Drewry, *The Changing Constitution*, 2d ed., J. Jowell and D. Oliver, eds. (Oxford, 1989), 141

———, *The Changing Constitution*, 2d ed., J. Jowell and D. Oliver, eds. (Oxford, 1989)

du Plessis, Lourens M. and A.G. du Plessis, *An Introduction to Law* (Cape Town 1992)

———, *The Interpretation of Statutes* (Durban 1986)

——— and J.R. de Ville, "Bill of Rights Interpretation in the South African Context (1): Diagnostic Observations," *Stellenbosch Law Review* 4(1) (1993): 63-87

———, "Bill of Rights Interpretation in the South African Context (2): Prognostic Observations," *Stellenbosch Law Review*, 4(2) (1993): 199-218

———, "Bill of Rights Interpretation in the South African Context (3): Comparative Perspectives and Future Prospects," *Stellenbosch Law Review* 4(3) (1993): 356-393

Duguit, Léon *Les constitutions et les principales lois politiques de la France depuis 1789*, 7th ed. (Paris, 1952)

Duncan, Richard F., "Religious Civil Rights in Public High Schools: The Supreme Court Speaks on Equal Access," *Indiana Law Review* 24 (1991): 111

Dunn, Dennis J., ed., *Religion and Communist Society* (Berkeley, CA, 1983)

Durham, W. Cole, Jr., "Religious Liberty and the Call of Conscience," *DePaul Law Review* 42 (1992): 85

———, "Treatment of Religious Minorities in the United States," in European Consortium for Church-State Research, *The Legal Status of Religious Minorities in the Countries of the European Union* (Thessalanica/Milan, 1994), 323

——— and Alexander Dushku, "Traditionalism, Secularism, and the Transformative Dimension of Religious Institutions," *Brigham Young University Law Review* (1993): 421

———, Pieter van Dijk, Lauren B. Homer, and John Witte, Jr., "The Future of Religious Liberty in Russia: Report of the De Burght Conference on Pending Russian Legislation Restricting Religious Liberty," *Emory International Law Review* 8 (1994): 1

Dwight, Timothy, *The Duty of Americans at the Present Crisis, Illustrated in a Discourse Preached on the Fourth of July, 1798* (New Haven, 1798)

Dwyer, Kevin, *Arab Voices: The Human Rights Debate in the Middle East* (Berkeley, 1991)

Eastland, Terry, ed., *Lowering the Wall: Religion and the Supreme Court in the 1980s* (New York, 1991)

———, ed., *Religious Liberty in the Supreme Court: The Cases that Define the Debate over Church and State* (Washington, 1993)

Eckardt, A. Roy, ed., *Christianity in Israel* (New York, 1971)

Eckenrode, H.J., *Separation of Church and State in Virginia: A Study in the Development of the Revolution* (Richmond, Va., 1910)

Eisgruber, Christopher L., "Madison's Wager: Religious Liberty in the Constitutional Order," *Northwestern University Law Review* 89 (1995): 347

Elliot, J. ed., *The Debates in the Several State Conventions on the Adoption of the Federal Constitution*, 2d ed. (Washington, 1836)

Ellis, James, *A Narrative of the Rise, Progress, and Issue of the Late Law-Suits Relative to Property Held and Devoted to Pious Uses* (Warren, RI, 1795)

Englard, Itzhak, "Die Stellung des judischen Rabbinats im Rahmen des Staat Israel," in *Festschrift zum 70. Geburtstag von Werner Kagi* (Tübingen, 1979), 101

———, "Law and Religion in Israel," *American Journal of Comparative Law* 35 (1987): 185

Ermacora, Felix, "The Protection of Minorities Before the United Nations," *Recueil des Cours* 182/IV (Alphen, 1983): 247

Esbeck, Carl H., "Table of United States Supreme Court Decision Relating to Religious Liberty 1789-1994," *Journal of Law and Religion* 10 (1993-1994): 573

———, "The *Lemon* Test: Should it be Retained, Reformulated, or Rejected," *Notre Dame Journal of Law, Ethics, & Public Policy* 4 (1990): 365

European Consortium for Church-State Research, *Conscientious Objection in the EC Countries* (Milan, 1992)

———, *The Legal Status of Religious Minorities in the Countries of the European Union* (Thessalanica/Milan, 1994)

Evans, Israel, *A Sermon Delivered at Concord, Before the Hon. General Court of the State of New Hampshire at the Annual Election* (Concord, 1791)

Fallon, Richard H., Jr., "What is Republicanism, and is it Worth Reviving?" *Harvard Law Review* 102 (1989): 1695

Fawcett, J.E.S., *The Application of the European Convention on Human Rights* (Oxford, 1987)

Englrad, Itzchak, *The Legal Status of the Holy Places, Jersalem: Aspects of Law* (Jerusalem, 1973)

Filippov., B., "The Role of the Church in Restoring a Civil Society in USSR," *Occasional Papers on Religion in Eastern Europe* (January, 1992)

Finke, Roger, "Religious Deregulation: Origins and Consequences," *Journal of Church and State* 32 (1990): 609

Fisher, Hugh, *The Divine Right of Private Judgment, Set in a True Light* (Boston, 1731, 1790)

Földesi, Tamás, "Gedanken über die Gewissens und Religionsfreiheit," *Kirchliche Zeitgeschichte* (1990): 80

———, "Reflections on Human Rights: An Eastern European Perspective," *Israel Law Review* (1989): 27

Foster, Isaac, *A Defense of Religious Liberty* (Worcester, 1780)

Fox, M., *A Spirituality Named Compassion* (San Francisco, 1990)

Francis, John G., "The Evolving Regulatory Structure of European Church-State Relationships," *Journal of Church and State* 34 (1992): 775

Franklin, Benjamin, *Benjamin Franklin: Representative Selections*, C. Jorgenson and F. Motts, eds. (New York, 1962)

Freedom of Religion: Hope for Lasting Peace and Unity. Proceedings of the All African Religious Liberty Congress (Nairobi, September 1991)

Freund, Paul and Robert Ulich, *Religion and the Public Schools* (Cambridge, 1965);

Frey, Barbara A. and Carl E.S. Söderberg, *Human Rights in The Socialist Republic of Albania* (Minneapolis, 1990)

Friedmann, Y., *Prophecy Continuous* (Berkeley, CA, 1989)

Friedrich, C.J., *Trends of Federalism in Theory and Practice* (New York, 1968)

Frost, J. William, *A Perfect Freedom: Religious Liberty in Pennsylvania* (Cambridge, 1990)

Fuchs, Lawrence H., *The American Kaleidoscope: Race, Ethnicity, and the Civic Culture* (Middletown, CT, 1990)

Gabriel, Ingeborg, *Minderheiten und nationale Frage* (Vienna, 1993)

Gaffney, Edward M., *Private Schools and the Public Good: Policy Alternatives for the Eighties* (Notre Dame, 1981);

Gans, Chaim, *Philosophical Anarchism and Political Disobedience* (Cambridge, 1992)

Garay, Alain, "Liberté religieuse et proselytisme: l'experience Europeene," *Revue trimestrielle des droits de l'homme* 17 (1994): 7

Garrard-Burnett, Virginia and David Stoll, eds., *Rethinking Protestantism in Latin America* (Philadelphia, 1993)

Gaustad, Edward S., "Colonial Religion and Liberty of Conscience," in Merrill D. Peterson & Robert C. Vaughn, eds., *The Virginia Statute for Religious Freedom: Its Evolution and Consequences in American History* (Cambridge, 1988), 23

———, *Liberty of Conscience: Roger Williams in America* (Grand Rapids, 1991)

Gedicks, Frederick M., "Public Life and Hostility to Religion," *Virginia Law Review* 78 (1992): 671

———, "Toward A Constitutional Jurisprudence of Religious Group Rights," *Wisconsin Law Review* (1989): 99.

Gellner, Ernest, *Nations and Nationalism* (Ithaca, NY, 1983)

Gerber, Haim, *State, Society, and Law in Islam: Ottoman Law in Comparative Perspective* (Albany, NY, 1994)

Gerstenblith, Patty, "Civil Court Resolution of Property Disputes Among Religious Organizations," *American University Law Review* 39 (1990): 513

Gibb, H.A.R., "Constitutional Organization," in M. Khadduri and H.R. Liebesny, eds., *Law in the Middle East* (Washington, 1955), 3

———, "The Heritage of Islam in the Modern World," *International Journal of Middle East Studies* 1 (1970): 11

Glendon, Mary Ann, "Law, Communities, and the Religious Freedom Language of the Constitution," *George Washington Law Review* 60 (1992): 672

——— and Raul F. Yanes, "Structural Free Exercise," *Michigan Law Review* 90 (1991): 477

Goadby, Frederic M., "Ethnic Segmentation, Western Education, and Political Outcomes: Nineteenth-Century Ottoman Society," *Poetics Today* 14(3) (1993): 517

———, *International and Inter-Religious Private Law in Palestine* (Jerusalem, 1926)

——— and M.D. Baer, "Social Boundaries of Ottoman Women's Experience in Eighteenth-Century Galata Court Records," in M. Zilfi, ed., *Women in the Ottoman Empire* (Bloomington, IN, 1995)

Goldstein, S., "The Teaching of Religion in Government Funded Schools in Israel," *Israel Law Review 1* (1992): 36-64.

Gormley, W.P., "The Right to Life and the Rule of Non-Derogatability: Peremptory Norms of *Jus Cogens*," in B.G. Ramcharan, ed., *The Right to Life in International Law* (Dordrecht/Boston/Lancaster, 1985), 120

Green, S.J.D., "Beyond the Satanic Verses," *Encounter* (June, 1990): 15

Green, Steven, "The Misnomer of Equality under the Equal Access Act," *Vermont Law Review* 14 (1990): 369

Greenawalt, Kent, *Conflicts of Law and Morality* (Oxford, 1987)

Greenfeld, Liah, *Nationalism: Five Roads to Modernity* (Cambridge, 1992)

Greer, Donald, *The Incidence of the Emigration During the French Revolution* (Cambridge, MA, 1951)

———, *The Incidence of the Terror During the French Revolution* (Cambridge, MA, 1937)

Gregory, David, "The Role of Religion in the Secular Workplace," *Notre Dame Journal of Law, Ethics & Public Policy* 4 (1990): 749;

Güldner, Gerhard, *Das Toleranz-Problem in den Niederlanden im Ausgang des 16. Jahrhunderts* (Lübeck/Hamburg, 1968)

Gutiérrez, Armando Méndez, ed., *Una Ley para la Libertad Religiosa* (Mexico City, 1992)

Hairi, A.H., *Shi'ism and Constitutionalism in Iran* (Leiden, 1977)

Hale, Frederick, "The Development of Religious Freedom in Norway," *Journal of Church and State* 23 (1981): 47

Hall, Timothy, "Religion, Equality, and Difference," *Temple Law Review* 65 (1992): 1

Hamburger, Philip A., "A Constitutional Right of Religious Exemption: An Historical Perspective," *George Washington Law Review* (1992): 915

Hamilton, Marci A., "The Belief/Conduct Paradigm in the Supreme Court's Free Exercise Jurisprudence: A Theological Account of the Failure to Protect Religious Conduct," *Ohio State Law Journal* 54 (1993): 713

———, "The Religious Freedom Restoration Act: Letting the Fox into the Henhouse under the Cover of Section 5 of the Fourteenth Amendment," *Cardozo Law Review* 16 (1994): 357

Handy, Robert T., "Why it Took 150 Years for Supreme Court Church-State Cases to Escalate," in R. White and A. Zimmermann, eds., *An Unsettled Arena: Religion and the Bill of Rights* (Grand Rapids, 1990), 54

Hannum, Hurst, "Contemporary Developments in the International Protection of the Rights of Minorities," *Notre Dame Law Review* 66 (1991): 1431

———, ed., *Guide to International Human Rights Practice* (Washington, 1992)

Harris, D. and S. Joseph, eds., *The International Covenant on Civil and Political Rights and the United Kingdom* (Oxford, 1995)

Hart, Levi, *Liberty Described and Recommended* (Hartford, CT, 1775)

Hatch, Nathan O., *The Sacred Cause of Liberty* (New Haven, CT, 1977)

Havighurst, Robert James, *Anthropology and Cultural Pluralism: Three Case Studies, Australia, New Zealand, and USA* (Wellington, New Zealand, 1974)

Heckel, Martin, *Die theologischen Fakultäten im weltlichen Verfassungsstaat* (Tübingen, 1986)

———, *Gesammelte Schriften. Staat, Kirche, Recht, Geschichte* (Tübingen, 1989), 2 vols.

———, *Gleichheit oder Privilegien? Der Allgemeine und der besondere Gleichheitssatz im Staatskirchenrecht* (Tübingen, 1993)

———, *Korollarien zur Säkularisierung* (Heidelberg, 1981)

———, *Organisationsstrukturen der Theologie an der Universität* (Berlin, 1987)

———, *Staat, Kirche, Kunst. Rechtsfragen kirchlicher Kulturdenkmäler* (Tübingen, 1968)

Helmreich, Ernst C., *Religious Education in German Schools: An Historical Approach* (Cambridge, MA, 1959)

Henkin, Louis "Human Rights," *Encyclopedia of Public International Law* (Amsterdam/New York/Oxford), 8:268

——— and John Lawrence Hargrove, eds., *Human Rights: An Agenda for the Next Century* (Washington, 1994).

Henriques, H.S.Q., *The Jews and the English Law* (Oxford, 1908)

Herskovitz, Frances, ed., *Perspectives in Cultural Relativism* (New York, 1972)

Herskovitz, Melville J., "Cultural Relativism," in Frances Herskovitz, ed., *Perspectives in Cultural Relativism* (New York, 1972), 15

Heuston, R.F.V., *Lives of the Lord Chancellors 1885-1940* (Oxford, 1987)

Higham, John, *Strangers in the Land: Patterns of American Nativism, 1860-1925* (Westport, CT, 1981)

Holdsworth, W.S., *A History of English Law* (London, 1938)

Hollenbach, David, *Justice, Peace, and Human Rights: American Catholic Social Ethics in a Pluralistic Context* (New York, 1988)

Holmes, Oliver Wendell, Jr., *The Common Law* (Boston, 1881)

Holwerda, David, ed., *Exploring the Tradition of John Calvin* (Grand Rapids, 1976)

Hopkins, James K., *A Woman to Deliver Her People: Joanna Southcott and English Millennarianism in an Era of Revolution* (Austin, TX, 1982)

Horkheimer, Max, *Die Sehnsucht nach dem ganz Anderen; ein Interview mit Kommentar von Helmut Gumnior* (Hamburg 1970)

———, *Verwaltete Welt? Ein Gespräch* (Zürich 1970)

Hageman, Alice L. and Philip E. Wheaton, eds., *Religion in Cuba Today: A New Church in a New Society* (New York, 1971)

Horwitz, Robert H., ed., *The Moral Foundations of the American Republic* 3d ed. (Charlottesville, Va., 1986)

Howarth, P., *Questions in the House* (London, 1956)

Howe, John R., *The Changing Political Thought of John Adams* (Princeton, NJ, 1966)

Howe, Mark D., *The Garden and the Wilderness: Religion and Government in American Constitutional History* (New York, 1965)

Human Rights Watch/Asia, *Freedom of Religion in China* (New York, 1992)

———, *Persecuted Minorities and Writers in Pakinstan* (Washington, 1993)

Humphrey, John P., "The U.N. Charter and the Universal Declaration of Human Rights," in E. Luard, ed., *The International Protection of Human Rights* (New York, 1967), 41

———, *Human Rights and the United Nations: A Great Adventure* (Dobbs Ferry, NY, 1984)

———, "Political and Related Rights," in Theodor Meron, ed., *Human Rights in International Law* (Oxford, 1985), 176

———, "The Universal Declaration of Human Rights: Its History, Impact and Judicial Character," in B.G. Ramcharan, ed., *Human Rights, Thirty Years after the Universal Declaration* (The Hague, 1979), 21

Hunter, I.A., R. St. MacDonald, and J.P. Humphrey, eds., *The Practice of Freedom: Canadian Essays on Human Rights and Fundamental Freedoms* (Toronto, 1979)

Hyneman, Charles and Donald S. Lutz, eds., *American Political Writing During the Founding Era 1760-1805* (Indianapolis, 1983)

Instituto de Investigaciones Juridicas, *Estudios Juridicos en Torno a la Ley de Asociaciones Religiosas y Culto Publico* (Mexico City, 1992)

International Campaign for Tibet, *Forbidden Freedoms: Beijing's Control of Religion in Tibet* (Washington, DC, 1990)

International Perspectives of Church and State (Omaha, 1993)

Iqbal, M., "Education and Islam in Britain—A Muslim View," *New Community* (1976-1977): 397

Ireland, Joel T., "The Transfiguration of the *Lemon* Test: Church and State Reign Supreme in *Bowen v. Kendrick*," *Arizona Law Review* 32 (1990): 365

Isensee J. and P. Kirchhof (hrsg.), *Handbuch des Staatsrechts der Bundesrepublik Deutschland: Bd. VI. Freiheitsrechte* (Heidelberg, 1989)

Ismael, Tareq and Jacqueline S. Ismael, eds., *Politics and Government in the Middle East and North Africa* (Miami, FL, 1991)

Ivers, Gregg, *Lowering the Wall: Religion and the Supreme Court in the 1980s* (New York, 1991)

Jack, Homer A., *WCRP: A History of the World Conference on Religion and Peace* (New York, 1993)

Jacobs, Francis G., *The European Convention on Human Rights* (Oxford, 1975)

Jacqueney, Theodore, "The Yellow Uniforms of Cuba," *Worldview* (New York, January, 1977): 4

James, A., *Sikh Children in Britain* (Oxford, 1974)

James, Charles F., *Documentary History of the Struggle for Religious Liberty in Virginia* (New York, 1971)

Janis, Mark Weston, "Panel on Religion and International Law," *American Society of International Law Proceedings* 82 (1988): 195

———, ed., *The Influence of Religion in the Development of International Law* (Dordrecht/Boston/London, 1991)

Jefferson, Thomas, *The Complete Jefferson, Containing His Major Writings,* Saul K. Padover, ed. (Freeport, 1943)

———, *The Papers of Thomas Jefferson*, Julian Boyd, ed. (Princeton, 1950)

Jelavich, Barbara, *History of the Balkans: Twentieth Century* (Cambridge, 1983)

Jennings, R.C., "Dhimmis (Non-Muslims") in the Early Seventeenth-Century Ottoman Judicial Records; The Shari'a Court of Anatolian Kayseri," *Journal of the Economic and Social History of the Orient* 21(3) (1978): 250

Jimenez, Frank R., "Beyond *Mergens*: Ensuring Equality of Religious Speech Under the Equal Access Act," *Yale Law Journal* 100 (1991): 2149

Johnson, Philip, "Concepts and Compromise in First Amendment Religious Doctrine," *California Law Review* 72 (1984): 817

Jordan, Wilbert Kitchener, *The Development of Religious Toleration in England From The Accession of James I To The Convention of the Long Parliament* (Oxford, 1908)

Kamali, Mohammed Hashim, "Freedom of Religion in Islamic Law," *Capital University Law Review* 21 (1992): 63

Kamen, Henry, *The Rise of Toleration* (New York, 1967)

Kauper, Paul B. and Stephen B. Ellis, "Religious Corporations and the Law," *Michigan Law Review* 71 (1973): 1499

——— and Rudolf Halberstadt, "Religion and Education in West Germany: A Survey and an American Perspective," *Valparaiso Law Review* 4 (1969): 1

Kedourie, E., *The Chatham House Version and Other Middle Eastern Studies* (Hanover and London, 1984)

Keyter, Elise, ed., *Official Yearbook: South Africa 1993* (Pretoria 1993)

Khadduri, M. and H.R. Liebesny, eds., *Law in the Middle East* (Washington, 1955)

Khan, Ilyas, "The Ahmadiyya Movement in Islam," *Proceedings of the Third World Congress on Religious Liberty* (IRLA, 1989)

Khan, M.W., ed., *Education and Society in the Muslim World* (London, 1981)

Kiss, Alexandre C., "Permissible Limitations on Rights," in Louis Henkin, ed., *The International Bill of Rights* (New York, 1981), 290

Kiteme, K., *We, The Pan-Africans: Essays on the Global Black Experience* (New York, 1992)

Klein, Claude, *Le charactere juif de l'etat d'Israel* (Paris, 1977)

Koch, A., ed., *The American Enlightenment: The Shaping of the American Experiment in a Free Society* (New York, 1976)

Kommers, Donald P., *The Constitutional Jurisprudence of the Federal Republic of Germany* (Durham/London 1989)

Kooijmans, P.H., "The Non-Governmental Organizations and the Monitoring Activities of the United Nations in the Field of Human Rights," in *The Role of Non-Governmental Organizations in the Promotion and Protection of Human Rights* (New York, 1990), 15

Korson, J.H., ed., *Contemporary Problems of Pakistan* (Leiden, 1974)

Kossmann, E.H. and A.F. Mellink, *Texts Concerning the Revolt of the Netherlands* (London, 1974)

Kothari, Rajni, "Human Rights as a North-South Issue," in Richard Pierre Claude and Burns H. Weston, eds., *Human Rights in the World Community: Issues and Actions* (Philadelphia, 1991), 134

Kramer, Hilton, "Angry History: Richard Pipes on the Bolshevik Revolution," *The New Criterion* 12(9) (May, 1994): 8

Krishnaswami, Arcot, *Study of Discrimination in the Matter of Religious Rights and Practices* (New York, United Nations, 1960)

Kuper, Leo, *Genocide: Its Political Use in the Twentieth Century* (New Haven, 1981)

———, *The Prevention of Genocide* (London, 1985)

Kurland, Philip, "Religion and the Law: Of Church and State and the Supreme Court," *University of Chicago Law Review* 29 (1961): 1

Lambton, A.K.S., *State and Government in Medieval Islam* (Oxford, 1981)

Laoust, H., *Le traité de droit publique d'Ibn Taymiya* (Beirut, 1948)

Lapidoth, R., "Jerusalem: The Legal and Political Background," *Justice* 3 (1994): 7

Lash, Joseph P., *Eleanor: The Years Alone* (New York, 1972)

Lash, Kurt T., "The Second Adoption of the Free Exercise Clause: Religious Exemptions Under the Fourteenth Amendment," *Northwestern University Law Review* 88 (1994): 1106

Lathorp, John, *A Discourse on the Peace* (Boston, 1784)

Lauterpacht, Herssch, *International Law and Human Rights* (London, 1950)

Laycock, Douglas N., "Formal, Substantive, and Disaggregated Neutrality Toward Religion," *DePaul Law Review* 39 (1990): 993.

———, "Free Exercise and the Religious Freedom Restoration Act," *Fordham Law Review* 62 (1994): 883

———, "Non-Preferential Aid to Religion: A False Claim About Original Intent," *William and Mary Law Review* 27 (1986): 875

———, "RFRA, Congress, and the Ratchet," *Montana Law Review* 56 (1995): 145

———, "Summary and Synthesis: The Crisis in Religious Liberty," *George Washington Law Review* 60 (1992): 841

———, "The Religious Freedom Restoration Act," *Brigham Young University Law Review* (1993): 221

———, "The Remnants of Free Exercise," *Supreme Court Review* (1990): 1

———, "Toward a General Theory of the Religion Clauses: The Case of Church Labor Organizations and the Right to Church Autonomy," *Columbia Law Review* 81 (1981): 1373

id. and Oliver S. Thomas, "Interpreting the Religious Freedom Restoration Act," *Texas Law Review* 73 (1994): 209

Layish, Aharon, "The Muslim Waqf in Israel," *Asian and African Studies* 2 (1966): 41

Lecler, Joseph and Marius-Francois Valkhoff, *Les premiers defenseurs de la liberte religieuse* (Paris, 1969)

Lee, Rex E., "The Religious Freedom Restoration Act: Legislative Choice and Judicial Review," *Brigham University Law Review* (1993): 73

Lee, S., *The Cost of Free Speech* (London, 1990)

Leland, John, *The Writings of the Late Elder John Leland: Including Some Events In His Life Written By Himself With Additional Sketches By L.F. Greene* (New York, 1845).

Lemkin, Raphael, "Genocide as a Crime in International Law," *American Journal of International Law* 41 (1947): 172

Leniaud, Jean-Michel, *L'Administration des cultes pendant la période concordataire* (Paris, 1988)

Lerner, Natan, "Ethnic Cleansing," *Israel Yearbook on Human Rights* 24 (1994): 103

———, *Group Rights and Discrimination in International Law* (Dordrecht, 1991)

———, "Incitement in the Racial Convention: Reach and Shortcomings of Article 4," *Israel Yearbook on Human Rights* 22 (1992): 1

———, "Individual Petitions Under the International Convention on the Elimination of all Forms of Racial Discrimination," in Irwin Cotler and F. Pearl Eliadis, eds., *International Human Rights Law* (Montreal, 1992), 435

———, "The Evolution of Minority Rights in International Law," in Catherine Brolmann et al., eds., *Peoples and Minorities in International Law* (Dordrecht/Boston/London, 1993), 77

———, "The 1992 UN Declaration on Minorities," *Israel Yearbook on Human Rights* 23 (1993): 111

———, *The UN Convention on the Elimination of All Forms of Racial Discrimination*, 2d ed. (Alphen aan den Rijn, 1980)

Lesch, Ann Mosley, "The Republic of Sudan," in Tareq Ismael and Jacqueline S. Ismael, eds., *Politics and Government in the Middle East and North Africa* (Miami, FL, 1991), 365

Leuprecht, Peter, "Conflict Resolution and Alternative Forms of Dispute Resolution," in Kathleen E. Mahoney and Paul Mahoney, eds., *Human Rights in the Twenty-First Century: A Global Challenge* (Dordrecht/Boston/London, 1993), 959

Levy, Leonard W., *Blasphemy: Verbal Offense Against the Sacred, from Moses to Salman Rushdie* (New York, 1993)

Lindholm, Tore and Kari Vogt, eds., *Islamic Reform and Human Rights: Challenges and Rejoinders* (Copenhagen, 1993)

Liskofsky, Sidney, "The UN Declaration on the Elimination of Religious Intolerance and Discrimination: Historical and Legal Perspectives," in James E. Wood, Jr., ed., *Religion and the State: Essays in Honor of Leo Pfeffer* (Waco, TX, 1985), 441

Little, David, *Ukraine: The Legacy of Intolerance* (Washington, 1991)

———, *Sri Lanka: The Invention of Enmity* (Washington, 1994)

———, "The Nature and Basis of Human Rights," in Gene Outka and John P. Reeder, Jr., eds., *Prospects for a Common Morality* (Princeton, NJ, 1993), 82

——— and Scott W. Hibbard, *Sino-Tibetan Co-Existence: Creating Space for Tibetan Self-Direction* (Washington, 1994)

Locke, John, *A Letter Concerning Toleration* (Buffalo, NY, 1990)

Luchterhand, Otto, "The Human Rights and Freedom of Religion and Soviet Law," in Leonard W. Swidler, ed., *Religious Liberty and Human Rights* (Philadelphia, 1986), 93

Lupu, Ira C., "Free Exercise Exemption and Religious Institutions: The Case of Employment Discrimination," *Boston University Law Review* 67 (1987): 391

———, "Statutes Revolving in Constitutional Orbits," *Virginia Law Review* 79 (1993): 1

———, "The Lingering Death of Separationism," *George Washington Law Review* 62 (1994): 230

———, "Where Rights Begin: The Problem of Burdens on the Free Exercise of Religion," *Harvard Law Review* 102 (1989): 933

Macartney, C.A., *National States and National Minorities* (New York, 1934)

Macaulay, T.B., *The History of England* (Harmondsworth, 1979)

Macchi, A., "Vatican-Israel Relations: The Catholic Perspective," *Justice* 3 (1994): 26

Macdonald, R. St. J., et al., eds., *The European System for the Protection of Human Rights* (The Hague, 1993)

———, F. Matscher and H. Petzold, eds., *The European System for the Protection of Human Rights* (Dordrecht/Boston/London, 1993)

Madison, James, "Detached Memoranda (c. 1817)," *William and Mary Quarterly* 3(3) (1946): 554

———, *The Papers of James Madison*, William T. Hutchinson and William M.E. Rachal, eds. (Chicago, 1962)

Maehl, William H., *Germany in Western Civilization* (Birmingham, 1981)

Mahoney, K.E. and Paul Mahoney, eds., *Human Rights in the Twenty-First Century* (Dordrecht/Boston/London, 1993)

Maitland, F.W., *The Constitutional History of England* (Cambridge, 1908)

Malbin, Michael, *Religion and Politics: The Intentions of the Authors of the First Amendment* (Washington, 1978)

Maldonado-Denis, Manuel, "The Situation of Cuba's Intellectuals," *The Christian Century* (January 17, 1968): 80

Malik, Charles Habib, "Reflections on the Origin of the Universal Declaration of Human Rights," in O. Frederick Nolde, *Free and Equal: Human Rights in Ecumenical Perspective* (Geneva, 1968), 10

Maoz, Asher, "Constitutional Law," in Itzhak Zamir, ed., *Introduction to Israeli Law* (Jerusalem, 1995)

———, "On the Legal Status of the Golan Heights: Application of Israeli Law or Annexation? Application of Israeli Law to the Golan Heights is Annexation," *Brooklyn Journal of International Law* 20 (1992): 365

———, "The Rabbinate and the Rabbinical Courts Between the Legal Hammer and the Halachic Anvil," *Shenaton Ha-Mishpat Ha-Ivri* 16-17 (1990-1991): 289

———, "State and Religion in Israel," in *International Perspectives of Church and State* (Omaha, 1993), 239

———, "Who is a Jew?" *Midstream* 35(6) (1989): 11

Maritain, Jacques, *Les droits de l'homme et la loi naturelle* (Paris, 1942)

———, *Man and the State* (Chicago, 1951)

Marshall, Paul, "Ignoring Religion Distorts All Human Rights," *World Perspectives* (Santa Ana, CA, July 6, 1994)

Marshall, William P., "In Defense of *Smith* and Free Exercise Revisionism," *University of Chicago Law Review* 58 (1991): 308

———, "The Case Against the Constitutionally Compelled Free Exercise Exemption," *Case Western Reserve University Law Review* 40 (1990): 357

———, "The Inequality of Anti-Establishment," *Brigham Young University Law Review* (1993): 63

Martin, David, *Tongues of Fire: The Explosion of Protestantism in Latin America* (Oxford, 1990)

Marty, Martin E., "On a Medial Moraine: Religious Dimensions of American Constitutionalism," *Emory Law Journal* 39 (1990): 9

——— and R. Scott Appleby, eds., *Fundamentalisms and the State: Remaking Polities, Economies, and Militance* (Chicago, 1993)

———, eds., *Fundamentalisms Comprehended* (Chicago, 1995)

Mathieson, W.L., *Politics and Religion: A Study in Scottish History From the Reformation to the Revolution* (Glasgow, 1902)

May, Henry, *The Enlightenment in America* (New York, 1976)

Mayer, Ann E., "Current Muslim Thinking on Human Rights," in Abdullahi Ahmed An-Na'im and Francis M. Deng, eds., *Human Rights in Africa* (Washington, 1990), 133

———, "Law and Religion in the Muslim Middle East," *American Journal of Comparative Law* 35 (1987): 127

———, "Moroccans—Citizens or Subjects? A People at Crossroads," *Journal of International Law and Politics* 26(1) (1993): 63

———, "Universal versus Islamic Human Rights: A Clash of Cultures or a Clash of Constructs?" *Michigan Journal of International Law* 15(2) (1994): 358

Mazrui, A., "Africa and Other Civilizations: Conquest and Counterconquest," in J. Harbeson, ed., *Africa in World Politics* (Boulder/San Francisco, 1991), 77

———, *The Satanic Verses or a Satanic Novel?* (Greenpoint, NY, 1989)

Mbiti, J., *African Religions and Philosophy* (Garden City, NY, 1970)

McCarthy, Rockne M., James W. Skillen, and William A. Harper, *Disestablishment a Second Time: Genuine Pluralism for American Schools* (Grand Rapids, MI, 1982)

McConnell, Michael W., "Accommodation of Religion," *Supreme Court Review* (1985): 1

———, "Accommodation of Religion: An Update and a Response to Critics," *George Washington Law Review* 60 (1992): 685

——— "Free Exercise Revisionism and the *Smith* Decision," *University of Chicago Law Review* 57 (1990): 1109

———, "Religious Freedom at a Crossroads," *University of Chicago Law Review* (1992): 115

———, "The Origins and History of Free Exercise of Religion," *Harvard Law Review* 103 (1990): 1473

McDonagh, Edna, *Freedom or Tolerance*? (New York, 1967)

McDonald, R. St. J., and F. Matscher and H. Petzold, eds., *The European System for the Protection of Human Rights* (Dordrecht, 1993)

McDougall, Myres S., Harold D. Laswell and Lung-chu Chen, *Human Rights and World Public Order* (New Haven, 1980)

McGoldrick, Dominic, *The Human Rights Committee* (Oxford/New York, 1991)

McGrath, Marcos, c.s.c., "Democracy and Christianity in Latin America," in John Witte, Jr., ed., *Christianity and Democracy in Global Context* (Boulder, CO/San Francisco, 1993), 173

McKean, Warwick, *Equality and Discrimination under International Law* (Oxford, 1983)

McKeen, Joseph, *A Sermon, Preached on the Public Fast in the Commonwealth of Massachusetts* (Salem, MA, 1793)

McLoughlin, William C., *New England Dissent* 1630-1833 (Cambridge, MA, 1967)

McMillan, Richard C., *Religion in the Public Schools* (Macon, 1987)

McWilliams, W.C., *The Idea of Fraternity in America* (Berkeley, 1973)

Mead, Sidney E., *The Lively Experiment: The Shaping of Christianity in America* (Berkeley, CA, 1963).

———, *The Old Religion in the Brave New World: Reflections on the Relation Between Christendom and the Republic* (New York, 1977)

Mecham, J. Lloyd, *Church and State in Latin America*, rev. ed. (Chapel Hill, 1966)

Mellen, John, *The Great and Happy Doctrine of Liberty* (Boston, 1795)

Meron, Simha, "Freedom of Religion as Distinct from Freedom from Religion," *Israel Yearbook on Human Rights* 4 (1974): 219

Meron, Theodor, ed., *Human Rights in International Law* (Oxford, 1985)

———, *Human Rights Law-Making in the United Nations* (New York, 1986)

Metz, Allan, "Mexican Church-State Relations under President Carlos Salinas de Gortari," *Journal of Church and State* 34 (1992): 111

Meyer, Alfred W., "The Blaine Amendment and the Bill of Rights," *Harvard Law Review* (1951): 939

Meyers, Marvin, ed., *The Mind of the Founder: Sources of the Political Thought of James Madison*, rev. ed. (Hanover, NH, 1981)

Middle East Watch, *Guardians of Thought: Limits of Freedom of Expression in Iran* (New York, 1993)

Miller, J., *The Glorious Revolution* (London, 1983)

Miller, Perry, "The Contributions of the Protestant Churches to Religious Liberty in Colonial America," *Church History* 4 (1935): 65

——— and Thomas Johnson, *The Puritans* (New York, 1938), 2 vols.

Miller, William Lee, *The First Liberty: Religion and the American Republic* (Charlottesville, 1986)

Minerath, Roland, "Freedom of Religion: A Challenge for Peace in the Teaching of the Catholic Church," in *Freedom of Religion: Hope for Lasting Peace and Unity. Proceedings of the All African Religious Liberty Congress* (Nairobi, September 1991), 47

———, "The Doctrine of the Catholic Church," *Proceedings of the Third World Conference on Religious Liberty* (IRLA, 1989), 49

Minnesota Advocates for Human Rights, *Human Rights in the Socialist Republic of Albania* (January, 1990)

Mojzes, Paul, "Religious Liberty: Definitions and Theoretical Framework," in Leonard W. Swidler, ed., *Human Rights: Christians, Marxists and Others in Dialogue* (New York, 1991), 173

———, *Religious Liberty in Eastern Europe and the USSR: Before and After the Great Transformation* (Boulder, CO, 1992)

———, "Religious Liberty in Yugoslavia: A Study in Ambiguity," in Leonard W. Swidler, ed., *Religious Liberty and Human Rights in Nations and in Religions* (Philadelphia, 1986), 23

———, "War between Religions," *Religion in Eastern Europe* (February 1993): I-II

———, *Yugoslavian Inferno: Ethnoreligious Warfare in the Balkans* (New York, 1994)

——— and Gerald Shenk, "Protestantism in Bulgaria and Yugoslavia Since 1945," in Sabrina Petra Ramet, ed., *Protestantism and Politics in Eastern Europe and Russia* (Durham, NC, 1992), 209

Momen, M., "The Trial of Mulla 'Ali Bastami: A Combined Sunni-Shi'i Fatwa against the Bab," *Iran* 20 (1982): 113

Moore, E.G., *An Introduction to English Canon Law* (Oxford, 1967)

Morgan, Edmund S., *Puritan Political Ideas, 1558-1794* (Indianapolis, 1965)

Mortensen, Reid, "Establishment and Toleration: The British Pattern of Secularism," *University of Queensland Law Journal* 17(2) (1993): 187

Mottahedeh, Roy P., "Toward an Islamic Theology of Toleration," in Tore Lindholm and Kari Vogt, eds., *Islamic Reform and Human Rights: Challenges and Rejoinders* (Copenhagen, 1993), 26

Munro, F., *Colonial Rule Among the Kamba: Social Change in the Kenya Highlands 1889-1939* (Oxford, 1975)

Nafziger, James A.R., "The Functions of Religion in the International Legal System," in Mark W. Janis, ed., *The Influence of Religion on the Development of International Law* (Dordrecht, 1991), 147

Nanda, Ved P., ed., *Global Human Rights: Public Policies, Comparative Measures, and NGO Strategies* (Boulder, CO, 1981)

———, "The Protection of the Rights of Migrant Workers," *Asian and Pacific Migration Journal* 2 (1993): 161

Nasr, S.V.R., *The Vanguard of the Islamic Revolution* (Berkeley, CA, 1994)

Nduru, Moyiga Koroto, "Taha's Martyrdom," *New African* (March, 1985): 28

Neff, Stephen C., "An Evolving International Legal Norm of Religious Freedom: Problems and Prospects," *California Western International Law Journal* 7 (1977): 543

Newman, John Henry, *An Essay on the Development of Doctrine*, Charles F. Harrold, ed. (New York, 1949)

Niblett, W.R., "Neutrality or Profession of Faith," in *Science and Freedom. The Proceedings of a Conference Convened by the Congress of Cultural Freedom* (London, 1955), 234

Nips, Jack [John Leland], *The Yankee Spy* (Boston, 1794),

Nolde, O. Frederick, *Free and Equal: Human Rights in Ecumenical Perspective* (Geneva, 1968)

Noonan, John T., Jr., *Believers and the Powers That Are* (New York, 1987)

———, "Development in Moral Doctrine," *Theological Studies* 44 (1993): 662

Norrie, K. and E. Scobbie, *Introduction to Scots Law of Trusts* (London, 1991)

Nowak, M., *UN Covenant on Civil and Political Rights: CCPR Commentary* (Kehl a Rhein, 1993)

Nsereko, Daniel, "Religion, the State and the Law in Africa," *Journal of Church and State* 28 (1986): 269

O'Brien, F. William, "The Blaine Amendment, 1875-1876," *University of Detroit Law Journal* 41 (1963): 137

Oakes, Urian, *New England Pleaded with, and Pressed to Consider the Things Which Concern Her* (Boston, 1673)

Oakley, A.J., *Parker and Mellows, The Modern Law of Trusts*, 6th ed. (London, 1994)

Oberholzer, Emil, *Delinquent Saints: Disciplinary Actions in the Early Congregational Churches of Massachusetts* (New York, 1956)

Oduyoye, Mercy, *Who will Roll the Stone Away?* (Geneva, 1990)

Ogden, John Cosens, *A Short History of Ecclesiastical Oppressions in New-England and Vermont* (Richmond, VA, 1799)

Oloyede, I.O., "A Muslim's Response," in John S. Pobee et al., eds., *Encounter of Religions in African Cultures* (Geneva, 1991), 122

Ong, B.N., "James Madison on Constitutional Interpretation," *Benchmark* 3 (1987): 1

Oosthuizen, G.C., et al., *Religion, Intergroup Relations and Social Change in South Africa. Work Committee: Religion, Human Sciences Research Council (HSRC) Investigation into Intergroup Relations* (Pretoria, 1985)

Orlin, T., "Religious Pluralism and Freedom of Religion," in *The Strength of Diversity* (Dordrecht, 1992)

Orsolic, Marko, "Religious Freedom as a Civil Right," in Leonard W. Swidler, ed., *Human Rights: Christians, Marxists and Others in Dialogue* (New York, 1991), 209

Ortega, Victor Hugo Acuna, ed., *Historia General de Centroamérica. Las Repúblicas Agro-exportadoras* (Proyecto elaborado por FLACSO, La Sociedad Estatal V Centenario y la Comisión de las Communidades Europeas, 1993)

Orwell, George, *Animal Farm* (London, 1951)

Outka, Gene and John P. Reeder, Jr., eds., *Prospects for a Common Morality* (Princeton, NJ, 1993)

Paine, Thomas, *The Complete Writings of Thomas Paine*, P.S. Foner, ed. (New York, 1945), 2 vols.

Papanek, H., "Purdah in Pakistan: Seclusion and Modern Occupation for Women," *Journal of Marriage and the Family* 33 (August, 1971): 517

Parpworth, N. "Defining Ethnic Origins," *New Law Journal* (April 30, 1993): 610

Parsons, Jonathan, *Freedom from Civil and Ecclesiastical Slavery* (Newbury-port, 1774)

Partsch, Karl Josef, "Freedom of Conscience and Expression, and Political Freedoms," in Louis Henkin, ed., *The International Bill of Rights* (New York, 1981), 209

Pasa, Ahmed Cevdet, *Tezakir* (Ankara, 1986)

Paulsen, Michael Stokes, "*Lemon* is Dead," *Case Western Reserve Law Review* 43 (1993): 795

Penn, William, *A Collection of the Works of William Penn* (London, 1726), 2 vols.

Peoplessen, Kirsten, *The History of the Ethiopian Community in the Holy Land from the Time of Emperor Teodorus II Until 1974* (Jerusalem, 1983)

Pepper, Stephen L., "The Case of the Human Sacrifice," *Arizona Law Review* 23 (1981): 897

Pfann, H., *A Short History of the Catholic Church in Ghana* (Cape Coast, 1965)

Pfeffer, Leo, *Church, State and Freedom*, rev. ed. (Boston, 1967)

———, *Religious Freedom* (Skokie, IL, 1988)

Picarda, H., "New Religions as Charities," *New Law Journal* (April 23, 1981): 436

Pobee, John S., "An African Christian in Search of Democracy," in John Witte, Jr., ed., *Christianity and Democracy in Global Context* (Boulder, CO/San Francisco, 1993), 278

———, "Images of the Enemy," *One World* 178 (August/September, 1992): 15

———, *Kwame Nkrumah and the Church in Ghana 1949-1966* (Accra, 1988)

———, "Mission from Below," *Mission Studies* 10 (1-2) (1993): 159

———, ed., *Ministerial Formation for Missions Today* (Asempa, 1993)

———, et al., eds., *Encounter of Religions in African Cultures* (Geneva, 1991)

Pollock, F. & F.W. Maitland, *The History of English Law* (Cambridge, 1895)

Poppel, Stuart D., "Fundamentalism, Fairness, and the Religion Clauses," *Cumberland Law Review* 25 (1994-1995): 247

Post, R., "Cultural Heterogeneity and Law: Pornography, Blasphemy, and the First Amendment," *California Law Review* 76 (1988): 297

Poulter, S., *Asian Traditions and English Law* (Trentham, 1990)

———, "Towards Legislative Reform of the Blasphemy and Racial Hatred Laws," *Public Law* (1991): 375

Prasad, Maya, "The Role of Non-Governmental Organizations in the New United Nations Procedures for Human Rights Complaints," *Denver Journal of International Law and Policy* 5 (1975): 460

Priestly, Joseph, *An Address to Protestant Dissenters of all Denominations* (Boston, 1774)

Prinsterer, Groen van, *Ter Nagedachtenis van Stahl* (Amsterdam, 1862)

Progress Reports of the Technical Committee on Fundamental Rights during the Transition (Kempton Park, 1993)

Ptacek, Kerry, "Waging Words," *Action* (Wheaton, IL, September/October, 1983): 8

Rahman, Fazlur, "Islam and the Constitutional Problem of Pakistan," *Studia Islamica* 32 (1970): 277

———, "Islam and the New Constitution of Pakistan," in J.H. Korson, ed., *Contemporary Problems of Pakistan* (Leiden, 1974), 40

Rahman, S.A., *Punishment of Apostasy in Islam* (Lahore, 1978)

Raikin, Spas, "The Bulgarian Orthodox Church," in Pedro Ramet, ed., *Eastern Christianity and Politics in the Twentieth Century* (Durham, NC, 1988), 160

Raikin, Spas T., "Schism in the Bulgarian Orthodox Church," *Religion in Eastern Europe* 13(1) (February, 1993): 19

Ramcharan, B.G., ed., *Human Rights, Thirty Years after the Universal Declaration* (The Hague, 1979)

———, "The Concept and Dimensions of the Right to Life," in B.G. Ramcharan, ed., *The Right to Life in International Law* (Dordrecht/Boston/Lancaster 1985), 1

———, "Towards a Universal Standard of Religious Liberty," in *Religious Liberty. Commission of the Churches on International Affairs* (Geneva, 1987), 8

———, ed., *The Right to Life in International Law* (Dordrecht/Boston/ Lancaster 1985)

Ramet, Pedro, ed., *Catholicism and Politics in Communist Society* (Durham, NC, 1990)

———, ed., *Eastern Christianity and Politics in the Twentieth Century* (Durham, NC, 1988)

———, *Religion and Nationalism in Soviet and Eastern European Politics* (Durham, NC, 1988)

Ramet, Sabrina Petra, ed., *Protestantism and Politics in Eastern Europe and Russia* (Durham, NC, 1992)

Rawls, John, *Political Liberalism* (Cambridge, MA, 1993)

Raz, Joseph, *The Authority of Law* (Oxford, 1970)

Redman, Barbara J., "Sabbatarian Accommodation in the Supreme Court," *Journal of Church and State* 33 (1991): 495

Reichley, A. James, *Religion in American Public Life* (Washington, 1985)

Reuther, Rosemary R., "Some Well-Guarded Secrets About the Churches in Cuba," *National Catholic Reporter* (August 30, 1985): 14

Reynolds, Laurie, "Zoning the Church," *Boston University Law Review* 64 (1984): 767

Richards, N.J., "Disestablishment of the Anglican Church in England in the Late Nineteenth Century: Reasons for Failure," *Journal of Church and State* 19 (1988): 193

Robertson, A.H., *Human Rights in Europe* (Manchester, 1977)

Robertson, G., "Blasphemy: The Law Commission's Working Paper," *Public Law* (1981): 295

———, *Freedom, the Individual and the Law*, 7th ed. (Harmondsworth, 1993)

——— and A. Nicol, *Media Law*, 3d ed. (London, 1992)

Robertson, Mike, ed., *Human Rights for South Africans* (Cape Town, 1991)

Robilliard, John, *Religion and the Law* (Manchester, 1984)

———, "Religion in Prison," *New Law Journal* 130 (1980): 800

———, "Report of Committees. Offences Against Religion and Public Worship," *Modern Law Review* 44 (1981): 556

Robinson, Nehemiah, *The Genocide Convention* (New York, 1960)

———, *The Universal Declaration of Human Rights* (New York, 1958)

———, et al., *Were the Minorities Treaties a Failure?* (New York, 1943)

Rodley, Nigel S., "United Nations Non-Treaty Procedures for Dealing with Human Rights Violations," in H. Hannum, ed., *Guide to International Human Rights Practice* (Philadelphia, 1992), 71

Romero, Archbishop Oscar, *A Shepherd's Diary*, Irene B. Hodgson, trans. (Cincinnati, 1993)

Rooter, Z., "The Position of Believers in Socialist Countries," *Occasional Papers on Religion in Eastern Europe* (June, 1989): 5

Rosen, D., "Vatican-Israel Relations: The Jewish Perspective," *Justice* 3 (1994): 22

Rossi, Gianfranco, "Violations of Religious Freedom in Various Parts of the World," *Conscience and Liberty* 4(2) (1992): 58

Rossiter, Clinton, *The Political Thought of the American Revolution* (New York, 1963)

Rothman, Stanley and Linda S. Lichter, *The Media Elite* (New York, 1986)

Rubinstein, Amnon, "The Right to Marriage," *Israel Yearbook on Human Rights* 3 (1973): 233

Ryan, James E., "*Smith* and the Religious Freedom Restoration Act," *Virginia Law Review* 78 (1992): 1407

Ryskamp, George R., "The Spanish Experience in Church-State Relations: A Comparative Study of the Interrelationship Between Church-State Identification and Religious Liberty," *Brigham Young University Law Review* (1980): 616

Sadurski, W., *Moral Pluralism and Legal Neutrality* (Dordrecht/Boston, 1990)

———, "On Legal Definitions of 'Religion'," *Australian Law Journal* 63 (1993): 834

Sandoz, Ellis, *A Government of Laws: Political Theory, Religion, and the American Founding* (Baton Rouge, LA, 1990)

———, ed., *Political Sermons of the American Founding Era, 1730-1805* (Indianapolis, 1991)

Sarwar, G., *British Muslims and Schools* (London, 1994)

Schacht, Joseph, *Islamic Law* (Oxford, 1964)

Schaff, Philip, *Church and State in the United States, or the American Idea of Religious Liberty and Its Practical Effects* (New York, 1888)

Schall, James V., *The Church, the State and Society in the Thought of John Paul II* (Chicago, IL, 1982)

Schama, Simon, *Citizens* (New York, 1989)

Schanda, Balazs, *Religious Freedom in Hungarian Law* (Ph.D. Diss., Budapest, 1988)

Scheinin, Martin, "Article 18," in Asbjorn Aide et al., eds., *The Universal Declaration of Human Rights: A Commentary* (Oslo, 1992), 263

Schwarz, Karl, "Der Begriff Exercitium Religionis Privatum," *Zeitschrift der Savigny-Stiftung (Kan. Ab.)* 105 (1988): 495

Schwebel, Stephen, "The Effect of Resolutions of the UN General Assembly on Customary International Law," *American Society of International Law, Proceedings of the 73rd Annual Meeting* (1979): 301

Secretariat, Bishops' Committee for the Church in Latin America, National Conference of Catholic Bishops, *New Evangelization, Human Development, Christian Culture* (Washington, 1993)

Shapiro, Barbara, "Sir Francis Bacon and the Mid-Seventeenth Century Movement for Law Reform," *American Journal of Legal History* 24 (1980): 331

Shaw, Malcolm N., "Freedom of Thought, Conscience and Religion," in R. St. J. Macdonald, et al., eds., *The European System for the Protection of Human Rights* (The Hague, 1993), 445

Sheleff, Leon Shaskolsky, "Rabbi Captain Goldman's Yarmulke, Freedom of Religion and Conscience, and Civil (Military) Disobedience," *Israel Yearbook on Human Rights* 17 (1987): 197

———, "Tribal Rites and Legal Rights," *Israel Yearbook on Human Rights* 18 (1988): 153

Shell, D. and D. Beamish, *The House of Commons at Work* (Oxford, 1993)

Sher, R., *Scotland and America in the Age of the Enlightenment* (Princeton, NJ, 1990)

Shestack, Jerome J., "Sisyphus Endures: The International Human Rights NGO," *New York Law School Law Review* 24 (1978): 89

Sheuner, Ulrich, "Erörterungen und Tendenzen im gegenwärtien Staatskirchenrecht der Bundesrepublik," *Essener Gespräche zum Thema Staat und Kirche* 1 (1969): 108

Shimonek, Douglas C., "Using the *Lemon* Test as Camouflage: Avoiding the Establishment Clause," *William Mitchell Law Review* 16 (1990): 835

Shirley, Eugene B., Jr. and Michael Rowe, eds. *Candle in the Wind* (Washington, 1989)

Shropshire, D., *The Church and the Primitive Peoples* (London, 1938)

Sieghart, Paul, *The International Law of Human Rights* (New York, 1983)

Sigmund, Paul E., *Liberation Theology at the Crossroads: Democracy or Revolution?* (New York, 1990)

Sillitoe, A.F., *Britain in Figures* (Harmondsworth, 1973)

Sirico, Louis, "Church Property Disputes: Churches as Secular and Alien Institutions," *Fordham Law Review* 55 (1986): 335

Skakkebaek, Christian, *Article 9 of the European Convention on Human Rights* (Strasbourg, 1992)

Smith, D.J. and G. Chambers, *Inequality in Northern Ireland* (London, 1991)

Smith, Huston, *Religions of Man* (New York, 1958)

Smith, Rodney K., "Getting Off on the Wrong Foot and Back on Again: A Reexamination of the History of the Framing of the First Amendment and a Critique of the *Reynolds* and *Everson* Decisions," *Wake Forest Law Review* 20 (1984): 569

———, *Prayer and the Constitution: A Case Study in Constitutional Interpretation* (Wilmington, 1987);

Smith, Steven D., "Idolatry in Constitutional Interpretation," *Virginia Law Review* 79 (1993): 583

———, "The Rise and Fall of Religious Freedom in Constitutional Discourse," *University of Pennsylvania Law Review* 140 (1991): 149

Smith, T.A., *A Short Commentary on the Church of Scotland* (Edinburgh, 1962)

Soifer, Aviam, "Freedom of Association: Indian Tribes, Workers, and Communal Ghosts," *Maryland Law Review* 48 (1989): 350

Soriá, Julio César Pinto, ed., *Historia General de Centroamérica. El Regimen Colonial* (Proyecto elaborado por FLACSO, La Sociedad Estatal V Centenario y la Comisión de las Communidades Europeas, 1993)

Souchal, François, *Le vandalisme de la Révolution* (Paris, 1993)

South African Law Commission, *Working Paper on Group and Human Rights* (Pretoria 1989)

Spurlin, P., *The French Enlightenment in America: Essays on the Times of the Founding Fathers* (Athens, 1984).

Spykman, Gordon, "Sphere Sovereignty in Calvin and the Calvinist Tradition," in David Holwerda, ed., *Exploring the Tradition of John Calvin* (Grand Rapids, 1976), 163

Stendel, Ori, *The Minorities in Israel: Trends in the Development of the Arab and Druze Communities 1948-1973* (Jerusalem, 1973)

Steiner, Henry, "Ideals and Counter-Ideals in the Struggle over Autonomy Regimes for Minorities," *Notre Dame Law Review* 66 (1991): 1552

Stern, Sol, "Cuba and Repression: Castro's Victims," *The Village Voice* 28(49) (New York, December 6, 1983): 1

Stohlman, Martha Lou, *John Witherspoon: Parson, Politician, and Patriot* (New York, 1976)

Stokes, A.P., *Church and State in the United States* (New York, 1950)

——— and Leo Pfeffer, *Church and State in the United States*, rev. ed (New York, 1964)

Stoll, David, *Is Latin America Turning Protestant?* (Berkeley, CA, 1990)

Stone, R., *Textbook on Civil Liberties* (London, 1994)

Story, Joseph, *Commentaries on the Constitution* (Boston, 1833)

Strickland, Reba C., *Religion and the State in Georgia in the Eighteenth Century* (New York, 1939)

Strong, William, *Two Lectures Upon the Relations of Civil Law to Church Polity, Discipline, and Property* (New York, 1875)

Strossen, Nadine, "A Constitutional Analysis of the Equal Access Act's Standards Governing Public School Student Meetings," *Harvard Journal on Legislation* 24 (1987): 117

Sullivan, Donna J., "Advancing the Freedom of Religion or Belief Through the UN Declaration on the Elimination of Religious Intolerance and Discrimination," *American Journal of International Law* 82 (1988): 487

———, "Gender Equality and Religious Freedom: Toward a Framework for Conflict Resolution," *New York University Journal of International Law and Politics* 24 (1992): 795

Sultanhussein Tabandeh of Gunabad, *A Muslim Commentary on the Universal Declaration of Human Rights,* F.J. Goulding, trans. (New York, 1970)

Swidler, Leonard W., ed., *Human Rights: Christians, Marxists and Others in Dialogue* (New York, 1991)

———, ed., *Religious Liberty and Human Rights* (Philadelphia, 1986)

Tabory, Ephraim, "Religious Rights as a Social Problem in Israel," *Israel Yearbook on Human Rights* 11 (1981): 256

Talbi, Mohammed, "Religious Liberty: A Muslim Perspective," in Leonard W. Swidler, ed., *Religious Liberty and Human Rights* (Philadelphia, 1986), 175

Teson, Fernando R., "International Human Rights and Cultural Relativism", in Richard Claude and Burns H. Weston, eds., *Human Rights in the World Community,* 2d ed. (Philadelphia, 1992), 42

The Freeman's Remonstrance Against an Ecclesiastical Establishment (Wiliamsburg, VA, 1777)

The International Federation of Human Rights, *Vietnam: Violations of Religious Freedom and Freedom of Conscience* (February, 1993)

"The NCC Takes Another Beating," *Christianity and Crisis* (October 1, 1984): 349

The Palladium of Conscience, or, The Foundation of Religious Liberty Displayed, Asserted and Established, Agreeable to its True and Genuine Principles (Boston, 1773)

The Canons of the Church of England (Convocations of Canterbury and York, 1964, 1969)

Thornberry, Patrick, *International Law and the Rights of Minorities* (Oxford, 1991)

Traer, Robert, *Faith in Human Rights* (Washington, 1991)

True Light (Boston, 1731)

Tumin, Melvin M. and W. Plotch, eds., *Pluralism in a Democratic Society* (New York, 1977)

United Nations, *Human Rights: A Compilation of International Instruments* (New York, 1993)

Universal Islamic Declaration of Rights (London, 1981)

Valticos, N., "The International Labor Organization," in Karl Vasak, ed., *The International Dimensions of Human Rights* (Westport, CT, 1982), 2:405

van Boven, Theo, "Advances and Obstacles in Building Understanding and Respect Between People of Diverse Religions and Beliefs," *Human Rights Quarterly* 13 (1991): 437

van Bueren, Geraldine, *International Law and the Rights of the Child* (Dordrecht/Boston/London, 1993)

van der Vyver, Johan, "Law and Morality," in Ellison Kahn, ed., *Fiat Iustitia: Essays in Memory of Oliver Deneys Schreiner* (Cape Town/Wetton/Johannesburg, 1983), 305

———, *Die Juridiese Funksie van Staat en Kerk: 'n Kritiese Analise van die Beginsel van Soewereiniteit in eie Kring* (Durban, 1972)

———, "The Function of Legislation as an Instrument of Social Reform," *South African Law Journal* (1976): 56, 62-67

———, "The Private Sphere in Constitutional Litigation," *Tydskrif vir hedendaagse Romeins-Hollandse Reg* 57 (1994): 378.

———, *Reformed Christians and Social Justice* (Sioux Center, IA, 1988)

———, "Religion," in W.A. Joubert and T.J. Scott, eds., *The Law of South Africa* (Durban/Pretoria, 1986), 23:175

———, "Sphere Sovereignty and the American Concept of Religious Freedom," in id., *Reformed Christians and Social Justice* (Sioux Center, IA, 1988), 1

———, "Sovereignty and Human Rights in Constitutional and International Law," *Emory International Law Review* 5 (1992): 321

———, "The State, the Individual and Society," *South African Law Journal* (1977): 291

van Dijk, P. and G. van 't Hoof, *Theory and Practice of the European Convention of Human Rights*, 2d ed. (Boston, 1990)

van Zyl, Liezl L., *Gesondheidsorg en Geregtigheid: 'n Filosofies-etiese Ondersoek* (Stellenbosch, 1993)

Vasak, Karl, ed., *The International Dimensions of Human Rights* (Westport, CT, 1982), 2 vols.

Vatican II, *The Documents of Vatican II*, Walter M. Abbot, trans. (New York, 1966)

Vecsey, Christopher, ed., *Handbook of American Indian Religious Freedom* (Washington, 1991)

Verdery, Katherine, "Whither 'Nation' and 'Nationalism'?" *Daedalus* 122(3) (Summer, 1993): 38

Vidler, Alec, *The Church in an Age of Revolution* (Harmondsworth, 1961)

Vierdag, E.W., The *Concept of Discrimination in International Law* (The Hague, 1973)

Villa-Vicencio, Charles, *The Spirit of Hope* (Johannesburg, 1993)

Vincent, R.J., *Human Rights and International Relations* (Cambridge, 1986)

Vitita, Edoardo, *The Conflict of Laws in Matters of Personal Status in Palestine* (Tel Aviv, 1947)

Volf, M., "Exclusion and Embrace: Theological Reflections in the Wake of Ethnic Cleansing," *Religion in Eastern Europe* (December, 1993): 6

Walkate, J.A., "The Right of Everyone to Change his Religion or Belief: Some Observations," *Netherlands International Law Review* 30(2) (1983): 146

Walker, Williston, ed., *The Creeds and Platforms of Congregationalism* (Boston, 1960)

Ward, Nathaniel, *The Simple Cobler of Aggawam in America*, 5th ed. (Boston, 1713)

Ware, Timothy, *The Orthodox Church* (Baltimore, 1969)

Washington, George, *The Writings of George Washington From the Original Manuscript Sources, 1745-1799*, J.C. Fitzpatrick, ed. (Washington, D.C., 1931), 39 vols.

Weber, Max, *Economy and Society: An Outline of Interpretive Sociology* (New York, 1968), 2 vols.

———, *From Max Weber: Essays in Sociology*, H.H. Gerth and C. Wright Mills, eds. (New York, 1958)

Weber, Paul J., "James Madison and Religious Equality," *Review of Politics* 44 (1982): 163

Weisbrod, Carol, "Commentary on Curry and Firmage Articles," *Journal of Law and Religion* 7 (1989): 315

———, "Minorities and Diversities: The 'Remarkable Experiment' of the League of Nations," *Connecticut Journal of International Law* 8 (1993): 359

Weissbrodt, David, "The Role of Nongovernmental Organizations in the Implementation of Human Rights," *Texas International Law Journal* 12 (1977): 293

West, Ellis, "The Right to Religion-Based Exemptions in Early America: The Case of Conscientious Objectors to Conscription," *Journal of Law and Religion* 10 (1994): 367

White, Lyman Cromwell, *International Non-Governmental Organizations: Their Purposes, Methods, and Accomplishments* (New York, 1968)

White, R. and A. Zimmermann, eds., *An Unsettled Arena: Religion and the Bill of Rights* (Grand Rapids, 1990)

Williams, Elisha, *The Essential Rights and Liberties of Protestants: A Seasonable Plea for The Liberty of Conscience, and the Right of Private Judgment in Matters of Religion, Without any Controul from Human Authority* (Boston, 1744)

Williams, E.N., *A Documentary History of England* (Harmondsworth, 1965)

Williams, Roger, *The Complete Writings of Roger Williams*, Perry Miller, ed. (New York, 1963), 7 vols.

Wilson, James, *The Works of James Wilson*, R.G. McCloskey, ed. (Cambridge, 1967)

Wilson, John K., "Religion Under the State Constitutions, 1776-1800," *Journal of Church and State* 32 (1990): 753

Winchester, Elhanan, *A Century Sermon on the Glorious Revolution* (London, 1789)

Wiseberg, Laurie S. and Harry M. Scoble, "Recent Trends in the Expanding Universe of Nongovernmental Organizations Dedicated to the Protection of Human Rights," V. Nanda, ed., *Global Human Rights* (Washington, 1981)

Witherspoon, John, *The Selected Writings of John Witherspoon*, Thomas Miller, ed. (Carbondale, Ill., 1990)

Witte, John, Jr., "Blest Be the Ties that Bind: Covenant and Community in Puritan Thought," *Emory Law Journal* 36 (1987): 579

———, ed., *Christianity and Democracy in Global Context* (Boulder, CO/San Francisco, 1993)

———, "How to Govern a City on a Hill: The Early Puritan Contribution to American Constitutionalism," *Emory Law Journal 39* (1990): 41

———, "Tax Exemption of Church Property: Historical Anomaly or Valid Constitutional Practice," *Southern California Law Review* 64 (1991): 363

———, "The South African Experiment in Religious Human Rights: What Can Be Learned From the American Experience," *Journal for Juridical Science* 18(1) (1993): 1

———, "The State of Religious Human Rights in the World: A Comparative Religious and Legal Study," *Preliminary Documents of Religious Human Rights Project* 1 (1993)

———, "The Theology and Politics of the First Amendment Religion Clauses: A Bicentennial Essay," *Emory Law Journal* 40 (1991): 489

———, *Towards an Integration of Law and Religion* (Pretoria, 1993)

———, "Toward an Integration of Religious Liberty," *Michigan Law Review* 92 (1992): 1363

——— and Johan van der Vyver, eds., *Religious Human Rights in Global Perspective: Religious Perspectives* (The Hague/Boston/London, 1995)

Woben, H., *Grundproblemen der Staatkirchenrechts* (Zürich, 1978)

Wolff, Robert Lee, *The Balkans in Our Time* (Cambridge, MA, 1956)

Wood, Gordon S., *The Creation of the American Republic, 1776-1787* (Chapel Hill, NC, 1969)

Wood, James E., Jr., "Editorial: Church and State in England," *Journal of Church and State* 9(3) (1967): 305

———, *The First Freedom: Religion and the Bill of Rights* (Waco, TX, 1990)

———, ed., *Religion and the State: Essays in Honor of Leo Pfeffer* (Waco, TX, 1985)

World Conference on Religion and Peace—South African Chapter, *Believers in the Future. Proceedings of the National Inter-Faith Conference on Religion-State Relations, December 2-4 1990, Johannesburg* (Johannesburg, 1991)

Zander, Walter, "Jurisdiction and Holiness: Reflections on the Coptic-Ethiopian Case," *Israel Law Review* 17 (1985): 245

———, On Settlement of Disputes About The Christian Holy Places," *Israel Law Review* 3 (1978): 331

Zilfi, M., ed., *Women in the Ottoman Empire* (Bloomington, IN, 1995)

Zoller, Adrien-Claud, "The Political Context of the World Conference," *Human Rights Monitor* 21 (May, 1993): 2

Zollman, Carl F.G., *American Civil Church Law* (New York, 1917)

Biographical Sketches of Contributors

Said Amir Arjomand, Ph.D. (Chicago), is Professor of Sociology at the State University of New York at Stony Brook, and Visiting Professor of Islamic Studies at the University of Chicago. Dr. Arjomand is an expert on Shi'ism and the sociology of religion and politics in Iran. He serves on the editorial board of *Iranian Studies*, and is Editor of the State University of New York Press Series on the Near East, which includes the 38 volume *History of al-Tabari*. Dr. Arjomand has published some 60 articles and book chapters and eight books, including *The Shadow of God and the Hidden Imam: Religion, Political Organization and Societal Change in Shi'ite Iran from the Beginning to 1890*, *The Turban for the Crown: The Islamic Revolution in Iran*, and *The Political Dimensions of Religion*.

Harold J. Berman, LL.B. and M.A. (Yale), is the Robert W. Woodruff Professor of Law at Emory University, Russian Studies Fellow at the Carter Center of Emory University, and James Barr Ames Professor of Law, *Emeritus*, at Harvard University. Professor Berman is the founder and co-director of the American Law Center in Moscow, and serves on the Board of Directors of the Council on Religion and Law. He is a world authority on Soviet law, international trade, legal history, and law and religion and has published more than 300 articles and 25 books, including *The Interaction of Law and Religion*, *Justice in the U.S.S.R.*, *The Russians in Focus*, *Law and Revolution: The Formation of the Western Legal Tradition* and *Faith and Order: The Reconciliation of Law and Religion*.

Jimmy Carter has devoted much of his career to political and social service. After naval duty, he served as Senator of Georgia, Governor of Georgia, and President of the United States, where he successfully negotiated the Panama Canal treaties, the Camp David Accords, and SALT II. Throughout his political career and thereafter, he has advocated greater human rights protection, democratic reform, and peace negotiation throughout the world, most recently in North Korea, Bosnia-

Herzegovina, and Haiti, and he has substantially advanced these causes through the work at The Carter Center at Emory University. His advocacy and accomplishments have won him numerous awards and honorary degrees from institutions around the world. President Carter has several books, including *Keeping Faith: Memoirs of a President, The Blood of Abraham, Negotiation: The Alternative to Hostility, Turning Point: A Candidate, A State and A Nation Come of Age*, and *Always and Reckoning and Other Poems.*

Peter Cumper, LL.M. (Essex), LL.B. (Queen's University, Belfast), is Senior Lecturer in Law at the Nottingham Law School and Visiting International Scholar at the University of Minnesota and has taught at Wolsey College, Oxford and the University of Hull. A specialist in international human rights, civil rights, and comparative constitutionalism, Professor Cumper has written some two dozen articles and book chapters, and has three books forthcoming, including *Textbook on Constitutional and Administrative Law.*

Lourens M. du Plessis, LL.B. and LL.D. (Potchefstroom University), is Professor of Public Law at the University of Stellenbosch and Professor Extraordinaire of Comparative and Public International Law at the University of the Western Cape. A distinguished authority on South African politics and constitutional law, Professor du Plessis played a leading role in drafting the famous *Koinonia Declaration* against apartheid and in drafting current constitutional and statutory provisions on religious rights for South Africa. He has published a number of articles and books, including *The Professional Conduct of the Jurist, The Interpretation of Statutes,* and *Ten Perspectives*.

W. Cole Durham, Jr., J.D. (Harvard), is Professor of Law at the J. Reuben Clark Law School of Brigham Young University, Secretary of the American Society of Comparative Law, and serves on the Board of Directors of the International Academy for Freedom of Religion and Belief. An expert in comparative law and religious freedom, Professor Durham has given lectures and advised constitutional conventions throughout Eastern Europe and Latin America. He has prepared 40 professional articles, an English translation of Viehweg's *Topik und Jurisprudenz* and is co-editor of a new volume, *Religious Liberty in Western Thought*.

James Finn, M.A. (Chicago), is Chairman of the Board of The Puebla Institute, Senior Editor of Freedom House's *Freedom Review*, and editor of *Freedom in the World: The Annual Survey of Politics Rights and Civil Liberties.* An expert on religion, politics, and culture, Mr. Finn is a member of the Council on Foreign Relations, and serves on the board of the Institute on Religion and Democracy and the World Without War Council. He is a frequent contributor to public policy volumes and journals, and has served as editor of *Commonweal, Freedom Review*, and *Worldview*. His books include *Protest: Pacifism and Politics, Global Economics and Religion* and *Private Virtue and Public Policy: Catholic Thought and Public Policy*.

Tamás Földesi, Ph.D. (Eötvös Loránd University), is Professor of Law and Head of the Department of Philosophy at Eötvös Loránd University in Budapest. He is also a member of the Committee for Elaboration of Human Rights in the Hungarian Constitution and Board Member of the Hungarian Human Rights Institute. Dr. Földesi is an expert on human rights and on legal philosophy and ethics, and has lectured on these topics around the world. Among his many publications are three prize-winning volumes, *The Dilemmas of Justice, Ethics for Everybody*, and *Truth About Truth*

M. Christian Green, J.D. (Emory), Ph.D. Candidate (Chicago), is a specialist in law, religion, and ethics, with an focus on feminist social thought as well as on Russian and international legal developments. She has written a number of articles on each of these themes, and has prepared two source collections on "The Protestant Reformation and Law" and comprehensive annotated bibliographies on "Law, Religion, and Violence" and "Religious Human Rights."

T. Jeremy Gunn, J.D. (Boston University), Ph.D. (Harvard), is Director of the Review Board for the United States Government, General Counsel for the National Committee for Public Education and Religious Liberty, Member of the International Advisory Board for the World Report on Freedom of Conscience, Religion, and Belief, and a participant in the United States Institute of Peace Working Group on Religion, Ideology, and Peace. Dr. Gunn also serves as counsel to the National Coalition for Public Education and Religious Liberty. He has argued a number of religious liberty cases in the United States, published several articles and book chapters on religious liberty, and recently published *A Standard for Repair: The Establishment Clause, Equality, and Natural Rights*.

Martin Heckel, Dr. iur. (München), is University Professor of Public Law and Church Law at Eberhard-Karls-Universität, Tübingen, member of the Historical Commission of the Bavarian Academy of Sciences and is editor of both the *Ius Ecclesiasticum* book series and the *Zeitschrift der Savigny-Stiftung (Kanonisches Abteilung)*. An eminent authority on Western legal history and church law, Professor Heckel has lectured throughout the world, written numerous articles and a dozen books, including *Gesammelte Schriften. Staat, Kirche, Recht, Geschichte, Staat, Kirche, Kunst. Rechtsfragen kirchlicher Kulturdenkmäler, Korollarien zur Säkularisierung, Die* *theologischen Fakultäten im weltlichen Verfassungsstaat,* and *Organisationsstrukturen der Theologie an der Universität.*

Alexandre Kiss, Ph.D. (University of Paris), Dipl. (Hague Academy of International Law), is Professor of Law at the Robert Schuman University of Strasbourg, Vice-President and Former Secretary-General of the International Institute of Human Rights, and Director of Research, *Emeritus,* of the French National Center for Scientific Research. A specialist in human rights, European community law, and environmental law, Professor Kiss has published some 300 articles and 15 books, including *La protection internationale des droits de l'homme, International Environmental Law,* and a seven volume work, *Répertoire de la pratique francaise en matère de droit international public.*

Natan Lerner, Ph.D. (Buenos Aires), Dipl. (Hague Academy of International Law), is Professor of Law, *Emeritus,* at Tel Aviv University and former Director of the Israel branch of the World Jewish Congress. Dr. Lerner is a world recognized authority on international law and human rights, and has participated in panels and conferences on the subject around the globe. He has served as a consultant to the UNESCO Division of Human Rights, Advisor to the Delegation of Israel to the General Assembly of the United Nations, and is active in the Association for the Study of Ethnicity and Nationalism and the Study Group on Ethnicity and Law in Latin America. In addition to his many articles and book chapters, Dr. Lerner's books include *Group Rights and Discrimination in International Law, The U.N. Convention on the Elimination of All Forms of Racial Discrimination, The Crime of Incitement to Group Hatred* and *In Defence of Human Rights.*

David Little, Th.D. (Harvard), is a Senior Scholar at the United States Institute of Peace and Director of its Working Group on Religion, Ideology and Peace. He has taught at Yale, Brown, Amherst, Haverford, and for nearly twenty years served as Professor of Religious Studies at the University of Virginia. An expert in law and religion, comparative religious ethics, and religious liberty, Dr. Little has written nearly 100 professional articles and book chapters, and 10 books, including *Religion, Order, and Law: A Study in Prerevolutionary England, Ukraine: Legacy of Intolerance, Sri Lanka: The Intervention of Enmity,* and *Human Rights and the Conflict of Cultures: Freedom of Religion and Conscience in the West and Islam.*

Asher Maoz, LL.B. and LL.M. (Hebrew University, Israel), M. Comp. Lit. (Chicago), J.S.D. (Tel Aviv), is Senior Lecturer of Law at Tel Aviv University, member of The Institute for Research of Family Law, and co-director of the Temple-Tel Aviv summer law program. Dr. Maoz is an expert in Israeli law, human rights, and family law, and has received numerous scholarships and awards for his work. He has published more than three dozen articles and book chapters in both Hebrew and English, and is co-author of *The Law of Succession*.

Paul B. Mojzes, Ph.D. (Boston University), is Professor of Religious Studies at Rosemont College, and former Professor and Dean at the Graz Center, Graz, Austria. A native of Yugoslavia, Dr. Mojzes is editor of *Religion in Eastern Europe*, co-editor of the *Journal of Ecumenical Studies*, and serves as President of Christians Associated for Relationships with Eastern Europe. He is an expert on church history and religious life in Eastern Europe, and has lectured widely in the United States and abroad. He has published numerous articles, and his books include *Religious Liberty in Eastern Europe and the USSR: Before and After the Great Transformation* and *Yugoslavian Inferno: Ethno-Religious Warfare in the Balkans*.

Stanley Muschett Ibarra, Ph.D. (Notre Dame), is Rector of Universidad Santa Maria La Antigua in the Republic of Panama, Chairman of the Catholic Church's Commission on Justice and Peace, a member of the Church's National Commission on Education, and Secretary General of the Government's Interoceanic Regional Authority. A native of Panama, Dr. Muschett is an expert on the philosophy of law and the social teachings of the Catholic Church and a frequent lecturer on political developments in Latin America. His publications include *Bolivar: From Utopia to Reality*, *The Church's Social Teaching and Society*, and *Eschatology and Politics*. His work has earned him the distinguished Presidential Award for Distinguished Services to the Country.

Makau wa Mutua, LL.M. (Dar-es-Salaam, Tanzania), S.J.D. (Harvard), is Projects Director of the Human Rights Program at Harvard Law School and former Director of the Africa Project of the Lawyers' Committee for Human Rights. A native of Kenya, Dr. Mutua also serves as Chairman of the Kenya Human Rights Commission and the African Studies Association Human Rights Committee, and conducts human rights fact-finding and diplomatic missions throughout Africa, Eastern Europe, and Latin America. Dr. Mutua recently participated in monitoring the elections in South Africa. His many publications and reports include *Zaire: Repression As Policy*, *Ethiopia in Transition: Strengthening the Rule of Law*, and *Sudan: Attacks on the Judiciary*.

John T. Noonan, Jr., Ph.D. (Catholic University), LL.B. (Harvard), is a Judge on the United States Court of Appeals for the Ninth Circuit, and former Professor of Law at the University of California School of Law at Berkeley. A distinguished public servant, Judge Noonan has served on numerous governmental, academic, and church societies, including the Canon Law Society, the Catholic Bishops Committee, and the National

Right to Life Committee. He is currently President of the Thomas More and Jacques Maritain Institute, among other appointments. Judge Noonan is a world class scholar of medieval canon law, legal history, legal philosophy, and religious liberty, and has written more than 150 professional articles and book chapters and 18 books, including *The Believer and the Powers That Are, Bribes, A Private Choice: Abortion in America in the Seventies, Persons and Masks of the Law*, and *Contraception*. He holds 22 honorary doctorates and distinguished service awards.

John S. Pobee, Ph.D. (Cambridge), is Associate Director of the Programme for Theological Education and President of the International Association for Mission Studies of the World Council of Churches in Geneva. A Ghanaian native and ordained Anglican priest, Dr. Pobee has taught and lectured throughout the world, has received numerous awards and honorary degrees, and has emerged as one of the preeminent authorities on theological education and church development in Africa. He has published some 160 articles and 37 books, including *Beyond an Issue of Legitimacy or Illegitimacy, Religion and Politics in Ghana*, and *Skenosis — A Tabernacling of Christian Faith in Africa*.

Michael Roan, M.A. (Lutheran-Northwestern Seminary), is Director of Project Tandem, Inc. (PTI), Coordinator of the Peace Prize Forum, Coordinator of the American Refugee Committee Health Clinic, and Director of the Minnesota Programs of the American Refugee Committee. He is an expert and activist in the fields of human rights and freedom of thought, conscience, and belief. As Director of PTI, Mr. Roan has organized three international conferences in Minnesota, Poland, and India on strategies for promoting the implementation of the 1981 United Nations Declaration on the Elimination of All Forms of Intolerance and of Discrimination Based on Religion or Belief.

Dinah L. Shelton, J.D. (Berkeley), is Professor of Law at Santa Clara University Law School, Director of the Budapest Summer Session, and Professor of International and Comparative Human Rights Law at the International Institute of Human Rights. Professor Shelton has worked as an expert consultant for the United Nations, European Community, and the Council of Europe, and has served on the National Advisory Council of Amnesty International's Legal Support Network. She has long been a behind-the-scenes force for the development of a United Nations declaration on religious liberty. In addition to her many articles, Professor Shelton has co-authored several books, including *Preventive Detention: A Comparative and International Law Perspective, European Environmental Law, Protecting Human Rights in the Americas: Selected Problems*, and a report for the European Community on legal measures to combat racism, xenophobia and incitement to hatred and racial violence.

Paul E. Sigmund, Ph.D. (Harvard), is Professor of Politics and former Director of the Latin American Studies Program at Princeton University and Executive Member of Americas Society, the Carnegie Council on Ethics and International Affairs, the Latin American Labor Institute, and the Woodstock Theological Center. Dr. Sigmund is a world authority on Latin American religion and politics, the history of Western political thought, and liberation theology. In addition to more than 200 articles, he includes among his numerous books, *Natural Law in Political Thought, The Democratic Experience, Multinationals in Latin America, Liberation Theology at the Crossroads: Democracy or Revolution*, and *The United States and Democracy in Chile, 1961-1991.*

Johan David van der Vyver, LL.D. (Pretoria), is I.T. Cohen Professor of International Law and Human Rights at Emory Law School, Fellow in the Human Rights Program at the Carter Center, and formerly Professor of Law at the University of Witwatersrand in Johannesburg, and Professor of Law and Dean of Pochefstroom University. Dr. van der Vyver is a widely-known authority on international human rights and comparative constitutionalism, and was one of the leading scholarly proponents for constitutional and human rights reform in his native South Africa. He is the author of more than 200 articles and eight books, including *Seven Lectures on Human Rights, Reformed Christians and Social Justice, The Juridical Function of Church and State*, and *The Republic of South Africa Constitution Act.*

John Witte, Jr., J.D. (Harvard), is the Jonas Robitscher Professor of Law and Director of the Law and Religion Program at Emory University, and member of the Project on Religion, Culture and the Family at the University of Chicago. A specialist in legal history, church-state relations, and law and religion, he has published 50 professional articles and book chapters, edited *Christianity and Democracy in Global Context, A Christian Theory of Social Institutions* and *The Weightier Matters of the Law: Essays on Law and Religion*, and is author of three forthcoming volumes, *From Sacrament to Contract: Law, Religion, and Family in the West, The Law and the Protestants: The Lutheran Reformation*, and *The American Experiment in Religious Rights and Liberties.*

Index